# HISTORY
## OF
# THE QUEEN'S ROYAL REGIMENT

Printed and bound by Antony Rowe Ltd, Eastbourne

[Photo: J. Russell & Sons, 73, Baker Street, W.

**GENERAL SIR CHARLES MONRO, BT.,**
**G.C.B., G.C.S.I., G.C.M.G.**
Colonel of the Regiment.

# HISTORY
## OF
# THE QUEEN'S ROYAL REGIMENT

COMPILED BY
COLONEL H. C. WYLLY, C.B.

*Printed and Published for the Regimental Committee by*
GALE & POLDEN, LTD.,
WELLINGTON WORKS, ALDERSHOT
ALSO AT LONDON AND PORTSMOUTH

# PREFACE

BY MAJOR-GENERAL SIR WILKINSON D. BIRD, K.B.E., C.B., C.M.G., D.S.O.

A MERE glance at this volume, in which is continued, where Colonel Davis left it, the great history of The Queen's, will show at once how difficult, how most invidious, was the task which has so ably been fulfilled by Colonel Wylly.

A history of a regiment is, of course, the narrative of the deeds of its components. But as the whole is always greater than the parts, so the requirements of space, of cost, and above everything of producing a book which will be readable from end to end by all into whose hands it comes, imperatively oblige the historian to make a firm rule ; and the rule is this—that only those things which are altogether essential in the broad regimental outlook can and must find a place in the text. The tale that was to be told was one of the endeavour of a whole regiment, not one of wearying detail of the hard, grinding task so efficiently performed by the tools used in the well-built machine ; for a story devoted solely to their actions would only have been obscure because swollen to too large a size by the mere superfluity of detail.

The History, then, sets out to tell us how brilliantly all the battalions worked and contributed both to maintain and to increase the already high reputation of The Queen's in barrack, billet, camp and bivouac, and in hard fight.

The English are a warlike, not a militarist race ; they fight rather to uphold their rights than in aggression. For centuries they have struggled—as in the Great War—in the defence of liberty, their greatest right ; and in the future, as in the past, the English, it is safe to say, will stubbornly resist all who attempt either to dictate or to oppress. This, then, was the reason why in 1914 our people, who were almost unarmed for great warfare on the land, so confidently stood out to keep their word ; to defend the weak, and to uphold the freedom of Belgium, even though this involved them in a bitter conflict with a great nation which was already most strong in arms.

In time of war the best policy must always be to hit the enemy as hard as possible, to hit so as to hurt, for war is made to win by doing harm, and in the most vulnerable place. But to resolve which is this place is perhaps the greatest test of high capacity ; for interests will ever diverge, and some strong interests will always tend to draw judgment in directions apart from the best course. This is especially so in Britain's case, whose naval strength has long endowed her with the power not only of strangling the sea trade of her enemies, but also of striking blows whenever ships can carry troops and whenever troops can gain a footing on the shore. We might in 1914, then, well have waited to see where our small Expeditionary Force of six divisions could best deliver an effective stroke against our German foes. But France now made a claim for such direct assistance as could be given by these troops, and the decisive point on land for us was held in consequence to be on the left flank and on the eastern frontier of our great ally.

To set the good standard, to show the best way, is a hard, an onerous duty, and it was this, as Colonel Wylly tells, that in 1914, both in Belgium and in France, Britain confided to the older battalions of her regiments.

The past history of The Queen's has shown that Britain in former times has more than once called on her few fully trained troops to face outnumbering enemies, and, as was the case in 1914, a retreat has followed. And dully to march and march, one's back to the foe, is the far heavier, the more oppressive strain, for none of the fierce excitement of the fight then lends it aid. It was in such a hard test of disciplined efficiency during that long retreat from Mons that the men of our 1st Battalion proved themselves to be the " best marchers " in the 1st Division ; and then they turned again and helped to win, when the Germans were checked and driven back at the great battles on the Marne and Ourcq.

Before the year 1914 a few had said—more, perhaps, may have thought—that England's proverbial toughness had been drowned in a great wave of luxury. England, it was whispered, " is being smothered in her own fat, and is no longer capable of severe exertion." These deeds of the men of the Old Army, with its Special Reserve, gave, however, the lie to this gross calumny ; yet had the event been otherwise, the spirit of the nation could surely not have risen to the full height required for its most heavy task.

An objective, we are authoritatively told, is essential in every operation of war ; and to fix on and hold fast to a resolve as to the decisive point, where all is to be won or lost by victory or defeat, is evidently one of the strong pillars of success ; for frequent changes in the plan both waste effort, scatter force, and also disturb the troops and shake their confidence—and without confidence victory cannot be won. The walls of great buildings must, as is well known, be buttressed up, or else they may disastrously collapse. In the same way the main endeavour of the nation's force—at this period it was to defeat the German invaders of France—must always be supported by measures adequate to assure that her other interests shall not suffer deadly harm. Of these one of the most important was, and still is, the peace and the integrity of India, which rests, as is the case throughout the world, on a foundation of armed strength. But India, like the remainder of the Empire's states, had, early in the war, sent most of her trained formations over the seas to undertake tasks of more immediate urgency than that of local defence.

The Territorial Force in Great Britain had been embodied, on the declaration of war, for the purpose of carrying out the obligations undertaken by its members in regard to the direct protection of what was then the United Kingdom. But, as was always certain, so strong was the reply to a call for volunteers from this force for service beyond these limits, that first our 1/4th, and soon afterwards our 1/5th Battalion also, was sent to India to act as a firm buttress to campaigns in progress overseas, that could not otherwise have been continued.

For nearly five long years the men of the 1/4th were, then, alternately pinched by the cold and weighed down by the torrid heat of the wild Indian borderland. And into those years was also crammed a wider experience of tribal warfare than used to fall, in a whole lifetime, to the most hardened warriors of the Punjab Frontier Force.

The contrast is, of course, great even between the rough work of the settlers' year and the still cruder tasks of war. But to exchange for the bivouac and trench the comforts of the town and of the developed land must be an outrage to all acquired habit. Life, also, every man holds dear, for we could not live were this not so, but life was cheap when in the trenches. It is good, therefore, to know that not only was our Special Reserve Battalion filled and refilled and the 4th and

5th The Queen's trebled in size, but that nine Service Battalions of the Regiment were raised, and, later on in the war, Labour and Young Soldier units as well. Men of West Surrey came forward, in fact, in crowds : some ready to take up and skilfully to bear the dreadful weight of leading in battle, when blood is the currency that is paid out for error as death's long shadows are always near ; the many prepared to face, when in the ranks, greater hardships indeed, but yet less anxious and in consequence less arduous tasks ; others to shoulder the thankless but essential work of training men to take the field and of insuring that the fighting troops should never lack the disciplined and well-instructed drafts, without which victory could not be won ; others, again, to do their best in manual labour, an essential service in modern warfare where machines are now so largely used.

While this great business was in hand and England, with her extraordinary power of adaptation, was rapidly developing her fighting strength, the two older battalions of the Regiment were still stubbornly helping in Northern France to hold, at fearful cost of life, the Germans from the French Channel ports ; the loss of which might have enabled our enemies almost to close this great sea highway to the essential traffic of British merchant ships.

And here it was that our 1st Battalion fought literally to the last man : " the best battalion I have ever seen, or certainly (as a Guardsman you will forgive me for saying it) equal to the very best in the Brigade of Guards in every respect."

War, however, cannot be won merely by holding fast ; to win men must strike hard and at the enemy's most vulnerable point ; and little ground even had of late been gained in France by the fiercest blows of the Germans. Some of the leaders, therefore, whose difficult work it was to contrive how many hands should strike when fitness led them on, now, early in 1915, half believed that neither side would ever achieve more than to bend those strong armed fronts that had been stretched across North-Eastern France. It was, they urged, hard to kick against the pricks, and in such cases wise generals had been accustomed to reach out towards the ends of the enemy's lines, his flanks. Russia, also, who when but ill-prepared had in 1914 boldly attacked the Germans, drawing away for the defence of East Prussia the troops that might have brought victory in the Western theatre of war, was now in difficulties and holding out against the Germans, Austrians and Turks. Such being the case, Britain might use her sea power to the advantage of her cause by sending such new formations as were ready either to gain the German flank in Pomerania, from which a hand could be held out to help the Russian troops ; or by bursting through the narrow Dardanelles, the Greeks, Bulgarians and Roumanians would be drawn to our side, and the Turks would be cut off from their Germanic friends. These then could be closely besieged, shut in by an unbroken ring of steel ; and as a further gain, direct touch would have been established with our Russian allies.

In managing a war the sound foundation of an attack against the enemy's flank is that our own front must both be safe and able to keep that of the enemy in a close grip. It is essential also that the force which moves against the flank should be quite adequate to roll it up. Whether these two conditions were or could have been fulfilled in the spring of 1915 is not material to our history ; but only about twenty-seven divisions from Britain, the Dominions and India had taken the field in June, whereas some sixty were ready to fight at the end of the year. It was, however, now decided that the enemy's most vulnerable place was at Gallipoli. A force was sent there to help our Navy to drive its way through the

Dardanelles by capturing the steep hills that overlook the straits; and in the summer our 2/4th Battalion was one of those that was safely carried in our ships to dispute with the Turks for the mastery of mere brown scrub and sunbaked rocks, which nevertheless are hardly surpassed in military importance by any stretch of country in the world.

The only certain grip in time of war is by attack, for then the enemy must keep a strong guard. Apart from this, it is essential to deliver blows as soon as forces able to do so have been prepared; the reason being that, since the moral factors, the opinions, count for so much, our own troops, those of the enemy, and also the world at large must clearly see that we are not afraid and that we are the better men. Such, then, were the causes, and also later on the need for hindering the dispatch of newly raised German units against the hard-pressed Russian front, why in March, 1915, when the British Army had become powerful enough to do this, attacks in combination with the French were begun against the German lines in France. These culminated in September in the hard fight at Loos, where our 6th and 8th Battalions were first closely engaged, and well upheld, the latter at fearful cost of life again, the fighting tradition of the Regiment. And the reformed 1st and 2nd Battalions also then showed all their old gallantry and steadfastness.

In the meanwhile, for Britain has long walls to buttress, many interests to protect, British warfare had spread to Egypt and to the East and West Coasts of Africa. British troops were fighting, too, on the wide, burning Mesopotamian plains, where oil for fuel and for the manufacture of high explosives was obtained, where enemies who might harm India could be met far from her gates, and where ports must be closed against raiders who could harass our commerce on the seas.

In all this widespread fighting Britain's material successes had been but few, and of the few the most remarkable were those that had been won on the broad levels of Iraq. Nations, like individuals, become despondent in times of stress and danger when without cheering news, and a despondent people can never win a war. Sometimes, therefore, it may not be injudicious to undertake a venture which, if successful, will make good copy for the press; and such a thrust was the most daring march against Baghdad which was commenced in November, 1915. This failed, large reinforcements were required to repair the harm, and among these the 1/5th The Queen's were sent from India to undertake, and in the end to help to win, this difficult campaign.

When once her teeth have closed Britain most rarely leaves her hold. But troops that are strongly opposed on land cannot, in wintry, stormy weather, continue to face the foe from the precarious footing of a narrow strip of quite unsheltered coast; for loss of ground may be disastrous on a blustering day when vessels cannot approach the shore. Later in 1915, therefore, and again early in 1916, the army that was at Gallipoli was skilfully withdrawn by General Sir Charles Monro from its dangerous posts, and, as so often in our history, found a safe refuge in our ships.

If the security of India is an essential buttress of our Empire's structure, it is of equal moment that no enemy should be allowed to reach the delta of the Nile. For once in this place the foe can not only close the nearest routes from England to her possessions in the East; but rumour of our retreat might quickly rouse against us the millions living in the broad belt of land which stretches from Palestine and Egypt to the Indus, who still hold the tradition of prosperous invasions of the rich plains of Hindustan.

Some ten of the British and Dominion divisions as they left Gallipoli were carried, therefore, eastward to form a strong guard along the Suez Canal. And here the 2/4th Battalion remained even when France, where in future the greatest blows were both to be struck and met, had claimed the services of the larger portion of this force. Since summer heat and drought—and water is one of the essentials of our life—had soon shown that, owing to the physical difficulties which must be overcome, the danger to the safety of the Egyptian delta was no longer such as to require the presence of so many troops.

No sooner had the flame of war gone out on the Gallipoli peninsula than the fire roared up in France, in Lombardy, for the Italians had now joined in with the English and the French, in Serbia, where belated aid was sent by Britain and by France to the weakest of our allies, and never died down until it was finally quenched.

Having meanwhile repulsed the Russians, during the summer and autumn of 1915, far from the Prussian frontier, and driven them over the great plain of Poland, the Germans turned in February, 1916, savagely on the French, and tried at Verdun for almost half a year to beat them down. But Britain was soon to be ready to throw her full weight into the fight to the help of her Allies, to hit with all her might; for the Empire, which at first could send only some ten divisions into the field, could, in 1916, send seventy. And terrible indeed was the blow dealt in the summer and autumn of this year at the first great Battle of the Somme.

Opinions will differ as to which of war's always grievous tasks is the one which is most hard. Valour alone will not help men to make marches like those that were effected in 1914; mere bravery will not carry troops over the top after their courage has been cooled by waiting under the scream and burst of shells, and by tense expectation of the moment, inexorably drawing always more near, when they must go out from the cover of the trench to meet death in the open. In either case only a strong discipline and mutual confidence will give to human nature the requisite support; and it was with their aid that our 1st, 2nd, 6th, 7th, 8th, 10th, and 11th Battalions were enabled to play so glorious a part in what the Germans will long remember as the " blood bath " of that most fierce and long-continued fight. But, although the enemy were gravely hurt, the British and French were far from being unscathed, and failed therefore to win more than a half success.

The Germans, though shaken, had still sufficient power quite to check and then again throw back the Russian troops. Roumania also, who in September had joined our group of Powers, was beaten down, and then experienced the fate which had befallen Serbia by being almost overrun.

The strain of war was now beginning to drag heavily on all the fighters, and Britain and her Dominions and Allies proposed therefore, in 1917, to make great efforts to end the conflict. This was to be done by means of " a series of offensives on all fronts, so timed as to assist each other by depriving the enemy of the power of weakening any one of the fronts in order to reinforce another." The Russians, however, tired of an inefficiency that sent men into battle without even arms in their hands, replaced in March the Government of the Czar by a Republic, and therefore were not in a condition to make the most vigorous efforts in the fighting. The Italians were still not ready to play their part when in April the British first, and then the French, began to strike. The French stroke failed, partly because the counsels were divided, some thinking that the plan was good, others that it was too ambitious. And when France drooped England at once went to the assistance of her wounded friend by showering blows which drew off the attention of the foe. At Arras, Scarpe, Messines, and other actions our 6th, 7th, 8th, and 10th Battalions were sent, therefore, again and again into stubborn battle. The 1st fought both at Arras and at Scarpe, the 11th at Messines; and later on men of the 1st, 2nd, 3/4th, and 7th Battalions also waded desperately through the deep mud round Ypres to reach the German lines; and once again " our new and hastily trained armies " then showed " that they were capable of beating the enemy's best troops," yet could not finally defeat them.

But worse still was to come, for in October the Austrians, with German help, dealt the Italians so staggering a reverse that Britain and France were called on urgently to give willing support to their Allies. Our 2nd, 10th, and 11th Battalions were, in consequence, quickly moved with others to Lombardy, and here they held the line on the cold foot-hills of the Alps.

To make an attack is always the best defence, and Egypt, where some of our troops were during all this time on guard, could evidently best be protected, not by waiting on the slow movements of the Turks, but by chasing their forces far from its border-line. A not greatly vigorous advance made by the Turks in August, 1916, was, therefore, first repulsed, and when our preparations were complete the 2/4th Battalion was one of those who swept the enemy back out of the Sinai peninsula and over the frontier into Palestine. Hard hammerings had now been given to the Turks both by the Allies at Gallipoli, by Russia in the snowy uplands of Armenia, and on the hot banks of the Tigris by the Anglo-Indian force. The losses sustained by the Turks in these theatres of war seemed so much to have weakened them that, when it was still our hope shortly to end the war, it was decided, in the spring of 1917, that the time had come to wrest Jerusalem from their grasp and win it again for Christendom.

At first our effort was in vain. But in November the 2/4th patiently marching, under a burning sky and in the half-suffocating dust of a dry, barren, rolling land, took part in actions which first won Gaza; and then towards the very end of the year the Holy City itself. And Britain, holding Jerusalem, and Baghdad too, could cheer the spirits of the people by pointing to these as outward signs, at any rate, of partial victory.

The Russians had now almost ceased to fight, Roumania and Serbia had been crushed, Italy had received a crippling wound, and Germany and her allies had stretched the frontiers of their arms over the whole centre of the European continent. But as a counterpoise, or more than a counterpoise, the United States, obliged to go to war by the brutal disregard of German submarine commanders of the right of American subjects to sail safely on the sea, had joined the Western Powers. And not a single one of all Germany's great successes had served materially to lessen the dead-weight pressure of our naval blockade, for she had tried, but altogether failed, to weaken the firm hold that was kept by our fleet upon all movement over the seas.

The best remaining hope of victory, therefore, for the Germans, before starvation either forced surrender, or America's great armies could reach the Western Front, was through such a success as would break up the main land forces of the British and French. Germany collected, then, during the winter of 1917-1918, masses of troops, among them forty divisions freed from the Russian front, for this attack; in which it was designed " to shake the hostile edifice by closely connected partial blows in such a way that sooner or later the whole structure would collapse." At the same time Britain, following indeed the example of other belligerent Powers, had unfortunately been obliged to lower the establishment of her divisions. For she was now no longer able both to sustain the Navy and also a great merchant fleet in which was carried over the ocean not only food and raw materials for her own people, but reinforcements and munitions needed for all the many fronts of war, and also troops that had been raised in the United States; to build ships to replace those that were sunk at sight by the commanders of German submarines; to manufacture munitions, clothing and other requisites both for her own armies and for those of her allies; and to find men to fill the great gaps in the formations that were in the field, caused by the rapid waste of war. Opinion also, despairing after so many disappointments of a decision on the wide front in France, had again begun to veer towards the belief that further to the east, in Palestine or Macedonia, might still be found our enemy's most vulnerable point; and proposals were made for the dispatch in this direction of forces drawn from the weakened British armies that were on the Western Front.

The first great German blow fell in March, 1918, upon the right wing of the British line which stood in the area to the east of Amiens, and knocked all these opinions quite out of our minds. The troops of our Fifth Army were nearly overwhelmed, among them the 7th and 8th The Queen's, who fought as the 1st Battalion had fought in 1914; the line bent back and almost broke, and Britain was now obliged to lean heavily upon France. Thanks to stubborn courage; to the ready assistance of the French; to that of reinforcements, including the 10th The Queen's, who had returned from Italy at the beginning of March; and to the fact that our Third Army resisted strong attacks, the 6th The Queen's were among these troops, and the 11th, who had also come back from Italy; the line, though deeply dinted, did not give way.

The other blows, one directed against the British front near Armentières, where the 1st, 6th and 10th The Queen's were in the fighting, another on the area that was held between Soissons and Reims by French and British troops, met with no greater success. The sting had by this time largely gone out of the enemy's thrusts; fresh British troops, including the 2/4th The Queen's from Palestine, had reached our armies in France, clearly the vulnerable point; and numbers of Americans—one of whose battalions was attached for instruction to our 11th Battalion—would soon be ready to take the field. In the second half of July, therefore, the French Marshal, Foch, who was in chief command of all the allied forces serving on the French front, hurled French, British (our 2/4th Battalion took a strong part) and Americans in combination against the German formations standing in a deep bulge between Soissons and Château Thierry which had been driven into our line six weeks before.

This sudden, able stroke obtained a great success, and the enemy, crowded and confined in a narrow space, and so unable fully to use their strength, were soon forced back across the River Aisne. The turning-point had now been passed. Within three months our 1st, 2/4th, 6th, 7th, 8th, 10th, and 11th Battalions, advancing with strong and steady purpose, in spite of barbed wire, in face of well-handled machine guns, had helped to break through both the great Hindenburg line of defence and all the maze of trenches extending to the north of it, that had so long been an insuperable bar to all our efforts to drive the Germans from North-Eastern France. These blows were sharply followed up on the whole of the allied front in France, and at the same time great victories were also won in Italy, where the 2nd Battalion was still serving, in Serbia, in Palestine, and in far-distant

Mesopotamia; for everywhere the enemy's armies were crumbling and their best troops were giving way.

In late October and early in November men of our 1st and 7th Battalions were advancing over the battlefield of Le Cateau, and forcing their way in the thick woodland of the Mormal Forest, places at or near which the old small army had fought so desperately four years before. And on November 11th, when our greatest enemy collapsed, hard conditions were granted to the Germans, whose confederates in Austria, Bulgaria and Turkey either already had sought or were about to beg for peace.

Peace, then, was won—well won—freedom and safety; and peace has held for most but not for all of the Battalions of The Queen's, since in our widespread Empire peace rarely reigns supreme. The 2nd Battalion, therefore, soon found itself again in war, defending the Indian marches against the hardy, restless tribesmen of Waziristan—a petty war, perhaps, in contrast with the gigantic struggle that had just closed.

Still war persists, and who can see the end of it? This tale of which our Regimental mottoes are the epitome, of suffering and of courage, of hardship stoutly borne, of death most bravely faced, of sacrifices gladly made, must therefore rouse not only admiration and wonder at the deeds, but something more. A strong resolve, whenever England's safety shall be threatened, her rights again assailed, to follow in the unfaltering footsteps of those who served and marched, who toiled and fought throughout this deadly, long-drawn struggle, this so far greatest war.

*W. D. Bird*

# CONTENTS

CHAP.                                                       PAGE

## 1st BATTALION.

| | | |
|---|---|---|
| I. | 1904–1914 | 1 |
| II. | THE OPENING OF THE WAR | 10 |
| III. | THE BATTLE OF LOOS | 28 |
| IV. | THE BATTLE OF THE SOMME | 38 |
| V. | THE BATTLE OF ARRAS—THE THIRD BATTLE OF YPRES | 49 |
| VI. | THE BATTLE OF THE LYS AND THE VICTORY BATTLES | 61 |
| VII. | DEMOBILIZATION AND RECONSTRUCTION | 76 |

## 2nd BATTALION.

| | | |
|---|---|---|
| VIII. | THE FIRST BATTLE OF YPRES | 81 |
| IX. | THE SECOND BATTLE OF YPRES AND THE BATTLE OF LOOS | 94 |
| X. | THE BATTLE OF THE SOMME | 101 |
| XI. | THE BATTLES OF ARRAS—THE FLANDERS OFFENSIVE | 109 |
| XII. | THE CAMPAIGN IN ITALY AND THE END OF THE WAR | 118 |
| XIII. | HOME SERVICE—INDIA—OPERATIONS IN WAZIRISTAN | 127 |

## THE 1st/4th BATTALION.

| | | |
|---|---|---|
| XIV. | THE MOHMAND, WAZIRISTAN, AND AFGHAN OPERATIONS | 137 |

## THE 2nd/4th BATTALION.

| | | |
|---|---|---|
| XV. | GALLIPOLI AND EGYPT | 147 |
| XVI. | PALESTINE AND FRANCE | 157 |

## THE 3rd/4th BATTALION.

| | | |
|---|---|---|
| XVII. | HOME SERVICE AND FRANCE | 170 |

## THE 1st/5th BATTALION.

| | | |
|---|---|---|
| XVIII. | INDIA AND MESOPOTAMIA | 178 |

## THE 6th (SERVICE) BATTALION.

| | | |
|---|---|---|
| XIX. | THE BATTLE OF LOOS AND THE BATTLE OF THE SOMME | 188 |
| XX. | BATTLE OF ARRAS—BATTLE OF CAMBRAI—THE VICTORY BATTLES | 198 |

## THE 7th (SERVICE) BATTALION.

| | | |
|---|---|---|
| XXI. | THE BATTLE OF THE SOMME, 1916 | 211 |
| XXII. | THE ARRAS OFFENSIVE—THE BATTLE OF YPRES | 220 |

| CHAP. | | PAGE |
|---|---|---|
| | **THE 8TH (SERVICE) BATTALION.** | |
| XXIII. | THE BATTLE OF LOOS—THE BATTLE OF THE SOMME—THE BATTLE OF ARRAS—THE BATTLE OF THE SCARPE—THE BATTLE OF CAMBRAI—THE VICTORY BATTLES ... ... ... ... ... | 237 |
| | **THE 10TH (SERVICE) BATTALION.** | |
| XXIV. | THE BATTLE OF THE SOMME, 1916—BATTLE OF ARRAS—THE BATTLE OF MESSINES—THE BATTLE OF YPRES, 1917—THE OFFENSIVE IN PICARDY—THE ADVANCE IN FLANDERS—THE BATTLE OF COURTRAI | 252 |
| | **THE 11TH (SERVICE) BATTALION.** | |
| XXV. | BATTLE OF THE SOMME, 1916—THE BATTLE OF MESSINES—THE BATTLE OF YPRES, 1917—BATTLE OF THE SOMME, 1918—THE BATTLE OF YPRES, 1918—THE BATTLE OF COURTRAI ... ... ... ... | 267 |
| XXVI. | THE LABOUR BATTALIONS—THE YOUNG SOLDIERS' BATTALIONS—UNITS WHICH DID NOT SERVE OVERSEAS ... ... ... ... | 280 |
| POSTSCRIPT. | BY GENERAL SIR CHARLES MONRO, BT., G.C.B., G.C.S.I., G.C.M.G. | 287 |

## APPENDICES.

| I. | PARCELS FOR PRISONERS OF WAR ... ... ... ... ... | 289 |
|---|---|---|
| II. | THE PRISONERS OF WAR, SURREY REGIMENTS, RELIEF FUND ... | 290 |
| III. | WELCOME HOME TO REPATRIATED PRISONERS OF WAR OF THE QUEEN'S REGIMENT, HELD AT GUILDFORD ON JANUARY 24th, 1919 ... ... ... ... ... ... ... ... ... | 291 |
| IV. | REGIMENTAL WAR MEMORIAL ... ... ... ... ... ... | 292 |
| V. | REGIMENTAL OLD COMRADES ASSOCIATION ... ... ... ... | 293 |

# ILLUSTRATIONS

|  |  |
|---|---|
| General Sir Charles Monro, Bt., G.C.B., G.C.S.I., G.C.M.G., Colonel of the Regiment ... | *Frontispiece* |
|  | FACING PAGE |
| 1st Battalion on Mobilization, August, 1914 | 26 |
| 1st Battalion on November 9th, 1914 | 27 |
| The Uniform and Equipment (front and back views) Worn in France and Flanders during the Great War | 50 |
| Wire Defences of the Hindenburg Line near Bellicourt, October, 1918 | 70 |
| Gheluvelt Church | 88 |
| Men of 2nd Battalion at Ablainzeville, March, 1917 | 110 |
| Trenches and Dug-outs on the Banks of River Piave, Italy | 120 |
| Turkish Positions West of Jerusalem | 164 |
| Cavalry Hill, Ramadie, showing the Outpost Line after the Capture of Ramadie, 1917 | 184 |
| Men of the 7th Battalion after reaching their Objective on the Montauban — Mametz Road on the First Day of the Battle of the Somme, 1916 | 194 |
| A View of a portion of a Battlefield, showing Shell Craters filled with Water | 200 |
| General View of the Battlefield leading up to Passchendaele, Boesinghe, August, 1917 | 222 |
| Captured German Trenches on Messines Ridge, June, 1917 | 256 |
| A Communication Trench through a Wood | 268 |
| Regimental War Memorial | 292 |

# MAPS

|  | FACING PAGE |
|---|---|
| BATTLE OF VITTORIO VENETO ... ... ... ... ... ... ... | 122 |
| BATTLE OF SOISSONNAIS-OURCQ ... ... ... ... ... ... | 166 |

# "The Queen's" in the Great War

## CHAPTER I.

### 1st Battalion.

#### 1904–1914.

The fifth volume of Colonel John Davis' monumental history of the Regiment closed with the account of the arrival of the 1st Battalion at Sialkote towards the end of 1904, from which station a detachment of two companies was furnished at Amritsar.

During the hot weather of the year 1905 Headquarters and five companies—" A," " B," " C," " D," and " E," strength 14 officers and 546 warrant and non-commissioned officers and men—were accommodated at Thobba in the Murree Hills, returning early in November to Sialkote whence the Battalion, 907 all ranks, proceeded by rail on the 29th to Rawal Pindi, moving out from there to a concentration camp prior to taking part in manœuvres before His Royal Highness the Prince of Wales. On December 4th a guard of honour, composed of 4 officers and 136 other ranks, was found by the Battalion for duty at the camp of the Commander-in-Chief during the stay there of Their Royal Highnesses the Prince and Princess of Wales. The following letter from the Military Secretary to the Commander-in-Chief was received a few days later by Colonel F. J. Pink, C.M.G., D.S.O. :—

*" The Commander-in-Chief desires me to express to you his high appreciation of the very representative guard of honour furnished by the Battalion under your command during the stay of Their Royal Highnesses the Prince and Princess of Wales at His Excellency's camp.*

*" The manner in which all duties were performed, and the smart and soldierlike bearing of the officers and men at all times, were worthy of the distinguished Regiment to which they belong."*

At the conclusion of the manœuvres and the review which followed them, the Battalion entrained for Sialkote and arrived there on December 11th.

The following are the remarks made by Brigadier-General B. Mahon, C.B., D.S.O., on his inspection of the Battalion, dated March 30th, 1906 :—

*" This is the second time I have had the honour to inspect this grand Regiment. I can say nothing except praise for them. They won the competition for the best Regiment in India last year, and in my opinion are better this year.*

*" The system on which the Regiment is worked is thoroughly good. A very strict discipline is maintained. There is great esprit de corps in the Regiment which is encouraged. The officers of the Regiment are both good at their work and good sportsmen. The Regiment is in every way fit for active service."*

On this Lieutenant-General J. Wodehouse, C.B., C.M.G., commanding 2nd (Rawal Pindi) Division, made the following general observations :—

"*I have nothing to add to Brigadier-General Mahon's expressions of the highest praise of this Regiment.*

"*I have known the Battalion now since 1897 in the field and in cantonments and what Brigadier-General Mahon says is thoroughly well deserved.*"

The summer of this year Headquarters and four companies spent at Barian, and in the succeeding hot weather six companies of the Battalion were accommodated at the same place.

On December 9th, 1907, the Battalion, less two companies which had moved earlier to Delhi, strength 26 officers, 2 warrant officers, 31 sergeants, 16 drummers, 24 corporals, and 509 privates, left Sialkote by rail for Agra, on change of station, arriving there on the 11th; and early in the following year while quartered here the following extract from Army Order No. 208 of 1907 was published in Battalion Orders :—

"*His Majesty the King has been graciously pleased to approve of the dates being added to the honorary distinctions already awarded as enumerated below :—*

\*     \*     \*     \*     \*

"*The Queen's (Royal West Surrey) Regiment.*

"*Ghuznee, 1839.*"

This distinction recalls, of course, one of the leading events of the first Afghan War, when the Regiment took part on July 23rd, 1839, in the storming of the great fortress of Ghuznee, on which occasion 4 men of the Regiment were killed, 6 officers and 27 other ranks were wounded. Rather more than a year later—in the *London Gazette* of July 27th, 1840,—the Regiment, in common with other units concerned, was granted the Honours of " Afghanistan " and " Ghuznee," now followed, sixty-seven years later, by the addition of the year " 1839 " to the last-named Honour.

During the summer of 1908 three companies were sent to Kailana.

The Battalion was now under orders to leave India for Aden, ordinarily the last station for a British infantry battalion preparatory to returning home, and on November 29th the Battalion paraded to enable Lieutenant-General Sir J. Wodehouse to bid farewell to officers and men; then on the 30th Headquarters and six companies (strength, 18 officers and 668 other ranks) left Agra, and embarked at Bombay on December 2nd in the *Rohilla*, arriving on the 8th at Aden, where it relieved the 1st Battalion The Bedfordshire Regiment. The two remaining companies, " B " and " D," remained on at Agra after the departure of the rest of the Battalion, and proceeded on December 6th to Deolali for detachment duty at that station.

Shortly after arrival of Headquarters at Aden, Lieutenant-Colonel A. W. Taylor joined from home and assumed command in relief of Colonel F. J. Pink, C.M.G., D.S.O., who was placed on half-pay on the expiration of his period of command of the Battalion.

At the end of the preceding year the new scheme of Army reorganization devised by Mr. Haldane had been promulgated in Army Orders, and was given effect to in the year 1908. Under this scheme the old Militia was abolished and was thenceforward to be known as the Special Reserve, while the Volunteer Force became the Territorial Force.  These changes, and the rearrangement of the units of the Army to which they gave rise, caused an alteration in the composition of The Queen's (Royal West Surrey) Regiment, and may be seen in the official Army List for July, 1908, and following months.  In the first of these publications we find under the title—

*Line and Militia Battalions.*

1st Battalion ...  ⎫
2nd    ,,    ...  ⎬ 2nd Foot.    3rd Battalion (2nd R. Surrey Militia).

*Volunteer Battalions.*

1st Croydon.                3rd Bermondsey.
2nd Guildford.              4th Kennington Park.

In the August Army List the 3rd Battalion is described as " Special Reserve," and the Volunteer Battalions of the Regiment are reduced from four to two, the 1st and 2nd only being retained and being therein designated as the 4th and 5th Territorial Battalions of The Queen's (Royal West Surrey) Regiment; while in succeeding Army Lists the Bermondsey and Kennington Park Battalions are shown respectively as the 22nd and 24th " County of London Battalions, The London Regiment (The Queen's)," retaining the badge of the Paschal Lamb, and so preserving to the present day their former connection with the parent regiment.

During the year 1909 the Regiment was awarded an addition to a Battle Honour commemorating even earlier war services than those recently recognized, as may be seen from the following extract from Army Order No. 180 of this year :—

*" His Majesty the King has been graciously pleased to approve of the following regiments being permitted, in recognition of services rendered during the operations at Tangier in the years 1662 to 1680, to bear upon their Colours and appointments the distinction (with dates where specified) as follows :—*

\*   \*   \*   \*   \*

" *The Queen's (Royal West Surrey) Regiment.*

" *Tangier, 1662—80,*"

This was followed later in the same year by the receipt of the following announcement contained in War Office Letter No. 6/913/A.G. 1 of November 15th, 1909 :—

" *His Majesty the King has been graciously pleased to approve of the Cypher of Queen Catherine within the Garter being borne on the Regimental Colours of the Queen's (Royal West Surrey) Regiment in place of the Royal Cypher within the Garter.*"

Another War Office letter followed—No. 55 (Infantry) 188, Q.M.G. 7, of November 22nd :—

" *I am commanded by the Army Council to inform you that sanction is given for the addition of a Silver Scroll, bearing the title ' The Queen's,' to the helmet plate worn by the Officers of The Queen's (Royal West Surrey) Regiment.  This Scroll will be placed below the Crown and above the Badge, across the ends of the Laurel Wreath.*"

Again in the same year, in Army Order No. 312, the connection of the Regiment with certain naval actions of past years was recognized in the following:—

"*His Majesty the King has been graciously pleased to approve of the following regiments being permitted, in recognition of services rendered as Marines on board vessels of the British Fleet during engagements stated, to bear upon their Colours a Naval Crown superscribed in each case with the date of the action.*

\* \* \* \* \*

"*The Queen's (Royal West Surrey) Regiment.*
"*Admiral Howe's Victory on the 1st June, 1794.*"

This announcement drew a letter from Captain R. Tupper, A.D.C., and the officers of H.M.S. *Excellent*, "congratulating the Regiment on having received the Honour, '1st June, 1794,' surmounted by a Naval Crown on the Colours," and stating that an entry to this effect had been made in the records of H.M.S. *Excellent*.

The Battalion, having been ordered to England, embarked at Bombay and Aden in the R.I.M. ship *Dufferin* as under:—

At Bombay, on January 26th, 1910, "B" and "D" Companies, strength 6 officers and 174 other ranks, and at Aden, on February 3rd, the remainder of the Battalion, viz., 19 officers and 630 warrant officers, non-commissioned officers and men, embarked, the whole then proceeding to Southampton, which was reached on February 20th. On arrival at Gibraltar on 16th February, the 1st and 2nd Battalions met for the second time, the first meeting having taken place at Malta in 1894. One officer and 206 other ranks were handed over to the 2nd Battalion.

On arrival in England the 1st Battalion proceeded by train to quarters at Warley, and there took over 7 sergeants, 4 corporals and 172 privates, left behind by the 2nd Battalion. Of the 23 officers and 597 other ranks who landed at Southampton, only 1 officer and 7 non-commissioned officers and men had embarked with the Battalion on its departure for foreign service in December, 1891, remaining with it during the whole period of its absence from England, viz., Captain F. B. B. Pickard, Regimental Sergeant-Major Balne, Regimental Quartermaster-Sergeant E. Rattey, Colour-Sergeants Mawditt, Fenn and Stacey, Pioneer-Sergeant Owen and Private W. Rolph.

In this year again Army Orders (No. 45) announced the bestowal of another "Honour" in recognition of services in the old wars in which the British Army was engaged:—

"*His Majesty the King has been graciously pleased to approve of the following regiments being permitted to bear the honorary distinction 'Namur, 1695' upon their Colours, in recognition of services during the siege and capture of that town.*

\* \* \* \* \*

"*The Queen's (Royal West Surrey) Regiment.*"

It will be remembered that at the close of the South African War the health of King Edward had given rise to considerable anxiety, and that certain festivities whereby the making of peace was to have been celebrated had had to be indefinitely postponed. In the years that immediately followed it was hoped that the health of the Sovereign was completely re-established, and that he would be spared to his people for very many years to come to continue his labours for the advancement and general good of his country. Of him indeed all men and women felt—

"In his right hand he carries Gentle Peace ; he is just and fears not :
The ends he aims at are his Country's."

His Majesty had spent the greater part of March and April, 1910, at Biarritz, in order to avoid the risk of bronchitis from the March winds in England, and while abroad he had for at least a week been more seriously ill than the British public suspected; but he seemed to have recovered and returned to London on April 27th. On May 1st he went to Sandringham, where he was confined to his rooms, but continued to transact business as usual, and as he did indeed almost up to the last ; then on the afternoon of May 5th a bulletin was issued stating that his condition " causes some anxiety." By the evening of the day following it was announced that His Majesty's condition was critical, and before midnight it was known that King Edward the Peacemaker had passed away, the announcement being made to a waiting and anxious crowd at the gates of Buckingham Palace, by whom it was received with manifold and heartfelt expressions of grief.

King George V was proclaimed on May 9th, and three days later he issued the following message to his Army :—

*"My beloved Father was always closely associated with the Army by ties of strong personal attachment, and from the first day that he entered the Service he identified himself with everything conducive to its welfare.*

*"On my accession to the Throne I take this the earliest opportunity of expressing to all ranks my gratitude for their gallant and devoted services to him.*

*"Although I have always been interested in the Army, recent years have afforded me special opportunities of becoming more intimately acquainted with our forces both at home and in India, as well as in other parts of the Empire.*

*"I shall watch over your interests and efficiency with continuous and keen solicitude, and shall rely on that spirit of efficiency and devotion which has at all times animated and been the proud tradition of the British Army."*

The funeral of His late Majesty took place on Friday, May 20th, when the 1st Battalion The Queen's proceeded from Warley to Windsor on duty in connection with it, returning the same day to Warley ; and during the lying-in-state in Westminster Hall a detachment of the Battalion was employed.

On May 16th, 1911, a representative detachment composed of 5 officers—Lieutenant-Colonel A. W. Taylor, Major W. J. T. Glasgow, Captain and Adjutant C. E. Koebel, and Second-Lieutenants W. Hayes and R. A. M. Basset—with the Colours and 53 other ranks, took part in the unveiling ceremony of the memorial to Her Most Gracious Majesty the late Queen Victoria, in London, when the following was published :—

*"His Majesty was much pleased with the appearance and steadiness under arms of the representative detachments from the Naval and Military Forces present on that occasion.*

*"The G.O.C.-in-C. has much pleasure in conveying this appreciation of His Majesty to the troops in the Eastern Command. The marching, generally, was very satisfactory, especially in the case of detachments of the 4th Hussars and of the 1st Battalion Royal West Surrey Regiment."*

On June 21st of this year Captain G. H. Neale, Lieutenant B. C. Quill, and

Second-Lieutenant M. W. H. Pain and 50 other ranks representing the Battalion, proceeded to London for duty in connection with the Coronation Ceremonies. While there they were encamped in the Regent's Park and formed part of " C " Composite Battalion, 19th Provisional Infantry Brigade.

During August the Battalion was sent for some three weeks to Leicester on duty connected with the strikes.

In the autumn of 1912 the Battalion left Warley for Bordon, and here in the following March Lieutenant-Colonel D. Warren took over command of the Battalion from Lieutenant-Colonel Taylor, that officer's period of command having come to an end. The 1st Battalion The Queen's was now in the 3rd Infantry Brigade, containing, besides themselves, the 1st Battalion Somersetshire Light Infantry, the 2nd Battalion The Welch Regiment, and the 2nd Battalion The Essex Regiment, commanded by Brigadier-General H. J. S. Landon, C.B., and in the 1st Division, under Major-General S. H. Lomax.

On October 4th, 1913, the Battalion, 381 strong all ranks, was taken by special train from Bordon to Guildford, there to take part in the ceremony of unveiling the window in the Queen's Chapel, Holy Trinity Church, dedicated to the Regiment in commemoration of the 250th anniversary of its formation. The subject of the window, installed at a cost of £315, represents " Three Christian Soldiers ": the centre light—St. Martin—was given by the 1st, 2nd and 3rd Battalions; the one on the left—St. Alban—was presented by all ranks of the Territorial Battalions; while the right-hand light—St. George—was a memorial gift from Colonel A. W. Taylor, lately commanding the 1st Battalion.

The unveiling ceremony was performed by Major-General C. C. Monro, C.B., of the Regiment, and the address was by the Right Rev. the Lord Bishop of Lewes.

For some time past the question of organizing our infantry battalions in fewer and larger companies, in view of the changed conditions of modern warfare, had been much debated, and on October 1st, 1913, under a Special Army Order dated September 16th, 1913, the Battalion was reorganized in four companies, under the new arrangement " A " and " C " Companies becoming " A " Company, " D " and " F " Companies becoming " B " Company, " B " and " H " Companies becoming " C " Company, and " E " and " K " Companies becoming " D " Company.

Then in May, 1914, a Divisional Cyclist Company was formed, when the Battalion furnished it with the following *personnel*—Captain R. G. Clarke in command, Company Sergeant-Major, 4412 Sergeant N. Potter, Company Quartermaster-Sergeant, 6186 Sergeant A. Taylor, and four private soldiers—two cooks, one batman, and one sanitary squad.

On July 25th, 1914, instructions were received that His Majesty had been graciously pleased to approve of the addition of certain dates to the honorary distinctions enumerated below :—

*" The Queen's (Royal West Surrey) Regiment.*
*" Afghanistan, 1839—Pekin, 1860."*

Thus the Regiment was in the act of receiving additions to Honours won in the wars of long ago at the very moment when it was preparing and arming for the greatest war in which during its two hundred and fifty years of splendid history it was to take part, adding to its laurels, acquiring increased honour and very many battle " Honours," and suffering cruel losses.

Throughout the whole of the first four or five months of the year 1914, people in England were wholly taken up with the consideration of their own domestic affairs; there had been a recrudescence of the old trouble in Ireland, and to this there was added a threat of civil war in that country, with the possible result that the British Army might conceivably be called in to redress the balance between the two parties—the men who wanted home rule and those whose only wish was to stay in the Union. There probably has hardly ever been a time in the history of Great Britain when its inhabitants were less concerned with the affairs of Europe than in the spring and early summer of 1914.

The murder at Sarajevo on June 28th of the Archduke Franz Ferdinand, the heir of the Emperor Francis Joseph, and of his consort, seemed a terrible affair enough, but few people, and still fewer Englishmen, perceived in it anything of really international importance, or that it could by any conceivable possibility become the prelude to a war in which nearly all the civilized nations would take part. But it was not long before it became abundantly clear that Austria-Hungary was determined to exploit the murder of the Archduke as a providential chance which made it possible to enlist the sympathy of Europe for an assault on Serbia. The Austrian and Hungarian journals began at once and continued during the next three weeks to pour insults upon Serbia, to proclaim that the Serbian Government was implicated in the murders, and to clamour for war without delay and without further inquiry; but it was not until July 23rd that the Austrian Government addressed what was virtually an ultimatum to the Serbian Cabinet, and the contents of which constituted, less an indictment for complicity in the Sarajevo murders, than a violent complaint that for years past Serbia had been an unfriendly neighbour to Austria.

Nearly a month had gone by between the date of the murders and the presentation of the Austrian ultimatum, but thereafter events moved with really startling rapidity, and within no more than a fortnight practically all the nations of Europe were at war. On July 25th Serbia replied to the Austrian demands, of which two were conceded in full and three in part, and suggesting in regard to the remainder that they should be referred to the International Tribunal of The Hague. It is, however, quite evident that the Austrian Minister in Belgrade had been instructed to declare any reply insufficient which did not amount to an unconditional acceptance of the full terms of the ultimatum, for the Minister and Legation staff left the Serbian capital within an hour after the handing in of the reply; while on July 27th the Vienna Cabinet published a document stating the Serbian terms to be unacceptable and declaring war.

In the meantime Sir Edward Grey, the British Foreign Minister, had made proposals for convening a conference of Ambassadors to discuss the matters in dispute, but Germany had refused to attend, and it now seeming impossible that the coming war could be prevented or even localized, Russia on July 28th mobilized fourteen of her army corps nearest to the Austrian frontier.

On August 1st the European situation became more menacing, for Germany had proposed mobilization and had dispatched an ultimatum to Russia; on the 3rd Germany declared war on France; and on the 4th a Royal Proclamation was issued in London calling out the Army Reserve and announcing the embodiment of the Territorial Force; while on the same day the British Cabinet demanded of the German Government an unequivocal assurance that the neutrality of Belgium would be respected, a satisfactory reply to be returned by midnight.

While these events were transpiring, the 1st Battalion The Queen's was in camp for brigade training at Rushmoor, near Aldershot, whither it had gone on June 29th; but about midday on August 1st sudden orders were issued to return to Bordon at once, and at 6 p.m. on the 4th the order for General Mobilization was issued. By Wednesday morning early, August 5th, all men knew that Germany had refused to give the assurance demanded of her by the British Cabinet, and that the two countries were consequently in a state of war.

On August 4th a council of war, attended by Field-Marshal Sir John French, the Commander-in-Chief designate of the Expeditionary Force, had been held in Downing Street, and it was decided that in the event of war a cavalry division and four infantry divisions should be sent to the assistance of France to operate on the left flank of the armies of the Republic, and that their detraining area should be between Maubeuge and Le Cateau.

The Expeditionary Force which proceeded to France in the early days of August consisted of a cavalry division under Major-General Allenby, of the I Army Corps, containing the 1st and 2nd Infantry Divisions, under Lieutenant-General Sir Douglas Haig, and of the II Army Corps, composed of the 3rd and 5th Divisions, commanded at the outset by Lieutenant-General Sir James Grierson, who was succeeded in command of the Army Corps, on his death very shortly after arrival in France, by General Sir Horace Smith-Dorrien.

The Battalion was still in the 3rd Infantry Brigade, under the same commander, but the Brigade was now composed of the 1st Battalions of The Queen's, the South Wales Borderers and the Gloucester Regiment, and the 2nd Battalion The Welch Regiment.

August 5th was the first day of actual mobilization, though a condition of so-called "Emergency Mobilization" had existed during the preceding forty-eight hours. On the evening of this day conferences of officers were held to ascertain the extent of the Battalion's readiness for war, and late that night 450 reservists joined from the Depot. On the afternoon of the following day 130 more reservists arrived, and by 5 p.m. on the 7th mobilization was completed and a report made to Brigade headquarters, the Battalion being the first in the Brigade to be ready.

On the 8th the Battalion was sent by wings to the rifle range, where all the men of the Reserve fired a modified course, and next day The Queen's marched out to Oxney to practise an attack; and in such manner the two following days were passed, Major-General Sir E. O. F. Hamilton, K.C.B., the Colonel of the Regiment, visiting Bordon on the 11th and addressing the Battalion.

"The Battalion paraded in two parties for the rail journey," we read in the diary of an officer then serving, under date of August 12th, "the right half ('A' and 'B' Companies) at 9 a.m., and the left half ('C' and 'D') at 10.30 a.m. The greatest secrecy was maintained as to our destination, and even the engine-driver did not know, when leaving Bordon, where we were due to embark. Eventually we reached Southampton at about 2 p.m. and commenced to embark on board the s.s. *Braemar Castle*. Curiously enough, it was in this ship that the 2nd Battalion had gone out to Gibraltar in December, 1909. After we were all on board, the 2nd Battalion The Welch Regiment and the Headquarters 3rd Infantry Brigade also embarked in the same boat, and we were packed like herrings in a barrel. . . The approaches to the docks had been screened by high hoardings, so that the

## 1st BATTALION LEAVES FOR FRANCE

general public could not see what troops were being moved by rail. Eventually our ship left the wharf at 8.15 p.m., and passed down an unbuoyed channel through a boom and a minefield to the open sea. At first we were escorted by destroyers, but later on we were left to ourselves."

The 1st Battalion The Queen's embarked for the Great War at a strength of 27 officers, 6 warrant officers, 44 sergeants, 42 corporals, 16 drummers, and 863 privates.

The following are the names of the officers who accompanied the Battalion, and it may be seen how heavy were the losses sustained by the commissioned ranks, and within how very short a time the officer-corps of the Battalion had to be wholly reconstructed.

Lieutenant-Colonel D. Warren, in command : killed, September 17th, 1914.
Major H. C. Pilleau, D.S.O. : died of wounds, September 19th, 1914.
Captain C. E. Wilson : killed, September 17th, 1914.
Captain and Bt. Major E. B. Mathew-Lannowe : wounded, September 14th, 1914.
Captain M. G. Heath : wounded, September 14th, 1914 ; killed, September 25th, 1915.
Captain A. E. McNamara : wounded, September 14th, 1914.
Captain C. F. Watson : wounded, 1918.
Captain S. F. Stanley-Creek : wounded, September 14th, 1914 ; killed, October 31st, 1914.
Captain H. N. A. Hunter : wounded, October 23rd, 1914.
Captain F. C. Longbourne : wounded, October 11th, 1914.
Lieutenant R. L. Q. Henriques : killed, September 14th, 1914.
Lieutenant M. V. Foy : killed, October 13th, 1914.
Lieutenant B. M. Kenny : wounded, September 14th, 1914.
Lieutenant R. S. Pringle : died of wounds, September 17th, 1914.
Lieutenant J. D. Boyd.
Lieutenant M. W. H. Pain : wounded, August 26th, 1914.
Lieutenant W. Hayes : wounded, September 14th, 1914 ; died 1918.
Lieutenant H. E. Iremonger : wounded, September 17th, 1914.
Second-Lieutenant E. D. Drew : wounded, September 18th, 1914.
Second-Lieutenant F. M. Eastwood : killed, October 29th, 1914.
Second-Lieutenant H. B. Strong : killed, October 30th, 1914.
Second-Lieutenant T. O. M. Buchan : wounded, October 29th, 1914.
Second-Lieutenant H. J. P. Thompson : wounded, September 26th, 1914.
Second-Lieutenant C. Bushell : wounded, September 14th, 1914 ; killed, August 8th, 1917.
Second-Lieutenant V. Cooper : Evacuated sick, September 6th, 1914.
Lieut. and Quartermaster G. H. Wallis : died of wounds, September 20th, 1918.
Captain A. M. Rose, R.A.M.C. : taken prisoner, October 31st, 1914.

The following warrant officers accompanied the Battalion :—No. 4283 Regimental Sergeant-Major C. J. M. Elliott, No. 4537 Regimental Quartermaster-Sergeant R. Nevins, Company Sergeant-Majors Nos. 5225 A. Stemp, 5033 E. Sweeney, 5311 P. Foster, and 5736 A. Hodgson, Company Quartermaster-Sergeants Nos. 3275 A. McArtney, 4858 A. Perkins, 5625 J. F. Grundy and 5218 W. H. Bush.

Maps 1, 2, 3, 5, 6 and 7.

## CHAPTER II.

### 1st BATTALION (*continued*).

### 1914.

#### THE OPENING OF THE WAR.

##### BATTLE HONOURS:
"Mons," "Retreat from Mons."
"Marne, 1914," "Aisne, 1914," "Ypres, 1914," "Langemarck, 1914," "Gheluvelt."

LE HAVRE was reached soon after 9 a.m. on August 13th, and the unloading of all baggage, transport, etc., began immediately and went on steadily until about five in the afternoon, when the Battalion fell in and marched some eight miles, the Drums playing, to No. 6 Camp—most of the way through crowds of enthusiastic French men, women and children, who became tremendously excited when the drums and fifes struck up the "Marseillaise." March discipline suffered somewhat from the crowd rushing in and shaking hands all the way, shouting "Guillaume fineesh," and drawing their forefingers across their throats in token that this unpopular potentate was as good as done for!

The heat was very great, and some of the reservists, who were unused to marching and had not worn a pack since their soldiering days, found the eight miles to camp about as much as they could manage, but not a man fell out.

There was a battalion parade at 10 a.m. on the 14th, when the King's message to his troops was read out, and copies of Field-Marshal Lord Kitchener's letter were distributed to all present. The former ran as follows:—

"*You are leaving home to fight for the safety and honour of my Empire.*

"*Belgium, whose country we are pledged to defend, has been attacked, and France is about to be invaded by the same powerful foe.*

"*I have implicit confidence in you, my soldiers. Duty is your watchword, and I know your duty will be nobly done.*

"*I shall follow your every movement with deepest interest and mark with eager satisfaction your daily progress; indeed, your welfare will never be absent from my thoughts.*

"*I pray God to bless you and guard you and bring you back victorious.*"

The letter from Lord Kitchener, who on August 6th had been appointed Secretary of State for War, to the intense satisfaction of the nation, was as under:—

"*You are ordered abroad as a soldier of the King to help our French comrades against the invasion of a common enemy. You have to perform a task which will need your courage, your energy, your patience. Remember that the honour of the British Army depends on your individual conduct.*

"*It will be your duty not only to set an example of discipline and perfect steadiness under fire, but also to maintain the most friendly relations with those whom you are helping in this struggle. The operations in which you are engaged will, for the most part, take place in a friendly country, and you can do your own country no better service than in showing yourself in France and Belgium in the true character of a British soldier.*

## MOVING UP TO THE FRONT

*" Be invariably courteous, considerate and kind. Never do anything likely to injure or destroy property, and always look upon looting as a disgraceful act. You are sure to meet with a welcome and to be trusted; your conduct must justify that welcome and that trust.*

*" Your duty cannot be done unless your health is sound, so keep constantly on your guard against any excesses. In this new experience you may find temptations both in wine and women. You must entirely resist both temptations, and, while treating all women with perfect courtesy, you should avoid any intimacy.*

*" Do your duty bravely.*

*" Fear God.*

*" Honour the King."*

The Commanding Officer also addressed the Battalion and spoke of the probable hardships which all ranks would have to face, saying that The Queen's were expected to do so cheerfully and without grumbling.

At 3 o'clock on the morning of the 15th the Battalion marched from camp in heavy rain, but again through cheering crowds, entrained at Havre station at 5.30, leaving some four hours later, the whole Battalion in one long train, for " an unknown destination." Rouen was passed through at 1 p.m., Amiens at 7 p.m., and Arras at 10 o'clock at night, finally arriving at 2.30 a.m. on August 16th at Le Nouvion, where the train was left, and after some three hours' rest the Battalion marched to Leschelles, where all were accommodated in billets.

" On the 14th and following days," we read in the Official History of the War,* " the troops began to move up by train to the areas of concentration, which were arranged so that the army was assembled in a pear-shaped area between Maubeuge and Le Cateau, about twenty-five miles long from north-east to south-west, and averaging ten miles wide. The cavalry was at the north-eastern end, ready to join hands with the Fifth French Army.

" In detail the areas were :—

" I Corps : East of Bohain ; Headquarters, Wassigny.

       1st Division : Boué, Esqueheries, Leschelles.

       2nd Division : Grougis, Mennevret, Hannappes."

The village of Leschelles was divided into four company sectors, and outposts were mounted in the outlying portions ; an officers' mess was established in an estaminet in the centre of the village, and the afternoon was spent in lecturing the men on the methods of challenging in the French and German armies as compared with ours. The night passed quietly, though there was some firing in the sector occupied by the South Wales Borderers.

August 17th, 18th and 19th were spent in Leschelles, but on the 20th the Battalion marched by way of Le Nouvion and Barzy to Le Sart in readiness for the general advance which was to commence on the day following, and for which orders were issued this evening. " The general effect of these orders when executed would be that on August 23rd the Army would be aligned on a front, roughly facing north-east, from Estinne-au-Mont (near Binche) on the south-east to Lens, eight miles north of Mons, on the north-west, with the Cavalry Division on the left ; while the 5th Cavalry Brigade, having covered the right flank during the movement, would find itself finally in advance of the right front. The daily moves were to be as follows :—

" . . . Covered by the cavalry, the rest of the Army was to advance :

\* Vol. I, pp. 47, 48.

"On the 21st the I Corps to the line Avesnes—Landrecies; on the 22nd north-east to the line Hautmont—Hargnies; on the 23rd the I Corps was to incline north-east and come up on the right of the II, on a line from Estinne-au-Mont west to Harmignies (immediately south-east of Spiennes)."*

Leaving Le Sart at 7.15 a.m. on the 21st, the Battalion marched fourteen miles through Barzy, Beaurepaire, Cartignies and Dompierre to Les Bodelez, and then, moving off next morning at 5 o'clock, the Battalion marched through St. Aubin and along the main north road towards Maubeuge; this march was almost entirely on the cobbles and was very trying, the more so that the men had started without food, and got their first meal that day at 1 p.m. The march was resumed at 3.30 to Bettignies, where a halt was called, and where for the first time distant artillery fire was distinctly audible. At 6.45 the Battalion moved on again, crossed the frontier into Belgium within the next half-hour, and reached Croix—Rouveroy at 7.45, finding billets in "several good barns with plenty of straw in them."

Soon after 3 a.m. on the 23rd the 1st Battalion The Queen's began entrenching a line 300 yards to the north of the Convent and on a ridge immediately north of the village, the remainder of the 3rd Brigade being also entrenched some 800 yards in front, and by 2.30 p.m. the trenches were completed and head cover provided.

"The ground on which the British Army had taken up its position is a narrow belt of coalfield which extends roughly for rather more than twenty miles west from Maurage (six miles east of Mons) along the Mons Canal, and has an average breadth, from the Canal south, of two miles. South of this belt the country gradually rises to a great tract of rolling chalk downs, cut into by many streams and with numerous outlying spurs. . . . In describing the general disposition of the troops, it must be remembered that, as the Army had halted whilst in the course of wheeling or forming to face towards Nivelles, the front of the I Corps was already turned north-east, whereas the II Corps, upon the wheeling flank, still mainly faced to the north. The general front, therefore, formed an obtuse angle, the I Corps being on the right half of the south-eastern arm, and the II Corps round the apex and along the western arm. The south-eastern arm from Peissant to Mons was about ten miles long, and the arm along the Canal from Mons to Condé seventeen miles. The I Corps was extended, roughly speaking, from the Sambre to the Haine; the 1st Division being on the right, with the 3rd Infantry Brigade in front between Peissant and Haulchin (about four miles); the 1st (Guards) Brigade in rear of its right at Grand Reng and Vieux Reng; and the 2nd Infantry Brigade in rear of its left at Villers Sire Nicole and Rouveroy." †

Up till about 2 p.m. on August 23rd all remained quiet opposite the I Corps, the front of which was held by the 3rd and 6th Infantry Brigades. "Throughout the afternoon," so we learn from the private diary of an officer of the Battalion, "a continuous artillery duel was in progress on our left front in the vicinity of Mons, where the 2nd Division was being hotly engaged. . . . At 6 p.m. orders were received to reinforce the 2nd Infantry Brigade on the Mons front. We moved along to the left flank for about a mile, and then forward to a position about a quarter of a mile from the town of Mons. Here we lay in an open field awaiting orders, but dusk came on and the firing gradually died down. Eventually the Battalion returned to its original position for the night.

"August 24th. The whole Battalion manned the trenches at 3 a.m., and shortly afterwards the 3rd Infantry Brigade started to withdraw, covered by our

\* Official History, Vol. I, pp. 49, 50.   † Official History, Vol. I, pp. 52-64.

Battalion. This was our first experience of being under shell fire, but all the bursts were well over our heads and aimed at the batteries behind us. All three of the other battalions of the Brigade were clear by 7.30 a.m. At 8.15 a small Uhlan patrol was fired on by 'B' Company, on the left of the Battalion line; all the men of the patrol except one were hit, as they had been allowed to ride to within about 400 yards of our trenches. The medical officer rode out to examine these scouts, and found that all three were dead; he had to finish off the horses, which had only been badly wounded. Shortly after 8.30 a.m. 'D' Company received the order to withdraw, being the last to do so, and the whole Battalion was soon on the move, having suffered no casualties. My platoon retired through the Convent grounds, and shells were bursting in the village just behind us as we left it. Cooper, who had sprained his ankle, was obliged to remain in the Convent for another hour, when he got a lift with some of the nursing sisters in a trap, just as the German infantry were approaching the village. The retreat, which was to take us south of Paris, had begun."

Passing through Bettignies, the Battalion spent the night of the 24th-25th in billets in Neuf Mesnil, and then, resuming the retreat on the 25th, marched through Hautmont, Limont Fontaine, St. Rémy, Dompierre and Marbaix to Le Grand Fayt, where the Brigade had no sooner settled down than there was an alarm that German cavalry was in the vicinity, and all had to turn out again and occupy alarm posts until it was established that the rumour was a false one. "Rouse" was at a very early hour on the 26th, when all the packs and greatcoats were packed on lorries and sent in charge of the Drum-Major to Etreux, while the Brigade moved off in accordance with orders received overnight from Sir John French, which directed the I Corps to march to the Busigny area; but it immediately received fresh instructions to move on Favril and reinforce the 4th (Guards) Brigade, which had been fighting all night at Landrecies, and the 3rd Brigade eventually entrenched itself at Sambreton to cover the retirement of the Guards, who came through the position taken up in the course of the morning. At 2 p.m. the Battalion was ordered to fall back by companies, and did so in the order "B," "C," "A," "D," handing over the duties of rear-guard to the Scots Greys, of the 5th Cavalry Brigade, and then marching off through La Groise to Oisy, the fatigue of the march being heightened by the troops and transport all moving along the road in three columns. At Oisy the men bivouacked in a field, while the officers were in a large barn.

Our diarist remarks that "Pain was mistaken for a German spy to-day and got shot in the arm by a Frenchman when leading our transport; this was our first casualty among the officers."

"The position of the I Corps on the night of the 26th was in and around Etreux; in detail as follows:—

       1st Division: Fesmy, Petit Cambresis, Oisy.
       2nd Division: Etreux, Venerolles.
       5th Cavalry Brigade: Hannappes.
       Corps Headquarters: one and a half miles east of Hannappes.

"The II Corps and the 4th Division and remaining cavalry brigades were eighteen miles to the west, in retreat south-west to the Oise, on the front of St. Quentin—Le Catelet."*

* Official History, Vol. I, pp. 205, 206.

The march on August 28th was a long and tiring one—first through La Groise, then retracing their steps through that town to cover the retreat of the 1st Division, and so through Oisy, Guise and Montigny to Bernot, marching continuously from early morning until 11.15 at night with only one halt of twenty minutes, and covering in all some twenty-seven miles. There was, however, no respite: the Battalion was roused early on August 28th to trench a position immediately north of Bernot, and dug hard until midday, when it was relieved by the 2nd Royal Sussex, of the 2nd Brigade, and continued the retirement through Ribemont and Sery to Brissy, the German guns opening on the village of Bernot and the trenches within half an hour of the Battalion evacuating them. At Brissy there was a halt for two and a half hours, when most officers and men enjoyed a bathe in a very muddy tributary of the Oise, and then, moving on, did another seventeen miles to Barisis, arriving there at 5.15 on the morning of the 29th, and all, utterly wearied out, falling down asleep on the road until billets were allotted.

"The inhabitants of the villages through which we passed to-day," writes an officer of the Battalion, "were particularly resentful at our continued retirement, and one could catch many remarks to the effect that we were running away and leaving them to the mercy of the Germans. The whole of this march was carried out without leaving a single man behind. The officers had to kick the men awake after every halt, for they just dropped on the ground and were asleep at once. . . . At 5 p.m. on the 29th we paraded and rejoined the Brigade at Bertaucourt, where we bivouacked for the night."

And so the great retreat went on from day to day, the 1st Battalion The Queen's marching on August 30th by Gobain and Septvaux to Brancourt; on the next day to Missy through Anizy, Pinon and Soissons; on September 1st through the forest of Villers Cotterets to the neighbourhood of Le Ferté Milon, moving off again at 12.45 a.m. on the 2nd, after no more than two and a half hours' sleep in some straw, by Mareuil sur Ourcq and Varinfroy to Crégy; on the 3rd the Marne was crossed near Germigny, whence the Battalion moved on to Sammeron, "A" Company, under Captain Heath, remaining behind to cover the party preparing the bridge for demolition, and so on to Perreuse Château. On the 4th the march was to Mouroux through Aulnoy, and thence in the evening to a bivouac south of Coulommiers; and on the 5th via Maupertuis to Rozoy, where at long last the retreat from Mons came to an end and the British Army turned upon its pursuers.

At Rozoy Lieutenant W. A. Phillips joined the Battalion with the first reinforcement of 90 non-commissioned officers and men.

"The retreat of the British Expeditionary Force had continued, with only one halt, for thirteen days over a distance as the crow flies of 136 miles, and, as the men marched, at least 200 miles, and that after two days' strenuous marching in advance to the Mons Canal. The mere statement of the distance gives no measure of the demands made upon the physical and moral endurance of the men, and but little idea of the stoutness with which they had responded to these demands. . . . The troops suffered under every disadvantage. The number of reservists in the ranks was on an average over one-half of the full strength, and the units were, owing to the force of circumstances, hurried away to the area of concentration before all ranks could resume acquaintance with their officers and comrades, and re-learn their business as soldiers. Arrived there, they were hastened forward by forced marches to the battle, confronted with greatly superior numbers of the most renowned army in Europe, and condemned at the very outset to undergo the severest ordeal which can be imposed upon an army. They were short of food and sleep when they began their retreat; they continued it, always short of food and sleep, for thirteen days, as has been told; and at the end they were still an army, and a formidable army. They were never demoralized, for they rightly judged that they had never been beaten."*

The British Army in its advance was now to operate over a very open, highly cultivated country, dotted with woods and villages, and cut into from east to west by the deep valleys of the following rivers—the Grand and Petit Morin, the Marne, the Ourcq, the Vesle, the Aisne and the Ailette—none of them passable except at the bridges. The I Corps Operation Orders of September 5th stated that the front allotted to the Corps was from La Chapelle Iger to Lumigny, that the advance would be made on the 6th in the general direction of Montmirail, and that by 9 a.m. the 1st Division front would be from Courpalay to Rozoy, with one infantry brigade in reserve behind the right flank.

The Battalion marched off at 7 a.m. on the 6th as advanced guard to the 3rd Brigade, " D " Company under Captain Watson forming the point; but the march had been no more than an hour in progress when the farm of Les Hauts Grés was reached and the Battalion was directed to halt here and put the farm in a state of defence, the reason being that the cavalry of the advance had come up against a body of German infantry with guns and had been checked some two miles east of Rozoy.

At 3.30 p.m. Sir John French ordered the I Corps to advance to a line just short of the Grand Morin, from Marolles to Les Parichets, and at 4.30 the 3rd Brigade was directed to move forward again and take the village of Vaudoy, which was captured without opposition before dusk, The Queen's taking up an outpost position on the north of it. Then on September 7th and 8th the Battalion marched on by Dagny, Chevru, Coffery, Choisy, La Boullaise, Jouy, Camp Martin and Grand Marché to Hondevillers, where the second reinforcement, composed of 10 per cent. of the personnel who had been left at the base, 92 strong, arrived under Lieutenant F. W. H. Denton and Second-Lieutenant F. P. S. Rawson.

The orders issued on the night of the 8th directed the continuation of the northward advance of the British Army, and it had been expected that the enemy would offer a stubborn resistance on the line of the Marne; but later reports showed that the Germans were moving hurriedly northward, and had not even destroyed the bridges except at three places; and by early morning of September 9th the cavalry of the British Expeditionary Force had seized the bridges at Nogent, Charly and Azy. By 7.30 a.m. The Queen's, the leading battalion of the 3rd Brigade, the advanced guard of the 1st Division, had crossed the Marne at Nogent, followed by the Welch Regiment and South Wales Borderers, the last-named then going through and crowning the heights north of the river, and by 10.15 a.m. the 3rd Brigade had pushed on to Beaurepaire Farm, two and a half miles north of Charly, without seeing any sign of the enemy. The I Corps was now ordered to halt for a time until the situation could be cleared up, and did not advance again until 3 p.m., when both divisions moved forward until their heads reached the vicinity of the Château Thierry—Montreuil road at Le Thiolet and Coupru respectively. In this night's orders the Army was directed to continue the pursuit northwards, attacking the enemy wherever met, the I Corps to move by Le Thiolet, Lucy le Bocage, Torcy, Priez and Neuilly St. Front.

* Official History, Vol. I, pp. 260, 261.

There was heavy rain in the early hours of the 10th, and The Queen's did not move till 8 a.m., when they marched through Lucy, Torcy and Courchamps, and then, turning east, through Priez to Sommelans. The march of the next day was by Grisolles, Rocourt and Coincy to Villeneuve, and the weather having now turned very wet, the roads were heavy and the bivouacs most uncomfortable. The orders for September 12th were that the march of the Army should be continued to the Aisne, that all crossing-places should be seized and the high ground on the northern side of the river secured, the I Corps marching by Rocourt, Fère-en-Tardenois, Loupeigne, Bazoches, Longueval and Bourg on the eastern, and via Latilly, Ouchy le Château, Arcy Ste. Restitue, Jouaignes, Courcelles and Pont Arcy on the western road.

From the private diary of an officer of the Battalion we learn that on the 12th " 'Réveillé' was at 4.45 a.m. We marched through Fère, Loupeigne, Broys and Bazoches; at the latter place we heard that the retreating columns of the enemy in our immediate front were only one and a half hours ahead of us on the road, and some French artillery opened fire on them over our heads, from both flanks, as we advanced. We were sent forward and deployed, but encountered no opposition as the enemy's rear-guard had meanwhile slipped away. The advance was continued down a very slippery lane and at a very fast pace, with 'D' Company as advanced guard on the lane itself and 'C' Company on the left. We reached Vauxcère at 8 p.m., and were to have done outposts, but the 2nd Welch took on this duty instead."

On this night two of the three army corps composing the British Expeditionary Force halted two miles distant from the Aisne, and so far none of its bridges were in British hands; for this the nature of the country was mainly responsible, for the many streams running in deep, narrow valleys made delaying tactics easy for the enemy. It was, moreover, clear that the Germans intended here to make a stand, for the line of the river offered every facility for defence; the Aisne was some 200 yards wide and unfordable, while there was little cover for infantry seeking to force a passage from the south, and few positions for artillery support. The pursuit, however, was to be resumed early on the 13th, the I Corps marching again on two roads, the one leading by Longueval, Bourg, Chamouille and Bruyères to Athies the other through Braine, Presles, Chavonne and Lierval to Laon; and Sir Douglas Haig's orders directed that in the first instance patrols were to be pushed forward to the river crossings, of which there were seven between Bourg and Venizel, the divisions remaining closed up and well concealed and ready to act on such information as might come in. If the Germans seemed inclined seriously to dispute the passage of the river, attack orders would be issued; if the retirement were continued, the 1st and 2nd Divisions were to occupy ground beyond the Aisne at Bourg, Pont Arcy and at Chavonne, with their advanced guards covering the crossings and pushing out reconnaissances towards the enemy.

"The ground facing the British I Corps presented a series of high spurs projecting generally south from the Chemin des Dames ridge towards the Aisne. First, commencing from the east, are the Paissy—Pargnan and Bourg spurs, both extending nearly to the river, with the village of Moulins at the top of the valley between them. Next is the short Troyon spur, with Vendresse in the valley east of it, and Beaulne and Chivy west of it. Westwards of those again are the three spurs at the foot of which lie Moussy and Soupir and Chavonne respectively; only the last of these comes close down to the river."[*]

[*] Official History, Vol. I, p. 331.

On September 13th, writes the Battalion diarist, "we did not march off till 2.30 p.m., so all got a good clean-up and a rest. The Battalion marched through Longueval and Bourg, where we crossed the Aisne by the only road bridge left standing.* It was thanks to this bridge that the 1st Division was the first to cross the river. We concentrated under cover a few hundred yards north-west of the bridge for two hours, and then billeted in the northern outskirts of Bourg. The Germans had occupied this place for the last nine nights, and the town was sacked by them because one of their men had been killed by an inhabitant. The French were all overjoyed to see us, as a lot of them had been rounded up and were about to be shot, when a German patrol came running up to report our proximity.

"September 14th. We marched off at 7.10 a.m. through Moulins to Paissy. Here The Queen's were ordered to act as escort to our artillery on the extreme right of the British front, and accordingly we deployed north-east of Paissy and advanced across the Chemin des Dames and through a small wood about 150 yards north of the road. We were held up on the northern edge of this wood, and could see the enemy's trenches on the slopes facing us. The ground from our position sloped away into a valley which separated us from the enemy's main line of trenches. 'D' Company was well concealed from view, and the Germans could not bring much aimed fire to bear on us. We caused quite a considerable number of casualties among them, even at a range of 700-800 yards. Captain Stanley Creek was himself hit on the forehead by a bullet and stunned, but only for a few minutes. At about 3 p.m. the Commanding Officer directed that a counter-attack should be made on our extreme right so as to assist the French Zouaves who were there. Captain Hunter, with two platoons of 'D' Company, proceeded to this flank, but found it impossible to carry out the attack, the enemy being by this time in considerable numbers and the French having fallen back to the Chemin des Dames. Meanwhile on our left things were more serious, and it was on this flank that we suffered our chief casualties. At about 4 p.m. the Colonel gave the order to retire to the Chemin des Dames, where we could carry out our rôle of escort to the artillery equally well. 'D' Company fell back first, and was followed by the remaining companies, with Captain Longbourne bringing up the rear and supervising the carrying in of Captains Heath and Mathew-Lannowe, both of whom had been wounded. We lined the Chemin des Dames for four hours under enemy artillery fire; they were searching for our artillery, which was just in rear of us and had the road which we were lining pretty accurately taped. Our own guns were only 30 yards behind us, and nearly blew our heads off each time they fired. The Zouaves retired early from to-day's battle and did not put in an appearance again before dark, so our left was unpleasantly in the air. Eventually we held the road all night with 'D' and 'C' Companies in the line and 'A' and 'B' in support.

"Our casualties had been pretty heavy—Lieutenant R. L. Q. Henriques killed, Lieutenant-Colonel H. C. Pilleau and Lieutenant R. S. Pringle died" (later) "of wounds, Captains M. G. Heath, E. B. Mathew-Lannowe, A. E. McNamara and Creek, Lieutenants B. M. Kenny, F. W. H. Denton and W. Hayes, and Second-Lieutenant C. Bushell—all wounded. Our casualties in other ranks were 13 killed, 88 wounded, and 39 missing. We heard later that Major Jenkinson, who was our brigade major, was killed to-day too. Lieutenant Foy took over 'A' Company, Captain Hunter 'B,' and Captain Longbourne 'C.'"

* Another account says: "By the bridge carrying the Aisne Canal over the river," which is correct as the road bridge had been destroyed.

On the night of September 14th the 1st Division was disposed as follows :—
From a point on the Chemin des Dames about 1,000 yards east of Troyon factory, south-west behind the factory, over the ridge to Mont Faucon and into the valley south of Chivy, with two advanced detachments at the head of the Chivy valley.

The 15th and 16th there was no advance by the Battalion, and indeed it may be considered that on the last of these dates the long-enduring period of trench warfare actually commenced. The Queen's spent these two days under a tolerably heavy enemy shell fire, but on the 17th there was an increased German activity and resultant loss to the Battalion. The enemy made repeated but comparatively feeble attacks upon the British right early in the morning of this day; these were easily repulsed, but later on a more serious onslaught was made upon the 2nd Infantry Brigade, supported by a very heavy bombardment, and The Queen's were called up to redress the balance. "At 11.30," we read in an officer's diary, "there was a sudden alarm with more intense artillery fire, and Drummer Green came running back with verbal orders from the Commanding Officer to reinforce the right flank at once. The support companies were turned out by Captain Wilson and reinforced the right at the double under heavy shell fire. It was raining hard with a very cold wind, and we found it difficult to see very far as the rain was straight in our faces. We got several targets, however, after reaching the Zouaves' trenches, and the reinforcements effectually prevented any further advance on the part of the enemy. Captain Longbourne and I shared a scratch in the ground—the Zouave trenches were barely four inches deep, and consisted of stooks of corn piled round the scratch as a breastwork, but no good, of course, as cover from fire. At 2.30 p.m. Longbourne was informed by a runner that Colonel Warren had been killed at Battalion Headquarters, and that Captain Wilson had been mortally wounded by a shell just after bringing up the supports. Colonel Warren was shot by a sniper while looking through his field-glasses from the top of a haystack. Wilson was found some time after he was hit, lying in the field within a few yards of where he had left us to go and report to the Colonel. Creek now became O.C. Soon after this Sergeant Smith was killed by a sniper while on the top of a haystack on the look out. Wilson died at 8 p.m., and Watson returned this day from the 2nd Brigade* and assumed command of the Battalion."

Six men were killed and 48 wounded on the 15th, Lieutenant H. E. Iremonger among the latter.

By September 20th the Battalion was in bivouac at Vendresse, where a third reinforcement of 197 non-commissioned officers and men, under Lieutenants J. M. Rose-Troup and M. S. Pound, joined the service companies; but it was not until a week later that The Queen's marched to Œuilly with the remainder of the 3rd Brigade, which was now in divisional reserve. "This was our first experience of rest billets, and though we were well within enemy artillery range, it seemed to us like a haven of rest." Then on the 29th, General Lomax, commanding 1st Division, inspected the Battalion, and said that "*during the retreat he had especially noticed The Queen's as being the best marchers in the Division. He had thought to himself at the time that surely the Battalion would give a good account of itself when the time came for fighting. The 1st Division had been the first to cross the River Aisne and the first to top the ridge, and The Queen's on the extreme right had held their own for five days against great odds. If the Commanding Officer had lived he would have had a*

---

* This officer had left on the 12th to take over the appointment of brigade-major of the 2nd Infantry Brigade.

*decoration, Captain C. F. Watson had been recommended for a brevet and had also been granted the local rank of major. He had been obliged to keep the 3rd Brigade up in the firing line for fifteen days, though he had twice tried to get them back for a rest."*

On October 3rd Lieutenant-Colonel B. T. Pell, D.S.O. arrived at headquarters and assumed command of the Battalion.

"Towards the close of September Sir John French had suggested to General Joffre the transfer of the British Army to its former place on the left of the line. Other British troops were about to be landed in the north of France, and it was obviously desirable that all the forces of the nation should act in one body. The lines of communication also of the British Expeditionary Force would be greatly shortened by its being near the coast. The British were specially concerned in preventing the fall of Antwerp, and were interested, above all nations, in barring the way to the Channel ports, from which the Germans could threaten the transport of troops from England to France and block the vital avenues of water-borne traffic converging on London. That the Germans had not seized Ostend, Calais and Boulogne during their first triumphant advance, when they might easily have done so, had been due to lack of troops; and that omission they were now making every effort to make good. But apart from all question of those ports, it was obvious that if the British were restored to their old place on the left of the line, they could be reinforced with swiftness and secrecy impossible elsewhere. . . .

"General Joffre agreed to Sir John French's proposal; and on the night of October 1st-2nd was begun the withdrawal of the British troops from the Aisne. Their movements were carefully concealed; all marches were made by night and the men confined to their billets by day, so that no sign of their departure from the Aisne should be visible to enemy aircraft." *

The II Corps was the first and the I Corps the last to move, the last-named remaining in its trenches until the night of October 12th-13th, but the evacuation was not finally completed until forty-eight hours later, while it was the 19th when the I Corps detrained and concentrated at Hazebrouck, moving thence to Ypres.

The Commander of the British Expeditionary Force has told us† that "early in October a study of the general situation strongly impressed me with the necessity of bringing the greatest possible force to bear in support of the northern flank of the Allies, in order to effectively outflank the enemy and compel him to evacuate his position." Various plans were devised and set in action; the first, Antwerp being then considered as in no danger, was to extend the Allied left and hold the line from Antwerp to Arras and move against the enemy communications through Mons and Valenciennes. The fall of Antwerp, now certain, put an end to this plan, and it was then proposed that the Belgian Army and the British 7th Division should fall back to the line of the Yser, protecting the Allied left and assisting to meet any German coastal attack, while the British Army operating from La Bassée would menace the enemy communications on the north-west. As a last resort, an enveloping attack might be attempted from the line of the Lys against the German right flank, using Menin as a pivot. The essence of the whole plan of attack was speed, and unfortunately, since the Germans held the interior lines and had the shortest distance to travel, they were able to move more quickly than were the Allies.

The Battalion was at Œuilly until October 1st, and then held the trenches in front of Verneuil with two companies, the other two being in reserve in the village. The trenches and village were much shelled, and snipers were active. Captain

* Official History, Vol. I, p. 406.   † Despatch of November 20th, 1914.

M. V. Foy was killed by a sniper on the 13th, and Captain Longbourne was wounded on the 16th.

On the night of October 14th orders were received to roll up and hand in all blankets preparatory to a move, but this did not actually take place until 1.15 a.m. on the 16th, when The Queen's were relieved by a battalion of French Territorial troops, and then, concentrating in Verneuil, the Battalion marched by Pont Arcy, Vieil Arcy and Vauxtin to Courcelles, where the rest of the day was passed. Happily the day was misty, as part of the movement had to be conducted in full view of the enemy.

The Brigade now started by road and rail for Flanders, reaching Hondeghem on the 18th, and finally arriving on October 20th at Elverdinghe, just on the eve of the great and long-enduring struggle for Ypres, as to the initial share in which of the I Corps the following instructions had been issued to Sir Douglas Haig :* " The I Corps will advance via Thourout with the object of capturing Bruges. If this is proved to be feasible and successful, every endeavour must be made to turn the enemy's left flank and drive him back to Ghent. The situation, however, is very uncertain, and in the first instance it is only possible to direct the I Corps with its right on the line Ypres—Roulers. Should the forces of the enemy, reported to be moving west between Iseghem and Courtrai, seriously menace the IV Corps, it is left to the discretion of the Commander of the I Corps to lend this Corps such assistance as may be necessary."

The Allied line from Albert to the sea was now occupied as follows : the 10th French Army lay from Albert to Vermelles, then came the II Corps between Givenchy and Laventie, a corps of French Cavalry, the II British Corps astride the Lys east of Armentières, then Allenby's Cavalry Corps ; in the Ypres Salient the 7th Division with the 3rd Cavalry Division on its left, while between Zonnebeeke and Bixschoote the I Corps was coming up in line, with French cavalry and marines between it and the sea.

At 2.45 on the morning of October 21st The Queen's moved out on to the main road and assembled in the order " B," " A," " C," " D " Companies, the 3rd Infantry Brigade furnishing the advanced guard for the 1st Division and the Battalion leading the Brigade, the march being through Elverdinghe and Boesinghe to Langemarck on the north-eastern side of which last-named village The Queen's deployed for attack, the objective assigned being the line of road running north-west and south-east through Poelcappelle station. " B " and " A " Companies occupied the frontage from the road to the railway, with two platoons of " A " on the north flank of the railway and with " C " and " D " Companies in support. As the firing line advanced it came under heavy flank and frontal fire, so " A " and " B " entrenched where they found themselves about 10.30 a.m., while " D " pushed rather further forward. About 1 p.m. " A " Company made a slight further advance, and at the same time the South Wales Borderers attacked unsuccessfully on the right of the Battalion, and Captain Hunter, commanding " B " Company, then found it necessary slightly to withdraw the right of his company. Owing to a misunderstanding, the remainder of " B " also retired, and a message that they were doing so was passed to " A," which fell back also, accompanied by " D," and these sustained considerable loss while doing so. A fresh line was taken up and entrenched where the supporting company was found, and here the companies remained until 7.30 in the evening, when they were relieved by the French, and proceeded to a bivouac in a field just south-west of Langemarck.

* Field-Marshal Earl French, 1914, p. 226.

On this day Captain J. R. M. Thornycroft was reported wounded and missing, and was later found to have been killed; Lieutenant M. S. Pound died later of wounds received this day, while Second-Lieutenant O. V. Le Bas was wounded; of the non-commissioned officers and men, 13 were killed, 68 wounded, and 6 missing. The Officer Commanding "A" Company wrote that "I lost 29 men, including Company Sergeant-Major Bush, who was shot through both cheeks by a bullet which passed me on the way as I was walking beside him at the time. One of our poor fellows, Private Sullivan, who was shot through the stomach, behaved very well, and preferred to let us carry him in rather than that he should be taken prisoner; he died the same evening in the ambulance . . . Most of the casualties were from shelling."

The morning of the 22nd the Battalion spent "digging itself in," and at 3 o'clock in the afternoon the Brigade was attacked north of the railway and its front temporarily broken, but the supports coming up retook the trenches. Towards evening the Battalion occupied a fresh line facing north.

In his despatch from which quotation has earlier been made, the Field-Marshal says that it had now become clear to him that the utmost that could be done to ward off any attempts of the enemy to turn the British flank to the north, or to break in from the east, was to maintain the present very extended front and to hold fast the positions until French reinforcements could arrive from the south.

October 23rd was a day of considerable activity for The Queen's and many casualties, and what happened may perhaps best be recorded in the words of a private diary. This day the Battalion was lent to the 2nd Brigade and acted under its orders; the attack was led by Captain Stanley Creek.

"At 10.15 a.m. they started on our trenches with Black Marias and Coalboxes. The 2nd Infantry Brigade was attacking in front of us at this time, but at 11.30 we got orders to advance and capture the Inn due north of Pilckem. 'A' Company was on the right of the road, and 'D' Company on the left, and we advanced in four lines, reaching our front line of trenches, about 50 yards short of the Inn, without many casualties; most of the enemy's shrapnel passed harmlessly over our heads, and our own artillery were doing very good work. Sergeant Monk and a platoon of 'D' Company did the actual rushing of the Inn, and released some eighty-odd 'Jocks,'* prisoners, who came skipping out of the Inn in great delight. Sergeant Monk obtained a D.C.M. for this eventually. 'D' Company was then ordered to the next ridge, about 400 yards north of the Inn, and 'A' was directed to hold the line of the Inn—Langemarck road in support of 'D' Company.

"At 5.30 p.m., when it was getting pretty dark, there was a sudden burst of rifle fire in front, and after a few minutes' pause we saw a column of men in fours approaching from our right front, all dressed in khaki and shouting in English. They seemed to be making so much noise, shouting and blowing bugles, that I got suspicious, and with the help of glasses made out that they were Germans. Many of them had on helmets, and only a few of the leading ones were wearing putties. I gave the order for rapid fire, and evidently it came on the Germans as a complete surprise; they stood for about a minute, and we could see them dropping like sheep as we blazed into them. They all then lay down, but we could still pick them off in turn on the ground. . . . We stopped another counter-attack about half an hour later, and had no further trouble after that. At about midnight Captain Stanley Creek rejoined with about forty of 'D' Company; he had been cut off by the same party of Germans who had come round his right flank, and the only

* Some men of the 1st Cameron Highlanders of the 1st Infantry Brigade.

way he could rejoin us was by leading his men into the enemy's lines and making a detour, which eventually brought him in on the 2nd Brigade front. Eight hundred prisoners were taken to-day, but our casualties were pretty heavy :—Lieutenant M. D. Williams killed, Captains H. N. A. Hunter and C. B. M. Hodgson and Lieutenants J. B. Hayes and F. R. W. Hunt wounded, 16 men killed, 35 wounded, and 89 missing."

The following was forwarded to the Officer Commanding The Queen's in reference to the events of October 23rd :—

"*The Brigadier-General Commanding 2nd Infantry Brigade desires to thank the General Officer Commanding 3rd Infantry Brigade for the assistance rendered by The Queen's in the action of October 23rd, 1914. This Battalion attacked and captured the Inn on the Bixschoote—Langemarck road, and the houses surrounding it, and then advanced further and at the point of the bayonet captured the German trenches to the north of that place, taking over 100 prisoners and setting free about 60 British prisoners previously captured by the enemy.*

"*He considers that the Brigade Commander, 3rd Infantry Brigade, may congratulate himself on possessing in his Brigade a battalion which shows such determination and 'élan,' and trusts that he will convey to the Battalion his personal thanks and those of the 2nd Brigade for its valuable assistance in the engagement.*"

" QUEEN'S

"*I send the original of the accompanying message to you. This acknowledgment of the work done gives me as much pleasure as I am sure it will to you. I congratulate myself indeed on my association with your splendid Battalion, and am proud to think I have the honour of commanding it in the 3rd Brigade.*

(*Signed*) " H. J. S. LANDON, *Brig.-General,*
"*Commanding 3rd Infantry Brigade.*"

The night passed quietly, but there was a good deal of shelling by the enemy on the 24th, while in the evening he attempted two attacks, but was repulsed, and then at 11 o'clock at night the Battalion was relieved, 15 men at a time, by French troops, the operation being successfully carried out despite the fact that the opposing lines were no more than 100 yards apart. During the night The Queen's marched back to Hooge, where next day the fifth reinforcement, 40 strong, joined under Captains C. F. Soames and A. Wood, both of the 3rd Battalion Royal Sussex Regiment.

The 25th was a Sunday, and all were glad of what actually was a day of rest, for some of the Battalion had had no sleep since the morning of the previous Thursday. It was discovered that the 2nd Battalion of the Regiment was in the vicinity, in Veldhoek Wood on the side of the Menin Road, and visits were exchanged and notes compared.

Field-Marshal Earl French has described the days from October 27th to 31st " as more momentous and fateful " than any others during the time he was Commander-in-Chief, and that " October 31st and November 1st will remain for ever memorable in the history of our country, for, during those two days, no more than one thin and straggling line of tired-out British soldiers stood between the Empire and its practical ruin as an independent first-class Power."

## THE FIRST BATTLE OF YPRES

On the morning of October 29th the Battalion left its bivouac in a field near Bellewaarde Farm, being joined before starting by a sixth reinforcement of 95 non-commissioned officers and men under Captain T. P. Aldworth, 3rd Battalion Royal West Kent Regiment. At this time the 22nd Infantry Brigade held a line between Gheluvelt and Kruiseecke, and thence west towards Zandvoorde, and news now came in that this line had been penetrated and that part of the 3rd Brigade was to reinforce it. The Welch Regiment and South Wales Borderers advanced on the north of the Menin Road, and at the outset the Battalion was in support of the Welch, but about 10 a.m., on arrival at Gheluvelt, it was ordered to support the 2nd Battalion The Queen's, which was holding the line out to Kruiseecke, the 1st Battalion remaining near a windmill 500 yards south-east of Gheluvelt. "D" and "C" Companies advanced some 200 yards north of the windmill and there entrenched with "A" in support. About 3 p.m. "A" Company was ordered to advance and capture a German trench in the front, but the attempt when made failed, in spite of help given on the right by some companies of the Scots Guards. The enemy made a half-hearted counter-attack at 7 o'clock in the evening, but were repulsed, and some three hours later the Battalion was ordered to dig in on a new line near the Windmill.

In this day's fighting Second-Lieutenant F. M. Eastwood was killed and Second-Lieutenant T. O. M. Buchan was wounded.

On October 30th the 3rd Brigade was employed in covering the withdrawal of the 22nd Brigade and in repulsing the attacks whereby the enemy attempted to harass this operation, and during the day there were two more officer casualties, Lieutenant H. B. Strong being killed, while Second-Lieutenant R. S. Schunck was so badly wounded that he died a few days later in hospital.

October 31st was one of the worst days experienced by the 1st Battalion during the whole war, and its events may be described in the words of the War Diary.

"Before dawn an attack was made on 'C' and 'B' Companies and the King's Royal Rifles, but was repulsed, and the enemy dug in within 300 yards of our line and reoccupied the trenches vacated by the 22nd Brigade. At 7 a.m. our line was subjected to a very heavy bombardment, to which our guns were unable to reply. The enemy then worked their way into the orchard, and the platoon of the King's Royal Rifles, supported by one platoon of The Queen's under Lieutenant Tanqueray, was driven out. Colonel Pell ordered a counter-attack, but the attempt by the King's Royal Rifles failed, and thus the enemy was in possession of the orchard within 150 yards of our line. Major Watson went back for assistance, but none was available, and he then returned to find Colonel Pell wounded, and he assumed command. We were holding our own when, about 10 a.m., 'B' Company was driven out of its trenches by machine-gun fire from both flanks, and the reserve (two platoons King's Royal Rifles) was sent for, but could not be found.

"Soon after this Captain Stanley Creek sent a message to say that he had heard the Welch had vacated their trenches, but that he was quite all right and could hold on. Major Watson went to 'A' Company to arrange a counter-attack in the event of the enemy coming on, and himself moved up to the ridge to see how the left was faring. When there he met a second messenger from 'D' Company, from whose report the situation there seemed to be as follows :—Germans were about 'C' Company's trenches (no report was forthcoming from this company) ; 'B' Company's trenches were evacuated and the men were retiring from the farm as the Germans were entering it ; orders were sent to 'D' Company to retire, but before the order arrived the Germans were seen to be in the village behind 'D' Company.

"Major Watson and Lieutenant Boyd then reformed what men they could find about the houses, while the few men left of the King's Royal Rifles went back to rally on their own battalion. As the Germans were now in the village, the above rallying party moved towards the King's Royal Rifles, who were then actually moving back owing, it is said, to a report that hostile machine guns were being brought up to enfilade them. There was thus nothing at hand to rally on.

"It was now about 11.30 a.m., and Major Watson and Lieutenant Boyd rallied what men they could find of different regiments and got them into the trenches.

"The 2nd Division recaptured Gheluvelt during the afternoon, but the line of trenches was reconstructed on the western side of the village; and Major Watson and Lieutenant Boyd collected some 200 men of the battalions of the Brigade, and formed them on a line immediately east of Hooge. Here a very few more men of the Battalion rejoined from the trenches occupied by the Welch Regiment, while Second-Lieutenant Fowler came up with 8 more from hospital—*and then this Battalion of The Queen's, 32 strong, under Lieutenant Boyd, proceeded to reinforce the King's Royal Rifles on the southern side of the Château near Gheluvelt, remaining in support until dusk and spending the whole of the next twenty-four hours in the trenches!*"

The casualties this day had been terribly heavy: of the officers of The Queen's, Lieutenant-Colonel B. T. Pell, D.S.O.,* and Captain C. F. Soames were wounded and missing; Captains S. F. Stanley Creek, E. de L. Barton and A. M. Rose, R.A.M.C., and Second-Lieutenants J. M. Rose-Troup and W. R. Connor-Green were missing; while Captain A. Wood and Lieutenant T. Tanqueray were wounded. Of the other ranks, no fewer than 624 were killed, wounded or missing!

Some further details of the day's fighting are furnished by Lieutenant Boyd, who was with "B" Company, and was one of the few surviving officers of the Battalion:—

"At about 11 a.m. we could see the enemy advancing at about 1,000 yards' range. They advanced up the 2nd Battalion trench† under cover and mounted machine guns commanding our road; they commenced sapping this trench, and we could not get at them to stop it, as they remained under cover all the time. A further enemy machine gun was also brought up under cover of a spinney and brought into action about 75 yards away from us. Meanwhile our ammunition in 'B' Company was running short, and Wood sent back two orderlies, each of whom we saw shot before they had run 20 yards. Regimental Sergeant-Major Elliott eventually came up with some, and stopped for two minutes for a breather; he then started back for Battalion headquarters, zig-zagging as he ran, and we saw him pitch on the road after going a few yards, and I was certain he was killed as he lay quite still without a move. Fortunately the Germans thought the same, and to our relief he suddenly got up and ran on under cover without another shot being fired; he had been hit in the arm when he fell, but was otherwise all right. It was just about this time that Battalion headquarters was set on fire by incendiary shells.‡

---

\* Died on November 4th in German hands.
† The trench occupied on the day previous by the 2nd Battalion is meant.
‡ All the Battalion war diaries and other documents were destroyed on this occasion.

"Things now began to look pretty hopeless, as we were being plastered with machine-gun and rifle fire from the two flanks and front without being able to retaliate on any visible target. Wood ordered me to take what was left of the platoon at the roadside and report to Watson what was happening. It was not a cheery prospect having to double along the road for about 50 yards under heavy fire all the way. Three men were all I could muster from the platoon, and we all started together, but when I reached the farm I found the only survivor of the three who had started with me, together with Drummer Williams, who was able to tell me where Watson was, and I reported the situation to him. We collected 11 men of 'A' Company and lined a hedgerow about 150 yards behind the Battalion headquarters farm. Here Watson received a report from our left that the Welch had been forced back and that 'D' Company was being enfiladed from the north. Immediately following this message we saw the enemy coming over the hill in rear of 'D' Company, having apparently come right round their flank. The Germans were already entering Gheluvelt from the north, so our small party fell back to the western side of the village and held a line of hedge immediately south of the Menin Road. Watson went back to report the situation to Brigade Headquarters while I took charge of a motley throng of various regiments, with only Sergeant Butler and 13 men of The Queen's amongst them. Colonel Burleigh-Leech* was now commanding the 3rd Brigade, as General Landon had taken over the 1st Division when General Lomax was hit, and he ordered me to take my party across the road to the northern side, as our artillery was totally unprotected on this flank and was by this time in the front line. . . . We straightened out the defence and covered our guns for the rest of the day.

"There was an exciting duel between one of our field guns and a German gun during the afternoon. One of the 3rd Brigade gunner subalterns—Blewitt—saw the enemy bringing up a gun on the Menin Road at 1,000 yards' range and preparing to come into action. He whistled up an 18-pounder gun and got it on to the road, and both fired their first round simultaneously, but the Germans had over-estimated the range, and Blewitt got it just right ; our second round was high explosive, and it blew the German gun and detachment to smithereens. At 11 p.m. Watson came back, and we walked round the whole of the 3rd Brigade front in search of any more of The Queen's men, but with no success. We left Sergeant Butler and 12 men under Rees, of the Welch Regiment, for the time being, as he had only 20 men all told. We then went to Brigade headquarters to see if any of the men could have collected at the transport lines, which were known to all. On the way we met Wallis, who was coming up with rations, and told him of the day's events."

On November 1st the following were found to constitute the 1st Battalion The Queen's :—

"A" Company ... ... 2 corporals, 2 lance-corporals, 20 privates.
"B"    ,,    ... ... 4 privates.
"C"    ,,    ... ... 2 privates.
"D"    ,,    ... ... 1 lance-corporal, 1 private.

This total of 32 included cooks and transport men collected from the Quartermaster, as they could now be spared for front-line purposes.

On November 4th the following Order of the Day was published :—

"*The Field-Marshal Commanding-in-Chief has watched with the deepest admiration and solicitude the splendid stand made by the soldiers of His Majesty the King in their*

\* Of the 1st Battalion South Wales Borderers.

*successful effort to maintain the forward position which they have won by their gallantry and steadfastness. He believes that no other army in the world would show such tenacity, especially under the tremendous artillery directed against it. Its courage and endurance are beyond all praise. It is an honour to belong to such an army. The Field-Marshal has now to make one more call upon the troops. It is certainly only a question of a few days, and it may be only a few hours, before, if they only stand firm, strong support will come, the enemy will be driven back, and in his retirement will suffer at their hands losses even greater than those which have befallen him under the terrific blows by which, especially during the last few days, he has been repulsed. The Commander-in-Chief feels sure that he does not make the call in vain."*

The 3rd Infantry Brigade, and with it the 1st Battalion The Queen's, remained in the front until the night of November 8th, when it was relieved by the 6th Cavalry Brigade, and the Battalion then—all that was left of it—proceeded to I Corps Headquarters at Brielen, picking up *en route* at Zillebeke the seventh reinforcement of 49 non-commissioned officers and men. At Brielen the Battalion remained some ten days; it was now reorganized into a single company of 2 officers—Lieutenant Boyd and Captain Aldworth—and 179 other ranks, including attached. Quartermaster-Sergeant Nevins was appointed Regimental Sergeant-Major, while Sergeants Barnes, Baverstock and Stilwell and Corporal Birmingham were the platoon commanders.

The 1st Battalion The Queen's had now been definitely taken out of the 3rd Infantry Brigade, its place being filled by the 1st Battalion Royal Munster Fusiliers, which left the 1st Brigade on this becoming wholly a Guards Brigade.

The Brigade Major of the 3rd Brigade wrote as follows to Lieutenant Boyd :—

" My dear Boyd,

"*We have no news of you, but you must allow a comparative stranger to say how miserable I am at the Battalion leaving the Brigade for such a reason. I have only been about six weeks with the 3rd Brigade myself, but I can honestly say that your Battalion, officers and men, has impressed me enormously, and I often thought yours was the best battalion I had ever seen, or certainly (as a Guardsman you will forgive my saying it) equal to the very best in the Brigade of Guards in every way. I can hardly bear to think of its unhappy fate.*

"*Yours ever,*
(*Signed*) " Charles Grant."

Of the remainder of the activities of the 1st Battalion The Queen's during the last few weeks of the first year of the war there is not very much of importance to record—it is for the most part a chronicle of the gradual rebuilding of the Battalion.

On November 20th Captain R. Needham, Suffolk Regiment, joined and assumed temporary command, and on the following day the Battalion marched by way of Poperinghe and Steenvoorde to Hazebrouck, arriving there at 6 o'clock in the evening; and during the next few days two drafts of 50 and 34 other ranks respectively joined, with the following officers :—Lieutenant-Colonel H. St. C Wilkins, Captains H. W. Stenhouse, G. B. Parnell and C. E. New (3rd East Surrey Regiment), Lieutenant M. W. H. Pain, Second-Lieutenants H. E. Chandler, G. P. Thompson and G. H. Voisin (East Surrey Regiment).

1ST BATTALION ON MOBILIZATION, AUGUST, 1914.

1ST BATTALION ON NOVEMBER 9TH, 1914.

During the early part of December His Majesty the King was in France, and visited Hazebrouck on the 2nd, when the Battalion furnished a guard of honour of 100 rank and file, under Lieutenant Boyd, and contained in it were 83 of those who had originally arrived in France with the Battalion.

It was now possible to form a second company, Captain Parnell commanding " A " and Captain Stenhouse " B," and on the 21st a draft of 35 non-commissioned officers and men arrived from home, and another of 186 on the 24th, when the " present strength " of the 1st Battalion The Queen's stood at 17 officers (including 2 attached) and 435 other ranks (including 12 attached). At this time there was no difficulty in the recruitment of new officers, but drafts of non-commissioned officers and men came in more slowly, for the Service Battalions now being raised were absorbing the majority of the volunteers who were coming forward, while the 2nd Battalion had equally experienced considerable losses and needed reinforcement; so that while by the end of the year the number of officers with the 1st Battalion had risen to 26, the strength of the other ranks had increased by 15 only.

The following are the other officers who joined:—Captains M. G. Heath, R. L. G. Heath and P. C. Esdaile; Second-Lieutenants A. W. A. Bradshaw, C. B. Brooke (3rd Suffolk Regiment), O. V. Le Bas, J. B. Close, G. B. Colebrooke (5th Middlesex Regiment), A. Burton, P. R. O. Trench, M. I. B. Howell, B. M. Pickering (3rd Buffs) and W. L. J. Nicholas (3rd Buffs); and Lieutenant P. Walsh, R.A.M.C.

By Christmas the Battalion had marched via Merville to Hinges, sending a detachment of 3 officers and 67 other ranks to Béthune under Captain New, and another 46 strong to Lillers, commanded by Captain R. L. G. Heath. Christmas brought many gifts from friends at home, and presents were distributed to all ranks from Their Majesties the King and Queen and from H.R.H. Princess Mary; while the Commander-in-Chief published the following message of good-will to his Army in France and Flanders:—

*" In offering to the Army in France my earnest and most heartfelt good wishes for Christmas and the New Year, I am anxious once more to express the admiration I feel for the valour and endurance they have displayed throughout the campaign, and to assure them that to have commanded such magnificent troops in the field will be the proudest remembrance of my life."*

The sorrow which all ranks felt at the loss of so many good friends and comrades during the comparatively few weeks that the campaign had endured was increased, were that possible, by the news, which reached the battalions of The Queen's just after Christmas Day, of the death of the Colonel of the Regiment, General Sir Thomas Kelly-Kenny, G.C.B., G.C.V.O., who had joined The Queen's in 1858 as a boy of eighteen, had commanded it for the full period, and had been its honorary colonel since April, 1902. He was succeeded by Major-General Sir E. O. F. Hamilton, K.C.B.

Maps 4 and 7.

## CHAPTER III.

### 1ST BATTALION (*continued*)

#### 1915.

#### THE BATTLE OF LOOS.

BATTLE HONOURS:
" Festubert," " Loos."

AT the beginning of the year 1915 the 1st Battalion The Queen's was organized as under:—

|  | Officers. | Sergeants. | Corporals. | Privates. | Drummer. |
|---|---|---|---|---|---|
| Headquarters | 4 | 8 | 1 | 40 | — |
| " A " Company | 10 | 7 | 7 | 155 | 1 |
| " B " Company | 10 | 6 | 5 | 171 | — |
| Machine Gun Detachment | 1 | 1 | — | 15 | — |
| Attached | 2 | 1 | — | — | — |
| Total | 27 | 23 | 13 | 381 | 1 |

The 1st The Queen's was now Corps Battalion to the I Corps, up to the end of 1914 commanded by Lieutenant-General Sir Douglas Haig; but soon after the arrival of the Battalion at Hinges the Expeditionary Force was organized in two armies, General Haig assuming command of the First, and General Smith-Dorrien of the Second, while General Sir Charles Monro succeeded Sir Douglas Haig in command of the I Army Corps. As Corps Battalion the 1st The Queen's accompanied Corps headquarters, finding guards and escorts and being held in corps reserve during any operations in which the I Army Corps might take part.

The Battalion was not seriously engaged in any of the great battles which took place during the earlier portion of the year 1915, and page after page of the Battalion diary for these opening months contains little beyond the words, " ordinary routine." Casualties occurred, however, with sad regularity, and although drafts came out from home in parties of varying size, some of these contained men who had already been more or less seriously wounded in previous actions, and were consequently hardly yet fit for the prolonged strain of modern war; while on at least one occasion one draft seemed to contain so many men who were in not sufficiently good health for campaigning that a special medical board was convened to report upon them, with the result that 70 *per cent.* of this particular draft were sent straight back to England again. The strength of the Battalion consequently did not mount as rapidly as would appear from the numbers contained in the drafts which joined.

The events of the first six months or so of this year may perhaps best be recorded in the words of an officer who joined the Battalion about this time, and who was in the best possible position to know all that was going on and also the reason for anything which the Battalion was required to undertake.

" Early in January we moved with Corps headquarters into Béthune into billets near the railway station, and on the 10th a sudden call came to us to go into the trenches, and on a night of icy rain (we had marched ten miles that morning) we started off for Givenchy. In pitch dark we groped our way for the first time through Beuvry, Annequin and Cambrin, afterwards so familiar to us, and fetched up at the Brigade headquarters in Harley Street—so called because the first house was occupied by a field ambulance. Here General Butler told us we were to go to French Farm, an unholy spot, and relieve the London Scottish, whose guides were waiting to lead us there. The rifle strength of the Battalion was only 262, the London Scottish—all that remained of that gallant regiment—numbering 370. We had no machine guns and no hand grenades; there were a few grenades, chiefly of the jampot or hairbrush variety, in the trenches.

"The Battalion headquarters spent the night in the famous Givenchy Redoubt, an oblong farm building with a few strands of wire round it, and held by a company of the Coldstream Guards; it lay about 200 yards behind the front trenches and close to the church. Owing to its weakness the Battalion could furnish only a small support to the trench companies, and no reserve. The communicating trenches were completely waterlogged, so the only way to the fire trenches was by the main road through the village, and reliefs could consequently be carried out only after dark. The front-line trenches were narrow, muddy ditches, provided at this time with iron loophole plates. Across the main road alongside the Farm was a rough barricade, consisting of an overturned cart, a few bricks and sandbags, and a few strands of wire. Next morning the Battalion headquarters moved into a small house opposite the Redoubt, and here we remained three days and nights under a sniping fire which never ceased; there was also occasional shelling. We carried on in our novel surroundings until the third night, when our relief arrived, and thus ended our first experience of the trenches in 1915.

"A fortnight later the Huns made a fresh attack upon Givenchy, and, owing to the heavy simultaneous bombardment of Béthune, we accompanied Corps headquarters to Hinges, a small village three miles west of Béthune. The bombardment was a lively one, the enemy's objectives evidently being the railway station and the station road. As our Battalion headquarters was at the Café Alphonse, a hundred yards from the station, and the men's and officers' billets were in the station road, we had a fairly exciting time. We marched to Chocques that afternoon (February 3rd), and remained there until the morning of March 10th, when we marched out to the Pont Levis, east of Béthune, where we remained in corps reserve during the Battle of Neuve Chapelle. A printed leaflet had been issued by Army headquarters to each man announcing that the time of inaction was over and that the situation was favourable for a break-through. In high spirits we marched through Béthune as the preliminary bombardment by our guns crashed out. Our hopes, however, were destined to be disappointed, and the expected order to advance beyond Pont Levis never came. News trickled through that the primary attack, though successful, was not a break-through, and for two days we waited by the roadside, ready to move at ten minutes' notice, and finally moved into billets in the area immediately north of the canal.

"Between the Battles of Neuve Chapelle and Festubert in May we were billeted in Chocques, Vendin and Le Hamel, in the last-named place being scattered over a wide area in quaint Flemish farmhouses. It was a pleasant place in spring, with its orchards and grassy meadows, but the country was low-lying, the roads bordered by dykes, the home of innumerable frogs. We were not idle during this period of building up the Battalion; it meant incessant hard work for all, as fresh drafts were constantly arriving : but at this time there was a fair leavening of regular officers, warrant and non-commissioned officers ; moreover, in France in 1915 there was a good stiffening of experienced soldiers in the ranks."

By this the Battalion again contained four companies, which were early in May commanded as follows :—" A," Captain G. B. Parnell ; " B," Captain M. G. Heath ; " C," Captain P. C. Esdaile ; and " D," Captain R. L. G. Heath.

"The Battle of Festubert in May" (15th-25th) "found us still in reserve, being much below establishment ; we moved to east of Béthune and Locon during the operations. The Army at this time was fighting without adequate artillery or shells, and the casualties in the fighting line were terribly heavy. Our 2nd Battalion lost heavily, and out of five officers who had visited us at Vendin a few days before the battle, four were killed, including the Commanding Officer, Lieutenant-Colonel Bottomley. The 1st Battalion also suffered casualties during the operations, some companies* being sent up to help clear the battle-field. Their good behaviour under fire brought a letter of thanks from the General Officer Commanding the 2nd London Division, into whose area they had gone, and the warm commendation of our Corps Commander. We unfortunately suffered the loss of one of the most promising subalterns in the Battalion, Second-Lieutenant P. W. Johnson, and of a number of non-commissioned officers and men while carrying out this duty."

On June 1st the Battalion marched to Marles-les-Mines, and while here several changes took place owing to the arrival of senior officers : Major J. K. N. Versturme-Bunbury, 3rd Battalion, joining and taking over command of " D " Company, while Major L. M. Crofts, who had been posted to the Battalion, became Second-in-Command, and Captain M. G. Heath was sent to command the 2nd Battalion.

"Towards the end of June" (actually on the 30th) "we moved from Marles-les-Mines, where the Battalion had been made up to war strength, to Beuvry, two and a half miles south-east of Béthune and three miles in rear of the trenches, and while here the Battalion furnished daily working parties, frequently under shell fire, assisting in constructing second-line defences in the Cambrin and Annequin area, immediately in rear of the trenches. These works consisted largely of redoubts such as at La Tourbière and Cambrin, also of fortified houses—a great feature of these second-line defences. The Battalion won high praise from the Chief Engineer of the Corps for its work during this period. In case of attack we were allotted to the third line of defence, a series of breastworks extending for several miles through the woods north and south of the La Bassée Canal in the vicinity of Gorre, Beuvry and La Fréole.

"A distressing bomb accident cost the lives of two young officers—Second-Lieutenants A. C. Armitage and G. B. Goldberg—during our stay in Beuvry. The hand grenade then in use had a dangerous method of ignition, which caused many accidents, and it was not until some months later that the Mills bomb, which combined safety to the thrower with effective action, made its appearance in France."

For some little time past rumour had been busy that the 1st Battalion The Queen's would shortly return to active duty with a division, but it was not until July 18th that orders were received for the Battalion to hold itself in readiness to join the 5th Brigade of the 2nd Division, taking the place there of the 2nd Battalion The Royal Inniskilling Fusiliers transferred to Corps troops. The 2nd Division was at this time commanded by Major-General H. S. Horne, C.B., C.M.G., and the

* These were " B " and " D."

5th Brigade by Brigadier-General C. E. Corkran, C.M.G. The Brigade contained, besides the 1st Battalion The Queen's, the 2nd Battalions of the Worcestershire Regiment and of the Oxfordshire and Buckinghamshire and of the Highland Light Infantry, and also the 9th Battalion of the last-named corps. The Battalion came under the 5th Brigade orders from the 21st, and joined on July 25th at Cuinchy.

From this date until the last week in September there was relative quietude along the whole of the British line, except at those points where the normal conditions of existence comprised occasional shelling or constant mine and bomb warfare.

There is not very much to be gleaned from the despatch of October 15th, 1915, as to the reasons for the operations which began on September 25th and which are known as the Battle of Loos; all that the Field-Marshal tells us is that " I have had constant meetings with General Joffre, who has kept me informed of his views and intentions, and explained the successive methods by which he hopes to attain his ultimate object. After full discussion of the military situation a decision was arrived at for joint action, in which I acquiesced. It was arranged that we should make a combined attack from certain points of the Allied line during the last week in September. . . . The main attack was delivered by the I and IV Corps between the La Bassée Canal on the north, and a point of the enemy's line opposite the village of Grenay on the south." In addition, secondary and subsidiary attacks were made by the V, III, and Indian Corps; but so far as the 2nd Division was concerned, the September operations were mainly confined to the Givenchy and Cuinchy sections.

The I Corps Operation Order stated that " the general intention of the General Officer Commanding I Corps is to break the enemy's line south of the La Bassée Canal and to advance to the line of the Canal Pont-à-Vendin—Bauvin with his right on the Hulluch—Vendin-le-Vieil road. A main attack will be made by the 7th, 9th, and 2nd Divisions against the enemy's front from the Vermelles—Hulluch road, inclusive, to the La Bassée Canal, with the view to an immediate advance on Hulluch—St. Elie—Haisnes railway line from Haisnes to La Bassée Canal. A subsidiary attack will also be made by the 2nd Division from Givenchy."

The objectives are then detailed:—" 7th Division—the enemy's front trenches from the Vermelles—Hulluch road, inclusive, to Quarry Trench. 9th Division—from Hohenzollern Redoubt to Vermelles Triangle Railway, inclusive. 2nd Division—the enemy's front trenches from the left of the 9th Division to the La Bassée Canal. Subsidiary attack; the left brigade of the 2nd Division holding the line north of the canal—the enemy's trenches opposite Givenchy, and to push on to the line Chapelle St. Roel—Canteleux."

At this time the 5th Infantry Brigade occupied the Givenchy Sector north of the La Bassée Canal.

" The task allotted to the 1st Battalion The Queen's," writes the officer from whose account of this period quotation has before been made, " was to attack from the Givenchy Sector, the 2nd Oxford and Bucks attacking on our left, the two Scottish battalions (Highland Light Infantry) on our right, and the 2nd Worcesters in reserve. In the event, the latter were required elsewhere and we had no reserve. The objective of our brigade was to capture the block of German trenches facing ours and to hold them; also, if possible, to press on and capture the German second line trenches about a mile in the rear in the direction of Violaines. Gas was to be employed by our troops for the first time,* and the attack was carried out in the gas mask then in use, a somewhat primitive grey-blue head cover which gave the wearer the appearance of a member of the Spanish Inquisition ! We moved into our attack sector twenty-four hours before zero, *i.e.*, in the early morning of September 24th, and thus had time to put the finishing touches to the preparations for the assault and to make the junior non-commissioned officers and men acquainted with the geography of the sector. The officers and senior non-commissioned officers knew it well from previous visits. On the afternoon of the 24th Battalion headquarters moved up to their advanced headquarters at Hilder Redoubt. The eventful day dawned at last, it was a great relief when it came, for one's nerves were at tension from three weeks of expectancy, and never was anything more welcome than the cessation of the deafening noise of our 96 hours' bombardment.

"I have mentioned above that ours was a subsidiary attack. There were no troops in reserve to us between our brigade and Béthune, five miles away, and I had received orders not to engage the whole of the Battalion in the first instance. I decided to send forward two companies abreast, each on a platoon front; the front of our trench sector being 300 yards, this gave each platoon a frontage of about 150 yards, or roughly four yards a man. Each company was thus to attack in four waves. These companies—'B' and 'D,' under Captain C. B. Brooke, 3rd Suffolks, and Major Versturme-Bunbury, 3rd Battalion The Queen's, respectively—were to carry forward their telephone instruments and cables and to establish the former in a pre-arranged spot in the enemy trenches. Immediately the two leading companies were over the top, their place in the front trenches was to be taken by the support company, 'C '—Major Weeding—which was to occupy our entire front-line trench. (This company had spent the previous night in Mairie Redoubt, adjoining the support trenches, and had lost some men from shell fire before they quitted the Redoubt.)

"Zero hour arrived—6.7 a.m.—and the attack started. Reports came in thick and fast, I soon learnt that we were in possession of the enemy trenches, but that most of the officers were casualties. It was also soon evident from the enemy's machine-gun fire that our gas was not having the effect anticipated. Major Bunbury was knocked out before reaching the enemy wire; Second-Lieutenant Joynson-Hicks of the same company was also wounded but carrying on, but two of his subalterns were killed and also the machine-gun officer (Second-Lieutenant Bradshaw) who had joined us at Hazebrouck. As soon as I gathered that most of the officers were casualties and that more grenades were required, I ordered half ' C ' Company to advance, taking forward as much S.A.A. as possible and 20 to 30 boxes of hand grenades. The enemy's fire was heavy, there were hidden machine guns away on the flanks, and the shell fire was also heavy. Soon came news that we were holding our own in the enemy's trenches, and that the work of consolidation was progressing, but that no further reinforcements were required as the trenches were somewhat congested.

"What I have narrated did not happen all at once—it was spread over several hours during which a constant stream of messages arrived over the telephone. Three or four hours after we had seized the enemy's trenches a message came back that the whole brigade was falling back and that men were streaming back over ' No-Man's Land.' I at once ordered up our reserve company—' A,' Captain Parnell—to our support trenches. We now had half of ' C ' and the whole of ' A '

* In the 5th Brigade from sixty emplacements, each of three cylinders.

intact. It transpired that the enemy had been reinforced and had made a strong bombing attack which had forced our brigade back. The result was undoubtedly disappointing. Officers, non-commissioned officers and men had advanced with great dash, had gallantly captured the enemy trenches, inflicting heavy losses on him and making a general havoc of his trenches, dug-outs, cables, and communications."

Of the 5th Brigade attack the Divisional History, after describing the capture of the enemy's front line, states :—*" A move was then made towards the enemy's second line, but the attacking battalions had been weakened, first, by the loss of men temporarily out of action suffering from the effects of gas, and secondly, by the enemy's fire from machine guns and snipers, which had gradually increased and was of deadly accuracy. Moreover, the number of bombs issued to the 5th Infantry Brigade—ten to each bomber—had been totally inadequate for the conduct of a bombing attack. And what was even more disastrous, many of these bombs could not be used. They were of the ' ball ' pattern and had to be ignited from a kind of match-box striker attached to the wrist of the bomber. The damp atmosphere and the falling rain made ignition impossible. The enemy used the stick grenade, a much better and more formidable weapon, which could be thrown further. Thus the advance towards the enemy's second line was begun under the most unfavourable conditions. The result was that although the attack was pressed with great gallantry, the three battalions were bombed back, first to the enemy's first-line trenches, and later to their own original trenches from which the attack had been launched.

" However, in spite of failure to maintain itself in the enemy's trenches, the 5th Infantry Brigade had succeeded in the task allotted to it—that of containing the enemy on his front and preventing him sending reinforcements elsewhere where the principal attacks were being made."

The casualties in the 1st Battalion The Queen's had been heavy ; of the officers, Second-Lieutenants A. W. A. Bradshaw, C. D. M. Fowler, M. I. B. Howell and F. G. Plant were killed or died of wounds ; Major J. K. N. Versturme-Bunbury, Captain C. B. Brooke, Lieutenants E. D. Drew, H. P. Foster, and Second-Lieutenant R. C. Joynson-Hicks were wounded ; while of the non-commissioned officers and men 19 were killed, 21 were missing, believed killed, 138 were wounded, and 80 were missing and wounded, while 7 were suffering from gas, and one of those wounded died of his wounds.

" We remained in our trenches that night, receiving a warning in the afternoon that an enemy counter-attack was in course of preparation. I fancy, however, that the enemy had been too severely punished, while our main attack towards Loos drew away their reserves—at any rate it did not materialize. The next morning we marched back along the canal to Le Prèol, a pretty village on a branch of the La Bassée Canal about one and a half miles behind the trenches. The next day we received reinforcements " (these were only 38 strong) " and now reaped the advantage of having the services of the four Company Sergeant-Majors and four Company Quartermaster-Sergeants who, according to the usual practice, had remained with the Regimental transport during the action. As the two companies which had attacked had lost all their officers and no officers of any experience were forthcoming as reinforcements, it was doubly necessary to have these valuable warrant officers available at this time of reorganization. After three days we

* *The History of the 2nd Division,* Vol. I, p. 224.

marched to a new trench sector, south of the La Bassée Road and opposite the grim skeleton of the village of Auchy. The weather was now bad, very cold with constant rain; the trenches were approached by a truly villainous communication trench about one and a half miles long, the bottom full of holes and with greasy mud above one's boots; at every step one floundered into a hole or caught one's foot in the network of telephone cables which lay buried in the mud. It took our machine guns five hours to get to the front that night. A number of men who had fallen in this sector on the 25th were still unburied, and in burying these men the Battalion lost the services of Major Weeding who was shot badly through the arm, a serious loss to the Battalion and the third company commander since the 25th."

After a few days spent in Vermelles, where the 6th Battalion The Queen's was met, "our next move during the Battle of Loos brought us, on October 10th, to the trench sector opposite Fosse 8 and a little north of the famous Hohenzollern Redoubt. Here we relieved the 1st Battalion Irish Guards and commenced digging by night a trench extending from our front line obliquely towards the Hohenzollern Redoubt; this trench we named the Guildford Trench. Facing us was the German trench known as Little Willie, which abutted further south on the Hohenzollern Redoubt. A sap nearly 100 yards long ran out from our front trench towards Little Willie, from which a German sap ran out towards ours, the intervening space being about seventy yards. I was informed that on October 13th an attack on the Hohenzollern Redoubt, a strong earthwork thrust out some 500 yards in front of the German trenches and close to ours, was to be made by the 46th Division. The 1st The Queen's, being the right flank battalion of our Division, was next to the 46th. A brigade bombing attack was to be made on the 13th from the long sap in our Battalion front, the brigade bombers being employed, and the Battalion was to furnish two platoons under Lieutenant Abercrombie in support of these and also a working party with tools.

"The scheme was that under cover of our bombardment and of the gas, which was to be discharged from our front trenches, the bombers, followed by the two platoons and working party, were to dash out of our sap-head and across the intervening seventy yards to the German sap and thence into Little Willie. A block was to be established on the left (north) in the latter trench, to prevent the Huns from emerging from their rear trenches into Little Willie, and the bombers were to bomb down Little Willie south into the Hohenzollern Redoubt and join up with the bombers of the 46th Division, who would bomb up towards them.

"About 11 a.m. our preliminary bombardment crashed out, and as our gas was discharged the rifle fire from the enemy's trenches died down, giving the impression that our gas was effective. The 46th Division now went forward to the attack and the enemy barrage came down—of the 5·9 variety, the right half of our Battalion sector, the Quarry where Battalion headquarters was, and the main communicating trench leading up from Brigade headquarters to the front line, being persistently bombarded with precision. Telephone communication with the front line trenches held for a time, but that with Brigade headquarters soon went, and for three hours was cut off; soon after communication with the front trenches followed suit, and runners came into use who had to run the gauntlet of heavy shell fire. About 11.30 a.m. an abortive attempt to launch the bombing attack was made, and it soon became obvious that our gas had had little effect on the enemy's machine gunners and that the exit from our sap was covered by them from Mad Point, a salient in the German trenches to the north of us, and from elsewhere.

"Owing to numerous casualties the bombing attack wavered. Three officers then very gallantly went to the head of the Brigade bombers, one of these being the subaltern in charge of The Queen's digging party—Second-Lieutenant A. Tweedie-Smith. Led by these officers, a party of the bombers dashed into the open, to be met by a withering fire, when every officer and man except two was knocked over, two of the three officers being killed—Tweedie-Smith and Leicester of the Worcesters. The third officer, Lieutenant Abercrombie, accompanied by a private of The Queen's by a miracle got across untouched into Little Willie and found it weakly held. Abercrombie then sent the man back with a request for reinforcements, but he was killed on the way back, and Abercrombie, remaining on alone in the enemy's trenches, did a little bombing on his own account, smashed up a machine gun which he found there unattended, and having kept the enemy at arm's length until dark, he then regained our lines and appeared in the Battalion headquarters dug-out, hours after he had been given up for lost."* Second-Lieutenant Carslake led a second bombing attack on the western face of the redoubt to cover some digging operations and withdrew after expending his bombs.

"Meantime the 46th Division in its attack had varying success. As often happened, the attack prospered in its earlier stages, but later on counter-attacks by enemy reserves resulted in our men holding at nightfall only the southern fringe of the Hohenzollern Redoubt, by which time the situation was uncertain and confused. An officer I sent to the redoubt returned and reported our men holding on to the southern trench, but that the work of consolidation was not progressing very rapidly, no doubt owing to heavy losses in officers and the severity of the fighting."

Thus ended the operations which commenced on September 25th; of them the Commander of the British Expeditionary Force wrote as follows:—†" The position assaulted and carried with so much brilliancy and dash by the I and IV Corps on September 25th was an exceptionally strong one. It extended along a distance of some 6,500 yards, consisted of a double line, which included works of considerable strength, and was a network of trenches and bomb-proof shelters. Some of the dug-outs and shelters formed veritable caves thirty feet below the ground, with almost impenetrable head cover. The enemy had expended months of labour upon perfecting these defences."

During the nineteen days that the Battle of Loos endured the 2nd Division sustained casualties amounting to 137 officers and 3,259 other ranks, while those suffered by the 1st Battalion The Queen's were 6 officers and 30 non-commissioned officers and men killed or died of wounds, 5 officers and 192 other ranks wounded or gassed, and 84 missing and wounded, while 21 non-commissioned officers and men were wounded believed killed.

"Soon after the events above described we marched back to Annequin, a ghost of a village, about one and a quarter miles behind the trenches and billeted there in support, sending up working parties at night to the trenches where we continued the excavation of the Guildford Trench which eventually joined up with the southern face of the Hohenzollern Redoubt, and the general line of our trenches was advanced to the level of the Guildford Trench. This work cost the Battalion

* He was awarded the D.S.O., which he had won with the M.C., at the age of 19. He was killed in the last year of the war.   † Despatch of October 15th, 1915.

the life of a valued officer, Lieutenant H. C. Williams, M.C., who was accidentally killed one night in this trench when in close proximity to the enemy. . . .

"There followed for the rest of the year 1915 a period of trench warfare in which the worst enemy was the climate. The toil involved in keeping the trenches *in situ* was unceasing, it meant twenty hours' work out of the twenty-four. The trench sectors south of the La Bassée Road were particularly bad, they were very badly built, the sand-bags having been laid perpendicularly and without breaking joint, and consequently they slid away in sections. The sector north of and adjoining the La Bassée Canal was also a shockingly bad one. Here the 1st Battalion in December held perforce a front of 700 yards with two platoons, or about seventy men, one platoon at each extremity of the front line, the intervening space being untenable owing to water and mud. At night a few men waded out breast high through the water and furnished an 'island post' about the centre of the front line. We managed to keep open two communicating trenches leading up to each end of the front line. Supports were posted at two small redoubts on each flank, about 300 yards in rear of the front trench. Headquarters were in the cellars of a ruined house on the canal bank known as Lock House.

"The communicating trench on the right—south—was three feet deep in mud and water, although the canal lay thirty feet below, separated from it by a thick bank. Much of our time here was spent in cutting channels through this bank at night to enable the water to drain off into the canal; had it been cut through every fifty yards the trenches would have been dry, but as it was, it took twenty minutes of exhausting effort to get through the last 200 yards up to the front line. Each foot had to be put down in turn into the greasy mud and then pulled out by force leaving one's gum boot stuck in the mud as often as not. At night it was possible to walk up to the front line along the canal bank—by day the attempt brought a shower of 'whizz-bangs.'"

By the end of this year many of the new formations were arriving in France from home, and it was realized that the troops of the New Army needed the guidance and the support of those who had experience of modern continental warfare, and battalions and even brigades were transferred to the new divisions to give them the necessary stiffening. On November 25th the 19th Infantry Brigade was transferred to the 33rd Division, which sent its 99th Brigade to the 2nd Division in its place; while on December 8th the 2nd Battalion Worcestershire Regiment, and on the 15th the 1st Battalion The Queen's, were transferred to the 33rd Division, their places in the 2nd being taken by the 13th Battalion The Essex and the 17th Battalion The Middlesex Regiment.

On December 14th the Battalion, then in Béthune, paraded in the morning for a farewell inspection by Major-General W. G. Walker, V.C., C.B., commanding the 2nd Division, and marched next day to St. Hilaire, west of Lillers, the 2nd Divisional Band accompanying The Queen's as far as Chocques. At Lillers the commander of the 33rd Division, Major-General H. J. S. Landon, C.B., C.M.G.—the same who had taken the 3rd Infantry Brigade out to France, was waiting to see the Battalion go by and seemed very glad to have it under his command again.

"General Twigg, who commanded our new brigade, the 100th," we read in the diary of an officer, "came out to meet us at Bourecq, and we had a triumphal march from there, headed by the band of the 16th Middlesex, which had been sent out to meet us. . . . They had given us the best billets in St. Hilaire, in the main street, and we settled down very comfortably. We had twelve days' rest here, right out of sound of even the artillery, which was a very acceptable change, especially at Christmas time."

At this time Field-Marshal Sir John French resigned the command of the British Armies in France into the able hands of General Sir Douglas Haig, and on December 19th the former drove through St. Hilaire paying a farewell visit to his troops, on which occasion the 1st Battalion The Queen's was employed lining the streets ; the following was the Special Order of the Day in which the Field-Marshal took leave of the Army :—

*" In relinquishing the command of the British Army in France, I wish to express to the officers, non-commissioned officers and men with whom I have been so closely associated during the last sixteen months, my heartfelt sorrow in parting with them before the campaign, in which we have been so long engaged together, has been brought to a victorious conclusion. I have, however, the firmest conviction that such a glorious ending to their splendid and heroic efforts is not far distant, and I shall watch their progress towards this final goal with intense interest, but in the most confident hope.*

*" The success so far attained has been due to the indomitable spirit, dogged tenacity which knows no defeat, and the heroic courage so abundantly displayed by the rank and file of the splendid Army which it will ever remain the pride and glory of my life to have commanded during over sixteen months of incessant fighting.*

*" Regulars and Territorials, Old Army and New, have ever shown these magnificent qualities in equal degree. From my heart I thank them all.*

*" At this sad moment of parting, my heart goes out to those who have received life-long injury from wounds, and I think with sorrow of that great and glorious host of my beloved comrades who have made the greatest sacrifice of all by laying down their lives for their country.*

*" In saying good-bye to the British Army in France, I ask them once again to accept this expression of my deepest gratitude and heartfelt devotion towards them, and my earnest good wishes for the glorious future which I feel to be assured."*

At the end of 1915 the following officers appear to have been serving with the 1st Battalion The Queen's :—Major L. M. Crofts, Captains F. B. Storey and G. B. Parnell, Lieutenants F. Godfrey, H. L. Harrison, H. E. A. Hodgson, H. E. Chandler and A. R. Abercrombie, D.S.O., M.C., Second-Lieutenants W. L. J. Nicholas, A. J. Crichton, R. E. C. Harland, R. Faulkner, G. Wheeler, O. S. Flinn, H. H. Richards, J. G. Buckner, C. W. Farwell, A. Mundye, L. H. Bennett, C. W. Roffe, I. W. S. Symonds, J. G. S. Morrison, W. Stranger, R. P. Slatter and S. E. Lukyn ; Lieutenant and Quartermaster G. H. Wallis, and Captain R. J. Clausen, R.A.M.C., in medical charge of the Battalion.

During this year the Drums and Fifes, which had been sent home in 1914, were brought out again and the Drums were reformed under Sergeant-Drummer Winter. Under him the Drums attained a state of smartness and efficiency quite up to the pre-war standard, and made a name for themselves wherever the Battalion went. Their playing on the march and in billets contributed greatly to keeping up the *esprit de corps* of the Battalion.

## CHAPTER IV.

### 1ST BATTALION (continued)

#### 1916.

##### THE BATTLE OF THE SOMME.

###### BATTLE HONOURS:
"Somme, 1916," "Bazentin," "Delville Wood," "Pozières," "Ancre Heights."

THE 33rd Division, of which the 1st Battalion The Queen's now formed part, had been constituted in December, 1914, but was broken up into independent brigades in the following April; at the end of this month, however, it was reconstituted and went to France in November of the year 1915, composed entirely of New Army units; but, as already stated, it was realized that the efficiency of these new formations would be enhanced if certain of the war-experienced Regular and Territorial battalions could be included in them. As a result, the 33rd Division was once more reconstituted, the 19th Brigade from the 2nd Division replacing the 99th, while certain veteran battalions of the 5th Brigade replaced an equal number of the New Army. At the date then when the 1st Battalion The Queen's was transferred to the 33rd Division this comprised the 19th, 98th, and 100th Infantry Brigades; the last-named of these three—commanded by Brigadier-General R. H. Twigg, C.B., of the Indian Army—contained the 1st Battalion The Queen's, 2nd Battalion Worcestershire Regiment, 9th Battalion The Highland Light Infantry, the 16th Battalion The King's Royal Rifle Corps, and the 16th Battalion The Middlesex Regiment (Pioneers); it was thus an eminently representative brigade, composed as it was of 2 Regular, 1 Territorial, and 2 Service battalions. Later, Brigadier-General A. W. F. Baird, C.M.G., D.S.O., relieved Brigadier-General Twigg in command of the 100th Brigade.

At the time when The Queen's joined the Division, it was occupying the line on the La Bassée front, holding the trench system round the canal, Cuinchy, the Brickstacks, and Cambrin. "It was a time when the antagonists had expended the full force of their power in the opening clash of war. The first round was over. After a ding-dong battle both sides were exhausted."* Below ground both sides were busily engaged in mining, while, above the surface, raids from the British lines were the order of the day.

The following is taken from the report of one of these raids carried out by the 1st Battalion The Queen's on March 22nd when up in the front line near Beuvry:—

"At 6 p.m. No. 3 Company under Captain Godfrey, less the raiding platoon, moved from the reserve trenches in Wimpole Street and took over the Twin Sap and front-line trench in rear of it. At 7 p.m. the raiding platoon, consisting of four sections each of 1 non-commissioned officer and 8 men, under Second-Lieutenants Lukyn and Morrison, started from Wimpole Street and at 7.30 commenced to get out of the sap, joining the Twin Craters, by a gap cut a few minutes previously. They were formed up in three shallow columns with reserve section in rear; this

---
\* *The 33rd Division in France and Flanders*, p. 5.

took some time and it was not until 7.55 p.m. that they commenced to crawl forward, reaching the German wire about 8.5 p.m.

" During this they were subjected to a good deal of casual rifle fire, and Second-Lieutenant Morrison was wounded. Second-Lieutenant Gurrey, who was sent to take his place, found the reserve platoon which had temporarily lost direction, and reached the German wire as the remainder of the platoon entered the trench. A German sentry at the corner where the wire had been cut fired two shots and then bolted; he was fired at and wounded, but managed to get away.

" The men on entering the trench at once sorted themselves as previously practised; one section worked to the right, one to the left, one up the communication trench, and the fourth remained in reserve at the point of entrance. The trenches were exactly as depicted in the air photo, and entrance was made at the exact spot decided on. The wire was absolutely cut by the artillery and wire cutters were not required. The reserve section found two deep dug-outs, one on each side of the island traverse, dug under the front parapet, and about twelve steps deep. Grenades were thrown down these, and much groaning was heard, and from one of them grenades were thrown back. The entrance to the dug-outs was completely blown in by the grenades. The right and left section each treated a dug-out in similar fashion, and groans were heard in each case. The centre platoon chased three Germans up the communication trench, but were unable to overtake them. A side trench, about seventy yards up, which was thought from the photo to be a bombing post, was found to be a latrine. The notice board we brought away, but lost.

" After the party had been in the trenches about ten minutes the barrage commenced. The officers described it as ' absolute hell,' especially north of the La Bassée Road, and its effect on the Germans must have been very great. One German was killed in the trench by the left section, but no papers, etc., could be found on him, and the barrage starting just then, the men were a bit startled and forgot to bring away the body. The smoke from the bursting bombs drifted down the trench and made it very difficult to see. After being in the trenches about twenty minutes the parties were recalled and ran back to our crater, hardly a shot being fired at them, which shows how completely the Germans were surprised by the barrage. The left party had a few grenades thrown at them as they were retiring, and one burst among the section without doing any harm.

" The platoons regained our craters at 8.30 p.m., less four men, who came in afterwards. The German trench was eight to nine feet deep, with fire platforms at intervals; it was floor-boarded, and firing platforms were revetted with wood. There were no machine-gun emplacements, but one sniper's loophole; no signs of mining."

The following congratulatory messages followed; from the Brigadier :—

" *Congratulate you and your platoon on success.*"

From General Haking, C.B., the Corps Commander, came :—

" *Congratulations on successful raid.*"

While General Sir Charles Monro, the Army Commander, wired as under :—

" *Please convey to my old Regiment the pleasure it gives me to hear of the successful raid last night.*"

And it was no doubt by reason of this, and other equally good services of a like nature, that the Battalion was mentioned in General Haig's first despatch, covering the period from December 19th, 1915, to May 19th, 1916, wherein he wrote :—

*"While many other units have done excellent work during the period under review, the following have been specially brought to my notice for good work in carrying out or repelling local attacks or raids :—*

\* \* \* \* \*

*" 1st Battalion The Queen's Regiment."*

During May and June it became every day more apparent that some great offensive was likely shortly to take place, and considerable attention was given to practising all arms of the British Army in the attack whenever these were out of the line. Considerable reinforcements had reached our armies during the last six months, and the labour of finding men had been lightened by the recent introduction of compulsory service. In the spring there had been very severe fighting on our front at Ypres, while in March the French had been heavily pressed at Verdun, and to give some much-needed help to their Allies, the British had taken over some twelve miles more of front. March saw much fighting about St. Eloi, and April about Loos ; and it seemed evident that the Germans were trying to hold the British while they prosecuted their offensive at Verdun.

The Allied Commanders had determined upon an offensive campaign during the summer of this year, but were only in doubt as to when the attack should commence. It was eventually decided that it should not be delayed much beyond the end of June, and that it must be a combined one, since neither of the Allies was sufficiently strong to attack unaided. There were now four British armies in the field—the Second in the Ypres sector, the First about Neuve Chapelle, the Third about Arras, and the Fourth, under General Rawlinson, between Albert and the Somme, joining on to the left of the French. The offensive, then, was to be carried out by the Fourth British Army, holding the front from Gommecourt across the Ancre Valley to Maricourt ; and by the Sixth French Army, commanded by General Fayolle, whose force lay from Maricourt, astride the Somme, to opposite the village of Fay.

The position to be attacked consisted of two strong defence systems, the first running north for 3,000 yards from the Somme near Curlu, then west for 7,000 yards to near Fricourt, and then due south. The second system, between the Somme and the Ancre, was at a distance of from 3,000 to 5,000 yards behind the first. Both contained several lines of deep trenches, with bomb-proof shelters, all protected by broad belts of barbed wire.

The first phase of the Somme battle began on July 1st and ended on July 14th, and of the results obtained by our troops Sir Douglas Haig wrote that " the enemy's second main system of defence had been captured on a front of over three miles. We had again forced him back more than a mile, and had gained possession of the southern crest of the main ridge on a front of over 6,000 yards. . . . Our line was definitely established from Maltz Horn Farm, where we met the French left, north along the eastern edge of Trônes Wood to Longueval, then west past Bazentin-le-Grand to the northern corner of Bazentin-le-Petit Wood, and then west again past the southern face of Pozières to the north of Ovillers."

The gain had been great, but much remained to be done ; the salient about Delville Wood and Longueval required to be widened, the villages of Pozières and

Thiepval, and the trenches all about them and on the main ridge in rear, had still to be carried, and it was to assist in these operations, and to give relief to the troops which had already been severely tried, that the 33rd Division was now called up.*

"At the beginning of July, 1916, the Division moved down to the Somme area to take part in the great offensive battle. Having detrained near Amiens, it proceeded by march route to Fricourt in intense heat, and bivouacked there on the night of July 13th. . . . Through dust and heat and a myriad flies, the sweating Division moved up through Fricourt across the captured German trench system on July 14th, with the 100th Brigade leading, followed by the 98th Brigade, and with the 19th Brigade in reserve, up the road through Montauban, where the enemy still grinned in his ghastly sleep, and eastwards to Caterpillar Valley, through the Valley of Death, just west of Bazentin-le-Grand. On the evening of the 14th, orders were received for a further general attack upon a wide front, the 100th Brigade being allotted the task of capturing Martinpuich and High Wood on the Flers Ridge, this being part of the German Switch Line, and of extending the attack eastwards. Patrols were immediately pushed into High Wood from the 9th Highland Light Infantry, under Lieutenant-Colonel Stormonth-Darling, and the 1st The Queen's Regiment, under Major Palmer,† accompanied by one section of the 100th Machine Gun Company. Very little time was possible for reconnaissance. At dawn on July 15th a thick ground mist covered the whole of the valley lying east of the village of Bazentin, and completely obscured High Wood and Martinpuich." Thus the 33rd Division History, and we may now take up the story from the 1st Battalion diary.

On the morning of July 14th the 1st The Queen's moved to an assembly position south of Mametz main road close to Fricourt Cemetery; the 16th King's Royal Rifles were close to The Queen's, while the 2nd Worcesters and 9th Highland Light Infantry were on the northern side of the road. Lieutenant-Colonel L. M. Crofts, as understudy to the Brigadier, remained with the transport, which was parked behind the Battalion bivouac, and had with him Captain Harrison (transport officer), Lieutenant Wallis (the quartermaster), and Second-Lieutenants Flinn, Faulkner, Roffe, and Mundye, while Second-Lieutenant Lukyn went as liaison officer to the Brigade. Major G. B. Parnell assumed command of the Battalion, the companies of which were thus officered:—

"A" *Company*.—Temporary Captain H. P. Foster, Lieutenant C. G. D. Thrupp, Second-Lieutenants J. G. Buckner, J. H. Rouquette and H. J. Buist.

"B" *Company*.—Temporary Captain R. P. Slatter, Second-Lieutenants H. H. Richards, R. E. C. Harland, G. D. G. Bottomley and W. A. L. Robinson.

"C" *Company*.—Temporary Captain P. Gurrey, Second-Lieutenants J. Burrell, A. Fairlie, G. R. Bower and W. C. Butterworth.

"D" *Company*.—Lieutenant G. A. Pilleau, Second-Lieutenants G. E. Wheeler, C. W. Farwell, R. Foley and J. S. Milner.

At Battalion headquarters with Major Parnell were Captain and Adjutant W. B. Carslake, Lieutenant D. A. Brown (signalling officer), Second-Lieutenant L. A. Crook (bombing officer), and Second-Lieutenant A. J. Crichton (Lewis gun officer).

The strength of the Battalion going into action was 25 officers and 697 other ranks.

* In relief of the 31st Division, joining the II Corps in the Fourth Army.
† Evidently a mistake for Parnell.

At 6 p.m. the 1st The Queen's moved along the Fricourt—Mametz road to a point of assembly near Flat Iron Copse, and four hours later to the neighbourhood of Bazentin-le-Petit, where " A " and " B " Companies were ordered to dig in, while " C " and " D " remained in reserve near Bazentin-le-Grand Wood ; the 9th Highland Light Infantry were entrenching on the right. These latter had not been able to get as far forward as had been hoped, as the enemy were holding the wood in their front very strongly with machine guns, and it now became necessary to concentrate and deploy the 100th Brigade in the open valley, under enemy observation at a mile range, without any covered approaches or other cover. The Brigade was consequently concentrated in the valley about 800 yards west of High Wood, and at 5 a.m. on the 15th The Queen's received orders to attack the trench known as the German Switch, the 9th Highland Light Infantry being on the right, while the attack was to be supported by the 16th King's Royal Rifles with the Worcesters in reserve.

No very definite orders appear to have reached the 1st The Queen's, so that the company commanders could not be given much information, beyond that the left would be 200 yards east of the cross roads, that the frontage would be 500 yards, and the general direction north ; " A," " B," and " C " Companies were to form the firing line, with " D " in support, and the front companies were to advance in two waves of two platoons each, with the second wave 200 yards in rear of the first. The companies were to be in position at 8 a.m., the bombardment commencing at 8.30 and lasting for half an hour. At 8.55 the first wave was to advance ; the distance to the German trench was about 900 yards.

While the companies were getting into position the enemy opened a heavy enfilade shell, machine-gun and rifle fire from which several casualties resulted, and our artillery reply was not very effective ; then almost directly the first wave started it came under fire from both flanks and front, and the second wave suffered in equal measure. The line pushed on, however, until within about 200 yards of the enemy trench, when it came under especially heavy fire, while the slopes up which the Battalion pushed towards the village of Martinpuich were covered with long grass in which the enemy had laid two lines of thin trip wire ; this The Queen's reached, but were unable to pass, and in a few minutes the ground was a shambles. At this stage Major Parnell came up with the Adjutant, and in the most gallant manner started to lead the attack forward again, but he was almost immediately hit and killed.

At 9.25 Captain Foster, commanding " A " Company, sent back word that he had reached a point about 100 yards from the enemy's trench, that the wire was not cut and that the Highland Light Infantry were not up ; cunningly laid machine guns had prevented their advance, while a battery, lying to the west of Martinpuich, which had for a time been out of action owing to the advance of The Queen's, had now opened fire into the backs of the Highlanders. Shortly after ten Lieutenant Thrupp reported from the left that he was held up by wire and asking that the bombardment might be resumed and reinforcements sent up, but when the gun fire again opened the majority of our shells fell short, some even pitching behind our line.

The Queen's hung on where they were until 12.30 p.m. and, no reinforcements arriving, the surviving officers conferred together and finally decided on withdrawal, as there seemed considerable danger of being cut off ; and the retirement was then commenced and carried out by small parties, and the original position on the road reoccupied. This position was heavily shelled all that afternoon and evening and night, and by the end of the day it was found that the casualties in the 1st Battalion The Queen's amounted to 5 officers and 28 other ranks killed, 11 officers and 207 other ranks wounded, while 58 men were missing. The losses among the non-commissioned ranks were specially heavy, 20 sergeants and 58 other non-commissioned officers being among the casualties.

The officers killed were Major G. B. Parnell, Captain R. P. Slatter, Second-Lieutenants A. J. Crichton, J. H. Rouquette and G. R. Bower, while those wounded were Captains W. B. Carslake and P. Gurrey, Lieutenant D. A. Brown, Second-Lieutenants H. H. Richards, J. Burrell, R. E. C. Harland, G. D. G. Bottomley, W. A. L. Robinson, C. W. Farwell, A. Fairlie and R. Foley.

"It was apparent at 5 p.m. that the whole attack had been a most costly failure. General Baird wrote of his Brigade that it had behaved with the greatest gallantry. The slopes lying to the west of Martinpuich and High Wood were a grim slaughter house. Dead, dying, and wounded lay thickly upon the blood-stained turf. During the night the remains of the Brigade occupied a small trench just west of the wood. The enemy bombardment became so severe that it was decided to retire still further. Had this decision not been made there is no doubt the Brigade would have perished to a man. . . . On the morning of the 16th the 19th Brigade relieved the 100th and the remains of the Brigade returned to defensive positions on the northern side of Mametz Wood."*

The Battalion was engaged in renewed fighting up to the 22nd, and had another officer (Second-Lieutenant W. C. Butterworth) and 7 more men killed, 3 officers (Captain H. P. Foster, Second-Lieutenants R. Faulkner and L. A. Crook) and 55 other ranks were wounded, Second-Lieutenant J. S. Milner and 7 men were missing, while Second-Lieutenant H. J. Buist was gassed.

The total casualties in the 100th Brigade during the fighting between July 15th and 22nd were 1,697 of all ranks, killed, wounded, and missing.

Early in August the Division was withdrawn for a short rest, and was bivouacked in the battle area round Mametz Wood, finally moving for a few days to Albert, and then on August 18th, the Division having been reinforced, it resumed the offensive on High Wood and the high ground between High Wood and Delville Wood. The result of some minor operations during the days that immediately followed was the seizure of certain important trenches, preparatory to an attack on a wide front, which was planned for the 24th. This was to be covered, for the first time, by a machine-gun barrage, provided by the machine guns of the 14th, 23rd, and 33rd Divisions, and these were ordered to maintain rapid fire for twelve hours continuously. So well was this order carried out that ten guns fired just under one million rounds!

On August 23rd, the eve of the attack, the Battalion was occupying the front line trenches to the west of Delville Wood with one company in the front line, two in support, and one in reserve, the enemy keeping up a continuous shelling of the front and support lines during the day and night. On the afternoon of this day it was announced that the 100th Brigade would carry out the big attack next day on the front of the Division, with the Worcesters, King's Royal Rifles, and the 1st The Queen's in front and the 9th Highland Light Infantry in close support. The morning of the 24th passed more quietly and everything connected with the attack was arranged and explained—"D" and "C" Companies being the assaulting

* *The 33rd Division in France and Flanders*, p. 18.

companies, with "B" in immediate support, and "A" in reserve, all to be in position by 3 p.m. "D" and "C" Companies were to capture the new German position from the point where the new German line met Wood Lane on a front, going east, of 300 yards. A bombing post was to be established as far up Wood Lane in a northerly direction as possible, this task being allotted to the Battalion bombers under Second-Lieutenant Carpenter.

"Zero hour" was 5.45 p.m., preceded by a two hours' bombardment and a final barrage of intense fire thirty minutes before the assault, which was to start sixty-five minutes after zero hour, the barrage lifting as the troops in front drew up to it.

At 8.30 p.m. the objective was reported taken, and the work of consolidation in progress, but reinforcements being asked for, two companies of the Highland Light Infantry were sent up; and messages now received stated that The Queen's had suffered very heavy officer casualties from shell fire, chiefly prior to the commencement of the assault. Colonels Crofts of The Queen's and Darling of the Highland Light Infantry were sent up about midnight with a view to clear up the situation, and relieve The Queen's by the Highlanders; but Colonel Crofts was wounded before reaching the front line, leaving Captain Brodhurst-Hill in command of the Battalion, and this officer having arranged details of the relief with Colonel Darling, the 1st The Queen's was withdrawn to the reserve line about five on the morning of August 25th.

The Battalion had succeeded in capturing its objective, while the bombers had advanced about 100 yards up Wood Lane Trench and seized a German block, establishing their own about ten yards in front of it.

Delville Wood was in our possession, but the north-eastern corner of High Wood still remained in the hands of the enemy.

The following is a copy of a Fourth Army telegram, dated August 25th :—

"*Please convey to the 33rd Division, and especially to General Baird, the Army Commander's congratulations on their performance yesterday, which he thinks was especially creditable to all concerned at the end of such a long period in the front line as the 33rd Division have now had.*"

The success had been great, but had not been achieved without heavy losses in all ranks of the 1st The Queen's; during the operations commencing on the 23rd 5 officers and 24 non-commissioned officers and men had been killed, 6 officers and 87 other ranks had been wounded; the officers were—killed, Second-Lieutenants E. d'A. Collings, J. A. Rope, L. E. Bennett, A. W. E. Long and A. M. Campbell; wounded, Lieutenant-Colonel L. M. Crofts, Captains O. S. Flinn, and S. E. Lukyn, Second-Lieutenants L. H. Bennett, W. J. Howell and J. W. Carpenter.

On leaving the reserve trenches the Battalion marched back to trenches in Fricourt, and thereafter had very many moves, during which Major-General Landon, commanding 33rd Division, took an opportunity of seeing and addressing The Queen's, praising all ranks in warm terms for their conduct throughout the operations in the parts from which they had just come, under the most trying circumstances, during the great offensive on the Somme. "He wished them all the best of luck and expressed his confidence in them to carry on in the future as they had done in the past, upholding themselves as a fine example of England's best troops."

During these days a large number of young officers joined from England or from the base, Second-Lieutenants A. C. Allen, H. D. Taylor, N. B. Avery, D. E. H.

Millard, T. R. G. Cowan, L. Perkins, R. S. Walker, K. M. East, R. C. Lloyd, B. C. Selfe, P. R. Hope, G. H. V. Burghope, J. Barnard, E. H. Langhorne, K. V. Norman, F. J. Bower, G. Stevenson, A. McN. Austin and J. Holliday.

At the end of September the 33rd Division was withdrawn from the forward area and proceeded by train to Longpré in the Longpré—Airaines area, where it was billeted, taking over for a very short period the line opposite Gommecourt Park; during the period Major-General R. J. Pinney relieved General Landon in command of the 33rd Division. On September 19th Major H. N. A. Hunter joined the 1st The Queen's, and assumed command of the Battalion, but a month later this officer was transferred to the headquarters of the 7th Division, and his place was taken by Lieutenant-Colonel S. T. Watson, D.S.O.

Towards the end of October the Battalion was occupying bivouacs between Bernafay Wood and Trônes, where, on the 30th, orders were received that the 100th Brigade would now move up to the front line—the 2nd Worcesters and 9th Highland Light Infantry in the front line, the 1st The Queen's to Guillemont, and the 16th King's Royal Rifles to the Hog's Back, respectively in support and reserve. While the 33rd Division had been away from the forward area and on the Gommecourt front, High Wood and Flers Ridge had been captured by our troops.

The weather had now entirely broken, the roads were deep in mud, and every yard of ground was pitted with deep shell holes, while the bivouacs chiefly consisted of shell holes, the greater number of which were half full of water; material for the building of shelters was non-existent.

On November 1st "A" and "B" Companies were moved forward to Ox Trench to be in close support during an attack by the 9th Highland Light Infantry on Baritska Redoubt, but these companies were not called upon to act though none-the-less they suffered some seven casualties. Next morning the Battalion was ordered to relieve the Highlanders on the right front, thus becoming the right battalion of the British line and joining up with the 66th Regiment of French infantry. Later, verbal instructions were received to the effect that the 1st The Queen's were to attack Baritska Trench on November 3rd at an hour to be fixed by the commanding officer; the Battalion left Guillemont at 4.15 p.m., meeting guides at Cuinchy Corner, and not reaching the front line until about 8 p.m. The Brigade had been asked to provide a working party to continue a trench already partly dug parallel to Baritska and about half-way between that trench and Antelope Trench; this was not done, however, as the digging party missed the guides. That portion of the trench already dug was known locally as New Trench.

The companies were ordered to occupy the following positions: "B" Company, New Trench; "A" Company, Antelope Trench; "D" German Trench; and "C," Muggy Trench; the Battalion headquarters being in the sunken road south-west of Les Bœufs. The ground was in so bad a state that "B" Company took no less than nine hours getting into position after leaving Battalion headquarters, while the trenches were so terribly wet that men were standing in mud and water up to well above their knees. Some found it quite impossible to move about, and had to be dug out of the mud after remaining in it for any length of time.

The orders issued by the Brigadier directed that the attack upon Baritska Trench was to be carried out by the 1st The Queen's, the 2nd Worcesters finding one company ready to provide carrying parties for The Queen's, while the 16th King's Royal Rifles was to assist by opening an intense fire with rifles and Lewis guns upon Hazy Trench in their immediate front; there was to be no preliminary bombardment by our heavy guns of Hazy and Baritska Trenches, but only of objectives further to the rear of these. There was, however, to be a field artillery barrage on Baritska, Mirage and Hazy Trenches. Once Baritska Trench was taken, the right of the attack was to swing round through Mirage Trench, while a communication trench was to be dug as soon as possible from the point of junction of Baritska and Hazy Trench to the present front line.

Zero hour was to be 4 p.m. on the 3rd. The field artillery barrage was carried out by the French, but this did not appear to be especially effective, for the north-western end of the trench was not touched, and the shelling of the remainder of the trench mostly went over, while the barrage lifted at 3.50 instead of, as arranged, at 4 p.m., at which hour the Battalion left the trenches, going forward in splendid style in spite of the adverse conditions of ground and weather. After getting about half-way to the first objective, the advance was held up by heavy rifle and machine-gun fire from the left front, when most of the officers became casualties and the losses in other ranks were serious. When it was found that no further headway could be made, the three companies withdrew and occupied their original positions.

During the night orders were received for the two companies in the front to fall back to the neighbourhood of German Trench, to permit of a further bombardment of Baritska Trench, while " C " Company was also ordered to withdraw to the Sunken Road, where was Battalion headquarters, in order to be as fresh as possible for further operations on the 5th. All reports received spoke of the exhausted state of the men owing to the condition of the ground.

The companies remained throughout the 4th under heavy enemy fire, and this day orders were issued for a renewed attack on Baritska Trench to be carried out at 11.10 a.m. on the 5th, the whole Brigade taking part instead of only one battalion as on the preceding occasion—with the 1st The Queen's on the right and 16th King's Royal Rifles on the left, while the other two battalions were to assail the right flank through the French lines. This was later modified, and the 9th Highland Light Infantry, less two companies, was held in Brigade Reserve, the two companies of this corps being attached for the operation to the 1st The Queen's, of which only one company was to take part in the attack.

The Battalion Operation Orders, after stating that there was to be a general attack on the 5th by the Fourth and Fifth British and Sixth French Armies, goes on to say that Baritska and Hazy Trenches were to be attacked from the front by The Queen's and King's Royal Rifles respectively, the attack by The Queen's being carried out by " C " Company, " A," " B " and " D " remaining in their present positions, but " D " being held in readiness to support " C " should the attack fail. " C " Company was to occupy New Trench on the night of the 4th-5th in preparation for the attack. " The artillery barrage," so runs the order, " will creep at 25 yards' interval in a north-westerly direction—that is, in the direction in which the Worcesters are attacking. At the time of the first lift the right platoon of ' C ' Company will advance in a north-westerly direction in conjunction with the advance of the 2nd Worcesters. On the next lift of barrage the right centre platoon of ' C ' Company will advance, and so on."

Before leaving Battalion headquarters, the Officer Commanding " C " Company had the scheme explained to him, but he was also given verbal instructions not to advance until and unless he saw the attack of the Worcesters developing on his right and unless he had enough men to attack with. It was considered that the main attack was to be made by the Worcesters, seeing that a whole battalion was employed and that the artillery barrage was lifting parallel to their front. " C " Company, however, arrived in Antelope Trench about 5 a.m. on the 5th only about 70 strong, the remainder having lost their way by reason of the darkness and the appalling state of the ground, and the Company failed to find New Trench before day broke.

Early on the morning of the 5th two companies of Highland Light Infantry reported, and one was ordered to occupy Antelope Trench in support of " C " Company of The Queen's, while the other was held at Battalion headquarters to furnish carrying parties.

At 11.10 a.m. the attack commenced, and the infantry were seen to be advancing in good order. The Officer Commanding " C " Company, however, acting on his verbal orders, did not advance, but unfortunately his inaction was not known until 3 p.m., but in the meantime the Worcesters and King's Royal Rifles had gained their objective and had pushed on further without meeting much opposition or incurring many casualties. One of the Highland Light Infantry companies attached to The Queen's was sent forward at 1.10 p.m. to help consolidate the line, and at 3.15 p.m. " C " Company of The Queen's was ordered to advance and also assist in consolidating the line gained ; this was done, the Company moving to the left of the King's Royal Rifles to prolong the line to the left and join hands with the next brigade.

At 4 p.m. it was known that the Brigade would shortly be withdrawn, and that night the Battalion was relieved and moved back to Ox Trench, about 800 yards in rear of Les Bœufs, and was there tolerably heavily shelled, but suffered no loss. From here the 1st The Queen's moved back through Carnoy to Guillemont, where the following message from the Divisional Commander was published :—

*" The Corps Commander wishes me to convey to you and your troops his high appreciation of your splendid effort which though not successful was none the less glorious. These efforts, even if not always successful, have the desired effect of keeping Germans on this front instead of allowing them to reinforce Roumania. We must also support the French in their attacks."*

In these operations, beginning on November 2nd and coming to an end on the 6th, the losses of the 1st The Queen's had again been considerable, 3 officers and 41 other ranks being killed, 4 officers and 131 non-commissioned officers and men being wounded, while 1 officer (also wounded) and 54 men were missing, but of these last 18 were traced. The officers' names are—killed, Second-Lieutenants L. Perkins, W. H. B. Gross and R. C. Lloyd ; wounded, Second-Lieutenants R. V. Norman, W. Stranger, A. McN. Austin and E. H. Langhorne ; and missing, Lieutenant C. W. Eltham.

During the Somme Battle, which commenced on July 1st and which was carried on with scarcely any check and with prodigious loss on both sides until the middle of November, the three main objects with which the offensive had been undertaken had been achieved : " Verdun had been relieved ; the main German forces had been held on the Western Front ; and the enemy's strength had been very considerably worn down. . . . The total number of prisoners taken by us in the Somme battle between July 1st and November 18th is just over 38,000, including over 800 officers. During the same period we captured 29 heavy guns, 96 field guns and field howitzers, 136 trench mortars and 514 machine guns."*

* Despatch of December 23rd, 1916.

During the rest of the month the Battalion was in the neighbourhood of Liercourt, where drafts totalling 207 joined—the greater number of these from the 4th and 5th Battalions of the Regiment—and where No. 4537 Regimental Sergeant-Major Nevins and No. 11247 Sergeant A. McCabe were granted commissions.

In the first week in December the 33rd Division " moved south and took over from the 30th French Division in the Rancourt—Bouchavesnes sector, opposite St. Pierre Vaast Wood, with its rear echelons and transport lines in the Maurepas ravine about three miles behind. The conditions in this area were even worse than those of the previous month in the Les Bœufs sector. Roads did not exist ; not a stick of vegetation was living, nothing but stunted trees and tangled scrub remained of the vast boar forests and pleasant parks of this district in pre-war days. Only one communication trench, three kilometres long, existed, and this was subjected from morning till night to a heavy bombardment ; and in any case the waterlogged condition of the ground made it almost impassable. . . . Over and over again men were stuck in the mud, often up to their shoulders, for many hours. Some lived for two days in this bitter cold, buried round the neck in mud, under continuous shell fire, it only being possible to render them assistance, or give them hot stimulants, under cover of darkness, until they were dragged out with ropes, almost insane and hideously frostbitten. A new plague, which in a minor form had revealed itself in 1914-15, now descended upon the Division, to be known as ' Trench feet.' . . . The number of cases during the first two eight-day tours, where each company performed forty-eight hours' duty in the wet, were as under :—

| 100th Brigade | 1st The Queen's | 209 | 2nd Worcestershires | 104 |
| | 9th H.L.I. | 259 | 16th K.R.R.C. | 82." |

The Battalion diary gives some idea of the extent of this scourge, for therein we read that on December 12th 65 men, on the 13th 64, and on the 14th 30 men were sent to hospital suffering from " trench feet " after a tour of duty in the front line.

During the month 90 men arrived in three drafts, and several officers—Major R. M. Grigg, 8th Battalion Hampshire Regiment, joined as Second-in-Command, and there also came out Second-Lieutenants H. J. Buist, L. P. Smith, C. G. Kemp, G. P. S. Jacobs, and C. H. Plowman-Brown—the last three from the 3rd Battalion.

Christmas cannot have been an especially festive season under the circumstances, but the day was at least spent happily out of the line, and in the manner in which —" it's a way they have in the Army "—the British soldier has from time immemorial found pleasure and even relaxation—in " cleaning up " !

Maps 5 and 9.

## CHAPTER V.

### 1st BATTALION (*continued*).

### 1917.

#### THE BATTLE OF ARRAS—THE THIRD BATTLE OF YPRES.

**BATTLE HONOURS:**

" Arras, 1917," " Scarpe," " Bullecourt," " Ypres, 1917," " Menin Road," " Polygon Wood."

IN January, 1917, the 33rd Division side-stepped rather further to the south, and took over the line from Bouchavesnes inclusive to the bend of the Somme at Clery, including the island of Ommiécourt in the river itself. Here the Division relieved the 17th French Division commanded by General Lancrenon.

In his despatch of December 25th, 1917, the Field-Marshal thus describes his plan of action for the general offensive proposed to be launched in 1917 :—" In the spring, as soon as all the Allied armies were ready to commence operations, my first efforts were to be directed against the enemy's troops occupying the salient between the Scarpe and the Ancre, into which they had been pressed as the result of the Somme battle. It was my intention to attack both shoulders of this salient simultaneously, the Fifth Army operating on the Ancre front, while the Third Army attacked from the north-west about Arras. These converging attacks, if successful, would pinch off the whole salient, and would be likely to make the withdrawal of the enemy's troops from it a very costly manœuvre for him if it were not commenced in good time.

" The front of attack from the Arras side was to include the Vimy Ridge, possession of which I considered necessary to secure the left flank of the operations on the southern bank of the Scarpe. The capture of this ridge, which was to be carried out by the First Army, also offered other important advantages. It would deprive the enemy of valuable observation and give us a wide view over the plains stretching from the eastern foot of the ridge to Douai and beyond. Moreover, although it was evident that the enemy might, by a timely withdrawal, avoid a battle in the awkward salient still held by him between the Scarpe and the Ancre, no such withdrawal from his important Vimy Ridge positions was likely. He would be almost certain to fight for this ridge, and, as my object was to deal him a blow which would force him to use up reserves, it was important that he should not evade my attack."

Certain modifications had subsequently to be made in this plan, but these did not materially affect the Arras operations in which the 33rd Division was engaged.

For the first three months of the year the 1st Battalion The Queen's remained comparatively inactive in the Clery sector, and at the end of March was occupying billets in the town of Corbie, where on the 31st it was announced that the 33rd Division was about to be transferred to the Third Army and that the 100th Brigade would make an early move from Corbie to the Villers-Bocage area. On April 2nd the move commenced, the Battalion marching via Villers-Bocage, Beauval, Ransart, Grenas, Souastre to St. Amand, where the Battalion remained two or three days under orders to move at three hours' notice, moving again on the 12th by way of Bienvillers, Monchy au Bois, Adinfer, and Boiry to the neighbourhood of Mercatel, where the Brigade was in divisional reserve. Then on the 15th the Brigade marched to a position north of Croisilles, there relieving the 110th Brigade. The 1st The Queen's were now in brigade reserve, the Battalion headquarters being at Hamlincourt.

Here on the 18th Lieutenant-Colonel L. M. Crofts, D.S.O., joined from home on recovery from his wounds, and assumed command of the Battalion, while Lieutenant-Colonel C. F. Watson, C.M.G., D.S.O., left to take command of the 7th Battalion.

By this date the British offensive had already commenced satisfactorily with the capture of the Vimy Ridge and villages further south, while a footing had been gained in the Hindenburg Line. From north to south the battle had gone well; on April 9th the Canadians had gained all their objectives on Vimy Ridge, the XVII Corps had also obtained all objectives and formed a defensive flank to the north, the VI Corps had equally gained all it had set out to do south of the Scarpe, but the VII Corps had got no further than the Hindenburg Line, and had incurred many casualties. When the 33rd Division arrived at the front to resume the offensive, the enemy had recovered from the surprise of the initial attack, and had already greatly strengthened his defence, particularly with artillery.

During the past ten days or so the 19th Brigade had been acting with the 21st Division, and when the 33rd Division took over the 19th Brigade was established in the Hindenburg Line, while to the south, the 100th Brigade occupied posts east of Croisilles, with patrols gradually moving across the Sensée River by night and pushing forward posts towards the Hindenburg Line, as far south as the Hump near Bullecourt.

"An attack on a very large scale was planned for April 23rd. In this attack the 98th Brigade to the north was ordered to force its way south down the Hindenburg Line, chiefly with bombs, and make a junction with the 100th Brigade in the Sensée Valley; the 100th Brigade delivering a frontal attack upon the Hindenburg Line. The attack was particularly difficult to carry out. The Hindenburg Line consisted of a highly fortified front and second line, with concrete machine-gun emplacements, some of them with two storeys, about every fifty yards along it. Both lines were defended in front by strands of the thickest wire to a depth of about twenty yards, and were connected by the most complete system of tunnels and dug-outs that has ever been seen in the history of warfare."*

"Sunday, April 22nd," so writes an officer then serving with the 1st The Queen's, "Battalion went off under Weeding† to a position of assembly in quarries half a mile north-east of Croissilles, east of the Sensée River. They are to advance across 800 yards of open in the dark and attack the Hindenburg Line on a front of about 400 yards to the south of the Sensée River, and to hold the line until the 98th Brigade, who are attacking down the Hindenburg Line from the north, have joined up; their right flank is to be protected by two tanks. A mad scheme in my opinion, as if the 98th *don't* join up, they will be left in the middle of the German line with both flanks in the air, and it will be impossible to get up reinforcements or

---

* *The 33rd Division in France and Flanders*, p. 35.

† The following officers remained behind:—Colonel Crofts, Captains Faulkner and Battiscombe, Lieutenant Thrupp, Second-Lieutenants Ribton-Cooke, Cowan, Barnard, Hughes and Kemp.

THE UNIFORM AND EQUIPMENT (FRONT AND BACK VIEWS) WORN IN FRANCE AND FLANDERS DURING THE GREAT WAR.

ammunition till dark. In addition the advance to within 200 yards of the enemy in the dark is a most difficult and dangerous operation ; the wire in front of the enemy is very strong, in three lines radiating from a centre, and only gaps have been cut by the artillery. Two companies of the King's Royal Rifles are following the Battalion with bombs, ammunition, etc."

The 1st The Queen's passed through Hamlincourt about 7.30 p.m. on the 22nd, picked up extra ammunition and bombs near Judas Farm and reached the place of assembly at 11.30 p.m.; here twenty entrenching tools per company were distributed and hot cocoa was served out, and at 3.30 on the morning of the 23rd The Queen's moved on from the Quarry to the position of deployment, deploying on a front of 300 yards on tapes previously laid down, 150 yards on each side of the Croisilles—Fontaine road.

The first two waves were composed of " D " Company, Captain Brodhurst-Hill, on the right of the road, and " A " Company, Second-Lieutenant Carpenter, on the left, with " mopping-up " platoons of " C " and " B " Companies forming a third line to the first wave. The third and fourth waves, moving at fifty yards' interval, were made up of " C " and " B " Companies on right and left, under Captain Ball and Second-Lieutenant Holliday; the two companies of the King's Royal Rifles attached composed the fifth and sixth waves.

The advance from the position of deployment was over 1,000 yards of open country, along the valley of the Sensée River, which was only a trickle running in a water-course giving a certain amount of cover, but commanded generally from the high ground on either side. The front German trench was protected by at least two rows of barbed wire radiating from where the trench crossed the road, with more thick wire between the first and second lines. The German front line trench was much knocked about, and for the most part not more than four feet deep. It was enfiladed from the north.

At twenty minutes before zero hour, the force was to advance to the line of a sunken road, crossing the Croisilles—Fontaine road, which had been picqueted during the night by the 2nd Worcesters, and was to lie down there and wait for the barrage to fall ; this was to dwell for eight minutes on the front line, for ten minutes on the second line, and then to continue behind the second line until ninety minutes after zero, by which time it was expected that the 98th Brigade would have joined up. " D " and " A " Companies of The Queen's were to cross the German first line and occupy and consolidate the second line. " C " Company was to make blocks on the right of the first line and form a defensive flank along the communication trench ; " B " was to do the same on the left along the Sensée River. The King's Royal Rifle companies were to form a central dump of bombs, etc., and occupy and consolidate the German first line ; the two tanks were to follow on the right of the attack and work down the enemy's line towards the river.

The 1st The Queen's advanced at 4.15, and moved in good order to the sunken road and there lay down to wait for zero—fixed for 4.45 a.m.—without detection by the enemy, and then when the attack began, they worked up to within fifty yards of the barrage, entering the front trench with few casualties ; this was found to contain only a few of the enemy who were quickly disposed of. The leading companies then went forward to the German second line, but were now held up by very strong uncut wire, and the barrage on lifting was taken too far back and rested *beyond* instead of *on* the second line, and the Germans were consequently able to man their parapet. Only a small party of " A " Company had managed to reach the second line, and the remainder of the attackers took cover in the many shell holes between the two lines.

The two tanks which should have arrived by this and given material assistance at a critical moment, never turned up, having broken down before zero.

Telephonic communication with Battalion headquarters was established and maintained until 5.30, when the lines were cut, and communication thenceforward was possible only by runners.

In the German first line on the right of the road two " strong points " were captured, and bombing parties pushed 100 yards forward until held up by a third " strong point," and a double block was here made and established ; this was maintained until 11 a.m., when the Germans made a determined attack with rifle grenades and bombs, but they were driven back by parties under Company Sergeant-Major Elderkin. On the left a block was at first made at the river, but on the " box barrage " lifting the enemy attacked ; he was, however, repulsed by the use of rifle grenades, and a party under Corporal Spooner, following him up for 150 yards, captured a concrete blockhouse and machine gun ; on the enemy counter-attacking this was destroyed by a bomb, and a block was then made fifty yards from the blockhouse, and held till the end. The first line very soon became completely filled with wounded men, and it was then very difficult to pass bombs to the five different points where bombing was incessant.

At 5.8 a.m. Second-Lieutenant Holliday reported the first line taken, but the second strongly held by Germans, while the tanks had not arrived.

At 5.25 five prisoners of the German 99th Regiment were passed back.

At 7.10 Second-Lieutenant Carpenter arrived at Battalion headquarters wounded, and reporting that the front-line companies were running out of bombs ; this was later confirmed by a message from Captain Godfrey, timed 6.45 a.m., reporting the shortage of bombs and Lewis-gun ammunition, and saying that the situation was then critical. During the next few hours parties from the King's Royal Rifle companies carried up nearly 1,500 bombs. Then at 10.10 Captain Godfrey was able to send a better report—that the advance of the 98th Brigade had relieved the pressure, and though the casualties were heavy the men were cheery and confident, but—bombs, more bombs, were wanted. Two hours later came news that the enemy was pressing the defence with repeated bombing attacks, while the supply of bombs was again running low, and now at 1.20 p.m. the last lot of 800 bombs was sent up, but before the carrying party had reached the front line the enemy had started strong bombing attacks from five different points, and five and twenty minutes later the Germans, having massed on the right, rushed the blocks under a barrage of aerial torpedoes and rifle grenades, the defenders' supply of bombs having here given out. The enemy pressure on the right flank now forced a retirement here, causing the cutting off of the men in the centre communication trench.

Many casualties occurred during this retirement, but the men rallied at the Battalion headquarters, which was heavily shelled, and further losses incurred. Then at last, at 8 p.m., orders were received to fall back to the railway cutting near Judas Trench.

The retirement was mainly due to the following circumstances :—
1. The fact that the 98th Brigade was held and failed to join up.
2. The non-arrival of the two tanks.
3. The wire being uncut between the first and second German lines.
4. The difficulty in keeping up the bomb supply.

As to this last, the 1st The Queen's were ably assisted during the action by the King's Royal Rifles, who performed valuable service in bringing up bombs and ammunition across the open under heavy fire, suffering severe losses in doing so.

Of the latter part of the action the divisional history relates that " it was apparent that The Queen's, for the time being at any rate, were cut off from the rest of the Brigade, it being impossible to move up to the Hindenburg Line owing to the very heavy shell and machine-gun fire, without incurring the heaviest possible casualties. Moreover, both tanks with the 100th Brigade had failed to leave their starting point. By 10 a.m. the situation of The Queen's was desperate. Their bombs were exhausted and it seemed an impossible task to supply them. . . . About 11 a.m. a determined counter-attack by the enemy, who seem thoroughly to have appreciated the awful plight of The Queen's, drove them and elements of the 16th King's Royal Rifle Corps from the Hindenburg Line. The 98th Brigade then, losing touch, were themselves driven back from their objective. As the men came back, the well-posted enemy machine guns picked them off like rabbits, and scarcely a man returned unwounded, whilst many were shot down in their tracks. The Queen's after the attack, mustered only 43 men."

Of the 14 officers of the Battalion who had gone into action, 13 were killed or wounded or missing, while the losses in non-commissioned officers and men totalled 26 killed, 101 wounded, and 308 missing. The officers killed were Second-Lieutenants D. E. H. Millard, A. C. S. Fowler and G. H. V. Burghope; wounded were Second-Lieutenants H. J. Carpenter and F. J. Bower; while the following were missing :— Captains F. Godfrey, F. S. Ball and R. Brodhurst-Hill, Second-Lieutenants O. V. Botton, J. Holliday, wounded, R. S. Walker, G. P. S. Jacob, wounded, and H. M. Thompson, wounded. Second-Lieutenant H. V. Lacey was the only officer who got back unhurt from the German line, while of the 8 missing officers all except Captain Brodhurst-Hill* were later reported to be prisoners of war in Germany.

The following messages were received by the Division; from the Commander-in-Chief :—

"*The fierce fighting yesterday has carried us another step forward. I congratulate you and all under you on the result of it and on the severe punishment you have inflicted on the enemy.*"

Then on the Division being relieved by the 21st Division, and being transferred to the Bienvillers—Pommier area to refit and reorganize, the Corps Commander, General Snow, wrote as follows to Major-General Pinney :—

"*On the occasion of the Division leaving the line for a well-earned rest, the Corps Commander wishes to record his appreciation of the high fighting qualities of your Division. The fighting of the last few days has been severe, and in open fight your Division, in a difficult situation, outfought and inflicted severe losses on the enemy.*"

During the fortnight or more that the 33rd Division was now out of the line— the 1st The Queen's in turn at Blaireville, Boiry St. Martin and Moyenneville— fighting had been carried on with great violence, the 7th, 21st, 58th, and 62nd Divisions all being engaged with greatly varying success; and when on May 16th the 33rd Division relieved the 21st it was found that not much ground had been won during the absence of the 33rd Division and that the enemy on this front had not withdrawn as had been rumoured. An attack was ordered for May 20th, by the Third Army under General Allenby, and by the Fifth Army under General

* This officer was taken prisoner but information was only received at a much later date.

Gough, on a wide front. The 98th Brigade was ordered to carry out an attack on pretty much the same lines with that of April 23rd, while the 100th Brigade was given a more ambitious scheme of a frontal attack on the Hindenburg Line between the Sensée River and "the Hump," just north of Bullecourt. The attack on this occasion was not, as usual, to be made at dawn, but at an hour when it was hoped that the enemy would be busy with his breakfast; further, there was to be no previous bombardment, but, for four minutes covering the initial assault, there was to be a hurricane bombardment, followed by a protective bombardment for two hours covering consolidation.

In the 100th Brigade the battalions of the Worcesters, King's Royal Rifles, and Highland Light Infantry were to attack from the Sensée River to Heudicourt Road with the 1st The Queen's providing carrying parties; the 98th Brigade was working down towards these from the left; while a battalion of the 19th Brigade formed a defensive flank on the right.

The attack commenced at 5 a.m. on the 20th, and the carrying party of The Queen's attached to the Worcesters sent forward ammunition in small quantities regularly and continuously at intervals until the afternoon of the 21st; the party with the Highland Light Infantry moved in two lots of 1 officer and 20 men each, but both officers (Second-Lieutenants Barnard and Howcroft), and half their men were wounded, and only one journey could be made; the party of The Queen's with the King's Royal Rifles carried continuously in small parties of two and three. The stores taken up to the front by The Queen's carrying parties included 55 boxes S.A.A., 140 boxes of bombs, 900 sand bags, 100 petrol tins of water (*i.e.*, 200 gallons), 40 picks and shovels, and 4 boxes of Very lights.

The enemy counter-attacked repeatedly, but the line captured was held, though with heavy losses among the defenders. "During the height of the bombardment and at a time of extreme peril, when our troops in the line were short of both bombs and ammunition, Captain Harrison of The Queen's, acting as Brigade Transport Officer, galloped the whole of the Brigade ammunition limbers up the Sensée Valley along the Fontaine Road, and succeeded in replenishing with bombs and ammunition the whole line, with the loss of only one limber. This feat was not only very spectacular, but needed the highest qualities of resource, initiative, and daring. Undoubtedly, Captain Harrison's act saved the 100th Brigade from again being driven out of the Hindenburg Line as on April 23rd."\*

At four in the afternoon the 19th Brigade was ordered to continue the attack, passing through the 100th, with special orders to capture Tunnel Trench, which connected the Sensée Valley through Fontaine, but the attack upon Fontaine Village was again a failure, although the whole of the Hindenburg front line was now entirely in our hands.

The casualties in the carrying parties of The Queen's were Captain R. Battiscombe, Second-Lieutenants J. N. F. Barnard and S. M. Howcroft, and 40 other ranks wounded, and on the following day when the Battalion took over the portion of the Hindenburg Line captured by the Highland Light Infantry, these casualties were increased by the loss of 11 men killed, Second-Lieutenant C. G. Kemp was wounded, while 8 men were missing.

There was further fighting on May 26th-28th and June 19th, and a special attack had been ordered for June 25th, but was cancelled at the last moment after the troops of the 100th Brigade were already in position. Finally, on the 27th,

\* *The 33rd Division in France and Flanders*, p. 41.

instructions were received for the Battalion to carry out an attack on the 29th, with the object of securing the enemy block in the northern end of Tunnel Trench, and, by establishing a post on high ground in Tunnel Trench, clearing Kitten Trench of the enemy. This operation was entrusted to a composite company made up of 73 men from " A," 23 from " B," 54 from " C," and 37 from " D " Company, under the following officers :—Lieutenant W. B. Carslake, Second-Lieutenants H. Ribton-Cooke, H. J. Trythall, G. F. Ashpitel, J. E. Shipton, and W. H. Baynes.

At 6 a.m. on the 29th the parties began to move into their appointed places in Lump Lane, each man having two bombs and an extra bandolier of rifle ammunition. The trenches were in places nearly knee-deep in mud and water from the heavy rain of the previous evening and the going was very heavy. Zero was fixed for 8.30 a.m., and at 8.15 all were in their places. The attack was to be a bombing attack up Tunnel Trench, starting from three points in Lump Lane, and crossing the broken ground between this and the objective in waves. Saps had been dug out from the Nebus and No. 5 Sap, and it was intended to join these up to form a " jumping off " place, but the time available was very short and these arrangements could not therefore be made, so that the attack had to be arranged to start from Lump Lane. It was hoped, however, to effect a surprise and accordingly the barrage of Stokes mortars, machine guns, and field and heavy artillery, was timed to commence at zero hour *plus* five minutes.

The ground between Lump Lane and the objective was very broken, being nothing but a mass of shell-holes ; while a ridge, about seventy yards from the Nebus, and 120 yards from the junction of Lump Lane and No. 5 Sap, commanded Lump Lane. The enemy was believed to be holding Kitten Trench, and a special patrol, composed of a Lewis gun section and bombers under No. 10683 Sergeant A. Spooner, was detailed as a right flank guard.

The advance began at zero—8.50 a.m., but at only some twenty yards from our trenches the leading waves of the left party came under a rain of bombs, and the leader, No. 22842 Corporal W. Brooks, and several men were wounded ; the centre wave was met with rifle grenades ; and only the right wave succeeded in advancing, a small party of bombers under Second-Lieutenant Baynes managing to reach a shell hole. Sergeant Spooner seems to have got rather too much to the left, and now reported that he was with his party below the crest with a German post on both right and left. As it was now evident that the surprise had failed, that any further advance could only result in heavy losses, while success was doubtful as the enemy was obviously in strength, it was decided not to proceed with the attack.

At this time, however, Second-Lieutenant Ashpitel, in the centre, was pushing on covered by the fire of rifle grenades from the left, but Second-Lieutenant Baynes and four men were known to be isolated in a shell-hole, having run out of bombs or grenades, so Second-Lieutenant Ashpitel was called back and then sent with a party of picked men to the right and end of Sap 5 to cover Second-Lieutenant Baynes' withdrawal. This party did admirable work and by putting a grenade barrage over the heads of the enemy, Second-Lieutenant Baynes and his party were able to retire to Lump Lane.

At 3 p.m. the men holding Lump Lane were sent back a few at a time to Moyenneville, and by the afternoon of the 30th the Battalion was concentrated at Berles-au-Bois.

In the above operations the composite company of The Queen's had 6 men killed and 16 wounded.

On July 1st the 33rd Division was relieved by the 50th, and proceeded to the Hamlincourt area to rest, refit, and obtain reinforcements, the latter being especially much needed, since the recent losses experienced by the Division amounted to 240 officers and 5,431 other ranks killed, wounded, and missing.

The 1st Battalion The Queen's spent the whole of July in billets at Picquigny, engaged in training of various kinds, and then on August 1st, in consequence of sudden orders which had been received, the Battalion marched to Longpré and, there entraining, left at 9.40 a.m., and passing through Abbeville, Etaples, Boulogne and Calais, reached Dunkirk docks the same night and marched thence to Ghyvelde. Something must now be said as to the reasons why the 33rd Division had been transferred to the coastal area.

The Battle of Arras had scarcely come to an end when the Field-Marshal turned his attention and directed the bulk of his resources to the development of his northern plan of campaign, and General Plumer, commanding the Second Army, had been ordered to attack and capture the Messines—Wytschaete Ridge as a preliminary to the completion of preparations for his principal offensive east and north of Ypres. The Battle of Messines once over, a complete redistribution of the armies had become necessary, and the Third Army having extended its front and taken over all the ground between Arras and the French, the Fourth and Fifth Armies became available for employment further north; the Fourth took the place of the French on the Yser Front, and in order from north to south came the First French and the Fifth, Second, and First British Armies.

The appearance of the British troops on the coast caused the Germans much alarm and they at once commenced there to be very active; about the middle of July the enemy attacked the British front in great strength and practically annihilated a brigade of the 1st Division, and it was to fill its place that the 33rd Division had been sent up here, taking over the line from Nieuport to Lombartzyde with the Belgians on the right. On August 14th, when in billets at Coxyde, the Battalion was ordered up to the front line and Major Weeding, Lieutenant Clenshaw, Second-Lieutenants Cooke and Cowan were sent on in advance to reconnoitre the sector allotted to the Battalion. On the way up the party was caught in an enemy barrage, and Major Weeding was killed, and Lieutenant Clenshaw and Second-Lieutenant Cowan were wounded. Early in September, however, the Division was withdrawn from the Nieuport to the Eperlecques training area, and then on the 15th started to march down to the Dickebusch area, where the Division was concentrated by the 18th ready to take part in the Third Battle of Ypres, which had already commenced on July 31st.

After describing all that had taken place from the beginning of the great battle until the date when the 33rd Division came up into line, Sir Douglas Haig wrote:—
*" All this heavy fighting was not allowed to interfere with the arrangements made for a renewal of the advance by the Second and Fifth Armies on September 26th.

" The front of our attack on that date extended from south of Tower Hamlets to north-east of St. Julien, a total distance of rather less than six miles; but on the portion of this front south of the Menin Road only a short advance was intended. North of the Menin Road, our object was to reach a position from which a direct attack could be made upon the portion of the main ridge between Noordemdhoek and Broodseinde, traversed by the Becelaere—Passchendaele road. The assault was delivered at 5.50 a.m., and . . . Australian troops carried the remainder of

---
\* In his despatch of December 25th, 1917.

# THE THIRD BATTLE OF YPRES

Polygon Wood together with the German trench line to the east of it, and established themselves on their objective beyond the Becelaere—Zonnebeke road. On the left of the Australians, English troops took Zonnebeke Village and Church, and North Midland and London Territorial battalions captured a long line of hostile strong posts on both sides of the Wieltje—Gravenstafel road.

"South of Polygon Wood an obstinate struggle took place for a group of fortified farms and strong points. English, Scottish, and Welsh battalions of the same divisions* that had borne the brunt of the enemy's attacks in this area on the previous day, gallantly fought their way forward. . . . It was not until the evening of September 27th, however, that the line of our objectives in this locality was completely gained."

The divisional history states that "by 12 midnight, September 24th-25th, both the 98th and 100th Brigades were concentrated for the attack. . . . In the 100th Brigade the 9th Highland Light Infantry and the 1st The Queen's were the leading battalions, concentrated on a line running from the south across the Tower Hamlets Ridge, thence across the Reutelbeeke, and to the east of Cameron Copse. These battalions were strongly supported by the machine-gun groups of their Brigade companies. . . . The attack of the Second Army, including the 33rd Division, was ordered for dawn on September 26th. At 3.30 on the morning of the 25th the enemy opened a bombardment of hitherto unparalleled intensity. So vicious was this bombardment, and in such great depth upon our rear communications, that it was impossible to move transport or troops along the roads. Following up their bombardment, the enemy counter-attacked in massed formation upon our lines, no less than six divisions being used in this attack upon our divisional front. On the right, the posts of the 1st The Queen's were overwhelmed, the enemy debouching from the village of Gheluvelt armed with flame-throwers; the stream of burning oil thrown from these devilish weapons reached a length and height of 100 yards and set fire to the trees, which, being as dry as tinder, immediately took fire. In Inverness Copse was concentrated the 2nd Worcestershire Regiment; two companies of this regiment had already been destroyed by the bombardment. The Glasgow Highlanders moved forward, and with great dash covered up the exposed flank of the 1st The Queen's; whilst the 2nd Worcesters consolidated their position. . . .

"Except for a lull of about twenty minutes, the intensity of the bombardment continued during the whole of the 25th and the night of the 25th-26th. At 9 p.m. orders were received from the Higher Command that the original attack would be carried out according to plan on the morning of the 26th. The Division by this time had suffered 5,000 casualties. . . . At dawn on the 26th the attack, which had been reinforced by the 19th Brigade, swept forward along the whole 33rd Divisional front with extreme bitterness. Very few prisoners were taken."

So far the divisional story; we now take up that furnished by the Battalion diary. On the morning of September 25th the Battalion, having taken over the front line the previous evening, had "B" and "D" Companies in the front line, and the remaining two in immediate support. The morning was misty, and at 7.30 a message was received at Battalion headquarters that the enemy had penetrated the front line, and this was shortly after confirmed by Second-Lieutenant Hughes, who came back wounded, and who also said that the front line had been practically obliterated by heavy "Minnies," but that "D" Company was holding out. A

---
* 33rd and 39th Divisions.

message was now made out directing " C " Company to be ready to counter-attack, but the barrage was so heavy between Battalion headquarters and the front line that it was impossible for any runner to get through. At 7.48 Company Sergeant-Major Tipper arrived badly wounded, and reported that only the headquarters of " D " Company was now holding out, but shortly afterwards, the barrage slightly slackening, " C " Company was able to advance in good order under Captain Carslake on the north of the Menin Road ; " A " Company was kept in hand as there were no other troops available to stop a possible break-through on the Menin Road, and though a request for reinforcements had been sent back to the Brigade by pigeon, nothing had yet materialized.

At ten o'clock Captain Carslake managed to get back a message to the effect that his company had reached the support line, was in touch on left and right with the Highland Light Infantry and a battalion of the 39th Division respectively, and that he was preparing to attack the front line held in strength by the enemy. At 11.30 a.m. a company of the King's Royal Rifles came up and took over the reserve line, less a strong point on the Menin Road, held by a platoon of " B " Company of The Queen's, and now " A " Company was sent forward, under Captain Burrell, to support " C."

By shortly after two in the afternoon both the officers commanding " A " and " C " Companies were wounded, their places being taken by Second-Lieutenants Howcroft and Lacey, while the companies were now reduced to about fifty rifles apiece. Happily matters quieted down somewhat about dusk, and some reorganization could be attempted, but at midnight orders were received that the attack was to be resumed at 5.50 a.m. on the 26th, and that for the present nothing more than the recapture of the original line was to be attempted.

The Queen's were to advance on the right and left of the Menin Road with the King's Royal Rifles in support, and arrangements were made with the artillery for a barrage of five minutes on the original line for 100 yards north of the cross roads, this barrage then conforming to the remainder of the barrage. It must have been disturbing to the Officer Commanding The Queen's to get a message at 4 a.m. on the 26th from the Highland Light Infantry that they had had no orders to attack, but fortunately the Brigade Major turned up at this time, and this little misunderstanding was put right !

At 5.50 a.m. on the 26th the barrage opened, and the troops advanced in conjunction with the 39th Division on the south of the Menin Road, but ere long the advance of The Queen's was held up by a strong point and machine gun on the left, and no further progress could for the present be made as the left was in the air, so the line reached was consolidated. The enemy counter-attacked more than once, but was driven off, and, a company of the Cameronians of the 19th Brigade now coming up, things began to look brighter, especially as the British guns had opened and maintained a very heavy fire, which endured for two hours. Lieutenant Preston, of the Cameronians, then organized a party of men of various battalions, and rushed the strong point above-mentioned, capturing a machine gun, killing some 70 of the enemy, and taking prisoners 16 others. " A jolly fine performance," writes an appreciative officer of The Queen's.

The line was now advanced to the original position, the enemy dug-outs were cleared, a further 28 prisoners secured, and the line consolidated.

The night of the 26th-27th passed without incident, and at 8.30 on the night of the 27th the Battalion was relieved, and marched back to camp in rear.

In the following messages superior officers recorded their satisfaction with the fine performance of the 33rd Division; the Commander-in-Chief telegraphed to the Army Commander :—

"*The ground gained by the Second Army yesterday, under your command, and the heavy losses inflicted on the enemy in the course of the day, constitute a complete defeat of the German forces opposed to you. Please convey to all Corps and Divisions engaged my heartiest congratulations, and especially to the 33rd Division, whose successful attack, following a day of hard fighting, is deserving of all praise.*"

From the General Officer Commanding X Corps came the following :—

"*Following received from General Plumer :—Please accept my congratulations on success of to-day's operations, and convey them to the troops engaged. The 33rd Division have done fine work under extraordinarily difficult circumstances, and the 39th Division have carried out their task most successfully. The Corps Commander adds his own congratulations.*"

In circulating the above messages, the divisional General wrote :—

"*I wish to congratulate all officers, non-commissioned officers, and men of the Division on having gained by their fine fighting qualities such marks of appreciation, from the Commander-in-Chief and from the Army and Corps Commanders.*"

The losses in the 1st The Queen's had again been very heavy; 4 officers and 59 other ranks had been killed, 9 officers and 109 non-commissioned officers and men had been wounded, while 1 officer and 219 men were missing. The officers killed were Captain L. A. Crook, M.C., Second-Lieutenants C. G. Kemp, F. D. Tucker and G. T. Purchase; wounded were Captains R. F. Faulkner, M.C., W. B. Carslake and J. Burrell, Lieutenant J. S. Milner, Second-Lieutenants I. T. P. Hughes, H. J. Trythall, C. W. C. Charles, W. H. Baynes, and W. L. Atkinson; missing, Lieutenant W. F. Clenshaw.

Early in October the 1st Battalion The Queen's moved to Wizernes, and there entrained for Bailleul, whence it marched to Aldershot Camp, some 1,200 yards south-west of Neuve Eglise, where it was accommodated in huts, and was mainly employed during the next few days in finding working parties for the Royal Engineers. This was a place of practical inactivity for the ground was very heavy, the River Douve having overflowed its banks, but there was a certain amount of intermittent shelling by the enemy. Then, early in November a further move was ordered, and the Division was transferred to the north of Ypres where, on the 6th, it relieved the Canadians in the Passchendaele Salient; this extended to a depth of about 3,000 yards, and a width of only 1,000 yards, it was overlooked by the enemy from Westroosbeke, and suffered from shell fire and gas of all descriptions continuously both by night and day. The Ravibeeke, the local stream flowing from the neighbourhood of Passchendaele, had overflowed its banks, the shell-holes by which the ground was pitted, were full of water, and the communications consisted of a single duckboard track, which had been carefully "registered" by the Germans, and was under constant shell fire.

During the month of December there were several minor moves, but by the 20th the 33rd Division was relieved by the 50th, and moved back to the Steenvoorde area, and in this neighbourhood Christmas Day was spent.

The closing days of the year were marked by a most unfortunate accident, Lieutenant-Colonel L. M. Crofts, D.S.O., who at the time was officiating as Brigadier, being very severely wounded in both hands while witnessing a trench mortar demonstration near Winnezeele ; Lieutenant S. F. Prior was also wounded, while one man was killed.

Of the Battle of " Ypres, 1917," which lasted for three and a half months, under the most adverse conditions of weather, it may be said that it only just missed being entirely successful, and that this partial success was due rather to the state of the ground than to the strength of the enemy's resistance. " Notwithstanding the many difficulties, much has been achieved," wrote the Field-Marshal in his despatch. " Our captures in Flanders since the commencement of operations at the end of July amount to 24,065 prisoners, 941 machine guns, and 138 trench mortars. It is certain that the enemy's losses considerably exceeded ours. Most important of all, our new and hastily trained armies have shown once again that they are capable of meeting and beating the enemy's best troops, even under conditions which favoured his defence to a degree which it required the greatest endurance, determination, and heroism to overcome."

Maps 1, 6, and 8.

## CHAPTER VI.

### 1st BATTALION (*continued*).

### 1918.

#### THE BATTLE OF THE LYS AND THE VICTORY BATTLES.

##### Battle Honours:
" Cambrai, 1918," " Lys," " Hazebrouck," " Bailleul," " Kemmel," " Hindenburg Line," " Epéhy," " Selle," " Sambre."

From the early autumn of 1917 negotiations had been in progress with the French military authorities having in view an extension of the front held by the British armies, and it was finally agreed that the French troops on the right of the British should be relieved by the British as far as the town of Barisis, immediately south of the River Oise, and that the French should again assume responsibility for the coastal sector at Nieuport. These reliefs should have been completed in December, but actually the place of the French up to Barisis was taken at the end of January, by which time the British armies were holding 125 miles of active front.

About the same time a change took place in the organization of the British forces, and under orders from the Army Council infantry divisions were reduced from 13 to 10 battalions, and the number of battalions in a brigade from 4 to 3. This change was completed during the month of February, 1918, with the result that, as stated by the Field-Marshal, " the fighting efficiency of units was to some extent affected. An unfamiliar grouping of units was introduced thereby, necessitating new methods of tactical handling of the troops and the discarding of old methods to which subordinate commanders had been accustomed."

In the reshuffling of brigades and divisions consequent upon this reorganization, three infantry battalions were taken from the 33rd Division, and the 1st Battalion The Queen's was transferred from the 100th to the 19th Infantry Brigade, which now contained the 1st The Queen's, the 1st Cameronians, and the 5th/6th Scottish Rifles ; the Brigade was commanded by Brigadier-General C. R. G. Mayne, D.S.O.*

In the first week in January the Division was moved back into its old sector at Passchendaele, the conditions of existence in which had now been much improved, the communications were very much better, and many of the old " pill-boxes " had been made quite habitable. On many occasions the divisional front was raided by the Germans, who seemed to come from the " gasometers " or from the direction of Passchendaele railway station. One such raid occurred on The Queen's front on January 11th at about 1.30 a.m., when a German fighting patrol numbering from 12 to 15 men, which had secreted itself near one of the advanced posts of " D " Company of the Battalion, rushed the listening post consisting of two men—Privates Purdie and Henson—who had been stationed some twenty yards in front of the post, overpowering and gagging them. The men were able, however, to give the alarm, and the post at once opened fire, with rifles and a Lewis gun, in charge of Corporal F. E. Clark, upon the enemy who were dragging away the two men of

---

* Lieutenant-Colonel St. B. R. Sladen, 5th Battalion, had assumed command of the 1st The Queen's, *vice* Lieutenant-Colonel Crofts.

The Queen's. The fire caused casualties in the patrol and Private Purdie, with a blow of his fist, knocked out the German who was left with him and escaped.

A patrol which went out later discovered the bodies of seven of the Germans, and there is no doubt that further casualties were caused. Private Henson was reported as "missing," and four men of the post were wounded, three of them, however, remaining at duty.

At the end of January the 50th Division relieved the 33rd, which moved to the Esquerdes area, and on arrival here, the Battalion, which for some time past appears to have been under the orders of the 19th Brigade, was, on February 4th, definitely transferred to it from the 100th Infantry Brigade, and then moved to join it at Longuenesse.

On March 12th Lieutenant-Colonel St. B. R. Sladen was killed by shell fire while going round the line; his place was taken by Major H. E. Iremonger, and on the 25th by Lieutenant-Colonel M. Kemp-Welch, D.S.O., M.C., both of the Regiment.

For some weeks past there had been persistent rumours that the enemy was concerting measures for an attack upon an especially large scale, and both Russia and Roumania now being to all intents and purposes out of the war as regarded the rendering of assistance to the Western Powers, Germany was able to transfer many divisions from the eastern to the western theatre, and it was upon the front covered by the Third and Fifth Armies, between Arras and Barisis, that the weight of the German onset was to fall. The storm broke on March 21st on the front of the Fifth Army, and arrangements were almost immediately made to relieve the 33rd Division and send it down to the southern area.

The 19th Infantry Brigade moved first in anticipation of relief, proceeding to the Arras area at Lattre St. Quentin, and on relief by the 49th Division the remaining two brigades of the 33rd Division followed, the whole being concentrated by April 8th. On the eve of the departure of the Division for the south, the following message was received from Lieutenant-General Sir A. Hunter-Weston, the Corps Commander:—

"*It is with great regret that I part temporarily with the 33rd Division. Throughout the time that it has been in the VIII Corps, it has done good service to the State, and the conduct, spirit, and resolution of all ranks has been beyond all praise.*

"*You are now going to bear your share in the greatest battle of all history. You go as the champions of Right and Justice, and the defenders of our homes and liberties and all that makes life worth living.*

"*The Empire is fortunate in having in you a well-disciplined, resolute, and determined Division, which can be trusted to 'stick it out,' to carry on, and win through to victory. I hope it may be my good fortune to have the 33rd Division under my command again.*

"*Wherever you go I shall follow your doings with the greatest interest, and wherever you are my thoughts and best wishes will be with you each and all.*"

As the troops moved down, very little news, and that mostly of an exaggerated kind, was forthcoming; that the enemy had made many attacks upon a stupendous scale; that he had broken through both the British and the French fronts, and was marching on Paris; and that he had captured tens of thousands of prisoners and very many guns, and the whole of the Somme and Arras battlefields.

The Division had barely arrived in the Arras area, when on the evening of the 10th orders were received that it was to entrain forthwith for the neighbourhood of Caestre; but the journey was greatly prolonged owing to the fact that the enemy had accurately ascertained the range of the railway line near Doullens and obtained a direct hit on a troop train containing a battalion of the 98th Brigade, doing much damage to the permanent way, and killing 40 men.

Before the 33rd Division had arrived at the new front, to which it had so hastily been dispatched, the great enemy offensive had been checked, and actually by April 5th the Somme battle had ceased, though German progress had been stopped only by the sacrifice of a considerable amount of ground in British possession and the expenditure of valuable and not easily replaceable reserves. The enemy had now turned his attention to Flanders, where the front was somewhat weakly held owing to the fact that many of the divisions in this part of the line had been withdrawn to the neighbourhood of the Somme, while if these had been replaced at all north of the La Bassèe Canal it was only by divisions exhausted in the Somme fighting.

The German offensive in Flanders opened on April 9th and was made in great strength, and on Saturday the 13th, when the 19th and 98th Brigades of the 33rd Division were nearing the scene of action, to quote the words of Sir Douglas Haig's despatch, " a situation which threatened to become serious had arisen north of Merville. At about 8 a.m. the enemy attacked in great strength on a front extending from south of the Estaires—Vieux Berquin road to the neighbourhood of Steinwerck. After very heavy fighting he succeeded in the afternoon in overcoming the resistance of our troops about Doulieu and Le Becque, forcing them back in a north-westerly direction. As a result of this movement, a gap was formed in our line south-west of Bailleul, and bodies of the enemy who had forced their way through, seized Outtersteene and Merris "; but when the two brigades of the 33rd Division came up all that was reported was that the enemy had captured both Merville and Estaires, some seven miles south of Meteren, and had succeeded in getting further west of Doulieu; it was supposed, however, though not known, that in this area the enemy's advance had been arrested.

On April 12th the following officers were serving with the 1st Battalion The Queen's:—

*At Battalion headquarters.*—Lieutenant-Colonel M. Kemp-Welch, D.S.O., M.C., Major H. E. Iremonger, Captain and Adjutant R. H. Nevins, Lieutenant K. M. East, and Second-Lieutenant P. Jakes; Captain G. C. Gaynor, M.C., R.A.M.C. (medical officer).

*With No. 1 Company.*—Captain H. J. Carpenter, Second-Lieutenants G. F. Ashpitel, L. O. Parkes, M.C., C. W. Elliott and H. G. Sweet.

*With No. 2 Company.*—Captain A. M. Allan, Lieutenant I. T. P. Hughes, Second-Lieutenants T. Crompton and E. de W. Green.

*With No. 3 Company.*—Captain H. Ribton-Cooke, M.C., Lieutenants H. Mallett, and G. Stevenson, Second-Lieutenants R. J. Brooks and F. Russen.

*With No. 4 Company.*—Captain N. B. Avery, Lieutenant J. A. Dickinson, Second-Lieutenants J. E. Corry and H. B. Denny.

On the night of April 11th-12th the Battalion was close-billeted in huts at the western end of Meteren, which was under a continuous shell fire all night, but fortunately only one casualty resulted; here it was under orders to move at ten minutes' notice. At 1.5 p.m. on the 12th the 1st The Queen's were ordered to fall in and at once take up a defensive position of 3,000 yards in length covering Meteren, as the 31st Division was reported to be retiring north in the direction of that place.

The companies moved out at 1.15 p.m., "B," "C," and "D" occupying the front, while "A" was held in reserve.

"C" Company appears to have been leading, and the Officer Commanding was given direct orders by the Brigade-Major to take up ground rather more to the south than had originally been intended, with the right of the Company at Hoegenacker Mill, the remainder deploying on a line facing east-south-east; and the other two companies were directed, "B" to take up ground from the mill to the southern end of an enclosure, "D" prolonging this line to the south-west. As the Battalion about 1.45 p.m. came up to the high ground it was to occupy, this was found to be held by enemy machine guns; these, however, inflicted but few casualties during the advance, carried out though this was through very enclosed country. "C" Company, while moving into position, came under enemy machine-gun fire from the mill, but this was immediately engaged and captured by Second-Lieutenant Russen and eight men, and the company then took up its ground and dug in; while "B" Company, moving on to the ridge south of Belle Croix Farm, encountered enemy machine-gun fire and riflemen in enclosures; these were never satisfactorily accounted for owing to the length of front the company had to occupy.

Lieutenant-Colonel Kemp-Welch now reconnoitred to the flanks, and found no formed body of British troops in rear of or on the right flank of The Queen's, and, deciding that it was inadvisable to have a flank in the air between Belle Croix Farm and Outtersteene, he ordered "B" to find a defensive flank on the right with one platoon under Second-Lieutenant Denny. The Battalion was now strung out on a front of 2,100 yards, no touch had been gained on either flank with other troops, while the sole artillery support was provided by two anti-aircraft guns; but the machine guns of "A" and "C" Companies, 33rd Battalion Machine Gun Corps, were disposed behind the Battalion, and rendered valuable service throughout the operations that followed.

One company of the 5/6th Scottish Rifles was, at 4 p.m., ordered by the Brigadier to hold a position astride the Meteren—Bailleul road, and to get connection with the left of The Queen's at the cross roads; but as there was still no touch with any troops on the right, a platoon under Second-Lieutenant Ashpitel was sent to a bridge on the right with another in support under Second-Lieutenant Parkes.

From 5 p.m. onwards the front line companies reported that the enemy was collecting and preparing to advance, and about six o'clock the Battalion official account says: "enemy attacked in waves several times, but was stopped without difficulty, and suffered many casualties"; but one who was there elaborates this account, as follows:—

"Presently over the ridge came a battalion of Germans marching in column of fours with company officers mounted. There was an officer in front—probably the Commanding Officer—on a grey horse. Undoubtedly, the Germans thought they had only now to walk through to the coast. British infantry had never had a better target—every Lewis gun, every rifle was trained on that slow-moving body—not a shot rang out yet; it would be murder when we did fire, we could not miss them. . . . The whole line vomited out a blaze of fire; ahead of us Germans reeled and fell, the grey horse reared up on its hind legs and horse and rider fell in a heap. The whole column broke and fled helter-skelter, but still the hail of bullets ceaselessly sped from Lewis gun and rifle, and bigger and bigger grew the heaps of corpses in front. 'Charge!' and the line, with bayonets uplifted, went forward over that road where pools of blood lay thick and slimy and as plentiful as leaves on an autumn day. Germans groaned and yelled, Germans lay dead in heaps, and those who had hesitated too long became involved in our advancing line. . . .

" ' Steady,' shouted the officers, for there was a fear that the line might advance too far. Company Sergeant-Major Jones, of ' B ' Company, went a bit too far, got surrounded, and had to surrender. He was put in charge of a young German to be taken to the rear, but this German was evidently in a hurry to get to the rear as he led the way himself. Passing through a farm gate he went first and Jones gave him a terrific blow with his fist, slammed the gate behind him, doubled along a hedge, and in ten minutes was back with his company. The charge, as a charge, was finished . . . the line was fixed, and men dug themselves into rifle pits, later to be connected up as trenches."

During the night the enemy was reported digging in in small posts, and certain localities in the Battalion front line were shelled from the direction of Outtersteene and Merris, both of which places were held by the enemy in strength all night. At 10 p.m. enemy patrols tried to get through " B " Company's front under cover of a fairly heavy bombardment, but were driven off; British patrols established that the Germans were digging in all along the Battalion front, and at a distance of some 400 yards only from it; there appeared to be much enemy activity in Outtersteene, and the Battalion right was still in the air. In consequence, about 12.35 on the morning of the 13th Colonel Kemp-Welch reported that he considered his position precarious and asked that Outtersteene might be captured as also Merris, that he himself was not sufficiently strong to attempt this, while, even if successful, to hold these places would unduly lengthen his front.

From 5.30 a.m. onwards very many attacks were made against the Battalion front, and at 8.45 certain posts of " B " Company were overwhelmed, when the enemy pressed on down the road towards Belle Croix Farm in rear of " D " Company, and both these companies had consequently to be withdrawn and the Germans occupied the farm. Two very gallant attempts, led by Second-Lieutenants Dickinson and Corry, were made to recapture the farm, but were unsuccessful in restoring the situation, these counter-attacks not having sufficient weight behind them.

In the early afternoon of the 13th the situation was most critical; The Queen's had incurred heavy casualties but reinforcements were either in the line or were rapidly coming up, and by the evening matters were easier. The night of the 13th-14th was quiet except for intermittent shelling and machine-gun fire, and it was possible to bring up S.A.A. and the infantry was able to reorganize.

" The 14th," we read in the Divisional History, " was probably the most critical day of these operations . . . at dawn on the 14th the enemy launched very heavy attacks against our positions from the south-east and south of Meteren. A gap was made in the centre of The Queen's line covering the Meteren Becque*; a second gap was made on the left of the 5/6th Scottish Rifles covering the approach to Meteren from the east; another gap was made between the right of The Queen's and the 1st Cameronians, north-east of Merris. The enemy exploited these gains to full advantage, pushing forward light machine guns with great rapidity. . . Between 6 and 7 p.m. another determined attack was made by the enemy on the front held by the 19th Infantry Brigade. The Queen's fell back and the retirement of our troops became fairly general. . . . By dawn on the 15th a very good line

* A slow-running stream about eight feet wide, with firm bottom, and banks about three to four feet high; fordable everywhere, and no great obstacle to infantry.

had been dug . . . the infantry had been reinforced by the 11th Field Company, Royal Engineers, disposed on the right of The Queen's, and by the 22nd Corps Cyclists disposed on the left of the same battalion. The situation during the 15th remained unaltered, the night was quiet."

The 1st The Queen's had been, however, relieved on the morning of the 15th, and was then concentrated in the Nooteboom area, being billeted in farms, and on the night of the 18th-19th the 33rd Division, on relief by the Australians, was withdrawn into the area about the Benedictine Monastery of the Mont des Cats.

The losses in the Division during the comparatively brief period that these operations endured, totalled 181 officers and 3,760 other ranks, while the 1st Battalion The Queen's had 4 officers and 36 non-commissioned officers and men killed or died of wounds, 8 officers and 161 other ranks were wounded, and 1 officer and 160 men were missing. The names of the officer casualties were :—Killed or died of wounds—Captain A. M. Allan, Lieutenant J. A. Dickinson, Second-Lieutenants E. de W. Green and C. W. Elliott ; wounded, Captain H. J. Carpenter, Lieutenant I. T. P. Hughes, Second-Lieutenants W. J. C. Morgan (employed at Brigade headquarters), H. B. Denny, F. Russen, L. O. Parkes, M.C., R. J. Brooks and H. G. Sweet ; missing, Second-Lieutenant T. Crompton.

On April 21st, the 33rd Division was reviewed by M. Clémenceau, and of his visit *The Times*' correspondent wrote :—" Of the comradeship between the two Armies nothing too much can be said, and a fine symbol of it was seen this morning when Monsieur Clémenceau, at a point not far behind the front line, reviewed the battle-worn men of a British division who have borne a noble part in the recent fighting. Monsieur Clémenceau was visibly moved by what he saw and what was told him of the men's achievements, and the enthusiasm with which the British soldiers cheered the French Prime Minister, their voices hoarse with the strain of battle, was extremely impressive."

Between April 25th and May 4th, desperate fighting took place for the possession of Montnoir, the Scherpenberg and Kemmel Hill, and on May 1st the 33rd Division was hurried up to Abeele and on the 6th took over from the French 14th Division of Chasseurs the line running through Ridge Wood and Scottish Wood east of Dickebusch Lake ; here on the right was the XVI French Corps.

Early on the morning of May 8th the enemy opened a very heavy bombardment with high explosive and gas, and the 32nd French Division attacked on the British right, but did not get very far forward, and the Germans, counter-attacking, succeeded in effecting a lodgment behind the French left and the British right, where lay the 30th Composite Brigade. About 10.30 a.m. a verbal message reached the 1st The Queen's and other battalions of the 19th Brigade to " stand to," as the situation on the front of the 30th Composite Brigade was very obscure ; this was followed by an order to move, when the 1st Cameronians were directed to occupy the Vlamertinghe Line from the southern divisional boundary to Hallebast Cross Roads, while the 5/6th Scottish Rifles were to occupy certain trenches which were pointed out on the map. At 3.15 p.m. came orders for a counter-attack to be delivered on a point penetrated by the enemy and this was made by the 19th Brigade on the right and 98th on the left ; there was some very heavy fighting, and the Cameronians in particular had many casualties—at one time, so the Divisional History states, their whereabouts were a complete mystery. The Queen's were held in support and suffered less than some other battalions engaged.

but had some 32 men killed, wounded, and missing. Of the results of the action the Corps Commander wrote :—

*"The Corps Commander congratulates the 33rd Division and 30th Composite Brigade on a very successful day. The stubborn defence put up and successful counter-attack reflect the greatest credit on all concerned."*

The 33rd Division remained in the sector between Ypres to the north and Kemmel Hill to the south, including Dickebusch Lake, from April until the middle of August, engaged in refitting and in training American troops attached to it; and then on August 17th orders were issued for the relief of the Division by the 50th American Division, and for the former to proceed to the Eperlecques sub-area for training preparatory to taking part in the final acts of the great war drama.

The events of the ensuing few weeks can best be given in the words of the Divisional History :—" The Division was now moved to a very scattered area west of Arras near Saulty, and was, within a few days, transferred at night in hundreds of lorries from this area via Albert and Bapaume to Rocquigny, the scene of our very bitter fighting on November 2nd-5th, 1916. It ' debussed ' in the early morning and occupied tents and such old Nissen huts and German stores as had not been entirely destroyed in the recent fighting. An enormous amount of material and salvage had been left behind by the retreating enemy at this point ; this included millions of bottles of soda water, of which everybody availed themselves.

" About August 25th, 1918, the Battle of Bapaume was victoriously expending itself, and on the 26th the Commander-in-Chief launched a new attack. The First Army, advancing, swept up on both sides of the Scarpe, and the battle went on until September 1st, when a pause for breath ended the great conflict begun on August 21st. Bapaume, a name only for a few jagged walls and heaps of rubbish, had been avenged and reparation exacted. From somewhere south the peasantry dribbled back to rebuild a ruined home, to plough up the shell-torn land.

" In nine or ten days most of the First Army and the whole of the Third and Fourth Armies had swept across the old Somme battle grounds of 1916 in one long continuous battle without a pause. Early in the morning of September 2nd the infantry of the First and Third Armies drove the enemy from the famous Drocourt—Quéant Line, and by September 22nd the Germans were defeated at Havrincourt, and the British forces were now faced with the formidable Hindenburg Line. . . . Further south the French had reached the Crozat Canal in their advance past Noyon from the Oise to the River Aisne, while Pershing's Americans had won St. Mihiel."

The 33rd Division was moved up to the Equancourt area as far east as Heudecourt on September 19th, taking over from the 21st Division the trenches which had formed the old front line at the end of the Cambrai reverse ; these included Poplar Trench and Beech Walk, lying west of Villers Guislain and just east of Epéhy ; and an attack was now ordered upon the outer defences of the Hindenburg Line, including the network of trenches and posts commanding the approaches to the St. Quentin Canal. Artillery support was weak, and no tanks were available to assist the assault, and Villers Guislain in particular was exceptionally strong, being defended by machine guns at every point, and by concrete " pill-boxes." The attack was to be made at dawn on September 21st by the 19th and 98th Brigades on the right and left respectively.

The following officers were this day present with the 1st The Queen's :—
Lieutenant-Colonel P. C. Esdaile,* Major G. K. Olliver, M.C., Captain R. Nevins, M.C. (adjutant), Lieutenant J. S. Milner (scout officer), and Lieutenant H. Mallett (signalling officer).

*With " A " Company.*—Captain K. A. Brown, Second-Lieutenants J. G. Harker, L. J. Brooker, D.C.M., M.M., and H. Basset.

*With " B " Company.*—Captain E. W. Bethell, Second-Lieutenants P. J. Jakes, M.M., M. B. Blagden and W. J. Pratt, M.M.

*With " C " Company.*—Lieutenants A. J. R. Haggard and H. L. C. Whittaker, Second-Lieutenants E. A. Field and J. A. Brooks.

*With " D " Company.*—Captain E. S. Bingham, M.C., Second-Lieutenants R. F. Higgs, W. J. C. Morgan and A. E. Saunders.

The disposition of the Battalion for the attack was as follows : " A " and " B " Companies in the front line, each on a two-platoon frontage, " C " in support, and " D " in local reserve. Zero hour was 5.40 a.m., and the attack started to time, but no information as to its progress was received until near an hour and a half later, when the Officer Commanding " C " Company came back to report that the right company had inclined too much to the right and was held up in front by machine-gun fire from the direction of Meath Post and Limerick Post ; while a few minutes later a message was received from the Cameronians saying that they were also held up ; and the Officer Commanding " D " Company of The Queen's was now ordered to send two platoons up to the ridge and to try to find out the situation in Pigeon Ravine. Along the whole front the line was now prevented from going forward by intense machine-gun fire, so it dug in on the line reached and held on there until dark.

The Queen's was now reorganized and small parties of isolated men were collected, and " C " and " D " Companies dug in on a line parallel to and about 400 yards east of the Sunken Road, while " A " and " B," now greatly reduced in numbers, were withdrawn to the Sunken Road itself. The absence of information early in the action is probably due to both the company commanders and many of the company officers having early become casualties.

The Cameronians on the left having been checked a short distance from where they started, the 5th Scottish Rifles were now brought up, and an operation carried out by this battalion during the night resulted in the capture of Meath Post and Limerick Trench south to a distance of 200 yards, whereby the enemy's activities, and especially his sniping, was appreciably reduced. With the object of exploiting any success gained by the Scottish Rifles, Captain Bingham reconnoitred the ground, but nothing could then be done. Apart from heavy shelling, the night of the 21st-22nd passed quietly. In the morning, however, the enemy artillery fire increased in volume, and early in the afternoon " C " Company was shelled out of its trench. Orders were then issued to Captain Bingham to endeavour with " D " Company and portions of " B " and " C " to capture Limerick Post, the 5th Battalion Scottish Rifles bombing southwards. " D " Company managed under cover to make good its way to Kildare Avenue and advanced along it ; it reached a block some 150 yards from the Post, which was gallantly scaled by a platoon led by Second-Lieutenant Higgs, the Post itself being engaged by men with rifle grenades, and Second-Lieutenant Higgs managed to get within 50 yards before this brave officer was killed.

* Lieutenant-Colonel Kemp-Welch had been promoted on June 24th to the command of the 123rd Infantry Brigade.

The men of "B" and "C," under Lieutenant Haggard, were checked in Pigeon Avenue, and Captain Bingham, recognizing the futility of further effort, established a post on the Block and withdrew his men to a line north and south-east of Poplar Avenue. That evening the 1st Battalion The Queen's was relieved and marched to bivouacs in rear.

Again had the Battalion suffered very heavily; during the attack, or operations connected with it, 6 officers and 39 non-commissioned officers and men were killed or died of wounds, 5 officers and 184 other ranks were wounded, while 89 men were missing. The officers were, killed or died of wounds:—Captain E. W. Bethell, K. A. Brown, and G. H. Wallis, D.C.M., quartermaster*; Lieutenant H. L. C. Whittaker, Second-Lieutenants M. B. Blagden and R. F. Higgs; wounded— Second-Lieutenants W. J. Pratt, M.M., L. J. Brooker, J. G. Harker, P. J. Jakes, and S. Yeo, attached.

On the 30th the Battalion was heavily shelled with gas shells, and 6 officers, including the medical officer and 139 other ranks, were sent to hospital for treatment, the officers being Lieutenants H. Mallett, A. J. R. Haggard, and W. A. North, Second-Lieutenants J. E. Shipton and W. J. C. Morgan, with Lieutenant A. C. Patterson, R.A.M.C.

During the last few days of September the 98th and 100th Brigades captured Villers Guislain, but the casualties suffered in what was a frontal attack were terribly heavy, two battalions of the 100th Brigade being practically wiped out; but when at dawn on the 30th the 33rd Division again advanced, it was to find that the enemy had evacuated Pigeon Trench, had destroyed the bridges over the Canal, and had fallen back on a wide front, leaving only rearguards east of the Canal and occupying the Hindenburg Line.

The Division was concentrated in a forward position on October 2nd, and on the 3rd patrols succeeded in crossing the Canal, over which bridges were thrown on the following day, so that on the 5th the Division was able to pass over the St. Quentin Canal in force, and the 19th Brigade occupied the Hindenburg Line without any very serious fighting. On this day The Queen's were in support to the other two battalions of their Brigade.

On October 6th orders were received that the 19th Brigade, as vanguard of the 33rd Division, would keep touch with the 38th Division, which was in front, and conform to any advance made by it; on this same day Lieutenant-Colonel H. H. Lee, D.S.O., The Cameronians, arrived at Battalion headquarters and took over command from Captain R. H. Philpot.

It was not, however, until the night of the 8th that the Brigade moved, when the 1st The Queen's marched off to La Pannerie north and, moving forward again from here, crossed a road running north-west and south-east, expecting every moment to come in touch with the enemy. Passing early on the morning of the 9th through Aubencheul-aux-Bois and Villers Ontreau, it was then discovered that the road had been mined and that it was impossible to get the transport any further; Lewis guns were thereupon unloaded and the march continued through Malincourt, the Battalion arriving at the spot whence the serious advance was to commence soon after 5 a.m.

* Wounded by shell, and died of wounds, while in charge of ration limbers bringing up supplies to the Battalion. Captain Wallis had come out with the Battalion in 1914, and had served continuously with it. His energy, courage, and resource in rationing the men under all conditions made his loss one that was very greatly felt by the Battalion.

A list of the officers serving this day with the 1st Battalion The Queen's shows how startling and numerous were the changes in the officer corps of an infantry battalion in those days:—Lieutenant-Colonel H. H. Lee, D.S.O. in command, Lieutenant K. M. East, adjutant, and Lieutenant D. V. Bernard, signalling officer.

With "A" Company: Second-Lieutenants J. E. Corry, M.C., and H. C. Crawley.

With "B" Company: Captain G. E. Ashpitel, M.C., Lieutenant R. O. V. Thomas, and Second-Lieutenant J. A. Rudkin.

With "C" Company: Captain A. R. Abercrombie, D.S.O., M.C., Second-Lieutenants W. R. Rudland and C. S. Clark.

It will be seen by the above that not only was the Battalion now reduced to three companies, but that it contained very few officers who had fought with it only a very few weeks previously.

On the morning of the 9th the Battalion was formed up to the west of Clary, "A" and "C" Companies in front and "B" in support, and on the advance commencing no gun fire was experienced, but the enemy machine guns were active from the Elincourt direction; "C" Company, pushing on, however, succeeded in outflanking these and forced the machine guns to withdraw. A thick fog now came down, making it very difficult to distinguish the objective and to keep direction, but all pushed on, and by 8.45 a.m. the whole Battalion had reached the final objective and was in touch with the 5th Scottish Rifles on the left, while the right was in the air. The Battalion now dug in under a considerable amount of fire from machine guns and snipers about Gattigny Wood, which appeared to hinder the advance of the 66th Division on the right. A squadron of cavalry now, however, rode forward through the Battalion position, clearing away the snipers and machine guns and collecting 24 prisoners, who were sent to the rear.

At 2 p.m. orders were received for The Queen's to support the Cameronians, who were to continue the advance via Bertry and Troisvilles to Neuvilly, and after passing through Bertry the Battalion took up a position for the night, the 98th Brigade passing through next morning and continuing to advance towards Troisvilles. In the operations of October 9th 3 men of The Queen's were killed, Captain Abercrombie and 16 other ranks were wounded.

For some few days now the Battalion was in billets at Malincourt, but these were left on the 19th and a move made by cross-country tracks, avoiding the villages of Clary and Bertry, to Troisvilles; and while here Lieutenant-Colonel Lee left to take command of the 1st Battalion of his own regiment, the Cameronians, his place being filled by Lieutenant-Colonel the Hon. H. Ritchie, D.S.O., of the Scottish Rifles.

At this time the situation was as described in the Field-Marshal's despatch:—
"The enemy was holding the difficult wooded country east of Bohain and the line of the Selle north of it in great strength, his infantry being well supported by artillery. During the first two days his resistance was obstinate; but the attacking British and American troops made good progress. By the evening of October 19th after much severe fighting, the enemy had been driven across the Sambre et Oise Canal at practically all points south of Catillon, whence our line followed the valley of the Richemont east and north of Le Cateau."

It was at this time that the 33rd Division was again brought forward with orders to cross the Selle River on the night of October 22nd, concentrating east of the river, and getting into position ready to attack on the 23rd. "The passage of the Selle was an exceedingly difficult and dangerous operation. The enemy was

WIRE DEFENCES OF THE HINDENBURG LINE NEAR BELLICOURT, OCTOBER, 1918.

[*Copyright: Imperial War Museum.*

within 2 miles of the river. The frontage allotted to the Division was little over 1,700 yards long, so that during this night it was necessary to concentrate the whole of the infantry, with its first line transport, in an area under one square mile and almost in the outpost line. The risk was great, but no great result can ever be achieved without the taking of great risks. The concentration was not detected by the enemy. . . . Such shelling as there was was intermittent and light, and the casualties sustained by the Division exceedingly few."*

On October 21st the 17th and 36th Divisions were established north-east of the Selle River, and the advance of the Third and Fourth Armies was to be continued by the 33rd Division, with the 21st on the left and the 18th of the Fourth Army on the right. The following were the orders received from the 19th Brigade Headquarters by the 1st Queen's, then billeted in houses in Troisvilles :—" The 1st Cameronians will relieve the 115th Infantry Brigade in the forward line, and the 5th Scottish Rifles and 1st Queen's will assemble in Quarry K.9.d. and Ravine and banks in K.16.a. and b. respectively. On completion of the move, the Battalion headquarters to be established at K.15.6. The 98th Infantry Brigade is co-operating on the right flank, and the first, second, third, and fourth objectives are to be captured by the 19th and 98th Brigades, the 100th Brigade eventually going through and capturing the fifth objective. The attack will be supported by artillery and machine-gun barrage and by one tank attached to the 19th Infantry Brigade." The Battalion's objective was the third, to be attacked when the Scottish Rifles had captured the first and second. Zero hour was to be 2 a.m. on October 23rd for the 33rd Division, 1.20 a.m. for the 18th.

The Battalion was now again organized in four companies, and moved out of Troisvilles on the evening of the 22nd in the following order :—" B," " C," " D," and " A " Companies in platoons at 50 yards distance, and, led by Second-Lieutenant Jakes, followed the route by a cross-country track by La Sottière and the main Le Cateau—Inchy road to a bridge over the Selle, and thence to the shelter of a ravine on the further bank, where, however, some casualties were experienced from a heavy barrage put down by the enemy.

This was repeated during the night, and more casualties resulted, but early on the 23rd the 1st Queen's moved to the position of deployment on a tape running north-west and south-east on a frontage of 850 yards—" B " and " C " Companies in the front line on right and left respectively, and " A " and " D " in support ; but by the time the tape was reached " C " had suffered such loss that " A " took its place in the front. The weather was very misty and direction was kept by compass.

On approaching the enclosures of Croisette and Richemont still heavier shelling was met with, and the Battalion was halted about 6 a.m. in a sunken road, and it was now realized that the enemy was still holding Richemont and Forest, and the 1st The Queen's suffered from a heavy enfilade machine-gun fire at 900 yards range down the road. To meet this, " B " Company, under Lieutenant Thomas, was ordered to form a defensive flank and open fire on the enemy. At this junction Lieutenant-Colonel the Hon. H. Ritchie went down the road towards Forest to reconnoitre, and was badly wounded by a machine-gun bullet ; two attempts were made to reach him, but without success, but a few minutes later the enemy machine gun was dealt with and the Colonel was attended to and carried to the rear ; troops were now seen coming back over the ridge, and the situation appeared

* *The 33rd Division in France and Flanders*, p. 145.

to be somewhat critical; the right brigade now, however, advancing, the enemy was seen streaming out of Forest in a north-easterly direction, affording an admirable target for anything but rifle or Lewis-gun fire. Captain Avery now assumed command of the Battalion and withdrew it south-west of the road, organizing it into three companies—" A," " B," and " C "—there being at this time no survivors of " D."

At 8.15 a.m. the advance towards the second objective was resumed, and, though some shelling was encountered, the Slaughter House was reached, where the 5th Scottish Rifles were found to be in position, and The Queen's took up the line on their right, subjected to heavy fire from machine guns and 77-mm. guns at close range from the direction of Harpies Mill. The Tank attached to the Brigade now arrived on the scene, but proved to be broken down and unable to get any further. Reinforced now by the Cameronians, the advance was renewed and the third objective reached at 9.50; here The Queen's dug in at the south-western edge of the Bois de Vendegies, while the Cameronians passed on towards the fourth objective. The Queen's remained during the night of the 23rd-24th near the wood, and about midnight rations, water, and spare ammunition were all sent up and distributed.

Early on the 24th the Battalion was ordered to go forward in reserve to the Cameronians and Scottish Rifles to a position in a sunken road, and provide a left-flank guard to the Brigade. During the rest of this day and night the enemy shelling of the area was heavy and sustained, and when the morning of the 25th broke the enemy was reported to be still holding the village of Englefontaine; and while the 1st Cameronians were facing the fifth objective, with the Scottish Rifles in support, they were not yet actually on it; so at midday The Queen's, with The King's of the 98th Brigade, were ordered to capture the final objective next morning, being subsequently relieved by the 100th Brigade. The 4th King's were the left Battalion of the 98th Brigade, and the 16th King's Royal Rifles were to support The Queen's, protect their right, and take over the position when captured. Zero hour was to be at 1 a.m. on the 26th; " B " Company, under Second-Lieutenant J. Rudkin, was on the left; " A," with Second-Lieutenents F. J. F. Moultrie and O. Jackman, M.M., was on the right; while Lieutenant F. W. Pelling and Second-Lieutenant C. S. Clark were in charge of special left and right-flank patrols.

The attack was entirely successful and the casualties light, the enemy appearing to be taken by surprise and demoralized by the suddenness of the attack, which was vigorously pressed home; the Germans surrendered readily, and the only difficulty experienced was in " rounding up " the prisoners. By 2.30 a.m. all objectives had been taken, Second-Lieutenant Clark doing great work in protecting the right, while he personally destroyed a German machine gun. Touch was established with the 9th Highland Light Infantry, and the position having been handed over to the 16th King's Royal Rifles, The Queen's moved back that evening to billets at Troisvilles, a distance of some miles.

The country fought over was undulating, all under cultivation, and without any trees or hedges and few enclosures until the Bois de Vendegies was reached; there were a few sunken roads running at right angles to the line of advance.

The casualties totalled 109 all ranks: 1 officer—Lieutenant-Colonel the Hon. H. Ritchie, D.S.O., Scottish Rifles—and 20 other ranks were killed or died of wounds, 8 officers and 78 other ranks were wounded, 1 man was missing, and 1 officer and 1 man were gassed.

The Divisional History relates that "there were extraordinary scenes in Englefontaine immediately the enemy were driven out. While the prisoners were being collected the inhabitants came out of their cellars and literally fell round the necks of the British troops. Coffee was very freely distributed, and general rejoicing took place, while hundreds of French flags appeared as from a conjuring hat." Then the intense gratitude of the people found expression in the following message, which was issued to the troops on October 26th:—

*"The Mairie of Englefontaine, which met this afternoon in a cellar of this village, begs to express to you in the name of the 1,200 inhabitants freed by the British Army its deepest feelings of hearty gratitude."*

From the General Officer Commanding the V Corps came the following:—

*"Please convey to all ranks under your command my congratulations on the gallantry and endurance they have shown during the recent hard fighting. They may well be proud of the advance from Malincourt to the River Selle, where all resistance was overcome until the final objective was gained, and the assault and capture of Englefontaine, with 500 prisoners, after 56 hours of continuous fighting and hard marching over most difficult country, was a magnificent piece of work well organized and gallantly carried out. The present nature of fighting was a little new to the Division, which made their task harder and more costly; yet, in spite of heavy casualties, their plucky determination to win, and splendid soldier-like spirit, carried them through to success.*

*"Please convey to them my personal thanks for all they have done."*

On October 27th Major and Brevet Lieutenant-Colonel H. W. Green, D.S.O., The Buffs, assumed command of the 1st Battalion The Queen's.

The 98th Brigade now went forward and took up the pursuit. The enemy had fallen back to the high ground on the further side of the Sambre, destroying the only remaining bridge; the river was unfordable, and the Germans kept up a heavy fire upon the river banks, and especially upon the ruined bridge-heads. The passage of the river was, however, forced by the 98th Brigade at Berliamont and by the 100th a mile further to the right; and by the morning of November 6th the villages of Aulnoye, Petit Mauberge and Leval, all on the east bank, had been taken and ground for manœuvre made available. The 19th Infantry Brigade was now called forward to take up the pursuit, and The Queen's were ordered to advance across the Sambre and deploy east of the river.

At 11 a.m. on the 6th the Battalion marched off and deployed as directed, "A" and "B" Companies in the front line on left and right and "C" and "D" in support, following the 5th Scottish Rifles, who captured that portion of the village of Aulnoye round the station, when The Queen's in turn passed through them and took the objective designated; few shells were fired by the enemy, but his machine guns were very active, and "B" and "D" Companies here suffered some loss. For the 7th the orders were that the Scottish Rifles would go through the Battalion and the line of the villages Ecuelin and Pot de Vin, The Queen's following 1,000 yards in rear, and, on the Scottish Rifles taking their objectives, advancing north of and through the northern edge of the Bois du Temple, thence pushing forward on to high ground east of the Mauberge—Avesnes road

The morning of the 7th was very misty, the Scottish Rifles lost direction, only one company reaching the line of The Queen's, so these now went forward in touch with the 21st Division on the left; about 1,000 yards west of Ecuelin the 21st Division was held up and touch with it was lost, but The Queen's continued steadily to advance, the two leading companies entering Ecuelin without encountering any opposition. So soon, however, as the enemy realized the village was in British occupation, fire was opened upon it by machine guns in the wood to the east and from sunken roads and quarries to the west.

On " C " and " D " Companies closing up to Ecuelin, " A " and " B " advanced east and north of it, and in the afternoon two attempts were made to capture the north-west corner of the Bois du Temple; the first failed, but at the second the enemy was found to have fallen back. In the evening The Queen's were relieved and went back for the night to Le Toque.

On the preceding days and on this day—the last on which the 1st Battalion The Queen's was in action during the war—Second-Lieutenant O. Jackman and 5 men were killed, 4 officers—Lieutenant-Colonel H. W. Green, D.S.O., Captain R. H. Nevins, M.C., Lieutenant F. W. Pelling and Second-Lieutenant F. H. E. Whittaker—and 43 other ranks were wounded, while 6 men were missing.

On the Battalion coming out of action, the undermentioned were present; they had embarked for France in August, 1914, with the Battalion, and had served continuously throughout the four years of the war :—Captain and Adjutant R. Nevins (R.Q.M.S. on embarkation), 9583 R.Q.M.S. H. Marsh, 5307 C.Q.M.S. G. Bayford, 5872 Sergeant-Drummer J. Winter, 9367 Sergeant E. Streeter, 9678 Drummer C. Wilson, 9303 Private H. Beacon, 9421 Private J. Coad, 8519 Private W. Earl, 9378 Private W. Gibson, 8885 Private W. Hollis, 10295 Private G. Lawson, 10296 Private T. Mills, 10325 Private J. Privett, 9561 Private W. Stevens, 10300 Private J. Wanstall, and 10360 Private S. Willis.

On November 9th the 33rd Division was withdrawn to the Berliamont—Aulnoye area.

For some days past all ranks had felt that the surrender of Germany was at hand, and early on this date it was strongly rumoured that the enemy had sent plenipotentiaries to Marshal Foch pleading for an armistice. This was officially confirmed at noon, when it was made known that very severe conditions had been imposed upon the enemy which he must accept, lest fighting be resumed at noon on the 11th. The excitement amongst all ranks was intense.

The next morning, November 11th, the following official order was received :—

"*Hostilities will cease at* 11.00 *hours to-day, November* 11*th. There will be no intercourse of any description with the enemy.*"

With his customary acumen the British soldier fittingly expressed what all men felt :—" Foch has put it across them," was the way he stated it.

One who was present writes :—" Quietly we gripped each other by the hand, and silence came and inward prayers went silently up to Him who had given us the victory and had spared us to see this day. Then cheers broke out and were taken up by troops in the distance. The roads were lined with guns, and the gunners and drivers took up the cheering. What it all meant was deeply realized by us who had been face to face with the Hun, and jubilation with any display of boisterousness was impossible."

Of the many well-deserved congratulatory messages received at this time from commanders and others by armies, corps, divisions, brigades, and individuals, it may be sufficient to select two only with which to close this chapter; the first came from the Commander of the V Corps to those he had led :—

# VICTORY

"*On the signature of the Armistice I wish to convey to all ranks of the V Corps my most sincere and cordial congratulations on their gallantry and endurance. No task has been too arduous, no difficulty too great for you to surmount. You have always been in the forefront of the advance. The prominent part taken by the V Corps in the defeat of the enemy has only been rendered possible by the gallant and unselfish manner in which every officer, non-commissioned officer and man in the Corps has played up for the common good. To command such troops has been an honour which I shall always remember.*"

The other message was from His Majesty the King, whose interest in the Army, his sympathy in its sufferings, and his appreciation of its achievements had never waned; to the Field-Marshal he telegraphed as follows :—

"*No words can express my feelings of admiration for the glorious British Army whose splendid bravery under your leadership has now achieved this magnificent success over the enemy. You have fought without ceasing for the past four years. My warmest congratulations to you and your undaunted Army, where all ranks with mutual confidence in each other have faced hardships and dangers with dogged resolution and have fought on with an irresistible determination that has now resulted in this final and overwhelming victory.*"

## CHAPTER VII

1st BATTALION (*continued*).

1918–1923.

#### DEMOBILIZATION AND RECONSTRUCTION.

DURING the days immediately following the announcement of the Armistice the 1st The Queen's made several moves—from Berliamont to Loquignol, thence to Forest, and from there to Clary; from Clary a party consisting of Captain R. H. Philpot, M.C., Second-Lieutenant H. Basset, 1 warrant officer, 1 colour-sergeant, and 6 selected privates, was sent via Boulogne to England to bring out the Colours.

Then on December 10th the 33rd Division began to move back to the Harnoy area west of Amiens, and by the 17th the Battalion was settled down in camp in the neighbourhood of Hallevillers, where Christmas Day was passed. Some few weeks were spent here, and then tolerably early in the New Year the 1st Battalion The Queen's was sent to No. 2 Reception Camp at Harfleur, where demobilization, which had already commenced, was proceeded with as expeditiously as was possible, consistent with the orderly return to civil life of several millions of men; and the diary now contains news of the departure of large and small parties of non-commissioned officers and men for "dispersal." A demobilization scheme had been drawn up in embryo before the war had been very many months in progress, and this had now been perfected, and all men were offered:—

    (*a*) A furlough, with pay and separation allowance for four weeks from date of demobilization.
    (*b*) A railway warrant to their homes.
    (*c*) A twelve months' policy of insurance against unemployment.
    (*d*) A money gratuity in addition to the ordinary Service gratuity.

While non-commissioned officers and men were daily undergoing demobilization, and officers who had engaged "for the duration" were returning to civil life, young officers and men, newly recruited for the post-war army, or for limited service in the Army of Occupation, were constantly joining, so that the Battalion was still at a fair strength when, on April 14th, orders were received that "all volunteers and retainable men of the Battalion were to proceed to Rouen and there join the cadre of the 6th Battalion of the Regiment." These orders were carried into effect on the 22nd, when the 1st Battalion The Queen's (less the cadre), strength 20 officers and 731 other ranks, was posted to the 6th Battalion. Then on May 7th instructions were received for the cadre of the 1st Battalion to be reduced from 4 officers and 46 other ranks to 3 officers and 36 other ranks.

The end of the stay of the 1st The Queen's in France was now very near, and on the 15th the cadre was directed to embark that day in the s.s. *Lydia*, and, parading at 5 p.m., the cadre and band embarked from the Quai d'Escarle. The following formed the cadre: Major N. B. Avery, M.C.; Captain and Adjutant R. Nevins, M.C.; Lieutenants A. J. R. Haggard, A. E. Saunders and W. Routley, D.C.M., Quartermaster; 4061 Regimental Sergeant-Major W. E. Reid, M.C.; 9583 Regimental Quartermaster-Sergeant W. H. Marsh; 8560 Company Sergeant-

Major J. Phillips; 5307 Company Quartermaster-Sergeant A. Bayford; 10253 Sergeant (Orderly-Room Clerk) C. D. Wakeford; 240184 Acting/Sergeant G. Selmes; 74 Corporal J. Sewell, M.M.; 10698 Lance-Corporal E. S. Hawes; Privates 5852 E. W. Morrish, 10296 T. Mills, 5972 J. Pullinger, 9328 A. Povey, 13461 A. G. Rance and 10360 S. H. Willis.

The following joined the cadre from the 6th Battalion a few hours only before embarkation: 1912 Acting/Sergeants S. R. Hawkins and 201895 A. W. Griffen; 69247 Lance-Corporal A. Harwood; Privates 2314 J. Burchett, 61142 J. Broadhead, 213 R. Chamberlain, 7139 E. Davies, 15489 H. Field, 437 R. Gilby, 3903 A. Hastings, 206160 C. W. Hawkes, 208058 R. Hall, 208057 A. W. Holland, 201120 W. C. Jewson, 67 H. Kitchen, 672 E. Sines, 331 F. Smith, 8277 F. F. Smith, 15455 A. J. Smith, 39434 B. Vaux, 654 G. Woodcock, 2421 J. Watling, 13948 J. W. Ware and 61663 J. Wilkinson.

The strength of the band was 1 warrant officer, 1 sergeant, 1 corporal, and 31 privates and boys.

The cadre and band disembarked at Southampton and proceeded by rail the same day to camp at Fovant, but here orders were received directing the party to hand in all mobilization stores and then move to the depot at Guildford. This was carried out on May 19th, the cadre reaching Guildford at noon, and being there met by Lieutenant-Colonel L. M. Crofts, D.S.O., and Major H. F. Warden, D.S.O., with the band of the 2nd Battalion from Aldershot. After detraining the cadre marched to the Town Hall, where the Mayor welcomed all ranks in the name of the people of Guildford, and then moved on to the Depot, where during the next few days demobilization was completed and furlough was opened. On June 23rd Lieutenant-Colonel H. F. Warden, D.S.O., assumed command, and rather less than a month later Battalion headquarters was sent by rail to Clipstone, where on August 5th the personnel of the 3rd Battalion—less headquarter staff—was absorbed by the 1st Battalion, which then, as part of the London Reserve Brigade, was located at Wakefield, in Yorkshire, for duty in connection with the coal strike—" C " and " D " Companies, under Captain F. W. H. Denton, being on detachment at Silkstone.

The strength of the Battalion was now 79 officers and 1,169 other ranks.

No doubt The Queen's, like other units of the Army, had hoped and even expected that the termination of the four years' war would mean for them the opening of a period of comparative ease and relaxation, or at least a time during which all ranks might take up again the tolerable burden of peace soldiering; but they were to find that there was no rest for the British soldier. The coal strike lay heavy on the 1st Battalion The Queen's while stationed, when yet in the throes of reorganization, at Clipstone Camp; on September 27th the Battalion was placed under orders to be ready to move at six hours' notice to protect the railways in consequence of the railway strike; and on October 2nd The Queen's actually moved up to Nottingham on this duty, providing detachments in several parts of the city, returning to Clipstone a week later. On the 25th the Battalion trained to Aldershot, and was accommodated in Tournay Barracks.

On May 15th, 1920, Lieutenant-Colonel H. F. Warden, D.S.O., gave up command and retired from the service, Major G. N. Dyer, D.S.O., commanding until July 15th, when Lieutenant-Colonel H. C. Whinfield arrived and assumed command.

The Battalion strength in officers remained very high until well into 1920, but when towards the end of June of this year the 1st The Queen's was ordered to Ireland for temporary garrison duty, it embarked at Fleetwood and landed at Belfast at a strength of 27 officers only and 630 other ranks. From Belfast the Battalion went by special train to Londonderry, and marched to a hutment camp in the Waterside area of the city known as Clooney Park Camp; while here The Queen's were concerned either in garrisoning the posts in the city area or in sending out detachments of varying strengths to Lifford, Strabane, Cookstown, Dungannon, Magilligan, Buncrana, Malin Head, Magherafelt, Luddan Camp, Carrowkeel, Letterkenny and Carrickmore. The duties of the detachments were the restoration and maintenance of order and the affording of assistance to the Royal Irish Constabulary. There were many raids carried out on the houses of prominent Sinn Fein leaders, and several arrests were made from time to time.

On October 13th, 1920, Major-General Sir E. O. F. Hamilton, K.C.B., having resigned the appointment, the Colonelcy of the Regiment was conferred upon General Sir C. C. Monro, G.C.B., G.C.S.I., G.C.M.G., A.D.C. General to the King.

With effect from January 1st, 1921, the title of the Regiment was changed to The Queen's Royal Regiment (West Surrey).

In the early part of this year there were no signs of any decrease of outrage in Ireland, and life was scarcely more secure in Dublin than it was in Cork and Kerry. In all parts of the country there was rioting, while trains were derailed and elaborate attempts were made to ambush police and military patrols. On January 14th " B " and " D " Companies were engaged under Major G. N. Dyer, D.S.O., in operations in the Dungloe—Burtonport area, and " C " Company was similarly engaged at Donegal with a battalion of the Rifle Brigade; while during three days in March the whole Battalion took part, under command of Lieutenant-Colonel H. C. Whinfield, in operations against Sinn Fein rebels about Crolly and Cresslough, in North-West Donegal, when trains conveying the troops were twice derailed, and in reprisal some 70 civilians from neighbouring villages were taken into military custody.

On March 28th the 1st Battalion The Queen's was transferred to the 6th Divisional area in Cork, moving thither by sea in the s.s. *Rathmore*, and by rail on disembarkation to Fermoy and thence to Kilworth Camp, where the Battalion came under the orders of the 16th Infantry Brigade. The county of Cork was at this time in an especially disturbed state, and crime was rampant. On May 1st a patrol of 4 officers and 12 other ranks of The Queen's, together with 16 men of the Green Howards and Royal Irish Constabulary, went out in the direction of Kildorrery and came upon a party of 30 rebels at Ahapuce Bridge. Lieutenant A. W. E. McCabe, who was in command of the party, showed great coolness and ability in dealing with the situation, with the result that of the rebels, 2 were killed, 2 wounded and 3 captured, while there were no casualties among the soldiers engaged. The rest of the month was spent in sending out numerous cycle and motor-car patrols to scour the country, but not much success resulted. The Queen's also furnished temporary detachments to Ballincollig and Glanworth.

On July 10th the Military and Police Barracks at Mitchelstown were attacked by some men of the so-called Irish Republican Army, when No. 6078040 Private Danby, transport driver, of the Battalion, who was fetching water for the detachment, was wounded in three places, but with great gallantry and devotion to duty galloped his mules back to barracks, a distance of a quarter of a mile.

Next day a truce was proclaimed, when the forces of the Crown and of the Irish Republican Army ceased hostilities and arranged an armistice, pending the result of a conference held in London between the Prime Minister and de Valera, the Republican leader.

In the middle of February, 1922, something of the nature of an agreement for the settlement of Irish affairs having been arrived at, Kilworth Camp was handed over to the Irish Provisional Government, and the 1st The Queen's moved into the Old Barracks at Fermoy, where on the 21st the Battalion was inspected by Major-General Sir E. P. Strickland, K.C.B., C.M.G., D.S.O., commanding the 6th Division, who expressed his very high appreciation of the work done by the Battalion during its twenty months' service in Ireland. He remarked that " never before, and probably never in the future, would soldiers be called upon to perform such repugnant duties and suffer such provocation as had been the case during the operations in Ireland. During these the discipline of the Battalion had been sorely tried, but had never been found lacking. He had always held a very high opinion of The Queen's Royal Regiment, and from the smart turn-out of all ranks on parade that day he could see that the efficiency of the Battalion was still maintained."

On March 23rd the Battalion was sent by train to Newtownards, marching from there to Clandeboye Camp, but had not been here more than a few weeks when it was ordered to prepare to cross over to England to be stationed at Aldershot. It was not, however, until January 22nd, 1923, that the 1st The Queen's left Clandeboye Camp for Belfast by march-route. The conditions were bad, it was raining, but all ranks were glad to leave Ireland and to have finished with a disagreeable task. Belfast was reached at 5.15 p.m., and the Battalion at once embarked, reached Fleetwood early in the morning of the 23rd, and left again in two trains at 10.45 and 11.50 a.m., reaching Aldershot the same evening.

The Battalion had arrived in Ireland at a strength of 27 officers and 590 other ranks, while on its departure from the country the strength was 32 officers and 540 other ranks, including 100 non-commissioned officers and men in Aldershot, awaiting passage for India to join the 2nd Battalion.

The following letter relative to the services of the Battalion in Ireland was received from the headquarters of the Northern Ireland District :—

"*On the departure of the 1st Battalion The Queen's Royal Regiment, the Divisional Commander desires me to express his appreciation not only of the high standard of discipline maintained by the Battalion during the long tour of service in Ireland under difficult and trying conditions, but also of the willing and the cheerful spirit displayed by all ranks during the time the 1st Battalion The Queen's Royal Regiment was under his command. The Divisional Commander wishes me to express his best wishes to all ranks for the success of the 1st Battalion The Queen's Royal Regiment under the new Command to which they are about to be transferred.*

"*The Brigade Commander 15th Infantry Brigade desires to associate himself in every way with the remarks of the General Officer Commanding Northern Ireland District.*"

At Aldershot the Battalion formed part of the 6th Brigade, 2nd Division, and shortly after the arrival of The Queen's the command of the 2nd Division was assumed by Major-General Sir E. P. Strickland, under whom they had served in Ireland.

On July 27th the Battalion was inspected by the Colonel of the Regiment,

General Sir Charles Monro, Bart., G.C.B., G.C.S.I., G.C.M.G., prior to his embarking for Gibraltar, where he had been appointed Governor and Commander-in-Chief. The General presented the Long Service and Good Conduct Medal on parade to Company Quartermaster-Sergeant Thompson, inspected the barracks and Sergeants' Mess, and lunched with the officers, and after parade issued the following complimentary order :—

"*As Colonel of the Regiment I was very glad to renew my acquaintance with the 1st Battalion, and as an officer who joined this Battalion forty-four years ago, it was very gratifying to me to notice the steadiness and smartness of all ranks under arms. The men were well dressed and well turned-out, the marching was conducted with accuracy and precision, the barrack-rooms and the comfort of the men are evidently the subject of careful attention. The Sergeants' Mess showed all the qualities of self-respect for which it was always noted in the old days ; an inspection of this mess afforded clear testimony of the high standard of esprit de corps prevailing in the Battalion. I regard the result attained as reflecting the highest credit on all concerned, and congratulate you, Colonel Whinfield, the officers, non-commissioned officers and men on the high standard of efficiency to which you have attained.*"

On December 31st, 1923, the strength of the 1st Battalion The Queen's Royal Regiment at Aldershot was 28 officers, 9 warrant officers, 5 colour sergeants, 23 sergeants, 11 lance-sergeants, 31 corporals, 72 lance-corporals, 7 drummers, 367 privates and 17 boys, a total of 570 all ranks.

Maps 1, 4 and 5.

## CHAPTER VIII.

### 2ND BATTALION.

### 1905–1914.

#### THE FIRST BATTLE OF YPRES.

##### Battle Honours:
"Ypres, 1914," "Langemarck," "Gheluvelt."

THE conclusion of the final volume of Colonel Davis' History of the Regiment, carried up to October, 1904, left the 2nd Battalion of The Queen's at Shorncliffe, whither it had been sent on its return from the campaign in South Africa.

For this war an Army Order dated December 21st of this year sanctioned the Honours, "South Africa, 1899–1902" and "Relief of Ladysmith," being borne on the Colours.

On January 1st, 1905, the Battalion was composed of 28 officers, 2 warrant officers, 40 sergeants, 35 corporals, 14 drummers, and 654 privates. The following are the names of the officers:—Lieutenant-Colonel H. D. Robson (in command), Majors (Brevet Lieutenant-Colonel) F. J. Pink, C.M.G., D.S.O., A. W. Taylor (Depot), M. C. Coles and G. G. Whiffin, Captains G. E. R. Kenrick, D.S.O., R. H. Mangles, D.S.O., W. D. Wright, V.C., I. L. B. Vesey (adjutant), P. Whetham and C. F. Watson, D.S.O., Lieutenants J. Rainsford-Hannay, P. J. Fearon, R. G. Clarke, S. T. Watson, F. J. Roberts, E. C. Feneran (Depot), H. F. H. Master, and R. T. Lee, Second-Lieutenants F. C. Longbourne, P. C. Esdaile, W. B. Haddon-Smith, F. G. A. Henderson, R. L. Q. Henriques, R. L. G. Heath, J. R. Walpole and A. P. Hamilton, with Lieutenant C. H. J. Wort (quartermaster).

On January 3rd the people of the County of Surrey presented the Battalion with a handsome silver cup in appreciation of its services in the late war.

From June 2nd to September 2nd, the Battalion, at a strength of 461 all ranks, was away at manœuvres in Sussex; and this year's inspection report was endorsed as under by the General Officer Commanding-in-Chief Eastern Command:—

*"There is no better battalion in my command. An excellent commanding officer and an admirable tone throughout the Battalion."*

On March 17th, 1906, the sum of £100 was sent from Battalion funds to "the Union Jack Club" for the provision in the Club of a room to be known as "The Queen's Regiment Room," the Club having been established as a memorial to those who fell in the recent campaign in South Africa, and for providing accommodation for soldiers and sailors staying in London on leave or furlough.

In the following month the Lee-Enfield short rifle Mark I with the new leather equipment was issued to the Battalion; and at the end of July the 2nd The Queen's, strength 20 officers and 800 other ranks, left Shorncliffe with the 10th Infantry Brigade for manœuvres in Sussex, returning to Shorncliffe early in September, but leaving again on the 21st by rail for Colchester, where it occupied quarters in

Meeanee Barracks, now forming part of the 11th Infantry Brigade. Here, on the 29th, Colonel H. D. Robson relinquished command and retired from the Service, his place being taken by Lieutenant-Colonel R. Dawson.

At the end of this year the establishment of the Battalion was reduced from 710 to 680 privates.

During the late summer of 1907 the 2nd Battalion The Queen's was moved about a good deal; in the first week in August it proceeded by rail to camp near Ringwood in Dorsetshire for brigade training with the 11th Infantry Brigade, followed by training with the 4th Division. This was succeeded by a week's manœuvres with the troops of the Eastern Command, and the Battalion then went for a week to a standing camp at Lark Hill, finally being moved by rail on September 14th to London to find the guards while the Brigade of Guards was away on manœuvres. The Battalion was quartered for a week in Chelsea Barracks while so employed, then returning to Colchester, from where a party of 8 officers, 10 sergeants, and 140 rank and file was sent up to London on November 13th to assist in lining the streets on the occasion of the visit of Their Imperial Majesties the Emperor and Empress of Germany.

The autumn of 1908 saw the Battalion taking part in the manœuvres held this year in the New Forest, returning on the conclusion of these exercises to Colchester, where the 2nd The Queen's remained until New Year's Day, 1910, when it embarked at Southampton in the *Braemar Castle* for Gibraltar, strength 22 officers, 1 warrant officer, 41 sergeants, 36 corporals, 12 drummers, 551 privates, 8 officers' wives, 3 officers' children, 45 soldiers' wives, and 60 soldiers' children; 1 warrant officer, 5 sergeants, 5 corporals, and 177 privates remained at Colchester to join the 1st Battalion of the Regiment on its arrival in England. The following officers embarked with the Battalion :—Brevet Colonel R. Dawson, Majors J. G. King-King, D.S.O. and M. C. Coles, Captains L. M. Crofts, Brevet Major H. R. Bottomley, G. E. R. Kenrick, D.S.O., and H. W. Stenhouse, Lieutenants P. J. Fearon (adjutant), F. J. Roberts, H. F. H. Master, R. T. Lee, F. C. Longbourne, W. B. Haddon-Smith and A. N. S. Roberts, Second-Lieutenants J. R. Walpole, A. P. Hamilton, M. Kemp-Welch, J. D. Boyd. G. C. O. Oldfield, C. Jackson and J. A. Lang-Browne, Lieutenant C. H. J. Wort (quartermaster).

At Gibraltar, Headquarters occupied Buena Vista Barracks with detachments, each of two companies, at North Front and Windmill Hill.

On May 9th the Battalion furnished a guard of honour at Government House on the occasion of the Proclamation of the Accession of His Most Gracious Majesty King George V, strength 3 officers, 4 sergeants, and 100 rank and file; and later in the same month the 1908 pattern web equipment with sword bayonet pattern 1907 was issued.

When in the autumn of this year, the King of Portugal, the Queen Mother, and the Queen Grandmother were driven from Portugal, consequent upon the revolution in that country, and took refuge in Gibraltar, the 2nd Battalion The Queen's provided special guards over their Majesties during their stay. The Battalion addressed a letter to His Majesty conveying the sympathy of all ranks of the 2nd Battalion The Queen's, and calling His Majesty's attention to the fact that after a lapse of nearly 250 years the Regiment was again employed guarding the interests of the House of Braganza. The special guards were found as under :—

October 12th : Captain H. W. Smith, D.S.O., 1 sergeant, 1 corporal, and 12 men.

October 14th: Lieutenant P. C. Esdaile, 1 sergeant, 1 corporal, and 12 men.

October 16th: Captain H. W. Stenhouse, 1 sergeant, 1 corporal, and 12 men.

On this latter date, when their Portuguese Majesties embarked on leaving Gibraltar, the Battalion furnished a guard of honour at the Governor's landing stage, under Major H. R. Bottomley, with Lieutenant R. L. G. Heath carrying the King's Colour, Second-Lieutenant J. D. Boyd, 4 sergeants, 100 rank and file, the Band and Drums, the remainder of the Battalion lining the streets on the same occasion under command of Lieutenant-Colonel J. G. King-King,* D.S.O., with whom were Captain and Adjutant G. E. R. Kenrick, D.S.O., Captain H. W. Smith, D.S.O., Lieutenants R. T. Lee and W. B. Haddon-Smith, and Second-Lieutenant C. Jackson.

On June 22nd, 1911, the Battalion was selected to troop the King's Colour on the occasion of the Coronation of His Majesty King George V, when the following order was published by His Excellency the Governor and Commander-in-Chief:—

"*The trooping of the Colour by The Queen's Regiment to-day was of a high standard of excellence in marching, drill, handling of arms, music, and saluting.*"

The time had now come for the 2nd The Queen's to proceed on another stage of their tour of foreign service, and consequently on January 3rd, 1912, the Battalion, having been inspected on the Alameda by His Excellency the Governor-General, Sir Archibald Hunter, G.C.B., D.S.O., embarked on board the hired transport *Soudan* for Bermuda, under command of Lieutenant-Colonel J. G. King-King, D.S.O. There also embarked 24 other officers, 2 warrant officers, 43 sergeants, 37 corporals, 14 drummers, and 744 privates—these numbers including 1 sergeant and 49 privates who had arrived from home in the *Soudan* on transfer from the 1st Battalion—11 officers' wives, and 6 children, 51 soldiers' wives, and 76 children. The officers were:—Lieutenant-Colonel J. G. King-King, D.S.O., Majors M. C. Coles and B. T. Pell, D.S.O., Captains L. M. Crofts, F. B. B. Pickard, Brevet Major H. R. Bottomley, W. H. Alleyne, P. J. Fearon and H. F. Lewis, Lieutenants F. J. Roberts, H. F. H. Master, P. C. Esdaile, W. B. Haddon-Smith, R. L. Q. Henriques, A. N. S. Roberts, R. L. G. Heath, A. P. Hamilton, J. D. Boyd, G. C. O. Oldfield, J. D. Mackworth and J. A. Lang-Browne, Second-Lieutenants C. R. Haigh and E. W. Bethell, Captain and Adjutant G. E. R. Kenrick, D.S.O., and Lieutenant and Quartermaster C. H. J. Wort.

The Battalion landed at Bermuda on January 15th, 1912, and was thus distributed:—

    Headquarters with "A," "C," "D," "G," and "H" Companies at Prospect.

    "B" and "F" Companies at St. George's Island.

    "E" Company at Boaz Island.

On Sunday, February 25th, His Excellency Lieutenant-General Sir F. W. Kitchener, K.C.B., Governor and Commander-in-Chief, presented the Certificate of the Royal Humane Society to No. 9359 Private A. Perry of the Battalion, awarded for gallantry in saving life from drowning at Gibraltar. This must have been one of the Governor's last official acts, for very shortly afterwards he died, and was succeeded by Lieutenant-General Sir George Bullock, K.C.B.; in October

---

* Colonel R. Dawson had retired on half-pay on September 29th previous.

Lieutenant-Colonel King-King retired on retired pay, and was succeeded in command by Lieutenant-Colonel M. C. Coles.

The Battalion had been barely two years in Bermuda when a change of station was ordered, and on January 21st, 1914, it left in the *Somali* for Durban, touching *en route* at St. Vincent and Cape Town, and on arrival in South Africa proceeding at once by rail to Pretoria, which was reached on February 19th, being quartered at Roberts' Heights. It had, however, barely settled down here when it left as part of the Pretoria District Infantry Brigade for Potchefstroom to take part in manœuvres, marching 110 miles in six days; and at 2 a.m. on August 1st, while lying out on the veldt waiting to attack a position at dawn, sudden orders were received to return to camp, and thence to Roberts' Heights, Pretoria, and it became known that war was about to break out between France and Germany. This was the first intimation that any of the Battalion had received that any European trouble was expected. The Commanding Officer appears to have been at first informed that the Battalion would next day be hurried to Cape Town, there to embark for England, but this seems to have been cancelled, and the 2nd The Queen's was now directed to stand fast, and await further orders. These were received some days later, it not being until the 19th that the Battalion left Pretoria, arriving at Cape Town on the 22nd, when it was at once embarked, together with the 2nd Battalion Bedfordshire Regiment, in the *Kenilworth Castle*, which then put out into Table Bay, and remained there till early on the morning of the 27th. The transport then joined the rest of the fleet, consisting of the *Astraea, Goorkha, Balmoral Castle, Dunluce Castle*, and *Briton*, with H.M.S. *Hyacinth* as escort, when the whole steamed off homewards. The wives of the officers accompanied the Battalion, but the married families of the other ranks came home in November in the *Dover Castle*.

At St. Helena, which was reached on September 2nd, the *Hyacinth* was replaced by H.M.S. *Leviathan* and H.M.S. *Europa*, and later the *Leviathan* by the *Carnarvon*, and finally the fleet of transports and its escort reached Southampton on September 19th, when the 2nd The Queen's disembarked and marched to a camp at Lyndhurst in the New Forest, there joining the 22nd Brigade of the 7th Division, then in process of formation. The 7th Division was commanded by Major-General T. Capper, and the 22nd Brigade by Brigadier-General S. T. B. Lawford. The 22nd Brigade was composed of the 2nd Battalions of The Queen's and the Royal Warwickshire Regiments and of the 1st Battalions of the Royal Welch Fusiliers and South Staffordshire Regiment.

The 2nd The Queen's had come home at full strength, 28 officers, 2 warrant officers, 40 sergeants, 48 corporals, and 855 privates, the officers being Lieutenant-Colonel M. C. Coles, Majors L. M. Crofts and H. R. Bottomley, Captains H. C. Whinfield, W. H. Alleyne, T. Weeding, H. F. Lewis, H. F. H. Master, T. C. Esdaile and W. B. Fuller, Lieutenants A. N. S. Roberts, R. L. G. Heath, J. A. Lang-Browne, C. R. Haigh, A. C. Thomas, D. R. Wilson, E. W. Bethell, and H. C. Williams, Second-Lieutenants G. K. Olliver, E. K. B. Furze, G. S. Ingram, R. K. Ross, J. G. H. Bird, G. M. Gabb, C. H. B. Blount and J. G. Collis, with Lieutenant and Quartermaster C. H. J. Wort. Within a very few days of disembarkation, however, three more officers joined—Lieutenant G. A. White, Second-Lieutenants D. Ive and J. Brown—with 253 non-commissioned officers and men from the 3rd Battalion, while Second-Lieutenant Olliver left on being posted to the Divisional Cyclist Company.

On Sunday, October 4th, at 3.30 p.m., the Battalion suddenly received orders to march to Southampton at 3.45 for embarkation, and the men having all been given leave to go into Lyndhurst it was no easy matter to collect them at such very short notice. Eventually, however, the first party, Headquarters and "A" and "B" Companies, marched off under Colonel Coles at 5.30, the remaining companies following with Major Crofts at 6.20 p.m. Lieutenant Roberts, Colour-Sergeant Shales, Band-Sergeant Burrows, and 97 non-commissioned officers and men remained behind at Lyndhurst as a first reinforcement. The strength of the 2nd Battalion The Queen's on embarkation totalled 30 officers and 988 other ranks; the staff and companies were officered as follows:—Lieutenant-Colonel M. C. Coles, Major L. M. Crofts, Lieutenant C. R. Haigh (adjutant), Captain C. H. J. Wort (quartermaster), Lieutenant A. C. Thomas (transport officer), Lieutenant R. L. G. Heath (machine-gun officer), Lieutenant F. G. Thatcher, R.A.M.C. (medical officer), Regimental Sergeant-Major W. Smith, and Regimental Quartermaster-Sergeant W. Routley.

"*A*" *Company*.—Captains H. C. Whinfield and P. C. Esdaile, Lieutenants J. A. Lang-Browne, E. K. B. Furze and G. S. Ingram, Second-Lieutenant R. K. Ross, Company Sergeant-Major C. H. Pascoe, and Company Quartermaster-Sergeant H. Sillence.

"*B*" *Company*.—Major H. R. Bottomley, Captain H. F. H. Master, Lieutenant D. R. Wilson, Second-Lieutenants G. M. Gabb, C. H. B. Blount and J. G. Collis, Company Sergeant-Major W. Martin, and Company Quartermaster-Sergeant W Puddicombe.

"*C*" *Company*.—Captains W. H. Alleyne and H. F. Lewis, Lieutenants E. W. Bethell and H. C. Williams, Second-Lieutenants R. H. Philpot and D. A. Brown, Company Sergeant-Major T. Lucas, and Company Quartermaster-Sergeant J. Burfield.

"*D*" *Company*.—Captains T. Weeding and W. B. Fuller, Lieutenant G. A. White, Second-Lieutenants J. G. H. Bird and D. Ive, Company Sergeant-Major W. Horsell; the Company Quartermaster-Sergeant did not embark, being sick in hospital.

The first party embarked at Southampton in the *Cymric* on the evening of October 4th, and sailed at dawn the next morning, reached Dover in the afternoon, and steamed on again as soon as it was dark. The second party embarked in the *Turkoman* at midnight on the 4th, but did not get away until dawn on the 6th, arriving just twenty-four hours later at Zeebrügge to find that the right wing had landed the previous day and had gone on by train to Oostcamp, a suburb of Bruges, getting into billets after dark. The wing under Major Crofts followed as soon as the disembarkation of the men and transport had been effected, and joined headquarters at Oostcamp at 9 p.m. on October 7th.

Something must now be said as to the reasons why the 7th Division had effected its landing in the theatre of war at a different port to those used by the divisions of the Expeditionary Force which had preceded it to the front.

By this date the German invaders had experienced a severe and wholly unexpected check at the Battle of the Marne, and this had drawn the attention of their leaders to the increased importance of Antwerp as a place of arms, whence the British and Belgian forces, supported by the English ships of war, might fall upon the flank, and even rear, of the German armies. "Antwerp," Mr. Churchill, then First Lord of the Admiralty, has reminded us,* "was not only the sole stronghold of the Belgian nation; it was also the true left flank of the Allied left front in the

* *The World Crisis*, Vol. 1, p. 332.

west. It guarded the whole line of the Channel ports. It threatened the flanks and rear of the German armies in France. It was the gateway from which a British army might emerge at any moment upon their sensitive and even vital communications."

The, for the Germans, untoward sequence of events had made the capture of Antwerp an absolute necessity for the Central Powers, and as early as September 9th, orders had been issued from the High Command that immediate steps should be initiated for the reduction of the fortress. On the 28th, therefore, fire was opened from giant howitzers upon the exterior forts, and although a strong Belgian army was engaged in the defence of the place, the situation soon became very grave, and the Allied governments were fully alive to the serious effect which its fall might have on the result of the campaign in the west. The Belgian Government appealed for assistance to England and France, and from the former the answer came that a cavalry division under General Byng, an infantry division under General Capper, and certain naval detachments would shortly be sent to Antwerp; while from France came promises of a French Territorial Division, and a strong brigade of Marines, making up a total force some 53,000 strong. The British contingent began disembarkation at Ostend and Zeebrügge on October 6th, while about the same date the French division and Marines were embarking at Havre or entraining for Dunkirk.

The Allies had at this time many and heavy commitments in the main theatre of war, the fear of invasion had retained a considerable army in the United Kingdom, while the Indian and Dominion Army Corps had not yet arrived in Europe; so that under the circumstances these reinforcements may be regarded as tolerably liberal, as all that at the moment could well be spared; the only matter in doubt was whether Antwerp could hold out until these forces arrived.

Early on the 8th the Battalion marched to Bruges and there joined the remainder of the 22nd Brigade, and in company with this the 2nd The Queen's moved along the main Bruges—Ostend road, turning south through Zandvoorde Brugge by the Nieuport Canal; and by 4 p.m., having at that time marched in all some 18 miles, the Battalion was directed to take up a position covering the Canal, " C " Company occupying the village of Istilles, 1½ miles in the front. During the night that followed orders came to hand for the Battalion to march via Ondebrugge to the railway station at Ostend early on the 9th, but shortly after setting out the bridge at Ondebrugge was found to be broken down by the Belgians, and The Queen's had to move along the railway line, while the transport proceeded by way of Leffinge. Ostend was reached by 11 a.m., and the Battalion went on by train to Ghent. Next day, the 10th, the march was to Heywyk, 1½ miles west of Melle, where all fell out by the roadside for the greater part of the day; then at dusk The Queen's moved a mile further to the south and went into billets for the night.

During this day the Belgian infantry were in action about a mile off only, and these held during the night an outpost line south of Melle; about 9 p.m. heavy firing breaking out in the outpost line, The Queen's were ordered to stand to, and first " B," and then " C " Company, was sent up to reinforce the Belgians, while the other two companies held a village.

Nothing transpired during the rest of the night or during the early part of the 11th, but in the afternoon orders were issued for The Queen's to relieve the Belgians in front of Melle, preparatory to a general retirement on Ghent. The Queen's held the outpost line until 8.30, when they in turn fell back upon Ghent, arriving there about midnight. The next day—the 12th—was a trying one for the Battalion; Ghent was left early in the morning and, marching west, the troops reached Hansbeke, about eight, and here went into billets, but before breakfasts were ready orders came to fall in again, and the 22nd Brigade started for Thielt, The Queen's providing the advanced guard; the road lay by Lootenhulle and Roysselede, Thielt being reached after dark, by which time the Battalion had marched 26 miles and been on the move 24 hours out of 26.

The march was continued on the 13th, Roulers not being arrived at till the evening, the day's march being made all the longer by reason of many protracted halts in the rain. Next day many of the men were found to be very footsore, and for this reason 400 of The Queen's were sent on to Ypres by train. Here the rest of the Battalion arrived in the course of the afternoon. There had been considerable enemy aircraft activity over the town during the early part of this day, but a Taube had been brought down by rifle fire from men of " C " and " D " Companies, falling some three miles off, and the occupants and the damaged machine were brought in by a cavalry patrol.

The 15th was passed in Ypres, but on the 16th the 22nd Brigade marched on to Zonnebeke, where during the day The Queen's took up a position north-west of the town covering the Zonnebeke—Langemarck road, and this day and the 17th were passed in strengthening and improving the position.

Up to some few days previous to these happenings, the 7th Infantry Division under Major-General Capper and the cavalry commanded by General Byng had formed an independent corps under General Rawlinson, directed by orders issued from the War Office, but it had now been placed at the disposal of Sir John French, who had issued the following orders :—*" Rawlinson was to move with his right on Courtrai, keeping generally level with the III Corps in the subsequent operations, should that prove possible; his cavalry under Byng was to move to the north of him. I had told Rawlinson that, whilst conforming to the general move east, he must keep an eye on the enemy's detachments known to be at Bruges and Roulers." Then a few pages further on in his book the Commander-in-Chief writes that having good reason to believe that Menin was very weakly occupied on the 17th, he issued orders to General Rawlinson to attack that place on the 18th, but that General Rawlinson " did not move."

This statement is not borne out by the war diary of The Queen's, wherein we read as follows under date of the 18th :—" Information Germans entrenched in position covering Menin. Brigade ordered to seize forward positions they (the enemy) had entrenched at Klythoek, preparatory to general attack on Menin, while 21st Brigade covered movement on right. Brigade marched through Becelaere to Dadizeele, Queen's in reserve at Dadizeele, ' B ' and ' C ' Companies supporting cavalry covering left flank. On reaching main Roulers—Menin road, Brigade swung to right and ' A ' and ' D ' sent to reinforce left of Royal Welch Fusiliers. Meanwhile heavy firing going on north of Ledeghem, though our cavalry had apparently been through it. North of town number of bicycles seen outside a house and party under Captain Lewis and Lance-Corporal Philips sent to bring them in. They advanced on house when fired on by Germans hidden in house. Captain Lewis shot in head and most of party killed. Sergeant Manning, just commissioned, was severely wounded and probably killed. Meanwhile ' A ' supported by ' D,' had crossed railway by level crossing south of Ledeghem and moved about one mile

* 1914, p. 219.

south; here a party of 'A' Company under Lieutenant Ingram surprised party of six Germans, killing and wounding most of them. German infantry now suddenly enfiladed 'A' and 'D' at close range.

"Battalion now ordered to retire and in this Captain Master was shot and had to be left. The whole Brigade now fell back, 'A' and 'B' covering right flank, to Zonnebeke, reached about 8 p.m."

The 19th was occupied in improving defences, and on the 20th the French were engaged to the east of the Passchendaele Road and had to fall back, while " A " Company of The Queen's also came under fire. The night of the 20th-21st was quiet, but in the morning of the 21st the enemy began shelling the line held by " B " and " D," and the infantry attack developed all along the line; at ten o'clock, by some mistake, " B " Company began to retire, but " A " was very strongly dug in, and held on till 1 p.m., when, with their right in the air and enfiladed by a German machine gun which had been brought across " B " Company's abandoned trenches, " A " also fell back, and the ridge along the Zonnebeke—Langemarck road was held by parts of " A " Company and some of the Life Guards on the left, and by others of The Queen's on the right. At 4 p.m. The Queen's were relieved by the Irish Guards, and were withdrawn to the railway embankment, there taking up a new position.

So soon as it became dark, however, the Battalion was ordered up to the Passchendaele road, there to fill a gap between the Royal Welch Fusiliers and the South Staffords. It was now, however, pitch dark, and the whereabouts of the South Staffords was not accurately known, and The Queen's finally took possession of some empty trenches on the east of the road in rear of the line originally held which was now in German hands. Here " C " Company was found still hanging on, having remained when the other companies retired.

Fresh orders now came for The Queen's to rendezvous near the cross roads in the centre of Zonnebeke, and the Battalion accordingly moved thither about 9 p.m., later being directed to take up a line on the right of the Warwicks, running south-east from the level crossing south-west of Zonnebeke. By the time this new position was reached it was 4.30 a.m. on the 22nd and entrenching was once again commenced, but much had to be done in clearing the foreground while the field of fire was found to be very limited, so a ridge 150 yards to the front was occupied by picquets.

On the 23rd Major Crofts took out 250 men who made up a party of 1,000 under Lieutenant-Colonel Cadogan of the Royal Welch Fusiliers, who was ordered to occupy again the trenches in Zonnebeke and collect abandoned equipment. The party came at once under very heavy fire, and Colonel Cadogan decided to fall back.

On the 24th the following order of the day was issued to the troops :—

*"The Field-Marshal Commanding-in-Chief wishes once more to make known to the troops under his command how deeply he appreciates the bravery and endurance they have again displayed since their arrival in the northern theatre of war."*

On this day the Battalion was split up for employment; " A " and " C " Companies moved to Veldhoek on the Ypres—Menin road, and were disposed under cover south of the road near the Château; and near here and in the adjacent woods they bivouacked for the night. In the morning of this day " C " Company had been sent to reinforce the Brigade, which was entrenched in thick woods on the right, and on arrival was ordered to relieve a battalion of the Guards, but on the 25th, which

GHELUVELT CHURCH.

[Copyright: Imperial War Museum.

passed quietly, mainly taken up with escorting prisoners to the rear, the Battalion was all together again near the Château.

Next day, the 26th, The Queen's marched to the cross roads west of Gheluvelt, and after a halt here of several hours, were ordered to advance parallel to and south of the Gheluvelt road. They came at once under heavy shell fire, and after continuing the advance for about one mile, the Battalion was directed to retire to a position in front of the Gheluvelt—Zandvoorde road, and there entrench. Later, however, The Queen's were sent to form up, in company with another battalion of the Brigade, on the Gheluvelt road, and found the enemy entrenched in their front in three lines, and at about 400 yards distance.

During the night of the 25th-26th the enemy had succeeded in making a considerable advance, and was concentrated in some strength in the woods and broken ground in the front of the 20th Brigade; he then launched an attack about 9 a.m. on the 26th, and after some hard fighting, succeeded in capturing the British front line trenches and the defenders had here to fall back. To re-establish the situation, at eight on the morning of the 27th, The Queen's, then north-east of Zandvoorde, were ordered to recapture the trenches abandoned about Kruiseecke. There was a wood here in the Battalion front, and " D " Company moving by the left, and " B " by the right of it, the trenches were occupied without opposition, and connection established with the brigade on the left. The enemy kept up a continual sniping, and a few casualties resulted.

The Battalion spent the 28th in the woods about Klein-Zillebeke, but early on the 29th it was again on the move, being first sent up to Veldhoek, and then at 8 a.m. being ordered to move half a mile further along the Gheluvelt road, and from there to reinforce the Guards at Gheluvelt. " A " Company moved off first with Major Crofts, and on reaching the high ground half a mile west of the Windmill, one subaltern and one machine gun were there found, the officer stating that there was no one in his front. " A " Company then lined the road facing the Gheluvelt—Menin road from which direction a hot fire was now coming. In the meantime " D " Company had extended to the right, while " B " had prolonged the line in the Kruiseecke direction, and during the morning these companies occupied various farms east of the Gheluvelt—Kruiseecke road. About midday the 2nd Battalion was reinforced by the 1st Battalion The Queen's under Lieutenant-Colonel Pell, and a party under Captain Soames came up on the right of the farm then occupied by " A " Company, 2nd Battalion; this line was held till the evening, and in the meanwhile " C " Company came up on the left near Gheluvelt—Kruiseecke road. The line was reformed after dark, the 1st Battalion holding the line from the Gheluvelt—Menin road round the Windmill to the Farm, while the 2nd Battalion held that onwards to the cross roads north of Kruiseecke, where it joined on to the Yorkshire Regiment.

On the 30th the Battalion was under very heavy shell fire from guns on the high ground south-west of Kruiseecke and from infantry posted east of the cross roads; and next day the companies were shelled out of their trenches and forced back into the woods, where they dug fresh trenches near the Guards. The fighting all day was very heavy, but the general line was held till night—Lieutenant Haigh,* Lance-Corporal Cooper, and Private Hartwell defending a trench from 1.30 p.m. till dark—when the remnants of The Queen's under Captain Alleyne retired to the Château and " dug in " on the edge of the wood.

* In a letter home Lieutenant Haigh, who was a very fine shot, describing this incident, said : " My Bisley training was not in vain."

In his despatch of November 20th, 1914, the Field-Marshal wrote :—" On October 27th I went to the headquarters of the First Corps at Hooge to personally investigate the condition of the 7th Division. Owing to constant marching and fighting ever since its hasty disembarkation, in aid of the Antwerp garrison, this Division had suffered great losses, and was becoming very weak. I therefore decided temporarily to break up the IV Corps and place the 7th Division with the I Corps under the command of Sir Douglas Haig. . . . On receipt of orders, in accordance with the above arrangement, Sir Douglas Haig redistributed the line held by the I Corps as follows :—

" (a) The 7th Division from the Château east of Zandvoorde to the Menin Road. . . ."

The 7th Division, and each of the brigades composing it, had by this been so greatly reduced by the losses sustained that on November 1st the 22nd Brigade was formed into two battalions, No. 1, consisting of the remnants of The Queen's and Royal Welch Fusiliers, was placed under command of Captain Alleyne, while No. 2 Battalion, containing non-commissioned officers and men of the Royal Warwickshire and South Staffordshire Battalions, was commanded by Captain Vallentine ; to No. 1 Battalion the following officers of the 2nd The Queen's were attached for duty :—Captain Fuller, Lieutenants White, Ross and Smith.

November 2nd and 3rd the 2nd The Queen's spent in reserve, and then next day they were sent into Ypres to the Hotel de Ville, where presumably the Battalion was intended to enjoy a complete rest. Unfortunately, however, owing to exceptionally heavy shelling opened by the Germans, The Queen's had to be moved on the 4th to a field $1\frac{1}{2}$ miles distant in the Dickebusch direction, remaining here until dawn on the 5th.

On this day Captain A. N. S. Roberts arrived with a draft of 110 other ranks.

The next two days witnessed the temporary close of these long-protracted and very costly operations. Early on the 6th the Brigade moved to bivouacs by the cross roads $1\frac{1}{2}$ miles due north of Dickebusch, but in the evening a message being received from the Officer Commanding 4th (Guards) Brigade at Zillebeke stating that he was in need of assistance, the Division marched in that direction and was at first placed in corps reserve. At 5 a.m. on the 7th the Brigade moved off to take up a position in view of an attack, proceeding by paths through the woods, and, screened by some rising ground, deployed for attack, timed to begin at 6.15 a.m. It was a very misty morning, and at this hour it was only just becoming light enough to see objectives.

The first two lines of The Queen's advanced over the rise when heavy machine-gun fire at once opened upon them ; the two lines then charged the German trenches, the Germans leaving them in all haste and bolting to the rear. The advance was continued, and a further German trench was taken with three machine guns, but the position could not be held by reason of the enfilade fire now experienced, while no further advance could be made owing to the fire from the houses and trenches held by the enemy.

The line gained was maintained all day under continuous fire of all kinds, which caused much damage, and in the evening the Brigade was relieved, and French reinforcements had come up in line. On the 8th the Brigade was at long last withdrawn from the front, and marched by way of Dickebusch to Locre, and from there on the 9th to Bailleul.

## THE LOSSES OF THE 7TH DIVISION

The losses suffered by the 2nd Battalion The Queen's had been very heavy in all ranks. Of killed or died of wounds there were 8 officers and 68 non-commissioned officers and men, wounded were 22 officers and 415 other ranks, while 163 men were missing, a total of 676 casualties in all. The officers killed or died of wounds were :—Captains H. F. Lewis and H. F. H. Master, Lieutenant and Adjutant C. R. Haigh,* Lieutenants A. C. Thomas and D. R. Wilson, Second-Lieutenants G. S. Ingram, J. G. H. Bird and D. Ive ; the names of those wounded are :—Lieutenant-Colonel M. C. Coles, Majors L. M. Crofts and H. R. Bottomley, Captains H. C. Whinfield, W. H. Alleyne, T. Weeding, P. C. Esdaile and A. N. S. Roberts, Lieutenants R. L. G. Heath, J. A. Lang-Browne, C. R. Haigh* (adjutant), E. W. Bethell, H. C. Williams, and E. K. B. Furze, Second-Lieutenants R. H. Philpot, G. M. Gabb, J. G. Collis, G. A. White, D. A. Brown, W. Smith and C. H. Pascoe, with the medical officer, Lieutenant L. H. F. Thatcher.

The First Battle of Ypres did not come officially to an end until November 22nd, but the 7th Division had nobly played its part in it, and had done all, and more than all, that was asked of it. " Day after day," writes the historian of the deeds of the original Expeditionary Force,† " the same British divisions, jaded, depleted of officers, and gradually dwindling into mere skeletons, were called upon to withstand the attacks of fresh and fresh troops. It was not merely that the Germans had the superiority in numbers on each occasion when they attacked, but they had also the unspeakable advantage of being able at any time to direct a stream of fresh troops against any part of our thin, weary, battered line." Then General Rawlinson, the commander of the IV Corps, which included the 7th Division, wrote as under :—

" *After the deprivations and tension of being pursued day and night by an infinitely stronger force, the Division had to pass through the worst ordeal of all. It was left to a little force of 30,000 to keep the German Army at bay while the other British corps were being brought up from the Aisne. Here they clung on like grim death, with almost every man in the trenches, holding a line which of necessity was a great deal too long—a thin, exhausted line—against which the prime of the German first-line troops were hurling themselves with fury. The odds against them were about 8 to 1 ; and when once the enemy found the range of a trench, the shells dropped into it from one end to the other with terrible effect. Yet the men stood firm and defended Ypres in such a manner that a German officer afterwards described their action as a brilliant feat of arms, and said that they were under the impression that there had been four British Army Corps against them at this point. When the Division was afterwards withdrawn from the firing line to refit, it was found that out of 400 officers who set out from England there were only 44 left, and out of 12,000 men only 2,336.*"

The 2nd Battalion The Queen's was only one day at Bailleul, marching on November 10th to Merris and remaining here until the early morning of the 14th. On arrival at Merris the strength of the Battalion was no higher than 3 officers and 311 other ranks, the officers being Lieutenant Buchanan, R.A.M.C., Second-Lieutenant Ross and Captain and Quartermaster Wort, but on the 12th Captain F. S. Montague-Bates, East Surrey Regiment, arrived with a draft of 207 non-commissioned officers and men, and assumed command, being, however, almost at once relieved by Major E. Monteagle-Browne, 1st Loyal North Lancashire Regiment, who within twenty-four hours was transferred to command a battalion of the Royal Warwickshire Regiment.

* Wounded on October 21st, killed on November 7th.
† Hamilton, *The First Seven Divisions*, pp. 274, 275.

On the 14th the 2nd The Queen's marched by Sailly and Fleurbaix to trenches at La Boutillerie, and here, or in billets at Rue de Bataille or Rue de Biache, the Battalion saw out the rest of the month of November. Many more officers and another strong draft joined during this time—the officers nearly all of comparatively junior rank and the majority drawn from other regiments and corps:—Capt A. S. Hewitt, Royal West Kent Regiment, Lieutenant W. V. T. Gripper, 3rd East Surrey, Second-Lieutenants A. M. Allan, The Queen's, D. G. Ramsay, Royal Sussex, P. C. Wort, Buffs, J. D. Burrows, Royal West Kent Regiment, H. Butterworth, The Queen's, C. F Austin, H. Messom, C. G. Rought and D. F. Humphreys—all these four from the Artists Rifles.

During December the weather changed very much for the worse, and the state of the trenches was appalling, on the 9th a man of the 2nd The Queen's being discovered who had remained stuck fast all night in the mud of the trenches. All the same, there was very considerable activity among the British troops, many raids were carried out by small parties led by enterprising subalterns, and one of these which took place on the night of the 14th-15th seems to deserve special mention.

At midnight Second-Lieutenant Ramsay took out 23 volunteers with the object of raiding an enemy picquet and capturing a prisoner so as to secure identifications. The party was divided into two, 16 men advancing with the officer, while Lance-Corporal Middleton was in charge of the remainder, who were to be used to draw fire. The two parties naturally lost sight of each other in the darkness, and presently Second-Lieutenant Ramsay noticed some men whom he thought must belong to Lance-Corporal Middleton's party, so sent No. 942 Private A. Knowles to find out. Knowles got right among these men before he discovered them to be Germans, when he shouted—wholly regardless of the consequence to himself—"Here they are, open fire!" He was then at once wounded by the enemy, when Second-Lieutenant Ramsay's party fired and charged, killed two of the enemy and wounded two others, one of whom was sent to the rear. No. 9169 Private H. Abbott carried Knowles back to our lines, whither, the fire from the main German trench having now become very heavy, Ramsay withdrew, No. 8468 Corporal F. Lamond covering the retirement. Private E. Viney was sent to tell Lance-Corporal Middleton that the party was falling back, but was unfortunately taken for one of the enemy in the darkness and mortally wounded. He delivered his message, saying: "The Queen's; Mr. Ramsay told me to tell you to retire as we have caught a German," the poor fellow then becoming unconscious and dying a few moments later.

The prisoner proved to belong to the 4th Königin Augusta Garde Regiment, and was at the time of his capture attached to the 9th Company, 55th Regiment, 13th Division of the VII Corps.

From the General Officer Commanding 7th Division came the following message to Second-Lieutenant Ramsay and his men: "They are to be congratulated on the success of the enterprise."

On the 18th two companies of The Queen's supported the Warwicks in an unsuccessful and costly attack, and at daybreak on the 19th the Germans in the opposite trenches initiated a local armistice for the purpose of collecting the wounded and burying the dead; but, as might almost have been expected, they managed to entice Second-Lieutenants Rought and Walmisley and seven stretcher bearers into the enemy trenches where they were made prisoners. The armistice was ended by a sudden opening of fire by the British guns, and in the course of this and the previous day Second-Lieutenant Ramsay and 7 men were killed, Captains P. J. Fearon and R. T. Lee, Lieutenant A. M. Allan, Second-Lieutenants H. Butterworth and F. T. Burkitt and 39 other ranks were wounded, besides the 2 officers and 7 men made prisoners.

On Christmas Day and also on the 26th there was again an informal armistice, when the German officers provided lists of British officers recently captured and promised to try to effect the release of Second-Lieutenants Rought and Walmisley so basely captured and detained on the 19th.

By the end of the month the 2nd The Queen's was once again tolerably strong in non-commissioned officers and men, but the officers were still something under 20 in number, though during December the following had joined :—Captains H. F. Kirkpatrick, R. C. Slacke, R. T. Lee and P. J. Fearon, Second-Lieutenants J. B. Coates, A. E. Walmisley, R. H. O'Brien, R. G. Heinekey and F. T. Burkitt ; Major L. M. Crofts rejoined on the 20th and assumed command.

The following appreciations of the services of the 22nd Infantry Brigade in general and of those of the 2nd The Queen's in particular were published during this month :—

"*In forwarding the remarks of the General Officer Commanding 7th Division on the part taken in the present campaign by the 22nd Infantry Brigade, I wish to convey to all ranks of the Battalion under your command my high appreciation of the good service done by them. All ranks have shown the same spirit and endurance which have in former years made the Regiment famous, and have now added to honour already gained. The heavy losses in both officers and men bear witness to the efforts made by this Battalion to uphold the honour of the Army and Empire. I am proud to have had the honour of having this Battalion in my Brigade.*

(Sgd.) "SYDNEY LAWFORD, *Brigadier-General.*

"*2nd Battalion The Queen's (Royal West Surrey Regiment).*

"*The Battalion has distinguished itself on several occasions. On October 31st this Battalion made a gallant counter-attack in combination with units of other brigades, driving back the enemy and gaining a considerable amount of ground.*

"*On November 7th the Battalion, though very weak after nearly three weeks' incessant fighting, took a leading part in a counter-attack against the enemy, who was pressing hard on the right of the I Corps. The counter-attack was successful, the enemy was driven back, and 3 machine guns were captured.*

"*It is to be noted that near Gheluvelt and Kruiseecke this Battalion found itself during the action alongside its own 1st Battalion of the 3rd Infantry Brigade. The two Battalions became intermingled and, together, carried forward a counter-attack and offered stubborn resistance to the enemy.*"

## CHAPTER IX.

### 2ND BATTALION (*continued*).

### 1915.

#### THE SECOND BATTLE OF YPRES AND THE BATTLE OF LOOS.

##### BATTLE HONOURS:
"Aubers," "Festubert, 1915," "Loos."

THE 2nd The Queen's remained during January and February, 1915, where the end of the year had left them, suffering from the continued inclemency of the weather, the discomforts and hardships and horrors of trench life, and sustaining daily a few casualties from the enemy's big guns and from the rifles of his snipers.

Drafts continued to come out and new officers joined, while some of the latter came back again who had earlier been invalided by reason of wounds or sickness, so that when on March 1st the 22nd Infantry Brigade marched from the neighbourhood of Fleurbaix to Laventie, on relief by the Canadians, the 2nd The Queen's moved at a strength of 29 officers and 824 other ranks.

"Our new line of trenches," we read in the Battalion diary of this date, "extends over a front of 1,400 yards, and as regards comfort to the officers and men is very much superior to that we have just left. Headquarters are in a house in the Rue Tilleloy; on our right the Royal Welch Fusiliers carry on the line, and on our left half a battalion of the 8th Royal Scots. The trenches are all high reintrenchments and the German lines are on an average 230 yards from us. Brigade headquarters are at Laventie. Order of Companies in trenches from right to left—'A,' 'B,' 'C,' and 'D.' There is no parados at present and 'D' Company's portion of trench will require a lot of work, the parapets are not bullet-proof in most places and are not high enough."

The Germans here seemed an unenterprising lot, and evinced a disposition to surrender over-easily, several being captured wandering about on the Battalion front and having no satisfactory explanation for their appearance—sometimes with unloaded rifles.

In his despatch of April 5th Sir John French states the reasons which had led him to believe that a vigorous offensive should be early carried out; he enumerates the objects of such an attack—the capture of Neuve Chapelle and the establishment as far forward as possible of the British line, and he states that the main offensive was entrusted to the First Army, supported by troops of the Second and by certain units of the general reserve. In these operations the 7th Division, now serving in the IV Corps, was actively engaged, particularly about the village of Aubers, and the importance of all that it was hoped to achieve was impressed upon those participating in the following order issued by the General Officer Commanding the Corps :—

"*The attack which we are about to undertake is of the first importance to the Allied cause. The Army and the Nation are watching the result, and Sir John French is confident that every individual in the IV Corps will do his duty and inflict a crushing defeat on the German VII Corps which is opposed to us.*"

The following account of the operations of the ensuing days is taken from the diary of the 2nd Battalion The Queen's:—" March 10th. In the trenches. At 7.30 a.m. our artillery bombardment commenced and was maintained incessantly until 8.15 a.m. At 8.45 we received information that the 8th Division attack, launched at 8.5, had taken the enemy's front line of trenches with but slight loss to us. At 8.55 the enemy's artillery shelled vigorously the Rue Tilleloy in which our headquarters are situated. At 9.25 we heard that the Indian Division had taken the enemy's trenches opposite them. At 9.55 information received from Division that fighting was progressing favourably at Neuve Chapelle. At 10.50 information reached us that the 25th Brigade had reached the main street of Neuve Chapelle and was in touch with the Gurkhas on the right; the 23rd Brigade was hung up by wire, but was in touch with left of 25th Brigade. At 1.30 p.m. the 8th Division was on a line through and to the north of Neuve Chapelle, and the 21st Brigade was about to attack. Aubers church in flames. 6.30. Information received that the 21st Brigade had captured the line of enemy trenches about 1,000 yards to our right front. 7.20 p.m. 21st Brigade consolidated on line of Moulin du Piètre.

" 11th March. In trenches. 4.30 a.m. Germans holding a line of trenches in front of us, a position facing south-west of Aubers. Our troops facing the enemy on line of our present trenches and line facing Moulin du Piètre. IV Corps to continue the attack to-day and attack Aubers; 21st Brigade attacking Les Mottes Farm; 20th Brigade passing Piètre with Le Plouich as its objective; our Brigade to assist the advance of other troops by vigorous fire and, as soon as its front becomes clear, to assemble in divisional reserve on our right flank. It appears that the enemy is in no great strength. 6.25 a.m. our artillery opened fire. 10.30. 21st Brigade attacking the line Les Mottes—Trevelet, is being hung up and cannot get on. 2 p.m. Our Brigade ordered to support by rifle and machine-gun fire the assault by 21st Brigade. 4 p.m. Assault not delivered; enemy appear to be hanging on to two strongly defended points and holding up our attack.

" 12th March. In trenches. Enemy holding a line through Moulin du Piètre and southwards, 21st Brigade facing them about 200 yards distant. Orders for an assault have been issued but no action taken. Morning very misty. The 20th and 21st Brigades have taken 600 prisoners in their successful assault on the Moulin du Piètre.

" 13th March. In trenches. On our front all is quiet except for intermittent shelling. At 6.30 orders received for us to move down the line and take over the line occupied by the two left companies of the Royal Welch Fusiliers. ' A ' and ' B ' Companies remain where they are and ' C ' and ' D ' take over new line.

" 14th March. We are holding our line, otherwise taking no action; the enemy shelling heavily all approaches to our position all night and most of the morning. We moved again this evening, ' A ' and ' B ' Companies remaining in their old position, ' C ' and ' D ' into billets."

The 2nd The Queen's remained in their trenches until the 18th, when they were relieved and marched back to Estaires. During these days in the trench line the Battalion had had 1 officer, Second-Lieutenant C. F. Austin, and 2 men killed, and 24 non-commissioned officers and men wounded.

During the month of April the Battalion remained in much the same neighbourhood, the usual tours of duty in the front line being varied by spells in billets in Estaires, Laventie or La Gorgue, but on May 8th we find the Battalion, then billeted at La Gorgue, engaged in final preparations for taking part in the closing operations of the Second Battle of Ypres, which had already been some time in progress, having commenced on April 22nd, while it endured until May 24th. The opening of the battle had gone rather in favour of the enemy who had introduced his new weapon of poison gas, and the British counter-attacks had not been specially successful, so that, as stated in his despatch of June 15th, the Commander-in-Chief directed the Commander of the First Army to concentrate all effort on the southern point of attack. " To this end the 7th Division had been brought round from the IV Corps area to support this attack, which was timed to commence on the night of the 15th, the 7th Division being placed on the right of the 2nd, and advancing with it and the Indian Division against the German trenches extending from Richebourg l'Avoué in a south-westerly direction."

At 1 p.m. then on May 8th the Brigade marched up to support trenches on the north side of the Rouge de Bout, just in rear of the Rue du Bois. The plan of attack for the next day was as follows :—The 8th Division was intended to break the German line approximately opposite Rouges Bancs and, having effected an entrance, was to advance on Fromelles, while the 7th Division was to follow through the gap thus made and deal with certain defended localities, then moving on to Aubers, Le Plouich, and Le Cliqueterie, where it was to effect a junction with an Indian division advancing from a point further south; it was hoped that in this way the Aubers Ridge would be secured. The 1st Division was to move on the right of the Indians. The 22nd Infantry Brigade was to provide the advanced guard of the 7th Division, The Queen's and Royal Warwicks being in the first line, the Royal Welch Fusiliers and South Staffords in support, and the 8th Royal Scots in reserve.

The attack by the 8th Division on the 9th was only partially successful, and the 22nd Brigade did not in consequence move further forward than the support trenches where the battalions remained throughout the day under continuous shell fire, and for the next six days no further advance was made, but of the events of the 16th the Field-Marshal wrote : " The 7th Division, on the right of the 2nd, advanced to the attack and by 7 a.m. had entrenched themselves on a line running north and south halfway between their original trenches and La Quinque Rue, having cleared and captured several lines of the enemy's trenches, including a number of fortified posts."

The plan of attack by the 7th Division was as follows :—This was to be delivered, in company with the 2nd Division, in the direction of Violaines, viz., south and south-east, the 2nd Division having its left on Richebourg l'Avoué, the 7th with its right some 150 yards south of the Rue de Cailloux. The 2nd Division was to attack at 11.30 on the night of the 15th and if unsuccessful, again at 3.15 on the following morning, the 7th Division attacking at the same hour on the 16th, preceded by half an hour's artillery bombardment ; the final objectives of both divisions were so arranged that, when arrived at, the two should connect along a semi-circular line running roughly from a point just west of Richebourg l'Avoué ; the advance was one of about 1,000 yards.

The 20th and 22nd Brigades, on left and right respectively, were to attack, while the 21st Brigade was to be held in reserve ; the Royal Welch Fusiliers and The Queen's were on left and right of the first line of the 22nd Brigade, the right of the Fusiliers resting on the Rue de Cailloux, while the left of The Queen's was on the orchard just to the right of the Rue de Cailloux, the Battalion frontage being one of 200 yards. " A " and " B " Companies were to lead the attack of

The Queen's, the Battalion being disposed in eight lines with 50 yards' interval between lines.

The strength of the 2nd The Queen's on going into action on May 16th was 22 officers and 773 non-commissioned officers and men, and the following were the officers engaged:—Major H. R. Bottomley (in command), Major H. F. Kirkpatrick, 3rd Buffs (acting adjutant), Lieutenant E. K. B. Furze (assistant adjutant), Second-Lieutenants R. G. Heinekey and I. W. Brooks (machine guns), Second-Lieutenant C. Taylor-Jones (bombing officer), and Lieutenant W. A. Stewart, R.A.M.C. (medical officer).

"A" *Company*.—Captain J. A. Lang-Browne, Second-Lieutenants A. McCabe, A. M. Hiller and D. F. Humphreys.

"B" *Company*.—Captain W. B. Fuller, Second-Lieutenants H. Messom and L. H. Fairtlough.

"C" *Company*.—Major R. C. Slacke, 3rd Buffs, Captain J. W. Garnier, Lieutenant R. H. Philpot, and Second-Lieutenant G. L. Pratt.

"D" *Company*.—Captain W. B. Haddon-Smith, Second-Lieutenants J. B. Coates, M. H. de Rougemont and F. T. Burkitt.

At 2.45 precisely on the morning of the 16th the bombardment of the enemy trenches began, continuing for half an hour, when the leading platoons of "A" Company climbed out of their trenches, formed up rapidly, and charged the German lines; it was now just daylight. As soon, however, as the heads of the attackers showed above their parapets, the enemy, apparently in no way affected by the intense British bombardment, opened a sustained rifle fire; none the less, the second line of "A" followed, and then the first of "C" Company, but the enemy fire seemed to gather volume rather than to lessen, so the British guns opened again with lyddite on the opposing trenches and the rest of "C" and "D," pushing on, forced the Germans out of their lines; most of them attempted to escape to our right, and in so doing afforded excellent targets to the Brigade Grenade Company.

Many officers and other ranks of The Queen's had now fallen, but the survivors—some 5 officers and 230 non-commissioned officers and men—charged on beyond the captured German trench over the 800 yards of ground separating them from their final objective, and two more German lines were passed, as also La Quinque Rue on the way, until about 6 a.m. the final objective was reached and captured, and here The Queen's connected up with the Staffords on the right and fragments of the other two battalions of the Brigade on the left. The position was a very open one, and consolidation in daylight was impossible, while, as the troops on the left had not been able to get on, this flank was exposed throughout the day. The enemy shelling was very heavy, the line was enfiladed and the left was still in the air, so at 7.30 p.m. the Brigade fell back and occupied the line of German trench captured in the morning.

The casualties in the 2nd Battalion The Queen's had been grievous, amounting to no less than 454 all ranks; 11 officers and 153 non-commissioned officers and men were killed or died of wounds, 8 officers and 231 other ranks were wounded, 42 men were missing, 2 were missing believed killed, and 1 man was wounded and missing.

The officers killed or died of wounds were Majors H. R. Bottomley, H. F. Kirkpatrick, and R. C. Slacke, Captains W. B. Fuller, W. B. Haddon-Smith and J. A. Lang-Browne, Second-Lieutenants A. M. Hiller, G. L. Pratt, D. F. Humphreys and M. H. de Rougemont; wounded were Captain J. W. Garnier, Second-Lieutenants F. T. Burkitt, R. G. Heinekey, I. W. Brooks, J. B. Coates, H. Messom,

A. P. P. McCabe, and L. H. Fairtlough, with Lieutenant W. A. Stewart (the medical officer).

Special acts of gallantry were performed by Major Kirkpatrick, Sergeant Cox and his signallers, and by Private Williamson. Major Kirkpatrick was hit first in the neck before leaving our trenches, but refused to go to the rear and insisted on advancing with the headquarters of the Battalion. He led the way to the final objective and there remained until hit a second time in the head by a fragment of shell which compelled him to retire.

Sergeant Cox, Corporal Morris, Privates Cleaver and Aldridge did excellent work throughout the day in maintaining telephone communication with the Brigade; the line was several times cut, but in every case it was repaired, however difficult and dangerous the work.

Private Williamson of " D " Company was reported by the Adjutant of the South Staffords for bringing in a wounded comrade, and although thoroughly exhausted he refused to rest, stating that " his place was in the firing line."

During the rest of May the 2nd The Queen's remained either in support or in reserve, and at Bourcq on the 31st the Battalion was inspected by General Monro, commanding the I Corps, who in the course of a speech said " how pleased he was to see that the 2nd Battalion was more than maintaining the exceptionally high standard of the Regiment. He knew how well they had done in the recent fighting and had the greatest confidence in their behaviour in the future. As a former officer of the Regiment he was more than gratified with their successes and he wished them always to remember the great and glorious traditions of the Regiment."

The 2nd The Queen's remained in these parts for something over three months, long days and hours of trying and costly duty in the trenches, varied by rests in rear in one or other of the little towns of France and Flanders; and it was in one of these last that, as a regimental diarist records, " Sergeant Botterill, who was the 2nd Battalion Mess Sergeant, made a name for himself as a French scholar. While doing his shopping one morning he entered a shop to buy eggs. Not knowing what the French for an egg was, he picked up a turnip and placed it on the floor. He then sat on it, to the astonishment of the shopkeeper, and began to cluck like a hen. He got his eggs all right !"

At the beginning of the third week in September the 2nd The Queen's were quartered in billets at Verquigneul near Bethune, the 7th Division now occupying the angle formed by the Lens—Hulluch and Vermelles—Hulluch roads, with the 9th Division on the left and the 1st on the right, the 7th being immediately opposite the gap between St. Elie and Hulluch. It was the eve of the Battle of Loos, as to the object and general results of which the Commander-in-Chief states in his despatch of October 15th, 1915 :—" It was arranged that we should make a combined attack from certain points of the Allied line during the last week in September. The reinforcements I have received enabled me to comply with several requests which General Joffre has made that I should take over additional portions of the French line. In fulfilment of the rôle assigned to it in these operations, the Army under my command attacked the enemy on the morning of September 25th. The main attack was delivered by the I and IV Corps between the La Bassée Canal on the north and a point of the enemy's line opposite the village of Grenay on the south. . . . The general plan of the main attack on September 25th was as follows :— In co-operation with an offensive movement by the Tenth French Army on our right, the I and IV Corps were to attack the enemy from a point opposite the little mining village of Grenay on the south to the La Bassée Canal on the north. . . . The attacks of the I and IV Corps were delivered at 6.30 a.m., and were successful all along the line, except just south of the La Bassée Canal."

On the evening of the 24th all greatcoats of the men of the 2nd The Queen's were collected and stored in a house in Verquigneul, the Battalion then marching off and some time after midnight was in position in the reserve trenches in Lancashire Lines. Next morning, the 25th, at about 5.50, an intense bombardment broke out against the enemy's trenches, this continuing for forty minutes, at the end of which the attack was launched. The 20th Brigade attacked on the right, the 22nd on the left, the enemy defences in the divisional front apparently consisting of two well-defined lines of trenches, the one running from Fosse 8 southwards to Loos, the other 1,500 yards in rear, running through Haisnes—Cité St. Elie—Hulluch.

The 2nd Battalion The Queen's was this day commanded by Captain (acting Lieutenant-Colonel) M. G. Heath, and the companies, from right to left, were disposed and commanded as follows :—" C "—Captain R. H. Philpot; " B "—Captain T. P. Brocklehurst; " D "—Captain R. L. G. Heath, and " A " Captain R. H. Maddock. The Bombing Officer was Second-Lieutenant C. Taylor-Jones, and the machine-gun detachment, commanded by Second-Lieutenant G. A. Pilleau, was placed in a forward position to support the advance and bring long-range fire to bear on the German communication trenches. The following officers were also present with the Battalion and took part in the attack :—Captain F. C. Longbourne, D.S.O. (adjutant), Second-Lieutenants J. A. L. Hopkinson, A. L. Brown, T. V. Chapman, J. B. W. Walsh, S. R. P. Walter, R. O. Sillem, C. G. D. Thrupp, M. G. Strode, and L. A. Crook.

On reaching the front line of British trenches the Battalion advanced in close support of the other three battalions of the Brigade, " C " Company directing just to the right of Fosse 8, and this company passed over the first and second German lines without much opposition; the other companies met with a sterner resistance, but, after making good these trenches, " A," " B," and " D " Companies were directed on Cité St. Elie, where they established themselves in the German trench 150 yards north of the same by 11 a.m., while half " C " Company, under Second-Lieutenant Chapman, carried " the Quarries," capturing in them 2 officers and some 40 men. Cité St. Elie was entered on the north about two in the afternoon by some of the 2nd The Queen's, but these had to fall back, and by this the men were somewhat disorganized and mixed up with the 9th Division on the left. The line arrived at was maintained until dark, when a fresh one was taken up and consolidated about 200 yards to the front of " the Quarries."

Both on the 26th and 27th the enemy made strong counter-attacks on Fosse 8 and on Cité St. Elie, but were driven back; fighting was renewed on the 28th, on the night following which the 2nd The Queen's were relieved and went back to billets at Sailly Labourse.

Again had the Battalion suffered serious loss, 5 officers and 24 non-commissioned officers and men were killed, 6 officers and 110 men were wounded, while 127 men were missing; the officers killed were Captain R. L. G. Heath, Second-Lieutenants J. B. W. Walsh, A. L. Brown and C. Taylor-Jones; while wounded were Captain T. P. Brocklehurst, Lieutenant J. A. L. Hopkinson, Second-Lieutenants L. A. Crook, M. G. Strode, G. A. Pilleau, and R. O. Sillem; Captain (Acting Lieutenant-Colonel) M. G. Heath was missing, believed killed.

Of the attack on September 25th the Field-Marshal wrote in his despatch that " the position assaulted and carried with so much brilliancy and dash by the I and IV Corps was an exceptionally strong one. It extended along a distance of some 6,500 yards, consisted of a double line, which included works of considerable strength, and was a network of trenches and bomb-proof shelters. Some of the dug-outs and shelters formed veritable caves thirty feet below the ground, with almost impenetrable head cover. The enemy had expended months of labour upon perfecting these defences. The total number of prisoners captured during these operations amounted to 57 officers and 3,000 other ranks. Material which fell into our hands included 26 field guns, 40 machine guns, and 3 Minenwerfer."

In this action the 7th Division sustained a very great loss in the death of its commander, Major-General T. Capper; he was succeeded by Major-General H. E. Watts, C.B., C.M.G.

The 2nd The Queen's spent the early half of October in the Cambrin area, where Major H. W. Smith, D.S.O., arrived and assumed command of the Battalion; and then on the 17th the Battalion marched back to the neighbourhood of Béthune, the end of the month finding it in the trenches near Givenchy—now at a strength of 22 officers and 738 other ranks.

There was no further change of quarters until December 5th, when the Division was transferred to the Third Army area, and the Battalion marched to Lillers and there entrained, arriving soon after midnight at Saleux, and marching from there to Molliens-Vidame, where Brigade headquarters, The Queen's, and the South Staffords occupied comfortable billets.

A fortnight later, on the 20th, a very considerable change took place; for reasons which have already been explained, connected with the enhancement of the efficiency of the New Army divisions now arriving on the Western Front, some of the new Service battalions were taken out of the divisions in which since their creation they had served, and were incorporated in the regular divisions which had been in France and Flanders since the early days of the war, these more experienced units going to the newer formations. In the case of the 7th Division, the 21st Brigade was taken bodily out of it, and was replaced by the 91st Brigade, formerly of the 31st Division. At this time the 91st Brigade was composed of the 20th, 21st, 22nd and 24th (Service) Battalions of the Manchester Regiment, but two of these, the 20th and 24th, were now transferred to the 22nd Brigade, taking there the places of the 2nd Battalion The Queen's and the 1st Battalion The South Staffordshire Regiment, which joined the 91st Brigade, commanded by Brigadier-General F. Kempster, D.S.O.

In consequence of the above rearrangements, The Queen's and South Staffords now marched to new billets at Riencourt, where Christmas Day, 1915, was spent. On December 31st the Battalion numbered 32 officers and 824 other ranks.

# CHAPTER X.

## 2ND BATTALION (*continued*).

### 1916.

#### THE BATTLE OF THE SOMME.

##### BATTLE HONOURS:
"Somme, 1916," "Albert," "Bazentin," "Delville Wood," "Guillemont."

THE 2nd Battalion The Queen's remained about Riencourt until January 28th, 1916, when the Brigade moved to a new area consequent on the 7th Division having been ordered to take over a part of the line near Fricourt. The distance being somewhere about 40 miles this necessitated a three-days' march by Poulainville and Corbie to Bray-sur-Somme, where the Brigade was to remain for some considerable time. Here many raids were carried out and useful information gained from time to time; many working parties were also constantly employed under the Royal Engineers.

This state of affairs continued until the end of June, when the Battalion was resting in huts in the Bois des Tailles some little distance to the south of Bray, but something of a very much more active nature was now evidently in contemplation, for under date of June 30th we read in the war diary: "Battalion packed up ready to move off at 11.15 a.m. to assembly trenches."

Something has already been said in Chapter IV about all that led up to the Battle of the Somme of this year, and this need not here be repeated; it will probably be sufficient to state the disposition of the British corps from south to north at the commencement of the battle; the order then was XIII, XV, III, X, VIII, and VII; the XV Corps now contained the 7th Division on the right, the 21st on the left, and the 17th in support.

The following operation orders were issued in the 7th Division on June 26th:—
"In conjunction with the French, who are operating from Maricourt southwards, the Fourth Army is about to assume the offensive. The attack will be developed to the north and south of Fricourt Village and Fricourt Wood by the 21st and 7th Divisions respectively, with the object of isolating the triangle formed by these localities, which will afterwards be dealt with in a subsidiary operation. The task of the 7th Division is to clear the trenches in front and seize and occupy the spur from the track at S. 25 to Willow Avenue at X. 29. Immediately on the right of the 7th Division, the left Brigade of the 18th Division will advance simultaneously and prolong the 7th Division line towards Montauban. On the left of the 7th Division, advancing on the north side and clear of Fricourt Village and Wood, will be the 50th Infantry Brigade, attached 21st Division, with their right on Fricourt Farm. That brigade will join hands with the 7th Division at Willow Avenue, and prolong the line north through the Quadrangle to Contalmaison.

"The 7th Division will be distributed as follows:—
    Right—91st Infantry Brigade.
    Centre—20th Infantry Brigade.
    Left—22nd Infantry Brigade (less 2 Battalions, and 2 sections M.G. Company).

"Main attack will be carried out by the 91st and 20th Infantry Brigades.

"Subsidiary attack will be carried out by the 22nd Infantry Brigade which will clear the German trenches north of Bois Français at an hour to be decided on later, when the main attack has reached its final objective. . . . This operation will take place in conjunction with the two battalions of the 50th Brigade, who will clear Fricourt village and wood.

"The object of the 20th Infantry Brigade will be to form a defensive flank facing north to cover the advance of the 91st Brigade. Its objective is the line from the bend of Bunny Trench (road inclusive) along Bunny Trench, thence along Sunken Road to the junction of Orchard Trench North with Orchard Alley—Orchard Alley to junction with Apple Alley, then along Apple Alley to the small salient in our present line."

Shortly after midnight on the night of June 30th-July 1st the 2nd The Queen's marched from their huts in the Bois des Tailles to the position of assembly, halting *en route* for the men to be furnished with an extra bottle of water and two bandoliers of S.A. ammunition, and then proceeding by companies via Norfolk Avenue and Minden Post to their positions which were taken up in the following order :—

"A" Company in London Road west, "B" in London Road east of Francis Avenue.

"C" Company in Cross Street, "D" in Cross Street and Portland Road.

The Battalion H.Q. was in Cross Street near junction of High Street.

The situation of the units of the Brigade from left to right was as follows :

Front line : 1st South Staffords and 22nd Manchesters.

Support : 21st Manchesters and 2nd The Queen's.

The objectives were Mametz Village and the high ground along the Montauban—Mametz Road—Fritz Trench—Bright Alley—Bunny Alley (all strong and well-made German trenches)—High ground 150 yards south of Mametz Wood.

The 21st Division, attacking on the north-western side of Fricourt, was to establish its front line on the northern side of Bottom Wood, with a strong point to the west to protect the left flank of the 7th Division.

At zero hour, 7.30 a.m., on July 1st, the two battalions advanced and captured the German front and support trenches on the southern edge of Mametz—Bulgar Alley, and on this the 2nd The Queen's occupied the front trenches vacated by the 22nd Manchesters on the east and west of the Mound. At 9.50 "A" and "C" Companies of The Queen's moved forward towards Danzig Alley east of Mametz, coming under enemy machine-gun fire from the eastern edge of Mametz and Danzig Alleys, and suffering numerous casualties, but they continued their advance to Bucket Trench, Bulgar Alley, and the trench running west of front of the latter to the eastern edge of Mametz. Some time later, about 1.30 p.m., "B" and "D" Companies began to move forward from the old front trenches east of the Mound, and made good the junction of Fritz Trench and Danzig Alley, Captain Foster and Second-Lieutenant Hobbs and a few bombers making their way to the Mametz end of Danzig Alley by way of Ferdinand Alley, capturing an officer, about 50 men, 2 machine guns, and 2 automatic rifles. "B" Company, under Second-Lieutenant Roberts, now began to clear Fritz Trench, and after taking here a few prisoners, found that that part of Danzig Alley near Fritz Trench was still in enemy occupation. A bombing post was thereupon placed in Fritz Trench and a party of bombers was collected who successfully bombed two lots of Germans, 20 and 25 in number, these giving themselves up without showing much fight. The officer of the enemy party, on seeing how weak in number were his captors, tried to get at his revolver, but on being shot in the shoulder surrendered a second time.

The rest of the companies of The Queen's were now collected and reorganized in Danzig Alley, Second-Lieutenants Hobbs, The Queen's, and Day, R.F.A., with a party of " B " Company having by now cleared Fritz Trench ; both these officers being killed in this operation. Corporal Shaw turned a captured automatic rifle on the enemy as they tried to escape from Fritz Trench.

By 7.30 p.m. Fritz Trench, held by the four companies of The Queen's and one of the 21st Manchesters, had been consolidated, three strong points made, and machine and Lewis guns placed in position to sweep the whole front, while during the night rations and water were brought up.

At eleven on the morning of the 2nd The Queen's moved forward by Beetle Alley, captured Cliff Trench, and occupied White Trench, Captain Foster with some of the Headquarter bombers again distinguishing himself by taking a machine gun and 5 prisoners, these last, as the diary is careful to explain, making very little resistance " after a few bombs had been thrown at them." In White Trench two abandoned 77 mm. field guns were found. This trench was only from 2 to 3 feet in depth in places, and much hard digging had to be done, and the work of consolidation and the placing in position of machine guns and Lewis guns was taken in hand.

When night fell on July 2nd the 91st Brigade was disposed as follows :—The 1st South Staffordshire and 21st Manchester Regiments—the latter less one company, were in Mametz ; the 22nd Manchesters occupied Fritz Trench ; the 2nd The Queen's held Cliff Trench and White Trench ; and one company of the 21st Manchesters was in the western end of Queen's Nullah.

On the morning of July 3rd, at three o'clock, the 21st Division attacked Fricourt Village and Wood, and the area west of the latter, including Railway Alley, Shelter Wood, and the Poodles, and during the course of these operations the 91st Brigade machine and Lewis guns successfully dealt with various units of the enemy who were moving about in front at ranges of from 1,100 to 1,500 yards, on one occasion the machine gun near Queen's Nullah wiping out a party of about 40 of the enemy who were advancing to reinforce near Shelter Wood ; while again from Cliff Trench The Queen's Lewis guns dropped from 40 to 50 Germans retiring from Bottom Wood to Quadrangle Copse.

During the night of the 3rd-4th again rations and ammunition came up to the trenches, one of the 77 mm. guns was salved, and material was brought in from an abandoned enemy dump in an embankment close to and south of Mametz Wood.

On the evening of the 4th the Battalion was relieved in the front line, and went back to bivouacs at Minden Post.

The casualties in the 2nd The Queen's during the operations of July 1st-4th were :—Killed, 6 officers and 40 other ranks ; wounded, 7 officers and 226 men ; while 41 men were missing. The officers who died were Second-Lieutenants (Temporary Captain) T. P. Brocklehurst, L. S. Ford, E. Hobbs, J. M. Foord-Kelcey, W. Crees and J. Gillies ; while the wounded officers were Captain R. H. Philpot, Lieutenant F. A. Jacob, Second-Lieutenants (Temporary Captain) E. C. Thornycroft, G. G. Smith, H. E. Harvey, E. E. Johnson, and W. A. L. Raeburn.

The following were brought to notice as performing specially good work :— Captain R. C. G. Foster, Lieutenant P. M. Turnbull, R.A.M.C., Second-Lieutenant J. T. Roberts, 7833 Sergeant P. Mawditt, 9215 Sergeant E. Constant, 990 Corporal

P. Pratt, 4989 Private S. Waite, 4940 Private P. Whibley, 1052 Private H. Morley, 330 Private J. Osborne, 4314 Private A. Bishop and 6714 Private E. Lover.

During the next few days the Battalion was quartered about Buire, but on the night of the 13th it marched to bivouacs north of Mansel Copse in anticipation of an attack to be made by the 20th and 22nd Brigades on the German trenches south of Bazentin-le-Grand Wood, the 91st Brigade to be held in divisional reserve ; and very early on the 14th The Queen's moved by companies at 100 yards interval to a position at the head of Mametz Wood and Flatiron Copse Valley where they dug themselves in.

On this day the following officers were present with the Battalion :—Lieutenant-Colonel F. C. Longbourne (in command), Lieutenant and Acting Adjutant L. M. Boddam-Whetham, Captain R. C. G. Foster (bombing officer), Second-Lieutenants C. Griffin (Lewis gun officer), and E. S. Bingham (sniping officer).

"*A*" *Company.*—Captain R. H. Maddock, Second-Lieutenants C. Pannall, T. J. Browning and A. Mundye.

"*B*" *Company.*—Second-Lieutenants J. T. Roberts, J. E. Lloyd, J. P. Howells and F. L. Rutter.

"*C*" *Company.*—Captain J. B Hayes, Second-Lieutenants K. A. Brown, F. G. C. Weare and H. B. Secretan.

"*D*" *Company.*—Second-Lieutenants V. C. Harvey, E. F. G. Haig and E. R. Ward.

It does not appear to have been till the late afternoon of this day that the Battalion came into action, when at 5.35 the 91st Brigade was ordered to attack and capture High Wood, and marched off in that direction by the north-western side of the Bazentin-le-Grand Wood, the South Staffords, followed by the 2nd The Queen's, moving by the cross roads and then deploying with the left on the cemetery, the right of The Queen's being on the road junction. The artillery barrage was timed to lift at 6.15 p.m., when the 33rd Division was to attack west of the cemetery and seize Switch Trench north-west of High Wood.

The 2nd The Queen's and the South Staffords deployed at 6.45, but there was some delay at the start as the 33rd Division was not yet up, and the South Staffords had to strengthen their left with a Lewis gun detachment, so that it was seven o'clock before the advance began from a road running north-west and south-east of the Windmill ; this was met with a volume of machine-gun fire from enemy sheltering in shell holes, but The Queen's were ordered to push on and endeavour to take the enemy machine guns in flank. Several prisoners were captured and very many of the enemy shot down in this advance which was materially assisted by our cavalry and an aeroplane, the former engaging the enemy on the right, while the aeroplane, dropping to 500 feet, fired into the Germans between our front line and the High Wood. At 8.45 p.m. the final objective, the north-eastern edge of the wood, was gained and the companies then dug themselves in.

During the night the position was wired and several strong points made, while " C " Company's bombers cleared several deep dug-outs on the north-eastern side of the wood, taking several prisoners. The enemy attacked " D " Company's left flank from the north-western corner of the wood shortly before midnight, but were driven back, and in the morning appeared to be so well-established on the north and north-east of the wood, that battalions of the 33rd Division made several unsuccessful attempts to drive them out. In these attacks our artillery endeavoured to help by shelling the wood, but unfortunately many of their shells fell among " C " and

"D" Companies of The Queen's, who, none the less, continued to hold on along the north-eastern edge of the wood. About six in the evening "A" and "B" Companies of The Queen's, together with other units of the 91st Brigade, worked along the southern side in High Wood and attempted to drive the Germans out. They lost heavily, however, from artillery and machine-gun fire, and after advancing a short distance had to fall back again to the east and south of the wood, where they dug themselves in.

The enemy shelling was heavy during the early part of the night of the 15th-16th, the lines were continually broken and great difficulty was found in keeping open the communications, but rations and water were sent up as also 19 boxes of ammunition.

At 2.20 a.m. on the 16th orders reached the 2nd The Queen's to evacuate the position, though by reason of the enemy fire this could only very slowly be carried out, but by 3.30 all were clear of High Wood and the Battalion marched back and bivouacked in the valley north of Mansel Copse.

The following did specially good work during these operations :—Captains Hayes and Maddock, Lieutenant Boddam-Whetham, Second-Lieutenants Roberts, Pannall, Harvey and Brown ; Lieutenant and Quartermaster Belcham in bringing up rations by night under heavy shell fire ; Regimental Sergeant-Major Routley, 5835 Company Sergeant-Major A. West, Sergeants 1111 H. Stanners, 8806 E. Ingham, 9177 J. H. Hooker, Privates 9854 C. Hasted, 330 J. Osborne, and 4606 Wallington.

The casualties sustained during these days had been very nearly as heavy as those suffered earlier in the same month, and amounted to 1 officer—Second-Lieutenant F. L. Rutter—and 47 non-commissioned officers and men killed, 10 officers and 211 other ranks wounded, and 47 men missing ; the names of the wounded officers were :—Second-Lieutenants (Temporary Captain) R. H. Maddock, E. S. Bingham, J. T. Roberts, K. A. Brown, H. B. Secretan, C. Pannall, J. P. Howells, T. J. Browning, E. R. Ward and E. F. G. Haig.

Towards the end of July the 2nd The Queen's moved by rail and march route by way of Mericourt, Hangest, Picquigny, and Aille-sur-Somme to St. Sauveur, which was reached about midday on the 22nd, when the men were billeted, and training of all kinds was engaged in. The 2nd The Queen's were now for upwards of a month out of the line, and during their absence from the front the second phase of the Somme battle had commenced. By the operations earlier carried out, and the successes gained by the British and their Allies, the Germans had been greatly shaken, and their *morale* had suffered, but the strength of their positions allowed them ample time to bring up fresh troops, while as Sir Douglas Haig wrote in his despatch : " We had indeed secured a footing on the main ridge, but only on a front of 6,000 yards. . . . West of Bazentin-le-Petit the villages of Pozières and Thiepval. . . had still to be carried. . . . On our right flank . . . at Delville Wood and Longueval our lines formed a sharp salient, from which our front ran on the one side west to Pozières, and on the other south to Maltz Horn Farm."

During the days immediately preceding the return of the 2nd The Queen's to the front, many further successes had been won, but progress was slow and achieved only by hard fighting.

At the end of August the Battalion was in camp at Vignacourt, when at noon on the 31st it was ordered to march up to Delville Wood and there relieve the 1st South Staffords at 7 p.m., this battalion having already that day withstood three very determined attacks. On arrival here " B " and " D " Companies of The Queen's at once reinforced the South Staffords, who were holding the eastern edge of the wood, occupying Devil Trench, Diagonal Trench, and Angle Trench, while " C " and half of " A " Companies were also sent forward from Folly Trench to reinforce, moving by Diagonal Trench, and by 11 p.m. on August 31st the companies were holding the line as follows :—

Two platoons " D " Company, two platoons " C," and four Lewis guns in Devil Trench from the south-eastern corner of Delville Wood to S. 18. 6. 85. 50. opposite Hop Alley.

Two platoons, " D " Company, in 22 Alley.

" B " Company and one platoon " C " in Diagonal Trench and trench south of Pilsen Lane.

Two platoons " A " Company in Angle Trench.

Two platoons " A " Company in Folly Trench in Battalion reserve.

The Company Commanders preceded their companies and were with the South Staffords at the time the enemy attacked, Captain Stovold reaching the company he was to relieve, but he was thenceforward never seen or heard of again. The 1st South Staffords now withdrew, and The Queen's held their trenches, whence at 5 a.m. on September 1st two platoons of " C " Company, led by Second-Lieutenant Weare (Buffs, attached), made a bombing attack along the eastern edge of Delville Wood, but the trench here was practically obliterated by shell fire, so that there was little or no cover, and after making ground as far as Hop Alley the party was held up by hostile machine-gun and rifle fire. The enemy guns fired on Delville Wood, Diagonal Trench, and York Alley from 9.40 a.m. to 8 p.m. this day, at times putting down no fewer than three barrages between the front line and the Battalion headquarters, making communication difficult and risky. The night that followed was fairly quiet, the enemy artillery firing in strong gusts of from half an hour to three hours' duration and then ceasing altogether for two or three hours.

The Queen's remained in the line until very early on the morning of the 3rd when, on relief by the 1st Royal Welch Fusiliers, they were withdrawn to camp near Montauban.

The casualties sustained seem nearly all to have occurred on the 1st, and amounted to 1 officer (Captain C. J. Griffin), and 28 other ranks killed, 4 officers and 74 men wounded, and 1 officer (Captain P. A. Stovold) and 11 men missing. The names of the wounded officers were Captain T. V. Chapman, Second-Lieutenants R. M. Burdon, E. G. Bickell, and F. G. C. Weare.

The Battalion was away from the front line for a very few hours only, since early on the morning of the 5th it marched via Fricourt and Mametz to Montauban Alley, there coming under the orders of the General Officer Commanding 20th Brigade, by whom The Queen's were directed to attack and capture the eastern edge of Delville Wood as far as the north-eastern corner inclusive, and the attack was, therefore, entrusted to " B " and " D " Companies. These, leaving Montauban Alley at 3.15 p.m., filed into Delville Wood by way of Diagonal Trench and here the two companies deployed, " B " with its left near Edge Trench, and " D " with its right on the south-eastern corner of the wood ; each company had two platoons in the first and two in the second line, while one Lewis gun was placed on each flank to give supporting fire and another was with the second line to assist in covering the front during consolidation.

Previous to the opening of the attack a medium trench mortar fired on Ale Alley for two hours, but does not appear to have done any material damage.

The attack commenced at 3.30 p.m., and the enemy at once opened a heavy machine-gun and rifle fire from the north-eastern corner of the wood, and also from Hop Alley, causing a good many casualties, and as a result of this fire both companies inclined too much to their right, so that, on reaching the edge of the wood, the left of " B " Company had made ground to about 30 yards north of the junction of Hop Alley and eastern edge of the wood, when a block was made and the eastern edge of the wood was consolidated from this point to the south-eastern corner, while touch was gained with the battalion holding Edge Trench by means of patrols.

Devil Trench was continually blown in, necessitating constant work to keep it open.

It was found very difficult to support any advance inside the wood with Lewis guns owing to the many obstacles encountered, and the gun detailed to cover the left of the attack had early been put out of action by shell fire.

During the morning of the 6th " A " and " C " Companies relieved " B " and " D," and the day was spent in consolidating the previous day's gains, in improving existing trenches, in burying the dead, and in clearing up the ground generally, but later in the day enemy fire rather interfered with work. Then during the afternoon of the 7th, in accordance with instructions, a bombing attack was made from the captured position to gain possession of the north-eastern corner of Delville Wood, but while the attacking party of " C " Company got into position, the rifle grenade section was able to put only a few grenades into the southern end of the enemy's trench, so that the occupants of this were able to command " C " Company's party from the start. The Germans indeed at this time—4.5 p.m.—were occupying the north-eastern corner of the wood for at least 70 yards along Edge Trench, and had a machine gun in position flanking the corner for about 20 yards to the south and 20 to the north.

On the 8th the 2nd The Queen's were relieved and withdrawn and for the next 48 hours or so the 91st Brigade remained in reserve to the 55th Division ; then on the 11th the Battalion marched to Albert and was sent by train to Oisemont, marching from there by Doudelainville to Huppy, where a few days were spent in training and in filling up the gaps caused by the fighting about Delville Wood. Here the 2nd The Queen's had suffered the loss of 21 non-commissioned officers and men killed, Second-Lieutenants J. E. Lloyd, A. T. L. Noble and N. A. Willis, and 40 other ranks wounded, and 5 men missing. Six subaltern officers joined—Second-Lieutenants M. P. Bennett, E. Schult, D. N. Ramage, E. E. F. Atall, E. D. Baily and W. T. Garyne—and several drafts, so that the strength of the 2nd Battalion The Queen's increased in a very few days from 22 officers and 658 other ranks to 28 officers and 1,026 non-commissioned officers and men.

On September 16th a warning order was issued to prepare for a move to the Ypres area, and on the evening of the following day the Battalion marched to Abbeville, and there entrained, and, proceeding by Etaples, Boulogne, and Hazebrouck, reached Bailleul early on the 8th, marching from there to huts in Aldershot Camp. Next morning the 2nd The Queen's relieved a battalion of the 57th Brigade, 19th Division, in the Douve sector of the line, " B " Company being in the front, " A " and " D " Companies in the subsidiary line, and " C " in reserve. This seems to have been a tolerably quiet sector except for raids which were carried out by both sides, and hereabouts the 7th Division remained until the beginning of November, when orders were received for the Division to move to the Second Army Training Area, west of Omer. The 2nd The Queen's marched on the 2nd to Steenwerck and on the day following to Meteren, where they seem to have discovered with some not unnatural dismay that " Training Area ' A ' was a long way from the billeting area and mostly water-logged plough."

The Battle of the Somme did not come officially to an end until November 18th, but the 2nd The Queen's took no further part in it ; much, however, of what had been attempted had been accomplished—Verdun had been relieved, the main German force had been held on the Western Front, while very heavy losses had been inflicted on the enemy. Of his soldiers Sir Douglas Haig stated that they had " shown themselves worthy of the highest traditions of our race and of the proud records of former wars."

The rest here, if rest it was intended to be, was a very short one, for on the 9th the 91st Brigade was on the move again, being recalled from the Second Army Area to that of the Fifth Army, to the neighbourhood of the Somme, where a certain amount of fighting was still in progress. Marching almost daily, the 2nd The Queen's arrived at Lealvillers on November 22nd and next day marched by Acheux, Forceville, and Mailly Maillet under orders to take over a portion of the line in front of Beaumont Hamel from troops of the Highland Division. On arrival at Mailly Maillet, however, it was found that the 32nd Division was engaged in an attack upon the enemy, so the relief was cancelled for the day, and The Queen's were directed to stand by. The relief was finally completed on the 24th.

The General Officer Commanding 7th Division, Major-General Watts, issued the following complimentary order on the marching of his troops from Meteren to the Somme :—"*The Divisional Commander wishes to convey to the troops his appreciation of the excellent march discipline displayed by all ranks during the march from the Second Army Area. He considers that the general behaviour of the troops and their marching are worthy of the best traditions of the Service, and reflect the greatest credit on all concerned.*"

While quartered in this neighbourhood a rather gruesome discovery is reported in the Battalion diary under date of December 11th :—" Large caves under Beaumont Hamel and north of Church opened in the morning, after having been closed since November 13th. About forty dead Germans discovered, mostly wearing gas helmets, and showing signs of having been gassed."

About the middle of the month the 2nd The Queen's moved back to rest about Bertrancourt and here, or rather in Louvencourt, Christmas Day was spent. Then next day the Battalion moved back to the trenches near Beaumont Hamel, described by an officer who served there as " surely without exception the most unpleasant bit of line on the Western Front. Constantly fought over and ploughed and reploughed by shells. Some peculiar quality of the soil had produced a stretch of mud which quite outdid anything that Flanders could produce. In most places it was literally impassable, and everywhere it was knee-deep. In this sector at various times during the winter of 1916-1917 several men were drowned in this morass in spite of all the efforts of their comrades to extricate them. In addition the enemy sprinkled it with shells, while his snipers, operating from higher and drier ground, were active and deadly. Both for danger and discomfort it was hard to beat."

None the less the 2nd Battalion The Queen's seems to have kept up its health and its numbers tolerably well, and throughout the month of December, 1916, the latter appear to have remained at a general average of 33 officers and some 930-940 non-commissioned officers and men. There is no mention of the arrival of any drafts during this month, but the admissions to hospital were few, all things considered.

Maps 4 and 9.

## CHAPTER XI.

### 2ND BATTALION (*continued*).

#### 1917.

##### THE BATTLES OF ARRAS—THE FLANDERS OFFENSIVE.

###### BATTLE HONOURS:
"Bullecourt," "Broodseinde," "Passchendaele.'
"Italy."

THE 2nd Battalion The Queen's does not appear to have made any move from the Beaumont Hamel Sector until February 20th, 1917, when it marched by bad roads and via Toutencourt, Vadencourt, Warloy, and Hennencourt to indifferent billets in Albert, where the main duty seems to have been the provision of working parties for the 2nd Division, necessitating the companies being much dispersed in billets adjacent to their tasks. Then five days later there was a further move to Bertranville where the Battalion was again called upon to furnish many working parties. Finally on March 13th the 2nd The Queen's marched to Puisieux and took over the front line south of the village, the companies being here disposed as follows:—

"A" Company in Fork Trench with posts 100 yards south of the junction of Fork and Bucquoy Trench on the left, with the right post in the valley north-east of Fork Wood.

"C" Company occupied a line from the Puisieux—Bucquoy road to the track running north and south, with "D" Company continuing the line to the railway.

"B" Company was in support in the sunken road with six posts 300 yards in front.

The enemy artillery was at this time paying a good deal of attention to Puisieux, shelling the village and the valley north-east of it with 4·9's and 77's during the day and using tear gas shells in the evening.

During this month operations were here to be carried out, the general effect of which was to cause the German front line to cave in to a depth of three miles north and south of the River Ancre, leading to the occupation by the infantry of General Gough's Fifth Army of the towns of Serre, Puisieux, Pys, Miraumont, Eaucourt, Warlencourt, and all the ground for eleven miles from Gommiécourt in the north, to Gueudecourt in the south.

So soon as the relief was completed and the companies of The Queen's were in position, patrols were sent out to reconnoitre the Bucquoy trenches and ascertain if they were still occupied by the enemy, and these on return reported that the Germans were still holding the Bucquoy Line with machine guns and in places by posts at fifty yards interval, while the wire in front of these was very thick and strong, the only gap being one twenty-five yards wide 250 yards north-west of the Puisieux—Bucquoy road. Second-Lieutenant Furze also obtained valuable information as to the siting of several enemy machine guns.

Late in the afternoon of the 13th orders for an attack by the 7th and 46th Divisions, respectively on right and left, were issued, the positions to be assaulted being the village of Bucquoy and Hill 155; the 62nd Division was on the right of the 7th. In these orders the attack of the 7th Division was originally to have been carried out by the 20th and 22nd Brigades, but later the scheme appears to have been modified in design and was conducted by two *battalions* only, the 2nd The Queen's taking the task allotted in the first instance to the 20th Infantry Brigade, and the 22nd Manchesters that of the 22nd Brigade. The operation orders of The Queen's then enacted that the Battalion boundaries should be the line of Fork Trench on the left and the railway on the right, the right of " B " Company directing along the railway line in close touch with the 22nd Manchesters. The first objective was the Bucquoy—Arnim Trench system, the second Crucifix Line.

" B " and " D " Companies were to advance in one wave in column of half-companies at a distance of 50 yards between lines, " C " following in the same formation at 100 yards distance and, on the first objective being captured, passing through the leading companies to the Crucifix Line. The first line of " B " and " D " was to go straight through to the second enemy trench, their second lines making good the first enemy line. " A " Company was to follow " C " at 100 yards distance in the same formation, and advance to the left corner of the village where bombers were to be posted. On arrival at the Crucifix Line, " C " Company was to form a block in the trench and consolidate the position; " A " was to reinforce " C," while " B " and " D " Companies were to reorganize in Bucquoy Trench and Road, thereafter getting into touch with " C " in the main Bucquoy—Ayette road. Then as soon as the second objective had been consolidated, a patrol, under Second-Lieutenant G. C. Smith, of 15 men was to proceed to Dierville Farm and hold and consolidate it, while " A " sent up a Lewis gun team to support the forward post.

Zero hour was 1 a.m. on March 14th.

Lieutenant-Colonel Longbourne's report gives us the following account of what this day occurred:—

At zero the companies were formed up on the tape previously put out by Second-Lieutenant Bingham in advance of the valley tramway line; they then advanced and succeeded in reaching the enemy's front wire, the enemy's artillery fire being intense while his machine guns were active the whole time. It was very dark and raining hard, the ground was very sticky and near the enemy wire it was full of shell-holes, into which many of the men fell and so became unarmed owing to the mud on their rifles preventing the bolts from working. Eventually small groups of men from " B," " C," and " D " Companies, with Captain Driver, Second-Lieutenants Furze, Burdon, Smith and Limbrick, succeeded in getting through two lines of barbed wire, only to find on arrival here that their rifles were useless; it was found impossible to penetrate the third line immediately in front of Bucquoy Trench. Finally at 3.45 a.m. on the 14th the companies of the 2nd The Queen's were ordered to withdraw and occupy their former positions which were successfully arrived at an hour later, eventually going back to camp near Mailly.

On March 28th the Battalion was brought up again to support two other battalions of the Brigade in an attack upon Croisilles, but the village was very strongly held with machine guns, while the wire had not been cut, so that the assaulting battalions were held up, and The Queen's were not called upon to act.

On April 1st, however, the Battalion being then at Courcelles, it was brought forward to take part in an attack to be made by the Division in conjunction with the Third Army on the left and the 4th (Australian) Division on the right, the task of the 7th Division being the capture of the villages of Longatte, Ecoust, and

MEN OF 2ND BATTALION AT ABLAINZEVILLE, MARCH, 1917.

[*Copyright: Imperial War Museum.*]

Croisilles, and the ground between them. Croisilles itself was not to be attacked in the first instance, the intention being to surround it at first and then to send troops in from the south to clear it. The attack on these places was entrusted to the 20th Infantry Brigade on the right and the 91st on the left. In the 91st Brigade three battalions were in the front line, each being given certain objectives marked on the map—The Queen's being on the left, the 21st Manchesters in the centre and the 1st South Staffords on the right; the 22nd Manchesters were in brigade reserve.

The Battalion was in position by 1 a.m. on the 2nd, having been shelled during the approach march, and its orders now were, with the 21st Manchesters on the right, to attack and capture the Factory Road and establish a forward line of posts.

Zero hour had been fixed for 5.15 a.m., but there was a short delay in advancing caused by part of the British barrage falling short, but "B" and "C" Companies of The Queen's pushed off, and were at once met by heavy machine-gun fire from the railway embankment and the cutting on the left. Covering fire was, however, at once opened by two Lewis gun sections, and the advance continuing the Factory Road Line was made good by about 7.30 a.m. Casualties were already heavy, all "B" Company's officers had become casualties soon after zero, but "C" and "B" were now reorganized and several strong points put out at the Factory and in front of the Factory Road by Second-Lieutenants Thomas, Gibson and Hullcoop, so as to cut off the retreat of the enemy from Croisilles.

In the meantime "D" Company's advance had been delayed by hostile enfilade machine-gun fire, but by degrees platoons were pushed forward and eventually Lewis gun posts were so established as to command the village of Croisilles and its northern exits, and the remainder of "D" Company was moved to a position in support of the Factory Road Line. At 7.55 a.m. the reserve platoon moved forward under Second-Lieutenant Gadner to reinforce "C" Company, and on arrival at the railway this party dispersed one of the enemy and drove others back to the village. Casualties were caused the Germans here by the action of our advanced posts which commanded the north-eastern exit from Croisilles; some of the enemy appear, however, to have made their escape from the north-western side.

At 10.50 p.m. The Queen's were relieved and moved back to Ervillers, having during the operations had Lieutenant F. C. Woods, Second-Lieutenants H. H. Richards, A. C. Fitch and J. C. How, and 25 other ranks killed, Second-Lieutenants E. J. Winnall, T. J. Bowring, and J. Innes and 42 non-commissioned officers and men wounded.

Of the operations in which the 2nd The Queen's were now in May called upon to take part, the Commander-in-Chief wrote as follows in his despatch :—

"To secure the footing gained by the Australians in the Hindenburg Line on May 3rd it was advisable that Bullecourt should be captured without loss of time. During the fortnight following our attack, fighting for the possession of this village went on unceasingly; while the Australian troops in the sector of the Hindenburg Line to the east beat off counter-attack after counter-attack. The defence of this 1,000 yards of double trench, exposed to counter-attack on every side, through two weeks of almost constant fighting, deserves to be remembered as a most gallant feat of arms. On the morning of May 7th, English troops (7th Division, Major-General Shoubridge) gained a footing in the south-eastern corner of Bullecourt. Thereafter gradual progress was made in the face of the most obstinate resistance."

On May 6th, the Battalion being then in billets near Courcelles, orders were received that for certain operations then in view The Queen's and the 22nd

Manchesters were to be attached to the 20th Infantry Brigade, and The Queen's accordingly moved this day to tents and shelters near Ervillers Road. From here they marched at 2 a.m. on the 7th to a position of readiness in the vicinity of L'Homme Mort north of Mory, arriving here at three in the morning, zero hour being 3.45. The Battalion seems to have remained here during the day, but at 8.30 p.m. " B " and " D " Companies were moved to Ecoust Village in support, while " A " and " C " were sent to the Sunken Road (Vraucourt—Ecoust), 500 yards north of the Sucrerie, and the companies were now called on to provide working parties to make strong points, and to carry up material to Bullecourt. Of this village but little now remained, but it formed a salient in the German front line, and was protected by very strong and well-built defences, while Riencourt Ridge and Quéant were both occupied by the enemy. On this day the 7th Division gained a footing in the south-eastern corner of Bullecourt, and by the 12th the greater part of it was in our possession, though parties of the enemy still held out in the southern and south-western outskirts.

On the 9th the 2nd The Queen's went back for one night to the neighbourhood of Mory, but came up again east of Ecoust next day, and on the 11th were in position for the final clearing of Bullecourt, the orders being that the 91st Brigade, in conjunction with the 15th (Australian) Brigade on the right, and the 62nd Division on the left, was to complete the capture. The Queen's and two companies of the 21st Manchesters were to capture, and consolidate, the Brown Line from the cross roads to the road junction north of the church. The Battalion order of attack was as follows :—

" A " and " B " Companies in front, each in column of half-companies at 30 yards distance, followed by four platoons of the 21st Manchesters as " moppers-up," these followed again by " C " Company in line of sections in file with Lewis gun sections in second line. " D " Company was to be in reserve, 100 yards in rear of and in the same formation as " C."

At zero hour, 3.40 a.m. on May 12th, the companies went forward following a creeping barrage which advanced at the rate of 100 yards in six minutes, and gained their objective by 4.15 a.m.; Lewis guns were now at once pushed out to the front and companies dug in in front of the Brown Line, the enemy severely shelling the Brown Line and the houses south of it. Close touch was maintained with the Australians on the right, and the 1st South Staffords on the left. Here the 2nd The Queen's remained until the early morning of the 15th, when they were relieved by a battalion of the 22nd Brigade, and were withdrawn first to reserve trenches and then to billets in Achiet-le-Petit. During the fighting at Bullecourt Captain T. V. Chapman, M.C., and Second-Lieutenant G. G. Smith, and 32 non-commissioned officers and men were killed, 4 officers (Second-Lieutenants F. Hakes, E. F. Hullcoop, C. M. Wright and J. B. Dimmock) and 121 other ranks were wounded, while 10 men were missing.

The 2nd The Queen's remained in these parts until August 29th when they marched to Mondicourt, and there entrained for Flanders, in view of taking their part in the Third Battle of Ypres which had by this been already nearly three months in progress, and particularly in the great struggle for the possession of Passchendaele Ridge, which was now in full swing. Passing by Frevent, St. Pol, Hazebrouck, and Lillers, Hopoutre, near Poperinghe, was reached at 9.30 p.m. on this day, and the Battalion finally settled down at Ouderdom at midnight in Ottawa Camp, described as " spacious but dirty and having quantities of flies."

## THE FLANDERS OFFENSIVE

The move to Flanders had been so hurriedly carried out that all ranks of The Queen's had confidently expected that the Division would take part in some big attack on the German position early in September; this was no doubt the original intention, but the weather had been very unsettled about the end of August, and it was decided to afford the 7th Division increased time for training. Accordingly on September 3rd the Battalion moved to the Zuytpeene area near Cassel, where it was met by General Sir H. Plumer, the Second Army Commander, and here some days were passed. There were then one or two minor moves, but by the end of September the Battalion was back again in the neighbourhood of Ouderdom; and late on the night of October 3rd The Queen's moved by Shrapnel Corner, Warrington Road, and Birr Cross Roads to a position of assembly between Château Wood and Tank Gun Post. The companies were here disposed in the order " D," " C," " B " and " A " from left to right along the line of Jargon Switch and Surbiton Villas. The Battalion was not made use of this day, but at noon on the 4th it was ordered to move to a position in reserve and dig in near the Butte—an artificial mound some 80 feet in height in the vicinity of Polygon Wood. Here The Queen's were exposed to very heavy shelling, and were unable to dig to a greater depth than two feet owing to the presence of water near the surface. About 5 p.m. " B," " C," and " D " Companies of the Battalion were placed at the disposal of the Officer Commanding 1st South Staffordshire Regiment—" C " and " D " being sent to Jetty Trench with orders there to dig in and hold themselves ready to counter-attack should the enemy gain a footing in the Red Line, while " B " was moved to a locality known as Jolting Houses facing south with directions to form a defensive flank if the 21st Division were held up; this happened, and " B " Company dug in on this line where they were in touch with the South Staffords, whose line was along Jolting Trench and Judge Trench.

At 3 a.m. on the 5th " A " Company of The Queen's also came under the orders of the Officer Commanding South Staffords, and dug in on the Judge Trench Line, and in these various positions the four companies of the 2nd The Queen's remained throughout the 5th under heavy rain and continuous shell fire. The situation remained unchanged on the morning of the 6th, and in the evening the Battalion was relieved and withdrawn to Bellewaarde Lake.

The following list gives the names of the officers engaged and the casualties incurred:—Major B. H. Driver, M.C. (killed), Second-Lieutenants E. D. Baily (wounded), and M. P. Bennett (died of wounds), Lieutenant W. G. McAfee, R.A.M.C.

" A " Company.—Second-Lieutenants J. P. Howells, M.C., C. O. W. Morgan, and R. E. G. Beavis (wounded).

" B " Company.—Captain R. L. Atkinson, M.C., Second-Lieutenants C. M. Wright, M.C. (wounded), G. W. Barley and M. Valentine.

" C " Company.—Captain W. G. Gibson, M.C., Lieutenant R. O. Sillem (wounded), Second-Lieutenants G. E. Wheeler and D. L. Inwood.

" D " Company.—Captain H. B. Secretan, M.C. (wounded), Second-Lieutenants R. W. Pinchbeck (wounded), and W. H. Aslin.

Of the other ranks, 38 were killed, 118 wounded, and 7 were missing.

On October 8th Major-General Shoubridge, commanding the 7th Division, issued the following order to his troops:—

"*Please accept and convey to all ranks my most sincere congratulations on our recent victory. Every man must feel proud that the Division captured all objectives and assisted in administering the best thrashing the enemy has so far received. Our success is entirely due to the untiring zeal and indomitable fighting spirit of all ranks, who, no matter what their arm and task have each contributed to our success. We have always had a reputation to live up to, we have a still higher one now.*

" *Remember the 7th Division never fails !*"

For a few days now the 2nd The Queen's were near Dickebusch, then near the Mont des Cats in the Thieushoek area, where some little time was spent in practising the attack over ground similar to that over which the Brigade was daily expecting to be called on to operate and for which final instructions were issued on October 24th.

Under these it was laid down that the 7th Division should attack Gheluvelt with the 91st Brigade on the right and the 20th on the left, with the 13th Infantry Brigade of the 5th Division on the left of the 20th. In the 91st Brigade the 1st South Staffords were to be on the right, the 21st Manchester Regiment in the centre, and the 2nd The Queen's on the left. In accordance with these orders the 2nd Battalion The Queen's "embussed" near Fermoy Camp at 2.30 p.m. on October 24th, "debussing" in the vicinity of Lock 8, and then, after a brief halt, moving off by platoons at 100 yards interval to relieve companies of the 16th and 17th Sherwood Foresters in the line in the Bodmin Copse area. The track, Morland Avenue to Canada Street, during this assembly march, was shelled but no casualties were incurred, though several shells fell between platoons ; and then, after some further delay of three-quarters of an hour in Canada Street, the Battalion followed the duck-board track through Bodmin Copse and the companies took up their positions in front of it, the relief of the Foresters being completed in rain and darkness by 1.30 a.m. on the 25th, Second-Lieutenant Wheeler, commanding "C" Company, being wounded just as the relief was completed ; the vicinity of the Basseville Beek was persistently shelled until dawn.

During the night of the 24th-25th the tape line and Battalion boundaries were staked out by Lieutenant Burdon of the Battalion.

The weather improved at daybreak on the 25th, and a strong wind which then got up did much to improve the state of the ground, which in advance of the ridge in front of the Basseville Beek was sandy and comparatively dry ; and in view of the fact that the enemy barrage line appeared to be through the Dumbarton Lakes area and as this usually came down about midnight, positions for "A" Company and an attached company of the 22nd Manchesters in the vicinity of the support line were selected during the day and arrangements made for their occupation before 11.30 p.m. October 25th passed without incident and on the whole the enemy's attitude was quiet, but about dusk Captain Atkinson was wounded while visiting his posts, having already been shot through the arm by a sniper, and so had to go back down the line.

Zero hour was 5.40 a.m. on the 6th, and an hour before this time the 2nd The Queen's were formed up on the tape on a three-company frontage—"D" right, "B" centre, "C" left, and "A" in support to "C." The Red Line was the objective for all front-line companies, the rôle of "A" being to pass through the Red Line and to establish posts to form a defensive flank to the 20th Brigade ; the enemy did not seriously interfere with the assembly, but shelled the Dumbarton Lakes area and the line of approach from midnight on the 25th to dawn on the 26th. A forward observation post was dug in the centre of the near tape and was occupied by Lieutenant Burdon, two runners and two signallers, Battalion headquarters being connected by a forward line with this post, but the line did not outlive the commencement of the advance and could not be maintained.

The weather became overcast and cloudy early on the 26th and at zero hour rain was falling; all started according to plan, and at 6.10 the attack appeared to be progressing favourably, but shortly after this hour the observation post was hit full by a shell and the garrison buried or temporarily stunned. They soon, however, came back and reported that the attack had suffered a check and that there was a certain amount of disorganization among the advancing troops, the result of the battalions on either flank converging on Lewis House where the main resistance had been met. As a result of this congestion it was impossible for the Stokes guns under Second-Lieutenant Schult to fire in reply to the pre-arranged signal of two white Very lights, while the hostile machine guns in Lewis House were afforded a target of confused units instead of meeting an organized assault by small controlled bodies.

By this time all the officers of the 2nd The Queen's, except Captain Streeter and Second-Lieutenant Howells, commanding "D" and "A" Companies respectively, had become casualties. Despite the confusion, these two officers pressed on and made several organized attempts to outflank the concrete structure of Lewis House, and when these failed they established themselves with a composite party from several battalions about 200 yards from the house. The loss of direction above noted resulted in gaps being formed in the general line to right and left of Lewis House, and these were filled as far as possible by organizing men who had drifted thither out of their alignment, and by bringing forward the two attached companies of the 22nd Manchesters to join up with the 21st Manchester Regiment on the right; further, two new Vickers gun sections were also sent in to cover the front.

By dusk the original front line had been re-established and touch with both flanks secured, though the enemy shelling of the area in rear of the front line became intense about noon and was kept up till after dusk. During the night of the 26th-27th what was left of the 2nd Battalion The Queen's, and of the two attached companies of the 22nd Manchester Regiment, was relieved and withdrawn to dug-outs at Lock 8; two posts of The Queen's, however, under Captain Streeter, being in advance of the old front line, could not be found until daylight of the 27th, being cut off from all communication, and so remained out another twenty-four hours.

It was no easy matter accurately to determine the casualties in the Battalion at the conclusion of this heavy and confused fighting, but the following may be accepted as approximately correct:—2 officers and 22 other ranks were killed or died of wounds, 9 officers and 189 non-commissioned officers and men were wounded, 14 men were wounded and missing, while 1 officer and 63 men were missing. Of the 12 officers Second-Lieutenant C. E. Green was killed and Second-Lieutenant E. Schult died of wounds; Captain R. L. Atkinson, M.C., Second-Lieutenants G. E. Wheeler, J. P. Howells, S. E. Tidy, D. L. Inwood, G. O. Hancock, P. G. Foster, W. H. O. Willmott and F. P. Shuter were wounded; and Second-Lieutenant M. Valentine was missing.

The following letter was sent round by the General Officer Commanding 7th Division :—

*"The Army Commander regrets we did not get our objectives on the morning of October 26th as much as we do ourselves, and he fully realizes that officers and men did all that was humanly possible in the face of great difficulties. He also wishes it known that the enemy had a railway between Menin and Passchendaele intending to employ it at the most threatened point. Our attack showed such determination that he retained*

*all reserves opposite us. This helped the Canadians materially to gain and hold their objectives. Therefore we did not fight in vain.*

"*The 7th Division has taken hard knocks before, but it never loses its splendid spirit, and the battle of October 26th will only be an incentive to get our own back on the next opportunity.*

"*The General Officer Commanding is very proud of the way in which officers, non-commissioned officers and men went forward under the worst conditions of mud and fire, and would not give in until they died or stuck in the mud.*"

For some days after coming out of the line the 2nd The Queen's were stationed in the Eblinghem area, where on November 8th the 7th Division was inspected by His Majesty the King of the Belgians, and then made one or two other moves; and it must have been while at Conteville and Betval in the Lens area about the 14th of the month that it became generally known that the Division was on the point of departure for a new theatre of war.

On the 18th the following message was received from the General Officer Commanding X Corps :—

"*On your departure from the X Corps I wish to thank you for all your good and gallant work whilst under my command. In bidding you good-bye, which I do with regret, I wish you all success and good fortune wherever you may find yourselves in the future.*"

From early in October onwards the Central Powers had made repeated attacks upon the Italians holding the Isonzo and Carnia fronts, but our Allies were able to repulse these, and though there was some not unnatural anxiety as to the issue, there seemed no reason to fear anything worse than mere local set-backs. On October 23rd, however, there was a very strong hostile concentration towards the Upper Isonzo and the Bainsizza Plateau, followed next day by a powerful attack by Austro-German troops in thick fog along a twenty-mile front, with the result that the Italian Second Army was broken through at Tolmino, Caporetto and Plezzo. The Italian Second and Third Armies fell back, abandoning the Bainsizza Plateau and the Carnia front, behind the line of the River Tagliamento, the enemy claiming to have taken 18,000 prisoners and 1,500 guns.

Appeals for help were sent out to the War Councils of France and England, and 12 divisions, 7 French and 5 British, were hastily dispatched to the assistance of the Italians from the Western Front; but before these had reached the scene of operations the Italians had suffered further reverses, and had fallen back to the line of the River Piave, where at last the Austro-German advance was held.

General Sir Herbert Plumer was taken from the Second Army which he had so long and so ably commanded, and placed in command of the five British divisions ordered to Italy, the Franco-British force being under General Fayolle. The five divisions, with the order in which they left the Western Front, were as under :—

The 23rd Division on November 9th.
The 41st      ,,         ,,      ,, 12th.
The 7th       ,,         ,,      ,, 19th.
The 48th      ,,         ,,      ,, 23rd.
The 5th       ,,         ,, December 1st.

The 2nd The Queen's—34 officers and 860 other ranks—entrained on November 18th at Anvins in two parties, "A" and "B" Companies in No. 1 train, and

"C" and "D" in No. 2; and the rail journey via Châlons, Marseilles, Oreglia, Parma, and Lenago, lasted the greater part of six days, it being noon on the 24th when the Battalion detrained at Montagnana and then marched by Pojana to Ponte de Masseno, and so on to Piazzola on the Brenta, which was reached on the 30th. December also saw many moves; on the 2nd to Rustaga, on the 3rd to Torreselle, then two days spent in training and on the 5th to Sala-di-Campagna; then on the 11th the 2nd The Queen's marched to Altivole, on the 19th to Paderno, on the 25th (Christmas Day) to Crespano, when the Battalion furnished working parties for a defensive line to the north of this place, and then on December 31st marching back to Altivole.

General Plumer had journeyed to Italy in advance of his divisions, and in his despatch of March 9th, 1918, he makes a report of the general situation as he found it on arrival. He describes it as " certainly disquieting. The Italian Army had just received a very severe blow, from which it was bound to require time to recover and reorganize. . . . The Italian retreat had been arrested on the River Piave, but it was uncertain whether they would hold this line, and in the first instance it was arranged that in conjunction with the French two of our divisions should move forward on arrival to the hills north and south of Vicenza, where a stand could certainly have been made. The forward march was well carried out. The marches were necessarily long, as time was, or might have been, important. . . . By the time we reached the above position the general situation had improved. . . . and it was suggested that we should . . . take over the Montello sector with the French on our left, to which we agreed. The Montello sector is a feature by itself and an important one. It acts as a hinge to the whole Italian line, joining as it does that portion facing north from Monte Tomba to Lake Garda, with the defensive line of the River Piave covering Venice which was held by the Third Italian Army. . . . We took over the line on December 4th and at once got to work to organize the defences in depth. . . . December was an anxious month. . . ."

It was certain Austrian successes in the mountains which had seemed likely to jeopardize the Italian positions on Monte Grappa and about the valley of the Brenta, which had summoned the 2nd The Queen's late in the month to Crespagno at the foot of the Alps, to prepare a defensive position to cover any possible retreat from the positions which our Allies were holding in the mountains.

On the 16th of this month there was a very largely attended meeting in the Albert Hall in London to commemorate the services of the First Seven Divisions of the original Expeditionary Force, " The Old Contemptibles "—" the little mighty force that stood for England "—when the following cable was received in Italy and published for the information of all ranks of the 7th Division :—

*" Those assembled to-day in the Albert Hall, London, at a meeting honoured by the presence of Their Majesties the King and Queen and Queen Alexandra to commemorate the heroic deeds of the First Seven Divisions, send their warmest greetings to all absent comrades, and wish them good luck and a victorious home-coming."*

Map 10.

## CHAPTER XII.

### 2ND BATTALION (continued).

### 1918.

#### THE CAMPAIGN IN ITALY AND THE END OF THE WAR.

##### BATTLE HONOURS:
"Piave," "Vittorio Veneto."

DURING the early part of the year 1918 the infantry divisions under General Sir H. Plumer's command did not take part in any fighting on the Italian front, although, as General Plumer tells us in his despatch, they might fairly claim to have had some share in the general improvement which during that time had taken place in the military situation. The Italians drove the Austrians from the western bank of the Piave, they had been tolerably successful in an attack upon Monte Asolona, while certain generally satisfactory operations had been conducted on the Asiago Plateau, and in some at least of these British guns had assisted.

When the New Year opened the 2nd Battalion The Queen's was still at Altivole, but on the 5th they moved to Castelcucco and were at once set to work digging a new defence line south of Possagna on the northern slopes of the hills facing Monte Tomba. The weather was at first very cold with hard frost and heavy falls of snow, but within a day or two this changed to thaw and rain, and the bivouac camp at Castelcucco was flooded out. The companies then moved into unoccupied houses about the villages of Rover and Cunial in the valley south of Monte Tomba, where the men made themselves very comfortable, firewood being plentiful. The stay here was only a short one for on January 11th the Battalion marched ten miles, over roads very slippery from ice, to Riese, and while here the Company Commanders were taken out in motor lorries via Montebelluno and Volpago to the Montello in view of the approaching relief there of the 41st Division. This relief took place on the 17th, when the 2nd The Queen's marched to the Montello—a curious flat-topped hill lying on the right bank of the Piave and covered with small woods, vineyards, and scattered farmhouses, and intersected by many roads. Here the Battalion occupied the left sector of the left brigade along the river bank, opposite Fontigo and Sernaglia, "D" Company, Captain Streeter, being on the right, "A," Captain Howells, in the centre, "B," Captain Jacob, on the left, and "C" Company, Captain Gibson, in support. The 21st Manchesters were on the right of The Queen's, while on the left was the right battalion of the 23rd Division. In rear of the 2nd The Queen's were the 22nd Manchesters in brigade reserve. Here there was "little enemy activity," but though visibility was bad, mists constantly rising from the river, our guns were firing all day, while during the night of January 20th-21st, two officer patrols from The Queen's crossed the river; one under Second-Lieutenant D. N. P. Squarey reached within fifty yards of the opposite bank, the current being very strong, the water icy cold, while many streams had to be crossed.

Activities of this sort went on most nights; on that of the 23rd a patrol of "A" Company under Captain Howells and Second-Lieutenant Cawston attempted to ford the Piave, but was held up by the fourth channel, which was both deep and rapid. Then very early on the 25th an escaped Italian prisoner being seen on " A " Company's front, Private Baker of that company swam a portion of the river and brought the man over.

On the 25th The Queen's went for a week into brigade reserve, the weather having now become fine, warm and clear. On the 28th the enemy dropped shells on the Montello, killing two pack-horses and the Adjutant's groom, Private Lowen. The two so-called pack-horses were the chargers of the Adjutant and Medical Officer, and that of the former had accompanied the Battalion from South Africa to France, and from France to Italy.

On February 2nd The Queen's marched back to billets at Volpago—" our stay in reserve in the Montello Sector," we read in the diary, " was a very interesting one, as from our position we had a really fine view of the Piave and surrounding country." Volpago was a large village to the south of the Montello and on the main Volpago—Montello road. On the 10th the Battalion moved forward again, occupying this time the Nervesa Sector of the Montello position. This was held by a system of small posts found by the two companies in the front line, which were manned by night only, the garrisons of the posts withdrawing to houses in rear connected up by communication trenches, while the front was watched by day by observation posts. The front was covered by Vickers guns, and of the two support companies that on the left was in dug-outs in one of the many dells found all over the Montello, while the right support company was in billets in Nervesa. The whole of the front system was under enemy observation from San Daniele, so all work had to be done at night.

On March 1st the 2nd Battalion The Queen's marched from Albaredo, where the last few days of the previous month had been spent, to San Martino, the roads being very heavy owing to rain; and on arrival it was found that the village was crowded with men belonging to units of the 41st Division and also with French troops, so that accommodation was hard to come by and the billets were very scattered. It was here that a rumour, which had for some days past been in circulation, seems to have crystallized, to the effect that the 7th Division was likely to be recalled to France together with the 41st, and the battalions of the former received orders in regard to arrangements for early entraining, while it was announced that all reinforcements, etc., for these two divisions were being detained in France. It was not until March 4th, when part of the 20th Brigade had already entrained, that it was announced that the move was cancelled, and the 2nd The Queen's then marched via Camposampiero and Mestrino to a training area at Toneglia, which was arrived at on the 9th, and where very scattered but comfortable billets were found.

On March 23rd the Division began to move to the north and the 2nd The Queen's marched by Secula, Quinto, Villaferra, Thiene, and Cariola, the last stage being accomplished in lorries, the whole brigade moving at once. The diary tells us that " it was a very interesting ride and the scenery was magnificent, especially when we started climbing up the face of the mountain. Billets are in wooden huts previously used by the Italians, they were awfully dirty and our men were very crowded; water was unobtainable and we had to melt snow to provide tea for our men. There is a great deal of snow about, and the roads on the top of the mountain were rather slippery."

The Battalion was here on the top of the Asiago Plateau—a country of fir forests, steep and rocky hills with snow peaks in the background. The line here was in the neighbourhood of Monte Lemerle, running along the edge of the pine forest and with some 2,000 yards of open ground between our front line and the Austrian trenches.

Lieutenant-Colonel Birkett had now left to take command of the 7th Division Machine Gun Battalion, and had been succeeded by Major H. D. Carlton, Royal Scots, who had taken his place with the 2nd Battalion The Queen's.

By this time the success of the great German offensive lately launched against the Western Front had made necessary the recall of certain of the Anglo-French divisions sent to Italy after the Caporetto disaster. General Sir Herbert Plumer was also sent for to resume his old place on the left of the British line and left early in the middle of March; while by April 3rd four French and two British divisions—these last being the 5th and 41st—had been withdrawn from Italy. While the departure of these two divisions made no difference in the strength of the *original* force sent to Italy, for they had only arrived in the country, the one early in December, 1917, and the other in November, they seriously depreciated the size of the Corps at the disposal of General Plumer's successor in command, Lieutenant-General the Earl of Cavan.

"During April," wrote Lord Cavan,* " signs continued to accumulate that the enemy contemplated an offensive astride the Brenta, but it was not until the middle of May that it appeared probable that this operation would be combined with an attack across the Piave. By the end of May the general plan of the enemy for their forthcoming attack could be clearly foreseen. Subsequent events proved that the Italian High Command had made a forecast correct in nearly every detail."

On June 15th the Austrians attacked on two fronts of 25 and 18 miles respectively, the one being from St. Dona di Piave to the Montello, the other from Monte Grappa to Canove, the whole of the British sector being involved and the 23rd and 48th Divisions being engaged. The enemy gained some initial success and secured some ground, but being counter-attacked the ground lost was recovered, and a portion of the right bank of the Piave, which had been in Austrian hands for some months past, was finally cleared of the enemy. The 7th Division was ordered to be ready to take part if required, and the 2nd The Queen's, then in the Thiene—Caltrano area, were at 4.30 p.m. on June 15th packed into lorries and rushed to the Plateau to the junction of the new Calvene and Marginal Roads at Monte Cavalleto. Here the Battalion bivouacked among the rocks in very cold and misty weather, and it was not until the next night that blankets, on the not extravagant scale of one per man, arrived and all were made more comfortable. On the 17th the Battalion moved out early and relieved the 21st Manchesters at Monte Brusabo, but at midday was ordered to be ready to move east again, and started at 1 p.m. for the Tezze Sciessere area, where the 91st Brigade was then concentrating. A very thick mist came down and it commenced to pour with rain, but the Battalion eventually got under cover, Headquarters and two companies in the small village of Marziele, and the other two companies in huts south of the Marginal Road. Here the Brigade was kept in readiness to hold the Marginal Line from Monte Corvo to the Montagnola Nuova in support to the French and Italians. On the 27th-29th there were signs that the enemy proposed to resume the offensive, and the 7th Division was again held in readiness, but nothing happened and the situation once more became normal.

* Despatch of September 14th, 1918.

[*Copyright: Imperial War Museum.*

TRENCHES AND DUG-OUTS ON THE BANKS OF RIVER PIAVE, ITALY.

The 2nd The Queen's, however, had no especial predilection for the quiet life, and if debarred from major operations for the time being, they found some solace in raids upon the enemy trenches. One such was carried out during the night of the 26th-27th with artillery co-operation. " C " Company, under command of Captain Gibson, made a raid upon a small salient in the enemy's front line at the junction of Guards and Gordon Trenches, immediately to the west of the village of Canove. The party consisted of 4 officers and 70 other ranks, while another party of 1 officer and 22 men advanced at zero and established themselves on high ground to the west and east of the raiders to assist with covering fire. The raiding party was formed up at 11 p.m. on a line running east and west across the Canove Road and about 250 yards from the enemy's line. The guns opened fire at 11.30 p.m., and five minutes later lifted on to a line of enemy dug-outs immediately in rear of the objective, remaining stationary on the front line to the right and left. The gun fire ceased at 12.4 a.m., and when the barrage lifted the raiders dashed forward and succeeded in capturing nine prisoners, but four of these resisted capture and were killed, while a fifth was mortally wounded; some 30 others of the enemy were seen lying killed and wounded from the effects of the barrage. The party of the 2nd The Queen's returned to the line about 12.30 on the morning of the 27th having had two men slightly wounded. Of the prisoners two were Germans, who seemed very glad to be captured and " all were *most* communicative," says the Battalion diary.

There is nothing of particular importance to chronicle for the months of July and August, except that during the latter month the 7th Division was billeted in the Trissino area, at the foot of the mountains skirting the Venetian plain, the 91st Brigade being billeted in and about the town of Arzignano.

At this time the question of sending troops from Italy to France seems again to have cropped up, for in his despatch of November 15th Lord Cavan wrote as follows : " Early in September, as it appeared unlikely that offensive operations would be undertaken in Italy in the near future, it was decided to assist France with some or all of the British troops in this country. . . . In accordance with this idea the 7th, 23rd, and 48th Divisions were reduced from 13 to 10 battalions, and the nine battalions thus released were dispatched to France on September 13th and 14th. The 7th Division was then at rest, and it was intended to dispatch this division as soon as a battle-worn division should arrive from France to replace it. . . . As a result of the tactical situation in France, and the subsequent demands on rolling stock, the proposed exchange of divisions was postponed from day to day. The situation in Italy also changed and finally all three divisions remained in this country."

In consequence of the reduction of the number of battalions in a division from 13 to 10, the 9th Battalion The Devonshire Regiment and the 20th and 21st Battalions The Manchester Regiment were taken out of the 7th Division, and were sent back to the Western Front, where they were later formed into the 7th Brigade of the 25th Division, and did very gallant work during the German retreat.

On September 7th the 2nd The Queen's were sent to Santa Margharita, a small village about five miles off, and situated in the hills, where it was intended the Battalion should remain for a week, there being here greater facilities for training than in the closely cultivated country round Arzignano.

Rumour had for some days past been very busy and equally contradictory ; on the one hand it was said that peace would shortly be proclaimed, and this supposition was based on the fact that Bulgaria had already thrown up the sponge, while it was known that Austria had officially implored President Wilson to arrange an armistice ; on the other hand, it was equally authoritatively asserted that an early offensive on the Piave was in view ; this latter view proved to be the correct one.

On October 3rd orders were issued for the 7th Division to move to the area north of Vicenza, and the 2nd The Queen's accordingly left Arzignano, whither they had returned at the end of their week's training, and marched to Creazzo ; and then on the 12th orders were suddenly issued for the immediate entrainment of the whole division and for it to proceed to the Treviso area, the entraining stations being Vicenza, Thiene, Morano, Dueville and Villaverle, of which Vicenza was the only one anywhere near the area in which the Division was billeted. The Queen's left Creazzo at 11 p.m. on the 13th, and marched to Morano, where they entrained for Treviso—a two-hours' journey, and on arrival marched to billets in the town ; only forty-eight hours were spent here and on the 16th the Battalion moved on to Casale, on the 19th to Santa Bona, on the 21st to Limbra, and so to the Brigade concentration area south of Maserada, where all bivouacked for the night, ready for the offensive across the Piave.

At this time General Diaz, the commander of the Allied Forces in Italy, had under him a particularly polyglot army, composed of one Czecho-Slovak, two French, three British, and fifty-one Italian divisions, and, in addition one American regiment, distributed as follows :—The Sixth Army, in which was the 48th British Division, was on the Asiago Plateau ; the Fourth Army was in the Monte Grappa Sector ; along the Piave and as far south as the Montello was the Twelfth Army ; at the Montello itself was the Eighth Army ; while south of this was the Tenth Army, of which General Lord Cavan was in command, and which contained one Italian and one British Corps, this last being the XIV, composed of the 7th and 23rd Divisions under Lieutenant-General Sir James Babington ; while between the Tenth Army and the sea was the Third Army.

The plan of attack devised by General Diaz was as under :—A feint attack by the Tenth Army on the Grappa, the Twelfth, Eighth, and Tenth Armies striking at the two Austrian armies in their front, driving a wedge between them and severing their communications ; thereafter the Twelfth Army was to advance on Feltre, the Eighth on Valmarino and Vittorio, driving the Sixth Austrian Army north, while the Tenth Italian Army was to move due east to the Livenza, guarding the flanks of the Eighth and Twelfth Armies and forcing back the remainder of the Austrians on a different line of retreat. The Army which included the 7th and 23rd British Divisions—the Tenth—had no easy rôle ; at the point of attack the Piave was about a mile and a half wide, and the stream consisted of several channels dotted with islands, the largest of these latter being known as the Grave di Papadopoli, some three miles long by one mile wide. In the larger of the channels the stream ran at a rate of never less than three miles an hour, while in flood time it might be as much as ten miles an hour. The Austrians held the Grave di Papadopoli as an advanced post.

The orders issued on October 23rd in the 91st Brigade directed that the XIV British Corps, in conjunction with other corps on both flanks, was to force the passage of the Piave and advance rapidly on the Livenza, the 7th and 23rd Divisions attacking on right and left of the Corps respectively, the 37th Italian Division being on the right of the British 7th Division. The initial attack against the main enemy defences was to be made with the 20th Brigade on the right, the 91st on the

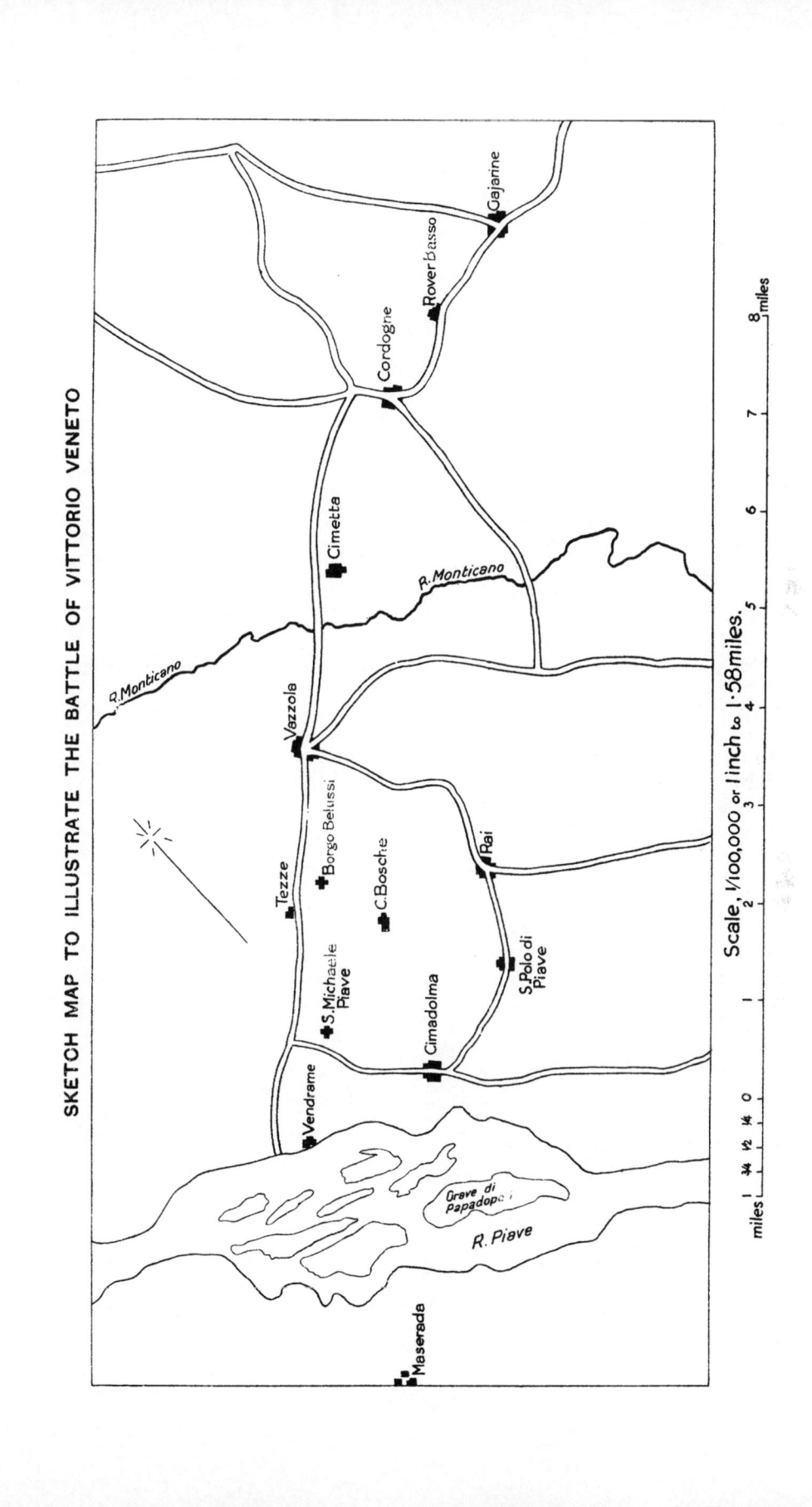

## SKETCH MAP TO ILLUSTRATE THE BATTLE OF VITTORIO VENETO

Scale, 1/100,000 or 1 inch to 1·58 miles.

left, and the 22nd in reserve. As a preliminary to the main attack the Grave di Papadopoli was to be captured either by surprise twenty-four hours before the main attack, or immediately previous to the main attack, the state of the stream determining which alternative should be adopted. If to be taken by surprise, the island was to be seized by the 22nd Brigade, the other two carrying out the main attack. In the 91st Brigade the attack was to be carried out by the 22nd Manchesters, supported by the 1st South Staffordshire Regiment, the 2nd The Queen's being in brigade reserve.

What follows is drawn from the Battalion account of the crossing of the Piave and Monticano and advance on the Livenza—operations which lasted from October 26th to 31st, and which brought about the surrender of Austria and, so far as the 2nd Battalion The Queen's Royal Regiment was concerned, the end of the war.

At 9.30 p.m. on October 26th, 1918, the Battalion left its bivouacs south-west of Maserada, and moved down to a pontoon bridge which had been thrown across the main stream of the Piave to the island of Papadopoli,* the Queen's crossing in rear of the 8th Devons of the 20th Brigade at eleven o'clock. The night was dark, and on reaching the island some difficulty was found in getting into the allotted assembly position, but this was completed by 1 a.m. on the 27th and the men began to dig in. The British guns had started the preliminary bombardment at 11.30, the retaliatory barrage falling an hour later, but only some 20 casualties were incurred. Heavy rain began to fall about 3 a.m.

At 6.15 a.m. The Queen's moved forward in artillery formation of platoons in rear of the 1st South Staffords, who were in close support to the 22nd Manchesters, the assaulting battalion. The country was difficult, being covered with scrub, and direction was kept by officers of each company marching on a compass bearing. On reaching the further bank of the river the centre of the Battalion found itself exactly opposite Vendrame, the centre point of the Brigade front, thus proving how well the direction had been maintained. From the very heavy machine-gun fire heard in front it was clear that the leading battalions were meeting with opposition, but the advance was slowly continued over streams and shingle, and about eight in the morning of the 27th The Queen's arrived on the edge of a broad, deep stream, which was forded in single file and the Battalion then lined the further bank and awaited orders.

These did not come until eleven o'clock, when The Queen's moved on again, and on arrival at an enemy trench line running north-west and south-east in front of San Michaele Piave, they consolidated the line, " B " and " D " Companies in front, and " A " and " C " in support. By this time the leading battalions had reached the Tezze—C. Bosche Line and were also consolidating, and about 6 p.m. rations and ammunition came up, and The Queen's settled down for the night. About 7.30, however, the South Staffords sent word that a prisoner had just been taken who stated that three Austrian regiments were then forming up for counter-attack outside Tezze, and assistance might be needed, so, on this being confirmed by the Brigade headquarters with which The Queen's were in telephonic communication, " C " Company of The Queen's was sent up to assist the South Staffords, lined a road in rear of Tezze, and there dug in. The rest of the Battalion stood to all night, but it passed quietly though in bitter cold.

The morning of the 28th broke quietly and about 9.30 orders came for the 91st Brigade to move forward to a line running north-west and south-east in front of

* The greater part of the island was taken by surprise on the night of the 23rd-24th.

Borgo Belussi, the South Staffords on the left and the Manchesters on the right. This was done about midday, and then in the evening about 9 p.m. The Queen's went forward and relieved the line, the enemy having everywhere fallen back. Consolidation was then proceeded with, and patrols sent out to try to get touch with the enemy. No rations came up, apparently owing to the bridges in rear breaking down.

About 10 p.m. orders came directing The Queen's and South Staffords to advance to the line of the Vazzola—Rai road, and this was reached, through very close and difficult country, by four on the morning of the 29th. Consolidation had hardly commenced when fresh orders for a move came up, the Brigade advancing by Vazzola, Cimetta, and Cordogne on Gajarine, the Battalion finding the advanced guard. It had been hoped that the rear-guard would be able to cross the Monticano River about 10.30 that morning, but the Vazzola—Cimetta road was found to be very congested, and it appeared that the 69th Brigade of the 23rd Division on the left had already been attacking the bridge over the Monticano for some time and was just commencing to cross, but enemy machine guns on the further side and to the east of the bridge were causing some trouble. "D" Company of The Queen's was now ordered to work up through the close country to the east of the road and, by seizing the embankment, assist the crossing at the bridge, while the rest of the advanced guard moved directly up the Vazzola Road to the bridge, and came under very heavy machine-gun and rifle fire. By this time, however, some of the 69th Brigade had crossed and "A" and "B" Companies of The Queen's, deploying to the right, forced the passage. The advance continued for some 500 yards, the resistance at first being slight and prisoners and machine guns were captured. Opposition then suddenly stiffened, touch was lost with the troops on the left, the country was close and cultivated, and by midday the enemy seemed to be working dangerously round the exposed flank. About 2.30 p.m. The Queen's were reinforced by the South Staffords, and the two battalions then rushed forward and took the village of Cimetta with many prisoners.

The three battalions of the 91st Brigade held the line in front of Cimetta for the night under a shell fire which at one period of the night was particularly heavy.

On the morning of the 30th the 22nd Brigade passed through the 91st, which about 1 p.m. followed in column of route down the Cordogne Road to Rover Basso, where the Battalion spent the night in billets.

During these operations 18 of The Queen's had been killed or died of wounds, Lieutenant L. H. Leckie and 83 other ranks had been wounded, and 5 men were missing.

On the morning of the 2nd The Queen's marched with the Brigade and, crossing the Livenza River at Cavolano by a pontoon bridge, which had replaced the permanent structure blown up by the Austrians, arrived at six in the evening in billets at Pordenone. The next day the 91st Brigade remained in reserve while the other brigades of the 7th Division were to advance to the line of the Tagliamento, but as the day went on news came back that the enemy with whom the advanced troops were in touch were refusing to fight, stating that an armistice had been signed and that its terms were to take effect from that morning.

The 91st Brigade moved off on the 4th, crossed the Meduna, and billeted in the San Martino area, The Queen's being in San Giorgio; and here about 4 p.m. information was received that the armistice had taken effect from three that afternoon, and that large numbers of prisoners were crowded on the banks of the

Tagliamento near the Gradisca Bridge, waiting to be passed to the rear. The Battalion now moved to Gradisca and was busily employed in sending back the captives.

" And so at 3 p.m. on November 4th, by the waters of Tagliamento, the part played by the 7th Division in the war came to an end. They ended, as their record deserved, in the front line of the advance, and the history of the last ten days made a fitting climax to their four years of toil. In those ten days the Division had advanced 91 kilometres, crossed five rivers, and captured prisoners to a number far in excess of their own entire strength."*

The following message was now received through the 91st Brigade Headquarters :—

" *From His Majesty the King to General the Earl of Cavan.*

" *With all my heart I congratulate you and the XIV Corps upon the splendid victory achieved fighting side by side with the Italian troops of the Tenth Army, resulting in the Armistice which takes effect to-day. For your great service I thank you.*"

From the Brigadier, Brigadier-General R. T. Pelly, C.M.G., D.S.O., came the following :—

" *Officers, non-commissioned officers and men of the 91st Brigade,*

" *I wish to make some attempt to express my admiration of your conduct during the recent battle. The Brigade has taken a leading part in the crushing defeat inflicted on the Austrians. Not only the fighting, but the hardships entailed by the fording of the Piave, the long period without rest or sleep, the constant attacks and advances by night and day, called for skill, endurance, and soldierly spirit of the very highest order. I was always proud of the 91st Brigade, but your conduct in our recent victory has made me prouder than ever of commanding a brigade composed of such men.*"

By November 11th the Battalion had recrossed the Piave for the San Biago area and was in billets at Cavrie, where the following General Order was on the 13th published by General the Earl of Cavan :—

" *The Germans have signed the Armistice and fighting ceased in the whole vast area of the Great War at eleven o'clock on Monday, November 11th.*

" *I thank you all, from the highest to the lowest, with all my heart for the way in which you have upheld British honour in Italy, not only in battle but in billets.*"

On the 13th the 2nd The Queen's moved by train to Costalunga, and then a very few days later to Montecchio Maggiore, the Battalion having been selected to form one of the units of a composite brigade representative of the 7th Division to be reviewed by H. M. the King of Italy. The next ten days were spent in the practice of ceremonial drill and the inspection duly came off on the 27th, and The Queen's marched back to Costalunga on the 29th, when the following message was promulgated :—

" *His Majesty the King of Italy was graciously pleased to express his delight at the parade to-day and the real pleasure it gave him to see the British troops. The Commander-in-Chief was extremely pleased with the parade, and all ranks deserve the highest praise for their turn-out, steadiness, and march past. He considers that no better war review has ever been held, and sincerely thanks all staffs, officers, warrant officers, non-commissioned officers and men for their efforts.*"

* Crosse, *The defeat of Austria as seen by the 7th Division,* p. 96.

During November and December military training of all kinds went steadily on, there were many inter-company and inter-battalion competitions in sport and rifle shooting, while the new Educational Scheme was inaugurated and classes were held in useful instruction of all kinds; while later on lectures were given explaining the Government plans for the demobilization of the army now about to take place. During December, and from that onwards, men began to leave the Battalion in parties of varying strength on return to civil life, while men were also invited to re-enlist for limited periods of engagement for the post-war army, and quite a number thus extended their army service. In January there was a considerable decrease in the strength of the Battalion, which on the 1st of the month contained 737 other ranks, while on the 31st there were 488 only; during the same period 8 officers also left.

In the month of February these numbers decreased further and even more rapidly in all ranks; the number of the companies was reduced by making two into one. On the 15th 1 officer and 87 other ranks, ineligible for demobilization, were transferred to the 22nd Battalion Manchester Regiment, which was being reformed in view of forming part of the Army of Occupation in Austria, and was now nearly up to establishment again; and several officers and men were from time to time detailed to accompany supply trains running to Austria-Hungary for the relief of the distress in that country.

Finally on the 19th orders were received that the cadre of the 2nd Battalion The Queen's would start for England on the 21st, while of the men who were on this date still remaining in excess of the cadre strength, 36 were transferred to the 6th Battalion Royal Warwickshire Regiment, while others still awaiting demobilization were to follow home on February 22nd, 23rd, and 24th.

On February 21st the cadre proceeded to Tavernelle in six lorries, and starting by train at five in the afternoon left on its long rail journey by Voghera, Turin, Montmelian, Lyons, Malesherbes and Versailles for Havre—and Home.

## CHAPTER XIII.

### 2ND BATTALION (*continued*).

### 1918–1923.

##### HOME SERVICE—INDIA.

##### OPERATIONS IN WAZIRISTAN.

THE cadre of the 2nd Battalion The Queen's was composed of the following :—

Acting Major J. B. Coates, M.C., Acting Captain E. J. G. Webb, M.C. (adjutant), Lieutenants R. H. Short and D. N. P. Squarey (quartermaster), and 48 other ranks. It arrived at Havre on February 25th, 1919, and remained for two nights in the reception camp at Harfleur, then being administered by the 1st Battalion of the Regiment, and embarked for England in the s.s. *Yale* on the 27th, landing next day at Southampton and proceeding direct to the Regimental Depot at Guildford.

By March 5th all the cadre had been dispersed except Major Coates, Lieutenant Squarey and Orderly-Room Sergeant Hammond ; but during the next few days 4 officers (Captains G. F. Courreaux and G. M. Gabb, Lieutenants R. E. C. Harland and R. C. Wilson), joined as a " temporary nucleus," while from time to time men were posted from the Depot, until it was at last possible to form two companies and also the nucleus of two more.

On March 25th Lieutenant-Colonel L. M. Crofts, D.S.O., arrived and assumed command, and during the weeks that followed the Battalion was gradually completed with officers and men ; while on April 24th it moved to Tournay Barracks, Aldershot, where on May 14th intimation was received that the 2nd The Queen's was to be prepared to embark for India some time after July 15th. On July 18th, the advance party, consisting of Lieutenant J. H. Sillem, Second-Lieutenant E. Mushett and 20 other ranks, left Aldershot for Liverpool, and there embarked for India in the *City of Calcutta*.

The remainder of the resuscitated Battalion remained long enough in England to be represented in the Victory March on July 18th, when the undermentioned went up to London as part of the Composite Battalion from the Aldershot Command :—Lieutenant-Colonel L. M. Crofts, D.S.O., Captains R. K. Ross, D.S.O., M.C., C. J. M. Elliott, D.C.M., and G. K. Olliver, M.C., and 22 other ranks.

The first party—7 officers and 338 other ranks—left Aldershot under command of Major S. T. Watson, D.S.O., on August 7th for Liverpool, there embarking in the steamer *Stephen*, while the second party did not leave Aldershot until September 6th, embarking in the *City of Marseilles* next day under Lieutenant-Colonel L. M. Crofts, D.S.O. ; the total embarking strength was 28 officers and 742 other ranks. The following officers accompanied the Battalion to India :—Major S. T. Watson, D.S.O., Captains G. K. Olliver, M.C., R. K. Ross, D.S.O., M.C. (adjutant), R. H. Philpot, M.C., R. C. G. Foster, M.C., J. B. Coates, M.C., and C. J. M. Elliott, D.C.M., (quartermaster), Lieutenants F. A. Jacob, R. E. C. Harland, T. C. Filby, D.S.O., F. T. Badcock, B. C. Haggard, H. J. Carpenter, G. D. G. Bottomley, P. L.

Leighton, M. S. Shuldham-Legh, R. C. Wilson, J. H. Sillem, C. O. W. Morgan, I. T. P. Hughes, M.C., C. C. Prescott, R. E. Pickering and E. Mushett, Second-Lieutenants A. P. Block, H. P. Combe, E. C. W. Cumberlege and R. M. Burton.

The 2nd Battalion The Queen's disembarked at Bombay on September 5th, and entrained for Bareilly, where it arrived in the morning of October 5th, and on November 6th was inspected by His Excellency the Commander-in-Chief, General Sir Charles Monro, Bart., himself an old officer of The Queen's.

On Christmas Day, 1919, the Battalion was ordered to mobilize by wire from Army Headquarters.

The country against the inhabitants of which the 2nd Battalion The Queen's was now in expectation of being actively employed is known as Waziristan and forms the connecting link on the Afghan Frontier between Kurram and Zhob; on its north and north-west lie the Afghan districts of Birmal and Khost, on the north-east and east are Kurram, Kohat, Bannu, and Dera Ismail Khan, while on the south lies Zhob. The country is very mountainous and rugged, the chief highways being through the Tochi and Gumal Valleys, and the most important of the tribes inhabiting it are the Darwesh Khel Wazirs and the Mahsuds.

From the close of the Sikh Wars of the first half of the last century, the tribesmen of Waziristan have been the cause of innumerable expeditions—in 1852, in 1859, in 1870, in 1881, in 1894, in 1897, in 1900 and in 1902; while from 1914 onwards there was frequent trouble and movable columns were constantly marching into and through their country. Then from 1884 up to quite recent years the Amir of Afghanistan had put forward claims that Waziristan belonged to him, and he had made more than one attempt to establish his supremacy over the Wazirs, culminating in 1892 in the occupation of Wana by Afghan troops. When in May, 1919, the Afghans invaded our territory, they were actively supported by the tribes of Waziristan, but it was not until hostilities ceased with Afghanistan in the late summer of this year that the Indian Government was able to concert measures for the due punishment of the Wazirs for the many wanton attacks they had made upon our troops. The Tochi Wazirs and Mahsuds were summoned to attend a jirga to be held in November when certain terms would be announced to them. The response to the invitation was quite unsatisfactory and consequently in November British columns entered this country with orders to deal first with the Tochi Wazirs and secondly with the Mahsuds, our troops advancing first to Datta Khel in the Tochi Wazir country, and then operating in the Derajat area against the Mahsuds. The first phase of these operations came to a close on December 28th, by which date the majority of the sections of both tribes had accepted our terms, but much remained to be done, and it was for the second phase of the operations that it was considered necessary, not only to employ fresh troops, but to have at call a limited number of British infantry battalions to be used on or beyond the frontier, should the necessity arise.

As matters turned out, however, the necessity did not arise, and the 2nd Battalion The Queen's remained on at Bareilly, being for many weeks held ready to move at forty-eight hours' notice, and, as we shall see, did not actually proceed to the frontier until another year had gone by. The operations of this year in Waziristan were carried out wholly with young Indian troops, except for certain units of the Royal Air Force and a battery of British Mountain Artillery, and the 2nd Battalion The Queen's spent the whole of the spring and hot weather of 1920 at Bareilly with a detachment in the hills at Kailana.

On August 5th, 1920, the following letter was received from the headquarters of the Bareilly Brigade :—" I am directed to say that the Battalion under your command has been specially selected by His Excellency the Commander-in-Chief to be present for duty at Delhi during the visit of His Royal Highness the Prince of Wales to the capital " ; but, as we shall presently see, recurring trouble on the North-West Frontier caused this order to be eventually cancelled.

Early in September Lieutenant-Colonel L. M. Crofts, D.S.O., left the Battalion for home on completion of his period of command, Major S. T. Watson, D.S.O., assuming charge pending the arrival of the new Commanding Officer, and one of Major Watson's first duties was to prepare and send a detachment of the 2nd The Queen's in aid of the Civil Power to Pilibhit in the north-eastern portion of the Bareilly District. This party, composed of Captain R. C. G. Foster, M.C., Lieutenants C. C. Prescott and R. E. Pickering with 70 other ranks taken from " B " Company, left Bareilly by train on September 24th and came back on the following day ; the following is an extract from a letter received by the General Officer Commanding from the Commissioner of the Rohilcand District :—" I sent back the troops to Bareilly last night after having performed a night and a day's very good service. I must thank you for the prompt way in which you sent them off to our assistance here. We were very short of police, and reinforcements were not expected until the next day. The situation at 10 a.m. on Friday was really very bad. . . . will you please convey to the Officer Commanding The Queen's Regiment my appreciation of their services while in Pilibhit and of the orderly conduct of the men. The coming of the troops was immensely appreciated by the bulk of the population, who, owing to their presence, were able to sleep safely in their beds on Friday night."

At this time there was very considerable unrest both within and without India, and the time was at hand when the Battalion was again to be employed beyond the North-West Frontier and against sections of the same tribe which had occupied the attention of our troops for many months past.

The trouble in Waziristan which had threatened to call the 2nd Battalion The Queen's to the neighbourhood of the Border at the end of 1919 had not yet been quelled, and although the raising of the blockade in favour of those sections of the Mahsuds that had submitted had tended to reconcile the tribesmen to our presence in the heart of their country, there were still very many irreconcilables who continued to be actively hostile against our occupation, although their activities consisted for the most part of sniping and petty raids. During August, 1920, matters considerably improved, the attitude of certain sections became distinctly more friendly, fines were paid and many of the rifles demanded were handed in ; while there were even hopes that the Mahsuds might themselves be induced, for the first time, to provide labour during the winter for working parties on the Ladha Road.

During September, however, the Wana Wazirs, who had committed very many outrages in 1919, again became more active, they ambushed parties of the Frontier Constabulary and even attacked certain of our smaller frontier posts. During the spring of 1919 it was intended to take steps for the punishment of the tribe, but this had to be postponed until the autumn, when the improvement in the Mahsud situation permitted of the concentration at Jandola of a force for dealing with the Wana Wazirs.

On October 9th the Battalion received orders that on a date to be notified later it would relieve the 2nd Battalion Norfolk Regiment in Waziristan, and in consequence of the above the intended move to Delhi was now cancelled. Then on the 23rd notice was received from the General Officer Commanding 18th Indian Infantry Brigade that in the event of any punitive expedition being sent against the Wana Wazirs the 2nd The Queen's would form part of the force; and during the next few weeks all necessary arrangements were put in hand for the departure of the Battalion to the Frontier.

An advance party, composed of Lieutenant E. C. W. Cumberlege, 2 sergeants, and 48 other ranks, left Bareilly on November 22nd to take over barracks at Rawal Pindi, to be occupied by the depot to be stationed there on the Battalion proceeding to the front, and on the same date the Battalion was warned to be ready to move on December 2nd. On the morning of this day the 2nd The Queen's entrained at a strength of 24 officers, 5 warrant officers, 27 sergeants, and 581 rank and file; the following was the composition of the staff and companies :—

Major S. T. Watson, D.S.O., commanding, Captain R. K. Ross, D.S.O., M.C. (adjutant), Captain C. J. M. Elliott, D.C.M. (quartermaster), Captain F. Rylands (educational officer), Captain T. H. B. Tabuteau (medical officer), and Regimental Sergeant-Major G. Sullivan.

"*A*" *Company*.—Captain R. H. Philpot, M.C., Lieutenants T. C. Filby, D.C.M., P. L. Leighton, M. S. Shuldham-Legh, R. C. Wilson, and J. H. Sillem (signalling officer), and Company-Sergeant Major Waspe.

"*B*" *Company*.—Captain R. C. G. Foster, M.C., Lieutenants C. C. Prescott and R. E. Pickering, Second-Lieutenant L. E. L. Maxwell (Indian Army Unattached List), and Company Sergeant-Major Boxall.

"*C*" *Company*.—Major A. N. S. Roberts, O.B.E., Captain J. B. Coates, M.C., Lieutenants F. A. Jacob, I. T. P. Hughes, M.C., and A. P. Block, and Company Sergeant-Major Hoare.

"*D*" *Company*.—Captain G. K. Olliver, M.C., Lieutenants F. T. Badcock, and H. P. Combe, Second-Lieutenant R. A. Harrild and Company Sergeant-Major Tedder, D.C.M.

A depot composed as follows was left at Bareilly on the departure of the Battalion, Lieutenants B. C. Haggard and C. O. W. Morgan, Second-Lieutenant R. M. Burton, Company Sergeant-Major Domoney, Bandmaster Adams, Regimental Quartermaster-Sergeant Holliman, Sergeant-Major Shales, and 296 other ranks; while the under-named officers, extra-regimentally employed, were also taken on the strength of the Depot, viz., Lieutenants R. E. C. Harland, S.S.O., Ranikhet, E. Mushett, R.T.O., and H. J. Carpenter, undergoing a course of signalling.

Travelling straight on without any real halt, the Battalion crossed the Indus on December 5th at Kalabagh, and then went on from here by the narrow-gauge railway in three parties to Tank, where the whole was concentrated by the 7th; and the 2nd The Queen's then marched on the 8th, and following days, by Manzai to Jandola, where the Battalion encamped and came under the orders of Brigadier-General W. F. Bainbridge, C.M.G., C.B.E., D.S.O., commanding the 23rd Infantry Brigade, which also contained the 28th and 2/30th Punjabis and the 1/4th Gurkha Rifles. Major C. D. Roe, D.S.O., of this last-named regiment was attached to The Queen's for instruction in frontier warfare, of which at this time no officer of the Battalion had any experience.

On the 11th the Battalion marched from Jandola to Haidari Kach and took over some eleven different picquets from the 58th Rifles, which then left for Sarwekai, where the remaining battalions of the 23rd Brigade joined it on the 14th. During the rest of the month of December The Queen's remained quietly at Haidari Kach, on the 20th Lieutenant-Colonel E. B. Mathew-Lannowe, C.M.G., D.S.O., arriving from the United Kingdom and taking over command of the Battalion from Major Watson.

It was now apparent that the stay of the Battalion at Haidari Kach was likely to be a prolonged one, and for some weeks nothing of an exciting character occurred. Leave for short periods was opened and all settled down to make themselves as comfortable as possible without relaxing anything of the necessary vigilance. On February 13th, 1921, the Battalion sustained its first casualty, one of the picquets being sniped by a small body of tribesmen, when No. 6078366 Bandsman J. Edwards was seriously wounded in the abdomen and died next day.

About this time The Queen's organized a mounted infantry section from the Lewis gun mule leaders, mounted on ponies belonging to the Field Hospital and Casualty Clearing Station. About fifteen mounted infantrymen could be mustered and they were found very useful in this kind of country, possessing as it did many fairly open stretches, and were especially handy for providing escorts for officers visiting distant picquets and for inspecting officers travelling up and down the line, while there can be no doubt that their presence had an excellent moral effect upon the enemy.

Early in March the garrison of Haidari Kach was increased by the arrival of No. 6 Pack Battery, R.G.A., No. 6 Company Machine Gun Corps and a Company of the 61st Pioneers ; and on the 20th The Queen's left Haidari Kach and marched via Jandola, Kotkai and Sorarogha to Ladha—being sniped without casualty *en route*—and reaching Ladha on the 25th. Here the Battalion joined the 9th Indian Infantry Brigade, commanded by Colonel Commandant H. M. W. Souter, C.M.G., D.S.O. The Brigade was composed as follows :—No. 6 British Pack Battery, 94th Company Sappers and Miners, 2nd The Queen's Royal Regiment, 2/25th Punjabis, 1/109th Infantry, two companies, 121st Pioneers, 2/6th Gurkha Rifles, and half No. 6 Company Machine Gun Corps.

At Ladha the Battalion was mainly employed in finding picquets and covering parties for road protection purposes, but occasions did arise when more formal exercises were practised, and even ceremonial, as on April 18th when His Excellency the Commander-in-Chief General Lord Rawlinson, G.C.B., G.C.V.O., K.C.M.G., A.D.C., arrived at Ladha and inspected the Battalion and details of the rest of the Brigade, of which at this time Lieutenant-Colonel Mathew-Lannowe was in command. On the 19th the following was published in Battalion Orders :—

"*His Excellency the Commander-in-Chief on his departure from Ladha spoke personally to the Commanding Officer expressing his appreciation of the turn-out and bearing of the Battalion. He was very pleased with the smartness with which the movements on parade were performed, the carriage of arms and the soldierlike bearing of the men. He made particular mention of his personal guard with whose appearance and conduct he was in every way satisfied.*

"*He added that, while he himself was far from the Frontier, he will always feel perfect confidence regarding the locality where the 2nd Battalion The Queen's Royal Regiment may be stationed.*"

The last week of April provided excitement of another kind ; on the 23rd the 2/25th Punjabis, who were this day engaged on road protection duty, were heavily attacked and " A " and " D " Companies of the Battalion were sent out from camp to support them. These did not, however, come into action, but provided the rear-guard during the final withdrawal. On the day following the Battalion accompanied a brigade reconnaissance, when some five men of the 2/25th Punjabis, wounded the previous day, were recovered and brought in ; and on the 25th the 2nd The Queen's had a very long day, being out for fourteen hours covering the establishment of two new picquets in the neighbourhood of Piazha, and providing the advanced guard and picqueting troops and the rear-guard during the retirement. Then on the 30th " A " and " D " Companies were out on road protection with the 2/4th Gurkhas when fire was suddenly opened on a picquet composed of one platoon under Lieutenant Combe from a wooded ridge some 300 yards to the south, when the under-mentioned non-commissioned officer and men, all of " D " Company, were wounded :—No. 6077313 Lance-Corporal G. Lockwood, No. 6076922 Private J. Webb, and No. 6077209 Private G. Twitchell. Fire was opened at once on the ridge with rifles and machine guns, the enemy was silenced, and the wounded were successfully evacuated.

The month of May passed quietly, and then on the morning of June 23rd the tribesmen showed a sudden increase of activity, a heavy sniping fire being opened on the camp at Ladha from the hills near the village, No. 6077325 Private W. Daniels, of " A " Company of The Queen's, being wounded by one of the first shots fired. The 3/11th Gurkhas, with " A " and " B " Companies, under Captain Philpot, in support, attacked and drove the enemy off the hills without further casualty.

There was sniping into camp again during several days in July, and the Battalion Lewis guns came into action on one or two occasions against small parties of the enemy seen on the neighbouring hills ; and on the 15th Private Pitter, of " C " Company, was wounded. During this month a good deal of extra labour was entailed on the troops by the river coming down in spate almost daily throughout the month, when the road required constant repair. As to these spates the despatch of the Commander-in-Chief, of May 24th, 1922, states :—

" During August there was heavy rain and the consequent spates seriously damaged communications throughout Waziristan and made the maintenance of troops in the forward area very difficult. On August 1st the new iron bridge above Jandola was washed away and great damage was done to roads and railways. As a consequence the troops had for a time to be put on reduced rations. . . . Above Jandola only pack transport could be used, and the progress of the new road was delayed. By the middle of September the question of supplies became less acute, and communications were again in good order."

Since June the enemy stronghold of Makin had been shelled almost daily by large-calibre howitzers, bombardment from the air having been found to be ineffective owing to the fact that practically every house in the district had its own caves and dug-outs into which the tribesmen could retire when enemy aircraft were reported to be in the vicinity. The resistance of the border people was now weakening, and about August 15th they made overtures for peace, and a small sub-section came in and surrendered all government rifles in their possession. By September 10th the Wana Wazirs had practically complied with our terms, and the blockade was raised four days later.

On the 30th the Commander of the 9th Infantry Brigade published the following Special Order of the Day to the troops at Ladha :—

" *The Abdullai Mahsuds of Makin have accepted the terms of peace and have surrendered the first instalment of Government rifles (including one Lewis gun) on the*

*29th instant. The following telegram from Advance Headquarters Wazir Force is published for the information of all ranks of the 9th Infantry Brigade :—*

*" ' The Force Commander wishes to convey to all ranks of the 9th Brigade his thanks for the part they have played in forcing the Abdullai Mahsuds to sue for peace. Owing to the dispositions adopted and the alertness of the troops, the Abdullai could lately find no opportunity to make a successful attack. The shelling carried out by the Section 10 Medium Mountain Battery R.G.A. combined with this was undoubtedly the main factor that caused the Abdullai to intimate their desire for peace and to accept the terms imposed by Government.'*

*" The Brigade Commander desires to add his own deep appreciation of the excellent work and devotion to duty by all ranks of the Brigade which he has the honour to command. Heavy and arduous calls have been a necessity in bringing about this very successful result and these calls have always been met cheerfully and with a high sense of discipline. The Brigade Commander heartily congratulates all ranks. He desires also to take this opportunity of sincerely thanking all troops, and especially the 121st Pioneers who have been working so continuously and under such difficult and heartbreaking conditions on the road and camel tracks during the long spate season now nearly passed.*

*" In spite of the present peace negotiations, the Brigade Commander wishes all ranks to fully realize that there are still many enemy and raiding gangs in the neighbourhood, who will always be on the look-out for opportunities, and that therefore all the present dispositions and alertness must never be relaxed in the very least."*

The 2nd Battalion The Queen's remained at Ladha until December 14th when the move to India commenced, " A " and " C " Companies moving first under command of Major Roberts, while the remainder of the Battalion marched on the following day under Lieutenant-Colonel Mathew-Lannowe. Moving by Sorarogha, Kotkai, Jandola, and Manzai to Tank, the 2nd The Queen's left this place in two trains on December 18th, and, crossing the Indus at Kalabagh, started off down country from Mari Indus in one train on the 21st and arrived at Lucknow, their new station, on Christmas Eve, 1921. The marching-in strength of the Battalion was 22 officers, 3 warrant officers, 25 sergeants, 29 corporals, 69 lance-corporals, and 451 privates. The officers were :—Lieutenant-Colonel E. B. Mathew-Lannowe, C.M.G., D.S.O., Majors P. J. Fearon, D.S.O. (Brevet Lieutenant-Colonel), and A. N. S. Roberts, O.B.E., Captains G. K. Olliver, M.C., R. H. Philpot, M.C., and J. B. Coates, M.C., Lieutenants R. F. C. Oxley-Boyle, M.C., B. C. Haggard, R. C. Wilson, C. O. W. Morgan, I. T. P. Hughes, M.C., R. E. Pickering, A. P. Block, H. P. Combe, E. C. W. Cumberlege, and R. M. Burton, Second-Lieutenant L. C. East, Captain R. K. Ross, D.S.O., M.C. (adjutant), Captain C. J. M. Elliott, D.C.M. (quartermaster), Lieutenant G. E. Buck, (Army Educational Officer), Lieutenant J. R. Wolfenden (New Zealand Staff Corps, attached), and Second-Lieutenant L. E. L. Maxwell (Indian Army Unattached List, attached).

At Lucknow the Battalion occupied Outram Barracks.

The following farewell order was published from Major-General T. G. Matheson, Commanding Waziristan Force, to the Officer Commanding The Queen's :—

*" I had hoped to be able to see you and address you before I leave this Force, but acting under doctor's orders I am, I regret to say, unable to do so. I therefore forward you what I had proposed to say.*

"Your Battalion has been in the force just over a year, first forming part of the Wana Column at Haidari Kach, and later joining the 9th Brigade at Ladha. Throughout the year you have stood to the whole force as an example of real efficiency and devotion to duty. The spirit of your Battalion has been remarked on by all who have been privileged to see it.

"Casualties, I am glad to say, have been few,* and the reason is not far to seek for the tribesmen of these parts soon find out which troops had best be left alone. In the case of The Queen's the fact that you have been here one year and that during that time the Battalion has never been seriously attacked is the highest praise that can be given you. You have defeated the enemy at his own game and in his own hills, and have set the standard of British infantry at a very high mark.

"Throughout my service I have always heard of the high standard The Queen's Royal Regiment has set in the past, but I have never before had the good fortune to serve with them. What I have seen of your Regiment during the last twelve months is quite sufficient to make me realize the truth of all I have previously heard, and I congratulate you, Lieutenant-Colonel Mathew-Lannowe, on your command.

"I cannot tell you how sorry I am that the time has now arrived for you and your Battalion to leave this force, and I wish you all the best of luck in the future."

To this the Commanding Officer replied in the following terms :—

"All ranks 2nd Battalion The Queen's Royal Regiment are grateful to you for your very kind appreciation of the work of the Regiment during the time it has had the honour of serving under your command. We much regret we were unable to say goodbye to you personally, but all ranks hope we may be able to serve under your command again."

On February 2nd, 1922, the Battalion, having been selected to form part of the troops concentrated at Delhi during the visit of His Royal Highness The Prince of Wales, proceeded thither at a strength of 27 officers and 732 other ranks, and was accommodated in Kingsway Camp; and while here a composite company composed as under moved into a special camp at Viceregal Lodge to find the guards here and at the Royal Pavilion during the Prince's stay at Delhi :—

Captains G. K. Olliver, M.C., and J. B. Coates, M.C., Lieutenants J. H. Sillem, R. E. Pickering, A. P. Block, and R. M. Burton, with 34 non-commissioned officers and men from each company of the Battalion.

The Battalion was employed to line the streets on February 14th, when His Royal Highness made his state entry, on the 15th at the unveiling of the All-India, King Edward VII Memorial, on the 16th on the occasion of a Durbar in Delhi Fort, and on the 17th when His Royal Highness laid the foundation stone of the Kitchener College. The Battalion left Delhi on the 23rd and was back at Lucknow on the 26th. Here the following letter was received from the Military Secretary to His Royal Highness the Prince of Wales :—

"I am directed by the Prince of Wales to write and say how glad His Royal Highness was to see the Regiment in Delhi and to express his appreciation of the smartness and discipline of the Battalion under your command and especially the guard of honour on the occasion of the Durbar.

* These were not, however, altogether negligible, the total casualties sustained in the force from April 1st to December 31st, 1921, amounting to, all ranks, killed 261, wounded 270, died of disease 467, total 1,098.

## BATTLE HONOURS COMMITTEE

*" His Royal Highness congratulates you and all in the Battalion on the very high standard of drill that is maintained and the smartness with which all duties have been carried out."*

Later His Royal Highness sent a copy of his photograph to the Officers' Mess as a memento of the Regiment having formed part of his guard at Delhi.

About this time every British Battalion in India had attached to it a number of Indian drivers for service with the Machine Gun Platoon, and this personnel now joined the 2nd Battalion The Queen's and shortly after Jemadar Karak Singh assumed charge of them.

On December 6th of this year in accordance with Army Order No. 338 of 1922, and Army Council Instruction of 1922, and also of a Memorandum from the Officer Commanding Depot The Queen's Royal Regiment at Guildford, who had been directed to commence preliminary work, in connection with the Regimental Committee, by General Sir Charles Monro, Bart., G.C.B., G.C.S.I., G.C.M.G., the Colonel of the Regiment, a Battalion Committee was formed composed of Lieutenant-Colonel E. B. Mathew-Lannowe, C.M.G., D.S.O., Major S. T. Watson, D.S.O., and Captain G. K. Olliver, M.C., and these compiled a report putting forward the views of the 2nd Battalion in regard to Battle Honours.

During the cold weather of 1923 His Excellency the Viceroy, Lord Reading, visited Lucknow when a special guard, composed as under, was mounted at Government House :—

Captain R. H. Philpot, M.C., Lieutenants C. O. W. Morgan and L. C. East, with 82 non-commissioned officers and men selected from the different companies of the Battalion. This guard was mounted from October 29th-31st, and the rest of the Battalion assisted in lining the streets on the occasions of the Viceroy's arrival and departure, while a special guard of honour was provided on the 29th when there was a grand Durbar at the Kaisarbagh ; this was composed of Captain G. K. Olliver, M.C., Lieutenants R. F. C. Oxley-Boyle, M.C. (with the King's Colour), and A. P. Block, 4 sergeants, and 100 rank and file. The following message from His Excellency the Governor of the United Provinces was published on October 26th in the 19th Indian Infantry Brigade Orders :—

*" His Excellency the Governor of the United Provinces desires to thank the officers and men of the Lucknow Garrison warmly for their services on the occasion of His Excellency the Viceroy's visit. He has separately conveyed to the Officer Commanding the Brigade his personal appreciation of the splendid work done."*

On December 16th a memorial tablet which had been placed in the Garrison Church, Lucknow, to the memory of the officers, non-commissioned officers and men who lost their lives on active service during the operations in Waziristan in 1920-21, was unveiled by Colonel Mathew-Lannowe, officiating in command of the 19th Brigade, at a memorial service.

The time had now come for the 2nd Battalion The Queen's to leave Lucknow for a fresh station ; an advance party had already proceeded to Allahabad under Lieutenant Hughes, with whom went Lieutenant Burton and Second-Lieutenant C. P. Murray and 133 other ranks, and on the morning of December 17th the rest of the Battalion followed, taking over quarters in Macpherson Barracks ; the strength of this party was 21 officers and 637 other ranks, and on the date of this move the following officers were on the strength of the 2nd The Queen's :— Colonel

E. B. Mathew-Lannowe, C.M.G., D.S.O., Majors S. T. Watson, D.S.O., and A. N. S. Roberts, O.B.E., Captains G. K. Olliver, M.C., R. H. Philpot, M.C., F. J. Jebens, M.C. (Brevet Major), R. C. G. Foster, M.C., J. B. Coates, M.C. (adjutant), A. S. Hodgson, and I. W. S. Symons, Lieutenants H. J. Carpenter, on leave in England, R. F. C. Oxley-Boyle, M.C., R. C. Wilson, C. O. W. Morgan, I. T. P. Hughes, M.C., C. C. Prescott, on leave in England, A. P. Block, H. P. Combe (acting quartermaster), E. C. W. Cumberlege, R. M. Burton, E. L. Behrens, G. Haggard, and L. C. East, Second-Lieutenants C. D. H. Parsons, D. H. Pearson, C. P. Murray, R. P. Shakespear, J. G. Bowman-Vaughan, A. M. Williams, K. W. Ross-Hurst, and W. W. A. Laing; the seven last-named officers were all on the unattached list, Indian Army.

On leaving Lucknow for Allahabad the following letter was received by the Commanding Officer from Major-General C. J. Deverell, C.B., commanding the United Provinces District :—

"*I wish to express to all ranks of the 2nd Battalion The Queen's Royal Regiment my appreciation of their very smart and soldierlike conduct and bearing whilst they have been serving in the United Provinces District under my command.*

"*They have at all times been an example and incentive to others, and have worthily upheld the splendid traditions of the splendid Regiment to which they belong.*

"*I part with the Battalion with the greatest regret and wish all ranks every good wish for the future.*"

## CHAPTER XIV.

### THE 1ST/4TH BATTALION.

#### 1914–1919.

##### THE MOHMAND, WAZIRISTAN, AND AFGHAN OPERATIONS.

###### BATTLE HONOURS:
" North-West Frontier, 1916–1917."

VARIOUS Corps of Volunteers have been raised and trained in this country when it was at war with other nations or when threatened with invasion, but it was not until the middle of the last century had gone by that the Force, now formed into and known as the Territorial Army, was established on a sound and permanent basis.

The 4th Battalion of The Queen's Royal Regiment dates from this period when, in the year 1859 a strong Volunteer Company was raised in Croydon, followed in the next year by another, the two companies then forming part of the 1st Surrey Administrative Battalion. It is impossible to over-estimate the public spirit which led to the creation of the early Volunteer Corps; the Government of the day did not believe in the importance of the movement, probably did not imagine that the enthusiasm, born in the days when the Crimean War and the Indian Mutiny were fresh in men's memories, would very long endure, and the Treasury was so unwilling to incur any unusual expense that at first the authorities would not promise to do more than provide rifles for 25 per cent. only of the enrolled strength of corps, so that the Volunteer of 1859 had—75 per cent. of him—to provide himself with his own uniform, arms, and equipment, and also to pay for his instruction in the military arts and sciences. The original cost to each man was consequently something like £8.

In 1867 the 1st Surrey Administrative Battalion was reorganized with an establishment of six companies and assumed the title of the 2nd Surrey Rifle Volunteers. The uniform then worn was rifle green, with a shako, which in 1877 was replaced by a helmet.

The Corps rapidly grew after its formation as an independent battalion, and in addition to the headquarter companies at Croydon, others were raised at the Crystal Palace, and at Norwood; but it was not until 1881, when the new Territorial scheme came into force, that the Battalion was joined to The Queen's and became the 1st Volunteer Battalion The Queen's Royal West Surrey Regiment. The only change in uniform which then resulted was an alteration in the helmet-plate when the crest of the Regular Regiment—the Paschal Lamb—was adopted.

In 1885 another company was added at Caterham, and detachments were later formed at Merstham and Oxted.

When in the autumn of 1899 it was realized that war was about to break out with the Transvaal and Orange Free State Republics, many offers were made to provide companies and battalions of Volunteers for service in the field, but these offers were declined by the military authorities of the day, who seem to have believed that the Army and the Militia Reserves would, with the active army, provide all the fighting men who could by any possibility be needed ; about the middle of December, 1899, however, the Government sanctioned the formation of a carefully-selected contingent of Volunteers for service in South Africa. This contingent was to be organized in Service companies of volunteers from existing Volunteer Corps, each company of a strength of 114 of all ranks, to be attached to Regular battalions at the front and take the place of such companies of each of those which in the early days of the war had been converted into mounted infantry. During the two years and more that the war lasted, some 16,500 Volunteers went out from home in these Service Companies, and the 1st Volunteer Battalion of The Queen's Royal West Surrey Regiment furnished 5 officers and over 200 non-commissioned officers and men for the Service company attached to the 2nd Battalion of the Regiment.

In 1908 the Territorial Force was formed under Lord Haldane's scheme of Army Reorganization, when the Battalion was renumbered and renamed, becoming the 4th Battalion The Queen's, and adopting the scarlet uniform of the Line Regiment ; while sanction was accorded for Territorial battalions to carry Colours, and it is a matter of Battalion tradition that the 4th Battalion The Queen's was the first Territorial unit to obtain this permission, due to the influence of Mr. Arnold Forster, M.P. for Croydon, and Secretary of State for War.

In this year two new companies were formed, the one at Lingfield and the other at Purley.

On July 10th, 1910, new Colours were presented to the Battalion at Duppas Hill, Croydon, by Field-Marshal Earl Roberts.

Four years later, on July 26th, 1914, the 4th Battalion The Queen's, under the command of Lieutenant-Colonel N. E. Cutler, proceeded to Bordon Camp for its annual training as part of the Surrey Infantry Brigade of the Home Counties Division, marching with it on the 31st via Alton, Kingsworthy, and Grately to Hamilton Camp on Salisbury Plain. It was at Amesbury on August 3rd, by which time the European situation was very serious, and next day the Battalion returned to headquarters at Croydon, arriving there late at night and receiving mobilization orders on the 5th. In accordance with these the 4th The Queen's left Croydon by train in the afternoon for Strood, where it was billeted for the night, and then marched on the 6th to Chattenden, the naval magazine on the hills north of the Thames, opposite Chatham Dockyard, from there furnishing guards for the naval airship shed at Kingsnorth, and for the various blockhouses, posts, and forts about the Thames Valley. Only three days were spent here, for on the 9th, on relief by the 3rd Royal West Kent Regiment, the Battalion marched to Maidstone, where the Battalion remained until the end of the month, busily engaged in prosecuting its war training. During September and October the Battalion was quartered at Canterbury.

The Territorial and Reserve Forces Act of 1907, Section XIII, had laid down that " no part of the Territorial Force shall be carried or ordered to go out of the United Kingdom," so it is clear that primarily the Force was intended for Home Defence only, and the scheme of Army Reorganization under which the Territorial Force was formed, provided for six months' home training should war break out prior to its dispatch on active service. It had, however, always been confidently expected that, should anything of the nature of a national emergency arise, a very large percentage of all ranks of the Force would volunteer for service overseas. As a matter of fact, it had been open to all members to accept such an Imperial obligation, but when war broke out in August, 1914, the percentage eligible for foreign and active service was very small indeed.

The mobilization order, No. 281 of August 4th, decreed the embodiment of the Territorial Force, and on the 10th Lord Kitchener, by then Secretary of State for War, had sent a note to the Director-General of the Force asking for early information as to what Territorial battalions would volunteer for service abroad, and what others desired only to belong to the Home Defence Force; and it was no doubt in consequence of this that volunteers for foreign service were now called for, the response by all ranks of the 4th The Queen's being very satisfactory.

At first, in accordance with instructions received, the Battalion was directed to be reformed as a foreign service unit, and to this end those of the 5th Battalion who had so volunteered were transferred to the 4th Battalion, while in like manner those who had not volunteered for foreign service were transferred to the 5th, the initial idea being apparently that the 4th should become a foreign service battalion, while the 5th should remain employed on home defence only. On October 13th, however, orders were received from the War Office that the 4th Battalion was to proceed at short notice to India with the Home Counties Division, and the instructions previously issued for the formation of Foreign Service and Home Service units of the 4th and 5th Battalions The Queen's respectively were now countermanded, the transferred personnel being sent back to their original units.

On September 21st, 1914, the County Associations had been authorized in Army Order No. 399 to form a home service unit for each unit of the Territorial Force which had been accepted for Imperial service, but this expansion was soon found to be insufficient and on November 24th it was enacted by the War Office that when an Imperial Service unit proceeded overseas and was replaced at home by its reserve unit, a *second* reserve unit should at once be raised at the depot or peace headquarters of the original unit.

In the case of the 4th Battalion The Queen's all home service personnel were returned to the 4th (Reserve) Battalion The Queen's, and it will probably now be convenient if the original 4th Battalion be henceforth referred to as the 1st/4th, by which it was known during the remainder of the war period, the reserve battalions as they were in turn raised becoming the 2nd/4th and 3rd/4th.

Prior to embarkation the Home Counties Division was inspected by His Majesty the King, and then on October 29th the 1st/4th Battalion The Queen's, strength 30 officers and 804 other ranks (including 5 R.A.M.C. details attached) left Canterbury at seven in the morning and embarked on the same day at Southampton in the *Grantully Castle*, joining the remainder of the Home Counties Division convoy off Plymouth on the 30th. Malta was reached on November 7th, Port Said on the 10th, and Suez on the day following. Here orders were received that the Division was to be detained pending further orders, in view of the situation in Egypt, but on November 18th the convoy continued its eastward voyage, H.M.S. *Minerva* accompanying it as escort.

Aden was passed on November 23rd, and Bombay was reached on December 2nd, the Battalion disembarking next day and proceeding by train to Secunderabad, which was reached on the 5th, and the 1st/4th The Queen's then took the place at Trimulgherry of the 1st Royal Inniskilling Fusiliers, who had already left for France.

When war broke out in August of this year 52 battalions of British infantry were serving in India, but so rapidly was the place of these taken by Territorial battalions* sent out from home, that before the war had been much longer than six months in progress some 40 of these Regular battalions had left India for one or other of the theatres of the war.

The Indian Army List for January, 1915, gives the following list of officers serving with the 1st/4th Battalion The Queen's :—Lieutenant-Colonel N. E. Cutler,† Majors S. D. Roper and C. W. Wise (adjutant), Captains H. R. Atkins, R. W. Potter, H. J. Gosney, L. G. Dibdin, W. S. Hooker, T. S. Keith and B. L. Evans ; Lieutenants J. C. Crowley, M. D. Helps, A. R. Jefferis, O. Featherstone, J. G. Fearon, E. L. Turner and A. G. Potter ; Second-Lieutenants R. R. B. Falcon, E. J. Brown, R. L. Moss, D. R. Potter, A. Dibdin, O. K. Caroe, G. L. Groves, H. D. R. Reilly, H. C. Gibsone, W. M. Maud and S. F. Bacon, with Hon. Major J. Greer as quartermaster.

On January 15th, 1915, the Battalion left Trimulgherry for Lucknow, and here on April 1st the double-company organization was adopted, " A " and " H " Companies forming the new " A " Company, " B " and " G " forming " B," " C " and " F " becoming " C," while " D " and " E " became " D."

During this year an officer, Lieutenant Jefferis, and 50 other ranks were sent to Mesopotamia as a reinforcement to the 2nd Norfolk Regiment, while at the end of October " A " Company proceeded on detachment to Fyzabad.

Lieutenant-Colonel Cutler rejoined the Battalion early in 1916, just in time to accompany it to Peshawar, for which place it started on January 15th, and on arrival occupying barracks then temporarily vacant and later moving into camp. On the 23rd, however, the 1st/4th was placed under orders to mobilize in readiness to proceed to Mesopotamia and there join Force " D." Preparations were at once set in hand, field service equipment was drawn and issued, and all men extra-regimentally employed were recalled, but the Battalion was already weakened by the reinforcements sent previously to Mesopotamia, there was then no hope or prospect of drafts coming out from England, and only some 600 other ranks were available for service. Consequently on February 4th the mobilization orders were cancelled, as were those of the 1st/9th Middlesex and 1st/5th East Surrey Regiments, three other battalions being warned for service instead, the Second Line or Reserve units of these being already in India and available to complete or reinforce those selected for mobilization.

On February 16th the Battalion marched from Peshawar to Nowshera, relieving here the 1st/4th Somersetshire Light Infantry, one of the battalions ordered to Mesopotamia. The 1st/4th The Queen's now formed part of the 2nd Infantry Brigade of the 1st Peshawar Division ; the Brigade was commanded by Brigadier-General W. G. L. Beynon, D.S.O., and contained, besides The Queen's, the 1st Durham Light Infantry, the 46th Punjabis, and 94th Russell's Infantry. Major-General C. J. Blomfield, C.B., D.S.O., commanded the Division. During this hot weather the Battalion was accommodated, by alternate wings, at Cherat, where in July two drafts, of 99 and 218 other ranks respectively, joined the Service companies ; so that when on October 1st The Queen's were again ordered to mobilize, this time for service on the North-West Frontier, the Battalion was once again at a tolerable strength. It joined the other regiments of the 2nd Indian Infantry Brigade in camp on the Jamrud Road, Peshawar, on October 25th.

---

* Some 55,000 Territorial soldiers in all served in India during the war.

† Lieutenant-Colonel N. E. Cutler came out in command of the Battalion, but was invalided home in January, 1915.

The tribesmen whose hostilities had now called the Peshawar Division into the field were the Mohmands, a tribe divided into two main branches of which the one dwells beyond and the other within the North-West Frontier. The country of the trans-frontier Mohmands extends from a little south of the Kabul River, on the line Girdikats to Fort Michni on the south, to Bajaur on the north, being on the east coterminous with the Peshawar district from three miles north of Jamrud to Fort Abazai, and thence for some twelve miles along the right bank of the Swat River; while on the west their country is bounded by the Kabul Tsappar Range and by the Kunar River. The settlements of the cis-frontier Mohmands lie immediately south of Peshawar and are bounded on the north by the Bara River, on the west, and south, by certain Afridi clans, and on the east by the Khattaks, the country being some twenty miles long by twelve broad. The Mohmands have not perhaps been so *generally* troublesome as certain of their neighbours, but their depredations have called for many punitive expeditions into their country, and as recently as 1915 operations had been undertaken against them; and it was confidently hoped that a severe defeat which had been inflicted on them in the neighbourhood of Shabkadar, some few miles above the junction of the Kabul and Swat Rivers, had brought the unrest among these turbulent people at least temporarily to an end, the more that in order to prevent raiding, and as a punishment, a blockade had been instituted, towards the latter half of 1916, along the Mohmand border, and a chain of blockhouses, connected by a wire fence, constructed and occupied. In this year again there was renewed disturbance and it had in the autumn been decided to concentrate on the blockade line the two brigades of the 1st Peshawar Division, now commanded by Major-General Sir F. Campbell, K.C.B., D.S.O., with a proportion of divisional troops and detachments of Frontier Militia and Constabulary.

The 2nd Brigade now marched by Adozai to Subhan Khwar which was reached on the 26th and from that date to the 30th was employed as a covering force to the 1st Brigade engaged about the blockade line from Abazai to Michni; but there being now a rumour of trouble in the Khaibar Pass, the 2nd Brigade was sent to Peshawar and remained there in camp while the trouble was dealt with by a flying column sent out from Peshawar. The Brigade then moved to Adozai and there camped, assisting the civil authorities in arresting offending tribesmen in the neighbouring villages.

On November 14th a Mohmand force, estimated at 6,000 men, concentrated near Hafiz Kor on the Panjpao, an affluent of the Kabul River, threatening Shabkadar, and Major-General Campbell issued orders for an attack on the morning of the 15th.

The action lasted all day, and was carried forward into the foothills occupied by the enemy in the vicinity of Hafiz Kor, casualties estimated at 100 killed and wounded being inflicted upon the Mohmands. The enemy gathering was completely broken up and subsequent reconnaissance showed that it had altogether disappeared, all dispersing to their homes; at 4 p.m. the British troops withdrew quite unopposed and having suffered very trifling loss. In this action, the first in which aircraft had been used in India, the armoured cars gave very effective support.

During the two following days reconnaissances were carried out in the direction of Hafiz Kor, and on the 18th the 1st/4th The Queen's and one battalion of Indian Infantry marched towards Michni before dawn, and at sunrise attacked and destroyed the village of Dewarzagai incurring no loss.

At the end of the month the 2nd Brigade was detailed to relieve the 1st on the Mohmand Blockade Line, and on the 30th Headquarters and "D" Company occupied Michni Fort, the remaining companies providing garrisons for blockhouses 33 to 46; certain isolated attempts were made by individual tribesmen to break through the line, but these had no real success. On December 22nd, however, Brigadier-General Beynon decided to make a sweep along the eastern bank of the Kabul River from No. 46 Blockhouse, using the Battalion as a striking force, and a most successful operation resulted. The Battalion was this day commanded by Major Roper, and from the western bank of the Kabul River a detachment of the Khaibar Rifles supported the left, while machine guns covered the right. The slight opposition offered was easily overcome, and some six villages along the river bank were destroyed. In January, 1917, several more villages were destroyed, while the construction of the blockhouses was improved and the barbed wire entanglements were strengthened.

On February 9th the 2nd Infantry Brigade was relieved by the 3rd, and next day the 1st/4th The Queen's marched back to Peshawar, and thence on the 11th to Jalosai for a fortnight's brigade training.

During the first half of March two more drafts, of a total of 95 other ranks, arrived from England, and then on the 18th and 19th the Battalion moved to Mian Meer, there relieving the 1st/5th Devons ordered thence to Egypt. The garrison duties here, already sufficiently heavy, were made all the heavier for the duty-men of the 1st/4th The Queen's by reason of the many demands made for men for extra-regimental employ, and for instructors for training the Indian Defence Units raised in and about Lahore, while the instruction of the new drafts had also to be carried on.

About this time the Viceroy, Lord Chelmsford, paid an official visit to Lahore, when the Battalion furnished a Guard of Honour at Government House under Captain Caroe, and other guards and escorts during his stay.

From the autumn of 1914 onwards there had been recurrent trouble on the North-West Frontier, especially in the Derajat Brigade area, consequent on the raiding propensities of the people of Waziristan.

"On the annexation of the Punjab in 1849 by the Indian Government, and our consequent occupation of Kohat, the inhabitants of Waziristan became our neighbours for 140 miles along the boundary line—from the north-western corner of the Kohat district to the Gomal Pass west of Dera Ismail Khan. Waziristan, the frontier Switzerland, is in shape a rough parallelogram, averaging 100 miles in length from north to south, with a general breadth of 60 miles from east to west. At the north-western corner a wedge of hilly country juts into the Kohat and Bannu districts. It is bounded on the west and north-west by Afghanistan; on the north-east and east by the British districts of Kurram, Kohat, Bannu, and Dera Ismail Khan; and on the south by Baluchistan."*

There are four main divisions of the people of this country, but by very far the most powerful and important are the Darwesh Khel and the Mahsuds, while all four have very little in common with each other, and for generations past have been in a perpetual state of feud. The Darwesh Khel and the Mahsuds can probably between them put some 40,000 fighting men in the field. The Wazirs have given us endless trouble; from 1852 up to the beginning of the present century some ten punitive expeditions have been sent against some section or other of the tribe; and our relations with them have of late years become all the more difficult and delicate, by reason of the claims to possession of Waziristan, which since 1884 have been put forward by the Amir of Afghanistan. For some few years no notice was taken of these

* *From the Black Mountain to Waziristan*, p. 418.

claims, and they were not indeed formally repudiated until 1892, when Afghan troops occupied Wana, in the heart of Waziristan, when the Amir was definitely informed that he had no right to occupy Wana, that under no circumstances was he to advance further into the country, and he was reminded that the Indian Government had always recognized and insisted on the independence of the Wazirs and upon its right to deal directly with them.

At the end of February, 1917, a large Mahsud force moved against Sarwekai, a post occupied by the South Waziristan Militia, which was practically besieged, and in view of the probability of the tribal movement developing further, Lieutenant-General Sir A. Barrett, K.C.B., K.C.S.I., K.C.V.O., commanding the Northern Army, was ordered to assume control of the operations considered necessary. He accordingly ordered a Movable Column to proceed at once to the relief of Sarwekai, while the 44th Infantry Brigade was to march to Tank, and on this the Mahsud gathering dispersed, and it was hoped that the tribesmen would now remain quiet. These hopes, however, were quickly dispelled, for during the next few weeks several attacks were made by the Wazirs upon convoys in country especially suited to their tactics, and it became necessary to increase the strength of the garrison of the Derajat, and it was in consequence of these measures that the 1st/4th The Queen's was now once more ordered to take the field across the Border.

On May 12th, then, the Battalion was ordered to mobilize as the British Infantry Battalion of the 43rd Indian Infantry Brigade for service with the Waziristan Field Force. This Brigade, commanded by Brigadier-General W. M. Southey, C.M.G., had been ordered very early in the month to proceed to Tank, and on the 6th the force now in the Derajat was constituted the Derajat Field Force, and was placed under the command of Major-General W. G. L. Beynon, C.B., C.I.E., D.S.O.; then a few days later the Bannu Brigade was also placed under General Beynon's command, and the whole was now designated the Waziristan Field Force.

The 1st/4th The Queen's left Lahore Cantonment, strength 750 all ranks, on May 15th, arrived next day at Mari Indus, and there crossing the river went on by the narrow-gauge railway from Kalabagh to Tank, which was reached on the 17th, and where the Battalion occupied the lines of an Indian Infantry battalion. During the ensuing days The Queen's were very busy preparing themselves to move forward and getting things ready for the reception of other British units shortly expected. But all hopes of seeing further service were soon dashed to the ground, for by the end of the month sickness increased in the Battalion at an alarming rate, malaria, sand-fly fever, and cases of heat-stroke being very prevalent; the quarters occupied were mud huts only recently vacated by Indian troops, who were possibly infected; and by June 6th, when the Battalion was to have moved out to join its brigade at Jandola, the ill-health was so general that the General Officer Commanding had no option but to replace the 1st/4th The Queen's by another unit, and under orders from Simla the Battalion was invalided out of the Force and ordered to move to the stations of Dugshai and Jutogh in the Simla Hills.

Never was Battalion more disappointed. It had left Lahore only three weeks previously, perfectly fit for service, but such a hold had the malaria and other climatic diseases got on all ranks, with a temperature often over 120° F. in the shade, that, despite all possible medical care and attention, only 350 other ranks were sufficiently fit and well to leave Tank on June 12th, while even of this small number over 100 were left sick at stations *en route*, and under 200 eventually reached their new stations in the hills, relieving here the 1st/9th Hampshire Regiment. The

Base depot at Tank was formed from men of the Battalion, under Major H. R. Atkins, and remained in being until August, 1917. It was well on towards the end of the year before the Battalion had regained a normal standard of health.

During the hot weather of 1917 two drafts, totalling 79 non-commissioned officers and men, joined; at the end of the year Major Roper proceeded on service to Egypt; while in January, 1918, Lieutenant-Colonel Cutler was appointed to command the convalescent depot at Wellington, Major H. R. Atkins then assuming command of the Battalion.

In the spring of 1918 the Battalion left the Hills and moved back again to Lahore, sending companies on detachment to Dalhousie and Amritsar; but at the end of the year the 1st/4th The Queen's was stationed at Lahore, where some loss was experienced—twenty good soldiers dying—from a terrible outbreak of influenza which swept India this year and carried off six millions of people in two months.

In January, 1919, demobilization commenced, and small parties of men had already started for home, when on April 12th the Punjab disturbances began, and the Battalion was called upon to find a flying column to proceed to Kasur, where a rising had taken place, the train from Ferozepore to Lahore having been held up by the mob and the European passengers attacked. While on this service Corporal Grinham and Lance-Corporal Battson were injured.

On April 13th the Battalion moved to Jullundur, and on arrival here many demands had to be met from the civil authorities for assistance and guards, and escorts were sent out from barracks at all hours of the day and night; while a number of civilians were accommodated in barracks during the period of unrest. Two armoured trains, manned by the Battalion, patrolled the line between Jullundur and Lahore. Then early in May the 1st/4th The Queen's was for a third time since arrival in India called upon to mobilize for field service.

In February of this year the Amir of Afghanistan had been murdered and the reins of power in Kabul were seized by Aman Ullah Khan, the third son of the late Amir, who began his reign well by declaring, among other promises, that he intended faithfully to preserve the tradition of friendship with the Government of India. This promise he did not long observe, and early in May a large Afghan army came pouring across the frontier and proceeded to pillage far and wide in the North-West Frontier Province. The Afghan army at this time was able to dispose of some 7,000 cavalry, 42,000 infantry, and 260 guns—the latter, however, largely immobile or obsolete. But the real danger attending upon any Afghan offensive lay not in the numbers of the Amir's regular army, but in the possible co-operation of the border tribes, amounting in all to some 120,000 men, all expert skirmishers and largely armed with modern rifles.

Towards the end of April the Afghan Commander-in-Chief arrived at Dakka, and the usual convoy proceeding through the Khaibar Pass was attacked on May 3rd by Afghan picquets; while it was at the same time discovered that the Afghan postmaster in Peshawar city was busily engaged in the distribution of leaflets, signed by the Amir, calling upon the Faithful to rise against the Infidel.

On May 5th the Field Army was mobilized, and was organized in three bodies—the North-West Frontier Force, the Baluchistan Force, and the Waziristan Force—and the plan of campaign was to advance against Jalalabad with the main striking force, thus dividing the Mohmands and Afridis, two of the most powerful of the border tribes, and cutting them off from Afghan support; to strike at any Afghan concentration within reach, and induce the withdrawal of enemy forces for the purpose of covering the Afghan capital.

On May 10th the Battalion left Jullundur for Peshawar, where it arrived in the early hours of the 12th, and while " A " and " C " Companies moved into Chitral Barracks, " B " and " D " were immediately dispatched into the city, then in a state of grave unrest, and here the duties of the two companies had to be carried out under extraordinary difficulties. All supplies had to come out daily from barracks under escort, only temporary arrangements could be made for cooking, the city garrison was divided into many picquets occupying various important points, and native buildings had to be made use of and made sanitary, while the heat by day at least was very great. The headquarter companies, too, in barracks were called upon to provide endless guards and escorts for armoured trains operating on the Peshawar—Jamrud line, while constant vigilance was necessary in view of recurring raids made by the tribesmen into the cantonment and city by night.

By May 28th more British battalions had been brought up to the frontier, and The Queen's, now being relieved by the 1st/4th West Kent and 2nd/4th Border Regiments, moved to Nowshera, where they took the place of the 1st South Lancashire Regiment, detaching a company to Risalpore as guard for the Royal Air Force aerodrome at that station. In June Major Gosney became Commandant, Landi Kotal section; and Captain Groves Commandant, Jamrud. At the end of July a peace conference attended by the Afghan delegates was opened at Rawal Pindi, and here a preliminary peace was signed on August 8th, and was duly ratified a month later, thus bringing the Third Afghan War at last to an end.

On September 5th the Battalion moved back to Peshawar, and here the demobilization which had been suspended was resumed, and the 1st/4th The Queen's were now placed under orders to proceed home, leaving in India with the 2nd Battalion of the Regiment all details not eligible for demobilization. Leaving Peshawar on October 3rd, the Battalion moved to and remained a few days at Jullundur, and at last left here by special train for Bombay, arriving there on the 18th, and embarking at once in the hired transport *Königin Luise*, which also accommodated the 1st/10th Battalion The Middlesex Regiment.

In the following words the Commander-in-Chief in India, General Sir Charles Monro, Bart., bade farewell to those units of the Territorial Force which had served in India during the four years' war :—

"*On your departure from India I desire to place on record my high appreciation of your services to the Empire during the period of the Great War.*

"*Many of you previous to the outbreak of war had, by joining the Territorial Force, already given proof of that patriotism and public spirit for which the Force has rendered itself so conspicuous. On the declaration of war your ranks were quickly filled by eager volunteers, animated by the same spirit of self-sacrifice ; when called upon to undertake the further obligation of service overseas your response was immediate and unanimous. By so doing you set free a large number of Regular units for service in the main theatre of war, at a time when every trained soldier was of the very greatest value. I share with you the disappointment which I know you all feel so keenly that it has not been your luck to fight the enemy in Europe. Many of you, however, have seen service on the Indian frontier, and by your conduct and bearing have added to the reputation of the famous regiments whose names you bear. For the greater portion of your service in India you have been engaged in the somewhat dull routine of garrison duty. The standard of efficiency which you attained both in training for war and in discipline, reflects the highest credit on you all.*

*" Since the termination of active fighting in all the theatres of war you have been subjected to the further stress of waiting for your relief. That you have appreciated the difficulties which the authorities have had to face in this respect is clear from the patience with which you have borne this trying period.*

*" You are now returning to your homes in the United Kingdom, and I bid you good-bye, God-speed, and a happy home-coming. As an old commander of a Territorial Division at home, I am proud to have again been associated with this Force in India."*

During its tour of Indian service the Battalion had suffered the following casualties :—Killed in action, 1 officer (Captain H. D. R. Reilly), and 1 man ; died of wounds, 2 officers (Captains J. C. Crowley and D. R. Potter) and 3 other ranks—2 in Mesopotamia and 1 in India ; died of disease, 61 non-commissioned officers and men, including 7 in Mesopotamia, 7 as prisoners of war in Egypt.

From first to last, the following officers served with the Battalion :—Lieutenant-Colonels N. E. Cutler, S. D. Roper and H. R. Atkins, Majors C. W. Wise, R. W. Potter, H. J. Gosney and L. G. Dibdin, Captains W. S. Hooker, T. S. Keith, A. R. Jefferis, W. H. Stacey, M. D. Helps, B. L. Evans, O. Featherstone, J. G. Fearon, J. C. Crowley, E. L. Turner, A. G. Potter, R. B. R. Falcon, E. J. Brown, R. L. Moss, D. R. Potter, A. Dibdin, O. K. Caroe, G. L. Groves, H. C. Gibsone, W. M. Maud, S. F. Bacon, H. D. R. Reilly and E. G. Frost, Lieutenants E. F. Charlesworth, L. L. Gosney, L. A. B. Edenborough, L. B. Howell, N. L. MacLennan, P. H. Cutler, H. C. Stone, D. G. K. Johnson, A. J. Sharpe, F. W. T. Hughes, J. S. Menhinick, H. E. Barrenger, A. V. Brandt, L. Bates, K. C. Groombridge, N. B. Greener, W. F. Hurry, R. E. Howell and H. Mason, Lieutenant-Colonel and Quartermaster J. Greer.

Attached officers : Captains F. M'G. Rodger and I. McI. Christie, Lieutenants T. M. Barclay, A. R. B. Wood, W. D. B. Read, L. Brotherton and A. H. Benson, Second-Lieutenants W. G. Endley, M. R. Riley, S. W. Lincoln and W. Stones.

The Battalion was constantly being drained of its efficient officers, non-commissioned officers and men for instructors at Training Schools, Indian Infantry regiments, signalling classes, machine guns, etc. ; while during the later half of the war three candidates per month had to be found for commissions.

On the night of November 12th the *Königin Luise* anchored in Plymouth Sound, and the 1st/4th Battalion The Queen's, disembarking, proceeded at once by train to Crowborough, which was reached on November 14th, and where the Battalion was accommodated in huts on Crowborough Beacon, the weather being exceptionally cold. Next day a party 150 strong was sent to Croydon, where it was accorded a civic reception and given a hearty welcome home.

During the next few days the Battalion was sent by small and larger parties to various dispersal stations, so that by November 18th only the cadre remained, and this was eventually removed from Crowborough to Croydon, where its duties were gradually closed down and the cadre of the Battalion was also dispersed.

Maps 11 and 12.

## CHAPTER XV.

### The 2nd/4th Battalion.

### 1915–1916.

#### Gallipoli and Egypt.

##### Battle Honours:

"Suvla," "Landing at Suvla," "Scimitar Hill," "Gallipoli, 1915," "Rumani," "Egypt, 1915–1916."

In accordance with the terms of an order quoted in the last chapter, the 2nd/4th Battalion The Queen's was raised in August, 1914, and was officially recognized on September 1st, when it was designated the 4th (Home Service) Battalion, a title later altered to that under which it was to be known throughout the war.

Originally raised and trained at Croydon, the Battalion was moved in the middle of November to Windsor, where it formed part of the Surrey Brigade of the 2nd Home Counties Division.

In April, 1915, the 2nd/4th and 2nd/5th Battalions of The Queen's formed between them a composite battalion for service overseas, each contributing an equal quota of officers and 540 and 460 other ranks respectively, the new unit being then at first known as "The Queen's Composite Battalion," and as such it proceeded to Cambridge under command of Colonel F. D. Watney, T.D., and there joined the 160th Brigade, commanded by Brigadier-General Hume, of the 53rd (Welch) Division. During the next two months the Battalion trained here and at Bedford, and from this last station was ordered to proceed overseas. Just prior to leaving, the title of the Battalion again became the 2nd/4th and so remained until the end of the war.

On July 16th the Battalion entrained for Devonport, embarking there two days later for "an unknown destination," in the steamship *Ulysses*, which also accommodated the Brigade staff, the 1st/4th Royal Sussex Regiment, and a detachment of the Royal Welch Fusiliers. Sailing the same evening, Malta was touched at and three days were spent first at Alexandria, and then at Port Said, 150 other ranks of the 900 comprising the strength of the 2nd/4th The Queen's being left behind at Port Said as a first reinforcement under Captain Twining. From Port Said the *Ulysses* sailed eastward to reinforce the army holding the beaches of the Gallipoli Peninsula.

Since the wonderful landing at Helles on April 25th the troops under General Hamilton's command had been hanging on to the toe of the Peninsula, suffering greatly from the fire of the enemy, and even more from the climate, and unable to force their way through to the possession of Constantinople, the aim and object of the expedition.

The troops now in Gallipoli had recently, however, been considerably reinforced, and with those now at his disposal and those on their way to him, Sir Ian Hamilton should have had available for any fresh operations a force of 13 divisions and 5 brigades, all, however, very considerably below strength and actually representing no more than 110,000 men. With the help of the newcomers, General Hamilton had decided to reinforce the Australian and New Zealand Army Corps at Anzac, to effect a landing in Suvla Bay, and from there to capture the hill known as Khoja Chemen Tepe, the main peak of Sari Bair, and so grip the Narrows of the Peninsula. In his despatch of December 11th, 1915, Sir Ian states that he proposed :—" (1) to break out with a rush from Anzac and cut off the bulk of the Turkish army from any land communication with Constantinople ; (2) to gain such a command for my artillery as to cut off the bulk of the Turkish army from sea traffic, whether with Constantinople or with Asia ; (3) incidentally, to secure Suvla Bay as a winter base for Anzac and all the troops operating in the northern theatre."

The operations in connection with this plan of campaign were to commence on August 6th, on which day the Army was distributed as follows :—

At Anzac : The Australian and New Zealand Corps, the 13th Division, an Indian Brigade, and a brigade of the 10th Division.

At Helles : The 29th, 42nd, 52nd, and Royal Naval Divisions, and 2 French Divisions.

At Mitylene : The 31st and half the 30th Brigades.

At Lemnos : The other half of the 30th Brigade.

At Imbros : The 11th Division,

while the 53rd and 54th Divisions, with the last of the promised reinforcements, were then approaching Mudros, and it had been originally intended that these should be landed there, remaining available as a general reserve, but actually on arrival off Mudros Harbour these were hurried on to Suvla Bay without disembarking.

From Port Said the 2nd/4th The Queen's prosecuted their voyage to Mudros and thence to Suvla, landing at " C " Beach on the night of August 8th-9th ; on this day the Battalion suffered its first casualty, one of the men falling down a hatchway and dying of his injuries.

Something should now be said about the features of the Peninsula and the dispositions of the invading army. The Australians held the edge of the plateau at the top of the long ravines or gullies which ran down to the sea. Eastwards the land rises in the uplands of Sari Bair till about a mile and a half north-east of the position the culminating point of Khoja Chemen Tepe is reached. On all sides the ground slopes away from the crest, distant some four miles as the crow flies from the waters of the Straits. North and west a jumble of ridges falls towards the Gulf of Saros, ridges wildly broken and confused, sometimes bare and sometimes matted with scrub, and separated by dry nullahs. From a point on the shore of the Gulf of Saros south of the Fisherman's Hut, a fairly well-marked ridge runs up to the summit of Khoja Chemen Tepe. North of this spur is a watercourse called the Sazli Beit Dere, and a little further north the Chailak Dere. Separating the two is a long spur which leaves the main range just west of Chanuk Bair ; north of Chailak Dere is another ridge, and still further north a wide watercourse, the Aghyl Dere. From the Fisherman's Hut the flat ground between the hills and the sea widens north as the coast sweeps round towards Niebrunessi Cape, and beyond it is the half-moon of Suvla or Anafarta Bay, two miles wide, enclosed between Niebrunessi and the Cape of Suvla Burnu, the north-western extremity of the Gallipoli Peninsula.

The hinterland of Suvla Bay consists of a rectangle of hills lying north of the Azmak Dere watercourse, and connected towards the east with the outflankers of the Khoja Chemen Tepe system.

The north side, lining the crest, is the ridge of Karakol Dagh, over 400 feet high. The south side, lining the Azmak Dere and breaking down into flats two miles from the sea, is a blunt range, rising as high as 800 feet, of which the western part is Yilghin Burnu, called by our troops Chocolate Hill. The eastern side of the rectangle is a rocky crest, rising in one part to nearly 900 feet, and falling shorewards in two well-marked terraces. Between the three sides of the hills, from the eastern terraces to the sea, the ground is nearly flat. Along the edge of Suvla Bay runs a narrow causeway of sand, and immediately behind it is a large salt lake, partly dried up in summer, but always liable to be converted by rain into a swamp. East of it the hills and flats are patched with farms and scrub, mostly dwarf oak, and on the edge of the terraces the scrub grows into something like woodland; everywhere the plain is cracked with dry watercourses.

Two villages are points in the hinterland, Little Anafarta, on the slopes of the south-eastern angle of the enclosing hills, and Big Anafarta, two miles south across the watercourse of the Azmak Dere and just under the northern spurs of Khoja Chemen Tepe. The road connecting the two villages runs south to Boghali Kalessi on the Straits.

The British plan of attack involved four separate actions: a feint was to be made at the head of the Gulf of Saros, as if to take in flank and rear the Bulair Lines; a strong offensive was to be assumed in the Helles area against Achi Baba, in the hopes of attracting the Turkish reserves to Krithia; the Anzac Corps was to attempt to gain the heights of Khoja Chemen Tepe and the seaward ridges; and simultaneously a new landing was to be made at Suvla Bay. If the Anafarta Hills could be captured and the right of the new landing force linked up with the left of the Australians, the British would hold the central crest of the uplands running through the western end of the Peninsula, cutting the enemy communications and resulting in the capture of Achi Baba and the Pasha Dagh tableland.

The following order was now issued by the Commander of the Expeditionary Force :—

"*Soldiers of the Old Army and the New!*

"*Some of you have already won imperishable renown at our first landing, or have since built up our footholds upon the Peninsula, yard by yard, with deeds of heroism and endurance. Others have arrived just in time to take part in our next great fight against Germany and Turkey, the would-be oppressors of the human race.*

"*You, Veterans, are about to add fresh lustre to your arms. Happen what may, so much at least is certain.*

"*As to you, Soldiers of the new formations, you are privileged indeed to have the chance vouchsafed you of playing a decisive part in events which may herald the birth of a new and happier World. You stand for the great cause of Freedom. In the hour of trial remember this, and the faith that is in you will bring you victoriously through.*"

On August 6th the attacks commenced by the forces at Helles and by the Australians at Anzac; the former were successful in so far that they distracted the attention of the enemy from the main operations in the north, while the Australians, after severe and costly fighting, secured touch with the right wing of the Suvla Bay force at Susuk Kuyu on the Azmak Dere on August 12th.

The force intended to land at and advance from Suvla Bay was made up of the 10th, 11th, 53rd and 54th Divisions of the new IX Corps, and was commanded by Lieutenant-General Sir F. W. Stopford.

On August 6th the 11th Division embarked at Imbros, and the transports conveying it entered Suvla Bay the same night without attracting the attention of the Turks. Three landing places had been selected where the troops were to be put on shore—" A," north of the Salt Lake, and " B " and " C " to the south-west of it. The 11th Division landed before dawn on August 7th, and held both sides of the Bay and the neck of land between them, and at daybreak six battalions of the 10th Division arrived from Mitylene, followed a little later by the remainder of the Division from Lemnos. These were also put on shore, under some enemy opposition, but by 2 p.m. the two divisions held a line east of the Salt Lake and running from the Karakol Dagh to a point near the ridge of Yilghin Burnu; but though the latter hill was carried that night and the flanks were practically safeguarded, matters now came to a standstill and the elements of a surprise had vanished.

During the days that immediately followed many attempts were made to advance, but very little ground was gained, and it was soon abundantly clear that enemy reinforcements had arrived.

The 53rd British Division landed on the 8th, and the 54th on the 11th, and the next few days were passed in consolidating the front line, which then ran from Azmak Dere across Chocolate Hill to the 11th Division on the left.

For the next ten days the Suvla operations languished, and we must now turn to the part played up to this time by the 2nd/4th The Queen's.

At dawn on August 9th the Battalion, with the 1st/4th Royal Sussex, was ordered to proceed to a spot west of Chocolate Hill and there entrench, but very shortly afterwards The Queen's were directed to report to the 31st Brigade on Hill 53, the Sussex Battalion being held in reserve behind Lala Baba. The Battalion marched accordingly in artillery formation across the southern side of the Salt Lake, coming *en route* under shell fire and incurring several casualties. But on arrival at Hill 53 instructions were received that The Queen's were to be attached to the 33rd Brigade, and they were then ordered to move round the northern slope of Hill 53, there consolidate a position and support the troops in front, who at the time were being very hard pressed. So at 9 a.m. this day The Queen's joined the headquarters of the 6th Dublin Fusiliers, of the 10th Division, who were in reserve to the Border, Stafford and Lincoln Battalions of the 33rd Brigade of the 11th Division.

The 2nd/4th The Queen's accordingly pushed forward and gained the top of Hill 53, where they came under heavy fire and were for a time forced to retire; but, advancing anew, the crest was reoccupied and held until the position had to be abandoned owing to the scrub catching fire. Up to this time the Battalion had suffered a loss of 8 officers and about 250 other ranks in killed, wounded and missing.

At noon the Battalion was concentrated in an old Turkish trench, and the position was strengthened and a line of defence organized; no further orders were received that day, but in the afternoon a battalion of the Royal Sussex Regiment came up and prolonged the line to the left. The enemy kept up a heavy fire all night, but showed no disposition to attack. Then on the morning of the 10th a message came through the 33rd Brigade that the 53rd Division was to attack

Hill 70, and that in the event of success The Queen's were to move forward and take up ground further east. This attack, however, failed, and the Battalion was ordered to hold the original trenches at all costs; this was a line some 400 yards in length opposite Hill 70. Finally, on the night of the 12th, the Battalion was relieved, and rejoined its own brigade on the north-western side of Lala Baba.

After only one day spent on the beach The Queen's returned to the trenches, and were now continuously in the firing line up to the end of the month. Here the daily routine was the digging of trenches, and the intense heat by day coupled with the great drop in temperature at sundown produced the inevitable sickness among men who were without greatcoats, blankets or ground sheets.

In the meantime preparations were in hand for another attempt to advance. The 29th Division was brought round from Helles and added to the large force at Suvla, as was also the 2nd Mounted Division, and the whole Suvla force was now placed under General de Lisle.

The objective now was the circle of hills behind the Suvla plain, extending from Hill 70, now in possession of the Turks, to Ismail Oglu Tepe. All advantage of surprise had by this gone, the enemy position was held in equal or even superior strength, and all that remained to be attempted was a frontal attack.

On the afternoon of August 21st the 11th and 29th Divisions attacked under the cover of a great bombardment of the ridges, and when the gallant attempts made by these troops failed, the Mounted Division was sent in, but by daylight on the 23rd all these divisions had been obliged to fall back to the positions whence they had started, and the final effort against Anafarta had failed. All that had been achieved in the course of three weeks of desperate and very costly fighting was the gain of a little more room in the Anzac zone.

During the attack by the 11th and 29th Divisions on August 21st, the 160th Brigade was on the right of the 53rd Division, which was between the 10th and 29th, the 2nd/4th The Queen's being on the right of the Brigade and having on their right the King's Own Scottish Borderers, the left battalion of the 29th Division; and the Battalion did all possible to assist the advance of the 29th Division with machine-gun and rifle fire. From this day until the end of the month The Queen's held a portion of the front line trenches situated north-west of Hill 70, being throughout subjected to constant sniping and shelling by day and night, and suffering many casualties therefrom, until on the evening of August 31st the Brigade was relieved and went back into reserve on the eastern side of Hill 10, and even here was perpetually under shell fire.

When on September 2nd Brigadier-General Hume was invalided, Colonel Watney of The Queen's assumed temporary command of the 160th Brigade, and Major Few, and later Major Tredgold, that of the Battalion, but after three weeks, Colonel Watney was back again with the 2nd/4th. Invaliding, however, produced further changes—Major Tredgold being sent away sick on September 26th, Colonel Watney on the day following, and by the end of this month Captain Hull was in command, when only 5 officers and 335 other ranks remained out of the 27 officers and 900 non-commissioned officers and men who had landed on the Peninsula less than two months previously. Then, out of the 335 other ranks over 100 were on light duty, for the continued strain of days and nights under fire, coupled with dysentery which had by this become serious, had taken a heavy toll of the men, During September a few officers joined, and in November a very welcome draft, 100 strong, arrived from England under Lieutenant P. C. Duncan.

During these weeks the Battalion took its full share of duty in the front line, and when withdrawn from the immediate front was busily employed on the construction of various lines of defences about Lala Baba.

As the month of November wore on, it became apparent that the Turks had received heavier guns and ample stores of ammunition; and then at the end of the month the weather changed very much for the worse. On the 27th it rained torrentially for twelve hours, when the trenches became running streams and every gully a raging torrent. Next day the wind veered round to the north, and a bitter frost followed, succeeded in turn by a snow blizzard. The effects of the storm were especially severely felt at Suvla, where there were 200 deaths from exposure, sentries being found dead at their posts, and over 10,000 sick were evacuated in a week. The gale lasted three days and was then happily followed by a spell of milder weather. The 1st/4th Royal Sussex Regiment was now attached to the 2nd/4th The Queen's, when the combined strength of the two battalions amounted to no more than 350 non-commissioned officers and men. The losses in the Expeditionary Force had indeed been exceptionally heavy, totalling by December 11th, when the campaign had been some seven months only in progress, 25,000 of all ranks killed, over 75,000 wounded, and 12,000 missing, while the admissions to hospital in that time came to 95,000. The chief ailments were dysentery and para-typhoid, the type of the first-named of these diseases demanding very special nursing and entailing a prolonged period of convalescence.

Before this time, however, there had been a change in the command of the Force, while the decision had reluctantly been come to for the withdrawal of all troops from the Gallipoli Peninsula. The military authorities in England had by this time realized the excessive cost of the operations, the meagre chances of their ultimate success, and the increasing difficulty of providing the necessary reinforcements, due regard being had to the needs of the main theatre of the war. Early in October General Hamilton had been asked for an estimate of the possible losses to be expected should withdrawal be decided upon, and on receiving a reply that these might well amount to 50 per cent., Sir Ian was directed to return home to consult with Lord Kitchener and to hand over the command of the Force to General Sir Charles Monro.

On leaving for home General Sir Ian Hamilton issued the following farewell order :—

"*In handing over the command of the Mediterranean Expeditionary Force to General Sir C. C. Monro, the Commander-in-Chief wishes to say a few farewell words to the Allied troops with many of whom he has now for so long been associated. First, he would like them to know his deep sense of the honour it has been to command so fine an army in one of the most arduous and difficult campaigns which has ever been undertaken; secondly, he must express to them his admiration of the noble response which they have invariably given to the calls he has made upon them. No risk has been too desperate, no sacrifice too great. Sir Ian Hamilton thanks all ranks, from generals to private soldiers, for the wonderful way they have seconded his efforts to lead them towards that decisive victory, which, under their new Chief, he has the most implicit confidence they will achieve.*"

General Monro arrived on the Peninsula on October 30th, and reported very strongly against any continuation of the enterprise, urging immediate and complete evacuation; but before any decision was finally come to, Lord Kitchener visited the Dardanelles, interviewed all the naval and military chiefs on the spot, and then finally and with reluctance, decided in favour of withdrawal, for which the necessary orders were issued early in November. The evacuation could not, of course, immediately take place, for the operation was a very difficult one involving great risks, the opposing trenches being nowhere more than 300 yards apart and in some places less than one-tenth of that distance; while at Suvla and Anzac alone there were more than 83,000 men to be taken off, besides guns, horses, mules, carts, and stores of all kinds. The success of the withdrawal depended upon four conditions—good staff work, high discipline, fine weather and secrecy; happily, all these were available in high degree.

The evacuation at Suvla commenced on December 10th, and by 5.30 a.m. on the 20th the bay was empty, every man, gun, vehicle and animal being embarked, all that was left behind being a small stock of supplies which at the last moment was set on fire. The 2nd/4th The Queen's embarked on December 13th and proceeded direct to Mudros, where what was left of the 160th Brigade embarked in the transport *Haverfordwest*, reaching Alexandria on the 19th, and, on disembarkation, being sent to camp at Wardan.

The casualties suffered during the campaign by the 2nd/4th The Queen's amounted to :—Killed, died of wounds or missing, 4 officers and 78 other ranks; wounded, 9 officers and 198 other ranks; died of disease, 4 other ranks; invalided, 16 officers and 400 other ranks.

Of the manner of the evacuation General Monro said in a Special Order of the Day :—

"*The arrangements made for withdrawal and for keeping the enemy in ignorance of the operation which was taking place, could not have been improved. The General Officer Commanding the Dardanelles Army and the General Officers Commanding the Australian and New Zealand and IX Army Corps, may pride themselves on an achievement without parallel in the annals of war.*

"*The Army and Corps Staffs, divisional and subordinate commanders and their staffs, and the naval and military beach staffs, proved themselves more than equal to the most difficult task which could have been thrown upon them. Regimental officers, non-commissioned officers and men carried out, without a hitch, the most trying operation which soldiers can be called upon to undertake—a withdrawal in the face of the enemy—in a manner reflecting the highest credit on the discipline and soldierly qualities of the troops.*

"*It is no exaggeration to call this achievement one without parallel. To disengage and to withdraw from a bold and active enemy is the most difficult of all military operations; and in this case the withdrawal was effected by surprise, with the opposing forces at close grips—in many cases within a few yards of each other. Such an operation when succeeded by a re-embarkation from an open beach, is one for which military history contains no precedent.*

"*During the past months the troops of Great Britain and Ireland, Australia and New Zealand, Newfoundland and India, fighting side by side, have invariably proved their superiority over the enemy, have contained the best fighting troops in the Ottoman Army in their front, and have prevented the Germans from employing their Turkish Allies against us elsewhere.*

"*No soldier relishes undertaking a withdrawal from before the enemy. It is hard to leave behind the graves of good comrades, and to relinquish positions so hardly won and so gallantly maintained as those we have left. But all ranks in the Dardanelles Army will realize that in this matter they were but carrying out the orders of His Majesty's Government, so that they might in due course be more usefully employed in fighting elsewhere for their King, their Country, and the Empire.*

*" There is only one consideration—what is best for the furtherance of the common cause. In that spirit the withdrawal was carried out, and in that spirit the Australian and New Zealand and the IX Army Corps have proved, and will continue to prove, themselves second to none as soldiers of the Empire."*

The 2nd/4th The Queen's remained at Wardan until February 5th, 1916, by which time the men were refitted and drafts had arrived, and these brought the strength of the Battalion by the middle of February up to approximately 500 of all ranks; and on the 16th the 2nd/4th entrained for Deir el Azab in Fayoum, where training was vigorously carried out for some three months, by which time the weather had become very hot, and the heat was much felt by the men in their single-fly tents.

In January of this year General Sir Archibald Murray had assumed command of all the troops in Egypt, his task being to protect that country from attack from the east; and while there had at the end of 1915 been a large massing of troops in Egypt, added to by the arrival in January, 1916, of the Divisions from Gallipoli, the evacuation of the Peninsula had equally released the whole of the Turkish Fifth Army, and General Murray estimated that the enemy undoubtedly now had at his command 250,000 men, or even more, available for an attack upon Egypt. To meet this there were at one time as many as thirteen divisions in Egypt, but the re-embarkation of troops for service in other theatres commenced in February, and went on until the end of March—the 13th Division going to Mesopotamia, the VIII and the Anzac Corps to France—but there still remained a tolerably large force in Egypt and work was soon found for these troops on both western and eastern borders.

Trouble on the western frontier, in the country of the Senussi, had started in August, 1915, but activities here came to something like a close in March of the year following, by which time on the eastern border, in the Sinai Desert, Turkish forces from the Beersheba base continued operations in a spasmodic manner.

There are three main routes across the desert to the Suez Canal—the coast route by El Arish to Kantara, the central route from El Audja to Ismailia, and the southern route from Akaba to Suez, the last mentioned being the pilgrim road from Egypt to Mecca. British parties had been pushed out east as far as the oasis of Katia on the northern route about 30 miles from the Canal, and in the middle of April the Australian mounted troops raided Jifjaffa, about 60 miles from the Canal on the central route; and from this date onwards during the next few weeks the advanced troops on either side were constantly engaged in affairs of outposts.

In May the 2nd/4th The Queen's moved to Ismailia, thence to Ferry Post on the Canal, and then on June 20th a further move was made to railhead about 8 miles into the desert from the Canal, the Battalion becoming here brigade reserve; and on July 11th, when Colonel Watney had left the Battalion and returned to England, the 2nd/4th The Queen's took over the left of the line of works covering Ferry Post, some 13 miles out in the desert and situated among sand-hills. Here the Brigade had a frontage of more than 7 miles with five defensive posts, each of which had to be reconstructed and wired into defended localities; this work was very heavy owing to the shifting sand, while by reason of the heat, which was now very great, the men could only work after sundown and in the early morning.

The activity of German troops on the Baghdad and Syrian railways, and the accumulation of stores at various points from Alexandretta to Beersheba, pointed to another enemy advance against Egypt and the Suez Canal, but on June 9th the Grand Sherif of Mecca, supported by many Arab tribes, proclaimed Arab independence of Turkey, occupied Mecca and Taif, and besieged Medina. The revolt spread rapidly both on the Red Sea littoral and northward to Damascus, and these activities caused the Turks to divert part of the force which had been intended for the invasion of Egypt.

The Hedjaz revolt delayed and rendered less serious, but did not prevent, the attack on the defences of Egypt, which was delivered by the northern route on August 3rd by a Turkish force under the German soldier, von Kressenstein, who hoped to find the desert front weakly held and to break through by surprise. The British, however, were strongly entrenched on a line some 7 miles in length from Rumani, 23 miles east of the Canal, to the Mediterranean; the left was protected by British ships of war in the Bay of Tinah, while on the right were the Australian and New Zealand Mounted Troops. The attack ended in the rout and pursuit of the Turks and the capture of about 4,000 prisoners, while a loss of some 5,000 killed and wounded was inflicted on the enemy.

The launching of this attack caused the hurried move of The Queen's on August 5th to Kantara, and next day to Hill 40, some 6 miles nearer Rumani, but in view of the decisive defeat of the enemy the services of the 160th Brigade were not now needed, and no further advance was made.

On August 21st command of the Battalion was assumed by Lieutenant-Colonel H. W. M. Watson, K.R.R.C., and on the 24th the 2nd/4th The Queen's moved by Kantara to Ismailia, where during the next two months steady Battalion and Brigade Training was carried out.

During the autumn of 1916 the new railway was pushed steadily out into the desert, while a 12-inch water-pipe was laid from the Canal, eventually reaching as far as Southern Palestine. Kantara itself, where the railway and pipe-line started, became an important terminus, while in the desert were strong positions well entrenched and wired, with standing camps, tanks, and reservoirs, aerodromes, signal stations, and wireless installations.

Everything was now in train for making the advance which was to clear the Sinai Desert of all enemy troops up to the Egyptian frontier, and, if necessary, to push forward into Palestine; General Headquarters moved from Ismailia to Cairo on October 23rd, the headquarters of the Eastern Force coming into existence at Ismailia under Lieutenant-General Sir C. Dobell; the advanced portion of this latter body was the Desert Column, later commanded by Lieutenant-General Sir P. Chetwode, consisting for the most part of mounted troops and camel corps.

On November 22nd the 160th Brigade marched via El Ferdan to Kantara, where the mules in possession were replaced by camels; and on the 27th the Brigade commenced its march across the desert, bivouacking at El Abd, where work on the construction of defensive localities was carried out on a line sited for defence by a division.

On December 19th the Turkish garrison of El Arish evacuated the place and fell back on Magdhaba, out of which they were driven on the 23rd, retreating on the main enemy body which was entrenched near Rafa, 30 miles north-east of El Arish; from this place also they were ejected on January 9th, 1917, whereby the whole of the Sinai Desert was cleared of Turkish troops, and all was ready for an advance to the Gaza—Beersheba Line. For such an advance General Sir A. Murray now had the following troops at his command :—The 52nd, 53rd, and 54th Divisions, the Australian and New Zealand Mounted Division, the Imperial Mounted Division, and the Imperial Camel Corps.

Maps 12, 13 and 6.

## CHAPTER XVI.

### The 2nd/4th Battalion (*continued*.)

### 1917–1919.

#### PALESTINE AND FRANCE.

##### Battle Honours:

"Marne, 1918," "Soissonnais-Ourcq," "Gaza," "El Mughar," "Jerusalem," "Jericho," "Tell 'Asur," "Palestine, 1917–18."

" Situated at the point of an outlying westerly spur of the Palestine Ridge, and where the coastal plain is narrowest, Gaza forms a kind of gateway barring advance from Sinai to the north. Gaza had been converted into a fortress of the first class, surrounded by earth works among the sand dunes lying between the town and the coast, and by works on the heights behind it. All these defences were heavily wired in. But along the spur extending inland, and in the triangle of country between the Wadi es Sheria and the Wadi Ghuzze, other defences had been laid out. They extended, indeed, as far as Beersheba, nearly 30 miles from the sea. To Beersheba there is a mule track from Rafa, and then through the hills north to Hebron a mountain road, but too rugged for wheeled traffic. It is not until Hebron, 25 miles north of Beersheba, is reached that this road, continued to Jerusalem, becomes practicable for vehicles. Beersheba owes its existence to its wells."\*

On January 11th, 1917, the 2nd/4th The Queen's moved from El Abd to Mazar, and on the 22nd Colonel H. St. C. Wilkins, a Regular officer of the Regiment, assumed command of the Battalion in the place of Lieutenant-Colonel Watson, who had been invalided home early in the previous month; and then on the 30th a further move was made to El Arish which was reached on February 1st. Here for nearly three weeks the Battalion was employed in laying wire roads, in the perfecting of the El Arish position and in training generally, until on the 22nd an advance was made to Sheikh Zowaid, where an outpost line was taken up and digging and wiring began again. Here was now the headquarters of the Desert Column, in advance of which the mounted troops were covering the construction of the railway which was being rapidly extended along the coast towards Rafa. Preparations were now made for an attack upon the enemy in a strong position in front upon which for weeks he had been busily working, but in the first week of March he fell back from here, retiring until he was out of reach and distributing his troops between Gaza and Tel el Sheria with a small garrison at Bir Saba.

It was desirable to engage the enemy as soon as possible lest he fall back upon more favourable lines in rear, and two possible plans presented themselves; either to make for Beersheba and so reach the Central Palestine railway, or to move up the coast with Gaza as the objective, aiming at the Turkish right flank; the disadvantage of the first plan was that such an advance would have brought the British line of communications from Rafa parallel to the enemy's front and so given

\* Dane, *British Campaigns in the Near East*, vol. 2, p. 71.

him an easy target for a counter-stroke, while the advantage of the second plan was that the left flank would be covered by the sea, the pipe-line would provide water, and the railway could more easily be laid along the flats of the plain than among the sandhills of the interior. " I decided, therefore," writes General Murray in his despatch,* " to continue for the present a methodical advance up the coast, moving troops forward as the railway could supply them, together with energetic preparation of the force for an attack in strength as soon as the state of its communications should make that possible."

On March 8th the 2nd/4th The Queen's moved up to railhead, and on March 21st it crossed the frontier at Rafa, where the railway had arrived on the 15th. The Desert Column was now between Rafa and Sheikh Zowaid, the 52nd Division being at Sheikh Zowaid, the 53rd at Rafa, and the 54th between Sheikh Zowaid and El Arish.

March 24th and 25th were occupied in the preliminary operations, covered by the cavalry, for the attack on Gaza which began with a night march on the 25th over the Wadi Ghuzze. The enemy's front did not consist of a continuous line of trenches, and the greater part of his troops were well to the north-east of Gaza, but there was a considerable garrison in that town, and hostile posts were echeloned to the south-east as far as Beersheba.

The British plan of attack was as follows :—The Cavalry of the Desert Column was to advance early on March 26th and occupy the country east and north of the town to prevent the arrival of Turkish reinforcements, and to cut off the enemy's retreat. The 53rd Division was to follow the cavalry and attack Gaza in front ; the 54th Division was to move on the right rear of the 53rd holding the Sheikh Abbas Ridge in case of an attack from the east or south-east, with one brigade placed rather to the west in readiness to support the Desert Column ; the 52nd Division was to be held in general reserve. The objects of the advance were, first, to seize the line of the Wadi Ghuzze to cover the advance of the railway ; secondly, at all costs to prevent the Turks again falling back without a fight ; and thirdly, if possible, to capture Gaza by a *coup de main* and cut off its garrison. The main intention, in fact, was less the occupation of Gaza than the capture of the 7,000 Turks forming its garrison.

The mounted troops moved off early on the 26th, crossed the Wadi, and headed for Beit Durdis, 5 miles east of Gaza, the Imperial Mounted Division and Camel Corps moved due east for El Mendur ; from both places patrols were pushed out and these troops were heavily engaged all day. In the meantime the 53rd Division, under Major-General A. G. Dallas, C.B., C.M.G., having thrown out strong bridgeheads before dawn, crossed the Wadi Ghuzze at a point some three miles from the coast, with one brigade on the right directed on the Mansura Ridge and another on the left of El Sheluf, some miles south of Gaza on the ridge running south-west from that place. The third brigade was held in reserve and also covered the left on the coast. The 54th Division, less one brigade ordered to Mansura to assist the 53rd, took up a position on the Sheikh Abbas Ridge.

The 53rd Division deployed on the line El Sheluf—Mansura to attack the Ali Muntar position with the following objectives :—One brigade astride the El Sheluf—Ali Muntar Ridge on the enemy's south-western defences ; one brigade moving north from Mansura on the prominent Ali Muntar Ridge on the southern outskirts of the town ; and one brigade, less one battalion in divisional reserve, pivoting on

* Of June 28th, 1917.

## THE FIRST BATTLE OF GAZA

the right of the last-named brigade on the hill 1,200 yards north-east of Ali Muntar, in co-operation with the attack of that brigade.

The deployment of the leading brigades commenced at 11.50 a.m., and the brigade in reserve moved forward shortly afterwards to its assigned position. Assisted by our guns and long-range machine-gun fire, the left brigade pressed forward along the ridge, the others over the flat, open ground, practically devoid of cover. The final advance, which began just before 1 p.m., was very steady, and all the troops behaved magnificently, the enemy offering a stout resistance. At the same time General Sir P. Chetwode flung the whole of the Australian and New Zealand Mounted Division against Gaza to support the attack of the 53rd Division, bringing the Imperial Mounted Division further north to act as a screen against enemy reinforcements from the railway now seen to be rapidly coming up. By 4.30 p.m. the 53rd Division had carried the greater part of Ali Muntar, and was closing in on Gaza from the south, while the Australians and New Zealanders were in the eastern streets; the brigade of the 54th Division, placed at the disposal of General Dallas, now came up and after a hard struggle captured the remainder of the position and pushed on for nearly a mile beyond the crest.

When darkness fell the situation was as follows:—Gaza was enveloped; the 53rd Division was occupying the Ali Muntar position, but its flank was very much in the air; the 54th, less one brigade, was holding Sheikh Abbas with its left about $2\frac{1}{2}$ miles from the flank of the 53rd, while the whole of the mounted divisions were very much extended, their horses were greatly exhausted, and strong enemy columns with guns were moving to the relief of Gaza from three directions. There was not sufficient daylight remaining to complete the capture of Gaza, and the whole force was now ordered to retire. This it did, attacked in flank and rear, and nothing but the valour of the troops and the heavy losses inflicted on the Turks saved the situation. By daylight on the 27th the British line north of the Wadi Ghuzze ran in a sharp salient along the El Sire and El Burjalife ridges, the 53rd Division on the left, and the 54th on the right, with the Gloucestershire Hussars on the coastal flank, and the Camel Corps between the right flank and the Wadi.

The garrison of Gaza had now been strongly reinforced, and the British patrols sent forward were driven in, while the British rear south of Mansura was shelled by Turks who had succeeded in reaching the Sheikh Abbas Ridge. None the less, the 53rd and 54th Divisions clung to their ground until dark, when a further retirement was ordered, and the troops fell back to the other side of the Wadi Ghuzze, taking up there a strong position covering Deir el Belah. "The troops engaged," wrote General Murray, "both cavalry, camelry, and infantry, especially the 53rd Division and the brigade of the 54th, which had not been seriously in action since the evacuation of Suvla Bay at the end of 1915, fought with the utmost gallantry and endurance, and showed to the full the splendid fighting qualities which they possess."

The 2nd/4th Battalion of The Queen's took its full share in the first Battle of Gaza; on the first day it was in brigade reserve, except for one company, which was pushed up to support the firing line late in the afternoon; and on the second day it was in the fighting area until about 3 p.m., and even held a position until 8 p.m., only re-crossing the Wadi Ghuzze about three o'clock on the morning of the 28th, when at last it was able to rest and recuperate after two days and three nights of continuous marching and fighting, during which the excessive heat added greatly to the exhaustion of all ranks of the Battalion, which had suffered losses amounting to 106 officers and other ranks.

The casualties by ranks were :—1 officer (Captain R. W. Spicer) and 3 other ranks killed or died of wounds ; 11 officers and 87 non-commissioned officers and men were wounded, while 1 officer (Lieutenant C. G. F. Ingram) and 1 man were missing. The wounded officers were Major L. H. F. Beach, Captain P. C. Duncan, Lieutenant and Quartermaster I. S. Keen, Second-Lieutenants P. Fripp, A. R. T. Philips, R. J. Harrison, J. D. Hodges, P. H. Laughlin, T. F. Griffin, S. G. Hillyer, and F. W. T. Hughes.

From now until April 11th the Battalion was engaged in preparing various positions, subjected at all times to shell fire, and then made ready a line of trenches at the Red House by the Wadi Ghuzze which it moved to and occupied on the 16th. In the meantime the railway had been advanced to Deir el Belah.

The Gaza position was now very much more strongly held than when attacked at the end of March, when the line of posts was occupied by two Turkish divisions only ; there were now no fewer than five divisions opposing the British, with a cavalry division and very many heavy guns. The inner defences of the town also— the Ali Muntar Ridge—had been enormously strengthened, there was a powerful line of outer defences from the sea to Sheikh Abbas, and on the east a new trench system 12,000 yards in length had been constructed from Gaza south-east to the Atawineh Ridge.

As soon as the first Battle of Gaza came to an end, preparations were at once put in hand for a second attack upon the Gaza position in greater force, which in this case was to take the form of a frontal attack in two stages, the first to carry the outer defences, and the second to break through the Ali Muntar position and carry Gaza. For this purpose the 53rd Division, now under Major-General S. F. Mott, was to stand north of the Wadi Ghuzze and carry out strong reconnaissances along the coast ; the 52nd on the right was to advance against the ridge running south-west from Ali Muntar ; on the right again of the 52nd, the 54th was to attack the line Mansura—Sheikh Abbas ; one mounted division was to protect the right of the infantry, the other to watch any enemy movement in the direction of Hareira ; while the 74th Division was in reserve.

The attack began at dawn on April 17th and the first stage was successful, the line Sheikh Abbas—Mansura—Kurd Hill being taken by 7 a.m., and during the 18th the position was consolidated. It was now the rôle of the 53rd Division to push north along the shore against the trenches south-west of Gaza, its first objective being the line Sheikh Ajlin—Samson Ridge ; the 52nd was to take the ridge running south-east from Ali Muntar, while the 54th was directed against Ali Muntar itself, and the enemy position at Khirbet Sihan.

The 53rd Division attacked at 7.15 a.m. the remaining divisions fifteen minutes later, and the 53rd captured Samson Ridge and reached its first objective early in the afternoon, but the attacks by the other two divisions were only partially successful, and at nightfall while the 53rd held their gains, the 52nd and 54th had made little progress and the three divisions had between them suffered a loss of some 7,000 men. The position reached was, however, consolidated during April 20th.

During the second Battle of Gaza the 2nd/4th The Queen's was employed as the connecting link between the 53rd and 52nd Divisions, and at the close of the fighting on the 19th was in a position on Heart Hill on the edge of the sandhills ; its casualties during the day were not heavy, only 1 officer (Second-Lieutenant D. G. K. Johnson) and 38 other ranks being wounded, for the most part lightly. After digging in on Heart Hill the Battalion was withdrawn to a rest position on April 23rd, and on

# THE ADVANCE ON BEERSHEBA

the 26th Second-Lieutenant G. H. Mapleson was killed by a sniper. The Battalion moved forward again on May 2nd in rear of the trenches as brigade reserve. On the 7th the 2nd/4th The Queen's marched from the Wadi Ghuzze to Dorset House, arriving here on the 8th.

At the end of June General Sir E. Allenby arrived to take over from General Sir A. Murray the command of the Egyptian Expeditionary Force, when the main features of the situation on the Palestine front were as follows :—" The Turkish Army in Southern Palestine held a strong position extending from the sea at Gaza, roughly along the main Gaza—Beersheba road, to Beersheba. Gaza had been made into a strong modern fortress, heavily entrenched and wired, offering every facility for protracted defence. The remainder of the enemy's line consisted of a series of strong localities, viz., the Sihan group of works, the Atawineh group, the Baha group, the Abu Hareira—Arab el Teeaha trench system, and finally the works covering Beersheba. These groups of works were generally from 1,500 to 2,000 yards apart, except that the distance from the Hareira group to Beersheba was about $4\frac{1}{2}$ miles. The enemy's force was on a wide front, the distance from Gaza to Beersheba being about 30 miles, but his lateral communications were good, and any threatened point of the line could be very quickly reinforced.

" My force was extended on a front of 22 miles, from the sea, opposite Gaza, to Gamli."*

There was no further infantry action during the summer months, and on May 25th The Queen's took over the front line about El Mendur ; the position here consisted of five front-line posts, but besides holding and strengthening these, three others had to be constructed in rear and the whole wired in so as to form a defended locality, the perimeter of which was about $3\frac{1}{2}$ miles. During July the Battalion was twice moved, but by August 3rd the Brigade was back again in the front line, The Queen's being now, however, in brigade reserve.

By this time the line of supply and communication had been greatly improved and extended, the railway having been prolonged to Karm, while lines were under construction from Gamli, the extreme right of the British position, to El Buggar, and on the left from Deir el Belah to Wadi Ghuzze.

General Allenby had now " decided to strike the main blow against the left flank of the main Turkish position, Hareira and Sheria. The capture of Beersheba was a necessary preliminary to this operation, in order to secure the water supplies at that place and to give room for the deployment of the attacking force on the high ground to the north and north-west of Beersheba, from which direction I intended to attack the Hareira—Sheria line."

The date for the attack on Beersheba was fixed as October 31st and the troops detailed for the operations reached their positions of deployment by a night march, and were all in place by the time appointed. The plan was to attack the enemy works between the Khalasa Road and the Wadi Saba with two divisions, masking the works north of the Wadi Saba with the Imperial Camel Corps and some infantry, while a portion of the 53rd Division further north covered the left of the corps. The right of the attack was covered by a regiment of cavalry, while further east mounted troops took up a line opposite the southern defences of Beersheba.

The strength of the Egyptian Expeditionary Force had now been increased to seven infantry divisions and four divisions of mounted troops, the infantry having been grouped from early in August in two Army Corps, the XX under command

* General Allenby's despatch of December 16th, 1917.

of Lieutenant-General Sir P. Chetwode, and XXI under that of Lieutenant-General Sir E. Bulfin; the 53rd Division formed part of the XX Army Corps with the 10th, 60th, and 74th Divisions, the XXI Corps containing the 52nd, 54th, and 75th Divisions.

On October 24th the 2nd/4th The Queen's moved from the neighbourhood of Deir el Belah to the right near Shellal and thenceforward took its full share in all the operations in which the 53rd Division was concerned up to the fall of Jerusalem.

On the 27th a heavy bombardment of Gaza was opened both by land and sea with the object of inducing the enemy to believe that an attack on this flank was intended, and then early on the 31st the 60th Division rushed Hill 1070, followed at midday by the attack and capture of the main defences between the Wadi Saba and the Khalasa Road by the 60th and 74th Divisions.

" The next morning (November 1st)," writes Colonel Wilkins, " our outposts having been relieved by the 10th Division at 7 a.m. we marched south-east over the hills, and on reaching the main road turned east towards Beersheba which we entered about midday. The heat was intense, the country a desert and the dust colossal!

" There was every sign of the battle of the day before, when we reached the western defences of Beersheba, 3 miles west of the town, and passed through the formidable trenches which had been heavily wired. Broken wire entanglements, empty shell cases and débris of every kind lay around, while on all sides we heard explosions caused by the detonation by our troops, who were clearing the battlefield, of unexploded shells and bombs. As we passed beyond the wire entanglements we saw a Turkish heavy battery of four guns, skilfully hidden, which stood just as it had been captured a few hours before, limbers, shell stacks, etc, all complete, the dug-outs showing signs of hasty evacuation. Soon we passed the solitary mosque and the railway station where stood an abandoned train which the Huns had mined as a booby trap! . . . . We passed through the town and halted on a bare, open and very desolate plain beyond. To the north a few miles off was a ridge of bare, formidable looking hills, the foothills of the mountains of Judea. . . . Here we remained until 4 p.m. when an order came for us to march north to the line Abu Towal—Nuweilah. . . . For hours we stumbled on in the dark through rocky valleys and over desolate hills. The men were very exhausted, they were heavily laden, and before we reached our destination we had marched fully 20 miles since 7 a.m., the conditions of the morning march in intense heat and dust having been very trying.

" Two battalions went on outpost, the remainder, including the 2nd/4th Queen's, being in reserve." This day the Turkish shells caused some casualties, and Lieutenant Fripp of the Battalion was wounded, while attached to Brigade Headquarters.

The next stage in the operations was the frontal attack on Gaza, designed as a subsidiary operation to attract the Turkish reserves to that sector. The objective was the 6,000 yards front from Sheikh Hassan on the sea, north-west of Gaza, to the south-west of the town. The main attack was delivered before dawn on November 2nd with complete success, and all was then ready for the major operations on the eastern flank, but water and transport difficulties made events move more slowly than had been planned. On the 2nd the 53rd Division and the Camel Corps covered the flank of the main attack.

"On the night of November 2nd," to quote Colonel Wilkins, "we were relieved by a brigade of the 74th Division after dark, and received orders to march at 3 a.m. the next day towards Tel el Khuweilfeh. At that hour accordingly on November 3rd we were on the march again, this time in a north-easterly direction over bare, rugged mountainous country, which strongly resembled the Indian Frontier, though on a smaller scale. Beyond a few carts which the Turks had abandoned in their flight from Beersheba, and an occasional Bedouin encampment, there was no sign of life.

"At 9 a.m. we halted and a close examination of maps took place. General Mott pointed out a cleft in the hilly ranges to the north, through which the 160th Brigade was to march towards Khuweilfeh. The Queen's formed the advanced guard and two Arab guides mounted on camels accompanied us, as did also a party of Royal Engineers, who made the track passable for transport as we advanced. The advance was consequently slow, and the heat became intense. Soon after, we saw on the heights above us the outposts of the 158th Brigade, and passing through them we felt our way cautiously in the direction of the enemy. After an uphill climb of some 3 miles, the advanced guard halted, and I went on with the Brigadier and climbed a neck leading to a high, rocky hill, from the summit of which we obtained a wide view. About $1\frac{1}{2}$ miles to the west we saw through our glasses that the head of the 159th Brigade had reached a low hill abreast of us; to the north-north-west stretched a wide plain shimmering in the sun; we were now behind the Turkish defences at Kawukah and Sheria, and we could perceive dimly through the clouds of dust bodies of enemy troops moving in the direction from Sheria towards the high, steep hill of Khuweilfeh, which towered above us some $1\frac{1}{2}$ miles to the north. On the hill we met the commander of a mounted division who told us that a mounted division held the line of hills intervening between us and Khuweilfeh and the ground east to Dhaheriyah near the Hebron Road. . . . The Brigadier* arranged that our brigade headquarters should be on the hill on which we stood and that the Brigade should cross the neck behind us and descend into a small sheltered valley; the Battalion had to cross in small parties as the movement must have been visible from Tel el Khuweilfeh.

"The men though somewhat exhausted by the heat were in fine fettle, and I was very pleased when the divisional general came up to me shortly afterwards and said : ' I have been talking to your men, they are simply splendid.'

"The Brigadier now announced that the 2nd/4th Queen's and the 2nd/4th Royal West Kent Regiment were shortly to carry out a reconnaissance of Khuweilfeh each with one company and Battalion Headquarters, and gave us our directions. . . . With our glasses we could see a few Turks moving from a trench towards the crest of Khuweilfeh and half an hour later I saw the whole of the Kentish battalion advancing in attack formation on our left. Anticipating the order, I at once ordered The Queen's to advance on the objective previously given me—there was no time for detailed orders—and the Battalion moved promptly forward in attack formation.

"We soon topped the first of the three ridges between us and Khuweilfeh, and as we reached the crest a sputter of bullets came over. The Australian outposts doubled back, and we advanced steadily over the crest, doubling down the far side under a fairly heavy rifle fire. Soon after we topped another ridge, along which the Turks had established a regular barrage of bullets. Our right leading company

---

* Brigadier-General V. L. N. Pearson, D.S.O.

had now reached the only hill remaining between us and the enemy's position. Selecting a sheltered spot for Battalion Headquarters with the Adjutant (Duncan) and Acting Second-in-Command (Hooker), I climbed this hill and lying down searched the enemy's position with my glasses. After a quarter of an hour or so, during which little or nothing was visible of the enemy, there came a sudden burst of machine-gun fire from the enemy's position on our left front," and by this Colonel Wilkins, Captain Cunningham, and Lieutenant Roberts were all wounded, and thus Colonel Wilkins' account ends; Lieutenant-Colonel Roper now assumed command of the 2nd/4th The Queen's.

This day the 53rd Division was able to occupy part only of the enemy's position at Tel el Khuweilfeh, by reason of the stout resistance put up by the Turks, who had diverted a considerable proportion of their reserves to this sector of the front. The attack was, however, renewed day and night, and the 53rd Division finally secured possession of the Tel el Khuweilfeh lines on November 6th, and when the enemy screen was swept away on the 7th, it was found that Gaza had been evacuated.

The Turkish line had now been completely rolled up from the left, and the enemy had suffered losses amounting to 10,000, while half that number of prisoners had been captured. Rear-guard actions now ensued, and the pursuit of the Turks was vigorously pressed. On the 9th Ascalon was occupied, on the 13th the enemy was driven from Katrah, and on the 14th Junction Station was in British hands, the Turkish army having now broken up into two parts which had retired north and east respectively.

Ramleh and Ludd were captured on the 15th, Jaffa was entered unopposed next day, and by the 22nd the British were holding, in spite of determined resistance and many counter-attacks, the line Kustul—Nebi Samwil—Beit Izza—Beit Dukka—Beit Dur El Tahta. For two weeks now there was a halt until arrangements could be made for commencing the final advance on Jerusalem.

During this time the 53rd Division had been sitting down before Hebron, not having been engaged since November 6th, but on December 4th it advanced, occupied Hebron without opposition, and, continuing to move forward, was by the 8th to have reached Surbahir and Sherafat, 3 miles south of Jerusalem. On the 7th the weather broke and three days of incessant rain followed, causing some unavoidable delay, but by the 9th the Yeomanry and the 60th Division had occupied a line across the Nablus Road, 4 miles from Jerusalem, while on the south the 53rd Division cut the main road to Jericho, Jerusalem being thus isolated.

At noon this day the Holy City was surrendered.

On the night of December 26th-27th the enemy attacked with great determination astride the Jerusalem—Nablus road. The 60th Division was mainly engaged, but assaults were also made against various points held by the 53rd Division on the east of Jerusalem, and in the course of these the 2nd/4th The Queen's suffered many casualties. The two divisions beat off the enemy, however, and by noon of the 27th the 10th and 74th Divisions had counter-attacked and driven in the Turkish right. The attempt to recapture Jerusalem had wholly failed, and on the 28th the XX Corps made a general advance north which, by the end of the month, had progressed to a depth of from 2 to 3 miles on a 12-mile front. The 53rd Division protected the right of this advance, and the 53rd eventually occupied Hizmeh Jeba and the high ground north of it overlooking the Wadi el Midineh. Further progress north was now impossible until roads could be made and supplies

TURKISH POSITIONS WEST OF JERUSALEM.

[Copyright: Imperial War Museum

brought up, while it was necessary to secure the right by driving the enemy across the Jordan.

This last task was entrusted to the 53rd and 60th Divisions, while the Australian and New Zealand Mounted Division was for the time being attached to the XX Corps.

On February 19th El Muntar, Arak Ibrahim, and Ras et Tawil were taken, the 53rd Division extending its right to include Rummon. On the 20th Talaat et Dumm was captured, and next day the Australians rode into Jericho, pushing patrols forward to the banks of the Jordan. The XX Corps was now disposed in two parts; the right was to secure the Jordan to a point north of the Wadi el Auja, while the remainder of the Corps was directed along the Nablus Road to the line Sinjil—Deir es Sudan.

The ground to be advanced over was very rugged and in places even precipitous, and it was March 8th before the XX Corps reached the line En Nejmeh—Et Taigibeh—Ain Sinia on the Jerusalem—Nablus road, the 53rd Division being on the right, the 74th in the centre and the 10th on the left; and in the fighting which followed on the two succeeding days the enemy had to be driven from ridge to ridge before the final objectives were secured. The 53rd Division especially met with considerable opposition and great natural difficulties, especially on the extreme right and at Tel Asur, the enemy making repeated but unsuccessful attempts to recapture this place.

During the next two months or more there was renewed fighting but the 53rd Division was not employed.

On May 25th Lieutenant-Colonel W. J. M. Hill assumed command of the 2nd/4th The Queen's *vice* Lieutenant-Colonel Roper.

The Battalion was now, however, to be transferred from Palestine to the main theatre of the war, consequent upon the success of the March offensive carried out by the enemy and the difficulty in replacing, by seasoned troops, the heavy British losses incurred in these operations. The withdrawals from General Allenby's force were on a very comprehensive scale, though it must be said that to some extent these were made good by divisions withdrawn from Mesopotamia. During the first week in April the 52nd Division left Egypt for France, the 74th followed a week later, while 24 infantry battalions were taken from the remaining divisions, with 9 regiments of yeomanry, $5\frac{1}{2}$ batteries of siege guns, and 5 machine-gun companies. Among the 24 infantry battalions withdrawn from the divisions remaining in Egypt, the 160th Brigade of the 53rd Division lost the 2nd/4th The Queen's and the 1st/4th Royal Sussex Regiment, The Queen's leaving the Brigade on May 31st, and marching to railhead at Ludd, there entraining for Kantara. Here the Battalion was re-equipped and then proceeded to Alexandria on June 15th, embarking next day in the *Malwa* and sailing on the 18th with a convoy for France.

The *Malwa* put into Taranto on the 21st, narrowly escaping being torpedoed as she entered the bay, and on the 22nd the Battalion disembarked—curiously enough by the very same lighter by which it had embarked at Suvla Bay—and at once entrained for the Western Front, reaching Proven after a journey of seven days and nights in the train, and joining the 34th Division commanded by Major-General C. L. Nicholson, C.B.

This division, owing to lack of reinforcements, had, in April of this year, been reduced to cadres, so far as its infantry was concerned, but in June it was reconstructed, its batteries, Royal Engineers, and machine-gun battalions returning to it, while the infantry battalions were all new, some coming from India, others from Egypt and Palestine, and none of these had any experience of war as waged in France. The 34th Division now contained three brigades—the 101st, 102nd and 103rd, each of three battalions, and in the 101st, commanded by Brigadier-General W. J. Woodcock, D.S.O., were the 2nd/4th The Queen's Royal Regiment, the 1st/4th Royal Sussex Regiment, and the 2nd Loyal North Lancashire Regiment. All was complete by July 11th, when the Division passed into general headquarters reserve.

Until July 15th The Queen's were occupied in reorganizing and refitting, being at the same time responsible for various sectors of the East Poperinghe defences.

On the 18th the 34th Division was concentrated in the Senlis area, and marched thence via Largny to the Vivières—Puisieux—Soucy—Longavesne area, coming on the 20th under the XXX Corps (General Penet) of the Tenth French Army commanded by General Mangin. This move was occasioned by the need of assistance to be given to our Allies in the great counter-offensive which Marshal Foch had been preparing on the front between Château-Thierry and Soissons.

"On the 21st orders were received to relieve the 38th French Division in the line opposite Hartennes—Taux the next day, and before this was commenced came orders to take part in an attack early on the following day, July 23rd. Under the most favourable circumstances this would have been difficult for any troops, but for a newly-constituted division, composed, as regards infantry, of troops which had not yet been in action in France, and which had just completed a trying move by rail, bus, and march route, it was a very severe test. There was no time for reconnaissance. The country was entirely new; there were no organized trench systems on either side. The enemy's positions were never accurately known till they had been captured. To all these difficulties there were added those inseparable from acting for the first time with foreign troops."*

The 101st Brigade was at Puisieux on July 21st, from where at 4 a.m. next day it moved to Villers-Helon, the remaining brigades of the Division following later, and all then taking up positions of readiness in the valleys and woods to the north of that place.

The general plan now was that the XX Corps on the left was to turn the wood north of Hartennes and Taux, while the right of the XXX Corps was to turn the two woods of St. Jean and du Plessier; the 34th Division, with two French divisions on right and left, was to connect the two turning movements and advance due east to the high ground east of the Soissons—Château-Thierry road; the 34th Division was not to move, however, till the XX Corps on the left had crossed the Soissons—Château-Thierry road.

The 101st Brigade now relieved a French Corps in the right section, the 2nd/4th The Queen's and 2nd Loyal North Lancs being in the front line on left and right respectively, while the Royal Sussex were in brigade reserve.

The advance was to have commenced behind the barrage at 7.50 a.m., but the lines to the 101st Brigade being broken, it started some five minutes late, and was met with an intense machine-gun fire on the right, which practically wiped out the first wave of the North Lancs in the first fifty yards, but on the left " D " and " B " Companies of The Queen's, under Second-Lieutenant Lessels, got across the Coutremain—Tigny road, and exterminated some machine-gun posts, but they were counter-attacked and forced back. The only gain was an advance of the line about 1,000 yards on the 102nd Brigade front.

* *The Thirty-Fourth Division, 1915-1919,* p. 254.

SKETCH MAP TO ILLUSTRATE THE BATTLE OF SOISSONNAIS-OURCQ, JULY 28th—AUGUST 2nd

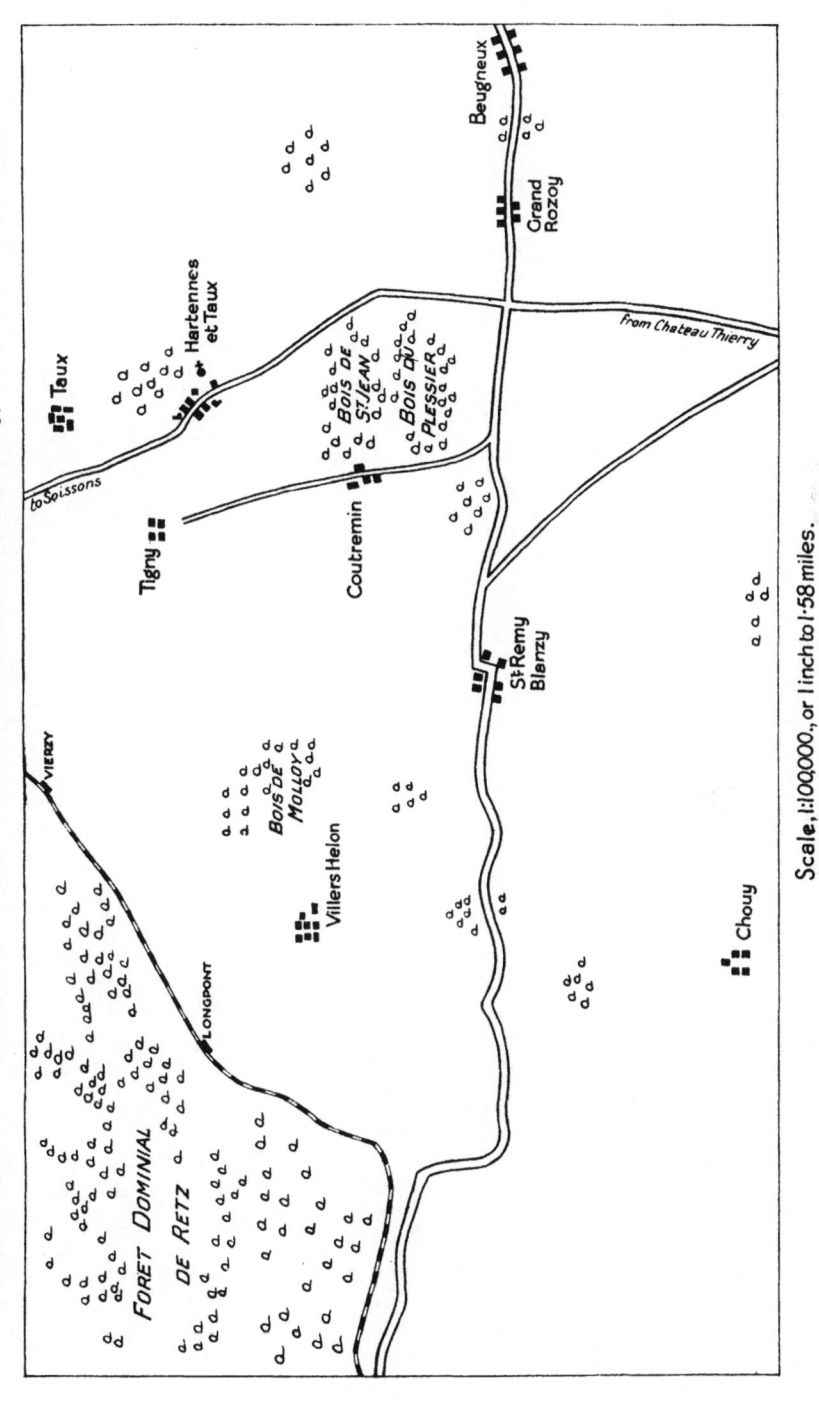

The 28th the Division spent in the rear line, but on the 29th it was sent up again to the front to take part in an attack on the Grand Rozoy Ridge, the 103rd Brigade attacking on the right and the 101st on the left; the 2nd/4th The Queen's were again in the front line of the Brigade with the Royal Sussex Battalion on the right. For some time the attack progressed satisfactorily and The Queen's got some way up the slopes north of the Beugneux woods, while the French took Grand Rozoy, but the Germans heavily counter-attacked the French who fell back and the rest of the line was obliged to conform. But the main line held and there was renewed fighting on the 30th and 31st, and on August 1st, when the advance was resumed, it was found that the enemy had fallen back; the French then passed through and pursued the enemy.

On the last day the 34th Division had less than 350 effectives per battalion, and between July 22nd and August 3rd had lost 153 officers and 3,617 other ranks.

The following Special Order of the Day was published by General Nicholson :—

"*The Divisional Commander has received the following and desires that it be read out to all ranks on parade :—*

"'*By direction of General Mangin, Commanding Tenth French Army.*

"'*General Mangin, the Army Commander, has instructed me to convey to you his personal thanks for the magnificent results achieved by your Division yesterday.*

"'*The General says that yesterday's battle worked out absolutely according to orders and times, and says that the general retreat taking place to-day is entirely due to the success of yesterday.*

"'*The General has instructed me to tell you of his gratitude and appreciation for the splendid success achieved by the 34th Division yesterday.*'"

The Division now went back for some two weeks or more to a rest area, but its units soon began to return to the front in the Ypres Sector, and on August 30th the 101st Brigade relieved a brigade of the 41st Division in the Scherpenberg Sector; the new front held by the Division extended for some 3,000 yards facing south-east about midway between Kemmel Hill and Scherpenberg, and was the left sector of the XIX Corps front. The 30th British Division was on the right and the 27th American on the left.

Early on the 31st a patrol of the 2nd/4th The Queen's established the fact that the enemy was withdrawing from Kemmel Hill, and this was accordingly occupied and our line advanced. On the 1st the forward move began all along the line, though the 2nd/4th The Queen's, as the Divisional History relates : " had a little trouble with some Huns in the Yonge Street dug-outs."* At dusk on September 2nd The Queen's and the Sussex had reached the outskirts of Petit Bois, and while the left of the 4th Division was at Frenchman's Farm, the line thence to the north was held as follows : Two companies of the Scottish Rifles to Spy Farm, two companies 2nd/4th The Queen's to Beaver Huts, and two companies of the Royal Sussex in Oak Trench.

There was now about a fortnight of comparative inactivity, and on September 20th the 34th Division was transferred from the XIX to the X Corps, and then on the 28th an advance began, the object of which was that the Division, assisted by a turning movement by the 41st Division, should capture the Wytschaete Ridge and establish itself on the Ypres—Comines Canal, south of the bend at Hollebeke.

These operations, and the movements which followed them, were entirely successful, and by October 16th the north bank of the Lys was arrived at. Next

* Here Captain E. A. Roe, M.C., was killed.

day it was crossed east of Menin, and on the 18th the 101st Brigade marched into Lauwe, the first inhabited Belgian town to be entered, and the inhabitants of which gave their deliverers a wonderfully enthusiastic reception. And so from day to day was the pursuit of the enemy pressed, his rear guards giving occasional trouble, but the main bodies making no real stand, and the advance finally ended on the Scheldt, when the 34th Division was drawn in to the reserve, marching on November 3rd back to the neighbourhood of Courtrai, where on the 11th the news of the Armistice was received.

Little more remains to be said; the Division was now with the X Corps, and the 2nd/4th The Queen's marched to the vicinity of Namur, arriving there on December 22nd, and early in the New Year was sent across the Rhine into Germany, where it was employed, until disbanded, in control posts in the areas of Allner, Seelescheid, Wahn, Kalk, Engelskirchen, Ehreshoven, Lindlar, Frankenfurst, and Michelsburg. In March the Battalion was transferred from the 34th (Eastern) to the 42nd (London) Division.

On April 7th General Sir H. Plumer, commanding the Army of the Rhine, presented the Battalion with the King's Colour.

Two days later Lieutenant-Colonel S. T. Watson, D.S.O., succeeded Lieutenant-Colonel Hill in command, and on the 11th the 53rd Young Soldiers' Battalion, The Queen's, about 1,000 strong, joined, and was absorbed into the strength of the 2nd/4th, of whom only about eight of the original members who had proceeded with the Battalion to Gallipoli, now remained.

On October 22nd, 1919, the Battalion was reduced to a cadre in consequence of the reconstruction of the Army of the Rhine, 374 men being sent to the 10th and 310 to the 11th Battalions The Queen's. Then on October 31st the cadre was disbanded, Captain Duncan and his office staff now returning to England and handing over the 2nd/4th Battalion The Queen's King's Colour to the Mayor of Croydon, by whom it was placed in the Town Hall with the Colour of the 1st/4th Battalion.

Few units, and certainly no second-line unit, had a more varied service or a more distinguished career in the war than the 2nd/4th The Queen's, and its casualties were very heavy as may be seen by the following figures of casualties in France alone:—

|  | Officers. | Other Ranks. |
| --- | --- | --- |
| Killed in action | 4 | 70 |
| Died of wounds | — | 29 |
| Wounded | 11 | 304 |
| Missing | — | 11 |
| Prisoner of war | — | 1 |
| Drowned | — | 2 |
| Accidentally injured | — | 12 |
| Died of disease | — | 4 |
| Total | 15 | 433 |

While, during the war, of the officers 17 were killed in action, 37 were wounded, 1 was missing, and 2 died of disease. Of the non-commissioned officers and men 145 were killed, 48 died of wounds, and 30 died of disease, while 681 were wounded, and 21 were missing.

# CASUALTIES

The following are the names of the officers of the Battalion who became casualties during the war :—Killed, Captains A. M. Hepworth, H. W. Hewett, D. R. Potter, M.C., J. Mc.G. McNaught, and R. W. Spicer, Lieutenants C. M. W. Jephson, P. H. Laughlin, and W. L. J. Longbourne, Second-Lieutenants G. T. Bray, R. M. Lessels, G. H. Mapleson, C. A. L. Pemble, F. C. L. Ridpath, H. G. Sweet, and D. J. Thomas, also the Rev. B. Kavanagh, chaplain ; wounded were Lieutenant-Colonel H. St. C. Wilkins, Captains L. H. F. Beach (twice), W. H. Cunningham, P. C. Duncan, J. G. Fearon, S. G. Hillyer, I. S. Keen, C. D. McIver, A. R. T. Philips, M. C. L. Porter, W. H. Pryce, G. H. Roberts, E. A. Roe, and E. H. Williams, Lieutenants A. K. Boyd, P. Fripp (twice), V. H. Galbraith, and R. J. Harrison (twice), Second-Lieutenants D. C. Braham (twice), L. B. Charles, E. D'Eath, T. F. Griffin, P. Harwood, B. G. E. Haywood (twice), G. H. Heyes, F. W. T. Hughes, J. D. Hodges, R. A. U. Jennings, D. G. K. Johnson, A. G. Robinson, A. G. Robshaw, J. L. Roger, H. M. St. George, G. F. Stringer, A. G. I. Thomas, and R. H. Twining ; died of disease, Captain L. H. F. Beach, and Second-Lieutenant B. B. Brodie, while Lieutenant C. G. F. Ingram was missing.

Maps 1, 4, 5, and 6.

## CHAPTER XVII.

### THE 3RD/4TH BATTALION.

### 1915–1918.

#### HOME SERVICE AND FRANCE.

##### BATTLE HONOURS:

" Ypres, 1917," " Broodseinde," " Passchendaele," " Cambrai," " France and Flanders, 1914–18."

THE date of the formation of the 3rd/4th Battalion The Queen's Royal Regiment was April 24th, 1915, on which date, as already explained in a previous chapter, a Composite Battalion for service overseas was created from the then already existing 2nd/4th and 2nd/5th Battalions of the Regiment, at that time stationed at Windsor with the Surrey Brigade, commanded by Brigadier-General J. Marriott, D.S.O., M.V.O., of the 2nd/1st Home Counties, later the 67th, Division, under Major-General J. C. Young.

The 3rd/4th was not then, however, a newly created unit, consisting as it did of the balance of the original battalion formed at Croydon under Colonel F. D. Watney in September, 1914. Actually it was on June 15th, 1915, that the "Composite Battalion," by which name it had been known, was re-named the 2nd/4th The Queen's, the existing 2nd/4th then becoming the 3rd/4th, and the Reserve Battalion the 4th/4th The Queen's.

On the Composite Battalion being formed at Windsor under Colonel Watney, the command of the 2nd/4th, as the 3rd/4th was then known, was given to Lieutenant-Colonel U. L. Hooke, who had previously been second in command; Major L. S. de la Mare became second-in-command with Major K. A. Oswald, adjutant, and Captain T. I. Birch, D.C.M., quartermaster, and the Battalion was made up to strength by the transfer from Croydon of men who had been recruited at the depot there.

Training was carried on in Windsor Great Park, the men being armed with Japanese rifles, with which a musketry course was gone through on the Runnymede ranges; while, when threats of Zeppelin raids were first made, the Battalion did picquet work in the neighbourhood of Slough. No raids seem to have been made in this vicinity, however, but in June the Battalion was transferred to the Tunbridge Wells neighbourhood, and in October part of this area was wrecked by bombs dropped from a German Zeppelin. It was while stationed near Tunbridge Wells that those men who had elected for Home Service only were separated from the others, and in June of this year some 400 officers and men were posted for Home Service duty to the 69th Provisional Battalion at Lowestoft. The deficiencies thus created were made up by drafts from the Depot, while commissions in the Battalion were given to eight aspirants from the Artists Rifles, and in addition twelve officers of the New Army were attached for training and duty.

From June 14th to July 21st the Battalion, or the greater part of it, was stationed at Halling, near Chatham, for work on the London defences; and from

October, 1915, to July, 1916, was at Reigate, and while here drafts from the Oxfordshire and Buckinghamshire Light Infantry and from the Somersetshire Light Infantry brought the strength of the Battalion up to about 1,200 of all ranks. After a few days in camp in Wildernesse Park, Sevenoaks, the 3rd/4th The Queen's marched to a camp at Westbere, near Sturry, which was reached in July, the 200th Brigade Headquarters being at Upstreet and the remainder of the Brigade at Gore Street. Training went steadily on, and a divisional musketry camp was formed at Sandwich, the course being fired with 1914 Enfield Mark W rifles, made in America, which by this appear to have replaced the Japanese rifles originally issued.

In August upwards of 300 men were sent overseas from the Battalion, the majority to the 22nd County of London Regiment and the remainder to the 6th County of London Regiment.

The 3rd/4th Battalion The Queen's remained under canvas at Westbere until November 2nd, and was then moved to Ramsgate in connection with the coast defences; when here the Battalion had experience of the heavy German bombardment of the town in the spring of 1917, and also of very frequent air raids.

While the Brigade was at Ramsgate, Brigadier-General E. H. Gorges took over the command of the 200th Brigade from Brigadier-General Marriott, and Major-General the Hon. C. E. Bingham relieved Major-General J. C. Young in command of the 67th Division.

For some time past every effort had been made to keep all ranks ready and fit to proceed on service overseas, and early in 1917, in order to complete the Battalion with men of " A " category, drafts were received from the Shropshire Light Infantry and from the Cambridgeshire Regiment, any men of the 3rd/4th The Queen's considered medically unfit being posted to the Labour Battalion of the Bedfordshire Regiment; but it was not until May, 1917, that the Battalion, then back again in Westbere Camp, was one of three battalions specially selected from the home serving brigades to proceed to France. But before leaving Westbere Camp the Mayor of Croydon, Alderman H. Houlder, accompanied by the Vicar, the Rev. Canon L. J. White-Thomson, and Dr. J. M. Newnham, Town Clerk, visited the Battalion and expressed the good wishes of the people of Croydon for the success of the 3rd/4th The Queen's in France. The Hon. Colonel, Sir Frederick Edridge, was, to the regret of all ranks, unable to visit the Battalion by reason of ill-health.

On May 30th the 3rd/4th The Queen's left Canterbury for Southampton, entraining in two parties, and reached the Docks Station at 3.30 and 5.20 on the morning of the 31st. The Battalion remained all day in sheds, and then embarked in the hired transport *La Marguerite*, in company with the 3rd/4th Royal West Kent, sailing that evening.

The strength of the Battalion was on embarkation 33 officers and 973 non-commissioned officers and men. The following was the disposal of the officers: Lieutenant-Colonel U. L. Hooke, in command; Major K. A. Oswald, second in-command; Captain V. F. Samuelson, adjutant; Lieutenant E. W. Preston, transport officer; Captain T. I. Birch, quartermaster; Lieutenant H. W. Carter, signalling officer; Lieutenant R. R. B. Bannerman, assistant adjutant and Lewis gun officer; Second-Lieutenant A. H. John, scout and sniping officer; Second-Lieutenant H. S. Gilliland, bombing officer, and Captain A. E. Mackenzie, R.A.M.C., in medical charge.

" *A* " *Company*.—Captain P. M. Hepworth, Lieutenant L. J. C. Vidler, Second-Lieutenants A. H. Lovell, H. E. Fisk, W. P. Thomas and J. C. Davie.

"*B*" *Company*.—Captains A. T. Latham and C. G. Moss, Lieutenant A. B. Frost, Second-Lieutenants J. Ost, A. E. Barrow and J. R. Skeet.

"*C*" *Company*.—Major F. T. Whinney, Captain G. A. Ionides, Lieutenants F. W. A. Buckell and A. H. A. Cooper, Second-Lieutenants W. A. Puddicombe and C. A. Freestone.

"*D*" *Company*.—Captain A. H. Harper, Lieutenants H. P. McCabe and G. A. Shaw, Second-Lieutenants E. H. Dakin and D. R. J. O'Connor.

Havre was reached at 3 a.m. on June 1st, and, disembarking, the troops marched to No. 1 Rest Camp, where a day and a half was spent; then at 3 p.m. on the 2nd the Battalion boarded the train at the Gare de Marchandise, and, moving by Bouchy and Abbeville, the 3rd/4th detrained early on the morning of the 3rd at Hesdins and marched thence to billets in the village of Laloge, about five miles from the station. Some forty-eight hours were spent here training in the forest of Hesdins, and then the Battalion went on by train to Duisans, which was reached in the early afternoon of the 7th, and here The Queen's found themselves attached to the South African Infantry Brigade in the 9th Division of the XVII Corps of the Third Army. At the date when the 3rd/4th The Queen's reached France the Arras offensive was just coming to an end and the Battle of Messines was about to open.

On the 9th the Battalion underwent something of an ordeal, being inspected at one and the same time by General Sir Charles Fergusson, Major-General H. T. Lukin and Brigadier-General F. S. Dawson—the Corps, Division and Brigade Commanders!

At the end of ten days the 3rd/4th Battalion was transferred from the 9th to the 4th Division, and moved to St. Nicholas, where the companies were attached for instruction in front-line duties in the sectors north and south of the River Scarpe to battalions of the 11th and 12th Brigades. Here on June 21st a great misfortune befell The Queen's, the Commanding Officer, Lieutenant-Colonel U. L. Hooke, being killed near the Chemical Works while going from the reserve to the front line with a small party of "C" Company. A shell burst on the party, wounding the Commanding Officer in the head and Lieutenant Buckell in the thigh, also Private Smith, Colonel Hooke's bâtman. After attending to the Commanding Officer, Lieutenant Buckell went on with his party to the front line, but was later compelled to return to the dressing station. Colonel Hooke died about five minutes after reaching the aid post without having regained consciousness. He was buried at Fampoux, and the command of the Battalion was assumed by Major Oswald, who was promoted Lieutenant-Colonel.

Lieutenant-Colonel Hooke was universally popular with both officers and men, and his labours during the long period of intensive training in England had been unceasing, and had contributed in large measure to the high standard of efficiency attained by the 3rd/4th Battalion The Queen's.

At the end of June the Battalion had yet another move and came under a new command, proceeding to Arras for work in the front line in the vicinity of Monchy, and being quartered in the Oil Factory at Arras, while from time to time companies were detached to Athies and Wancourt. Here The Queen's were attached to the 12th Division, and when on August 8th the Battalion again was "moved on," the following appreciative letter was received from the Divisional Commander, Major-General A. B. Scott:—

"*At the conclusion of their attachment to the 12th Division the Major-General Commanding desires to express to Lieutenant-Colonel Oswald and all ranks of the 3rd/4th Bn. The Queen's (R. W. Surrey) Regiment his appreciation of the good work they have done while under his command. Though not of a fighting nature, the work has been most important, and the Battalion can be assured that it will be highly appreciated by those who will profit by it.*

"*Major-General Scott wishes them all good luck with their new Division.*"

On August 9th the Battalion marched nine miles to Moyenneville, where it was accommodated in tents and huts, joining here the 62nd Infantry Brigade, commanded by Brigadier-General C. G. Rawling, of the 21st Division, then forming part of the VI Corps; the Divisional Commander was Major-General D. G. M. Campbell. The Division was at this time in the sector opposite Fontaine-les-Croisilles, and after spending some few days in reserve, the 3rd/4th The Queen's took over the left sector of their Brigade front consisting mainly of the old Hindenburg Line with its extensive trench system. Here, there was a broad "No-Man's-Land," and opportunity was taken for extensive and practical patrol training. Thus, on the night of the 25th-26th, a patrol of six other ranks under Second-Lieutenant Gilliland, carried out a bold reconnaissance to verify reports which had been received as to the positions of enemy machine-gun emplacements. Having cut through several lines of wire, the party lay under cover observing the movements of the enemy, and then the officer and Lance-Sergeant W. N. Goatcher managed to crawl under the wire and get on to the German parapet unseen. After remaining there for about three-quarters of an hour, these two rejoined the patrol, and commenced withdrawal, when a heavy machine-gun fire was at once opened on the party. Second-Lieutenant Gilliland and Private Homewood were wounded in the arm, and Lance-Corporal H. P. Matthews very severely in the abdomen. The latter refused help, and asked to be left where he was so that the patrol could get back, but he managed to crawl some 200 yards when he became exhausted, and the officer and lance-sergeant then in turn carried him on their backs. The withdrawal, the whole way under machine-gun fire, was covered by Lance-Sergeant Blakeman, Privates Rosenbaum and Painter.

Next day the Division was sent ten miles back to Warlus, west of Arras, for training, and was now transferred from the VI to the XVII Corps.

Rather over a fortnight was passed here, and then on September 16th, the 3rd/4th The Queen's moved again, marching from Warlus to Savy, where it entrained for Caestre, and on arrival here being accommodated in billets in the village of Le Peuplier, which was in the area of the X Corps (Lieutenant-General Sir T. Morland) in the Second Army commanded by General Sir H. Plumer. While here two drafts, amounting to 106 other ranks, were received.

The Battalion was now to take some part in the Battle of Ypres, which had been going on since July, and which was not to come officially to an end until the first week in November.

During the next few days many moves were made—on September 23rd to the Roukloshille area near the Mont des Cats for training; on the 28th via Berthen and Boesinghe to the neighbourhood of Reninghelst; and on the last day of the month by way of Westoutre, La Clytte, and Voormezeele to Zillebeke, where The Queen's went into shelters and trenches on the south bank of the Dickebusch Lake, and here the final arrangements were made for the offensive in which the Battalion was to take part. On October 1st the Battalion numbered 44 officers and 938 other ranks.

On the night of October 2nd-3rd, the 62nd Brigade relieved the 110th in the front line just east of Polygon Wood, the 3rd/4th The Queen's taking the place in the trenches of the 8th Leicesters; the journey up was of a trying nature owing to the very heavy shelling of the roads and tracks, while the moving troops were also silhouetted against the light of burning ammunition dumps. Of the Battalion, "A" and "D" Companies were in the front line, "B" in support, and "C" Company in reserve, and on the 3rd as much reconnaissance work was carried out as was possible, but since the enemy was in occupation of high ground in close proximity, little movement could be made without attracting heavy fire. On the day previous to relief the Germans had made a serious attack upon this part of the line which on the right had been bent back some 250 yards, so that the right of the 3rd/4th The Queen's was rather uncomfortably forward. The ground hereabouts was very muddy, and the constant shelling had churned the Polygon Beek into a broad and almost impenetrable morass; carrying parties had great difficulty in bringing up supplies and necessaries of any kind.

The attack of the Second Army on the enemy's position began at 6 a.m. on October 4th, a dark, damp morning, when the 21st and 7th Divisions on the right and left respectively were to assault and capture the enemy's defensive system on the Broodseinde—Becelaere Ridge. On the right of the 62nd Brigade was the 64th, while the 91st was on the left. The total depth to be captured by the 62nd Infantry Brigade was of about 1,200 yards.

At 3 a.m. on the 4th the Battalion commenced to assemble, when three companies were in the front line, the disposition from right to left being "A," "B," "D," each company having a frontage of 85 and an average depth of 30 yards, each being on a one platoon frontage; "C" Company was in close support, formed in one line of half platoons in file in rear of the centre of "B"; two reserve Lewis-gun teams were with "C."

At zero hour—6 a.m.—the British barrage came down 150 yards in front of the Brigade line, the attacking troops at once moving up to it. The first obstacle met with was a line of concertina and barbed wire along the whole front, while the advance came under heavy machine-gun fire from the right. The passage of the Polygon Beek and the adjoining marsh presented some difficulties, time was lost, and the men got too far behind the barrage, and there was a certain amount of confusion. Juniper Trench was then assailed, the wire in front of it offering no serious obstacle; many Germans emerged as The Queen's drew near, but in the darkness it was impossible to tell if they meant fighting or surrender, and they were all killed; and though an enemy concrete strong point made some resistance, this was overcome by a party of bombers under Lieutenant Frost, the rest of this portion of the German line of defence being captured with no very great difficulty.

On Judge Trench being taken, consolidation at once commenced, six posts were dug along the Red Line in front of which four Lewis-gun posts were formed, communication was established with the 1st South Staffordshire Regiment of the 7th Division on the left, and messages were sent back by runners and pigeons announcing the capture of the first objective.

The 62nd Brigade narrative of the events of this day states that "the offensive spirit of the 3rd/4th Queen's in this, their first fight, was beyond all praise, and their recent hard training enabled them to work those 'mebus' (concrete emplacements), and reduce them with skill and rapidity."

Two other battalions now advanced through The Queen's, and captured the second objective, whereupon the Battalion withdrew to Jetty Warren, and there dug in ; and the Germans now opening and maintaining so long as daylight lasted a continuous barrage over the whole of the captured area, great difficulty was experienced in clearing away the wounded ; then, during the night, their guns changed on to the back areas. The 5th was spent in improving the position, and though the enemy shelling was at all times heavy, and attacks were made on the right and left, there was no enemy infantry activity on the front of the 62nd Brigade. This day the following was sent round :—

"*Major-General Campbell, although severely regretting the heavy losses sustained by the battalions and units of the Brigade, heartily congratulates those who took part in the successful fight yesterday. The enemy was signally defeated although holding a commanding position, protected by an almost impassable bog and defended by concrete emplacements. Despite your heavy losses you must, from necessity, hold on to the ground won for four or five days.*"

Throughout the 6th and 7th The Queen's held on under tolerably persistent shelling, and then on the early morning of the 8th they were relieved and went back to shelters in rear, and thence by road and rail to Sercus near Ebblinghem, which was reached on the 9th, and where at last all ranks were able to rest, clean up, and reorganize.

In this, the Battalion's first fight, the losses had been very heavy, amounting to a full third of the strength. The casualties were :—Killed, 3 officers and 61 non-commissioned officers and men ; 17 officers and 241 other ranks wounded and 21 men missing. The officers killed were :—Lieutenants J. J. Brooke, A. H. A. Cooper, and A. E. Barrow, while the wounded were Lieutenant-Colonel K. A. Oswald, Captains P. M. Hepworth, V. F. Samuelson, C. G. Moss and L. J. C. Vidler, Lieutenants E. H. Dakin, A. B. Frost, A. H. Lovell, D. R. J. O'Connor, S. J. Mason, P. A. Curtois and G. A. Shaw, Second-Lieutenants J. Ost, J. C. Davie and C. A. Freestone, with Captain A. E. Mackenzie, R.A.M.C., and the Rev. M. Tron, M.C., the chaplain.

The captures made by the Battalion totalled 200 prisoners of all ranks, 8 heavy and 7 light machine guns, 5 trench mortars, and 5 granatenwerfers. No wonder that in a letter their Brigadier should have written as follows of the 3rd/4th The Queen's.

"*I always knew that any Queen's Battalion would be good, but it was a severe trial to take a new battalion through that terrific barrage fire, then across those bogs in the face of concrete emplacements, in each of which were three machine guns, it was a glorious feat. I am sorry to say the losses were dreadful ; you lost between 300 and 400 killed, wounded, and missing. The Bosche lost heavily, the place is littered with his dead. The Battalion has added another laurel to the Regiment's Battle Honours.*"

Little more than ten days later the Battalion was back again in the line near the scene of the recent fighting—east of Polygon Wood—relieving a battalion of the 69th Brigade, 23rd Division, in the front line on the night of October 22nd. It was fairly quiet during the darkest hours, but from 3.30 a.m. to daylight on the 23rd the hostile shelling was very heavy, the German gunners searching all the ground from just behind the front line to the east edge of the wood. On the left of The Queen's was the 29th Australian Infantry, and on the right the 10th Yorkshires ; there was no further advance by the Brigade, and no relief of the Battalion until the 26th, when it moved gradually back to the neighbourhood of Dickebusch Lake, where it remained until the end of the first week in November.

In these operations the 3rd/4th The Queen's had 36 other ranks killed and wounded, while two days after they came out of the line their Brigadier was killed by an enemy shell at his headquarters at Hooge Crater.

Until November 8th the Battalion remained in this area, usually doing duty in the line in the neighbourhood of Reutel, when at rest being in camp near Zillebeke or Dickebusch. It was then quartered for brief periods in the Westoutre and Ecurie Sectors, moving into the XIII Corps' area of the First Army, and while at Aubrey Camp, Ecurie, there seemed some likelihood that the Battalion might possibly be transferred to another theatre, and all preparations were actually set on foot with this end in view. As has already earlier been stated,* there was in the autumn of this year a decision come to, for the assistance of the British Army in France, to send thither some or all of the British troops then serving in Italy, relieving them there by battle-worn units from the Western Front. Some nine battalions were taken from the Army under Lord Cavan and sent to France in September, and the three divisions then serving under him were to have been exchanged. The relief was continually postponed, and the idea of exchange was finally abandoned, but apparently the 3rd/4th The Queen's was one of the battalions which would have gone from France to Italy had the original scheme been carried into effect. The success of the German attack south of Cambrai seems to have been the cause for the decision not to make any change in the disposition of the British armies.

On November 21st Lieutenant-Colonel G. H. Sawyer, D.S.O., 1st Battalion Royal Berkshire Regiment, was appointed to command the Battalion *vice* Major H. C. Cannon, M.C., who had exercised temporary command since the date of Lieutenant-Colonel Oswald being wounded.

On December 4th the 3rd/4th The Queen's were at Longavesnes, after which the 21st Division took over a sector on the front south of Gouzeaucourt, the Battalion going into the line near Vaucellette Farm—then a quiet enough part of the front. At Christmas time The Queen's were at Heudecourt, the weather at that time being intensely cold with heavy falls of snow and the trenches were consequently very wet. While in the line during this month a fighting patrol, under Sergeant W. G. Ford, obtained valuable identifications by the capture of German soldiers of the 1st Battalion 25th Regiment near Reudicourt.

The end of the 3rd/4th Battalion The Queen's Royal Regiment was very near, and it was not to see the war out. At the end of January the Battalion moved to Moislains, north of Peronne, and a few days later orders were received for the Battalion, the only Territorial unit in the Division, to be disbanded, and by February 20th this painful operation was concluded, all officers and other ranks being posted to battalions of The Queen's as under :—

To the 1st Battalion, 7 officers and 160 non-commissioned officers and men.
,, 6th ,, 7 ,, ,, 150 ,, ,, ,,
,, 7th ,, 10 ,, ,, 196 ,, ,, ,,
,, 8th ,, 10 ,, ,, 160 ,, ,, ,,

The Battalion transport was sent to the 8th Divisional Train.

To those who had the well-being of the Battalion at heart, the sudden termination of its career was a very bitter disappointment. It had earned a splendid reputation entirely due to the keen sense of *esprit de corps* among all ranks,

* See Chapter XII, page 121.

and it is satisfactory to know that the services of the 3rd/4th The Queen's are recognized and perpetuated by the presentation of a King's Colour, later deposited for safe keeping in the Parish Church, Croydon.

During the seven months that the Battalion served in France, it had 5 officers and 174 non-commissioned officers and men killed or died of wounds, 22 officers and 366 men were wounded, 6 men died of disease, while 7 only became prisoners.

In a letter to the President of the Surrey Territorial Force Association, Lieutenant-General Macready, Adjutant-General to the Forces, paid a fine tribute to the Battalion on its disbandment. He wrote :—

*" The recent reorganization of infantry in France involved the disbandment of certain battalions amongst which is the 3rd/4th Battalion The Queen's Royal West Surrey Regiment. This Battalion was a third line Territorial battalion, formed on April 24th, 1915, whose first and second lines were serving in India and Palestine.*

*" It was therefore raised to the status of an overseas unit, and was selected out of a Second Line Territorial Force Division serving at home to go to France in May, 1917. The Battalion was attached to the 12th Division in July, but in August was posted to the 21st Division, with which it served in the line near Croisilles, moving to Flanders in September, and taking part in a highly successful attack on Reutel on October 4th. Fifteen machine guns, 10 trench mortars, and 200 prisoners were taken, and the Chaplain, the Rev. M. Tron, M.C., was awarded the D.S.O. The Commanding Officer, Lieutenant-Colonel K. A. Oswald, D.S.O., was, however, wounded. The Battalion was again in action near Reutel on October 26th and November 5th, but moved south at the end of November, being in the line near Gouzeaucourt by December 10th. It continued in this area till disbanded in February, 1918. In every engagement in which this Battalion took part during its short career in the field, it upheld the brilliant and glorious traditions of The Queen's Regiment, and was awarded during the period that it was in France, two D.S.O.'s, four M.C.'s, two D.C.M.'s, and nineteen M.M.'s. Although the 3rd/4th Battalion has been disbanded, the officers, warrant officers, non-commissioned officers, and the men have not been lost to The Queen's Regiment; they have all been drafted into other battalions of the Regiment, and will continue to uphold the name and traditions of this Regiment, with the same spirit, loyalty, and ' esprit de corps ' as they have done in the 3rd/4th Battalion."*

## CHAPTER XVIII.

### THE 1ST/5TH BATTALION.

### 1914–1919.

#### INDIA AND MESOPOTAMIA.

##### BATTLE HONOURS:
"Khan Baghdadi," "Mesopotamia, 1915–1918."

DURING the years 1880–1882 the undermentioned Rifle Volunteer Corps were amalgamated and became the 4th Surrey Rifle Volunteer Corps:—

The 4th Surrey Rifle Volunteer Corps (Reigate), originally formed in September, 1859.

The 5th Surrey Rifle Volunteer Corps (Reigate), originally formed in September, 1859.

The 13th Surrey Rifle Volunteer Corps (Guildford and Godalming), originally formed in October, 1859.

The 24th Surrey Rifle Volunteer Corps (Guildford, Godalming, and Woking), originally formed in February, 1862.

In 1883 the title of the Corps was changed to the 2nd Volunteer Battalion The Queen's (Royal West Surrey) Regiment.

During the war in South Africa the Battalion contributed its quota to form the Service companies which fought beside the Regular soldiers of the 2nd Battalion of The Queen's.

On April 1st, 1908, under the Haldane scheme of Army Reorganization, the 2nd Volunteer Battalion was transferred to the Territorial Force, and became the 5th Battalion The Queen's (Royal West Surrey) Regiment, and it was now composed of eight companies located as follows:—" A," Reigate; " B," Camberley; " C," and " D," Guildford; " E," Farnham; " F," Godalming; " G," Dorking and " H," Woking—the headquarters being at Guildford. The Honorary Colonel at this period was the Right Honourable Lord Ashcombe, and the Battalion was commanded by Lieutenant-Colonel W. J. Perkins, V.D., the strength on transfer to the Territorial Force being 21 officers and 355 non-commissioned officers and men, but in 1914—the year the Great War broke out—the Battalion stood at 27 officers and 786 other ranks.

In this year the 5th Battalion proceeded to camp on July 26th with the Home Counties Division, marching from Bordon to Salisbury Plain, but the troops can scarcely have reached their training ground when the course of events brought them back again to Guildford, where the 5th Battalion arrived on August 4th, and was mobilized on the 5th, proceeding the same day to the war station at Strood near Chatham. Here, however, the 5th Territorial Battalion was very shortly relieved by the 3rd Special Reserve Battalion of the Regiment, and then went to Maidstone for training with the rest of its Brigade, until ordered to Canterbury on September 1st.

Having volunteered and been accepted for service abroad, the Battalion was ordered to proceed to India and embarked at Southampton on October 29th, 1914, in the s.s. *Alaunia*. The following are the names of the officers accompanying the Battalion abroad—Lieutenant-Colonel Hon. A. G. Brodrick, T.D.; Majors St. B. R. Sladen, T.D., and F. W. Smallpiece; Captains W. L. Hodges, C. E. H. Master, F. E. Bray and H. P. Gabb; Lieutenants P. R. Whittington, L. Whittington, L. M. Yetts, R. L. A. Atkinson, J. W. Shilcock, J. L. C. Mercer, W. P. Spens (adjutant), J. E. B. Jardine, G. C. Morton, E. W. Mountford and E. F. Evetts; Second-Lieutenants O. S. Cleverly, L. W. Jardine, F. D. Ardagh, K. F. Campion, C. R. Wigan, J. D. Gabb, G. C. Cleverly, A. D. Stoop, A. E. Clark-Kennedy and G. B. Harrison; Lieutenant and Quartermaster E. J. W. Reeder and Captain L. D. Bailey, R.A.M.C. (T.), in medical charge.

Bombay was reached on December 2nd, and, disembarking at once, the Battalion was sent by train to Lucknow, where it arrived on the 4th, and joined the brigade commanded by Major-General A. Wilson, C.B., in the 8th Division under Major-General E. S. May, C.B., C.M.G.

From here early in 1915 the 5th The Queen's, or the 1st/5th as the Battalion must now be called since its second line unit had been formed on its departure from the United Kingdom, sent two small drafts to the 2nd Battalion Norfolk Regiment in Mesopotamia; the first was made up of 29 non-commissioned officers and men under Lieutenant J. W. Shilcock, while the second contained 20 other ranks only.

On May 1st the double-company organization was introduced, " A " and " G " Companies becoming " A," " B," and " E " Companies being " B," " C " and " D," " C," while " F " and " H " became " D " Company.

At the end of October, 1915, the Battalion, exclusive of R.A.M.C. personnel attached, comprised 28 officers and 793 other ranks distributed as under:—

| | | |
|---|---|---|
| At Lucknow ... ... ... ... | 17 officers and | 432 other ranks. |
| At Lebong, near Darjeeling ... ... | 2 ,, ,, | 118 ,, ,, |
| At Fyzabad ... ... ... ... | 4 ,, ,, | 160 ,, ,, |
| At various courses, etc. ... ... | 4 ,, ,, | 20 ,, ,, |
| In Mesopotamia ... ... ... | 1 ,, ,, | 44 ,, ,, |
| *En route* to England ... ... ... ... | | 5 ,, ,, |
| Invalided ... ... ... ... ... ... | | 10 ,, ,, |
| Discharged ... ... ... ... ... ... | | 4 ,, ,, |

At 11 p.m. on October 26th the following was received from the Lucknow staff office:—

" Please hold in readiness to mobilize and concentrate 1st/5th Royal West Surrey Regiment to join the 34th Infantry Brigade. If Regiment eventually moves it will be relieved by half battalion 4th Border Regiment from Poona. Orders mobilization and concentration will issue later, pending receipt of which leave men should not be recalled. All subsidiary action to be taken in direct communication with branches concerned. Acknowledge."

This was followed at eight the next morning by a telephone message saying:—
" 1st/5th Royal West Surrey will mobilize at Lucknow as strong as possible. Field service clothing winter scale and field service scale of tentage. Movement orders will be communicated in due course."

There was very much to be done. On the 29th and 30th the Fyzabad and Lebong detachments rejoined, the Battalion was medically inspected, Captain C. E. H. Master

was told off to command the depot; but a check seemed given to all the arrangements in progress, and to the high hopes entertained by all ranks of the Battalion at the prospect of seeing something of active service, by the receipt on November 5th of a wire from divisional headquarters at Allahabad, which ran:—
"Chief General Staff wires that the mobilization of the 1st/5th Queen's is only a precautionary measure, and the unit should be informed accordingly."

In consequence of the above, matters now quieted down a bit; musketry and other routine work was resumed, when suddenly, on the 25th, came an order over the wires to the military authorities in Lucknow:—" Please be prepared to move 1st/5th West Surreys Lucknow to Bombay at few hours' notice." And then at last, on November 29th, Lieutenant A. E. Clark-Kennedy and two other ranks having left by the mail as an advanced party, the Battalion, strength 25 officers and 655 other ranks, marched to the railway station and there entrained, leaving at 10.10 a.m., and arriving at Bombay at 2 p.m. on December 1st. Here embarkation was proceeded with next day in H.M.T. *Elephanta*, which also contained Brigadier-General Tidswell and the headquarters of the 34th Infantry Brigade, and, sailing early in the afternoon of this day, the transport anchored at 5.15 p.m. on the 7th in the river just below Basrah.

The following officers arrived with the Battalion in Mesopotamia:—Lieutenant-Colonel Hon. A. G. Brodrick, T.D.; Majors F. W. Smallpiece, T.D., and W. L. Hodges; Captains F. E. Bray, H. P. Gabb, P. R. Whittington, L. Whittington, L. M. Yetts and R. L. A. Atkinson; Lieutenants J. E. B. Jardine, G. C. Morton, J. L. C. Mercer, E. W. Mountford, E. F. Evetts, O. S. Cleverly, L. W. Jardine, F. D. Ardagh, K. F. Campion, C. R. Wigan, J. D. Gabb, G. C. Cleverly, A. D. Stoop, A. E. Clark-Kennedy and G. B. Harrison; Lieutenant and Adjutant W. P. Spens, Lieutenant and Quartermaster E. J. W. Reeder and Captain L. D. Bailey, R.A.M.C. (T.).

In Mesopotamia much had happened during the weeks since the 1st/5th Battalion The Queen's had been placed under orders to prepare to proceed thither. Early in December, 1915, Major-General Townshend, after gaining success at Ctesiphon, had retreated to Kut with the remnants of his force, now only some 10,000 in number, and was here soon very closely invested; he had, however, supplies for some two months, and an assurance from the Commander of the Forces in Mesopotamia that within that time he should be relieved, and steps were at once taken far down the river to collect and start off the relieving force, of which at the moment only the remnants of General Gorringe's Indian Division was available. A new force, called the Tigris Corps, was formed under General Sir Fenton Aylmer, reinforced by a division from the Western Front, by part of another, by Indian troops from Gallipoli, and by Territorial battalions from India.

The Turkish Commander in Mesopotamia had not, however, been merely content to invest Kut; he had also made extensive preparations to bar the road by which any relieving force could arrive, and from Sheikh Saad, twenty-five miles east of Kut, right up to that place itself he had constructed or was engaged in preparing a succession of strong positions, mostly astride the river and with their flanks resting on impassable swamps.

In December General Sir John Nixon resigned the command of the Forces in Mesopotamia, and was relieved by General Sir Percy Lake.

On December 10th the 1st/5th The Queen's and other troops transhipped from the *Elephanta* on to barges, which were towed up the Euphrates by a steam tug to

Kurna, from which place the voyage was continued in forty-one *mahaillas* to Nasariyeh, which was reached on the 15th, the Battalion forming the advance of the 34th Indian Infantry Brigade, of which the other battalions were the 31st Punjabis, the 112th Infantry and the 114th Mahrattas. The Battalion was immediately employed in finding patrols and guards, in making a road to " Ur of the Chaldees," and in digging redoubts and other defensive works, finally in guarding the Turkish prisoners-of-war camp. All these duties required many duty men, and the following parties were supplied daily :—

    1 officer and 55 other ranks as guard on the prisoners-of-war camp ;
    2 officers and 2 platoons as guard at No. 9 Post ;
    1 double company road making ;
    1 officer and 20 other ranks as guard on prisoners working on the New Bund ;
    1 officer and 30 other ranks on patrol duty in the neighbourhood ;

while all other available men were employed constructing outpost works, and in such " spare time " as could be improvised detachments had to be trained for six extra machine guns, additional signallers had to be instructed, while all ranks had to be taught to pole and row *bellums* and even, so the war diary states, " to climb trees." But possibly this is " writ sarcastic !"

On January 5th, 1916, the Headquarters of the 12th Indian Division, commanded by Major-General Gorringe, arrived at Nasariyeh, and on the 11th the 1st/5th The Queen's were transferred to the 12th Brigade of this Division, their place in the 34th Brigade being taken by the 2nd Royal West Kent Regiment. The Commander of the 12th Brigade was Brigadier-General H. Brooking, and the Brigade contained the 1st/5th The Queen's, the 44th Merwara Infantry, and the 90th Punjabis. Next day General Gorringe, leaving a small garrison at Nasariyeh, moved with the bulk of his force, and including the 1st/5th The Queen's, to Butaniyeh, a village about twelve miles on the road to Kut, with the object of assisting the Kut relief force on the Tigris by a diversion, and on the 14th the Battalion was engaged in its first action.

The Battalion had been ordered to parade at 9 a.m. to accompany a reconnaissance made by the General Officer Commanding 12th Division, and the troops detailed were two squadrons 12th Cavalry, one section 30th Mountain Battery, and the 1st/5th The Queen's. General Gorringe moved off in front with the cavalry, leaving special instructions as to the protection of the survey party accompanying the reconnaissance, and the Battalion and guns came on in rear in the following order :—Half " D " Company under Captain Bray as advance guard, two guns, Battalion Headquarters, " C " Company, the machine-gun section, " B " Company, then two platoons of " A " Company under Major Hodges forming the rearguard, the flank guards being each of one platoon under Lieutenants Campion and Wigan on right and left respectively.

The column had marched some seven miles along the Suwaij Road without incident, when a mounted orderly came back with a message for the column to take up a defensive position on an irrigation channel 900 yards from Suwaij Village, and the " point " under Captain Yetts had just reached the place indicated when the cavalry were seen to be retiring. Moving on, Captain Bray with " D " Company and Captain Gabb with " C " lined the irrigation channel on right and left, and while this was being done considerable firing broke out from Arabs on the north, north-east and north-west. " B " Company now lined a second channel 200 yards in rear of the first, together with half " A," and the scouts then going forward under

Lieutenant Jardine ascertained that the enemy was all along the front and appeared to be getting round the flanks. The guns now opened and scattered some of the enemy grouped in front, while " B " Company of The Queen's was ordered to the right to support " D " and prevent the enemy getting round. At this time there was some anxiety as to what had become of the flank guards under Lieutenants Campion and Wigan.

At 11.45 General Gorringe ordered a retirement, but there was some delay, as " D " Company had several casualties and could not get these away till stretchers, which were not immediately forthcoming, could be brought up; and when this company at last began retirement the Arabs were close up to them, and the right platoon suffered some loss. News was now received that Lieutenant Wigan had taken up a position on the extreme right front, and there was some difficulty in withdrawing him, but the first position was successfully evacuated and the retirement to the second accomplished.

Retiring by alternate companies and platoons, the road was at last reached and the retreat on Butaniyeh continued until about 3.15 p.m., when the column reached a position occupied by the 34th Brigade, which had come out in support from camp on hearing news of the action, and the column now passing through proceeded into camp.

The 1st/5th The Queen's had been in action for some five hours, and the casualties numbered 14, 1 man being killed, another missing, believed killed, while Lieutenant L. W. Jardine and 11 other ranks were wounded.

The men were throughout very steady, fire control and discipline were excellent, especially considering that the ground was very broken and covered with scrub, of which the enemy took every advantage.

The weather now turned terribly cold and wet, and men on escorts and picquets had a truly trying time of it; while the Arabs were rather active about the picquets, firing into them at long range. On the 6th Private Burnett of the Battalion was severely wounded.

It had been now decided to withdraw the force from Butaniyeh back to Nasariyeh, and when this took place on February 7th the column was attacked and sustained some 300 casualties. The Queen's were on convoy escort duty, and took little part in the action, and on arrival at Nasariyeh resumed many of their former duties. Here also they found letters of four mails waiting for them, " together with 69 tins of plum puddings from the Women's Branch of the Bombay Presidency War Committee, and 86 parcels of comforts from Calcutta ladies. All were most acceptable to the troops, who had had little comfort at Butaniyeh."

On the 9th The Queen's formed part of a column which moved out under Brigadier-General Tidswell to punish those villages the inhabitants of which had given trouble on the 7th. There was some slight resistance, and as usual the retirement was followed up, but four villages of the fighting men concerned were burnt and the column was back in camp early in the afternoon, The Queen's having had two men wounded.

On February 25th the first war distinction earned by the Battalion was the D.C.M. conferred upon Private Drowley, " D " Company, for gallantry in action on January 14th.

During the next few weeks several drafts, varying in strength, arrived, until by June 3rd these amounted to 6 officers and 233 non-commissioned officers and men. The officers were Lieutenant P. F. A. Cocks, Second-Lieutenants F. C. de L. Kirk,

R. C. Ball, R. S. Lloyd and G. E. Peden; so that by this date the strength of the Battalion was 28 officers and 1,029 other ranks. During the early summer there was very heavy rain, and the river rose in flood, and the Battalion was very busily occupied in building bunds to keep out the flood water. There was also an outbreak of cholera in the native city, which was at once put out of bounds, and there were some isolated cases in the Battalion. Some of these ended fatally, as did also certain cases of enteric and heat apoplexy. In the middle of July the number of cholera cases rose appreciably, and " D " Company was moved out to a special camp; but by the end of this month the health of the Battalion improved considerably—cholera disappeared and also many of the less serious diseases from which the men had lately suffered. The temperature, which about the 20th went up to 123·5° F., and that too at a time when there was no breeze, improved during the last ten days of the month; the " Schamal " blew steadily and the nights were cool, while the days, though still usually up to 120° F., were, thanks to the breeze, not so deadly as earlier in July.

On July 31st the 1st/5th The Queen's contained 27 officers and 1,020 other ranks, distributed thus:—

|  | Officers. | N.C.Os. and Men |
|---|---|---|
| At Headquarters | 18 | 486 |
| Attached Brigade Machine-gun Section | 1 | 30 |
| Sick at Nasariyeh | 2 | 236 |
| Garrison and Battalion employment | 1 | 164 |
| At Basrah | 5 | 104 |

The Arabs having lately become unusually aggressive, coming close up to our picquets and sniping at the sentries, a column moved out on September 9th from Nasariyeh under Brigadier-General Dunsford to disperse a hostile concentration at Es Sahilan. The village was captured and destroyed, and all went well until the retirement began, when the column was followed up by some 7,000 Arabs, and the withdrawal was much pressed. The companies of the Battalion chiefly engaged were " A " and " D " in the centre and " C " Company as right flank guard, and during the later stages of the retirement the companies received but little support from our guns, possibly owing to the fact that signalling communication broke down between the rearguard and column headquarters. The column had 198 casualties, of which the 1st/5th The Queen's had their full share, 2 officers and 10 other ranks being killed or dying of wounds, while 3 officers and 32 other ranks were wounded. The officers who were killed were Captain J. C. Crowley and Second-Lieutenant F. Morris, while wounded were Captain H. P. Gabb, Lieutenants O. S. Cleverly and C. D. Ingram. Regimental Sergeant-Major Green did fine work in salving the equipment and rifles of the killed and wounded.

There is nothing special to record during the remaining months of this year, largely occupied with brigade training, and when the year 1917 opened the Battalion, while at a strength of 30 officers and 1,014 other ranks, was only in a tolerably satisfactory condition of health, the admissions to hospital being still between fifty and eighty daily. The men, however, were now well housed against the approaching bad weather, while rations had improved in variety and quality, and good and suitable clothing had been issued.

On March 27th news reached the Battalion by telephone from the Brigade Staff that the Division was under orders to proceed to Baghdad, and on the following day orders were received directing the 1st/5th The Queen's to move as strong as possible with all heavy baggage to Basrah, and it was found that "strong as possible" would mean 30 officers, 1,109 other ranks, 27 public and 46 private followers, with 32 transport drivers.

It was not, however, until June 23rd that the long-announced move actually took place, when the Battalion proceeded in four trains to Basrah, and there embarked on river steamers, voyaging up the Tigris to Baghdad, which was reached on July 1st, the 1st/5th The Queen's being camped at Hinaidi.

In the previous July the troops under the command of General Maude had carried out certain operations at Ramadie, against the Turks who then occupied an entrenched position covering the town from the east and south-east, but the great heat had caused these operations to be temporarily abandoned and the troops had fallen back, but little molested, to Sinn-el-Zibban. A month later, on the Dialah front, the enemy had been driven into the Jebel Hamrin, and a new line here taken up and consolidated. Then, as the weather grew cooler, plans were made for the capture of Ramadie, the garrison of which had been reinforced, but it was late in September before a column of adequate size could be concentrated within striking distance.

On September 17th the Battalion, strength 23 officers and 886 other ranks, left Baghdad with the 12th Infantry Brigade, Lieutenant L. F. Crane remaining behind in charge of details, and marched for Madhij, some eight miles from the Turkish outposts, arriving here on the 26th and bivouacking on the banks of the Euphrates.

"The enemy was found to be holding an advanced position four miles east of Ramadie on Mushaid Ridge, which runs north and south and rises some 60 feet above the plain. To the north of the ridge lies the Euphrates, and to the south the salt Habbaniyeh Lake. The Turkish main position was semi-circular in outline and was sited about one mile to the east and to the south of Ramadie. The eastern front ran along but behind the Euphrates Valley Canal, and the southern front across bare sandy downs extending from the Euphrates Valley Canal to the Aziziyeh Canal, which leaves the Euphrates one mile west of Ramadie and flows south.

"The plan of operations was to turn the southern flank of the Mushaid Ridge, secure a crossing over the Euphrates Valley Canal, and attack Ramadie from the south with the bulk of the column, whilst the cavalry operating west of the Aziziyeh Canal threw themselves across the enemy's communications with Hit by blocking the Aleppo road. Steps were taken to induce the enemy to expect the main attack against his left on the Euphrates, and with this intent the river was bridged at Madhij and a road was constructed thence up the left bank, whilst supplies were also collected there. The distribution of the troops until the night of the 27th-28th was also designed to give colour to such a movement.

"At 6 p.m. on the 27th two infantry columns" (under Generals Dunsford and Lucas, the 12th Brigade being with the former) "with the cavalry moved from Madhij to the position of assembly some five miles in front of our outposts, and the infantry subsequently made a night advance some two miles in a westerly direction to a position of deployment whence an attack on Mushaid could be delivered at dawn. An infantry detachment also skirted the northern edge of Lake Habbaniyeh, and before daybreak on the 28th had secured important tactical features on and behind the south flank of the Mushaid position, including a dam across the Euphrates Valley Canal, passable by all arms. This action compelled the enemy to withdraw from Mushaid Ridge, which he shelled heavily subsequently in anticipation of its

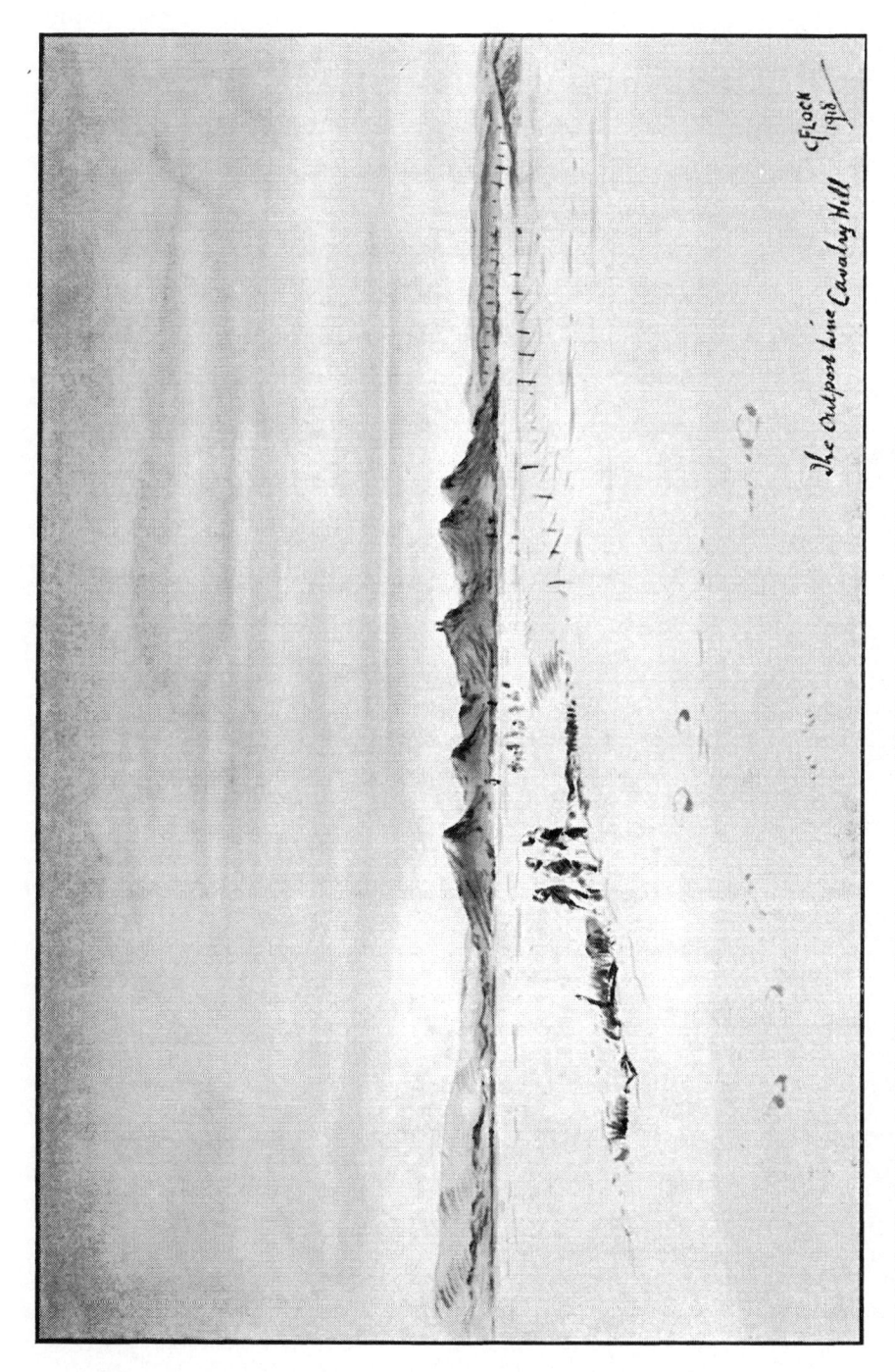

CAVALRY HILL, RAMADIE, SHOWING THE OUTPOST LINE AFTER THE CAPTURE OF RAMADIE, 1917.

## THE ATTACK ON AZIZIYEH RIDGE

occupation by our troops; but in this he was disappointed, as our infantry moved south of the ridge and crossed the dam. At 7 a.m. the cavalry were transferred from our right to our left flank, their march being secured from the enemy by Mushaid Ridge. They crossed the Euphrates Valley Canal by the dam and pushed west across the Aziziyeh Canal to a position astride the Aleppo Road so as to cut off the enemy's retreat.

"Meanwhile, to the west of the Euphrates Valley Canal, our left infantry column advanced against the enemy's southern front and occupied and consolidated a position under considerable opposition. . . . Under cover of the attack our right infantry column was withdrawn, and, passing in rear of the left column, was subsequently launched to an attack which secured a firm footing on Aziziyeh Ridge. Thus by nightfall the enemy was hemmed in on the south-east and south by our infantry and on the west by our cavalry, whilst to the north ran the River Euphrates."*

This attack on the Aziziyeh Ridge was carried out by the 39th Garhwalis and 90th Punjabis, with the 1st/5th The Queen's in support, and on the night of the 28th-29th the Battalion was ordered to dig in in two lines on the north-west side of the Rayan Knoll facing midway between the southern ends of Ramadie Ridge, then held by the 42nd Brigade, and Aziziyeh Ridge, held by the 39th and 90th Regiments. Then at 2 a.m. on the 29th orders were received to put two companies at the disposal of the Officer Commanding 90th Punjabis for an attack on Sheikh Farajah Ridge ordered to be made by the two Indian corps of the 12th Brigade at 6.30. "C" and "D" Companies were detailed, under Captain Bray, and as these moved up about 5 a.m. explosions were heard and fires started in Ramadie, while the enemy attempted to break through and retreat by the Aleppo road, but was driven back into the town by our cavalry.

At 6.20 Captain Bray was ordered by the Officer Commanding 90th Punjabis to advance between Aziziyeh Ridge and the canal and join the first line on the left of the 39th, and if Sheikh Farajah Ridge were taken, to occupy the western end of it so as to command the bridge; while if the attack failed, to work up towards Sheikh Farajah House. The companies then advanced in four lines of double platoons, "D" leading, extending in four waves on coming under rifle fire. They advanced with the 39th, and when within 200 yards of the ridge, the Turks ceased firing and began to surrender. Two platoons of "C" Company now halted and began to entrench on the ridge, while the remainder advanced, reaching the Palm Grove on the right of Aziziyeh Bridge. The consolidation of the line was now taken in hand from north-west of the bridge, where the Aleppo road crosses the canal, up to and along Sheikh Farajah Ridge. The 1st/5th The Queen's companies and the 39th had by this between them captured three guns and many prisoners.

Meanwhile the Headquarters and rest of the Battalion remained in their trenches under desultory shell fire till 10.30 a.m., when they were ordered to move to the south side of Double Hill and from there attack Unjana Ridge; but as deployment was taking place, a report came in that the ridge was already evacuated, and, moving on, the position was occupied without opposition, and here information was received that the enemy was surrendering *en masse*.

Ramadie was entered, and one company supplied a picquet to prevent looting, while the rest of the Battalion moved into camp some 500 yards downstream on the river bank.

* General Maude's despatch of October 15th, 1917.

General Maude wrote that "the units engaged displayed commendable dash and initiative," and that "throughout the operations, which were continuous, the endurance and fine fighting spirit of the troops were conspicuous, whilst the night operations so successfully carried out testified to the excellence of their discipline and training."

The casualties suffered by The Queen's may, under the circumstances, be regarded as slight, while the majority of the wounds were not serious: 11 men were killed or died of wounds, 3 officers—Captain E. W. Mountford, Lieutenant A. D. Stoop, and Second-Lieutenant C. H. Fison—and 63 other ranks were wounded.

From this time onwards the winter months were spent in digging on the defences of Ramadie, and it was not until February 3rd, 1918, that the 12th Brigade left here for Feluja, arriving on the 5th; it moved on again on the 21st with a force commanded by Major-General Brooking for certain operations which were to be conducted beyond Hit, into which place The Queen's marched on the 22nd.

Since the death from cholera of General Sir Stanley Maude at the end of November, 1917, the command of the forces in Mesopotamia had been assumed by Lieutenant-General Sir William Marshall.

The orders given to Major-General Sir H. Brooking were simple enough: he was to "drive the enemy as far as possible from Hit and inflict all possible damage on him," and the plan of operations arranged for this purpose was to make an attack against the enemy's left, and to send the cavalry and armoured motor cars round his right flank. Preparations for the attack on the 26th were nearly completed when it was found that the Turks had already began to withdraw from their forward position, but proposed making a stand north-west of Khan Baghdadi; they were, however, ejected from here the same evening with slight loss, while the cavalry gained their rear and cut off their retreat by road and river. An attempt by the enemy to break through was repulsed, and his losses amounted to 1,000 in prisoners alone.

The infantry followed up early next morning and completed the defeat, capturing many prisoners and supplies and much ammunition, while the mounted troops and cars pushed on in pursuit for seventy-three miles along the Aleppo road, and the rout of the Turks was finally consummated, General Brooking's force taking the Commander and Staff of the 50th Turkish Division, over 200 officers and more than 5,000 other ranks, with 12 field guns, 47 machine guns, and huge stocks of rifles, ammunition, and stores of all descriptions.

The 1st/5th The Queen's occupied the Turkish camp at Haditha on March 28th, while "A" and "B" Companies were placed in cars and assisted in the pursuit as far as Ana. The Battalion now marched back to Madhij for the hot weather, arriving there on the 16th.

On October 4th the 12th Brigade was moved to the Hillah area, the Battalion being stationed at Nejef and Kufa, and here the final break up commenced. At the end of November, Captain G. C. Morton, Second-Lieutenant J. Bentley, and 198 other ranks left as a draft for Salonika; and on December 22nd the first party to be demobilized left for the Base, when at intervals other parties followed.

On January 20th, 1919, the detachments at Kufa and other places rejoined headquarters at Nejef, and on March 3rd the Battalion marched to Hillah, arriving there on the 7th. From here a draft was sent to the 1st/5th East Surrey Regiment, with Captains H. D. Reilly and A. D. Stoop, M.C., Lieutenants E. Savereux, A. J. Taylor, H. W. Brown, H. T. Handscomb and B. G. Godlonton, and Second-

Lieutenants H. Gunner and F. E. Osmond ; and on the 10th the last party for demobilization left for the Base, when there remained only a cadre of 3 officers—Major P. R. Whittington, Captain and Quartermaster E. J. W. Reeder, and Lieutenant and Adjutant A. Gillott—and 43 other ranks, and these left Hillah on March 13th, embarked at Baghdad next day, and arrived at Makina on the 18th. Here the cadre boarded the *Aronda* on the 26th, and reached Bombay on April 2nd. At Bombay no delay was experienced ; the cadre—which had been joined at Amara by Lieutenant-Colonel F. E. Bray, M.C.—sailed from Bombay on April 4th in the *Port Lyttelton*, and landed on May 2nd at Plymouth, reaching Guildford on the following day, and being received by the Mayor and Corporation and accorded a civic welcome at the Guildhall.

On May 7th the non-commissioned officers and men, and on the 13th the officers of the cadre, were finally disembodied.

Captain Mountford and about 120 other ranks, forming the depot in India, came home separately.

The total casualties sustained by the 1st/5th Battalion The Queen's Royal Regiment amounted to 2 officers and 30 other ranks killed or died of wounds, 8 officers and 118 non-commissioned officers and men wounded, 1 officer and 93 men died of disease, while 6 men died while prisoners-of-war.

Maps 1, 4, 6, 7, and 8.

## CHAPTER XIX.

### THE 6TH (SERVICE) BATTALION.

### 1914–1916.

#### THE BATTLE OF LOOS AND THE BATTLE OF THE SOMME.

##### BATTLE HONOURS:
"Loos," "Somme, 1916," "Albert, 1916," "Pozières," "Le Transloy."

BEFORE proceeding to recount the part which was played in the European War by the Service battalions of the Regiment, something must be said about their creation—how and why they came into existence.

When Field-Marshal Lord Kitchener assumed office as Secretary of State for War he at once saw the urgent necessity for a very considerable increase of the Army, but he was faced with the fact that there was no regular Army basis upon which such an augmentation could be raised. Three schemes were considered in turn :—(1) To expand the Special Reserve, which was indeed in a measure regular owing to the inclusion in it of the regular depot establishments; (2) to use the organization of the Territorial Force; and (3) to create wholly new formations. The first of these was set aside for the reason that it would disorganize the Special Reserve already engaged in the provision of reserves for the Regular Army, and that the Special Reserve units were few in number and consisted almost entirely of infantry. The chief objection to (2) was the inadequacy of the framework for building up the hundred divisions upon which Lord Kitchener had decided; and it was then resolved to create new divisions at once, retaining the Special Reserve for its maintenance functions and at the same time fostering the training and recruiting and duplication of the Territorial Force. The new divisions were to be created as armies each of 100,000 men. Shortly before his death Lord Kitchener explained his methods of army manufacture to his countrymen of the House of Commons, telling them that it was necessary to feed the existing expeditionary force, to maintain adequate garrisons at home and in India, and also to produce a new army sufficient in numbers to count in a European War. "I had, rough hewn in my mind," he said, "the idea of creating such a force as would enable us continuously to reinforce our troops in the field by fresh divisions, and thus assist our Allies when they were beginning to feel the strain of the war. By this means we planned to work on the up-grade while our Allies' forces decreased, so that at the conclusive period of the war we should have the maximum trained fighting army this country could produce."

On August 8th the Field-Marshal asked for 100,000 men, and within a fortnight he had them in camp; on one day the enlistments totalled 30,000, and, as a matter of fact, the men came in more quickly than arms and clothing and equipment could be provided for them.

The 6th (Service) Battalion of The Queen's was one of the first of the New Army to be raised, and in Army Order 324, dated August 21st, 1914, was posted

## THE 6TH BATTALION GOES TO THE WAR

to the 37th Infantry Brigade of the 12th (Eastern) Division, quartered at Shorncliffe, Colchester, and Rainham. The Division was in the First New Army, commanded by General Sir A. Hunter, G.C.B., G.C.V.O., D.S.O. ; the divisional commander was Major-General J. Spens, C.B., the brigadier was Colonel C. A. Fowler, D.S.O., and the other battalions composing it were the 6th Battalion The Buffs, the 7th Battalion The East Surrey, and the 6th Battalion The Queen's Own (Royal West Kent Regiment). In the *Army List* for October,* 1914, the following are the names of the officers then belonging to the 6th (Service) Battalion The Queen's :—Lieutenant-Colonel H. F. Warden, Major C. H. Williams, Captains V. V. V. Sandiford, S. T. Watson, F. J. Roberts and C. Parsons ; Lieutenants H. C. E. Hull, H. D'A. M. Cooke and A. S. Herbert ; Second-Lieutenants C. H. E. Varndell, H. F. Orpen, E. C. L. Luxmoore, J. Sowrey, C. D. H. Wooster, R. B. Rutherford, R. E. M. Davidson, R. M. Clerk, A. J. Pike, A. R. Rawlinson, H. D. Taylor, J. E. Tollemache, W. J. Semple, H. A. R. Butler, M. R. Read, P. Cuddon, F. L. Simmons, H. C. Cannon, and T. L. Ormerod, with Lieutenant and Adjutant R. A. M. Basset and Lieutenant and Quartermaster O. K. Belchem. The 37th Brigade assembled at Purfleet.

The next nine or ten months were given up to very intensive training, and it was not until the end of May, 1915, that the Battalion received orders to prepare to proceed on service overseas. The 6th The Queen's was at that time quartered at Aldershot, and on June 6th it left that station in two trains at 5 and 5.45 p.m. for Folkestone, embarking immediately on arrival in the s.s. *Invicta* for Boulogne, which was reached at 10.35 p.m. The stay here was of the briefest, for on the following day the Battalion entrained and proceeded to Wizernes, marching thence in very great heat to Meteren, where all were accommodated in billets, and training again commenced and was carried on until, in the first week of July, the Battalion was accommodated in the Blue Blind Factory at Armentières.

At the time when the 12th Division—now commanded by Major-General Wing —arrived in France, the Battle of Ypres of this year had come to an end and the final operations of the Hooge fighting were just at this time taking place.

The Battalion spent the greater part of July, August, and September either in billets in Le Bizet or in the trenches about Le Touquet, learning all that their more experienced comrades could tell them about trench warfare, incurring a certain number of casualties and preparing to take part in their first general action. This was to be the Battle of Loos, which began on September 25th and, with its several subsidiary actions, endured until October 8th. The reason for undertaking these operations, and the results which thereby were achieved, are given as follows in the Commander-in-Chief's despatch of October 15th of this year :—" It was arranged," he wrote, " that we should make a combined attack from certain points of the Allied line during the last week in September. . . . In fulfilment of the rôle assigned to it in these operations, the Army under my command attacked the enemy on the morning of September 25th. The main attack was delivered by the I and IV Corps between the La Bassée Canal on the north and a point of the enemy's line opposite the village of Grenay on the south. At the same time, a secondary attack, designed with the object of distracting the enemy's attention and holding his troops to their ground, was made by the V Corps on Bellewaarde Farm, situated on the east of Ypres. Subsidiary attacks with similar objects were delivered by the III and Indian Corps north of the La Bassée Canal and along the whole front of the Second Army."

* No *Army List* was published for September of this year.

In these operations the 12th Division fought in the XI Corps of the First Army; and the actual strength of the 6th The Queen's at the beginning of September was 25 officers and 1,010 other ranks.

The Battalion remained in the neighbourhood of Armentières until the end of September, when it moved by rail and road to Corons de Rutoire, south of Vermelles, where the Brigade of which it formed part was in divisional reserve, the other two brigades being in the trenches along the Lens—Hulluch road; and the XI Corps was now to take part in what is known as "the actions of the Hohenzollern Redoubt," which may be regarded as included in the operations of the Battle of Loos, though, strictly speaking, these took place on dates rather outside those of the actual battle.

Lord French thus describes* certain notable tactical points in the British front:—

"Fosse 8" (a thousand yards south of Auchy), which is a coal-mine with a high and strongly defended slag-heap. "The Hohenzollern Redoubt." A strong work thrust out nearly 500 yards in front of the German lines and close to our own. It is connected with their front line by three communication trenches abutting into the defences of Fosse 8. "Cité St. Elie." A strongly defended mining village lying 1,500 yards south of Haisnes. "The Quarries," lying halfway to the German trenches west of Cité St. Elie. "Hulluch," a village strung out along a small stream, lying less than half a mile south-east of Cité St. Elie and 3,000 yards north-east of Loos. Half a mile north of Hill 70 is "Puits 14 Bis," another coal-mine, possessing great possibilities for defence when taken in conjunction with a strong redoubt situated on the north-east side of Hill 70.

Then later, in detailing the operations which commenced on October 13th, the Commander-in-Chief wrote:—†"The divisions chiefly engaged were the 1st Division (IV Corps) and the 12th and 46th Divisions (XI Corps). Speaking generally, the objective of the 1st Division was the enemy's trenches on the Lens—La Bassée road; that of the 12th Division was the Quarries; whilst the troops of the 46th Division attacked the Hohenzollern Redoubt and Fosse 8. The day's fighting commenced with an artillery bombardment of the objectives of the attack, and in this bombardment the French artillery on our right collaborated. Shortly before the attack was launched at 2 p.m. smoke was turned on all along our front from the Béthune—La Bassée road southwards, and under cover of this smoke the attack was delivered."

Major-General Wing had been killed by a shell on October 2nd, and the command of the 12th Division had next day been assumed by Major-General A. B. Scott, C.B., D.S.O.

On the morning of the 12th orders were received that the 37th Brigade, in conjunction with the 35th and 1st Brigades, would attack the enemy's line from the Hohenzollern Redoubt to the Lens—La Bassée road. The 6th The Queen's was simply to hold its own line, assist the attack on either flank with fire, and demonstrate as if an attack were about to take place. Seven hundred and fifty Threlfallite smoke bombs were issued to "C" and "D" Companies so as to enable these to make a smoke barrage.

The early morning of the 13th was quiet, and at noon the British guns opened and reply was immediately made by those of the enemy, which did considerable damage to the Battalion trenches, while all the telephone lines to the companies

* Despatch of October 15th, 1915. † Despatch of July 31st, 1916.

were cut and could not be repaired. The smoke bombs were lit at 1 p.m., but did not make a very good barrage, while they drew no small amount of fire from the enemy. "The attack on the right was carried out by the 37th Brigade (Fowler), the 7th East Surrey with the 6th Royal West Kent in support, against Gun Trench, and the 6th Buffs against a trench to the north of it."*

At 2 p.m., so the story in the Battalion diary runs, the East Surreys, on the immediate right, assaulted the German trench between G. 12 B. 22 and G. 12 D. 57 and got into it. At 4.30 p.m., after repeated appeals for assistance from the company of the East Surreys in the German trench, one platoon of " A " Company, under Lieutenant Pike, and one section of " D " Company were sent to its assistance. The platoon of " A " succeeded in blocking the German communication trench and held it. " B " Company, which was at the disposal of the Officer Commanding 7th East Surrey Regiment, was sent to support him at 4.30 p.m., and two platoons of this company moved into the three-foot trench behind the captured German trench, while two were kept in reserve. Our machine guns made good practice on some of the enemy who were running out of the trench when the East Surreys advanced. During the whole afternoon and evening the enemy kept up a lively artillery fire on our trenches, but did not do much damage. Second-Lieutenant Mann, who had been sent to act as liaison officer between the Buffs and the right of the 35th Brigade, did very good work.

The casualties in the Battalion were 1 man killed and 15 non-commissioned officers and men wounded.

"The day's fighting resulted in the capture of Gun Trench, the south-west face of the Quarries, with the exception of a portion in the centre, and the greater part of the north-west face, to be known later as the Hairpin Trench. . . . The following message was received by the General Officer Commanding the Division from the Corps Commander :—

" ' *Please convey to the officers, non-commissioned officers and men of the 12th Division my appreciation of their successful attack against Gun Trench on the 13th inst., and also the efforts to gain the Quarries, where they have made an important and successful advance. This advance was carried out by troops who had been for some days in the trenches, and reflects great credit on all.*' "

Next day the Battalion was relieved, incurring some 15 more casualties during the process of relief, and went back to the old British trenches; here it was in reserve to the 36th Brigade, the remaining three battalions of the 37th being at Noyelles-les-Vermelles.

" The 12th Division had thus passed through its first important engagement, gaining great experience from the twenty-one days on the battle front. It had been successful in attack and defence, had withstood heavy casualties—117 officers and 3,237 other ranks having been killed or wounded—and had given proofs of heroism in action. With increased training and experience, its future as a fighting unit seemed assured."

Five days were spent in reorganizing and refitting and in receiving reinforcements, and then on October 26th the Division took over the line facing the Hohenzollern Redoubt, and steps were at once taken to improve the trenches, dug-outs and shelters. Heavy rain came on and much discomfort was experienced, while many men were admitted to hospital suffering from " trench feet."

* This and the paragraphs which follow in inverted commas are taken from *The History of the 12th Division*, by P. M. Brumwell, pp. 20 *et seq.*

On November 1st the 12th Division was transferred to the I Corps, and at the end of the month was sent to the reserve area near Lillers, the 37th Brigade being at Ecquedecques and the 6th The Queen's at Lières; this was a welcome change, as the troops had been in the line since September 30th except for five days out. The period at "rest" was not, however, a long one, for "on December 10th the Division moved up and relieved the 33rd Division on the Givenchy sector, headquarters at Béthune. If the last front was bad, this one beggared description. In the Festubert section the country, principally water-meadows, was intensely wet and waterlogged; the rain had filled the trenches, and pumping had not overcome this trouble. Along a large portion of the front line the parapet appeared in the form of islands above the water. These islands became small defended posts holding from five to ten men, and were called 'keeps.' They could not be approached during daylight, and life was so intolerable in them that reliefs took place every twenty-four hours under cover of darkness. On the other hand, they were immune from attack except by artillery, and to that they offered a very small mark. Each keep was provided with bombs and ammunition, and the non-commissioned officer had two Very light pistols at his disposal. The actual islands were dry, though in many places the sentries stood in the water with their waders on. In other portions of the line the trenches were more or less normal, but inclined to be very wet."

Shortly after midnight on December 12th-13th, when the Battalion was up in the line, a mine was successfully exploded near the trenches then occupied, and the company of the Battalion received great praise for the promptitude and initiative shown in seizing the near lip of the crater and denying it to the enemy.

Christmas Day, 1915, was spent in the trenches, and was passed in pursuits of a kind not usually associated with this festival. "Christmas Day—Our artillery bombarded the enemy at 4 a.m. and kept it up most of the day; not much retaliation from the enemy. Gradually getting the water pumped out." So runs the day's entry in the diary; and in such manner was passed the first winter at the war by the 6th Battalion The Queen's.

Early in February, 1916—by which time the command of the 37th Brigade had passed from Brigadier-General Fowler to Brigadier-General A. B. E. Cator—the 12th Division was holding much the same line as in the previous November, from the Quarries to the north of the Hohenzollern Redoubt, but the general conditions had in the meantime been much improved.

The month of March was to prove a very trying period of mine warfare. The Germans in the course of their recent operations had formed four huge craters in "No-Man's-Land" in the neighbourhood of the Hohenzollern Redoubt, and the lips of each of these were held by the opposing forces. Then, by each side, mines were exploded and sapping was conducted out to the craters, and finally a scheme was prepared to destroy the whole of the German underground system, and four huge mines were made and charged in the Hohenzollern sector. A large amount of the preparatory work in connection with these was done by the 37th Brigade, and the mines were ready by the beginning of March, when the 36th Brigade attacked in the hope of gaining the enemy front trenches. These operations—attack and counter-attack, mining and counter-mining—went on all through March and up to April 23rd, and though no action on a big scale resulted, the work entailed continuous fighting and resulted in heavy loss, amounting to considerably over 4,000 casualties in the 12th Division.

Sir Douglas Haig "considered that the recent operations at the Hohenzollern Redoubt were well arranged and conducted, and agreed in the opinion of the Army Commander that, though the losses were heavy, the results gained justify the undertaking."

The Army Commander, General Sir C. Monro, wrote:—" The Army Commander will be glad if you will convey to Brigadier-Generals Boyd-Moss and Cator, and the troops who have been engaged in the recent operations at the Hohenzollern Redoubt, his appreciation of the determined and gallant spirit in which they have held to the craters under exceptionally arduous conditions."

On relief on April 25th the 6th The Queen's proceeded by rail and road by way of Nœux-les-Mines and Lillers to Allouagne, where it was accommodated in billets, and here or hereabouts the Brigade remained some weeks, engaged in training of a varied and very strenuous kind.

"On June 12th one Field Company Royal Engineers moved south to the III Corps near Albert, for already the Somme battlefield was casting its shadow before. Two more were to follow, and the General Officer Commanding the divisional artillery and some staff officers of the Division were ordered in that direction too. Our future destination, hitherto kept secret, was therefore revealed, and between the 16th and 18th the Division detrained at Longeau, two miles east of Amiens, marching to the Flesselles area, at which latter place the headquarters were located. The Division now belonged to the III Corps (Pulteney) of the Fourth Army (Rawlinson). The other divisions of the Corps were the 8th, 19th and 34th, and final training for the expected rôle of the Division took place—viz., the capture of Martinpuich, a village some three miles behind the German front line. . . . Kits were now reduced to a minimum, and on June 27th the Division commenced moving up to the front to take part in one of the biggest battles of the British Army, known to future history as the Battle of the Somme. The attack was to be made by the Fourth Army on a twenty-five mile front extending from Maricourt in the south to Gommecourt in the north. The Sixth French Army was operating on our right. In the opening phase the 34th and 8th Divisions of the III Corps were to attack La Boisselle and Ovillers, and the 19th and 12th were to pass through and push forward."*

The preliminary bombardment of and attack upon the enemy positions were to have begun on June 25th, but the weather was very inclement and operations were postponed for forty-eight hours; the 12th Division did not, however, move forward until the 30th, and it was late in the morning of July 1st when the infantry brigades reached Henencourt and Millencourt. By this time the attack had opened and the 8th Division had incurred very heavy casualties; it was therefore relieved by the 12th Division, which was ordered on the 2nd to push on to the capture of Ovillers, the 19th advancing on La Boisselle, while the X Corps on the left was to attack the Leipzig salient. As it, however, unfortunately turned out, the X Corps attack was postponed, with the result that the German machine guns on this flank were able to give their undivided attention to the 12th Division.

At 9.15 on the morning of July 1st the 6th The Queen's arrived at the intermediate line of trenches north-west of Albert, marching thence to the front line in relief of the 2nd Battalion Rifle Brigade. Here the next day was spent quietly except for some desultory shelling, and at 3.15 a.m. on July 3rd "the Division attacked on a two-brigade front, the 35th on the right. . . . the 37th on the left with the

* *The History of the 12th Division*, pp. 49, 50.

6th Queen's and 6th Royal West Kent Regiments in front, the 6th Buffs in support, and the 7th East Surrey in reserve. The 36th Infantry Brigade held the extreme left of the front line and was in divisional reserve. . . . The 6th Queen's, on the right of the 37th Brigade attack, only gained the front line in one place, elsewhere the Battalion was held up by uncut wire and machine-gun fire from Mash Valley."

Thus the Divisional History; the account taken from the Battalion diary now follows:—" At 3.12 a.m. the 1st Platoon of 'B,' the right company, closely followed by 2nd, 3rd, and 4th, advanced. The 1st Platoon got to the enemy parapet, where the officer in command was killed and the majority of the men were hit by machine-gun and rifle fire, but the bombers knocked out an enemy machine gun in an advanced sap. The 2nd Platoon also got to the German wire and was then stopped by the enemy fire, the 3rd was checked in rear of the 2nd, while the 4th Platoon got halfway, but lost heavily and went no further.

"The 1st Platoon of 'C,' the left company, went too far to the left; the 2nd caught up with the 1st with about five men only, the remainder being hit by machine-gun fire, while the Lewis-gun team entered the enemy trench with the Royal West Kent Regiment and was there captured. The 3rd Platoon suffered heavily, as did the 4th, and were stopped by the hostile fire.

"'A,' the left rear company, followed 'C' over the top, but went more to the right; the 1st Platoon got up to the German wire, but found it uncut and was brought to a halt; the 2nd and 3rd Platoons suffered from machine-gun and rifle fire, and the commander of the company was missing. The 4th Platoon, owing to the trench being blocked, got up late and was ordered not to advance further.

"Seeing the hopelessness of further attack, the advance of 'D,' the right rear company, was stopped, but on the receipt of orders at 4.30 p.m.—'Suffolks on your right have got in, endeavour to push on and support them'—they were sent forward again, but coming at once under heavy machine-gun fire the company did not get far, while all its officers were killed or wounded."

The reasons for the failure of the attack were generally as under:—
1. The fire of the enemy machine guns swept the whole ground.
2. The German wire was insufficiently cut.
3. The time available for the arrangement of the attack was too short, the ground was not known, and there was consequent loss of direction.
4. The enemy trenches were thick with Germans, so that the British bombardment must have been comparatively ineffective.

The losses in the 6th The Queen's were heavy, 10 out of 18 officers being hit, while 294 non-commissioned officers and men became casualties, 23 being killed, 154 wounded, while 117 were missing. Of the officers, Lieutenant C. W. Fitch and Second-Lieutenant C. S. Hall were killed, Captain H. A. R. Butler, Lieutenant R. E. Johnson and Second-Lieutenants T. L. Ormerod and F. W. Elliot were wounded, while Captains E. Wright (later reported killed) and R. B. Rutherford (later reported killed), Lieutenant M. G. L. Wallich, and Second-Lieutenant A. D. W. Ward were missing.

The 12th Division moved into the V Corps, Fifth Army, on July 5th, on which day Second-Lieutenant A. J. Sells and 5 more other ranks were wounded.

The following Order of the Day was received from the G.O.C. III Corps:—

"*As the 12th Division is leaving the III Corps, the Corps Commander wishes to thank all ranks and to express his appreciation of the gallantry and dash shown in the attack on Ovillers. He is also grateful for the very efficient support which the*

MEN OF THE 7TH BATTALION AFTER REACHING THEIR OBJECTIVE ON THE MONTAUBAN-MAMETZ ROAD ON THE FIRST DAY OF THE BATTLE OF THE SOMME, 1916.

*Division rendered to their comrades of the 19th Division, who were fighting in La Boisselle. The Commander-in-Chief desires Sir William Pulteney to convey his congratulations to General Scott and the Brigadiers of the 12th Division, and all ranks should be informed of his satisfaction."*

On the 7th the attack on Ovillers was resumed, on this occasion the 37th Brigade assisting by making a smoke screen on the left and by covering machine-gun fire, and certain positions were captured providing good starting points for a further advance, but on the 8th the 12th Division was relieved by the 32nd and moved back next day, the Headquarters to Contay and the 37th Brigade to Warloy.

" One of the main difficulties the troops had to contend with in the attack was the mud, which was very deep and sticky, in many places men being unable to move without assistance. . . . On capturing the enemy's trenches, a large quantity of tinned meat, cheese, butter, etc., was found, also mineral waters and packets of Iron Crosses done up in pink tissue paper !"*

The Division was now, during the next few days, a good deal moved about, first being transferred from the X to the VIII Corps, headquarters being at Bus-les-Artois ; then on the 20th it returned to the line near Beaumont Hamel, finally five days later moving back to the sector from which on July 9th it had been withdrawn, and coming under the orders of the II Corps. This portion of the line had been somewhat advanced since the 12th Division had left it, and it was now required, in company with other divisions on right and left, to push forward, secure the high ground north and north-east of Pozières, and destroy the German garrison in the Thiepval area. With the operations that followed the 37th Infantry Brigade was not greatly concerned, and the 6th The Queen's in particular had but little to do ; then, on August 14th, the Division was once again transferred and, leaving the II Corps and the Fifth Army, marched to the Arras Sector and joined the VI Corps of the Third Army, the 37th Brigade being on the right about Brétencourt and the Battalion in billets in Sombrin.

" The front now held was an interesting one, involving the defence of the south suburbs of the city of Arras and was some 9,000 yards in extent. The attitude of the enemy was reported quiet. The battle on the Somme " (in progress since July 1st) " occupied most of his attention, and this portion of the line was held by those of his troops who had been withdrawn from that struggle to recoup and enjoy a period of comparative rest. . . . Our position, running along the valley of the Crinchon, was very much dominated by that of the Germans on the rising ground to the east, especially by Beaurains, and whereas our communication trenches were all on the forward slope of the hill and so in full view of the enemy, his were over the rise and practically unseen."

The time spent here may almost be described as one of rest, and preparing to take part later on in the long-enduring Battle of the Somme ; but it was a period of many activities, and several raids were carried out against the enemy trenches. One of these was conducted by some of the 6th The Queen's on the night of September 17th, and is described as follows in the Battalion diary :—" At 9 p.m. a raiding party of one officer—Second-Lieutenant Robson—and 13 other ranks went out to Sap H. They found the wire cut and thrown about in confused masses, but had little difficulty in getting through. No opposition was offered, and two parties went up trenches right and left ; the left trench was found purposely blocked with wire and

* *The History of the 12th Division*, p. 60.

disused; the right party went up the main trench about 20 yards, and was also stopped by wire which had been blown into it, so was obliged to retire, and on doing so was fired on by a sentry, whom the party bombed but could not reach by reason of his being behind wire. Second-Lieutenant Robson and Sergeant Pentelow had proceeded in the meantime over the open to the north of the sap and reached the main German line, which they explored without result. On hearing the first shot and a bell ring, they returned to the sap-head, where Second-Lieutenant Robson was badly wounded in the head by a bomb. Sergeant Pentelow, on finding his officer hit, ordered the party to close and retire, while he helped Second-Lieutenant Robson in."

On September 26th and 27th the 12th Division was relieved by the 14th and commenced the move—mainly by bus—to the Somme area, leaving the VI Corps for the XV of the Fourth Army, and on the night of October 1st-2nd it had taken over a portion of the front line, the 37th Brigade being on the right in the north and east extremities of Gueudecourt, with the 36th Brigade on the left as far west as the Flers—Ligny—Thilloy road, while the third brigade of the Division was in reserve in Bernafay Wood. The 6th The Queen's relieved the 1st Lincoln Regiment in the support line behind Gueudecourt—" A " Company in Pioneer Trench, " B " and " D " in Grid Trench, and " C " with Battalion Headquarters in Bull's Road Trench.

An offensive had been planned for October 5th, but owing to bad weather it was postponed until the 7th, when the Fourth Army attacked, with the Fifth Army co-operating on its left and the Sixth French Army on its right. The objective of the 12th Division was Bayonet Trench, to be followed by an advance of some 500 yards; the 20th and 41st Divisions were on the right and left respectively.

The 37th Brigade attacked the enemy front-line trenches opposite Gueudecourt with the 6th Buffs on the right and the 6th Royal West Kent on the left, the 6th The Queen's being in support, and the 7th East Surrey Regiment in reserve; but the attack was held up by very heavy rifle and machine-gun fire, and both the front-line battalions suffered many casualties. At 6 p.m. two companies of the 6th The Queen's were ordered to advance and attack Rainbow Trench and drive the enemy out, but on arrival this was found to be impossible, as the position was not at all clear, so the two companies occupied part of the Buffs' line, these now being very weak; and later The Queen's took over the whole line from the Buffs, holding it until relieved about midday on the 9th.

From the 5th to the 8th the casualties in the 6th The Queen's totalled 11 killed, 4 officers and 72 other ranks wounded. The officers were Lieutenants C. E. S. Beadle and H. A. Parkinson, Second-Lieutenants A. G. Maisey and D. R. Sharman.

There was continued fighting, with a more limited objective, during the days that followed, but the 6th Battalion The Queen's does not seem to have been seriously engaged, and on the 19th the 12th Division was relieved by the 29th and returned to the VI Corps near Arras. The Battalion marched on the 20th to Ribemont, on the 21st to the Albert—Amiens road, whence buses took it as far as Wanquetin, when the 6th marched on to billets in Simoncourt. The move was not yet, however, fully completed, for on the 25th the Battalion marched from Simoncourt to Rivière, and here furnished the garrisons of the four " keeps " in F Sector, " A " Company providing the garrison for the Factory Keep, " B " Company for the Petit Moulin Keep, " C " for the Wailly Keep, and " D " Company for the Petit Chateau Keep.

The 12th Division was now occupying very much the same sectors which had been handed over at the end of September.

When out of the line the 6th The Queen's appear to have usually been billeted in Beaumetz, and from here on the night of December 5th-6th the Battalion carried out a raid upon Saps Z. 14 and Z. 15, the object being to kill Germans, to capture prisoners, and to obtain identifications. The raiding party was composed of 3 officers and 74 other ranks, and was under the command of Captain Clerk. At 6.30 p.m. on the 5th patrols went out to examine the wire, and reported that it presented no obstacle, being well broken in front of both saps, while there was a good gap in the wire between the saps. At 8.20 p.m. the tape layers started out, the moon being at the time obscured and the conditions favourable; these were followed fifteen and twenty minutes later by the covering, blocking and raiding parties. At 8.45 the moon suddenly appeared through the clouds and the whole sky became clear and visibility good, and Captain Clerk then decided that it was useless to go on and recalled the different parties. Second-Lieutenant Pym, in charge of the left party, was just about to withdraw at 9 p.m. when two heavy trench-mortar shells fell in the trench, burying and killing him and three other ranks, and partially burying twelve others, some of whom were badly shaken. It had been intended to try to carry out the raid at 3 a.m. on the 6th, but the scheme was abandoned as, under the circumstances, there did not seem any reasonable chance of success.

" On December 17th the Division was again relieved by the 14th Division, and proceeded to the Grand Rullecourt and Ambrines area, with divisional headquarters at Le Cauroy. This was the first real rest since the opening of the Somme battle on July 1st, and as it meant Christmas out of the line all ranks thoroughly appreciated the fact. The usual cleaning up, refitting and reorganizing took place, and the country round was scoured for the orthodox necessities for Christmas dinners. A ton of divisional Christmas cards arrived for dispatch to our friends. Tournaments, races and various competitions took place, the most successful being a horse show, a regimental drum competition, and a Marathon race, in which 117 out of 140 competitors finished the course."

Maps 4, 6, and 9.

## CHAPTER XX.

### THE 6TH (SERVICE) BATTALION (*Continued*).
### 1917–1919.

#### BATTLE OF ARRAS, BATTLE OF CAMBRAI, THE VICTORY BATTLES.

##### BATTLE HONOURS:
"Arras, 1917." "Scarpe, 1917." "Cambrai, 1917." "Somme, 1918." "Ancre, 1918." "Bapaume, 1918." "Amiens." "Hindenburg Line." "Epéhy."

"EARLY in the winter it had been settled that the offensive of the British Army in the spring of 1917 was to be carried out by the First and Third Armies on a front of about twelve miles, with Arras as the centre. In the beginning of January this information reached the divisions concerned, and on the 14th the 12th Division took over a sector of 2,000 yards extending from 700 yards south of Faubourg St. Sauveur to the River Scarpe. The enemy's trenches ran parallel to ours at a distance of about 200 yards, except on the extreme left of Blangy village, where, in one place, they approached as close as eight yards. From this sector the attack of the VI Corps was to be launched. The 37th Infantry Brigade took over this portion of the line, which was immediately on the left of that handed over by the Division in December. The other two infantry brigades remained in the training area, divisional headquarters moving to Agnez les Duisans."*

There was a very great deal to be done in preparation for the forthcoming offensive, and the three brigades had to find 2,500 men daily for fatigues. In consequence the arrangement was that one brigade was in the trenches, one other was in the training area, while the third found the working parties.

"In the third week in January the 3rd and 15th Divisions took over their sub-sectors of the trenches, the 12th retaining the centre one with a front of about 800 yards. Although there was so much to be done in preparation for the main battle, an aggressive spirit had to be maintained; and as the command of 'No-Man's-Land' was very important to us, raids were carried out frequently and with somewhat stronger forces than previously. On the night of February 3rd, which was very dark, the Germans, under cover of a bombardment, raided a sap manned by one non-commissioned officer and six men of the 6th Queen's. Two sentries on duty at the head of the sap observed the enemy approaching, and one ran back to warn those in the trench close by, but being wounded fell dead in the trench. The non-commissioned officer and the other men then rushed up the sap, and, opening fire with a Lewis gun, wounded and took one of the raiders prisoner. The original sentry was missing and taken prisoner. . . . The attack of the British forces, aiming at the capture of Monchy-le-Preux and the Vimy Ridge and the breaking through of the German line, was to be launched on April 9th. On the right was the Third Army with the VII, VI and XVII Corps; on the left, the First Army with the Canadian Corps.

* *The History of the 12th Division*, p. 90.

"The task of the VI Corps, with the 3rd Division on the right, the 12th in the centre, and the 15th on the left, was to gain the Wancourt—Feuchy line, entailing an advance of over 4,000 yards. . . . Of the 12th Division, the 37th Brigade on the right and the 36th on the left were to capture the Black Line (800 yards), consisting of the enemy's front system, as well as the Blue Line, a further distance of 1,000 yards, in which were a series of strong redoubts. The 35th Infantry Brigade was then to pass through and, going forward, attack the Brown Line, including the Wancourt—Feuchy trench, well wired and containing the strong post known as the Feuchy Chapel Redoubt on the Cambrai Road."*

As an idea existed that the Germans might be withdrawing from the 12th Division front, a raid was carried out by a party of the 6th The Queen's at 9 p.m. on April 7th. The party was divided into two, and that under Second-Lieutenant R. Harding was successful in capturing two prisoners; but that under Second-Lieutenant C. Bourne went forward with such dash that it passed through our own barrage and penetrated to the German second line, where the officer was wounded and captured with four of his men. Second-Lieutenant Harding was also slightly wounded. One non-commissioned officer of the raiding party crawled back and reported that the first and second lines of the enemy front system were hardly recognizable, and presented little or no obstacle.

At 5.30 a.m. on April 9th the leading waves of the infantry advanced under cover of a very effective creeping barrage, the 6th The Queen's and 7th East Surrey Regiment being respectively on the right and left of the 37th Brigade attacking line, and the attack was so sudden and the advance so rapid that many of the enemy were unable to issue from their dug-outs—deep and with very narrow exits—in time to oppose the British advance. The final objective of The Queen's was Glasgow Trench, and this was gained with comparatively little loss. The counter-battery work had practically silenced the German guns, and the assaulting battalions now halted on the so-called Black Line to clear up the captured ground and to allow the supporting battalions to pass through and form up for the second phase. At 4.30 p.m. Captain Pike with 250 men was sent up to support the 7th Suffolk Regiment of the 35th Brigade, who were attacking the Brown Line; this, however, was subsequently found to have been evacuated by the enemy. The rest of the Battalion remained in Glasgow Trench, where the detached party rejoined during the night.

On the 10th the 37th Division passed through the 12th and went on to the capture of Monchy-le-Preux, and on the night of the 12th-13th, the 12th, on relief by the 39th Division, moved back to Arras. Next day the Division was transferred to the XVIII Corps and moved to the neighbourhood of Doullens, the 37th Brigade being about the village of Humbercourt. In the Battle of Arras the 12th Division on its own front had penetrated to a depth of 4,000 yards, had captured over 1,200 prisoners, 41 field guns and howitzers and 28 machine guns, and had suffered casualties to the number of over 2,000 killed, wounded, and missing. The 6th Battalion The Queen's had 2 officers—Captain R. M. Clerk and Second-Lieutenant E. H. Aspden—and 4 other ranks killed, 7 officers and 88 non-commissioned officers and men wounded, while 19 men were missing. The wounded officers were Captain A. J. Pike, Second-Lieutenants J. P. Boden, J. S. Lewis, R. Harding, J. F. Henderson, C. L. Borst and A. S. Worman.

* *The History of the 12th Division*, pp. 93, 97.

The following Order of the Day was issued after the action:—

"*Lieutenant-General J. A. L. Haldane, C.B., D.S.O., commanding the VI Corps, desires me to express to all ranks his grateful appreciation of the brilliant work carried out by the 12th Division whilst under his command.*

"A. B. SCOTT, *Major-General,*
"*Commanding 12th Division.*"

During the action of the 9th and 10th the 6th The Queen's were commanded by Major N. T. Rolls.

The Battalion was only some ten days absent from the front line, for by April 24th the Division was again back at Arras, rejoining the VI Corps; but in the first instance the 35th Brigade only was engaged, endeavouring to gain a position on the south side of the River Scarpe, but these operations were not altogether successful, and preparations were now made for an attack on a more extended scale. This was timed to take place on May 3rd, and the Fifth, Third, and First Armies were all to take part, the 12th Division making an advance of nearly 2,000 yards on the right and 3,000 on the left, the latter including the capture of the village of Pelves: there were three objectives, known as the Brown, the Yellow, and the Red Lines.

The 12th Division attacked at 3.45 a.m. on May 3rd, the 37th and 36th Brigades on the right and left, and in the first-named the 6th Buffs and 7th East Surrey being in the front line, with the 6th Royal West Kent in support and the 6th The Queen's in reserve. The front-line battalions were repulsed and the West Kent Regiment moved up to reinforce, while The Queen's advanced to the Gun Pits, remaining here for the rest of the day. At 9.45 p.m. the Royal West Kent attacked Scabbard Trench, and "B" and "D" Companies of The Queen's came up to support them; but the attack failed and the Battalion was then sent up to the vicinity of Monchy Wood. The casualties this day were 3 men killed, Lieutenant E. T. Trend and 32 other ranks wounded.

"At 2 a.m. on the 4th," so runs the Divisional History, "it was evident that the 37th Brigade had made no progress, and as the village of Rœux had not been captured and Devil's Trench was strongly held by the enemy, General Scott ordered the 36th Brigade to withdraw from the north end of Gun Trench and consolidate Scabbard Trench. It had been a disappointing day and the gain was small, but the cause must be attributed to the advance having been attempted at such an early hour over a portion of ground abounding in small valleys, banks and shell-holes, where the objectives were ill-defined, also to the unfortunate overrunning and failure to mop up Devil's Trench in the dark."

This Devil's Trench was on the far side of a ridge, and when any attack reached the crest it came under a very heavy fire both from that trench and Gun Trench; a second attempt at its capture, made on the 12th by the 36th and 37th Brigades, was again unsuccessful, and on the night of the 16th the Division was relieved and moved back to the Le Cauroy area, where it arrived on May 24th and once more joined the XVIII Corps. It remained in these parts until the middle of June, the 6th The Queen's occupying billets in Ivergny. By June 19th, however, the Division had gone back to Arras and to the VI Corps, later joining the XVII, on this relieving the VI at the end of the month, and for some days after return to this area the 6th The Queen's occupied billets in Gouy-en-Artois.

[*Copyright: Imperial War Museum.*

VIEW OF A PORTION OF A BATTLEFIELD SHOWING SHELL-CRATERS FILLED WITH WATER.

From now on until well into October, a period of some eighteen weeks, the 12th Division held the Monchy-le-Preux sector ; it was a time during which very much useful work was done ; a great many raids were undertaken against an enemy who himself was by no means unenterprising, and the strain on all ranks was severe and constant. Early in October there were strong rumours in circulation that the Division would shortly be relieved, and it was thereupon decided to carry out one more raid on a larger scale than ever before. Some 750 infantry were to participate, and over 200 guns, large and small, with 20 trench mortars, were also to be employed, and those detailed for the raid were trained for a week over taped ground at Beaurains. The raid was divided into three phases : there was first the bombardment, commencing at 10.35 a.m. on October 10th, then the move forward of the selected parties of infantry of the 35th and 37th Brigades, and finally the opening of the raid at 4.55 p.m. There were three infantry parties—one on the right from the 6th The Queen's, a second in the centre supplied by the 6th Royal West Kent Regiment, while the left party was detailed from the 7th Norfolk Regiment. The raiding party from the 6th The Queen's consisted of four bodies each of 50 non-commissioned officers and men under an officer—No. 1 commanded by Second-Lieutenant Daly, No. 2 by Second-Lieutenant Manicon, No. 3 by Second-Lieutenant Borst, and No. 4 by Second-Lieutenant Bell, the whole under the direction of Captain Pike.

The several parties of The Queen's assembled in Hoe Support and Knife Trench, and, moving up to the assembly trenches from here, all were in position by twenty minutes before zero hour. Enemy opposition in the front line, except on the extreme right, was of a somewhat feeble character, but more resistance was met with in the German support line and in Beetle Trench, resulting in many Germans being killed, but more than one case occurred of Germans putting up their hands and then opening fire again ; " these men," says the diary tersely, " were promptly dealt with in the usual way." The operation was a decided success, and the 6th The Queen's estimated that they killed at least 100 of the enemy, took 44 prisoners, and blew up many of the German dug-outs. The Battalion loss was Second-Lieutenant C. E. St. F. Daly and 2 men killed, 22 other ranks wounded, 3 missing, and 4 " gassed."

On the 19th the 12th Division once more went back to the Le Cauroy area. By this date the command of the 37th Brigade had changed hands, Brigadier-General Cator being promoted to command the 58th Division and being succeeded by Brigadier-General Incledon-Webber.

Within a few days the 12th Division moved again, this time to the Hesduis area, well behind the front, and began training with tanks which had lately been very greatly increased in numbers and much improved in design. It was very clear, however, that this new weapon could not effect all that was hoped from it in the morassy fields of Belgium, and it was therefore resolved that new ground should be found for the fresh attacks which were contemplated, and that selected was south-west of Cambrai, an area where, while the enemy was not in especially great force, his defences were known to be very strong, consisting of three main lines, the Hindenburg, the Hindenburg Support, and the Masnières—Beaurevoir lines, all heavily wired and having concrete machine-gun emplacements.

Early on the morning of November 16th the 6th The Queen's left Villers l'Hopital, where for some days past it had been quartered, and marched to Bouquemaison, whence it proceeded by train to Peronne, which was reached in the course of the afternoon. Some few hours were spent here, and then the Battalion marched on by Haut Allaines to Heudecourt, where it arrived late on the 17th and was accommodated in hutments.

The attack now about to commence was to be carried out by the Third Army with the object of breaking through the enemy's line between the Scheldt Canal at Banteux and the Canal du Nord near Havrincourt, when the cavalry were to go through. On the south was the III Corps, with the 12th Division on the right, the 20th in the centre, the 6th on the left, and the 29th in reserve : 216 tanks were to operate with the III Corps, and 72 of these had been told off to work with the 12th Division. " There were two phases in the attack—namely, the capture of the Blue Line and of the Brown Line—and the special rôle of the 12th Division, after gaining its objective, was to form a defensive flank to the south-east, keeping in touch with the 55th Division of the VII Corps on its right, the attack to be carried out on a 1,700-yard front by the 35th Brigade on the right and the 36th on the left. In the opening part of the first phase the German outpost system of trenches with a strong position at Sonnet Farm were to be taken. Fresh companies were then to pass through, and, gaining some 1,500 yards of the Hindenburg Line, were then to establish themselves on the far side thereof. This was the Blue Line, an advance of 2,000 yards. After a pause of forty-eight minutes to allow the 37th Brigade and the 11th Middlesex Regiment to assemble, the attack was to be continued to the Brown Line, a further distance of 2,000 yards. This latter phase entailed the capture of the Hindenburg Support Trench, and the strong positions of Bleak House, Bonavis, Pam Pam Farm, Le Quennet, and Lateau Wood. As the advance proceeded, the new line of defence on the flank was to be formed, and, with the exception of some trenches in Lateau Wood, none of the German fire trenches faced in the required direction, thereby greatly increasing the work of consolidation. Forming this defensive flank was the most difficult portion of the 12th Division operation, and it entailed a particularly close study of maps, and most careful organization previous to the battle."*

The 6th The Queen's left Heudecourt at 12.5 a.m. on the 20th, and marched to the Brigade assembly position east of Gonnelieu, arriving there at 4 a.m. ; zero hour being 6.20, when it moved forward, following the remainder of the Brigade in artillery formation on a two-company frontage, " C " and " D " Companies being in the front line and " A " and " B " in support. The task assigned to the Battalion was to pass through the 6th Royal West Kent and occupy a defensive flank after the capture of the Brown Line by the 37th Brigade, the advance thereafter being continued by the 29th Division. When the 37th Brigade advanced to complete the capture of the Hindenburg Support Line, stern opposition was met with from Bonavis and Pam Pam Farm, and there was much hard fighting, in which the 6th Battalion The Queen's was called upon to assist, before Lateau Wood—a very important point—was finally taken. Here the Battalion captured several guns, including a 5·9 and a 4·2 howitzer, the latter being turned against the enemy.

Of this attack the Army Commander wrote to Major-General Scott :—" *Lateau Wood and Bonavis I look upon as being one of the finest achievements of the day. All good luck to you and that splendid division.*"

The casualties sustained by the 6th The Queen's were :—Second-Lieutenant M. S. Fox and 11 other ranks killed, Captain A. J. Pike, M.C., Second-Lieutenant R. C. Woodruffe and 41 non-commissioned officers and men wounded.

* *The History of the 12th Division*, pp. 135, 136.

The next three days the Division was busily engaged in consolidating the new line, The Queen's incurring some eight further casualties, including Second-Lieutenant C. L. Borst killed, and then on the 25th it was relieved and marched back for a few days' rest to Heudecourt.

Three days later, however, it appeared that the enemy was concentrating for attack about Villers Guislain in the 55th Division area, and this Division being weak and holding a long line, was considered to need support; when, therefore, the German attack commenced early on November 30th, reinforcements were ordered up, and early on the morning of November 30th the 6th The Queen's were ordered to concentrate at Vaucelette Farm and there consolidate a defensive position. The Battalion left Heudecourt at 9.5 a.m. and had at once to adopt artillery formation, as the enemy was already in Villers Guislain. On reaching the line Vaucellette Farm—astride Chapel Hill, the Battalion found it under shell fire and held by a small party of a battalion of the 55th Division, and at once dug in, establishing connection with the 11th Middlesex Regiment on the left and details of the 12th Division on the right. Five platoons under Captain Pash occupied the farm, and these repulsed an advance of the enemy; seven platoons took over the defence of Chapel Hill, leaving one company in support.

"The enemy by this time were holding the Beet Factory, Chapel Crossing, and Gauche Wood. The 11th Middlesex, moving from Heudecourt to Quentin Mill, reached the ridge half a mile north-east of Revelon about 10 a.m. Here the G.O.C. 35th Brigade was in position with a small number of men. Under his direction the 11th Middlesex took up a line astride the Revelon—Gouzeaucourt road, and, opening fire on the Germans, who were advancing up the slope, drove them back. Shortly afterwards a second attempt by the enemy was also repulsed. Touch was obtained with the Queen's at Chapel Hill, and about 11 a.m. two cavalry brigades extended the left of the Middlesex. By 1 p.m. Johnson's Provisional Battalion had taken over the defence of Vaucellette Farm and filled up a gap in the Queen's line. At this time the Northumberland Hussars were sent to Vaucellette Farm to keep touch with the 55th Division on the right, and the III Corps Cyclist Battalion to Revelon Farm to reinforce that part of the line. The advance of the enemy in this direction was now effectively checked. . . . A line had now been established from Vaucellette Farm along Irvine Lane, with a support through Chapel Hill, along Revelon Ridge, and then due north to west of Gouzeaucourt."*

Towards evening matters quieted down, and by then the 12th Division was holding its reserve line covering La Vacquerie, with a forward position across the Hindenburg Line south-west of Bleak House; portions of the Division were in Foster Lane and Green Switch, and also on the south from Vaucellette Farm along Irvine Lane to within 1,000 yards of Gouzeaucourt.

On December 1st the Germans renewed their attacks, which were continued during the greater part of the day, but the line held and was handed over intact on the 4th to the 61st Division, the 12th then reassembling at Heudecourt and marching thence to Albert. Then on the 7th the Division entrained—the 37th Brigade at Albert, the two others at Aveluy and Dernancourt—and moved to the neighbourhood of Aire (the 6th The Queen's being billeted at Steenbecque), the Division being now in the XV Corps of the First Army.

When the German attack opened on November 30th, the battalions were very weak, and the casualties incurred represented well over 50 per cent. of the actual

* *The History of the 12th Division*, pp. 144, 145.

strength; the losses sustained by the 6th Battalion The Queen's in the fighting on November 30th and December 1st and 2nd amounted to 2 officers and 8 other ranks killed, 6 officers and 56 non-commissioned officers and men wounded. The names of the officer casualties were :—Killed, Captain E. W. Edwards and Second-Lieutenant J. O. C. Knight; wounded, Captains R. G. Danks, W. Ord and A. L. Pash, Second-Lieutenants J. H. Manicon, M.C., E. H. Hudson and G. C. Middleton.

In writing to Major-General Scott, the Army Commander, General Sir Julian Byng, said : "*I wish to express to you and your Division how much I have appreciated the work done by them whilst forming part of the Third Army. During their long period in the line, and in the attack on the Hindenburg Line, and finally in the successful repulse of the German counter-stroke, the Division has fully lived up to its splendid reputation.*"

At Steenbecque the 6th The Queen's passed the Christmas of 1917.

By the opening of the New Year certain reinforcements had arrived from home or from the Base, but the infantry battalions of the Division were still anything but up to strength when early in January the 12th Division began to move up nearer to the front. The 36th and 37th Brigades marched first, relieving the 38th Division in the Fleurbaix sector, and by the 13th the 6th The Queen's was at Doulieu, whence next day they went up to the front-line trenches in the left sub-sector. Here the Portuguese were on the right and the 57th British Division on the left of the 12th, these three constituting the XV Corps. It was a quiet sector, and the trenches, situated in low-lying, marshy ground, were in anything but a satisfactory condition, necessitating much work being carried out upon them, several new trenches, reaching as far back as the west bank of the Lys, being dug; concrete machine-gun emplacements were built, and miles of wire entanglements were put up.

The question of man-power, already alluded to in an earlier chapter, soon became acute; each infantry brigade was reduced by one battalion, and the 37th Brigade lost the 7th Battalion East Surrey Regiment, which had been with it from very early days.

When in March, 1918, the great German offensive commenced, the Division had been relieved at the front and was then in the neighbourhood of Estaires; but on March 22nd warning orders for a move back to the front were received, and it appeared that the Third and Fifth Armies were falling back all along the line. Starting at nine o'clock on the morning of the 24th, the 6th The Queen's proceeded by bus and by march route via Fouquereuil and Bouzincourt to a position near Bazentin-le-Grand, but on arrival near La Boisselle on the afternoon of the 25th the Battalion was directed to push on and attack Pozières, reported to be in the hands of the enemy, the 6th Royal West Kent Regiment moving on the north-east side of the Albert—Bapaume road, and the 6th The Queen's on the south-east of it.

The 12th Division now formed part of the VIII Corps of the Third Army.

The 6th The Queen's and 6th Royal West Kent were about to launch the attack ordered, when the operation was cancelled and fresh instructions issued to take up a line of outposts through Ovillers. This was done by the 37th Brigade, which then covered the withdrawal of the 47th Division over the Ancre, and thereafter commencing its own retirement at 4.30 a.m. on the 26th, arrived at the Aveluy bridge and took up a position on the left of the 12th Division, which was now transferred to the V Corps.

The three brigades were now ordered to take up a line covering Albert along the west bank of the Ancre as far as Hamel; all three brigades were in line, but as there were no trenches in existence here and no time for digging any, the railway embankment formed the line of resistance for the greater part of the front occupied. The 37th Brigade was on the left holding as far as Hamel inclusive, the 6th The Queen's and 6th West Kent being in front with the 6th Buffs in reserve at Mesnil. The Ancre here was nowhere really impassable, and none of the bridges had been either destroyed or prepared for demolition.

The 6th The Queen's had its left in the village of Hamel and the right 600 yards north of the north edge of Aveluy Wood, " C " Company being in Hamel, " D " and " B " along the railway embankment, with " A " Company in support on the ridge 500 yards south-west of Hamel.

Early in the afternoon the enemy advanced into the Ancre Valley and attacked, The Queen's right flank being assailed about 8.15 p.m., but the Germans were driven back by Lewis-gun and rifle fire, The Queen's capturing several prisoners and two machine guns and killing many of the enemy.

During the morning of the 27th the enemy shelled " C " Company of The Queen's in the village of Hamel, and about 2.15 p.m. the Germans made a strong attack, driving in " C " and part of " D " Company, capturing Hamel and the road-junction south of it; a barricade, however, was formed 250 yards south of the road-junction, and here the enemy was held, while during the night that followed a series of strong points was organized to link up with what was left of " C " Company of The Queen's and the 6th Buffs. During almost the whole of the 28th the Battalion was heavily shelled, and in the afternoon the enemy was seen to be concentrating in front of The Queen's, but no attack resulted, and at 2 a.m. next day, on relief by troops of the 2nd Division, the Battalion fell back to billets in Martinsart, moving next day to Warloy.

During these days the losses in the Battalion had been very serious, 2 officers and 18 non-commissioned officers and men being killed, while 4 officers and 112 other ranks were wounded; the officers killed were Second-Lieutenants R. S. Flint and R. Harding, M.C., while those wounded were Captain F. R. McNair, Lieutenants E. E. Elliott and J. McCarthy, and Second-Lieutenant J. M. K. Strudwick.

The Division had no more than a very brief respite, for it was recalled to the front line on the night of April 2nd, relieving the 17th Division in the right sector of the Corps front due west of Albert. The 37th Brigade was at first in reserve, but the German attacks were so many and so persistent that on the 7th The Queen's were once more in the front-line trenches—" C," " B," and " A " Companies in line and " D " in support—remaining in the trenches until the night of the 11th, by which date the Germans had shot their bolt, and the 12th Division, having been relieved by the 38th, marched back to the Toutencourt area. " The whole of the 12th Division was now rested for a time," writes an historian of the war, " but they withdrew from their line in glory, for it is no exaggeration to say that they had fought the Germans to an absolute standstill."

During this last week's fighting the divisional losses amounted to 1,285, and of this total the 6th The Queen's contributed 66 killed and wounded, Second-Lieutenant W. J. Giles, D.C.M., and 6 other ranks being killed, Second-Lieutenant H. Northover and 58 non-commissioned officers and men being wounded.

A tolerably large draft now reached the Battalion, and by the end of the month, when the 6th The Queen's was training about Acheux, the strength was:—

In France, 33 officers and 822 non-commissioned officers and men.

At Headquarters, 24 officers and 660 non-commissioned officers and men.

The command of the 12th Division had now changed hands, Major-General Scott leaving to take up a command in India and being succeeded by Major-General H. W. Higginson, C.B., D.S.O.

The Division now made several moves—on May 25th to the Puchevillers—Beauquesne area; it was transferred on June 4th to the XXII Corps in reserve to the French, and on the 16th was transferred back to the V Corps and occupied the Bouzincourt sector, the 36th and 37th Brigades occupying ground which they had fought over in the preceding March and April; the 6th The Queen's was in the front line south of Aveluy Wood.

" An operation was now planned to gain the remaining high ground of the Bouzincourt Spur. The attack was to be made by the 37th Brigade in conjunction with the 18th Division on the right, and the troops were specially trained for the purpose. . . . Zero hour was 9.35 p.m. on June 30th and . . . the advance was to be made under a creeping barrage, the 6th Queen's attacking on the right and the 6th Royal West Kent on the left."*

Of this attack the Battalion diary records under date of June 30th:—" The assembly for the operation commenced at 3.30 p.m., and was complete by 5.45 p.m., the whole movement being carried out without casualties. Zero hour, 9.35 p.m. Stokes mortars opened barrage at zero *less* 1 minute. Artillery barrage opened at zero. Enemy barrage opened at zero *plus* 10 minutes. All objectives were reported as having been taken, and consolidation started at 11.40 p.m. Touch was obtained with the Royal West Kents on the left, but was not gained with the Bedfords on our right. About midnight the situation was obscure.

" July 1st. At 1.10 a.m. all objectives were still enemy-held. At 7.30 a.m. touch was obtained with the Bedfords by means of a small bombing raid. At 3.30 p.m. touch was lost with the Bedfords on the right. At 8 p.m. the Germans counter-attacked on our right, and we were forced back to the original German front line; in this line touch was regained with the Bedfords on the right and the Royal West Kents on the left.

" July 2nd. The Battalion was relieved by the 6th Buffs about 5 a.m. and marched to reserve line in front of Bouzincourt."

The position had been captured, but could not be held; many of the enemy had been killed and wounded and several machine guns had been captured; of the casualties sustained by the 12th Division, nearly one-half were in the 6th The Queen's, which had 3 officers and 28 other ranks killed or died of wounds, 9 officers and 190 non-commissioned officers and men wounded, while 8 were missing. Lieutenant C. R. McWhinnie died of wounds, Second-Lieutenants G. A. Flanagan and A. L. Ashton were killed, while Captains F. Hakes and F. A. G. Powell-Jones, Lieutenant A. S. Worman, Second-Lieutenants F. C. White, G. Turberville, C. W. Handford, A. H. D'E. Forbes, C. Franklin, and F. H. Aspden were wounded.

The rest of the month of July was spent first at Rubempre, then at Vers, and lastly at Pernois, where the 12th Division was in the III Corps and took over the centre sector of the Corps front. The trench warfare was now nearly at an end, the enemy was beginning to fall back, and in the advance to final victory the 12th Division was to play its part.

The Fourth Army, containing the III, Australian, and Canadian Corps, in conjunction with the First French Army, was to attack between Ribecourt and

* *The History of the 12th Division*, pp. 185, 186.

Albert, with the view of flattening out the Amiens salient. The III Corps, composed of the 12th, 18th, 47th, and 58th Divisions, was on the left, the 12th Division being astride the Ancre. The action actually commenced on August 8th, but on this day only the 35th Brigade of the 12th Division appears to have been seriously engaged, and when on the 9th the action was resumed, the 37th Brigade was ordered to assemble in rear of the 35th in readiness to pass through and carry on the offensive. The fresh attack began at 5.30 p.m., assisted by tanks and under a creeping barrage, The Queen's being in the centre, the Royal West Kent on the left, and the 6th Buffs on the right. All three battalions met with considerable opposition, " the 6th The Queen's, attacking to the north of Morlancourt, being held up by a strong point, but Captain Pash, seeing a tank a few hundred yards away, crossed the zone of the German machine-gun fire and obtained the assistance of the tank, which, destroying the strong point, permitted the Battalion to complete its task. Several prisoners, including a battalion commander, and 5 machine guns were taken. . . . Continuing the attack at 6 p.m. on August 10th, the 37th Brigade, with the 6th Buffs on the right, 9th Essex (attached from the 35th Brigade) in the centre, and the 6th Queen's on the left, supported by tanks, gained the old front line of the Amiens defences, the Buffs claiming to have captured a battery of 5.2 howitzers." The attack was completely successful, and by 8 p.m. the position was occupied.

In these three days' fighting the 6th The Queen's had Captain C. D. H. Wooster, M.C., Second-Lieutenants S. P. Wadson and W. G. Lippiatt, and 21 other ranks killed, Second-Lieutenant L. Donne-Smith and 95 other ranks wounded, 14 men missing, and 3 gassed; but the Battalion captured 1 field gun, 3 trench mortars, 4 heavy, and 20 light machine guns.

The operations continued during the next two or three days, and by the 13th Amiens was free from the German menace, and the 12th Division, on the extreme left of the advance, had moved forward some 3,000 yards. There was now a pause of some days, but on the 22nd the British offensive recommenced, although it was not until the 23rd that the 6th The Queen's were asked to undertake anything very serious. During the afternoon of this day " orders were received for a moonlight attack at 1 a.m. on the 24th instant to capture the high ground from which the advance of the Essex had been stopped on the 22nd. The left flank of the Division was also to be extended beyond the village of Bécordel to gain touch with the 18th Division. The attack of the 6th Royal West Kent and 6th The Queen's on the right failed, but that of the 7th Royal Sussex in capturing the village of Bécordel was successful. At 1.30 p.m. a second attempt was made on the right, assisted by three whippets, of which two were knocked out and the guns of the third jammed. This also failed. Later on the 47th Division having worked forward on the right, and the 36th Brigade on the left, the position became outflanked and the enemy withdrew, the 37th Brigade moving forward at once.

" The advance was renewed at 2.30 a.m. on the 25th, the 6th Buffs and 6th The Queen's on the right and 9th Royal Fusiliers on the left. A thick fog made it impossible to see more than fifty yards, but practically no opposition was met as the enemy was in retirement, and an advance of 3,000 yards was completed at 7.15 a.m. without any casualties. It was now open warfare. . . ."

During the operations of this week the 6th The Queen's had Second-Lieutenants Roberts and Stevenson and 24 other ranks killed, Captain A. L. Pash, M.C., and 73 non-commissioned officers and men wounded, while 3 men were gassed.

The Division now moved forward in pursuit of the retreating enemy, whose rearguards were holding strong positions, but it was not until the 29th, when east of Maurepas, that the 6th The Queen's were finally held up by a heavy 7·7 mm. and machine-gun barrage, which was kept up throughout the night. Next day, the 30th, the Battalion was withdrawn to Favière Wood, and thence to Talus Wood, the Division now becoming corps reserve. This day one man of the Battalion was killed, Lieutenant C. G. Herbert and 13 other ranks wounded, while one man was missing.

The next day was devoted to resting and cleaning up and to distributing among the Service companies a draft of 12 officers and 105 other ranks which now joined.

During the last few weeks the enemy had been pressed all along the front and his retreat hastened and molested in every way, and he was now falling back upon the Hindenburg Line, where he was in hopes of holding his ground during the forthcoming winter. The 12th Division was recalled to the front on September 5th to assist in overcoming the German resistance, and the special task assigned to it was the capture of Nurlu, in the initial operations connected with which the 37th Brigade was not actively concerned. Nurlu village and ridge were taken on the evening of the 6th, and the enemy pursued by our troops, who reached the line Lieramont Cemetery—Sorel Wood, the 47th Division being on the right and the 21st on the left of the 12th.

On the morning of the 6th The Queen's had moved up by easy stages from Combles, where training had been carried on, to an assembly position in Riverside Wood, and at 8 a.m. next day the 37th Brigade continued the advance with the object of gaining a line east of Epéhy and Peizières. The Battalion moved in support of the Buffs and Royal West Kent, and under considerable opposition the Division managed to advance 4,000 yards, and then consolidated a line some thousand yards west of Epéhy and Peizières, both of which were strongly held.

On this day the 6th The Queen's had 1 officer and 4 men killed, 1 officer and 40 other ranks wounded.

"The Division now had a short respite in the vicinity of Manancourt, with headquarters in Vaux Wood. This gave it the opportunity to reorganize and rehearse for the next task, the capture of Epéhy, which had become a very strong outpost of the Hindenburg Line, to which the Germans had now succeeded in retiring. The attack on Epéhy was to take place on September 18th, the 18th Division operating on the right, and the 58th against Peizières on the left.

"The 12th Division was disposed as follows: on the right, the 7th Royal Sussex and 9th Royal Fusiliers of the 36th Brigade, their objective being the Malassise Farm area; on the left, the 7th Norfolk and 9th Essex, with two tanks and two companies of the 1/1st Cambridgeshire (35th Brigade), for the capture of Epéhy. The 37th Brigade, with the 5th Royal Berkshire (36th Brigade), were in support east of Guyencourt, their rôle being to pass through and, pushing on, to take Little Priel Farm and Kildare Post, two miles east of Epéhy."*

The 6th The Queen's was in Guyencourt on the 17th, and moved up from here early next day to an assembly position south-west of Epéhy, where it was directed to stand by until Peizières and Epéhy had been " mopped up." It then advanced up to the railway east of Epéhy in preparation for an attack on Malassise Farm. This was carried out at 11 a.m. on the 19th, when the Battalion attacked with the

* *The History of the 12th Division*, p. 206.

6th Buffs on the right and the 35th Brigade on the left. The enemy offered a very stout opposition, his artillery and machine-gun fire being especially heavy from the farm and from Tétard Wood, while his wire was thick and comparatively intact, but The Queen's captured Malassise Farm and advanced a further 500 yards to the east. During the night of the 19th-20th the divisional boundary was extended to the right as far as the Ronssoy—Vendhuile road, but in the area now reached the enemy was found to have numerous posts well entrenched, heavily wired, and strongly held by machine gunners and infantry.

On the 20th the 6th The Queen's side-stepped to the right, taking up a position in Old Copse area, then attacking No. 12 Copse and Horse Post where little resistance was met with and the positions assailed were occupied. During the 21st-25th the Battalion was in brigade reserve at Prince Reserve, but was moved forward again on the latter date, and was attached to the 36th Brigade in the Kildare Post area, attacking Dados Loop at dawn on the 26th, capturing the objective, but falling back again before an enemy counter-attack. A second assault was equally unsuccessful, and the Battalion was withdrawn at nightfall, rejoining its own Brigade, then in divisional reserve. There was more fighting by the 12th Division before the month closed and the Division moved back to the Guyencourt area, but The Queen's took no very active part in this, although in the operations which commenced on the 18th the Battalion lost 1 officer (Second-Lieutenant F. H. Aspden) and 23 other ranks killed, 6 officers and 109 men wounded.

" Since August 8th an advance of twenty-six miles, from Morlancourt to the Escaut Canal, had been made, and many prisoners taken. In addition, 22 guns, 320 machine guns, 72 trench mortars, and 11 minenwerfers had been captured. On the other side of the register, we had suffered heavy casualties, 80 officers and 769 other ranks being killed, 204 officers and 4,466 other ranks wounded, 6 officers and 704 other ranks missing—a total of 6,229."

On October 1st the 12th Division left the III Corps and the Fourth Army, and, joining the VIII Corps and the First Army, occupied a line some 11,000 yards in length, from Oppy to Eleu-dit-Leauvette, on the Lens Canal. Here all three brigades were up in the line, the 37th being on the left with The Queen's and Buffs in front and the Royal West Kent in reserve.

The story of the events of October, 1918, is one of open warfare and steady and relentless pursuit of the retreating enemy, and by the 31st the 6th The Queen's had fought its last fight in the war and was in billets at Cattelet, the Division in corps reserve. The pursuit was not conducted without loss, and the Battalion, which began the month at a strength of only 22 officers and 406 other ranks present with headquarters, had by the end of it lost 6 men killed, 4 officers and 36 other ranks wounded. The wounded officers were Lieutenant L. H. Van der Pant, Second-Lieutenants G. C. Middleton, H. J. Matthews and H. Northover.

When on November 11th the news of the signing of the Armistice was made known, the 6th The Queen's was quartered at Rumegies, but moved on the 25th to Auberchicourt, in the area east of Douai, where all began—somewhat prematurely as it turned out—to look forward to demobilization and an early return to England. But some time was still to elapse before the army could be dispersed, since the peace terms had not yet been either settled or signed, and much time was devoted to salvage work and training of all kinds.

On January 11th a party, composed of Lieutenant J. T. Horsford, No. 9017 Company Sergeant-Major S. Atfield, and No. 22115 Company Quartermaster-

Sergeant H. Grove, was sent into Somain to fetch the King's Colour.* The actual ceremony of presentation took place on February 4th by H.R.H. the Prince of Wales, who handed the Colours to the various Service battalions of the Division, which paraded by brigades. The 6th The Queen's was this day commanded by Major D. Mann, M.C., and the Colour, having been consecrated by the Rev. H. P. Berkeley, M.C., Major W. C. Cook, M.C., handed it to His Royal Highness, who in turn handed it to Lieutenant R. Foley. The warrant and non-commissioned officers of the Colour party were No. 11425 Regimental Sergeant-Major G. Turl, No. 9807 Company Sergeant-Major H. Inman, No. 4337 Company Sergeant-Major Barnes, No. 5772 Sergeant Brewer, and No. 9594 Sergeant J. Brown.

His Royal Highness the Prince of Wales then addressed the Battalion as follows :—

"*It gives me very great pleasure to be here to-day and to have the honour to present the King's Colours to the battalions before me.*

"*You were raised in August, 1914, and came out to France in the 12th Division in May, 1915. Since that date, in addition to much hard fighting in minor engagements, and long periods of strenuous work in the trenches, you have taken a conspicuous part in the following battles—Loos, Hohenzollern Craters, Somme 1916, Arras, Cambrai, Somme 1918, Epéhy, and the German retreat to the Scheldt, which culminated in the final victory of our arms.*

"*I know full well that these Colours will always be honoured and cherished by you, and that you will worthily uphold in the future, as you have always done in the past, the glorious traditions of the regiments to which you belong. These Colours are emblems of the heroic deeds which have been performed by your battalions. I now entrust them to you, confident that you will guard them as worthy successors of the gallant soldiers who have so gloriously fallen in the service of their King and Country.*"

Soon after this the process of disintegration commenced, on February 16th 10 officers and 300 other ranks leaving for Havre to join the 1st Battalion of the Regiment, so that by the end of the month the numbers present with headquarters amounted to no more than 13 officers and 177 other ranks. Four more officers and 7 more men left early in March to join the 11th The Queen's, and on the 27th what was left of the Battalion went by train to Rouen and joined the 19th Brigade of the 33rd Division. Any hopes which may now have been entertained of an early return to England by reason of the small numbers of the Battalion must have been seriously damped by the arrival early in April of a draft—from the 1st Battalion The Queen's—of 11 officers and 412 non-commissioned officers and men, bringing the strength in France up to 29 officers and 845 other ranks.

In June the Battalion was moved to Calais, remaining here until the autumn of the year, when it at last came home to England for disbandment.

* As a curious example of official procedure, it may be mentioned that all reference to this Colour-issue must be sought—not in A.O., as might be expected, but in A.C.I., and not under "Colours," but under "Flags" : further, while the presentations were for the most part made in January and February, 1919, the A.C.I. sanctioning the issue is No. 444 of *July 21st* of that year !

Maps 1, 4, 6, and 8.

# CHAPTER XXI.

## The 7th (Service) Battalion.

### 1914–1916.

#### THE BATTLE OF THE SOMME, 1916.

##### Battle Honours:
"Somme, 1916," "Albert, 1916," "Bazentin," "Thiepval," "Ancre Heights," "Ancre, 1916."

The 7th Battalion came into existence within a very few days of the declaration of war against Germany, and in Army Order No. 382 of September 11th, 1914, it was posted to the 18th Division of the Second New Army, joining the 55th Infantry Brigade, composed of the following Service Battalions—the 7th The Queen's (Royal West Surrey Regiment), the 7th The Buffs (East Kent Regiment), the 8th East Surrey Regiment, and the 7th Queen's Own (Royal West Kent Regiment). The Division was assembled at Colchester and Purfleet, and was commanded by Major-General F. I. Maxse, C.V.O., C.B., D.S.O., while the commander of the 55th Brigade was Brigadier-General J. H. Poett, C.B.

Many months, spent in hard training, were to elapse before the 18th Division left England, and it was not until July 26th, 1915, that the 7th The Queen's, then stationed at Codford, in Wiltshire, sent off the battalion transport and 105 rank and file, under Major F. B. B. Pickard, with Lieutenants C. A. Haggard and N. C. Ingpen, to Southampton, where these embarked for Havre in the s.s. *Mount Temple*, crossing over the same night. On the following afternoon the Battalion left Codford in two trains for Folkestone, and there embarked for Boulogne in the s.s. *Victoria*. The embarking strength of the 7th The Queen's was 33 officers, 47 sergeants, 43 corporals, 51 lance-corporals, and 773 privates, a total all ranks of 947. The following were the officers who sailed for France with the Battalion:—
Lieutenant-Colonel W. J. T. Glasgow; Majors F. B. B. Pickard, C. A. Russell-Stower and H. C. Jeddere-Fisher; Captains R. S. Hebeler, C. W. M. Price, M. Kemp-Welch (adjutant), G. H. H. Scott, J. R. Walpole, H. L. Martin and R. S. Le Bas; Lieutenants S. C. Eastwood (quartermaster), J. M. Du Buisson, N. C. Ingpen, L. W. M. Howard, W. Wigham-Richardson, C. A. Haggard, I. P. W. Bennett, F. Travers, D. R. Heaton and B. C. Haggard; Second-Lieutenants D. Neilson-Terry, O. E. Saltmarshe, V. Hook, M. J. Penrose-Fitzgerald, H. Cloudsley, H. J. Tortise, M. S. Shuldham-Legh, J. S. Walter, G. Whittet, A. W. B. Kitchin and J. Farren; Lieutenant C. E. Sundall, R.A.M.C., was the medical officer.

The Regimental Sergeant-Major was C. E. Smith, the Regimental Quartermaster Sergeant was C. E. Punter, while the other warrant officers were Company Sergeant-Majors T. Hart, G. J. Denyer, F. Sageman and W. T. Mabe.

The night of the 27th-28th was spent in the rest camp at Boulogne, and next day the 55th Brigade proceeded to Bertangles by train, being now in the X Corps of the Third Army; but on August 6th the 7th The Queen's marched eastward, arriving on the banks of the Ancre and being billeted in La Neuville-en-Corbie.

From here it moved on to Dernancourt, whence " A " and " B " Companies went up to the trenches and were attached for instruction to the 1st Battalion Norfolk Regiment, coming for the first time under fire and sustaining the initial casualties, Lieutenant B. C. Haggard and Company Sergeant-Major G. J. Denyer being both wounded in the right arm by the same bullet.

The 18th Division had arrived in France while the Battle of Hooge was just drawing to a close, and for the remaining months of the year the battalions composing the Division took no part in any events of outstanding importance. " Though by the end of 1915 the Division had suffered 1,247 casualties, those four months proved to be the quietest and not the least pleasant in its history. Except for the winding ribbon of bare land that marked the opposing trench lines, the Somme country remained green and eye-pleasing. . . . No large attack had taken place for some time. Shells rarely descended beyond the rival trench systems. . . . The wagon lines and back areas were havens of rest, and neither side shelled transport. The trenches were well made and legibly labelled, so that reliefs were simple. Food was plentiful, and the men looked models of health. Three brigades were in the line at a time, and on each brigade front two battalions occupied the forward trenches with two companies. The remaining battalions were in show billets in Ville-sur-Ancre, Dernancourt, Meaulte and similar villages, with canteens and libraries, and a bed and a seat at table for each man. Eight days was the average tour of duty in the lines."*

During this period three officers—Captain Hebeler, Lieutenant Howard and Second-Lieutenant Kitchin—were killed.

On October 25th the Battalion, with the 10th Essex of the 18th Division, the 1st Norfolk and 1st Dorset of the 5th Division, the 7th Black Watch and 7th Gordon Highlanders of the 51st Division, were inspected by His Majesty the King and by M. Poincaré, the President of the French Republic, at 11 a.m., two miles north of Ribemont. H.R.H. The Prince of Wales was also present, and the troops were under the command of Major-General F. I. Maxse.

In February, 1916, Lieutenant-Colonel Glasgow was promoted to command the 50th Brigade, when the command of the 7th The Queen's devolved upon Major Pickard.

The German attack on Verdun commenced at the end of the winter of 1915-1916, and the Division was transferred on March 1st from the X to the XIII Corps of the Fourth Army; and when on July 1st the Somme battle of this year opened, the XIII Corps was on the right of the Fourth Army, next to the French, and was in front of the salient in the British line facing the villages of Maricourt, Hardicourt, Montauban and Mametz. The Division attacked at 7.30 a.m. with all three of its brigades in line, the 55th on the right, the 53rd in the centre, and the 54th on the left, and in the first named of these the 7th The Queen's—now commanded by Lieutenant-Colonel M. Kemp-Welch—were on the left, the East Surreys on the right, the 7th Buffs in support, and the 7th Royal West Kent in reserve. The objective of the Brigade was a trench line about 200 yards north of the Montauban—Mametz road, and also the west end of Montauban; the extent of the front attacked by The Queen's was some 409 yards.

" Lieutenant D. R. Heaton, who commanded the right leading company of The Queen's, found their advance checked at the Boche second line, because from the Boche third line came an unchecked hail of machine-gun fire. The Queen's

* Nichols, *The 18th Division in the Great War*, pp. 16, 17.

had already suffered heavy casualties. The company at this period was unsupported and there was no communication with the Norfolks on the left. The situation was critical. Lieutenant Heaton showed what a leader with initiative and confidence in himself can do. He organized a bombing party and led them up the communication trench, and the attack was carried through with such thrust that the German third line was cleared and 163 of the enemy surrendered. Heaton collected his forces, and, two platoons of 'D' Company, The Buffs, coming to his aid, a dash along the Montauban—Mametz road was made and the first objective was carried....

"Five minutes after 'going over the top,' Lieutenant C. A. Haggard, who commanded "C" Company of The Queen's, was wounded in the head. He lay unconscious for an hour, but afterwards took command of the remnants of his company, and by 1.45 p.m. had led them as far as the Montauban—Mametz road trench. Then his condition became serious and he had to be taken to the rear. There was also Second-Lieutenant H. J. Tortiss, who, on reaching Blind Alley, which he knew to be occupied by the enemy, took forward a bombing party. So many bombs had been thrown during the morning that only one bomb per man could be given out. But the party captured the trench and twelve Germans with it. In Montauban itself was a post held by three machine guns. For three hours it held out. Lieutenant Tortiss, who had the Maxse dictum—'Kill Germans'—ingrained in him, made a dash at them. He and his dozen men got right among the enemy, bayoneted several of them, and ended in possession of the post....

"Steadily the advance of the three brigades continued. By 1.30 p.m. the 55th Brigade were on their final objective, and, aided by three companies of the 8th Suffolks, were working west along Montauban Alley towards Loop Trench.... By 8 p.m. the Division had received a congratulatory message from General Congreve, commanding the XIII Corps, and in sending out this communication to his brigades General Maxse added:—'Well done, it's what I expected. Now hold on to what you have gained so splendidly.'" *

The 18th Division had suffered not far short of 4,000 casualties, to which total the 7th The Queen's, in this the first action in which it had taken part, had contributed its full share, 7 officers and 174 non-commissioned officers and men being killed, while 9 officers and 284 other ranks were wounded and 58 men missing—in all, 532. The officers killed were Captains J. R. Walpole and G. H. H. Scott, Lieutenants H. Cloudsley and O. E. Saltmarshe, Second-Lieutenants J. F. Miller, G. S. Dandridge and R. C. Herbert; while wounded were Lieutenants C. A. Haggard and A. J. R. Haggard, Second-Lieutenants E. F. Bennett, M. S. Shuldham-Legh, J. Farren and M. J. Penrose-Fitzgerald; Lieutenants V. Hook and D. R. Heaton, and Second-Lieutenant H. J. Tortise were also wounded, but remained at duty.

The line reached by the 7th The Queen's was held all night, the 8th East Surrey being on the right and the 8th Norfolk Regiment on the left; and when on July 3rd the Battalion moved back on relief to Bronfay Wood some nine officers joined—Second-Lieutenants G. F. Woollatt, G. Whittet, H. H. G. Ferguson, N. G. Wright, G. D. Currie, C. Lloyd, L. St. C. Legge, H. A. Blewchamp and H. Golding.

A highly important tactical point in the German position hereabouts was occupied by Trônes Wood for the possession of which the British had for some days been fighting, and on July 11th the 30th Division reported its capture, but stated that all of its three brigades were greatly exhausted and needed relief. In consequence,

* *The 18th Division in the Great War*, pp. 39 *et seq.*

the 18th Division was ordered to send one of its brigades to act as divisional reserve to the 30th Division in place of an exhausted brigade which had been withdrawn, and the 55th Infantry Brigade was moved to Maricourt and Trigger Wood Valley on the morning of July 11th and attached to the 30th Division. Major-General Maxse, in his notes on the Somme situation on this day, states :—" The task of the 30th Division was one of great importance in view of contemplated operations—namely, to safeguard the right flank of an attack northwards by two Army Corps—the XIII and XV—against the German second-line system of trenches between Delville Wood and a point north of Contalmaison Villa. This attack was timed for 3.20 a.m. on July 14th, and it was of vital necessity that Trônes Wood should be securely held on the flank of the attack. Indeed, the success of the Battle of the Somme may be said to have depended upon the retention of Trônes Wood and the trenches between it and Maltzhorn Farm at that particular moment. With Trônes Wood in German hands, the main attack northwards might be seriously delayed.

"It was therefore somewhat disconcerting to the higher command to learn from the 30th Division on July 12th that the Germans had retaken all Trônes Wood with the exception of a small portion of the south end of it. The result was that on the evening of July 12th the 18th Division was ordered to relieve the 30th Division. The relief was completed by 10 a.m. on the 13th. The XIII Corps Commander's orders were that the 18th Division must recapture Trônes Wood by midnight, July 13th-14th, at all costs.

"The 55th Infantry Brigade had already relieved the 89th Brigade of the 30th Division on the line Maltzhorn Farm—south end of Trônes Wood on July 12th ; it was accordingly detailed to recapture the whole of Trônes Wood. Also the 12th Battalion Middlesex Regiment and 6th Battalion Northamptonshire Regiment, both of the 54th Brigade, were placed at the disposal of the Brigadier 55th Infantry Brigade in case he should require them. They were quartered in Maricourt and north of it. At the time the 55th Brigade were ordered to capture Trônes Wood they were disposed as follows : The 7th Buffs, holding a line of trenches from the junction with the French (just south of Maltzhorn Farm) to near the south corner of Trônes Wood. The 8th Royal West Kents occupied the south end of Trônes Wood with two companies, one company was in the sunken road south of the wood, and the fourth company holding the south part of Bernafay wood. The 7th Queen's were in support in and about Dublin Trench. The 8th East Surreys were in brigade reserve in Silesia Trench in the original German system."

The Battalion report on the action of July 13th runs as follows :—" The Battalion was in brigade reserve, ' A,' ' B,' and ' C ' Companies in Dublin Trench, ' D ' Company in Casement Trench, and Battalion Headquarters at the junction of Favière Support and Briqueterie Road. Fighting strength about 300 all ranks. Dublin Trench was heavily shelled during afternoon of 13th, and Battalion suffered 20 casualties. The situation in Trônes Wood was not clear. The enemy was known to have received orders that it was to be held at all costs, they had suffered heavy casualties from previous bombardments and attacks by the 30th Division, while they were also known to have deep dug-outs in the wood and some strong points, and the wood would therefore be difficult to clear, but was not supposed to be strongly held.

"The orders for the 7th Queen's were to attack the wood from a point on the railway to its north extremity, to occupy and clear it, consolidating the east edge.

The Battalion front of attack was 730 yards. The guns were to bombard the west edge of the wood, lifting at zero hour, which was 7 p.m. The Queen's were to move up by a new trench from Nord Alley to the south-west corner of Bernafay Wood, thence along the west edge into Longueval Alley, whence the attack was to be carried out in two lines, 'A,' 'B,' and 'C' Companies in the first line, 'B' Company, 7th Buffs, and 'D' Company of the Queen's in the second line. One platoon of 'B' Company with a Lewis-gun detachment and a Battalion bombing party, all under Lieutenant B. C. Haggard, was given the task of capturing and consolidating at the north end of Trônes Wood.

"The Battalion moved off at 5.30 a.m., but on the headquarters arriving at the junction of Nord Alley and the new trench thence to Bernafay, it was found that a company of the Middlesex Regiment was already moving along it, thus causing confusion and delay, but the Queen's were in position ready to attack at 6.57. It was now, however, plain that the bombardment of Trônes Wood was not sufficiently heavy to neutralize the enemy holding the west edge of the wood, and he kept up from here a steady fire on Bernafay Wood and Longueval Alley. The telephone to Brigade Headquarters had been cut by enemy fire, and all attempts to repair it were in vain.

"At zero the artillery barrage lifted and the Battalion moved forward from Longueval Alley, but was at once met with a heavy machine-gun and rifle fire from the west of the wood and by a heavy barrage of 150 and 105 mm. howitzers and 77 mm. guns. The first line suffered immediate and heavy casualties, and the second line reinforced, but also suffered much, and, despite gallant leading by Captain Bennett and Second-Lieutenant Woollatt, was unable to get to within 100 yards of Trônes Wood.

"With the exception of the party under Lieutenant Haggard"—of which more will presently be said—"the attack was now definitely held up, and those who had not already become casualties took cover in shell-holes, unable either to advance or retire. Some more men of the 7th Buffs came up later, but were too few in number to send forward to the attack with any hope of improving the situation. Towards 9 p.m. the wood was again bombarded by our guns, but without much effect, and as it was obviously impossible to gain the objective, what was left of the 7th The Queen's was organized for the defence of Longueval Alley. Under cover of darkness those who had been lying out in the open began to come in, and from now on till 2.30 a.m. on the 14th, when the Battalion withdrew, Second-Lieutenant J. S. Walter and two men worked at bringing in all the wounded they could find under a continuous shell and rifle fire.

"When Lieutenant Haggard moved off with his party to carry out the orders issued to him, he almost at once encountered the enemy in Longueval Alley and was driven back by bombs. Advancing again, he reached his objective without serious opposition and at once began to consolidate, sending some men to the right to get touch with the remainder of 'B' Company of the Queen's; this company however, had been met with a heavy fire when crossing the open west of Trônes Wood and had failed to reach there, and consequently touch was not gained. Lieutenant Haggard and his party remained for the best part of an hour in the north part of the wood without interference by the enemy, and while there came across an abandoned heavy enemy howitzer. Later on strong parties of the enemy began to attack the right of the party, and after fighting for about an hour Lieutenant Haggard was wounded and Second-Lieutenant Blewchamp killed, the party suffering heavily and being split up into four small parties. Lieutenant Haggard and about eight men, mostly wounded, got back to Longueval Alley, while three other parties, each of three men, remained in the north part of Trônes Wood during the night, holding on to the positions gained and killing Germans wherever opportunity offered. Two of these parties were eventually relieved by the 12th Middlesex about noon on the 14th, while the third, under Sergeant A'Bear, starting to go back about 11 a.m., traversed the whole wood, meeting nobody but Germans, and assisted to bring in a wounded officer of the 7th Royal West Kent Regiment. Throughout the night of the 13th-14th no body of our troops reached these small parties."

The orders were peremptory that Trônes Wood should be taken, and this was ultimately done by the 54th Brigade, supported by the 53rd, but during this time the 55th Brigade was at rest in rear, the 7th The Queen's in camp at Grovetown Camp.

In this last fighting the Battalion had 4 officers and 22 men killed, 7 officers and 150 other ranks wounded, and 2 officers and 44 men missing. Killed were Captain I. P. W. Bennett, Second-Lieutenants P. R. Woollatt, G. Whittet and H. A. Blewchamp; Lieutenants B. C. Haggard and W. Wigham-Richardson, Second-Lieutenants H. J. Tortise, C. Lloyd, H. Golding, A. B. Marston and G. D. Currie were wounded; while missing, believed killed, were Second-Lieutenants N. G. Wright and L. St. C. Legge.

While the Battalion was in Grovetown Camp, Captain H. R. Longbourne, Second-Lieutenants A. N. Scott and J. G. F. Phillips joined for duty, while reinforcements—greatly needed—to the number of 315 arrived. Then on the 20th the Division proceeded by rail and march route to a new area, and by the end of the month the 7th The Queen's were stationed at Flêtre. Early in August the Division moved to a quiet training area in front of Armentières, joining here the Third Army. This quiet time came to an end on September 8th, when the 7th The Queen's moved to Puchvillers, the 18th Division now forming part of the II Corps, to which, with the Canadian Corps, was assigned the task of capturing the whole ridge running from the north-west of Courcelette to the Schwaben Redoubt, a ridge which provided the enemy with his last remaining observation points over the Albert area, and which entailed the assault and capture of Thiepval and the Schwaben Redoubt.

There was very much preparatory work to be done; assembly and communication trenches had to be dug and dumps laid down, while in addition the whole road from Authuille to Thiepval was cleared and a screen put up along its length. In this all the 7th The Queen's were almost throughout employed. There was a three days' preliminary bombardment, and then on September 26th Thiepval was assailed by the 53rd and 54th Brigades, the Battalion being ordered to stand by in readiness for employment if necessary; but it was not called into action until the following day, when the attack was made upon the Schwaben Redoubt.

On September 27th the 53rd and 54th Brigades were holding a line running north of Thiepval and along the Zollern Trench to the point where the 53rd Brigade was in touch with the 11th Division on the right. These two brigades had suffered greatly in the fighting for Thiepval, and it was arranged to reinforce them with fresh battalions from the 55th Brigade, leaving the original brigadiers to direct the further attacks. The 7th The Queen's was attached for the coming action to the 53rd Brigade, and was directed to attack the Schwaben Redoubt, with the 8th Suffolk on the right and a battalion of the 54th Brigade on its left.

The Battalion left Blighty Alley at 10.15 on the morning of September 28th, and on debouching from the north-east corner of Authuille Wood it was noticed that all movement between this and Thiepval was in full view of the enemy observation balloon.

Soon after noon the Battalion, with " D " Company, 8th Norfolks (" moppers-up "), were formed up in the open in their attacking lines—" B " Company, Captain Martin, on the right, and " C," Captain Longbourne, on the left, in front ; " D," Captain Walter, in support ; and " A," Captain Heaton, in reserve. The forming-up places were under fairly heavy shrapnel, machine-gun and long-range rifle fire. The British artillery barrage opened at 1 p.m., when the Battalion moved forward to the attack, and Bulgar Trench was found to be weakly held, its defenders being disposed of without much trouble. After crossing this, direction was found to be difficult to maintain, and the Battalion inclined slightly to its left. Some opposition was met with in Martin's Lane, while heavy machine-gun and rifle fire was coming from the south face of Schwaben Redoubt, causing casualties and checking the leading waves, which became somewhat mixed up.

The assaulting companies got over Market Trench with some difficulty, and were checked for over an hour by a strong point, but this halt was made use of to fill up a gap caused on the right, through the above-mentioned loss of direction, by bringing up part of Captain Walter's company, and this officer led a bombing party and cleared the trench and dug-outs in his front, capturing some fifty prisoners. The strong point had by this been reached by the left of the Battalion, chiefly owing to the action of Captain Longbourne, who stalked two machine guns in succession, moving from shell-hole to shell-hole with a bag of bombs ; he knocked out the whole of one gun team and captured the gun ; the second gun he bombed and put out of action, but the detachment managed to get away. While Captain Longbourne was thus employed, Sergeant Punter led a bombing party up the west face of Schwaben Redoubt, but was then driven back owing to his supply of bombs running out, but he finally established a bombing-post in the front. On the reduction of the strong point the Battalion secured a line in touch with the 8th Suffolk.

An enemy strong point was still holding out on the Battalion right, but no attempt to take it was feasible that night, and as night came on the Battalion was fairly established and consolidated the line gained. During the night, however, there was continuous bomb fighting on the west face of the Redoubt, and finally the left of the 7th The Queen's was driven back to Point 45, where touch was with some difficulty gained with the Royal West Kent Regiment.

On the night of the 29th the 7th The Queen's were relieved and proceeded to North Bluff, near Authuille, having in this last action had 1 officer—Captain H. L. Martin—and 45 other ranks killed, 10 officers and 252 other ranks wounded, while 87 men were missing. The wounded officers were Captain D. R. Heaton, D.S.O., Second-Lieutenants F. G. Fendall, C. C. Hammond, W. J. Short, J. G. F. Phillips, C. W. Rogers, A. G. Gadd, A. N. Scott, H. D. Thatcher and F. R. Lines.

Fighting—heavy bombing attacks by both sides—went on until October 5th, by which date the whole of Schwaben Redoubt, except a small strip along the north-west corner, had been captured, and the 18th Division was then relieved, the 7th The Queen's spending some weeks in the latter half of October and the earlier portion of November in the neighbourhood of Albert, where, while certain casualties occurred, several drafts of varying strengths joined the Battalion. During this period the command of the 55th Brigade was taken over by Brigadier-General G. D. Price.

During these months the rain was very heavy, and it was impossible to carry out any really large scale operations, but a number of minor attacks were made with a view of shaking the enemy's defence and causing him to loosen his grip upon the Somme area and retreat to his prepared positions in rear. Such an attack was that made in conjunction with the Canadians on the right and the 19th Division on the left on Desire Trench at dawn on November 18th. Of this attack the Divisional History records that "the Canadians gained their objective and advanced beyond it. The 55th Brigade, who attacked for the 18th Division, also reached the arranged line, but in their case touch was never gained with the assaulting companies of the 19th Division, who in the mist swerved to their left and descended towards the Ancre. The German machine gunners were hurried up into the gap thus made between the 18th and 19th Divisions, and two companies of the 7th Queen's vanished utterly, being overwhelmed by machine-gun fire."

On the night of the 16th-17th two companies of the Battalion—"C," under Second-Lieutenant Beswall, and "D," under Captain Walter—had moved up into the front line, from which the Battalion was to attack (Regina and Hessian Trenches), and these two were detailed to carry out the assault on Desire Trench, "C" on the right and "D" on the left, while twenty picked men were attached from "B" to "D" for the purpose of clearing dug-outs in Stump Road and to assist in keeping touch with the brigade on the left. On the night of the 17th-18th "A" and "B" Companies of The Queen's moved from the huts at Ovillers to Zollern and Hessian Trenches respectively, while the two other companies moved forward to their attacking fronts, all being ready by 2.30 on the morning of November 18th; this was very cold, snow, succeeded by rain, making the ground very slippery, while visibility was bad.

The companies moved off at "zero" hour, with the 7th Buffs on their right, but connection was not maintained with the troops on the left, while the party attached to the assaulting companies from "B" Company had both its non-commissioned officers knocked out by a shell, and failed in achieving all that had been hoped from it. The enemy was especially alert, and almost at once opened a barrage on Regina and Hessian Trenches.

At 8 a.m. some prisoners were sent back, stated to have been captured in Desire Trench, but from then up to 9.30 no news coming in from the assaulting companies, runners were sent out to try to get touch, but these were in every case held up after crossing Regina Trench by rifle fire, and beyond finding some of our wounded failed to see or hear anything of the front-line companies. It was not till 11 o'clock that a wounded sergeant of "D" Company was brought in, who said he had seen "C" and "D" almost reach Desire Trench, and that, in spite of heavy machine-gun and rifle fire, their losses had not been severe. However, at 4.15 p.m. Captain Du Buisson's company was sent forward with one of the 7th Buffs to clear the ground between Regina and Hessian Trenches, and the leading wave, under Second-Lieutenant Hewett, got to within about a hundred yards of Desire Trench and then met with very strong opposition from the enemy holding Stump Road, and the rest of this company was consequently not pushed forward to attack, but was used to hold Regina Trench for the night. Patrols sent out during the hours of darkness failed to gain any touch with "C" and "D" Companies of The Queen's, though some of them managed to get as far forward as the junction of

Desire Trench and Stump Road; further patrols were sent forward on the 19th, but only found dead and wounded of "C" and "D" Companies; no trace was discovered of any officer.

From such men as survived of these companies the following was gleaned: during the first 200 yards of the advance the assaulting companies had met with but little enemy fire, and all seemed to be going well; but about a hundred yards short of Desire Trench, it was seen that the left company, "D," was inclining to the left and losing direction, part of it crossing Stump Road, while the whole line was assailed by heavy rifle and machine-gun fire from both flanks, and was later taken in rear from Stump Road and overpowered, heavy casualties being suffered about Desire Trench. One survivor stated that "it was all over in ten minutes."

"There is direct evidence that the men of the 7th Buffs and 7th Queen's died game, for Lieutenant-Colonel Ransome, 7th Buffs, went over the same ground months afterwards, and found over fifty dead, the bodies having been preserved during the long intense frost of February, 1917."[*]

During the 19th the enemy evacuated Desire Trench as far west as Stump Road.

The losses of the 7th The Queen's were heavy, and the proportion of missing to killed and wounded was high: 10 men were killed, 2 officers—Captain J. M. Du Buisson and Second-Lieutenant A. P. Beswall—and 73 other ranks were wounded, while 5 officers—Captain J. S. Walter, Second-Lieutenants J. E. Russell, E. H. Nelson, C. G. Brown and W. Damer—and 173 non-commissioned officers and men were missing.

On the evening of November 21st what remained of the Battalion was relieved and returned to Ovillers, which was left again next day, the Battalion marching by Harponville, Longuevillette, Autheux, Prouville and Maison Ponthieu to Canchy, which was reached on the 27th, and where The Queen's were accommodated in billets. Here reinforcements to the number of 166 joined.

Then on December 14th the Battalion moved by march route to Drucat, in the Abbeville area, where training of all kinds was carried on, and where Christmas Day was spent.

[*] *The 18th Division in the Great War*, p. 134.

Maps 4, 5, 6, and 9.

## CHAPTER XXII.

### THE 7TH (SERVICE) BATTALION (*Continued*).

### 1917–1919.

#### THE ARRAS OFFENSIVE—THE BATTLE OF YPRES.

##### BATTLE HONOURS:

"Arras, 1917," "Scarpe, 1917," "Pilckem," "Passchendaele," "St. Quentin," "Avre," "Villers Bretonneux," "Amiens," "Hindenburg Line," "Epéhy," "St Quentin Canal," "Selle," "Sambre."

THE 18th Division remained where the end of the year 1916 found it until the middle of January, 1917, when it was sent back to the same section of the line which it had handed over the previous November, the 7th The Queen's marching by Coulonvillers, Bois Bergues and Raincheval to Varennes in readiness to help in the operations designed to " pinch off " the salient here formed by the German lines. But the further successes of the Division were to be won under a new commander, for on January 14th General Maxse, who had commanded the Division since its formation in 1914, was promoted to the command of the XVIII Corps, and was succeeded by Major-General R. P. Lee.

In the action of Boom Ravine, fought on February 17th, in which the Division deservedly won great distinction, and which helped to break the backbone of the German resistance on the Ancre, the 55th Brigade was in reserve, and does not appear to have been especially actively concerned; but none the less the casualties this month in the 7th The Queen's totalled 10 killed, 2 officers—Captain R. C. Burr and Second-Lieutenant T. C. Dickinson—and 48 other ranks wounded, while Second-Lieutenants H. W. Vaughan and P. E. Thorn and 8 men were wounded and missing, and 41 men were missing.

On March 21st the Battalion proceeded by rail and road to the Aire and Hazebrouck area, the Division having been ordered thither for a month's rest in G.H.Q. reserve. Here the battalions composing the Division remained until the last week in April, receiving orders on the 26th to move to the neighbourhood of Arras on transfer to the VII Corps. The 7th The Queen's actually started from the vicinity of Béthune on the 27th, and, proceeding by train and road via Bailleul-les-Pernes, Bryas, Dainville and Beaurains, finally occupied trenches at Neuville Vitasse, going up into the line on the 29th and taking over the left sector of the Division. Here the front trenches were very narrow, and those in the support line were shallow; there were no dug-outs, and as the position was overlooked by the enemy from Vis-en-Artois, all the work of deepening trenches and making firesteps had to be carried out at night, and movement by day was as far as possible avoided.

The attack in which the 18th Division was now to take part was included in a very large-scale battle, by which a wide sweeping advance was to be attempted from Bullecourt in the south almost to Lens in the north. General Allenby was in charge of the operations, and had units of no fewer than three armies under his command. So far as the share in it of the 18th Division was concerned, the attack, carried out on the Cherisy front, was conducted by the 54th and 55th Brigades, but with wholly inadequate preparation, since these had less than three days given them in which to become acquainted with the ground, while just previous to the attack there was an alteration of some 500 yards made in the Division line.

The action was timed to commence at 3.45 a.m. on May 3rd, the VII Corps, containing the 21st, 18th and 14th Divisions, on right, centre and left respectively, advancing with the VI Corps on its left and the Fifth Army on its right. " The first objective was along a line running through St. Michael's Statue on the north-eastern outskirts of the ruined village of Cherisy, across the Sensée river, and then south-west to where the river flowed east of Fontaine Wood. The final objective allowed for an average advance of 2,000 yards, and brought the British forces within 700 yards of the village of Vis-en-Artois. The 18th Division advance, preceded by a rolling barrage, was to be at the rate of 100 yards in two minutes to the western outskirts of Cherisy, a downhill advance ; through Cherisy to the line of the first objective at 100 yards in six minutes ; thence to the final objective, 100 yards in three minutes. . . . The Division attacked with the 54th Brigade on the right and the 55th Brigade on the left. The disposal was as follows :—

" 55th Brigade : 7th Buffs on the right, with three platoons of the Royal West Kents as ' moppers-up ' ; 8th East Surreys on the left, with one platoon of the Royal West Kents as ' moppers-up ' ; the 7th Royal West Kents (less two companies, one employed as ' moppers-up ' and one furnishing carrying parties) were in support ; the 7th Queen's were in reserve.

" The moon had set and there was much darkness at ' zero ' hour, so that it was impossible to see our waiting men until one came within two yards of them. It soon became manifest, too, that the enemy was standing by expecting our attack, for immediately our barrage opened he replied with heavy fire from machine guns and rifles. Still, our assaulting battalions were clear of our front line before the Boche reply barrage descended, about four minutes after ours had opened. The ground being hard and chalky, the shelling caused an enormous curtain of dust to spring up, making it still more difficult to see."*

At 2 a.m. on May 3rd the 7th The Queen's were assembled in the old British trenches and at 3.45 the assaulting battalions of the Brigade attacked, reaching their first objective, and there began to dig in. Matters had not, however, been going so well on the right of the Division, and a considerable gap had been formed between the two brigades ; this gap the enemy had been quick to seize and occupy, using it to pass through reinforcements, and, as it turned out, the existence of this gap had no inconsiderable influence on the course of the action.

Some time before noon it was realized by The Queen's in reserve that all was not going well, for numbers of our men were seen to be falling back from the front, and at 2.30 p.m. orders were received for The Queen's to reorganize the line and by a counter-attack to reoccupy Cable Trench ; but Lieutenant-Colonel C. F. Watson, who was commanding the Battalion, sent word to the Brigadier that no counter-attack was possible before 6 p.m. At 5.25 p.m. detailed orders were received for the Battalion to attack at 6.15, and the companies moved forward in readiness. " C," " A " and " B " Companies were to attack, " D " to be in support, the objectives being Cable Trench and the road through Cherisy. Just as the attack was commencing word was passed up that it had been postponed one hour, and at

* *The 18th Division in the Great War*, pp. 167 et seq.

7.15 p.m. a desultory shrapnel barrage opened, and the companies of The Queen's then advanced in two waves in extended order at four paces interval, meeting at once hostile machine-gun fire from the front and both flanks, especially the left, and the two left companies suffered many casualties, most of the officers being hit, and failed to reach their objectives. The right company, "B," was checked, but was reinforced by " D," under Captain A. S. Watson, who led his men through " B " and got into part of his objective, but was later directed to fall back at night.

Long before this it was clear that the attack had failed all along the VII Corps front, and the units of the three divisions composing it were back in their original front line ; the enemy had reoccupied his former trenches, but showed no disposition to advance beyond them.

On the night of May 4th the 7th The Queen's moved back to bivouacs in Beaurains.

The casualties among all ranks during the action at Cherisy numbered 142 ; 4 officers—Captains H. R. Longbourne, D.S.O., and V. Hook, Second-Lieutenants J. J. Garden and A. Roskilly—and 23 other ranks were killed or died of wounds, 6 officers and 105 non-commissioned officers and men were wounded, and 14 men were missing. The wounded officers were Captains J. M. Du Buisson and A. S. Watson, Second-Lieutenants R. T. Batchelar, J. Aston, C. E. St. F. Daly, and L. M. Robinson.

For some little time the Division remained in a more or less restful area, and then early in July it was sent to Flanders, the 7th The Queen's moving on the 2nd and proceeding by train and road to Hopoutre, near Poperinghe, where within a week of arrival Acting-Captain H. J. A'Bear and Second-Lieutenant O. J. F. Osborne were killed by a shell at their company headquarters.

The Division was now again in the II Corps of the Fifth Army, and on the night of July 7th the 55th Brigade took over the section of front running from the north boundary of Sanctuary Wood to Observatory Bridge Road. The 54th Brigade was in support at Dickebusch, while the 53rd was training for the coming attack at Steenvoorde. " Trips were made to a field between Ouderdom and Poperinghe, where a vast model of the area to be attacked had been prepared, and many explanatory lectures were given."

At the end of the month the 30th Division was to attack and capture the Black Line—one which ran east of Shrewsbury Forest at its southern extremity, east of Dumbarton Lakes and Inverness Copse and bisected Glencorse Wood. This line captured, the 18th Division was to leapfrog the 30th and pass on to the attack on Polygon Wood. The 30th Division was, however, held up just before reaching the Black Line, and, misleading information coming back as to the result of the 30th Division attack, the 53rd Brigade of the 18th Division advanced against an enemy and a position which the 30th Division should have, but had not, overcome.

The 7th The Queen's were ready to move forward in camp at Château Segard, but were not engaged on this occasion and suffered no casualties.

Now followed four days' heavy and incessant rain, but on August 4th the 18th Division again took over the front line, with the 55th Brigade on the right and the 54th on the left, and preparations were made for another attack upon the German positions, the 18th Division being detailed to attack the strong points in and about Glencorse Wood and Inverness Copse, while the 25th Division was to complete the capture of Westhoek Ridge.

" The Queen's had just had a draft when they went up with the West Kents and took over the old line at Sanctuary Wood. For the new-comers it was a frightful

GENERAL VIEW OF THE BATTLEFIELD LEADING UP TO PASSCHENDAELE, BOESINGHE. AUGUST, 1917.

[*Copyright: Imperial War Museum.*

apprenticeship to active service. Nothing went smoothly; it was a pouring wet night; there were casualties in the way, 'C' and 'D' Companies losing heavily; the trenches had been shelled or swilled away, and . . . an adjustment of some hundreds of yards was needed to put the line where it was by the official chart. . . .

"For the attack against Inverness Copse and Glencorse Wood on August 10th General Lee put in the 55th Infantry Brigade, with the 7th Queen's as the assaulting battalion on the right, and on the left the 54th Brigade, with the 11th Royal Fusiliers on the right and the 7th Bedfordshire Regiment on the left. . . . The enemy knew what was coming, and he had pushed out a fresh line of wired posts, which came very near to the 7th Queen's forming-up tape. Some of the Queen's, stealing forward in the darkness, collided noisily with these posts. Rifle shots rang out, up went green lights along the German front, and down upon the luckless Queen's came a Boche barrage. Disorganizing gaps appeared in the right company, and three platoons of the left company were also caught. The havoc was accentuated by a second German barrage that came almost on the stroke of zero hour. It says much for the surviving officers and non-commissioned officers that the fragments were welded into a line and jumped off at the given signal. . . .

"One section of the leading platoon of the right company of the Queen's reached the south-west corner of Inverness Copse. It was found to be protected by a machine-gun post and by a well-guarded tunnel. All but one of the Queen's who reached the wood at this point became casualties.

"Further north Second-Lieutenant J. H. Wilson, with two platoons, followed the barrage along the north edge of Inverness Copse to the Queen's objective. By this time he was the only unwounded officer of the assaulting companies of the Queen's, and, lacking support and being threatened on his left flank, he withdrew to the north-west corner of the copse. In the course of his withdrawal, he organized and carried out an attack on a concrete emplacement, the fire from which was causing many casualties among our men. Wilson then took a party into Jasper Lane, and their grip on this bit of trench was tightened by the arrival of two Vickers guns. Wilson held on here until relieved eighteen hours later. Lance-Corporal Jelly,* of the Queen's, who was in charge of a Lewis gun, did fine work all that morning. He was asked by another Lewis gunner, who was hard pressed, to come to his assistance; he took his gun across 40 yards of open ground, exposed to heavy machine-gun fire, and got it into action. Then he found another gun, which he caused to be fired. In spite of the great difficulties which the Queen's had to face, Jelly never lost heart, and kept his gun going until the Battalion was relieved next day,"†

The attack on Inverness Copse and Glencorse Wood failed, and it is difficult to see how success under the circumstances could well have been expected.

The attempt was renewed and fighting was carried on by the 18th Division for the best part of another week, and then on the 15th the 55th Brigade went to Wormhoudt, the 7th The Queen's being quartered about Eringhem.

During this last fighting the casualties in the Battalion amounted to 10 officers and 272 other ranks killed, wounded, and missing; but The Queen's had not been long at Eringhem before reinforcements in all ranks brought the strength up to 24 officers and 710 non-commissioned officers and men.

The Battalion diary for September closes with the following statement :—
"September has been a most enjoyable month. The Battalion has been out of

* No. 1109 Lance-Corporal S. Jelley.   † *The 18th Division in the Great War*, pp. 216-218.

the line the whole period, and the greater part has been spent in the agricultural country which lies north of St. Omer. The weather has been most favourable and has greatly facilitated the work of reorganizing the Battalion. Work and pleasure have been intermixed. Numbers of men have been sent on leave to England, and sports of all kinds—cricket, football, cross-country racing, boxing, and assaults-at-arms—have been arranged. Men have been allowed to assist the farmers to gather their crops; the whole Battalion has made trips in lorries to the Fifth Army musketry camp, and on special occasions men have been taken by lorry for a day at the seaside. Large reinforcements of officers and men have been received.

"The command of the Battalion has changed during the month. Lieutenant-Colonel E. W. Lennard, 6th Gloucesters, attached 5th East Lancs, and Lieutenant-Colonel O. C. Clare, D.S.O., M.C., have exchanged commands."

At the beginning of October the 7th The Queen's was at St. Jan-ter-Biezen, and here on the evening of the 4th news was "received," so states the war diary, "of the successful attack by the Second and Fifth Armies on the Poelcappelle area and the part of the Passchendaele Ridge from Broodseinde to the south, 4,446 prisoners and 6 guns captured, all objectives taken." On the 9th, however, the Brigade moved to Dirty Bucket Camp, and next day orders were received that, "owing to the failure of the 32nd Brigade on the 9th instant, the 55th Brigade will move forward to relieve that brigade and carry out the assault allotted to it."

The Division was again under its old commander, General Maxse, in the XVIII Corps of the Second Army, and that commander met the officers of his former division with the characteristic remark, "I have arranged a very nice battle for you, gentlemen, with lots of Huns to kill!" The battle was that of Poelcappelle, one of the very few solid gains in a year that had proved especially costly to the Allies.

The first attack was made on October 12th by the 4th Division on the left, the 18th in the centre, and the 9th on the right, and the attack of the 18th was made by the 55th Brigade, the 7th The Queen's being in reserve. The conditions were appalling; it had rained all day on the 11th, and to get through the mud was almost impossible, many men sticking fast and being unable even to reach the assembly positions, while the guns sank in the mud and could not be got forward, and it is not surprising that the attack failed, while the casualties in the Brigade were very heavy. The Battalion held the front line all the 13th, and then went back to Dirty Bucket Camp, having had Second-Lieutenant A. C. Swindell and 15 other ranks killed, Second-Lieutenants W. M. Watson, G. E. Step and J. B. Lancaster, and 86 men wounded, while 36 men were missing.

The time for reorganizing and clearing up was short, for on the 19th orders were received that the 7th The Queen's were placed at the disposal of the General Officer Commanding 53rd Brigade for the second—and successful—attack upon Poelcappelle, and next day the Battalion moved up to the front line and there relieved two battalions of the 53rd Brigade so as to enable them to attack with their brigade; The Queen's held the line until the afternoon of the 22nd, when they were again withdrawn to Dirty Bucket Camp, having sustained 75 casualties, including 2 officers wounded—Second-Lieutenants J. L. Caufield and L. T. S. Hawkins.

The good work done by The Queen's on this occasion was appreciated by the General Officer Commanding 53rd Brigade, who wrote to the Brigadier of the 55th as follows:—

"*I also wish to convey our thanks to the 7th Queen's for their valuable assistance in holding the line, which enabled the two battalions of this Brigade to go into the line quite fresh, and which in no small measure contributed to the success of the attack.*"

The rest of the month was passed at Petworth Camp, Proven, and in or about this area the Division remained until well into the new year. It was not, indeed, until February 8th that the Battalion moved by train to the Noyon area—a journey of some fourteen hours—and on arrival it settled down in Frières Camp. It was a greatly weakened division at this period, since, consequent on the recent reorganization, three battalions had been taken out of the Division—the 8th Norfolk and 8th Suffolk Regiments from the 53rd, and the 12th Middlesex from the 54th Brigade, while the 7th Royal West Kent had been transferred from the 55th Brigade to the 53rd. The total strength of the 18th Division was now not more than 12,000 men, while on February 1st, 1918, the numbers of the 7th Battalion The Queen's are given as 40 officers, including the Medical Officer, and 750 other ranks. The officers serving with the Battalion at the commencement of this epoch-making period upon which it was now entering were as follows :—Lieutenant-Colonels C. Bushell, D.S.O., in command, and E. M. Liddell; Major A. R. Grylls; Captains J. E. Snell, W. H. Laslett, M.C., R.A.M.C., and W. G. Simmons; Lieutenants W. R. Cohen and J. Norman; Second-Lieutenants D. C. Cottrell and S. J. Friend.

"*A*" *Company*: Captain H. J. Tortise; Second-Lieutenants P. Bessell, J. F. Henderson, L. P. P. T. Bartlett, W. G. Phipps and E. Ranger.

"*B*" *Company*: Captain T. C. Filby; Lieutenants G. C. Evans and J. G. S. Morrison; Second-Lieutenants J. S. Adams, R. T. Batchelar, A. A. Brookes and A. F. A. Hay.

"*C*" *Company*: Captain W. H. C. Grant; Lieutenant A. L. Haig; Second-Lieutenants J. Innes, R. H. Baylis, N. Freeman and C. E. Hall.

"*D*" *Company*: Captain P. V. Cooper; Lieutenants A. S. Watson and E. C. Evans; Second-Lieutenants W. J. Butler, W. F. Bower, E. V. Batten, K. A. H. Hassell, C. L. Harvey, H. Marshall, A. R. Mitchell and A. Ogden.

The 18th Division was now in the III Corps on the extreme right of the Fifth Army, next to the French, occupying a front that was some 9,000 yards in extent, stretching from a point just north of Travecy to Alaincourt, having the 58th Division on the right and the 14th on the left. The ground here occupied consisted of three defensive belts, known as the Forward Zone, the Battle Zone, and the Rear Zone, but so far little work had been done on the last-named of these. A German offensive was known to be imminent and was expected to fall on the Fifth Army sector with the object of capturing Noyon, and at 3 p.m. on March 20th a warning was issued for all to be in readiness for the attack which opened next morning, when the 18th Division was disposed as under :—

The front was divided into two brigade sectors, the 53rd Brigade being on the left and the 55th on the right; here the 7th Buffs were in the Forward Zone, the 7th The Queen's in the Battle Zone, while the 8th East Surrey Regiment was in divisional reserve in Haute Tombelle Camp.

The enemy bombardment began at 4.45 a.m. on the 21st, the shelling being intense, and Liez Village, Vieville, Vivier, Quenet and Verger Woods were heavily gassed. As dawn broke it was found that the whole area was enshrouded in a thick mist through which it was impossible to see further than 20 or 30 yards; the Battle Zone was so far untouched, with the exception of the Liez and Ronquenet Farm

Road. As the mist cleared and the day went on, it was ascertained that the enemy had broken through on both flanks. Some of the enemy who had apparently worked south-west under cover of the mist were in Ronquenet Wood, but the positions of the 7th Buffs both in Vendeuil Fort and the support and reserve areas were still intact. On the right of The Queen's the enemy broke through and fighting took place on the right flank of the Battle Zone, where "C" Company was involved, but nothing serious occurred, and the British guns caused numerous casualties among the enemy behind Travecy; later, however, German infantry was seen advancing towards Tergnier—apparently unopposed. No enemy attack was, however, made on The Queen's position in the Battle Zone.

One hundred and fifty men from the 5th Cavalry Brigade were sent up in support, and another body moved to form a defensive flank to the south of Fort Liez; but a patrol which went out from The Queen's left company to gain touch with the enemy or to reach the 7th Buffs was captured. The Buffs were attacked in and counter-attacked from about Vendeuil Fort, and a counter-attack was arranged and about to be launched to clear up the situation in Ronquenet Wood, when orders came from the Brigade for withdrawal to the west of the St. Quentin Canal about midnight, while it was directed that officers' patrols were to be sent forward to gain communication with the 7th Buffs and bring them back, if possible. This was successfully done, and then The Queen's companies fell back by platoons to the Battalion command post, and thence across the Canal and through Mennesis to Frières Wood, which was reached in the early hours of the 22nd, and where The Queen's halted and awaited orders.

The Battle Zone of the 18th Division had remained intact all through the 21st, but those of the 14th and 58th Divisions had gone; as many as eight enemy divisions had been identified on the III Corps front, while the attack on the 18th Division had been carried out by four enemy divisions.

At 8 a.m. on March 22nd the situation on the 18th Division front was as follows: the 54th Brigade held the line of the Canal from the east edge of Jussy to the north edge of Mennesis; the 3rd Cavalry Brigade and other details held the line of the Canal as far as Quessy; while the 55th Brigade had crossed the Canal and its battalions were posted, The Queen's in the valley to the north of Vouel, the remainder in Frières Wood; the 53rd Brigade was at Rouez.

The bridges over the Canal between Jussy and Mennesis had not been destroyed and were all passable for infantry.

During the morning the 7th The Queen's moved forward and took up a position near the canal, holding it all day; but later in the day the Germans crossed the canal at Tergnier in front of the 58th Division.

At 6 a.m. on the 23rd two battalions of French infantry came up with orders to counter-attack and recapture Tergnier, and two companies of The Queen's were directed to lend flanking assistance; the French moved confidently forward, but they did not know the ground, the fog still hung about, and—worst of all—the men were insufficiently supplied with ammunition—only 35 rounds per man.

"The fog was so thick that some of the Queen's also lost their way going to the attack. A gallant runner, Private C. W. Ponsford, found one wandering platoon and led it straight to its position, enabling it to be up in time to join in the attack. The Queen's, like the West Kents and the East Surreys, always had brave and resourceful runners. Though the attack failed, the Queen's did not fail, and glorious gallantry and leadership that gained him the Victoria Cross was shown by

Colonel Bushell. He took charge of the left of the French as well as of his own two companies, and led them to the assault under fierce and sustained machine-gun fire. He was struck by a bullet in the head, but again and again he rallied the troops, walking up and down in front of them, encouraging them to fresh efforts. Although little progress could be made, Colonel Bushell's uplifting bravery kept the line firm. Not until he had assured himself that his positions were intact did he go back to Rouez to report to General Wood. Even then, when his head had been bandaged, no one could prevent him from returning to command his battalion as it retired in front of Faillouel. . . . He carried on until he fainted from exhaustion. Then Major Tortise, his second-in-command, and Colonel Ransome, of the Buffs, persuaded him to go back. He fainted again and had to be carried out of action. . . .

"About 10 a.m., when the French had entirely run out of ammunition, the Germans poured forward to the attack. The Queen's had to fall back, but they retired in orderly fashion. Indeed, it was a retirement carried out according to the Manuals, with proper covering fire and companies falling back by sections."*

Finally, a defensive position was taken up by the Battalion on the west edge of the road running north and south through Frières Wood, and this was held for the rest of the day. Then as dusk came on the whole line withdrew and the remnants of the Battalion reassembled in Le Bosquet Wood, where orders were received to retire to the Chauny—Villequier Aumont road; here French troops took over the front and the 55th Brigade was withdrawn to billets at Berthancourt.

Early on the 24th the Brigade took up and entrenched a position on the Berthancourt—Neuflieux road, but only two hours later was ordered to withdraw to another east of Chaillouel, and here two of the enemy wandered into the lines of The Queen's and volunteered the information that fresh attacks were to be made each day by new German divisions. The retreat had to go on, for at 3 a.m. on the 25th it was learnt that ground had been lost on the left and a fresh retirement was made to a defensive position at Crepigny, but this in turn was abandoned and the Brigade fell back, after a rearguard action in which The Queen's took part, to the west of Babœuf, and from there via Selency to billets at Varennes, where the night was passed in comparative quiet. Marching on by Caisnes and Nampcel, The Queen's here embussed, and arrived at Boves on the 30th *en route* to rejoin the Fifth Army near Amiens, the Battalion immediately on arrival going up to the line west of Marcelcave.

During these days of fighting, marching, and retreat the losses in the Division had naturally been very heavy, and the casualties in the 7th The Queen's totalled from the 21st to the 29th, all ranks, 342. Of these, 1 officer, Lieutenant G. P. Cockburn, and 28 other ranks were killed, 6 officers and 121 non-commissioned officers and men were wounded, while 12 officers and 174 men were missing, the majority presumed to have been captured. The wounded officers were Lieutenant-Colonel C. Bushell, D.S.O., Captain P. V. Cooper, Second-Lieutenants J. A. Hunt, L. G. Cottrell, R. Charlton and E. Ranger; while missing were Captain T. C. Filby, D.C.M., Lieutenants A. B. Frost, W. R. Cohen, A. L. Haig and E. C. Evans, Second-Lieutenants W. G. Phipps, R. T. Batchelar, E. V. Batten, A. F. A. Hay, C. L. Harvey, A. Ogden, and A. A. Brookes.

"At the time of the 18th Division's arrival in the Amiens area, the advance of the Second German Army had been checked on the general line running from

* *The 18th Division in the Great War*, pp. 284, 285.

south to north by Demuin, Aubercourt, Marcelcave, Warfussée, Sailly, Albert and Beaumont Hamel. The portion of the front between Marcelcave and the river Luce was held by elements of four divisions, all of which, like the 18th, had been in action since March 21st, had suffered grievous casualties, and were now very exhausted. Their immediate relief was imperative, especially as the enemy was expected to make further and early attacks in this sector." At midday, then, on March 30th the 18th Division was ordered that night to relieve all the troops between the River Luce and the Marcelcave—Cachy road. By daybreak on the 31st the Division was in the line, the 53rd Brigade on the right, the 55th in the centre, and the 9th Australian Brigade, which had been placed under the General Officer Commanding 18th Division, on the left ; the 54th Brigade occupied the high ground between Hangard Village and Hangard Wood.

General Lee's orders were that all positions were to be held to the last ; if lost, they must immediately be retaken by counter-attack. During the days that followed the line was very severely tried, the pressure being exerted to a greater extent against the other two brigades of the Division than against the 55th, and the 7th The Queen's spent some days tolerably quietly at Riencourt ; but on April 25th they were at St. Fuscien, when a message was received stating that the Battalion had been lent to the 53rd Brigade, and that brigade again to the 58th Division, to take part in certain projected operations. The 53rd Brigade, *less* the 8th Berkshire and 7th Royal West Kent, but *plus* the 7th The Queen's, was, in conjunction with the French Moroccan Division on its left, to attack the Bois de Hangard on the 26th. The Queen's were to be on the right of the Brigade.

Zero hour was at 6 a.m. on the 26th, and by 10 the previous evening The Queen's were assembled at the Villers Bretonneux—Domart road, whence officer patrols were at once sent out along the Cachy—Hangard road to examine the forming-up line, to see whether any troops, hostile or allied, were in the vicinity and whether any trench line existed. Meanwhile the following dispositions were made : " A " Company, under Lieutenant Henderson, was to attack on a two-platoon front, with one platoon of " B " to protect the right flank and keep touch with the brigade on the right, and one platoon to be used to " mop up " the wood ; " D " Company, under Lieutenant Morrison, was to be in support ; " B," less two platoons, was battalion reserve under Lieutenant Evans ; while " C " Company was employed as brigade reserve. Considerable difficulty was experienced in getting the companies into position owing to the enemy shelling, the want of knowledge of the ground, and the mist which rose at night.

At zero hour the attacking platoons went over in two waves under a barrage, keeping up well with it though suffering heavily from machine-gun fire from the wood, all the drives and openings in which were covered by guns and snipers ; progress consequently was slow. The troops, however, advanced well past a drive running north and south through the wood and took up a line approximately on this drive, while Second-Lieutenant Hassell and Sergeant Wyatt pushed up their platoons into a gap which had formed between The Queen's and the Essex Regiment.

The Moroccan Division had advanced in splendid style, but met with very great resistance and suffered enormously, causing portions of the division to fall back towards Gentelles ; the Essex then were obliged to conform and withdraw to the drive, as their flank was now in the air.

Lieutenant Skeet came up at 8 a.m. from Battalion Headquarters to learn the situation, but was wounded before reaching the wood and was later killed by a shell; Lieutenant Evans then went forward and reconnoitred the Battalion front, reporting certain gaps which were at once made good. It was found to be very difficult to entrench owing to the want of tools and the chalky nature of the ground, while during daylight the enemy snipers and machine-gunners were active; there was, however, a low bank in rear of the drive which afforded cover, and after dusk consolidation was proceeded with. Unfortunately the field of fire was much restricted by the dense undergrowth.

From midday this day until 3 p.m. on the 26th the enemy subjected the whole area of Villers Bretonneux and Domart to a most intense bombardment by high explosive and gas, and while this was at its height troops holding the line south of the wood were forced to leave their posts, returning immediately it slackened.

Relief by the French had been expected on the night of the 26th, but this was postponed for twenty-four hours, and it was not until 1.30 a.m. on the 28th that the 7th The Queen's finally moved back, via Gentelles Woods, to bivouacs at Blangy Tronville.

The following incidents of the fighting are given in the Divisional History, pp. 231, 232 :—

"The 7th Queen's faced and overcame the same difficulties. When casualties from machine guns and snipers were so heavy that men were beginning to waver, Second-Lieutenant K. A. H. Hassell collected the remnants of his own platoons and other units, including the French, and dug in on a line that stood fast until relief came on the 27th. Second-Lieutenant H. P. Clarke, finding himself the only officer left on a 500 yards' sector, took command, and as his party still suffered losses from rifle and machine-gun fire, he led his men forward and cleared that part of the wood. He was hit in the head, but after having his wound dressed he returned to the front line and carried on the whole of the next day until the French relieved him. Lieutenant G. C. Evans not only made a reconnaissance that proved invaluable for securing the safety of the Queen's, he also guided a party forward and wired the wood in front of the Battalion's position."

The 7th The Queen's had again suffered casualties out of all proportion to their strength : these totalled 5 officers and 141 other ranks, 2 officers and 14 men were killed or died of wounds, 1 officer and 85 other ranks were wounded, 1 officer and 41 men were missing, while 1 officer and 1 man were wounded and missing.

For his services during these days Lieutenant-Colonel Bushell was awarded the Victoria Cross, the mention of which appears as follows in the *London Gazette* of April 30th, 1918 :—

"*Captain (T. Lt.-Col.) Christopher Bushell, D.S.O., Royal West Surrey Regiment.*

"*For most conspicuous bravery and devotion to duty when in command of his battalion. Lt.-Col. Bushell personally led 'C' Company of his battalion, who were co-operating with an Allied regiment in a counter-attack, in face of very heavy machine-gun fire. In the course of this attack he was severely wounded in the head, but he continued to carry on, walking about in front of both English and Allied troops encouraging and reorganizing them. He refused even to have his wound attended to until he had placed the whole line in a sound position and formed a defensive flank to meet a turning movement by the enemy. He then went to brigade headquarters and reported the situation, had his wound dressed, and returned to the firing line, which had come back a short distance. He visited every portion of the line, both English and Allied, in the face of terrific machine-gun and rifle fire, exhorting the troops to remain where they were and to kill the enemy. In spite of his wounds, this gallant officer refused to go to the rear and had eventually to be removed to the dressing station in a fainting condition.*

*"To the magnificent example of energy, devotion and courage shown by their Commanding Officer is attributed the fine spirit displayed and the keen fight put up by his battalion, not only on the day in question, but on each succeeding day of the withdrawal."*

During May, June, and the first half of July the Division held the line in front of Albert; it was a time of much patrol work and many raids, while during the latter part of the time spent here the officers and men of two American divisions were attached to the 18th for training—an outward and visible sign that America had really entered upon the war. Then on the 13th the 18th Division proceeded to the Picquigny area for a fortnight's rest, the 7th The Queen's occupying billets in Pissy; and by the beginning of August the Division had taken up a line astride the Bray—Corbie road south-west of Morlancourt in readiness to take part in the great attack east of Amiens to be launched on August 8th.

The Fourth Army at this time contained, in order from right to left, the Canadian Corps, the Australian Corps, and, north of the Somme, the III Corps, this last being composed of the 58th, 47th, and 18th Divisions in the front line, with the 12th in support. To the 18th Division was given the task of capturing the high ground along the Bray—Corbie ridge so as to form a protective flank for the main Fourth Army attack.

Six tanks had been told off to accompany the 7th The Queen's, who were especially concerned with the capture of the ground north of the Bray—Corbie road, but the tanks failed to arrive at the appointed time. By 3.40 on the 8th the Battalion was in position, one wave in front of and three behind Burke Trench, and almost at once a heavy enemy barrage came down, causing several casualties. For some time the situation was very obscure, and many officers and runners sent forward to report became casualties; and at 7 a.m. Lieutenant-Colonel Bushell went forward himself with his runner to deal with the situation. Collecting all available men, he led them forward from Croydon Trench to the assault, capturing Cloncurry Trench between Culgor and Cloud Support. He then proceeded along the trench to organize and encourage the men, and on his way to give orders to a tank, which had now arrived, as to the next move, he was mortally wounded by a sniper. "His runner, Private A. E. Morris, a gallant soldier whose knowledge of the country was instinctive, who earlier in the day had led the advance platoons to their assaulting positions and had been at Colonel Bushell's elbow when he first came to clear up the situation, rushed across the open to where his colonel lay, and though the ground across which he carried the colonel was swept by hostile machine-gun fire, he brought him in. But it was a heroism that counted for nothing. Colonel Bushell had been fatally wounded."

Colonel Ransome, of the Buffs, was now placed in command of all the troops in the forward area, and by his orders Captain Snell went forward and reported the situation as follows:—Captain Simmons, "C" Company of The Queen's, with Company Sergeant-Major Knight, "D" Company, and about 100 men were in Cloncurry Trench; the trench about the Bray—Corbie road was empty, and Captain Simmons was directed to dispose his men in Cloncurry Trench from Cloud Support to the Bray—Corbie road. Captain Snell formed the opinion that men of The

Queen's had reached their objective, and that if immediate action was taken the Battalion flank objective could be gained.

Captain Snell, being ordered to try to effect this, calling to the men in Cloncurry Trench to follow him, led them down the trench, he, with two men, working in the open to the north, while Captain Hayfield moved on the south, but his party was met by machine-gun and rifle fire. He then sent the men forward while he, with a non-commissioned officer and six men, went on down the trench running north to form a bomb stop, when the enemy commenced retiring and the line was occupied and organized. About five in the afternoon a brigade of the 12th Division passed through the line held by The Queen's, encircled Morlancourt, and captured the ridge beyond.

In the 7th The Queen's 4 officers and 24 other ranks had been killed, 6 officers and 140 non-commissioned officers and men had been wounded, 68 men were gassed, and 7 were suffering from shell-shock—a total of 275 all ranks. The officers killed were Lieutenant-Colonel C. Bushell, V.C., D.S.O., Lieutenant D. Holman (Middlesex Regiment, attached), Second-Lieutenants P. V. Cooper and H. M. Barber (East Surrey Regiment, attached). Wounded were Captain L. G. Stedman, M.C., Second-Lieutenants J. T. Lancaster, W. M. Watson, J. S. Adams, W. L. Atkinson and H. P. Clarke, M.C.

There was now a few days' pause, and then on August 22nd the offensive reopened on the front of the Fourth Army; on this day the 18th Division was holding the line in the Albert sector on a two-brigade front, with the 12th Division on the right and the 38th Division of the Third Army on the left, and the rôle assigned to the 18th Division was the capture of Albert and the high ground to the east of it. The Division attacked with the 54th Brigade on the right and the 55th on the left—The Queen's on the left of the attacking line of their brigade—and by 8.30 a.m. on the 22nd Albert was again in Allied hands. That afternoon the 7th The Queen's learnt that for the operations of the 23rd they had been placed at the disposal of the 53rd Brigade, which was detailed to attack Tara Hill at 4.45 that morning.

The Queen's left the railway cutting west of Albert at 1 a.m. and marched through the town to the assembly position on the east in front of the light railway and immediately south of the Albert—Bapaume road; " A " and " B " Companies were on the right and left, " C " in support and " D " in reserve, each 100 yards in rear of one another. The barrage came down at zero, and on this occasion the tanks arrived on time. There was at the start a certain mingling of units, and on the left the advance tended to become one in a long mixed line, but matters improved in this respect as the advance went forward. Hostile machine-gun fire was heavy, while some of the shells from the British howitzers fell among our own infantry, causing some disorganization ; but Lieutenants Coles and Hogg soon put things right, and as the line pushed on the enemy opposition became weaker. Tara Hill, the final objective, was reached at 6.30 a.m., and the infantry and tanks worked on over the crest, but, running into our own barrage, had to fall back to Tara Hill, where the trench line was consolidated while posts were sent out in front.

" Lieutenant Coles of the 7th Queen's," says the divisional historian, " when the objective on Tara Hill was reached, found himself the senior officer of the Queen's. Practically single-handed, he pushed on with the work of consolidation ; and his determination and leadership were the more astounding because his men, besides being extremely fatigued, were most of them new recruits, and only three young officers and very few non-commissioned officers were left to help him."

The line on Tara Hill was held all day under considerable shelling, and at five in the afternoon the General Officer Commanding 53rd Brigade came up and issued orders for further operations that night, two battalions pushing on to the capture of La Boisselle, the 7th The Queen's remaining in their present position, but sending forward " A " Company to form a line of resistance on which the assaulting battalions could fall back at need. By 10 p.m. La Boisselle had been captured, and at midnight the 7th The Queen's reverted to their own brigade. On this day the General Officer Commanding 55th Brigade, after thanking the battalions which had fought immediately under his command on the previous day, added that "*The Queen's, fighting with the 53rd Infantry Brigade, have gained all their objectives, captured many prisoners and an enemy field gun.*\* *The Hun is getting nearer ' beat' and more disorganized each day. I look to you all to get fit again as quickly as possible so that the Brigade, which has fought so gallantly in the early and stiff days of the gigantic battle, may be ready to take part in the pursuit for which they have been fighting so long.*"

There was renewed fighting on practically every one of the remaining days of the month, but the advance went on; on the 26th The Queen's were at Buire, next day at Bernafay Wood, the 28th and 29th at Fricourt; and then on the 30th they went to bivouacs on the Montauban—Guillemont road. In the ten days' fighting from August 19th to 28th many casualties had again been sustained by the 7th The Queen's: 2 officers—Second-Lieutenants C. L. Bearman and J. H. Sheppard —and 27 other ranks were killed, 10 officers and 147 non-commissioned officers and men were wounded, 2 officers and 1 man were gassed, 20 men were missing, and 3 otherwise injured—a total of 212. The wounded officers were Captain G. C. Evans, M.C., Lieutenants R. J. J. Hogg and G. E. Jenkins, Second-Lieutenants C. H. Davis, W. C. Gray, J. W. Bourne, F. J. McKinless, F. F. J. Claxton, J. C. Hedley and J. B. Lancaster; the two officers who were gassed were Second-Lieutenants E. E. Daniel and L. V. Richman.

On September 1st it was arranged that the 38th Division should capture Morval, the 47th was to take Rancourt and reach the south-east corner of St. Pierre Vaast Wood, while the objective of the 18th Division was to be the capture of the north-west portion of the wood and the formation of a line astride the Rancourt—Sailly Saillisel road. In the 55th Brigade the 8th East Surrey Regiment was to push forward to St. Pierre Vaast Wood, the 7th Buffs were to follow and secure the remainder of the objective, while the 7th The Queen's were to " mop up " the area north-east of Combles that was not attacked frontally. The advance was splendidly successful, and The Queen's, following up, collected all the Germans whom the other two battalions had encircled; some 700 prisoners were here taken. " In the attack and clearing of Fregicourt, Sergeant Cornwall, of the 7th Queen's, showed great coolness and bravery in leading his platoon. The enemy put down heavy trench-mortar and machine-gun fire. Cornwall walked in front of his platoon in full view of the enemy, firing as he walked, never once attempting to take cover, exhorting his men to ' fight like Queen's.' It was largely his splendid example to a platoon composed chiefly of a new draft that carried his little force forward, and resulted in the capture of trench mortars, machine guns, and over 200 prisoners. . . . The completeness of the Division's success on September 1st may be gauged by the swift advance that followed during the next few days."

\* The actual captures by The Queen's were 1 officer, 70 men, 1 field and 11 machine guns.

On September 7th General Lee received the following letter from Lieutenant-General Godley, commanding III Corps :—

*" I wish to congratulate and thank all ranks under your command for the very fine work which has been done by the Division since it went into the line practically a month ago. For the greater part of this month the Division has been fighting daily and incessantly, and has to its credit the crossing of the Ancre and the Canal du Nord and the making of bridges over them, the capture of Albert, Tara, and Usna Hills, the craters at La Boisselle, Montauban, Bernafay, Trônes and Leuze Woods, Combles, Frégicourt, Saillisel, St. Pierre Vaast Wood and Vaux Wood, and the whole of the country as far east as the Canal du Nord, a distance of 17 miles. 2,464 prisoners and 321 guns and machine guns have been captured by the Division during this period, and the fighting has been very heavy. You may well be proud of the valour and endurance which the Division has daily and incessantly displayed in order to enable it to add such a record to its already long list of notable achievements."*

For a fortnight now the 18th Division was at rest, not being called to the front again until September 18th, by which time the Fourth Army had fought its way further forward, and the sector now allotted to the 18th Division and those working with it, included Templeux-le-Guerard, Ronssoy, and Epéhy.

It is not easy to disentangle from the diaries any really consecutive account of the part which the 7th The Queen's took in the operations of this week, involving the attacks on the outposts of the Hindenburg Line, the fighting about Ronssoy, undertaken by a battalion which, like all those now contained in the 18th Division, was composed of young officers and men, and also greatly under strength—for few companies were now more than seventy in number ; but when on the night of the 24th-25th the Division went back to Nurlu—the Battalion to Leuze Wood—the 7th The Queen's had suffered a loss of 195 all ranks ; 3 officers and 27 non-commissioned officers and men had been killed, 6 officers and 124 other ranks had been wounded, 31 men had been gassed, and 4 men were missing. Captain E. F. Bennett, M.C., Second-Lieutenants J. J. Power and A. W. Servante were killed, while wounded were Captain J. E. Snell, M.C., Lieutenants F. H. Livesay, E. L. Coles and J. Innes, Second-Lieutenants W. T. Morris and T. F. Relf-West.

The rest-period was a very brief one, for the Division was called up once more to the front to take part in the main attack by the Fourth Army, which was fixed for September 29th, the attack on the III Corps front being entrusted to the 18th and 12th Divisions. The 55th Brigade was on the 29th in the concentration area just east of Guyencourt, when " in consequence of reported success of Americans and 54th Brigade, Battalion was ordered," so runs the entry in this day's diary, " to proceed at once down the Macquincourt Valley in order to take up a position, with the Buffs on our left, in order to carry out the ' mopping-up ' of Vendhuille. In accordance with these orders, the Battalion moved off towards Sart Farm—' B ' Company in front followed by Battalion H.Q., ' C,' ' D,' and ' A ' in artillery formation. Enemy having been seen in Grub Lane in a manner suggesting counter-attack, the Battalion was ordered to hold Doleful Post, but owing to congested state of the trenches only ' B ' Company could be accommodated, ' C ' and ' D ' being established in the bank and ' A ' in slits fifty yards west of the bank.

" At 1.55 p.m. information was received that the Buffs would advance against a pocket of the enemy reported as holding out in front, moving along the Knoll and getting into touch with the 54th Brigade, and a section was detailed from 'A' Company to co-operate with the Buffs, while another from 'B' was told off to help the Australians who were to deal with a similar enemy pocket round Guillemont Farm; the rest of the Queen's was to be ready to exploit success, 'mop up' Vendhuille or, if necessary, take it by assault from a south-westerly direction. As the movement by the Buffs did not take place, the Queen's were ordered at 5 p.m. to remain where they were, but to hold the line of posts, Egg Post—Doleful Post, with two companies in counter-attack position in rear.

"At 7.10 p.m. the Queen's were ordered to pass to the 54th Brigade as counter-attack battalion and to take up fresh positions, but it was by now very dark, rain was falling heavily, and the new position was only reached at four o'clock on the morning of the 30th, when 'A' Company occupied the south-east half of London Road, 'B' Lark Trench, 'C' was in the north-west half of London Road, while 'D' Company occupied Causeway Lane. Here orders came to hand from the 54th Brigade that the Royal Fusiliers and Northamptons would move forward on Vendhuille, while the Queen's were then to occupy the existing front line—viz., Spree Lane—Tino Support—Macquincourt."

Here The Queen's appear to have remained until the night of October 1st-2nd, when all three brigades of the 18th Division were relieved and moved back by omnibus to the Montigny area, The Queen's proceeding to Béhencourt and now rejoining the 55th Brigade.

The following message reached the Division from the III Corps Commander:—

"*It is with the greatest regret that I bid ' au revoir ' to the 18th Division. Throughout all the operations of the III Corps since March, 1918, the Division has not only fought with gallantry and determination, but also with the spirit of mutual co-operation and comradeship which ensure success. I also wish to convey my personal thanks to General Lee, the staff, and all ranks of the 18th Division for their loyal support and for the manner in which they have always ' played up.' I trust that it may be my good fortune, at no distant date, to have the Division in my command again in further operations.*"

On October 17th the Division received information that its services were again needed to assist in the battles of the Selle and Sambre Rivers, and as an initial operation the Fourth Army, in conjunction with the Third, was to gain the western edge of the forest of Mormal, forming a defensive flank facing east to protect the major operations to be carried out by the Third Army. The 18th Division was to attack, with the 25th and 33rd on its right and left respectively, on October 23rd, the 53rd and 54th Brigades in line, the 55th then passing through to the capture of the third, fourth and fifth objectives, all of which lay beyond Bousies.

In consequence of the above arrangements the 7th The Queen's left Béhencourt on October 17th and proceeded by rail and road to Maurois, which was reached on the 21st, and on the 23rd marched through Le Cateau to a forward position, where the Battalion remained for some time, the position in front being rather obscure. As it had been arranged that the 8th East Surrey and 7th Buffs were to capture the 3rd and 4th objectives, the 7th The Queen's (right) and 6th Northamptonshire Regiment (left) then leapfrogging the other two battalions and moving on to the capture of the fifth objective, these two battalions were not actively engaged until the morning of the 24th, when the advance to the fifth objective was proceeded with.

"By 8.25 a.m. the 7th Queen's had pushed far enough through the trees and hedges to gain a footing in the western outskirts of Robersart. But the enemy made great play with machine guns from the bedroom windows of the scattered houses. The Queen's continued to have casualties, and by this time the holding up of the 54th Brigade about Renouard Farm had caused the suspension of the whole advance." Later, successes in other parts of the line allowed the advance to be resumed, and by 6 p.m. two companies of The Queen's and East Surrey Regiment had got as far as the church in Robersart.

The 25th passed quietly, though constant and active patrolling went on, and there was a good deal of fighting about Robersart, and about 1 p.m. it was announced that the advance would be continued next day, the task of the 18th Division being the capture of Mount Carmel some 1,200 yards in front. The advance, through a very enclosed country, was a difficult one, but at the end of the month the 55th Brigade had been withdrawn to billets in Bousies.

The war had now entered upon absolutely its last phase, and on November 3rd began the advance through Mormal Forest; the starting point of the 18th Division was a line parallel with and slightly east of the Engelfontaine—Robersart road, and when the 53rd Brigade should have carried a line running through the western edge of the forest, the 55th Brigade was to pass through this line and capture another east of the road running from north to south on the east of the forest. The first of these lines was reached at 2.30 p.m., and the second at 7 p.m.; this was held as an outpost line, while the 7th The Queen's and 7th Buffs consolidated their positions slightly in rear. The night of the 4th-5th November passed quietly, and next day at 6.30 in the morning the advance continued swiftly, much as the enemy tried to delay the progress of the troops. Sassegnies, the last village from which the 18th Division drove the Germans, was reached, when the 7th The Queen's held the main line of resistance, the Route Tourtenale, with headquarters at Le Croisil Inn. The 53rd and 54th Brigades were now withdrawn, but the 55th remained in the forefront until the evening of November 6th, when the Battalion fell back to billets in Preux.

When on the 11th the Armistice was announced, the Battalion was in billets at Pommereuil, and on the news of the cessation of hostilities the brigade bugles sounded the "Cease fire" and the "Stand fast," and the massed bands paraded and played the "Marseillaise" and the British National Anthem.

The rest of the month was passed at Elincourt and for many weeks to come the battalions were very busily engaged in salvage work.

The following letter, appreciative of the services of the 18th Division, was received by its commander from General Sir H. Rawlinson, the Fourth Army Commander:—

"*I have not had time to come and see you, and therefore write these few lines to express to you, and to all ranks of the 18th Division, my warmest thanks for the splendid work that has been done by the Division, not only during these 100 days which have won the war, but from March, 1918, onwards. The fine spirit of discipline and fighting energy which has characterised the Division throughout these operations have filled me with admiration, and I offer to all ranks my warmest thanks for their gallantry and skill in so many hard-fought battles.*

"*I especially call to mind the strenuous times before Gentelles and Cachy, the taking of Albert and Meaulte, the capture of Bernafay and Trônes Woods, the forcing* of the Tortille River, the battles around and beyond Ronssoy, and finally the attacks on Boursies, Hecq, and the Forêt de Mormal.

"It is indeed a record that every officer, non-commissioned officer and man has a right to be proud of, and I very much regret that you are not marching to the frontier with the Fourth Army.

"The very best of luck to you all, and again a thousand thanks for the brilliant part which the Division has played in these battles of the Hundred Days."

On January 16th, 1919, the King's Colour was consecrated and presented to the 7th The Queen's at a brigade parade at Villers Outreaux. Major Tortise handed the Colour to the Corps Commander, who in turn handed it to Lieutenant A. N. Scott. Acting Regimental Sergeant-Major Cook and Sergeants Cooper and McGregor formed the Colour party on this occasion.

By the 27th of the month the progress of demobilization had so depleted the Battalion that companies were reduced to a 2-platoon strength; drafts were sent to other battalions, and on April 1st the 7th The Queen's contained 21 officers and 111 other ranks only; on May 1st these figures were reduced to 14 and 64 respectively; and finally on June 13th the Battalion Cadre, comprising Second-Lieutenant A. M. Sullivan and 2 other ranks, with the Colour, was dispatched to England, leaving behind in France an equipment guard of 2 other officers, Captain M. F. Barnard and Lieutenant L. T. S. Hawkins, and 12 non-commissioned officers and men, who in turn entrained for Dunkirk on the 21st, embarked on the 25th, and sailed for England two days later.

Maps 1, 4, 5, 6, 7, and 8.

## CHAPTER XXIII.

### The 8th (Service) Battalion.

### 1914–1919.

THE BATTLE OF LOOS—THE BATTLE OF THE SOMME—THE BATTLE OF ARRAS—THE BATTLE OF THE SCARPE—THE BATTLE OF CAMBRAI—THE VICTORY BATTLES.

**Battle Honours :**

" Ypres, 1917," " Loos," " Somme, 1916," " Somme, 1918," " Delville Wood," " Ancre, 1918," " Arras, 1917," " Scarpe, 1917," " Messines, 1917," " Pilckem," "Cambrai, 1917," " Cambrai, 1918," " St. Quentin," " Rosières," " Avre," " Hindenburg Line," " Epéhy," " Sambre," " France and Flanders, 1914-1918."

THE 8th (Service) Battalion of the Regiment was embodied early in September, 1914, and went into camp in the Oxen Field just outside the village of Shoreham on the Shoreham—Steyning road, joining the 72nd Infantry Brigade, commanded by Brigadier-General B. R. Mitford, C.B., D.S.O., in the 24th Division of the Third New Army ; this latter was commanded by Lieutenant-General Sir E. T. H. Hutton, K.C.B., K.C.M.G., and the Division by Major-General Sir J. G. Ramsay, K.C.B. The 72nd Brigade contained the following battalions :—The 8th The Queen's, 8th Buffs, 9th East Surrey, and the 8th Royal West Kent Regiments.

The companies were formed in rotation as the men joined, and by the middle of November all four companies had been formed under Major W. R. B. Peyton, " A," Captain Fox, " B," Major A. R. Grylls, " C," and Captain H. M. Drake, " D " Company ; the Battalion was commanded by Lieutenant-Colonel F. H. Fairtlough, C.M.G., who had commanded the 3rd Battalion of the Regiment in the South African War. The men, who had all joined in and for many weeks wore civilian clothing, had now been issued with blue uniforms, but they were still without rifles. On December 1st the 8th The Queen's moved to Worthing, and here some rifles of Japanese pattern were issued, and it was possible to train larger numbers of men in musketry. Khaki uniforms now also began to make their appearance, and early in the New Year a miniature rifle range was opened, company training was commenced, and lectures and staff rides began in earnest.

On Good Friday, 1915, the Battalion left Worthing for Reigate, where a fortnight was spent, returning to Shoreham and occupying a hutted camp which had now been built, and a very strenuous two months then followed, during which complete uniform and equipment was received, and service rifles arrived and were issued. At the end of June orders were received for a move to Blackdown, near Farnborough, the Battalion marching via Horsham and Guildford, and being met at the last-named place by the band of the 3rd Battalion. From Blackdown the musketry training was carried on at Bisley, while the proximity to Aldershot, where a large number of troops was concentrated, allowed of many brigade and divisional field days. While here the 24th Division was inspected by Field-Marshal Lord Kitchener, and later by His Majesty the King when engaged in digging an elaborate system of defence on Chobham Common.

It was not until August 21st, when the 8th The Queen's had been the best part of a year in existence, that information arrived that the Battalion was likely to leave for France in a few days' time. On the 27th all leave was stopped, and all who were absent were recalled, and then on the 29th The Queen's were finally warned for active service. At 10.20 a.m. on the 30th, Major H. J. C. Peirs, Lieutenants J. R. Smith and W. Q. Henriques, and 106 non-commissioned officers and men proceeded by rail as an advanced party from Farnborough to Southampton, while the remainder of the Battalion entrained twenty-four hours later at Frimley station for Folkestone, which was left at ten on the night of the 31st, Boulogne being reached at midnight. On disembarkation the 8th The Queen's marched to a camp on the heights to the south-east of the town, leaving again early on the morning of September 2nd for Montreuil, where the party, which had embarked at Southampton and landed at Havre, now joined. From Montreuil the Battalion marched some twelve miles to Herly, where the Division found itself in the XI Corps, and where nearly three weeks were spent. Herly was left on the 21st, and marching by Glem, Berguettes, and Béthune, Vermelles was reached on the afternoon of the 25th and the 72nd Brigade moved out to trenches west of Le Rutoire Farm, the Officer Commanding the Battalion being now directed to prepare for an attack on the ground south of Hulluch Village, the 8th West Kent and 9th East Surrey being in the front line, and the 8th The Queen's and 8th Buffs in support of these battalions. No written orders were given, and no zero hour was mentioned, and no objective pointed out, while dusk had now fallen, and the troops knew nothing of the country, the position of the enemy, or the whereabouts of our own forces.

At 11 p.m. the Battalion came under enemy shell fire, but happily experienced no casualties therefrom, and at 2 a.m on the 26th reached the old German communication trenches which had recently been captured and from which the attack was to be made. Here at 10.30 in the morning verbal orders were received that the attack was to start at 11.5, the objective being still anything but clearly defined, but at the hour named the advance began in lines of platoons in extended order. The Battalion came at once under heavy shrapnel and machine-gun fire, the latter growing heavier as The Queen's crossed the Lens—La Bassée road, and appearing to come chiefly from Hulluch which was supposed to be in British hands. On reaching the neighbourhood of the German trenches a broad belt of uncut wire was met with, and the Brigade line lay down while all possible effort was made to cut through it, but scourged by machine-gun fire from both flanks at the closest range, the task was manifestly impossible, and the 72nd Brigade fell back to its starting point. Next morning on relief the Brigade was concentrated west of Vermelles, and in the evening marched to and bivouacked for the night at Noeux-les-Mines.

Thus tragically ended for the Battalion its first experience of war—the Battle of Loos—in which it had suffered a great loss in all ranks, 12 officers and 409 other ranks having become casualties. Lieutenant-Colonel F. H. Fairtlough, C.M.G., Captain C. A. Cooke and Second-Lieutenant C. H. Cressy were killed, Captains W. H. Stacey (adjutant) and R. G. Thompson, Lieutenants J. C. Brooks, F. C. J. Lofting and W. H. Price were wounded; Lieutenant L. G. Duke was wounded and a prisoner, and Second-Lieutenants C. P. Waldie (wounded), E. G. Johnson and P. G. Burgess were missing.

Lieutenant-Colonel Fairtlough was one of the first to fall; he had commanded the Battalion since its inception, and had won the regard of every officer and man serving under him. The traditions of The Queen's were an inspiration to him, and he was able to instil those under him with the same keenness so that the *esprit de corps* of the Battalion was very high. On his death in action the command of the 8th The Queen's devolved, temporarily, upon Major H. J. C. Peirs.

At Noeux-les-Mines a draft of 82 non-commissioned officers and men was found opportunely waiting for the Battalion, which on the 28th was sent by train to Berguettes, where what remained of the month was spent in reorganizing.

On October 2nd the Brigade left Berguettes and went to Reninghelst, which was reached on the 5th and where, on the 10th, the following message was received from the Brigadier, and read out on parade :—

" 72nd Infantry Brigade.

" Last Sunday the Brigade went into action for the first time, only a year after they came forward at their country's call. The way the Brigade advanced under very heavy machine-gun fire from flanks and rear, has evoked the approbation of the Divisional and Corps Commanders ; you were an example of steadiness and determination to carry out your task, not only to the New Armies, but to seasoned troops who could not have done better than you did. As I say, you carried out your task, but had to retire. Yet, do not think it was a failure for it was not, as you caused sixteen of the enemy's battalions of reserve to be brought up into our area and taken away from the French just south of us, thereby enabling the French to make an appreciable advance. I should like all of you who know the relatives of those who are not with us to make known to them how gallantly they fought and how nobly they served their country in whose service they fell and what prestige they brought on the names of the regiments to which they belonged. Men of the Queen's, Buffs, East Surreys, Royal West Kents, you have added glory to the ancient regiments of which you are the children ; you have made for the 72nd Brigade a name which none of you can be anything but proud of and which, I know, in the future you will never allow to diminish. I feel it a great honour to have the chance of commanding such troops on service and I shall never forget the ground about Hulluch Village."

Next day the Brigade was inspected and addressed by Lieutenant-General J. Capper, who had now taken over command of the 24th Division, and who bade the troops " not to be disheartened at their recent losses, but rather to be urged to greater fury against the enemy who had caused them."

While at Reninghelst another draft of 60 men joined, also the following subaltern officers :—Second-Lieutenants Foard, Sanders, Wyndham, O'Connell, Wilcox, Tollemache, Carpenter, Payne, Reynolds, Hopgood and Vipan.

At the end of October Lieutenant-Colonel A. M. Tringham, D.S.O., arrived from the 2nd, and took over command of the 8th Battalion, and the 71st Brigade was transferred to the 6th Division, the 17th Brigade joining the 24th Division in its place, while at the same time the two other brigades of the 24th Division each lost one of their original battalions, the 8th Buffs leaving the 72nd Brigade, which received in its place the 1st Battalion North Staffordshire Regiment.

A draft of 200 men was now received, but as they had to be left behind to complete their training when The Queen's went up to the front line, the Battalion trench strength was little over 400. Towards the end of the month of November a move was made, the Battalion marching to Nordausques, a small, straggling village about four miles from St. Omer, and on the main St. Omer—Calais road. Here, the rest of the year was spent, the companies being accommodated in barns, and here the first Christmas at the war was passed by the 8th The Queen's. The Division was now in corps reserve.

During December 2 officers and 126 other ranks joined the Battalion.

Towards the end of the year 1915 the Division appears to have been warned to be ready to march to the Yser Canal near Brielen; these orders were, however, cancelled; and on January 3rd, 1916, it was rumoured that the destination of the 24th Division was the Hooge Salient. On the 4th the advance parties moved off, and on the afternoon of the 5th, the 8th The Queen's marched to Audriques, and there entrained for the neighbourhood of Poperinghe, marching from here to a hutment camp situated on the west of the Ouderdom—Vlamertinghe road, and about half a mile from the first-named of these places, one company being sent forward to a line of dug-outs, known as "Belgian Château," where the rest of the Battalion joined it next day. While up in the line Second-Lieutenant C. P. Burnley patrolled alone towards the German wire in front of the northern end of Trench "A," at Railway Wood, and brought back a small German flag, bearing an eagle upon it, which had been seen during the day. A private of the 8th Buffs had attempted to capture this flag on the previous day, but was wounded in so doing and, not being able to get back, was rescued under heavy fire by No. 3014 Private H. Homer, of The Queen's, with the assistance of a corporal of the man's own battalion, and brought under cover—an operation which took two hours. Some little time later Second-Lieutenants Burnley and Tollemache left "A" Company's lines with the view of exploring a new trench on which the enemy was supposed to be working, but unfortunately, no sooner had Second-Lieutenant Burnley dropped into the trench, which was very deep, than he was attacked, overpowered, and taken prisoner by a large party of the enemy, the other officer escaping.

On March 28th the Brigade left for the Dranoutre area, the Battalion here being accommodated in three large farms near Wulverghem; here the Battalion, though nominally in support, was within 30 yards' range of the German trenches, but the tour was a tolerably quiet one as the enemy was not very active. But later the enemy on one or two occasions discharged a lot of gas which, coming unexpectedly, caused a considerable number of casualties in the 8th The Queen's. By the beginning of June the trench strength of the Battalion was as low as 437, but within the next few days several considerable reinforcements arrived, so that by the middle of the month the fighting strength had risen to 36 officers and 865 non-commissioned officers and men. On the night of the 16th-17th, however, casualties to the number of 5 officers and 78 other ranks were caused by a heavy and prolonged gas attack delivered against the fronts of the 72nd and 73rd Brigades, accompanied by a heavy bombardment when the Battalion was up in the trenches. The gas attack continued for nearly an hour and a half, but the casualties sustained were not wholly due to gas, but also to the bombardment which was particularly heavy in and about Wulverghem, where "B" Company of the Battalion was in support. Of the officers who suffered from the effects of the gas—Captains G. F. Clayton and R. H. Rowland, Second-Lieutenants E. F. Sanders, A. F. M. Grant and H. M. N. Chatterton—the two last-named died.

At this time very few senior officers were present with the Battalion, the companies of which were now commanded as under:—"A" Company, Second-Lieutenant D. W. Lane-Nichols; "B," Second-Lieutenant J. L. Hopgood; "C," Second-Lieutenant J. M. Clarke; "D," Lieutenant G. A. Penrose.

On the night of June 28th a party of 70 non-commissioned officers and men of the 8th The Queen's, which had undergone special training at Dranoutre under Major Peirs, made a raid on the German trenches. The party was divided into four squads, under Second-Lieutenants R. H. Hoole, J. E. Tollemache, D. W. Lane-Nichols and F. D. Reynolds. The enterprise was wholly successful; 6 Germans were captured and some 24 of the enemy were accounted for in their dug-outs, at a total cost of 1 officer—Second-Lieutenant Reynolds—and 6 other ranks wounded, all of whom were brought in.

On July 1st the Somme battle commenced, and many moves took place within the next few days as fresh divisions were sent down to the battle raging in the south to take the place of others coming out to rest and refit. On July 1st the 72nd Brigade, in Dranoutre, was relieved and moved to a hutted camp at Locre, where it was responsible for the Kemmel defences in case of attack, and where every night the Battalion was called upon to supply working parties numbering 450 out of a trench strength of 618. This went on until the 9th of the month, when The Queen's relieved an Australian regiment in the sector on the right of that previously occupied. Here the trenches extended from the River Douve on the right to the Wulverghem—Messines road on the left, three companies being in front with one in support. Two days later The Queen's were themselves relieved and moved to a support position in rear, where they remained for a week, being again transferred on the night of the 18th-19th still more to the right, the Battalion headquarters being at a—no doubt, suitably named—place called "Stinking Farm"! Two nights later a fresh move took place, the Brigade moving back to Meteren, where for a very few days training was proceeded with, and where orders were issued that the 24th Division was shortly to leave Flanders for France and the Somme.

On July 24th, then, the 8th The Queen's left Meteren and, moving by march and rail, went by Bailleul, Longueau, Foudrinoy, Ailly-sur-Somme and Mericourt to Morlancourt, where they arrived on the 31st and went for the night into billets, moving up next day to the training area, where the actual front was within a short march. Here on the 8th orders were first received to relieve the 2nd Division near Guillemont, but these were cancelled the same afternoon, when it was directed that the Division would relieve the 55th Division in the right sector of the XIII Corps. These orders were also almost at once cancelled. Eventually, on the evening of the 10th, the Battalion did go up to the front trenches in front of Talus Boisée, the total trench strength being 382, the rest of the Battalion being in reserve at the craters in the old German front line.

At 4.30 p.m. on August 21st the 8th The Queen's attacked in conjunction with the 17th Infantry Brigade, which was on the left. The right of the attack was early brought to a standstill, as the enemy was found to be in force close at hand, and a very severe bomb fight ensued in which neither side could claim any advantage. Matters went rather better on the left for a time, and The Queen's established touch with the 1st Royal Fusiliers—the right battalion of the 17th Brigade—in the neighbourhood of the junction of Green Street and Hill Street. This battalion had not met with any very serious opposition and had reached the High Holborn Line without much difficulty, but during the night the action was broken off and the whole line fell back to its starting-point.

During the previous tour of the trenches the 8th The Queen's had already had some 86 casualties, but in this last action it suffered 89 more, in addition to the loss of 7 officers; these were Captain C. H. Woollatt and Second-Lieutenants (temporary captain) D. W. Lane-Nichols, J. E. Tollemache, R. H. Hoole and A. W. Powell killed, with Major H. J. C. Peirs and Lieutenant (temporary Captain) F. D. Higham wounded.

At the end of the month the Battalion was in brigade reserve in the Longueval area, and had by then received four drafts, totalling 1 officer and 224 other ranks, so that, except as regards officers, the recent losses had been more than made good.

On September 1st The Queen's moved into Delville Wood, " C " Company being in the Forward Trench, " B " and " D " in Inner Trench, and " A " Company in support in York Trench. Here the Battalion remained in vile weather for three days, during the whole of which time the enemy continued to batter all that was once Delville Wood; only the stumps of the trees remained, the whole centre of the wood being now a mass of tangled and rotting débris, still strewn with corpses and at intervals made more impassable by wire which both sides had thrown up during the confused and terrible fighting which had preceded the final capture of the ground. At night the place was a veritable maze, illumined only by the bursting shells and the pale rays of a Very light. Formed troops could only be moved through it at all after lights, carefully shaded from the enemy, had been hung at short intervals on the stumps of trees, and even then reliefs and ration parties only dribbled slowly through to the front line. It was very soon obvious that no troops could remain entrenched inside the wood without incurring very heavy losses, and accordingly " B " and " D " Companies were moved to positions beyond and on the enemy's side of the wood. This undoubtedly saved them many casualties, as they could lie in comparative safety while the enemy shelled an empty wood.

When on the night of September 5th-6th the 8th The Queen's were relieved, they had suffered losses in this tour of the trenches amounting to 1 officer—Second-Lieutenant T. R. Castle—and 25 other ranks killed, 104 non-commissioned officers and men wounded, and 13 missing; and this proved to be the last occasion on which the Battalion was to take part in the Battle of the Somme, which endured for some two months longer, since on the 8th it entrained at Longpré for Buigny-l'Abbé, in the Abbeville area, where some few days were spent, and then, moving on again, the rest of the month and the first three weeks of October were spent in the neighbourhood of Camblain l'Abbé, in divisional reserve for the most part. There were, however, occasional symptoms of liveliness, as on the early morning of October 9th, when a party of the enemy, from thirty to forty strong, raided Ersatz Crater, held by some of " D " Company of the Battalion, on Vimy Ridge. The German occupation only lasted for a hectic ten minutes, at the end of which time the enemy was ejected by a party of Battalion bombers, under Second-Lieutenant Hamilton and Sergeant A. Johnson. The Queen's had six casualties, two of these being " missing "; but at least two of the raiders were killed, including one officer whose body was recovered and who proved to belong to the 101st Regiment.

On the 24th the Division left this area and relieved the 40th Division about Noeux-les-Mines, the Battalion marching into billets at Mazingarbe, and in this neighbourhood the rest of the year was passed, without any incidents of unusual importance taking place on the front occupied by the 8th The Queen's.

Early in the New Year—1917—the Battalion was again up in the line, and, having during the previous month repulsed two raids by the enemy, it was considered only fair to give the Germans a chance of showing what they too could do on the defensive. Their wire was blown up by a carefully placed Bangalore torpedo on January 7th, and through the gap thus created a party of 45 non-commissioned officers and men of The Queen's, commanded by Second-Lieutenants Mosse and Allinson, penetrated on the night of the 9th into the German trenches, just after dusk and without artillery support. The raid was entirely successful; three of the enemy dug-outs were bombed, two of his sentries were killed, and a third was brought back alive. The raiding party suffered no casualties.

On February 12th the 37th Division relieved* the 24th, which moved by Noeux-les-Mines to Allouagne, where the troops remained until March 1st, engaged in various forms of training, and in reorganization under a scheme recently introduced whereby each platoon was to contain separate sections of riflemen, bombers and Lewis gunners respectively. Early in March the Battalion was moved up to the Calonne defences, when in reserve or at rest being in billets in Bully Grenay. Here some little time was spent, but on May 12th the Division moved by way of Hazebrouck and Steenvoorde to the Watou area, arriving on the 13th in camp at Brandhoek, and moving up next day to the right sub-sector of the Hooge—Observatory Ridge line. The whole salient was found to have greatly changed since the 8th The Queen's had left it more than a year previously; camps and dumps were everywhere springing up, long-range guns were in position, and the artillery on both sides was very active. Great preparations for an offensive were on foot, and there was a great deal of work on the roads in bringing forward rations and material. The enemy infantry here showed an enterprising spirit, and twice in this month attempted a raid upon the trenches occupied by the Battalion.

In June there were again several moves—on the 1st via Abeele to a training area near Watou, then after a day or two to Dominion Camp near Ouderdom, and then to the Canal Reserve Camp in reserve to the X Corps. The short summer night was almost entirely taken up in the march; at this time the Battle of Messines was just commencing, and gigantic mines were exploding and the barrage was beginning, so that there was little sleep on arrival in camp for any of The Queen's. During the next week the Battalion moved gradually up to the front, and by the 13th had taken over the Railway Dug-outs south-east of Zillebeke, being here in brigade reserve. The companies at this time were commanded as follows:— "A" Company, 131 all ranks, Captain Rider; "B," 131 all ranks, Captain Fellowes; "C," 122 all ranks, Lieutenant Samson, and "D" Company, 138 all ranks, Captain Yandell.

On June 27th the Battalion proceeded by train to Coulomby, a small village to the south of the St. Omer—Boulogne road, where some three weeks were passed very pleasantly, the weather being fine and warm, in training and musketry; and then in the middle of July special training over prepared ground commenced in view of an offensive proposed to be carried out north of Klein Zillebeke. On the 18th the Battalion left Coulomby to follow the rest of the Brigade to the Renescure area, the Battalion being attached temporarily to the 17th Brigade, the attack being intended to commence on the 31st, and to be carried out by a composite brigade made up from the three brigades of the Division. The march came to an end on the 21st at Reninghelst, where a draft of 99 men joined, who were, however, left behind, as insufficiently trained, when The Queen's went into action a few days later.

On the 29th the Battalion moved up to the trenches, under command of Major Peirs, occupying the right sector of the Brigade front, the right resting on Klein Zillebeke, and the left touching the 1st North Staffordshire Regiment at a point about 350 yards north of that place, the Battalion being on the extreme right of the Division, in touch with the 11th The Queen's, of the 41st Division. On moving up Second-Lieutenant E. J. Young was wounded and 28 other casualties

* One officer of the 8th The Queen's—Second-Lieutenant Gammon—was wounded during the relief.

were caused. The companies began to go forward to the assembly position on a taped line east of the front line, and all were in place by 3.45 a.m. on the 31st, " D " Company being on the right, " A " on the left, " C " in support, and " B " in reserve. The position to be attacked, though nominally divided into two objectives, really consisted of three lines ; the first, an outpost line, centred round a concrete dug-out called Job's Post, which lay in the centre, the rest of the position consisting of fortified shell-holes. Jehovah Trench, the first objective of The Queen's, was the German main line of resistance, and was a continuous trench in which were some rather poor dug-outs. From this ran Alarm Weg, a communication trench, marking the inter-company boundary. The final objective, Jordan Trench, was a small new trench, unsupported on either flank. For 200 yards beyond this the ground was clear ; the country had been wooded, but shell fire had thinned the trees, and on July 31st it was an open and desolate bog from which all landmarks had been obliterated.

At 3.50 a.m. the British barrage came down, and was almost at once replied to by the German guns. Four minutes later the advance started ; Job's Post fell after a stiff little fight, and Jehovah Trench was reached at schedule time—fifty-two minutes later. The two leading companies halted here for a short time, and then, leaving two platoons of " C " Company to " mop up," again advanced and captured Jordan Trench, the final objective. The " moppers up " collected sixteen prisoners, all of the 71st Regiment of German Infantry. During the afternoon heavy rain came on, making the work of consolidation very difficult ; while both flanks of The Queen's were in the air, as the battalions on right and left had not reached their final objectives, consequently " C " Company had to form a defensive flank, and " B " Company's Lewis gunners were brought up into support. Just before dusk the enemy counter-attacked a neighbouring battalion, gained some ground, and appeared to be massing for a general attack, but, the British guns turning on to them, this did not materialize.

Second-Lieutenant Frost and twenty of " B " Company, bringing up rations for the front line, were drawn into the fight on the right, and succeeded in recapturing a post lost by the 20th Durham Light Infantry.

Throughout the night heavy enemy shelling continued, one of the chief targets being the dug-out in Image Crescent used as Battalion headquarters ; here the adjutant, Lieutenant Hamilton, was killed. In front matters were in a bad way, the trenches gradually filling with mud and water as the rain continued, and Alarm Weg, the trench running from Jehovah to Jordan, now used as a defensive flank, being especially bad, and many of the wounded were drowned. All day on August 1st a barrage fell between Brigade headquarters and the front, and many runners and stretcher-bearers were hit. Even when the wounded reached Battalion headquarters they were little better off, as there was another barrage between here and the Brigade headquarters, and the Battalion medical officer, Lieutenant Lodge Patch, and a company of the Royal West Kent, detailed as stretcher-bearers, did splendid work.

On the night of August 1st the 8th The Queen's were relieved and went back to camp, having in the three days' fighting lost 3 officers and 32 other ranks killed, 9 officers and 156 non-commissioned officers and men wounded, while 105 men were missing ; these casualties reduced the Battalion to a strength of 24 officers and 653 other ranks. The officers who were killed were Lieutenant and Adjutant G. S. C. Hamilton, Second-Lieutenants L. Looker and L. S. P. Green, while wounded were Captains W. Yandell and F. S. Rider, Second-Lieutenants E. J. Young, L. G. Stedman, E. J. Millard, M. B. C. Lake, E. R. Scrivener, H. A. Stedman and L. N. Jonas.

The casualties had been heavy, but the Battalion was well pleased with itself; it had done all that had been asked of it, and all ranks had displayed a devotion to duty fully maintaining the high standard of the Regiment.

When on the 15th the Battalion moved up into the line again in front of Dickebusch, it had been organized, owing to casualties, in three companies; it was now, however, for a time in brigade reserve, and was mainly employed in finding carrying parties for other battalions—usually under heavy shell fire. In this area the Division remained until September 14th, when it moved by motor bus to Merris, The Queen's being accommodated in barns in Rouge Croix, a village south-east of Caestre, where they remained, engaged chiefly in company training, until the early morning of the 20th, on which day the Division entrained and steamed away to the south to the area of the Third Army, thus leaving "the Bloody Salient" for the last time. Quitting the train at Miraumont, The Queen's marched to Beaulencourt, which was reached late that evening. Three days were spent here in training, and then on the 25th the Battalion proceeded by march route and by bus via Haut-Allaines to Hancourt, whence it moved up to the front line and became the right support battalion of the centre sector east and south-east of Hargicourt. The new sector consisted partly of trenches dug when the German retreat ceased this year, and partly of those wrested from the enemy in many smaller actions during the summer. For the most part they ran along a low ridge lying to the east of Hargicourt, of which the highest points—Quennemont Farm and Ruby Wood—were still in the hands of the enemy. The front German trenches were in advance of the Hindenburg Line, as, at a point opposite the British front, the canal, which elsewhere formed a natural protection for the enemy, here ran underground.

The Queen's right formed a re-entrant in the line, and Turnip Lane was in the nature of a defensive flank for the centre and left companies; it was, however, under direct observation from the north, and had only recently been completed.

The village of Hargicourt was to the north-west of the Battalion left, while that of Villaret was in rear of the centre, and, standing as it did on a slight rise, was under direct observation from the German positions at Quennemont Farm and Ruby Wood. Templeux-le-Guerard was west of Hargicourt, while the village of Hervilly, where Brigade Headquarters was established from October to December, was some two miles behind the line and nearly due west of Villaret. Between Hervilly and the front line ran the Fervaque Ridge, the key of the whole position, commanding Villaret and the rise to the east of it. At its southern extremity stood the village of Le Verguier, to the west of which was Vendelles. The whole area had been systematically laid waste by the enemy in his retreat.

The 8th The Queen's remained some time in what was a tolerably quiet sector; the procedure followed was six days in the line, followed by six in brigade support, six again in the line, and then six in brigade reserve, and this routine was continued until November 30th, when the Battalion, then at Vendelles, was preparing to move to Haut-Allaines, but received sudden orders from the Brigade to proceed to Hervilly. While actually on the way thither another message was received directing the Battalion to move to Templeux, where it came under the orders of the 73rd Brigade. "A" and "C" Companies were now sent forward to hold a system of posts just east of Ronssoy, while "D" and "E" Companies took up positions on the high ground north-west of Templeux. Later these two companies were ordered to reinforce those in the front, and on this being done the Battalion was on a line immediately east of Lempire and Ronssoy, and came then under the orders of the 165th Infantry Brigade. During the night the Battalion was employed in digging a new trench and in putting up wire, and was ordered to be on the alert in view of a possible enemy attack. No attack was made, however, on the divisional front, and by the middle of December the Battalion was in divisional reserve at Vrignes, where Christmas was spent and the end of the year 1917 was passed.

The 8th The Queen's were still in this area at the beginning of February when, consequent on the newly-introduced reorganization of divisions, many changes took place; the disbandment of the 3rd/4th Battalion The Queen's brought a draft of 6 officers and 114 other ranks from that battalion to the 8th, the officers being Captain H. G. Garbett, Lieutenant R. B. Sparkes, Second-Lieutenants J. Howells, G. P. Phelps, S. Hall and E. B. Hogbin; then, of the 24th Division, the 12th Royal Fusiliers and the 8th Buffs were disbanded, with the result that on February 7th the 8th The Queen's were transferred from the 72nd to the 17th Infantry Brigade. On the 28th the Battalion, then under orders to move to the Villers-Bretonneux training area, was suddenly directed to proceed via Hancourt to Montecourt, in view of an anticipated enemy offensive round Cambrai and St. Quentin; The Queen's (and Division) passed here into corps reserve. The final and a much felt change which now followed was the departure of Lieutenant-Colonel A. M. Tringham, D.S.O., who left the Battalion to take command of the Fifth Army Group of Entrenching Battalions.

"Colonel Tringham had commanded the Battalion for two and a half years, and had won the respect and devotion of all ranks, who owed him a deep debt of gratitude. He had found the 8th The Queen's very raw soldiers, had taught them their 'job,' and had commanded them at the Somme and in the Ypres actions. On his departure Major H. J. C. Peirs assumed command."

When, early on the morning of March 21st the great German offensive opened, the 8th The Queen's were holding the left sub-sector of the divisional front on a line east of Le Verguier, "A" and "C" Companies being in the front line.

The enemy bombardment which commenced at 4.30 a.m. was at first directed solely on the intermediate and back areas and contained large quantities of gas shells, and a runner from one of the front companies who arrived at Battalion headquarters at 7 a.m. was surprised to find everybody wearing gas helmets, since when he left the front all was quiet. This bombardment lasted for eight hours, and the British guns suffered much. By seven o'clock all telephonic communication was gone with the forward companies, but the usual dawn patrols had by this come in with nothing unusual to report. The first intimation the Officer Commanding "A" Company had of the coming infantry attack was at 10.30 when four men of "C" Company's advanced right post arrived at "A" Company's headquarters, closely followed by German infantry advancing from the direction of Priel Farm. "A" Company then at once came under heavy machine-gun fire from the north, and the German infantry rapidly surrounded it, getting between "A" and "C" and on to "A" Company's line of retreat; but, fighting hard, the survivors of "A" made for and reached Orchard Post, on the north-east outskirts of Le Verguier, while the remnants of "C" struggled back to the village line.

About 3 p.m. the main attack on the village began; the 66th Division on the left appeared to be falling back, and the northern flank was fiercely attacked, while at dusk the bombardment was resumed and throughout the night a series of attacks pressed both flanks in towards the centre, despite repeated counter-attacks ably organized and often personally led by Colonel Peirs. By dawn on the 22nd the enemy seemed to have worked round from the south also, the prospects of getting clear appeared hopeless and all confidential papers were now destroyed.

At 7 a.m. " B " Company in Fort Dyce was rushed, and only " D " Company in Fort Greathead and Battalion headquarters were holding out, though both had been repeatedly attacked and only determined counter-attacks had prevented capture. At about 9.30 a.m. Colonel Peirs, realizing that the enemy was now all round the villages, and that, owing to the fog, the Battalion was unable to protect its line of communication, ordered a withdrawal and, covered by a Lewis-gun section, the remnants of the Battalion fell back in an orderly manner and rejoined the Brigade in trenches half a mile south-west of Le Verguier, whence a further retirement was made through heavily-shelled Vendelles to Montecourt, where some greatly-needed rest was obtained.

At 3 a.m. on the 23rd the retreat was continued to Douvieux, about a mile south of Montecourt, and all were just digging themselves in and thinking of breakfast, when a cavalry officer arrived with orders for the retirement to be resumed to Pargny on the Somme, and passing through here the Battalion went on to Licourt, where the 8th Division was met coming up from reserve to hold the river crossings. It had been hoped that a night's rest might be snatched at Licourt, but at 11.30 p.m. instructions came to march to St. Christ, and there assist the 1st Sherwood Foresters to hold the river crossing, the bridge being only partially destroyed, and some of the enemy already across it. These had been pushed back, but the Germans had established guns on the high ground dominating the bridge and effectually prevented any attempts to complete its demolition. At dawn on the 4th the Battalion moved on towards Chaulnes, being reinforced on the march by some 100 men of The Queen's who had been stopped at the base when going on leave, and it now took up a line of defence from Omiécourt to Hyencourt-le-Grand—a naturally strong position, well provided with " pill-boxes," part of the German defence system of 1917.

Early on the 25th the cheering news came to hand that it was now the turn of the Allies to take the offensive, that French troops had come up and that our soldiers were to co-operate with them in throwing the enemy back on the Somme. No offensive movement, however, took place this day, for the time for such had not yet come ; it was the enemy who this day advanced, making repeated attacks, and after holding on to the position all day the 8th The Queen's, ammunition now running very low, began to withdraw towards Omiécourt, Colonel Peirs being here wounded and Major R. H. Rowland taking his place. Another stand was made on the high ground east of Chaulnes, and then the retreat went on to Lihons and thence to Vrély, where on the 27th and 28th the enemy made repeated attacks, losing heavily, before the retirement was continued by Caix, Beaucourt, and Villers-aux-Erables to Castel. At Beaucourt advantage was taken of a short halt to reorganize the Battalion, with a number of stragglers from other corps, into two companies each about 100 strong.

Castel was left again on the 29th, and a move made to Hailles, where next day a position was taken up in a wood to the west ; finally, near Thezy, the 72nd and 17th Brigades were ordered to defend the crossing of the river. The share of The Queen's in staying the German advance was now ended, and though not actually relieved until April 5th, when, officially, the retreat ended, the Battalion, remained in support and was not again in action. In the 10 days' fighting the 8th The Queen's had suffered casualties to the number of 20 officers and 380 other ranks.

The Battalion had during these ten days put up a splendid fight; it had borne the brunt of the first onset in which it had lost the best part of two companies; it had held on to Le Verguier in a manner which had earned the commendation of the Commander-in-Chief, and after the first day its positions were never broken into by direct assault; while during the fatigues of a long retreat it could always be relied on to turn and check the advancing enemy. After March 21st the line of the Fifth Army was never broken by direct attack—it was pierced through gaps which there were not men enough to fill.

On the evening of the 5th the 8th The Queen's were at long last relieved by troops of the 58th Division, and marching to Longueau, moved thence by omnibus to Saleaux and there entrained for the coast, where they were billeted in two villages near St. Valery; here a draft of 299 other ranks joined the Battalion under Captain G. A. R. Slimming, while a few days later 5 more officers came—Lieutenant J. B. Sturgis, Second-Lieutenants W. E. Kaye, H. J. Stallard, E. Plowman and W. Parkhill—with some 85 more men. Most of these latter were very young—boys of 19, whose training had been of the briefest.

During the next few days there was a succession of moves—to Woincourt, to Pernes, to Houdain—and early in May the Battalion found itself in Maroc, in receipt of frequent warnings that the enemy was about to attack, and taking every possible opportunity of training and blooding the young entry. Practically the whole summer of this year was passed in a comparatively quiet part of the line, and it was not until October 1st that the 8th The Queen's left the neighbourhood of Maroc to take their part in the closing battles of the war. Moving by road and by rail and via Mesnil-les-Ruitz, Barlin, Le Souich, Bouquemaison, Havrincourt, Hermies, and Demicourt, Graincourt was reached on the 6th, and next evening The Queen's proceeded by cross-country tracks to the neighbourhood of Anneux.

On the 8th Cambrai was taken and the 24th Division now relieved the 63rd, the 72nd Brigade being in front, the 73rd in support, and the 17th in reserve, The Queen's moving from their bivouacs, via Cantaing and Noyelles, across the river and the Scheldt Canal to Rumilly Trench, a mile west of the village of that name. Continually advancing, the 17th Brigade was in front on the 11th, The Queen's in support, and soon after dawn had reached the south-western edge of the village of Rieux, which the enemy at once began to shell, causing some casualties. The enemy offered a stout resistance to the attack of the leading battalions of the Brigade and the Battalion was called up in support; the Division on the left was, however, held up, and soon after, the whole Corps front came to a halt. Later a determined effort to get on was again made and in this " A " Company of the Battalion took part, a platoon under Second-Lieutenant J. C. Brooks making a very gallant effort to rush an enemy machine-gun nest; this attack though beaten off inflicted heavy casualties on the enemy, as was seen when next day the line again went forward.

The 8th The Queen's were now sent back to Rieux for the night.

The enemy had now withdrawn his main body beyond the River Selle, and on the morning of the 12th the Brigade again advanced, The Queen's being in support, and by 12.30 p.m. had gained the outskirts of the village of Villers Cauchies where a halt was made. The Battalion was now ordered to pass through the leading battalions after dark and try to force the passage of the river under an artillery barrage. This barrage opened before The Queen's advanced and the enemy retaliation was very heavy, especially on the western edge of Montrecourt where the Battalion was assembling and some casualties resulted. "B" and "C" were ordered to go forward, cross the river, and endeavour to establish posts on the further bank, and get as far as the railway embankment, "D" being in support, and "A" in reserve. But on arrival at the river it was found to be too deep to cross, though some patrols reached the other bank by a broken bridge—all that remained of it being a six-inch iron rail. These were, however, too few in number to deal with the enemy counter-attacks, and only the west side of the river was for the present held. Throughout the night the position was under heavy fire of all kinds, and "C" Company suffered several casualties.

The greater part of the Battalion was withdrawn to Rieux in the early hours of the 13th, but "C" and part of "B" were in too advanced a position to be then relieved, and did not rejoin till nearly midnight, having taken part in a good deal of spasmodic fighting at the bridge-heads.

During these last three days the Battalion had suffered considerable loss and some 120 non-commissioned officers and men were sent to hospital suffering from gas poisoning, while there were also many killed and wounded. Of the officers, Second-Lieutenants L. A. MacDermott and E. P. Dorrell were killed or died of wounds, Lieutenants T. E. Swain and P. A. Reeves, and Second-Lieutenant A. B. Heffer were wounded, while the following were sent to hospital suffering from gas poisoning:—Lieutenant-Colonel H. J. C. Peirs, D.S.O., Captains E. A. Fellowes, M.C., E. A. Moore and C. H. T. Ilott, R.A.M.C., Lieutenant H. G. Veasey and Second-Lieutenant H. P. Combe.

Major H. H. Hebden, M.C., 1st Royal Fusiliers, now took over temporary command of the Battalion, which on the 16th marched via Cagnoncelles to billets in the Faubourg St. Druon, Cambrai, which was reached on the 19th, and where some days were spent in training and reorganization.

At 4 a.m. on November 4th, the 17th Brigade, then at Bermerains, moved forward in close support of the 73rd which was following the retreating enemy; ere long the Brigade was east of Sepmeries, whence it moved on to Maresches and from there to the north of Villiers Pol. The orders for the next day were that the 17th Brigade would pass through the 73rd, the 8th The Queen's being on the right and the 1st Royal Fusiliers on the left, the Guards Division advancing on the right of the Brigade. The first objective was the high ground east of Wargnies-le-Petit, believed to be still in enemy hands. At six on the morning of the 5th patrols of "D" Company on the right and "C" on the left, passed through the 73rd Brigade which had cleared the high ground east of Wargnies, and by eight o'clock the village of Le Bois-Crette had been captured, and a few stragglers taken.

After a short pause the advance was resumed, the village of Le Plat-du-Bois was in our hands, and by 10 a.m. the station to the west of St. Vaast was captured, but further movement was checked by machine-gun fire from the houses in St. Vaast itself, and from the houses and woods to the south of the village and to the west of the River Cambron. The Battalion front now extended from the Jenlain—Bavai road on the north to the Quesnoy—Bavai road on the south.

The Brigadier now decided to get our guns to fire on the high ground to the south-east of St. Vaast, and to resume the advance under their bombardment; in the meantime, however, "D" Company had worked forward across the Cambron stream and gained the high ground, but had to fall back again on the shell fire opening, and it was now decided to defer the continuation of the attack to the following day, but, as a preliminary, The Queen's were detailed to capture the high ground on which stands the village of Le Pissotiau. The operation was not an easy one; nobody knew the ground, the night was dark and wet, the enemy shell fire was heavy, and the assembly place was across a river. The operation was, however, well carried out by Captain Wyndham's company, the enemy only retaining possession of the broken bridge to the north of the village.

That night " B " Company was in touch with the Guards on their right, but, as it was in a pronounced salient, a platoon of " C " was directed to take up a position on the River Cambron near the hamlet of Le May to protect " B's " left flank, the remainder of " C " Company being still on the western outskirts of St. Vaast. At dawn on the 6th the attack commenced, and as it did not progress as rapidly as had been hoped, " C " Company of The Queen's was ordered, first, to push forward patrols into St. Vaast as far as the cemetery on the east, and, secondly, to cross the Cambron, gain the railway embankment north-east of Le May, and also the sunken road commanding the crossings of the Le Moulin River. As it happened, however, " C " was unable to debouch from Le Pissotiau and was engaged throughout the day in street fighting in the village, taking some few prisoners.

Later " D " Company relieved " C " which had been fighting for forty-eight hours, and the men of which were greatly exhausted, and by 2 a.m. on the 7th Captain Burrell, commanding the combined " A " and " D " Companies, was able to report St. Vaast clear of the enemy; at dawn the Rifle Brigade passed through finding the high ground north of Le Pissotiau clear of the enemy.

The 72nd Brigade now took up the pursuit, and the 17th Brigade concentrated in and about Le Pissotiau, moving on the 8th to billets in Bavai, and suffering its last casualty *en route* from a shell from a long-range high velocity gun. It was at Bavai that the news of the Armistice was received.

During these operations the casualties in the 8th The Queen's amounted to 3 officers and 35 other ranks; of the officers, Second-Lieutenants W. T. Everett was killed, Second-Lieutenant C. A. Field died of wounds, and Second-Lieutenant E. E. Plowman was wounded.

During the next few days the Battalion was much moved about, but the end of November found the 8th The Queen's at Baisieux, a frontier village on the main Lille—Tournai road, and here the Battalion stayed during the remainder of its stay in France. The time was taken up by parades and educational classes, and by the slow—all too slow, as it must have seemed—processes of demobilization; but by the end of January something like 50 men a week were being sent to England, either for final discharge from the army or on furlough pending re-enlistment in the post-war army.

On February 12th a ceremonial of great significance took place when the Corps Commander, Lieutenant-General Sir A. Holland, K.C.B., D.S.O., M.V.O., presented the King's Colour to the Battalion, the Divisional Commander, Major-General A. C. Daly, C.B., being also present. The Battalion was specially commended for its turn-out by the Corps Commander. The 8th The Queen's was by this reduced by demobilization to between 350 and 400 non-commissioned officers and men, and the ground was covered with snow, but all ranks earned the praise given them for the way they played their part in this historic ceremony. This Colour eventually went home with the Cadre, and after finding a temporary home at the Depot, was finally hung in The Queen's Chapel in 1921.

Soon after this orders were received to send away two large drafts—10 officers and 200 other ranks to the 10th Battalion, and 5 officers and 100 other ranks to the 11th Battalion of the Regiment, both of which were at the time serving in the 41st Division with the Army of Occupation in Germany; these defections practically reduced the 8th The Queen's to Cadre strength. At last, in June, the long-expected orders were received to embark for home, and, proceeding by train to Antwerp, the Battalion crossed to Tilbury, handed in all stores at Presheath, and demobilized all remaining officers and men, except the Commanding Officer, the Adjutant and their two bâtmen, all of whom had been with the Battalion in the autumn of 1914, at Shoreham, and though in each case entitled to wound stripes, all were lucky enough to see the beginning and end of the war. These then went to Mansfield, and so the 8th (Service) Battalion The Queen's Regiment was finally disbanded after a glorious existence of nearly five years.

Maps 1, 4, 5, 6, 8, and 9.

## CHAPTER XXIV.

### THE 10TH (SERVICE) BATTALION.

#### 1915-1920.

THE BATTLE OF THE SOMME, 1916—BATTLE OF ARRAS—THE BATTLE OF MESSINES—THE BATTLE OF YPRES, 1917—THE OFFENSIVE IN PICARDY—THE ADVANCE IN FLANDERS—THE BATTLE OF COURTRAI.

#### BATTLE HONOURS:

" Ypres, 1917," " Ypres, 1918," " Somme, 1916," " Somme, 1918," " Flers-Courcelette," " Morval," " Le Transloy," " Arras, 1918," " Messines, 1917," " Pilckem," " Menin Road," " St. Quentin," " Bapaume, 1918," " Lys," " Kemmel," " Courtrai," " France and Flanders," " Italy, 1917-18."

THE 10th Battalion The Queen's was raised in June, 1915, and was posted to the 124th Brigade of the 41st Division, which had come into existence on the 27th of the previous month. The 124th Brigade contained the 10th Battalion The Queen's, the 26th and 32nd Battalions of the Royal Fusiliers, and the 21st Battalion of the King's Royal Rifle Corps. After very nearly twelve months of intensive training, the latter part of the time at Aldershot, orders were received for embarkation for France, when, on the morning of May 5th, 1916, the Battalion left Aldershot in three trains for Southampton, and sailed thence the same night for Le Havre; on arrival here early on the 6th, disembarkation was effected, and the Battalion then marched to the Dock Rest Camp.

The following are the names of the officers who landed in France with the 10th Battalion The Queen's:—Lieutenant-Colonel R. Oakley; Majors T. McL. Jarvis and A. K. D. Hall, Captains M. Bessell, D. C. Johnston, A. Lawrence (adjutant), J. A. Worthington, G. F. Collyer, W. Barclay, F. Sutherland and J. B. Dodge, Lieutenants L. J. Petre, H. A. Dawson, A. F. Robson, E. H. S. Barter, C. H. Hastings and T. W. Brereton, Second-Lieutenants G. A. Webb, G. N. Gibbs, L. E. Andrews, H. G. D. Ereckson, H. V. Shortman, H. Raynham, F. L. W. Dowling, W. A. Pope, R. A. Hawes, F. R. Hoggett, W. G. B. Ellis, F. J. Heath, L. Inkster, J. W. F. Burgess, R. C. Burr, L. Bain, H. S. Brown, S. J. Ranson and E. H. Bird; Hon. Lieutenant G. King was quartermaster.

At five o'clock on the morning of the 7th the Battalion left Le Havre by train for Steenbecque, and marched from here to the Outtersteen area, where it was accommodated in billets and training of all kinds set in with renewed severity. On the last day of the month the 10th The Queen's marched to Steenwerck in the Ploegsteert area, where the first casualties were experienced, Privates A. J. Browett and H. E. Youl being wounded by shrapnel while at work improving the trenches; these were added to in the course of the next few days, particularly after June 4th, on which day the Battalion commenced its first tour of duty in the Ploegsteert trenches, and by the end of the month 6 men had been killed or had died of wounds, while 3 officers—Captain J. T. Bretherton and Second-Lieutenants L. E. Andrews and F. R. Hoggett—and 41 other ranks had been wounded.

Towards the end of June 140 volunteers were required to carry out a raid upon the enemy's lines ; the numbers asked for could have been obtained several times over, but eventually those needed were picked out and sent down by motor-bus to the neighbourhood of Bailleul to be trained over specially-prepared ground. The officers with the party were Captain F. S. Sutherland, Lieutenant J. A. L. Hopkinson, Second-Lieutenants S. J. Ranson, J. W. F. Burgess and W. F. Serley. The raid, while tolerably successful, was rather costly, all the officers except one being wounded, while of the other ranks 6 were killed or died of wounds, 37 were wounded, and 7 were missing.

About the middle of August a succession of moves commenced, first to Notteboom, then via Pont Rémy to Buigny l'Abbé, where several days were spent, then by way of Longpré to the Dernancourt area, and then to Meaulte, until on September 14th the Battalion had reached Pommiers Redoubt early in the afternoon, and was then guided to trenches on the north-east of Delville Wood, where orders for an attack next day were issued. Here the 10th The Queen's was distributed as follows :— " A " and " B " Companies in the front line on right and left, " C " in left, and " D " Company in right reserve. The Battle of the Somme had now been raging since the beginning of July and the 41st Division was called up to take the place of one of those which had been badly hammered in the continuous fighting, and the 41st was now, with the 14th and New Zealand Division, in the XV Corps, commanded by General Horne. In the plan of battle for the 15th the 14th Division on the right of the XV Corps and the 41st in the centre were to make good the ground east and north of Delville Wood, while the New Zealanders had Flers as their objective. The divisions on the left of those of the XV Corps were to attack Courcelette and Martinpuich and clear High Wood, while those on the right were to move against Les Bœufs and Morval, carry Bouleaux Wood, and form a defensive flank. In these operations the whole of the Fourth Army was to take part as well as one corps of the Fifth Army.

Preparatory to the attack the 124th Infantry Brigade was formed up in an assembly position with the 10th The Queen's on the right and the 21st King's Royal Rifle Corps on the left of the front line, distributed in depth, in eight waves, in " No-Man's-Land " and Brown Trench, the two battalions Royal Fusiliers in support in four waves in and between Green Trench and Inner Trench. There were four objectives, the first being the enemy trenches 800 yards south of Flers (Switch Line) from the junction with Cocoa Lane to junction with Coffee Lane ; the second was the German trenches running south-east on the south-western and southern sides of Flers (Flers Line) ; while the third was the village of Flers, and the line Cross Roads—northern edge of Flers to road junction. The fourth objective was a line marked on the map issued to the troops.

The Brigade moved forward to the attack at 6.20 a.m. on the 15th, the leading wave in extended order, those following in shallow columns, and within half an hour the first objective—Switch Trench—was captured, when, leaving parties to consolidate and to construct a strong point, the remainder pushed on, the second objective—Flers Trench and Flers Avenue—being in their hands by 8.50. No further news of the fight appears to have reached the Brigade headquarters until just after ten o'clock, when the Officer Commanding the 10th The Queen's reported that some 200 men of all battalions had reached a certain map point, where they were in touch with scattered parties of the 14th Brigade on the right, but could see nothing of the 122nd Brigade on the left. Ten minutes later, however, it was reported that the 122nd Brigade was apparently retiring from Flers and that the 124th was being then heavily shelled and might have to conform.

The fight then died down and about noon the Officer Commanding The Queen's ordered a withdrawal to the line of the second objective, and here and in various places between it and the third objective, the bulk of the Brigade was assembled and was reorganized; and about 3.20 p.m. the Brigadier arranged for an advance on the village of Flers and the line of Cross Roads—northern edge of Flers to the road junction. Reports as to the general situation and progress of the attack were not clear, but it was learnt that the enemy was counter-attacking, and it was not until 7 p.m. that it was definitely learnt from Colonel Oakley, Queen's, who came back wounded, that the remains of his battalion and of others were holding the third objective and that he did not think there were more than 50 unwounded men left. Orders now arrived from divisional headquarters to hold and consolidate the line reached, and the third objective was held during the night, and on the morning of the 16th the 124th Brigade was relieved in the advanced positions, returning to Flers and Switch Trenches.

During the 16th and 17th, when the Brigade was subjected to constant shell fire, the positions were consolidated, and then on the morning of the 18th the 124th Brigade was relieved in the trenches and withdrawn to the rear, to a support position in Green and Brown Trenches on the right of Flers.

The Brigade in this its first general action had suffered over 1,300 casualties, those of the 10th The Queen's numbering 5 officers and 26 other ranks killed, 13 officers and 211 non-commissioned officers and men wounded, while 66 men were missing—a total of 321 casualties all ranks. The names of the officers were :—Killed, Captain M. Bessell, Second-Lieutenants H. E. Mance and R. C. Javes, while the wounded were Lieutenant-Colonel R. Oakley, Captains A. Lawrence (died later of his wounds), D. C. Johnston, F. Hayley-Bell, J. B. Dodge and A. F. Robson, Lieutenant T. W. Sweetman, R.A.M.C., Second-Lieutenants R. F. Berrangé, F. J. Heath, F. Baker (died later of his wounds), E. Savereux, R. W. Scott, F. Cox, R. A. Hawes and J. S. Cashel.

On the 19th the Battalion moved back to the Dernancourt area, where it remained during the rest of the month, then returning to the front trenches. In the course of this relief Captain W. A. Pope was mortally wounded. The Brigade was now required to make a fresh attack upon the enemy position in conjunction with the 122nd Brigade on the left, the attacking line on this occasion being formed by the two battalions of the Royal Fusiliers with the remaining battalions of the 124th Brigade in support.

Of the companies of the 10th The Queen's " A " and " D " were in Gird Trench, " B " and " C " in Factory Trench, the two first-named having instructions to move up and occupy the positions of the 21st King's Royal Rifle Corps on these going forward. Soon after the opening of the action " D " Company received orders to move up to assist the front battalions, on which " B " and " C " advanced up to Gird Support. Communication early became very difficult, all sorts of rumours came back from the front—that " D " Company had been wholly wiped out—messages took as long as five hours to get through to the Brigade, and important orders as to movements were in some cases received hours after they had been anticipated and carried out on the initiative of those on the spot.

The Officer Commanding the Battalion, Major Jarvis, was wounded about 2 p.m., and was sent down at night to the dressing station, Lieutenant and Adjutant

## THE FLANDERS OFFENSIVE

Andrews assuming command of the Battalion, until relieved on the morning of the 8th by Major Clarke, Royal Fusiliers, and then on the evening of the 10th The Queen's were withdrawn and went back via Mametz to Bécordel.

In this action the casualties in " D " Company alone amounted to 1 officer and 9 men killed, 3 officers and 71 men wounded and 7 men missing.

During the next few days the 10th Queen's experienced several moves, first to Buire, then to Airaines, thence to Thieushoek, and thence again to La Clytte area, where the remainder of this the first year of the war for the Battalion was passed.

The Queen's were still in this neighbourhood during the first two months of 1917, and in February were detailed to take part in an important raid by daylight on the enemy's trenches in the Hollandscheschuur Salient on the afternoon of the 24th, the object of the raid being to take prisoners, inflict loss on the enemy, and destroy his dug-outs, defences, and material. Some 17 officers and 525 other ranks of the Battalion with a section of Royal Engineers and a party from a Tunnelling Company were to take part. This was a very important raid, being the second undertaken by a whole battalion, an earlier one having been carried out by a battalion of the 47th Division ; this raid was under the command of Major R. V. Gwynne, with Captain L. Andrews.

The Battalion reached its assembly position early in the afternoon, and ten minutes after the advance commenced the first objective was captured, and fifteen minutes afterwards the second was also in our hands, while many prisoners had been passed back. By 6.30 p.m. the enemy retaliation was very intense, but was effectually dealt with by our guns, and reports coming in from the forward companies stated that all dug-outs about the second objective had been destroyed, their garrisons had been killed or captured, and that of four enemy machine guns found embedded in concrete emplacements, one had been sent back and three destroyed. The raiders were back again in their lines within an hour and a half of the " push off," and a number of congratulations, from the Army Commander, the Commander-in-Chief, and H.R.H. the Prince of Wales, were received on the success of the operation, which had not, however, been conducted without considerable loss. Of The Queen's Captain E. Bird and 26 other ranks were killed, while Second-Lieutenant E. M. Fairclough died of wounds, Lieutenant F. J. Monk, Second-Lieutenant E. H. Edenborough and 91 non-commissioned officers and men were wounded and 11 men were missing.

The 10th The Queen's were not now seriously employed until called out, early in June, to take part in the Flanders offensive of this year, when it was announced in orders of May 24th that the Second Army was to be prepared to assume the offensive soon after the end of the month, the front of attack, occupied by the X Corps in which the 41st Division was serving, being from the Dieppendaal Beek to Observatory Ridge ; in the corps front the 41st Division was on the right, and the 47th on the left, while in that of the Division the 124th Brigade was to be on the right, with the 123rd on its left during the first stage of the attack and the 122nd during the later stage.

The 124th Brigade was to attack on a three-battalion front with the 10th The Queen's on the right, and all assembled in their allotted positions on the night of June 6th, when the men went to sleep, only to be awakened early next morning by the explosion of the mines at St. Eloi, upon which the whole Battalion advanced to the assault, and, the capture of the front German line presenting no particular difficulty, The Queen's were soon formed up on the Red Line in Oaten Wood, and from there advanced to the Black Line, the final objective, and there established themselves. Here they remained all through the 7th, on relief on the 8th moving back to Ridge Wood, having suffered casualties to the number of 1 officer and 11 men killed, 3 officers and 56 other ranks wounded, out of 16 officers and 610 non-commissioned officers and men who went into action.

At the end of June the Battalion moved to the Meteren training area, remaining here upwards of a fortnight and being joined by drafts amounting to 158 non-commissioned officers and men, and then moving to the Westoutre area, and finally back to La Clytte. The Second Army, fresh from its triumphs at Messines, was now called upon to take part in the Third Battle of Ypres in company with the Fifth Army, but in the plan of attack now arranged the Second Army was to play a somewhat restricted rôle, for its right was to capture La Basse Ville on the Lys, and its left to attack the village of Hollebeke and clear the ground north of the bend of the Ypres—Comines Canal and east of Battle Wood. This action fought by General Plumer's men was an unqualified success. On the right the New Zealanders carried La Basse Ville, while on their left the 41st Division advanced some 800 yards down the valley of the Roosebeek, captured the village of Hollebeke and the ruins of what had once been Klein Zillebeke.

Of the part taken by the 10th The Queen's the Battalion diary tells us that the Battalion was ordered to move on the morning of August 1st from Bluff Tunnels, and to advance to the Red Line, "B" and "C" Companies to "mop up" between the Red and Blue Lines at 3.10 a.m., while at 4.30 the remaining two companies were to pass through, capture, and hold the spur of the hill known as the Green Line. Only one guide was, however, provided for the whole Battalion, no officer or man had ever been over the ground, and finally the guide lost his way, so that the leading company only arrived at the Red Line at 4.30 a.m., whereas it should have "mopped up" between the Red and the Blue Lines at 3.10. The rear of the column was heavily shelled coming up, and Captain H. C. Wilders-Lewis was first wounded and then killed, while "A" Company became somewhat disorganized, owing to the fire and to casualties, and eventually only 50 men under Second-Lieutenant Parkes reached Battle Wood.

Lieutenant-Colonel Gwynne, now commanding the Battalion, went forward to reconnoitre at 4.40 a.m., to see whether it were possible to attack without the promised creeping barrage, the advantages of which had by now been lost; he was twice hit by machine-gun bullets and was eventually brought in by the stretcher bearers. Any movement over certain portions of the front was impossible by reason of the heavy fire from machine guns located in some dug-outs, and at 7 a.m. the disposition of the Battalion was as follows :—" C " Company was in shell holes and dug-outs along the eastern side of the railway embankment, " B " and " D " along the western side of the same, and " A " in Battle Wood; these positions were maintained until nightfall.

About 1.30 p.m. Major L. E. Andrews assumed command of the 10th The Queen's in Colonel Gwynne's place, and at eleven o'clock at night the 123rd Brigade relieved the 124th, the 10th being relieved by the 11th Battalion of the Regiment.

It had been hoped to advance upon and capture the Zandvoorde Line, but this unfortunately proved to be impossible, for the attack on the Green Line, which should have been carried out by the 123rd Brigade, and was afterwards allotted to the 124th, was not a real success owing to the fact that the only guide provided lost his way, and owing also to the pressure of the three enemy machine guns. The

[Copyright: Imperial War Museum.

CAPTURED GERMAN TRENCHES ON MESSINES RIDGE, JUNE, 1917.

weather during this and subsequent days was the worst imaginable, and the ground became so bad that some of the men who fell into shell holes died from sheer exhaustion.

August 2nd was a fairly quiet day, and on the night of the 3rd The Queen's went back to the front line, taking over a frontage of some 600 yards, which was held more or less as an outpost line, the front being covered by rifle and machine-gun fire from the railway embankment which commanded the greater part of it.

Soon after arrival two Germans, who had lost themselves, surrendered to Captain Berrangé.

During the 4th the line was heavily shelled, and the enemy counter-attacked Hollebeke, penetrating here and also through the battalion on the right, but was driven out again; there was fighting all through the 5th, the enemy attacks being very persistent, and when on the night of the 6th The Queen's were relieved and went back to camp in rear, they had suffered a loss, in killed, of Acting Captain H. C. Wilders-Lewis and 27 men; wounded, Acting Lieutenant-Colonel R. V. Gwynne, D.S.O., Second-Lieutenants R. C. Wilson and A. Wills, and 130 other ranks, and missing, 5 men.

On the 7th Acting Lieutenant-Colonel F. Hayley-Bell took over command, and a few days later the Battalion was sent to the Thieushoek area, and there disposed in tents and billets. Here a great misfortune overtook the 10th The Queen's; on the evening of the 18th a hostile aeroplane dropped a bomb in the middle of the camp, which was a very crowded one owing to the need for saving the small amount of land under cultivation by the French peasantry, and three companies of the Battalion were camped in a very small space, with the result that the one bomb dropped caused no fewer than 107 casualties, including 1 officer wounded, and 45 other ranks being killed or dying of their injuries.

At the end of August the Battalion was in billets in the village of Martinslaers.

The 10th The Queen's were now again summoned to the front to take part in the long-drawn-out battle of Ypres of this year, the front of the Second Army having now been extended further to the north, and General Plumer taking over the attack upon the southern portion of the enemy front on the Menin Road. Careful preparations for this attack had for some time past been made and special steps had been taken for dealing with the "pill-boxes"; the weather by this, too, was improving and the ground was drying fast. The new eight-mile front of attack ran from the Ypres—Staden railway north of Langemarck to the Ypres—Comines Canal north of Hollebeke.

The orders issued in the 41st Division prescribed that the X Corps was to take the offensive in conjunction with the IX Corps on its right and the I Australian Corps on its left, and the X Corps front being occupied from right to left by the 39th, 41st, and 23rd Divisions, with the 21st and 33rd in corps reserve; the 124th and 122nd Brigades were to be on right and left respectively of the 41st Division, with the 123rd in reserve, each brigade in front attacking on a line of two battalions, and in the 124th Brigade the 10th The Queen's and the 21st King's Royal Rifle Corps being the attacking battalions on right and left respectively for the first phase of the attack—up to the Blue Line, the second objective.

The whole area of attack was subjected to an intense bombardment for several days prior to the advance, but when moving forward at 5.40 on the morning of September 20th, The Queen's had hardly advanced fifty yards when they were met with a heavy fire from two machine guns which caught the Battalion when it was

s

moving in close formation in the hope of getting well forward before the German barrage fell. These machine guns wrought great havoc especially among the officers; Major Andrews, commanding the Battalion, was killed, but in spite of the losses and inevitable momentary confusion, Second-Lieutenants Hare and Toombs, with Sergeant Busby, were able to get some men together and succeeded in working round the machine-gun positions, silencing and subsequently capturing them. The Queen's then pushed on and reached both objectives though exposed to heavy machine-gun fire. About 8.30 the reserve brigade, the 123rd, came through and completed the morning's work, crossing the valley of the Basse Ville Beek and storming up the slope of the Tower Hamlets, a strong position just south of the Menin Road. Both the 123rd and 124th Brigades suffered much from machine guns east of Bodmin Copse, and were held up at the Tower Hamlet Plateau. In spite of repeated counter-attacks the evening of September 20th found the left of the Division well established in its new line, and only short of its full objective about the Tower Hamlets, where for the next two days it had to fight hard to hold a line.

Next day, the 21st, there was intermittent shelling, increasing in regularity and violence between 2 and 7 p.m., at which hour the Germans attacked but were bloodily repulsed. Matters were much the same on the 22nd, when the shells and snipers made it very difficult to communicate with the different posts, and men were hard put to it for supplies of food and water. The Queen's were relieved by wings on the nights of the 22nd and 24th, and withdrawn to the rear and sent by train to Ghyvelde, where the rest of the month was occupied with reorganization and clearing up.

On September 25th General Plumer, commanding the Second Army, wrote the following letter to Major-General Lawford, commanding the 41st Division:—

"*My dear Lawford.*

"*The 41st Division are shortly to leave the Second Army for a time and before they go, I should like to express to you and to ask you to convey to the Commanders and Staffs in the Division my appreciation of the excellent service they have rendered during the period they have been in this Army.*

"*They have taken a prominent and very creditable part in all the offensive operations in which we have been engaged and their work on the defensive has been equally satisfactory. Throughout the whole period the discipline has been excellent and all ranks have maintained a fine fighting spirit.*

"*I hope at some future time the Division may again be in the Second Army and wherever they may be I wish you and all the best of luck.*

"*Yours sincerely,*
(*Signed*) "HERBERT PLUMER."

The Division remained quietly throughout October in the training area of the XIV Corps, and towards the end of the month was warned to move to the Italian theatre of war under the circumstances described in Chapter XII, whereby five British divisions were transferred from the Western Front to Italy. On October 4th the 10th The Queen's marched to Wormhoudt and a few days later to Esquelbecque, where the Brigade commenced entraining and then proceeded to Mantova which was reached on the 16th and 17th; here the troops detrained and marched to billets at Gazzoldo, receiving next day a warning order to prepare for a five-days' march in view of taking up a defensive line from Vicenza to Grisignano. Instructions were also issued that all officers in excess of 30—including the Medical Officer—were to be sent to the base, and accordingly 12 officers were returned to Pavia.

Starting on the 19th the Battalion marched by Tormina, Tarmassia, Sabbion Zovencedo, Montegalda, Arsego, and Resana, Fossalunga being reached on the 29th; this was the final stage of the march of 120 miles. The Battalion had left Gazzoldo at a strength of 962 all ranks, and completed the march with exactly 900 officers, non-commissioned officers, and men. Of the 62 men who did not arrive, 30 were passed as unfit for service and of the remaining 32 many were men who had returned to the Battalion from employment at base camps, had had no recent experience in marching, or in carrying heavy packs. The march discipline and general bearing were excellent throughout. The Drums, which had been organized only a fortnight before leaving Flanders, did much to help to bring the men along. The health of the Battalion was very good, only one man reporting sick during the whole march.

The following table shows the composition of the 10th The Queen's at this date, and, incidentally, from how many corps a battalion was drawn at this period of the war:—

| | |
|---|---|
| Original Battalion | 196 |
| Sussex Yeomanry | 88 |
| Army Ordnance Corps draft | 42 |
| Surrey Yeomanry | 129 |
| 2nd/5th Battalion The Queen's | 155 |
| 2nd/5th Battalion The Buffs | 105 |
| In small drafts from 8 different battalions The Queen's | 216 |
| Total | 931 |

On December 1st the Battalion moved forward to Volpago by a villainous road—" Roman road-making unduly praised " is the comment in the diary—and The Queen's were here reserve battalion to the Brigade, which occupied the right sub-sector of a front including Nervesa and the bank of the Piave River for a distance of 3,500 yards north of the village. During the eight days the Brigade occupied this sector there was much to be done in the organization of its defence; the front appeared to be quiet, but there was occasional enemy artillery fire directed upon it, and The Queen's had one officer—Second-Lieutenant H. C. Phillips—killed, and three men wounded by shell fire near the church of Sovilla.

The Battalion remained in these parts throughout December, experiencing some loss and inconvenience from the enemy's shell fire and from the activities of his aircraft; and then early in 1918 the 10th The Queen's found themselves as right reserve of the left brigade of the right division in the Montello Sector, and here, when in the line, they held a front of some $3\frac{1}{2}$ kilometres in length consisting of posts on the side of a cliff face on the right and centre and on the left of posts in the river bed. Here they remained some eight days, experiencing very cold weather, the tracks leading to the various posts were covered with ice and the work of the ration and fuel carrying parties became one of great difficulty, time and even danger, and had there been any wounded they could hardly have been evacuated without sleighs. By day movement was impossible owing to enemy observation, and the Piave, which rose from one to two feet nightly, proved quite unfordable by the patrols owing to the current. There was a good deal of shelling of the front by the enemy, who could be heard at night busy on the construction of strong points.

During the last three weeks of January the Battalion was in a training area about Altivole, and at this time the sick-rate was rather high ; during the month some 80 men being admitted to hospital.

In February the Battalion made several moves, marching on the 7th to Crespano some 3,000 yards from the slopes of Monte Grappa, on the 17th to Riese, and next day to Biadene, where bombs were dropped on the billets from enemy aircraft, without, however, causing any injury to the troops. On the 24th the 10th The Queen's were once again on the road and marched by Ramon and Camposampiero to Bevaboro, but when *en route* to this place it was found that, owing to the movements of French and Italian troops and the consequent congestion at Bevaboro, no accommodation was there available, and the Battalion was accordingly diverted to Limena.

While here orders were received that the 41st Division was now to return to the Western Front, and that entrainment for France would commence very early in March, the entraining stations being Pojana, Fontaniva, Carmigliana, Padova, and Camposampiero.

The Queen's left Italy in two trains on March 1st, and, travelling slowly and with occasional halts for meals, arrived on the 5th at Mondicourt, where the train was left and the Battalion marched to Sous St. Leger. Here training of all kinds was again commenced and continued until the 20th, when orders were received that the Brigade was next day to entrain at Saulty for Senlis in the Acheux area, and there go on with the training.

In consequence of the orders governing the reduction in the numbers of the battalions per brigade, which had been issued before the 41st Division left Italy, but which had now come into effect, the 32nd Battalion Royal Fusiliers had been taken out of the 124th Brigade which was now made up of the 10th The Queen's, the 26th Royal Fusiliers, and the 20th Durham Light Infantry ; while on the disbandment of the 32nd Royal Fusiliers, Lieutenant-Colonel W. Clark, D.S.O., of that battalion, had been transferred to the command of The Queen's.

The Battalion left Saulty at 5.30 a.m. on the 21st, and heard news *en route* that a big German offensive had broken out and that many places, up to this far behind the front, were now under enemy gun-fire, while it was soon notified that the destination of the Division had been changed, and that it was now directed upon Achiet-le-Grand. The events of the next few days are taken from the Battalion narrative.

The 10th The Queen's left the train about 1.30 on the morning of March 22nd at Achiet-le-Grand, and marched from there to Camp No. 13, east of Favreuil, where the men were able to get hot tea, and then at 11.30 the Battalion moved out in artillery formation to dig itself in on the north-east of Beugnâtre, where it was disposed astride the Vaux—Beugnâtre road as follows :—" B " Company with its flank on the main road, " A " astride the road," " C " slightly in advance, and " D " in rear of " B " Company ; this position was held all day under some shelling, which caused half a dozen casualties, while slight attacks were being made upon the front line. About midnight orders were received to relieve the Durham Light Infantry, this necessitating a half-right movement, and by the time the Battalion was in position they discovered there were no British troops in front of them, while the 1st/7th Cheshires were now on the right and the 20th Durham Light Infantry on the left. About 80 yards in front of the position was a belt of old wire, and about 25 yards further on was another, while there were barricades on the main road and also on the sunken track forming the left flank of " C " Company.

The night of the 22nd-23rd was quiet, but about eight o'clock next morning the enemy attacked in two waves from the direction of Vaulx, but this attack was broken by artillery and rifle fire, although a small enemy party got as far as the cemetery, where they remained for the rest of the day, providing useful targets for the British Lewis gunners and snipers. Again, at 11 a.m., after a light barrage lasting for rather less than half an hour, the Germans came on, and on reaching the edge of the wire they were again stopped by our gun-fire; but after a slight pause they advanced once more, and managed to push two machine guns through the furthest belt of wire on " D " Company's front, and another on " A " Company's front, establishing them in rear of mounds some 100 yards in front of The Queen's. " A " Company also came under a fire of rifle grenades from the sunken track. There was no more enemy activity until 6 p.m., when a half-hearted attack was launched, centring chiefly on the barricade opposite " D " Company, but a Vickers' gun dealt with this.

The night of the 23rd-24th was again tolerably quiet until about 1.30 on the morning of the 24th, when a heavy bombardment, lasting a couple of hours, came down on the front and support lines, and at the end of this a strong attack was made on The Queen's front and also on the right. The Cheshires began to fall back, and the platoon of " B " Company of The Queen's on the right of the road also withdrew, when the Germans were seen working round the flanks and rear. " B " Company now fell back some 800-900 yards to the line it had occupied on the night of the 22nd, but " A," reinforced by " D," held out some half hour longer, and formed a defensive flank with platoons of " A " and " D " swung back. The enemy then entered " B " Company's old trench and successfully bombed up it, driving " A " out of their trenches in a north-westerly direction. By the time " A " Company retired the Germans had obtained possession of commanding positions on flank and rear and many casualties were sustained.

A little later, the 10th The Queen's, supported by the 26th Royal Fusiliers, reoccupied the original front line, but the order was received to withdraw, and about 6.30 p.m. the remnants of the now very scattered Battalion dug in on a line running north-west from the western edge of Favreuil to Sapignies; then during the course of the 25th a further withdrawal was ordered, and a fresh line taken up between Bihucourt and Achiet-le-Grand.

On the night of the 25th-26th the Brigade was ordered to concentrate at Gommecourt, and by 6 a.m. on the 26th 125 men of the 10th The Queen's had there reported, and been given a hot meal. A position was taken up in trenches south of Gommecourt, The Queen's having the 11th Battalion of the Regiment on its left, and the 26th Royal Fusiliers on its right. During the course of the morning an order was issued that every available man at the transport lines was to be armed and equipped and sent up to the firing line, but the majority of these were unable to get up to the Battalion and were formed into and employed as an unattached body to meet any emergency that might arise.

The Commanding Officer had been hit on the 23rd, Major Chichester, the second-in-command, and Captains Robson and Hart, the two senior company commanders, were put out of action on the next day, and Captain Mellor now took over command of the Battalion which was then organized in three companies each 113 strong.

Apart from machine-gun fire from enemy aircraft the 26th was fairly quiet, and early on the 27th The Queen's marched back for the day to Bienvillers-au-Bois, but at midday on the 28th were recalled to Gommecourt there to take up a position to the north-east of the town. The 29th passed quietly until the afternoon, when a heavy bombardment was opened on Gommecourt and on the Essarts Road, when, consequent on orders received to relieve a battalion of the 42nd Division in front of Bucquoy, it was decided that " B " Company of The Queen's should be attached to the 20th Durham Light Infantry and " A " Company to the 26th Royal Fusiliers, occupying the inner flanks of these battalions. " A " occupied the position allotted to it while " B " was placed in support to the Durham Light Infantry.

On March 31st these two companies reverted to their own Battalion, which then took over the centre sector of the Brigade front—400 yards in all.

During the period from March 1st to 31st the losses in the 10th The Queen's had been very serious; 1 officer and 26 other ranks had been killed, 11 officers and 145 other ranks had been wounded, and 4 officers and 184 other ranks were missing; so that while at the commencement of the month the strength of the Battalion was 44 officers and 858 other ranks, by the 31st this had fallen to 28 officers and 516 other ranks.

After the ten days' fighting in the Battle of Amiens the 10th The Queen's were relieved, and on April 1st " embussed " to Halloy, where they rested for twenty-four hours, and then passing on successive days through Bonnieries and Frevent entrained to Poperinghe in the Steenvoorde area, rested here again during two days, and then marched to Brandhoek, on the 7th relieving a battalion of the 29th Division in the Passchendaele sector; here the Battalion held 1,200 yards of front in 14 different posts south of the village—" B " and " D " Companies being in the front line, " A " in support at Mosselmark, and " C " Company in reserve at Bellevue.

The Queen's remained in these positions until April 14th, but on the night of this day, owing to the German successes south-west of Ypres, it was decided to hold the line lightly and draw one battalion back into reserve, and The Queen's then took over the front hitherto occupied by the withdrawn battalion as well as that they were themselves holding, and were now responsible for 2,200 yards of front. The Battalion's strength on April 1st was only 5 officers and 374 other ranks, and though reinforcements amounting to 20 officers and 577 other ranks joined during the month, these total numbers did not amount to anything like adequacy for the front held.

By April 16th the loss of Kemmel necessitated the retirement of the line nearer Ypres, and during the very early morning of this day the Battalion fell back quietly and unnoticed by the enemy to the defences in front of Ypres; here all were employed on the Intermediate Zone defences from the Sally Port to the St. Jean road, a distance of 1,200 yards, the line running through the cemetery which later became the main line of resistance. Conditions here were tolerably quiet, except for mustard gas shelling two or three times a week, which caused most of the casualties incurred.

The Division remained about the Ypres defences until early in May, when it was moved by rail to Watten, and then marched via Volkeringhove, Ganspette, Bayenghem, Nordausques, Tournehem, and Bonningues to Audrehem, where training in open warfare was practised, and where time for recreation was also provided. At the end of May the Battalion was at Oudezeele when Lieutenant-Colonel E. B. North, D.S.O., of the Royal Fusiliers, assumed command; here the

10th The Queen's relieved the 1st Battalion 102nd Regiment of the French 7th Division as reserve battalion of the right sub-sector of the XIV French Corps front.

The greater part of June was passed about the Scherpenberg in daily expectation of enemy attacks which did not materialize. The Battalion took part in several raids in the weeks which immediately followed, but there is no record of it having been seriously engaged until the end of September, by which date it had been moved up to the Brandhoek area where the 41st Division was to take part in an attack by the Second Army, and share with the XIX Corps in the final advance in Flanders and the last great Battle of Ypres. The force engaged in Flanders was placed under the command of H.M. The King of the Belgians and comprised the Belgian Army, some French divisions, and General Plumer's Second Army, and the course of the action which followed and the results achieved are thus epitomized in Sir Douglas Haig's despatch of December 21st, 1918 :—" At 5.30 a.m. on September 28th the XIX and II Corps of the Second Army attacked without preliminary bombardment on a front of some $4\frac{1}{2}$ miles south of the Ypres—Zonnebeke road. The 14th Division, 35th Division, 29th and 9th Divisions delivered the initial assault, being supported in the later stages of the battle by the 41st and 36th Divisions. On the left of the II Corps the Belgian Army continued the line of attack as far as Dixmude. On both the British and Belgian fronts the attack was a brilliant success. The enemy, who was attempting to hold his positions with less than five divisions, was driven rapidly from the whole of the high ground east of Ypres, so fiercely contested during the battles of 1917. By the end of the day, the British divisions had passed far beyond the furthest limits of the 1917 battles, and had reached Kortewilde, Zandvoorde, Kruiseecke, and Becelaere. . . . South of the main attack, successful minor enterprises by the 31st, 30th, and 34th British Divisions carried our line forward to St. Yves and the outskirts of Messines. Wytschaete was captured and after sharp fighting our troops established themselves along the line of the ridge between Wytschaete and the canal north of Hollebeke. . . . On September 29th our troops drove the German rearguards from Ploegsteert Wood and Messines, and captured Terhand and Dadizeele. By the evening of October 1st they had cleared the left bank of the Lys from Comines south, while north of that town they were close up to Wervicq, Gheluwe, and Ledeghem."

Such is the outline of the happenings of this period and it may now be filled in from the Battalion report on the operations which endured for many days.

On the morning of September 28th the 10th The Queen's marched from Brandhoek at 6.30, arriving at the bivouac area near Swan Château at 10.30. Here a halt of an hour was made, and then the Battalion moved on by way of Woodcote House, Bedford House, and Ravine Wood to the assembly position at Hill 60. Here it formed up on a bearing of 54°, " A " and " B " Companies in front and " C " and " D " in reserve. At zero hour—3 p.m.—The Queen's on the right and the 26th Royal Fusiliers on the left, advanced and met with but little opposition until the line of Opaque Wood was reached, and by seven in the evening the line ran through Kortewilde to Zandvoorde, when with a loss of no more than 16 casualties, the Battalion had captured 63 prisoners, 16 machine guns, a battery of field guns, a howitzer—and a motor omnibus !

On the following morning the 123rd Brigade passed through with orders to reach the line of the River Lys at Comines, and " A " and " C " Companies of The Queen's were detached and formed a flank guard to the 123rd Brigade along the Ypres—Comines Canal ; the 123rd Brigade failed, however, to reach its objective, owing to a strong counter-attack by the enemy. On the 30th The Queen's and Royal Fusiliers continued the advance, passing in turn through the 123rd Brigade, and by 10 a.m. had arrived on the banks of the Lys between Comines and Wervicq; here The Queen's were consolidated in depth on the line of the objective. This day the captures by the Battalion amounted to 29 prisoners and 25 machine guns. On October 1st The Queen's were relieved and remained until the 7th in brigade reserve in the Kruiseecke area, suffering a good deal from enemy shelling and from persistently bad weather; and on the evening of the 7th the Battalion marched to Birr Cross-roads on the Ypres—Menin road, where it was to entrain for Abeele, but the trains were greatly delayed, and the Battalion eventually arrived in Douglas Camp, Steenacker, about 9 a.m. on the 8th, remaining here some four days, and marching again for Rémy Siding *en route* to take its place in the Battle of Courtrai.

The Queen's detrained at Clapham Junction and remained there in bivouac until the evening, when it marched off to the attack in reserve to the other two battalions of the 124th Brigade.

The Belgian, French, and British forces in Flanders were now attacking on the whole front between the Lys River at Comines and Dixmude. " The British sector extended for a distance of between nine and ten miles from Comines to the hamlet of St. Pieter on the Menin—Roulers road. The assault was launched by the X, XIX and II Corps of General Plumer's Second Army, employing respectively the 30th and 34th Divisions, the 41st and 35th Divisions, and the 36th, 29th, and 9th Divisions. The Allied attack was again attended by complete success. The two southern British corps advanced their line according to programme to the southern edge of the rising ground overlooking Wervicq, Menin, and Wevelghem, in spite of very considerable resistance. Meanwhile, the II Corps, after heavy fighting, penetrated to a depth of between three and four miles east, capturing Moorsele and making progress beyond it to within a short distance of Gulleghem and Steenbeek. . . . During the ensuing days our success was vigorously exploited. By the afternoon of October 16th we held the northern bank of the Lys from Frelinghien to opposite Harlebeke, and had crossed the river at a number of points."\*

On the night of October 13th the 10th The Queen's seem to have marched off, two companies with each of the attacking battalions, and on arrival at the cross-roads at the Au Rossignol Cabaret the tail of the column was heavily shelled, causing some few casualties and a certain amount of temporary disorganization. The position of assembly was reached early on the 14th at Rifle Farm, but when at zero hour our barrage fell, the enemy put down a heavy retaliatory bombardment lasting for two hours. The morning was very misty and this, together with the smoke from the barrage, caused a dense fog entailing disorganization and loss of direction, so that when later the fog lifted the units were found to be considerably intermingled. Then also an enemy field battery and several machine guns were firing on the Brigade at point blank range, checking the advance and causing a number of casualties. But the units were reorganized, the objective was captured and consolidated, and the enemy battery was put out of action by two of our guns co-operating with the 26th Royal Fusiliers.

On the 15th the 10th The Queen's were relieved and marched back for a few days' rest to the Gulleghem area.

On the morning of October 21st the Division was again called to the front to attack the line of the River Scheldt east of the Courtrai—Bossuyt Canal between

\* Despatch of December 21st, 1918.

Bossuyt and Autryve, and The Queen's moved to an assembly position in the vicinity of Vamoennacker Farm, where it was on the left of the Brigade front with the 20th Durham Light Infantry on the right and the 123rd Brigade on the left. The attack, which commenced at 7.30 a.m., was successful until the tunnel along the Courtrai—Bossuyt Canal was reached. It had been intended that on crossing the canal near Keibergmolen The Queen's should advance with their right on the canal, but the tunnel could not be passed, as it was heavily wired and defended by many enemy machine guns; all movement here was impossible, the area being swept by fire from machine guns and mortars. Next day, the 22nd, The Queen's were relieved and marched back to the eastern side of the canal, where they still found themselves under heavy machine-gun fire. During the early afternoon orders came to resume the attack in conjunction with the 122nd Brigade, but this order was later cancelled—not before some of the companies had already advanced, and these went on and joined in the attack which was very successful, the tunnel being taken and the Battalion capturing 26 prisoners and 6 machine guns. The night was spent at Drie Linden Farm.

There was no further forward movement by the Brigade until the morning of the 25th, when there was a general advance covered by a barrage, the objective being the line of the Scheldt about Avelghem; The Queen's were in support of the other two battalions of the Brigade, and followed in rear of the advance, but on arrival at the line Kattestraat—Ooteghem found that the leading battalions were checked 600 yards in front of that line while the 9th Division on the left was also held up at Ooteghem. The main enemy opposition seemed to come from the left flank, and at 4.30 p.m. The Queen's were ordered to advance with two companies on the left and right respectively of the two leading battalions of their brigade. The advance on the left—where were " B " and " C " Companies—was stopped after some 300 yards by heavy machine-gun fire from just east of Ooteghem; while on the right the advance was met by short-range gun-fire as it reached the crest line and the line was stopped some 600 yards beyond. At dusk patrols were sent out and reported Ooteghem and Driesch clear of the enemy, and the Battalion then went forward to the line of the Driesch—Ooteghem road.

Next day patrols pushed forward unopposed to Kloosterhoek, Bosch, and Kaphoek, and on the left the situation was still obscure, but on this day the 10th The Queen's were relieved in the front line and passed to the Courtrai area, where all rested and reorganized. In these operations the losses amounted to 2 officers and 26 other ranks killed, 1 officer and 142 men wounded, while 1 man was missing.

This was the last general action in which the 10th Battalion The Queen's Regiment was engaged, for though it was called up again to take part in the pursuit of the enemy, now everywhere falling back, and incurred some few more casualties, there was, so far as the Battalion was concerned, no further fighting, and it had reached Terbosch near Nederbrakel when on November 11th the news of the signing of the Armistice was promulgated. There was not, however, to be any very prolonged period of rest yet awhile, for it was now given out that the 41st was to be one of the eight British Divisions intended to compose the Army of Occupation in Germany, and the advance was accordingly continued and the beginning of December found the 10th The Queen's, now at a strength of 38 officers and 645 other ranks, at Viane. Here, there was a halt for a few days, after which the march was renewed until Wanze was reached, where Christmas Day and the New Year were passed.

On January 6th, 1919, the Battalion crossed the frontier into Germany, and proceeded to Lindlar, where the men were billeted and certain outposts taken over. Demobilization had now commenced and already 55 men had been sent to England.

On February 10th the Battalion marched from Lindlar to Ehreshoven to receive, at the hands of the Army Commander, the King's Colour which had been sent from home; and next day The Queen's moved to Engelskirchen and later in the month to Ehreshoven, where the whole of March and April were spent. The beginning of May found the 10th The Queen's back at Lindlar—now under a new Commanding Officer—Lieutenant-Colonel R. O. H. Livesay having assumed command on April 18th—and on May 1st the strength stood at 65 officers and 1,275 other ranks.

There was no change of station until July 17th, when the Battalion moved to Bensberg and later again to Siegburg; there is not anything of special interest to record during the remainder of the year; training of all kinds—military, educational, and recreational—was steadily pursued, while at times there seems to have been an expectation of the outbreak of civil disturbance and measures were taken for nipping such in the bud. Then on December 31st, 1919, there appears the following entry in the Battalion diary—" Preparations started for disbandment of the Battalion."

On January 5th, 1920, the Colour was marched under escort of " B " and " D " Companies to Siegburg railway station, and left for the United Kingdom, under charge of Lieutenant Cadman, to be deposited in Holy Trinity Church, Guildford. In February the 10th The Queen's moved to Muhlheim Barracks, Cologne, and were busily employed on salvage work; and then on the 25th the end seemed very near, when an advance party of the 2nd Battalion Loyal North Lancashire Regiment arrived to take over barracks in relief of The Queen's, while two days later a notice appears in orders that " the Battalion will move to No. 1 Concentration Camp for dispersal on the afternoon of March 6th."

On March 5th 2 officers and 199 other ranks proceeded to No. 1 Concentration Camp, Cologne, for demobilization; next day, " the Battalion, less a rear party, proceeded to No. 1 Concentration Camp for demobilization. Before moving off the Battalion paraded on the barrack square, the Commanding Officer made a farewell speech, after which the Battalion gave a Royal Salute to the Union Jack and the band of the 1st Battalion Durham Light Infantry played the last Hymn. The Army Commander then made a farewell speech, and the Battalion marched past and proceeded direct to the concentration camp for dispersal "—and Home.

Maps 1, 4, 5, 6, 8, 9, and 10.

## CHAPTER XXV

### The 11th (Service) Battalion.

#### 1915–1920.

BATTLE OF THE SOMME, 1916—THE BATTLE OF MESSINES—THE BATTLE OF YPRES, 1917—BATTLE OF THE SOMME, 1918—THE BATTLE OF YPRES, 1918—THE BATTLE OF COURTRAI.

#### Battle Honours:

"Ypres, 1917," "Ypres, 1918," "Somme, 1916," "Somme, 1918," "Flers-Courcelette," "Morval," "Le Transloy," "Arras, 1918," "Messines, 1917," "Pilckem," "Menin Road," "St. Quentin," "Bapaume, 1918," "Lys," "Kemmel," "Courtrai," "France and Flanders," "Italy, 1917-18."

The history of the war services of the 11th (Service) Battalion of The Queen's is in many respects very similar to that of the 10th, since the two came into existence at very much the same time, both were posted to the same division, and served in it to the end of the war. While, however, the 10th Battalion joined the 124th Infantry Brigade, the 11th Battalion formed part of the 123rd, with the 10th Royal West Kent, the 23rd Middlesex, and the 20th Durham Light Infantry.

The 11th Battalion was serving at Aldershot when the 41st Division was placed under orders to proceed to France, and left that station for Southampton early on May 3rd, 1916. Owing to fog, embarkation in the *Cesarea* was delayed for twenty-four hours, and consequently Havre was not reached until the morning of the 5th. Disembarking here, the Battalion entrained the same evening for Godwaersvelde, and marched from there to Strazeele, where it was billeted in five different farmhouses, and at once entered upon training in trench warfare, parties of officers and other ranks being sent up to the trenches for instruction.

The following are the names of the officers who landed in France with the 11th Battalion The Queen's: Lieutenant-Colonel H. B. Burnaby, D.S.O.; Majors H. Wardell and R. C. Graham-Clark; Captains R. C. Smith (adjutant), C. J. Hogan, F. C. Vignoles, A. A. Langley, T. Kelly and W. C. Sharpe; Lieutenants E. G. Bowden, W. L. S. Cox, J. P. H. Cookson, W. J. Hedley, W. McDonald (transport officer), A. McKenzie, R. V. Peddar, M. C. L. Porter and G. P. White, R.A.M.C.; Second-Lieutenants W. H. G. Chapman, H. N. F. Cook, J. A. Cowan, H. A. Head, G. M. Lewis, C. A. Lindup, A. L. Keep, R. Love, O. J. Partington, G. E. Penman, T. B. Smith, J. Wardroper (signalling officer), C. W. Wiley and D. C. H. O'Byrne; with Lieutenant and Quartermaster B. W. Jordon and Regimental Sergeant-Major A. C. Middleton. The total strength of the Battalion was 33 officers and 924 non-commissioned officers and men.

The Battalion remained rather over three weeks at Strazeele, and as each party proceeded to the same trenches much useful instruction of a practical kind was obtained; but on the afternoon of the 29th the 11th The Queen's marched by way of Nooteboom to Le Bizet, the rest billets of the three battalions, in the left sub-sector of the Brigade sector of the front line of trenches. This was reached at 8 p.m. on the 31st without the opposition which had been expected, as the enemy had put up placards in the vicinity announcing that they were aware of the coming relief.

On the very next day the Battalion experienced its first casualty in the war, No. 9111646 Private F. W. Bartlett being killed while on a working party, and by the end of June 16 men of the 11th The Queen's had been killed, and 2 officers—Captain C. J. Hogan and Lieutenant M. C. L. Porter—and 33 other ranks wounded.

The Battalion remained in the Le Bizet area until well into August, when it marched by Steenwerck to Fontaine Houck, and thence by train to Longpré, and from there by march route to Bussus-Bussuel, where training in the attack set in with great severity. On September 6th, however, the 11th The Queen's marched back to Longpré, and went from there by train to a bivouac near Meaulte, arriving there at night. On the very next day a great loss befell the Battalion, Lieutenant-Colonel Burnaby being killed while reconnoitring the front line with his four company commanders. He was succeeded by Major Wardell.

On the night of the 10th the Battalion moved up to the trenches, where the 1st Battalion New Zealand Rifle Brigade was on the left and the 23rd Middlesex on the right. The disposition of the Companies was as follows:—

" B " Company in Tea Lane, with its right on Flers Road.
" A " Company in rear of " B."
" C " Company in Tea Trench.
" D " Company in Orchard Trench.
Headquarters in Carlton Trench.

The trenches occupied were bombarded intermittently throughout the 11th, and considerable damage was done to the parapets, while Delville Wood also came under heavy fire; but much good work was achieved in improving and repairing trenches and also in digging assembly trenches for the troops to be employed in an attack on Flers, projected to take place on the 15th.

Orders for the attack were received on the morning of the 14th, and by these it appeared that the 123rd Brigade would form the reserve brigade of the 41st Division, and the 11th The Queen's the reserve battalion of the Brigade.

During the night of the 14th-15th, Major Otter, Norfolk Regiment, arrived to take over the command of the Battalion, which at 11.30 a.m. on the 15th moved from Montauban Alley to Check Trench, and, after a brief halt here, on to Carlton Trench, where it remained until the evening. Here at 7.30 p.m. verbal orders were issued to the Commanding Officer for the Battalion to go forward and consolidate the position round Flers, won by the 124th Brigade during the day, Major Otter being directed to make himself responsible for the defence of the town. In accordance with the above, the 11th The Queen's proceeded to Milk Alley, and were led east of Flers to a position north-east of the village, where they at once began to dig themselves in. The work was completed by 6 o'clock on the morning of the 16th, communication being established with the Durhams on the right and Australians on the left by means of patrols. It was not long before the enemy began heavily to shell Flers, the road leading from Flers to Gueudecourt, and the Flea Trench with guns of all calibres, and when the Battalion was relieved on the night of the 17th and marched back to camp at Meaulte, it had experienced, during the three days' operations, a loss of 4 men killed, 3 officers and 40 other ranks wounded.

The next few days were spent in reorganization and training, but on the 27th the Battalion was back again in the trenches, and remained for the next forty-eight

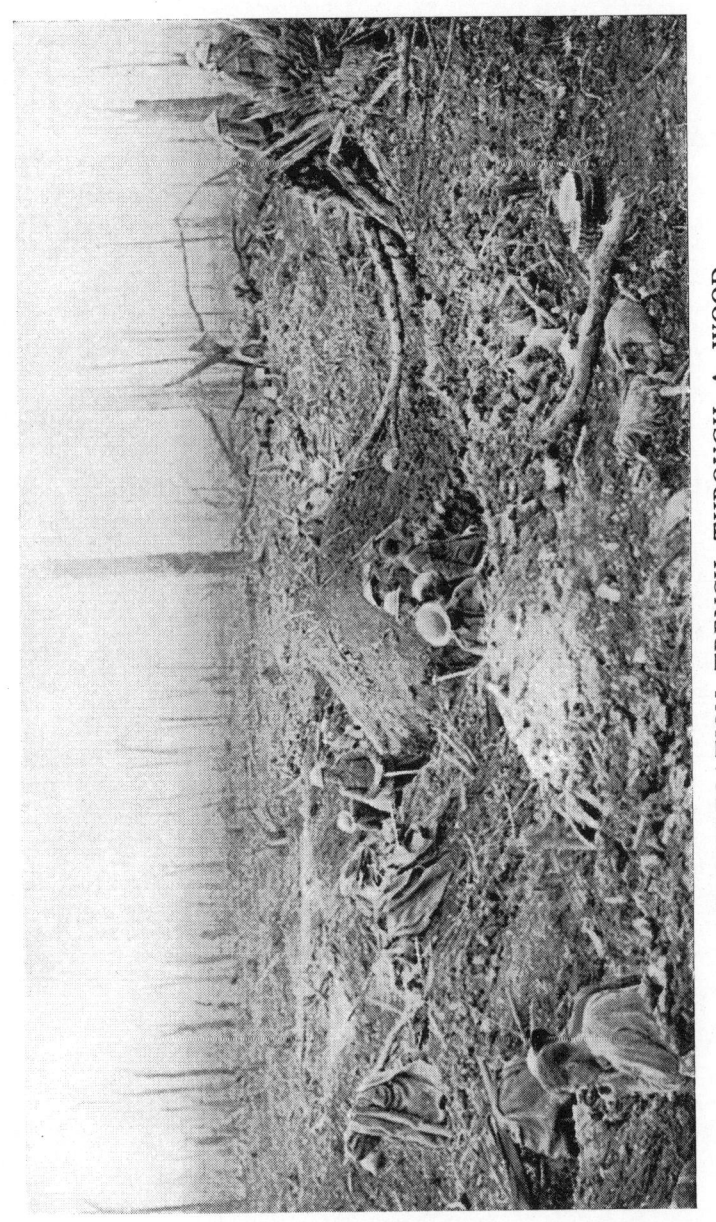

A COMMUNICATION TRENCH THROUGH A WOOD.

hours under very heavy shell fire, experiencing in this tour casualties to the number of 17 killed, 1 officer and 73 other ranks wounded, and 1 man missing.

During the first ten days of October the 11th The Queen's were alternately up in the trenches and back in bivouac near Mametz Wood, but on the morning of the 13th they were taken by train via Dernacourt to Oisemont, marched from here by Limeux to Pont Rémy, took the train again to near Godwaersvelde, and marched thence to Chippewa Camp, near Boescheppes, relieving here the 52nd Australian Infantry, and having a battalion of the 47th Division on the left and the 23rd Middlesex on the right. When out of the line here the Battalion was in huts near Reninghelst, and in these parts the whole of November and December was passed. The enemy was not specially provocative, but his artillery activity was at times considerable, and in these months the casualties amounted to 8 men killed, Second-Lieutenants H. M. Todd and F. W. Tugwell and 31 other ranks wounded. On the other hand, the reinforcements received amounted to 3 officers—Second-Lieutenants A. E. Joiner, W. T. H. F. Courthope and T. Martin—and 194 other ranks.

For some considerable time now there was no change, and it was not until the end of the first week in April, 1917, that the 11th The Queen's left Reninghelst and went for a fortnight to the training area at Houlle, returning to the vicinity of Reninghelst at the end of that time, and finding that the activity of the enemy artillery had to some extent increased during their absence.

The time was now, however, at hand when the Battalion was to take part in some larger operations, and on the night of June 5th-6th the 11th The Queen's—strength, 17 officers and 550 other ranks—marched by companies from Alberta Camp, Reninghelst, to an assembly area, where they occupied a position in Old French Trench; Lieutenant-Colonel Otter was at this time away sick, and Major Wardell was in command of the Battalion.

At 12.30 a.m. on the 7th the Battalion moved on to tapes laid out for a distance of 220 yards in rear of the front line, the right being on the Mud Patch and the left on the left of Triangular Wood; the 10th Royal West Kent Regiment was on the right, the 8th London Regiment on the left, while the 20th Durham Light Infantry was in support. The Queen's formed up on a double-company front with "A" and "B" Companies on the right and left respectively and "C" and "D" in support. Each company was in three waves and each wave in two lines, the distance between waves was 20 yards and between lines 10 yards. The objectives of the attack were two in number—the first, the Red Line just south-east of Eikhof Farm and about 100 yards in advance of it; the second, the Blue Line at Damstrasse.

At zero hour, 3.10 a.m., a large mine was exploded by the British on the right in the St. Eloi craters, and the barrage opened with great intensity on the enemy front line, and the leading wave, which had previously advanced to within 75 yards of the enemy trenches, moved forward and entered the front line without opposition, it appearing to be untenanted. The advance then continued to the German support line, where the first wave halted, as directed, for the purpose of "mopping up"; this was not, however, found to be necessary, as the trench was completely demolished and the advance was consequently resumed. The remaining waves now went straight on to the Blue Line, the second objective, which was carried with great dash, although the lines were enfiladed by machine-gun fire from the direction of the White Château and The Stables, and here about 30 Germans were captured and an equal number killed. A line was now rapidly dug in front of the Damstrasse, protected by Lewis-gun posts pushed well forward, and by 5 a.m. this line afforded good cover.

During the attack but very little resistance was met with, and such prisoners as were taken appeared to be totally demoralized, and the line must have either been very lightly held or was evacuated directly the attack commenced, as very few enemy dead were seen; the later enemy shelling was almost negligible, and it was possible to bring pack animals up to the Damstrasse even during daylight.

The Queen's and other battalions of their Brigade now halted, and the 122nd Brigade and the 24th Division attacked through them and captured the Black Line (Oblong Reserve and Obscure Trench).

The ground over which the Battalion attacked was very much cut up by shells and nearly all the trenches were obliterated, so that any landmarks were very difficult to recognize. The attack had hardly begun before Major Wardell was seriously wounded in the head, when Captain Cox assumed command of the Battalion until relieved by Captain Kelly, M.C., who came up from the reserve.

The losses incurred by the 11th The Queen's had been heavy enough, considering the strength on going into action—4 officers and 29 other ranks having been killed, 5 officers and 157 other ranks wounded. The officers who were killed were:—Captain W. J. Hedley, Lieutenant A. McKenzie, Second-Lieutenants T. B. Smith and T. Martin; while the wounded officers were Major H. Wardell, Second-Lieutenants W. T. H. F. Courthope, H. O. Love, A. E. Ryan and A. W. Price.

The Battalion remained in or near the line, enduring a considerable amount of shelling, until the evening of the 12th, when the residue moved back to billets near Voormezeele, remaining here resting and reorganizing until the 19th, when they returned to the line, and here on the evening of the 26th three more officers were killed, a 5.9 shell bursting on the dug-out occupied by Captain T. Kelly, M.C., Second-Lieutenants W. A. L. Robinson and H. N. F. Cook, and killing all three instantly.

When the Battle of Ypres of this year opened the 11th The Queen's were in occupation of Imperial Trench in the Westoutre area; this trench system consisted of groups of outposts, "A" and "B" Companies in advance, "C" in support, and "D" Company in reserve in the original British front line—Red Lane and Deansgate. Here the shelling was heavy, a 5.9 shell falling on a party of "B" Company, killing 6 and wounding 8 men. The back areas and lines of approach were also under artillery fire, and the transport suffered some loss while bringing up rations on the afternoon of July 27th, and Captain W. L. S. Cox was wounded.

In the early hours of the 28th tapes were laid out by Second-Lieutenant Darlington to mark the forming-up place for the Battalion in the attack now impending, but this work was much impeded by enemy machine-gun and rifle fire, and was not completed until the next morning, but in the meantime all the senior ranks had been over the ground to be traversed. July 30th passed quietly, and during the evening the Pioneers cut steps in the railway embankment over which The Queen's had to pass to reach the forming-up tapes later in the night. By 1.30 a.m. on the 31st the Battalion was in position, and at zero hour—3.50—moved forward with the barrage and, despite the very heavy nature of the ground, captured the first objective without any real difficulty. About 300 yards from the final objective, however, the Battalion came upon three concrete shelters strongly held by machine guns and picked riflemen; upon these the British bombardment appeared to have made little or no impression, and their capture by infantry bordered on the impossible. Nevertheless, two parties of The Queen's—one of 50 men under Second-Lieutenant Ryan, and another of much the same strength under Second-Lieutenants Ford and Martin—got to within some 50 yards of these " forts," but suffered heavily and had to withdraw during the night, joining the remainder of the Battalion at the second objective.

Captain Bowden, with " C " Company, had also been held up by these same concrete shelters, and had linked up with the Royal West Kent Regiment at the second objective. During this day's fighting the casualties in the 11th The Queen's numbered over 200, with Second-Lieutenant A. J. Smith killed, Second-Lieutenant C. L. Kitchingman wounded, and Lieutenant E. Apted missing.

The Battalion held the line all through August 1st, being relieved on the evening of that day by the 10th Battalion of the Regiment and moving back to the Ridge Wood area, having during the day experienced some 40 more casualties, including Second-Lieutenants A. E. Ryan, M.C., and A. P. D. Lodge, wounded.

On the 7th the Battalion returned for four days to the line, having another officer, Second-Lieutenant N. S. Ford, wounded, and then on the 12th was sent by bus to a camp at Meteren, where steady training was entered upon; the stay here was only a very brief one, for on the 20th the 11th The Queen's marched to Wizernes, where they were billeted, and where four days later the Division was inspected by Field-Marshal Sir Douglas Haig. At the end of some three weeks' steady training and the practice of the attack over prepared ground, the 11th The Queen's returned about the middle of September to the Reninghelst area, and marched on the 19th to Voormezeele, where, as the diary states with a somewhat grim humour, " Everything in preparation for to-morrow's attack—including motor and horse ambulances !"

At dawn on the 20th the barrage opened and the attack commenced, but, being in reserve, the 11th The Queen's did not move forward until nearly eleven o'clock, when they advanced to Hedge Street, and in the afternoon to a position in the trenches, which on the day previous had been our front line; during the course of the day reinforcements for the Battalion to the number of 213 other ranks closed up in rear, and when on the evening of the 21st The Queen's moved forward to Java Trench, some of these reinforcements were brought up to the line and employed to evacuate the many wounded. By the 23rd the Battalion was relieved in the front line, and was then sent by train, bus, and march route via Zevcoten, Caestre, and Hazebrouck to Fort des Dunes, near Oxem, and was there accommodated in tents on the beach.

During this tour in the front line the losses had been by no means light, 13 men being killed, while 2 officers and 45 other ranks had been wounded.

At Fort des Dunes the Battalion was employed on the coast defences.

The month of October was spent at various training camps, and at the end of the month The Queen's were at La Panne, where news must have been received of the proposed move of the 41st Division to Italy for the reasons and under the circumstances detailed in the last chapter; on November 4th, then, the Battalion commenced to move by easy stages to Esquelbecque, which was reached on the 13th, and on the next day it entrained in two parties at 8.55 a.m. and 1.30 p.m. respectively, and started off on its long rail journey through Southern France to Italy and the banks of the Piave. The frontier was crossed on the night of the 16th, and the Battalion finally left its trains on the afternoon of the 18th at Vigasio.

From here there was a long march of over 70 miles by way of Fagnano, Oppeano, San Gregorio, Barbarano, Vaccarino, Baglioni, and Fossalunga to Giavera, which was reached on the afternoon of November 29th, and here next day The Queen's took over the line from troops of the 1st Division of the Italian Army, the line running for 700 yards from the right of the village of Nervesa.

The line was found to be in a rather dirty, insanitary condition, and much work was required on it to provide the necessary cover from shell fire, and we read in the Battalion diary that " owing to the Italian regiment having more than twice the number of machine guns than a British battalion, it was impossible to relieve each gun with another gun. The Italian gunners, on being told that they were relieved, refused to move until a gun was placed in the position theirs occupied, and so remained with the Battalion for several days, and just lived on the rations we could spare them."

On December 6th the Commanding Officer, Lieutenant-Colonel Otter, was slightly wounded in the head by shell fire.

In this area the end of the Old Year and the beginning of the New Year, 1918, were spent, and already it must have begun to be rumoured that the Division was soon to return to the Western Front. Early in February the 11th The Queen's were at Castelcuoco, moving on the 7th to Altivole, where some days were passed. On the 25th the Battalion was on the march again, proceeding by Riese, Corregia, and San Michele delle Badesse to Padua, where it entrained for France in two trains at midday and 4 p.m. on March 1st. Travelling practically continuously, the frontier was crossed on the 4th, and on the morning and afternoon of March 6th the 11th The Queen's detrained at Doullens, marching thence to billets at Ivergny, the other units of the Brigade being quartered at Beaudircourt, Coullemont, and Humbercourt. In these parts several days were spent in training of various kinds, while in consequence of the divisional reorganization which had already affected the divisions of the British Army in France and Flanders, each of the brigades of the 41st Division was reduced by one battalion, and the 20th Durham Light Infantry was taken out of the 123rd Brigade and transferred to the 124th.

The commencement of the great German offensive of this year called the 41st Division from its training area, and on the 21st the Brigade was ordered to entrain at Mondicourt, and move to Albert, detraining there and marching to Bouzincourt, and its neighbourhood. The 11th The Queen's and 10th Royal West Kent Regiment seem to have got off first, and were taken on by train to Achiet-le-Grand, and there accommodated in camp at the south-eastern corner of Logeaste Wood ; but on the afternoon of the next day, the 22nd,* joined the remainder of the Brigade in the valley north-west of Bapaume, and The Queen's were set to dig a line 1,000 yards north of Beugny, running north-west from the Vaulx—Beugny road—" A " and " B " Companies in front, and " C " and " D " in support ; but at 7.30 a.m. on the 23rd the three first-named of these companies advanced in extended order to reinforce the Royal Welch Fusiliers, who were in a line about 200 yards in advance of the line then being dug by the Battalion. This position was heavily bombarded during the morning and early afternoon of the 23rd, and this was followed about 4.30 by an infantry attack, whereby the Battalion on the right of The Queen's was forced to withdraw, and at 5.30 p.m. " A," " B," and " C " Companies of The Queen's also fell back through Beugny, coming, as they did so, under intense artillery and machine-gun fire.

* The strength of the 11th The Queen's this day was 16 officers and 550 other ranks.

It was reported by a non-commissioned officer who got through that many men of these companies were unable to reach Beugny owing to a flanking movement by the enemy.

The remainder of the Battalion now rested and reorganized in Beugny, and with other units of the Brigade took up a position on a line south of the village, which was already partly dug; here these remained the night of the 23rd-24th.

When at 4.30 p.m. on the 23rd the enemy attacked, "D" Company retired from its support position on to the Bapaume—Beugny road, where it was reorganized and took up a position in the line then under construction across the railway; but the Battalion headquarters, which had been established on the Vaulx—Beugny road, appears, from the reports of runners, to have been cut off at the same time as was the portion of "A" and "B" when retiring on the village.

The casualties in the 11th The Queen's had been very heavy, 1 officer and 5 other ranks killed, 8 officers and 317 other ranks missing, 5 officers wounded, and 43 men wounded and missing. Second-Lieutenant T. A. Crozier, M.C., was killed, Captain C. T. Royle, Lieutenant E. Lansdowne, Second-Lieutenants J. M. Eagles, C. G. Sharp, and A. H. J. M. Titmuss were wounded, while missing were Lieutenant-Colonel R. Otter, M.C., Captains G. D. Henderson, D.S.O., M.C., A. E. Ryan, M.C., and S. J. Darke, M.C., R.A.M.C., Second-Lieutenants E. W. Spencer, R. S. Brown, A. E. Claret and L. T. M. Allen.

The position south of Beugny was heavily shelled from 9-10.30 on the morning of the 24th, and about noon, the units on the right of The Queen's beginning to fall back, these had to conform, and, in company with the Cheshires, took up a position on a line crossing the Bapaume—Cambrai railway; but about eight at night they were moved to another position in rear where they remained digging in all that night. On the 25th about 10 a.m. the enemy attacked east of Bapaume, and after much resistance broke through on the left, when the whole line was withdrawn; during this operation what was left of the Battalion—now 2 officers and 200 other ranks, with Second-Lieutenant L. C. E. Baker in command—joined up with the 23rd Middlesex, and on reaching Achiet-le-Petit was relieved by units of the 42nd Division, and, moving on to Bucquoy, there reorganized.

Retiring by Gommecourt and Bienvillers, the 11th The Queen's on the evening of the 27th took up an outpost position at Essarts, and then, on the 29th, joining the 10th Royal West Kents under Major Wallace, M.C., relieved a battalion of the 42nd Division in the front line west of Ablainzeville, remaining here throughout the 30th and 31st, and receiving certain reinforcements which brought up the strength of the Battalion, now commanded by Lieutenant F. G. Chitty, to 8 officers and 320 non-commissioned officers and men.

On April 1st, on relief by a battalion of the 42nd Division, the 11th The Queen's marched to Bienvillers, having suffered some more casualties, 3 men being killed, and Captain E. Jordan and 5 other ranks wounded.

On April 2nd the Battalion went by bus to Thièvres, on the next day by similar conveyance to Beauvoir, from there by train to Poperinghe, and thence again by omnibus to billets south of Steenvoorde, which was arrived at on the 5th, and here Captain Thompson assumed command. But after only a few hours' stay here, the 11th The Queen's moved again to Ypres, where Major Bowden, M.C., took over command of the Battalion from Captain Thompson, and from here The Queen's moved out to the battle zone, and commenced work on a line of resistance, "C" and "B" Companies being in front line, "D" in support at Bossaert Keep, and

T

"A" Company in reserve at Pickelhaube Keep; this line of resistance, when completed, ran from Jasper Keep, Uhlan Keep, Carte Keep to Hasler Camp. The work here was difficult and dangerous, having for the most part to be carried out under a very harassing fire, while the enemy infantry was also very enterprising.

There was no change during May, but early in June The Queen's moved by Proven and Watten to the St. Momelin area, and then on the 10th to billets at Tatinghem, and finally on the 30th the Battalion went up to the line in relief of the support battalion of the 104th Regiment of French Infantry in the centre sector of the Scherpenberg—La Clytte line. During the afternoon of July 2nd "D" Company's dug-outs were heavily shelled, many of them being destroyed, and Second-Lieutenant T. Darlington is reported as having done splendid work in digging out the occupants of these shelters under heavy gun fire. The patrol work here was very constant, and Second-Lieutenants Jackson and Moon showed great gallantry and initiative.

The 11th The Queen's were ordered to carry out a raid upon the enemy trenches on the night of June 18th-19th, and for this purpose Captain Furness and Second-Lieutenant Moon laid out preparatory tapes, in spite of considerable machine-gun fire, covered by a party composed of Second-Lieutenant Jackson and 6 other ranks.

The night was unfortunately unusually light up to midnight, which enabled the enemy to observe the assembly and open upon the party with machine guns. The right platoon, commanded and gallantly led by Lieutenant Trotter, left the tape line at zero, and went forward with great dash up to the forward shell hole posts, where the enemy held up the attackers with a machine gun, firing at very close range. Lieutenant Trotter at once grasped the situation, ordered a burst of rifle fire from his party and then charged, when out of the seven or eight of the enemy manning the lip of the shell-hole, one was shot through the head, three were bayoneted and killed, and three were taken prisoners. The enemy seemed prepared to fight, and when the charge was made most of them left the parapet to meet it. Two attacked Lieutenant Trotter with the bayonet, but Corporal Finlayson got in first and killed both Germans with the bayonet, whereupon the remainder dived into their dug-outs, constructed in a trench connecting up two shell holes, covered over with corrugated iron and camouflaged. One of the enemy—to use the simple yet expressive language of the diary—"had to be picked out of his shelter with the bayonet"—before his companions could be induced to surrender, and when asked why they had not done so earlier, they replied "English no take prisoners!"

By this time Lieutenant Trotter had lost several men, and was himself severely wounded, but he moved on to the next enemy position, fainting, however, from loss of blood before reaching it; then, recovering, he pushed on through the German wire, and he and his men did a considerable amount of execution in this trench.

Corporal Lakins, with his Lewis gun, had followed Lieutenant Trotter's platoon, and assisted greatly with its fire in keeping the enemy's heads down, while he had earlier engaged and silenced an enemy machine gun firing from the right. Corporal Finlayson brought in three prisoners and a machine gun which had been most gallantly captured by Lance-Corporal Nicholls; while Private Bullen, stretcher-bearer, carried in Lieutenant Trotter after he finally became unconscious, and throughout the raid did good and gallant work.

The left platoon was equally well led by Lieutenant Moon, who started from the tape as the first shells of the barrage came down. He met with but little opposition until arrival at the German second line, except for an enemy machine gun which opened from the direction of Kim Camp, but this was effectually silenced by Corporal Sandells, who worked his Lewis gun quite admirably. About the line of the shell-holes three Germans were now seen running back towards their line; Lieutenant Moon dashed forward, bayoneted two, and sent the third back, wounded, as a prisoner. On the left the enemy was seen to be bolting through a gap in his wire, when Corporal Sandells, though wounded in the leg, got his gun on to this group and accounted for several of them.

The wire was being cut all along the line, and the men of the 11th The Queen's were gradually getting through, but the whole of this platoon suffered much from the British barrage, Lieutenant Moon being himself hit three times, so that further progress became impossible and the platoon withdrew, the wounded corporal bringing his gun back with him. Sergeant Walsh was in charge of the "moppers-up," and filled a gap at the last moment, by his capable leadership rendering invaluable assistance to his officer, and, though badly wounded, would not give in. Private Webb carried Lieutenant Moon on his back from the enemy wire to the British front line, and did fine work throughout.

Captain Furness, who was in charge of the operations, estimated that the enemy casualties numbered at least 30; he himself was wounded about 1.30 a.m. Lieutenant Jackson rendered great assistance to Captain Furness; whilst the tapes were being put out on the previous evening he patrolled to the front and worked until daylight, thereafter remaining all day in the line guarding the assembly position, and was out again with his party in the evening. It was largely due to his efforts that the wounded were got back safely, and he himself passed three times through the enemy barrage. All the stretcher-bearers worked hard and well under Corporal Hazell.

The casualties sustained by the 11th The Queen's in this raid amounted to 4 men killed, 2 men missing, believed killed, and 3 officers and 38 other ranks wounded; the officers wounded were Captain F. L. Furness, Lieutenant D. Moon, and Second-Lieutenant B. Trotter.

The 11th The Queen's came out of the line on the 3rd, and on this day a misfortune befell the Battalion, Major E. G. Bowden, M.C., being killed about midday while riding through Steenvoorde.

During this month two companies of the 3rd Battalion 106th Regiment, United States Infantry, were attached to the 11th The Queen's for instruction; later on, in the early part of August, more American troops arrived for attachment, when the Battalion was organized on a two-battalion basis, half of each being British and half Americans, and the units being known as "A" and "B" Composite Battalions. "A" Battalion was composed of "A" and "B" Companies of The Queen's and "G" and "H" Companies of Americans, and "B" Battalion of "C" and "D" Companies of The Queen's and "E" and "F" Companies of the United States Infantry. The Composite Battalions were now in the La Clytte area. This arrangement did not remain very long in being, for at the end of the month the 123rd Brigade was relieved by the 101st—the 11th Battalion The Queen's being relieved by the 2nd/4th Battalion of the Regiment—and marched to the Loye area for entrainment to Tatinghem, in the St. Martin au Laert area, to join in "the advance in Flanders" and the Battle of Ypres with the XIX Corps of the Second Army.

On September 2nd the 123rd Brigade moved via St. Omer to Abeele, the two other brigades of the 41st Division going up into the front line and relieving the 27th American Division. The Battalion did not move again until the 6th, when it advanced in the afternoon to the right sub-sector of the support area, and was there disposed in the Vierstraat line of resistance, remaining at work on the position during the rest of the day. In this neighbourhood The Queen's remained until the early morning of September 28th, when the Battalion moved forward to Pulse Farm, and thence later to the ravine 2,000 yards east of Voormezeele, and so on to Klein Zillebeke, where it remained for the night; and it was not until 2 p.m. this day that orders came to hand announcing that the 123rd Brigade would attack at 7.30 a.m. on the 29th, with the Middlesex Regiment on the right, the Royal West Kent on the left, and the 11th The Queen's in support, and make good the Wervicq—Comines railway.

The Battalion advanced at 5.30, and on reaching the line gained consolidated a position in support. Considerable machine-gun and shell fire was encountered, but otherwise the opposition was not especially formidable. Late in the afternoon, however, the leading battalions had to fall back owing to the casualties sustained and to the fact that their flanks were exposed, when the old support line became the front line. This was reorganized and held during the night, and in the afternoon of the 30th the 123rd Brigade was relieved by the 124th passing through to continue the advance, the Battalion remaining in its position.

During these operations Captain J. A. L. Hopkinson and 16 other ranks of the 11th The Queen's were wounded.

On October 1st the Battalion marched early in the morning with orders to reach the Ypres—Menin road via Tenbrielen and America, but on arrival at Tenbrielen the 123rd Brigade halted, as the advanced guard of the 122nd Brigade, which was leading, was checked by fire at America. At 4.25 p.m. The Queen's and 23rd Middlesex were ordered to attack on left and right respectively and make good the Wervicq—Menin railway line. The Battalion advanced with " C " and " D " Companies in front and " A " and " B " in support, but after going forward some 1,500 yards it came under very heavy machine-gun fire from some tall crops, and owing to casualties and the gathering darkness it was impossible to get further forward, and The Queen's consequently halted and dug in on the line reached. This line was held all through the 2nd and 3rd, and at midnight the Brigade was relieved by units of the 34th Division, and went back to the support area.

The casualties both during the march to the assembly position and during the actual operations had been heavy, particularly in officers—Captain L. C. E. Baker, Lieutenant J. V. Cooke, M.C., and Second-Lieutenant F. G. Strawson were killed, while Major V. Holden, D.S.O., M.C., Lieutenant R. F. Edwards, Second-Lieutenants J. W. M. Denton and P. E. May were wounded. Captain Sir W. A. Blount, Bart., of the Royal Fusiliers, assumed command of the Battalion on the 4th, but was relieved on the next day when Lieutenant-Colonel Owen, M.C., returned from leave, and on the same date Second-Lieutenants Williams, Tasker and Price and 30 other ranks arrived as reinforcements.

When on the 14th the Second Army renewed the attack, the Battalion moved forward from the support area and advanced to Poulton Farm, remaining here until the 16th, when it relieved a battalion of the 36th Division in the left sub-sector about Courtrai. The enemy fire was now tolerably harassing, and there were attacks made on left and right, while the canal bank was carefully reconnoitred, and on the 18th a scout party, under Lieutenant Maudling, crossed the Lys north of Courtrai and patrolled the enemy bank, meeting no opposition.

Having been ordered to try to cross the Lys north of Courtrai, the 11th The Queen's went forward at 11 o'clock on the morning of the 19th, and at the first attempt to cross the river met with active machine-gun fire; this was soon, however, overcome, and "B" Company effected a crossing, followed by "A" and then by "C," "B" Company pushing boldly forward and making good the line of the railway and taking 7 prisoners; this company was reinforced by "C," while "A" proceeded as far as Bossunt, dropping flanking posts *en route*. An advance post was sent forward some 200 yards during the night, and rations and ammunition were passed over the river. This day 2 men were killed or died of wounds, and Lieutenant Abbot and 8 other ranks were wounded. On the 20th the Battalion was relieved and went back to brigade reserve.

The 11th The Queen's were up again in the forefront of the advance on the 25th, captured the village of Hustrêt after stiff fighting, and, continuing the advance, next day possessed themselves of Avilghem, and were then withdrawn by Knokke to Courtrai, where they remained until November 4th. On this day the Brigade was ordered to relieve the 124th Brigade in the front line, and late in the afternoon The Queen's found themselves occupying the Berchen Sector on the River Scheldt, with the Battalion headquarters about Kreyelstraat. Here there was occasional enemy shelling of the road junctions, while the British patrols were very active, and one sent out by the Battalion succeeded in locating three hostile machine guns. At 4 a.m. on the 6th a violent counter-preparation was put down by the enemy, causing several fires in the Battalion area; while a daylight patrol under Captain Powell ascertained that the enemy was still holding the east bank. His guns also were active, and the villages of Kerkhove and Tenhove received considerable attention.

The enemy shelling continued all the early part of the day, but in the afternoon Captain Hedley and a few men attempted to cross the Scheldt in a small boat, although the river was in flood owing to heavy rain. The boat had, however, been much damaged by shell fire and sank in mid-stream under its crew, when these swam over and gained the further bank; these men were later brought back with much difficulty. At the same time some of "C" Company attempted to cross by a ford near Grijkoort, but this attempt was foiled by heavy enemy machine-gun fire.

On the 8th many patrols were out and examined the river bank under enemy shelling, and it was decided to make another attempt to cross at dusk, so a strong patrol under Captain Hedley was directed to try to pass over near Meersche, reconnoitre that village, and, if unopposed, to occupy it and send forward reconnoitring patrols; if the enemy was met, to secure identifications and then fall back. A collapsible canvas boat was procured, and at 9 p.m., the situation being then fairly quiet except for some spasmodic machine-gun fire, the boat was launched and the crossing commenced, the occupants trying to paddle across by the aid of shovels—a task of much difficulty, as a very strong current was running. The passage was effected and a rope rigged so that the boat could be pulled backwards and forwards, and the patrol was put across in five journeys, the boat only accommodating eight men at a time. The whole patrol now pushed on to the village of Meersche, and by 11 p.m. on the 8th word was received from Captain Hedley that he had cleared the village of the enemy, when orders were issued for the whole of the 11th The Queen's to pass the river, and all had crossed over in the one boat by small parties by 3 o'clock in the morning of the 9th and were established in Meersche. Pushing on, patrols were well south of the railway by 3.50 and were advancing to the high ground near Nokerke ; these were in touch with the French troops on the left, but not with any of ours on the other flank.

By midday the Battalion was held up—now holding a line some 3,000 yards in length—by hostile machine-gun fire, and was then relieved on the outpost line by the other two battalions of the Brigade and recalled to Meersche.

The 11th Battalion The Queen's had fought its last fight in the World War and was occupying billets in various farms on the high ground south-east of Schoorisse, when at 9.45 a.m. on the 11th a message was received that the Armistice was signed, and that hostilities would cease at 11 o'clock.

The Queen's advanced on the 13th to an outpost line near Grammont, receiving next day a warning that in a very few days' time the 41st Division would be moving forward to the German frontier, but for the present it did not go further than Stroquy, where the last few days of the month and the first ten days of December were spent. It was not until December 13th that the march was resumed by Marcq, Waterloo—where the battlefield of 1815 was crossed—Loupoigne, Sombreffe and Lueze to Braines, the weather being wet and cold and the roads in a bad state. At Braines there was a longish halt, and here Christmas Day was spent ; and it was not until January 8th, 1919, that the 41st Division moved on to take the place of the 1st Canadian Division in the Cologne area. On this day the 11th The Queen's entrained, and, proceeding by Liège and Aix-la-Chapelle, arrived at Troisdorf on the morning of the 9th, and marched from there to the Seelscheid area, taking over part of the outposts as follows : " B," left front company, with headquarters at Oberhoven ; " C," right front company, with headquarters at Oberwennenscheid ; " A," right support company at Polhausen ; and " D," left support company and Battalion headquarters at Seelscheid. The ground in the area occupied by The Queen's was broken and hilly, intersected by water-courses, which at this season were flooded. The high ground was mostly occupied by villages and woods, connected by tracks and unpaved roads.

Before the month was out the Battalion had moved twice : on January 24th by Lohmar to Lind, where for a few days it supplied guards on the Rhine, and then on the 31st to Kalk-Cologne, where it was billeted in two schools, and at once commenced slowly the process of demobilization.

The King's Colour had now arrived from England, and this was presented to the 11th Battalion The Queen's on the Exerzier Platz on February 11th by the Army Commander, General Sir H. Plumer, G.C.B., who in a speech recounted the history of the Regiment. The Colour Party was composed of Second-Lieutenant G. N. Bradnock, Company Sergeant-Majors Garratt and Austin.

During March 5 officers—Captain H. D. Gardiner, Lieutenants W. J. Barre and E. F. Reeves, M.C., Second-Lieutenants P. C. Crowe and W. H. Williams—and 79 other ranks joined from the 6th Battalion ; and then on April 1st the strength of the 11th The Queen's was very substantially increased by the arrival of the 52nd Battalion of the Regiment, which joined as a reinforcement, and was composed of 39 officers and 903 other ranks, commanded by Lieutenant-Colonel J. W. Jeffreys, D.S.O., of the Durham Light Infantry, who now took command of the reinforced Battalion, but was relieved two days later by Lieutenant-Colonel R. T. Lee, C.M.G., D.S.O., at Lindlar, where the whole of this month was spent.

From this time on the diary contains continual announcements of arrivals from other battalions and of parties being sent away on demobilization or to join other units, so that the strength of the 11th The Queen's seems to have fluctuated from day to day. In the middle of June Lieutenant-Colonel Lee went home and Lieutenant-Colonel F. C. Longbourne, C.M.G., D.S.O., arrived and took his place ; but indeed there was from this time onward no real continuity of tenure of the appointment of commanding officer, for there were at least two more changes before the end of the year, Lieutenant-Colonel V. M. Fortune, D.S.O., of the Black Watch, assuming command on November 8th, and Lieutenant-Colonel E. FitzG. Dillon, C.M.G., D.S.O., Royal Munster Fusiliers, on the 17th of the same month.

The Battalion—or the gradually dwindling remains of it—stayed on in Cologne until the early months of 1920, being finally disbanded in March of that year. The last duty performed was the finding of a Guard of Honour at the Cologne railway station on the departure of Field-Marshal Sir William Robertson, the Guard being commanded by Lieutenant-Colonel E. FitzG. Dillon, C.M.G., D.S.O., with Lieutenant T. Newman, M.C., D.C.M., the adjutant, as subaltern.

On the final day of disbandment the Colour was trooped, and the 11th Battalion The Queen's then marched to the Demobilization Camp, where the career of the Battalion closed. The King's Colour was handed over to and is preserved by the Mayor of Lambeth.

# CHAPTER XXVI.

The Labour Battalions—The Young Soldiers' Battalions—Units which did not Serve Overseas.

### THE LABOUR BATTALIONS.

The rearward and construction needs of the Army in France and Flanders grew as the size of that Army increased, and necessitated the creation of special labour units for work behind the front ; the personnel of these was drawn from men who for one reason or another were unsuited for service in the firing line, or from individuals of special technical training or capabilities who were taken from corps already in existence. The Queen's supplied five such Labour Battalions which came into being between July and November, 1916, and the dates and places of raising of each were as under :—

The 13th Labour Battalion was formed at Balmer on July 6th, 1916, under Colonel L. J. Andrews, of the Indian Army.

The 14th Labour Battalion was formed at Crawley on August 16th, 1916, under Lieutenant-Colonel E. C. B. Cotgrave, late of the Indian Army.

The 15th Labour Battalion was formed at Crawley on September 12th, 1916, under Lieutenant-Colonel E. G. R. Wilkins.

The 17th Labour Battalion was formed at Crawley on November 8th, 1916, under Captain R. E. Wilson, and the 18th on the same date and at the same place, under Major L. R. Protheroe, 6th Battalion The Gloucestershire Regiment.

All these Battalions were finally handed over to the Labour Corps on June 1st, 1917.

### THE YOUNG SOLDIERS' BATTALIONS.

Of such battalions, many of which later supplied the nucleus of the British Army of Occupation in Germany, three — the 51st, 52nd, and 53rd — were known as Battalions of The Queen's (Royal West Surrey Regiment).

### *The 51st Battalion.*

Was originally raised in November, 1914, as the 8th (Service) Battalion of the Northamptonshire Regiment ; in April of the following year it became a reserve battalion of that regiment ; in August, 1916, it was renumbered and renamed as the 28th (Training Reserve) Battalion ; in July, 1917, it was known as the 245th Infantry Battalion Training Reserve ; in November of that year it became the 51st (Graduated) Battalion The Queen's (Royal West Surrey Regiment), and on February 8th, 1919, the 51st (Service) Battalion The Queen's (Royal West Surrey Regiment). On April 1st, 1919, it was absorbed by the 10th Battalion The Queen's, and ceased to exist as a separate unit.

### *The 52nd Battalion.*

This first came into being as the 9th (Service) Battalion The Buffs (East Kent Regiment) in October, 1914, at Dover. In April of the following year it became a reserve battalion of that regiment; was changed in August, 1916, to be the 29th (Training Reserve) Battalion; in July, 1917, it was known as the 255th Infantry Battalion Training Reserve; in November of the same year it became the 52nd (Graduated) Battalion The Queen's (Royal West Surrey Regiment), and on February 8th, 1919, the 52nd (Service) Battalion The Queen's (Royal West Surrey Regiment). On April 17th of that year it was absorbed by the 11th Battalion The Queen's, and then ceased to exist as a separate unit.

### The 53rd Battalion.

Originally raised at Chichester in October, 1914, as the 10th (Service) Battalion of the Royal Sussex Regiment, it became a reserve battalion of that regiment in the following April. In August, 1916, it was renamed and renumbered as the 23rd (Training Reserve) Battalion, and became in November, 1917, the 53rd (Young Soldiers') Battalion The Queen's (Royal West Surrey Regiment), and on February 8th, 1919, the 53rd (Service) Battalion The Queen's, finally, in April of the same year, being absorbed by the 2/4th Battalion of that Regiment, and so ceasing to exist as a separate unit.

#### UNITS WHICH DID NOT SERVE OVERSEAS.

### 3rd (Special Reserve) Battalion.

On August 8th, 1914, the 3rd Battalion mobilized at the Depot and within a week proceeded to its war station in the vicinity of Chatham—Thames and Medway Defences.

The Battalion was detailed for various duties—guarding magazines and vulnerable points in the area Chattenden—Belvedere—Lodge Hill—Strood—Chatham Dockyard, the headquarters of the Battalion being at Chattenden.

From Chattenden the Battalion fitted out and drafted over 1,000 reservists to the 1st and 2nd Battalions. In November, 1914, the Battalion moved to Rochester, where it was split up—Headquarters and "A" Company at Fort Clarence, and a company in each of the forts—Horsted, Berstal, Bridgewood. Companies were composed of Regular and Special reservists at this time, with a sprinkling of Expeditionary Force non-commissioned officers and men (wounded and unfits).

Men enlisting straight from civilian life were sent to the Lines, Chatham, to undergo training. Thus, the Battalion was divided into five groups. When considered sufficiently trained, the recruits from Chatham Lines were transferred to the Service companies in the forts where their training was rounded off, and the men made ready for drafting overseas.

In May, 1915, the Battalion moved to camp in the vicinity of Fort Bridgewood—Battalion headquarters being in Fort Bridgewood—and remained under canvas until the autumn when it moved back into the forts. Whilst at Bridgewood the first Zeppelin bombing raid over Chatham took place—the Zeppelin appeared to be hit by a shell and was driven off with its nose in the air. No damage was occasioned to the Battalion.

During the whole of 1915 drafts were constantly being prepared and sent over to France to 1st and 2nd Battalions; during the later months to 6th and 7th Battalions also.

On February 28th, 1916, in a snowstorm, the Battalion moved to Sittingbourne, where it remained until the end of the war. The Battalion was situated at Gore

Court—a fairly large mansion—the men being billeted on the inhabitants of the town until the summer, when camp was formed around Gore Court.

The recruits training at Chatham Lines joined the Battalion at Gore Court—the Battalion being composed : " A " Company (Expeditionary Force unfits, etc.), "B," " C," and " D " Service Companies (draft finding), Nos. 1, 2, 3, and 4 Training Companies.

On November 11th, 1918, the strength of the Battalion, exclusive of officers, was 152 warrant and non-commissioned officers, and 848 privates.

In March, 1919, the Battalion moved to Clipstone, and here on August 5th, 1919, the personnel, less the headquarters staff, was absorbed by the 1st Battalion.

The Battalion was commanded throughout by Colonel A. G. Shaw.

### The 4/4th Battalion.

After the 4th Battalion The Queen's had left Croydon for Windsor to form part of the " Composite " Battalion of the Regiment and eventually to produce, first the 2/4th, and later the 3/4th The Queen's, the Depot Company remaining behind in Poplar Walk, Croydon, became known as the 4/4th, and Captain K. W. Elder was appointed to the command in July, 1915, with Captain Pryce as adjutant.

The 4/4th was then essentially a draft-finding and training unit, training and sending out drafts to the 1/4th in India, to the 2/4th in Egypt and Palestine, and to the 3/4th in France and Flanders ; and when at last the regimental drafting system could no longer be strictly adhered to in view of the many calls for reinforcement, the Battalion provided levies wherever men were most urgently needed, to the Regulars, New Army, or to the Territorials.

The aim of the training afforded was rather physical fitness than mere smartness on parade, and gymnastics, trench digging, bayonet exercise, and machine-gun drill formed the chief items in the training syllabus.

In the autumn of 1915 the Battalion went into camp at Windsor, but in November moved into huts at Purfleet, and in the New Year was sent first to Crowborough and later to Cambridge, where the conscripted men began to come in.

By the middle of 1916 the pressure of recruiting due to conscription appreciably lessened, and training battalions, such as the 4/4th The Queen's, were brigaded ; Major Elder then joined the Brigade Staff of the Home Counties Reserve Brigade, and the Guildford men of the 5th The Queen's were added to the Croydon men of the 4th The Queen's, forming a fresh unit in the Brigade under the name of " the 4th Reserve Battalion The Queen's."

### The 2/5th Battalion.

The record of the 2/5th Battalion The Queen's presents an interesting phase in the scheme of Home Defence during the Great War.

When the 1/5th Battalion volunteered for service abroad and left for India in October, 1914, it was at that time generally supposed that Home Defence was the duty of the Territorial Force, and, to take the place of the 1/5th The Queen's, a new battalion was raised at Guildford ; this was at first styled " the 5th Reserve Battalion The Queen's " and it joined the newly-formed second-line Home Counties Division, being posted to the Surrey Brigade and joining it at Windsor on November 20th. The Brigade was then commanded by Brigadier-General Marriott, and it contained the 2/4th and 2/5th Battalions The Queen's, and the 2/5th and 2/6th Battalions The East Surrey Regiment.

Training was carried on in the Great Park, and the infantry of the Division was largely employed in picqueting all main roads.

On November 27th, 1914, the Battalion was made up of 25 officers and 981 non-commissioned officers and men, and of these 981 there were:—

| | |
|---|---|
| Trained Men | 407 |
| Trained men rejoined after a break in service of 12 months or more | 198 |
| Recruits of two months' service or more | 112 |
| Recruits of under two months' service | 264 |

While of these, 40 trained men and 208 recruits had volunteered for foreign service, leaving 367 trained men and 366 recruits engaging for home service only.

In May, 1915, volunteers were called for to proceed to the Dardanelles, when about 400 of the Battalion were formed into a separate unit, later known as the 2/4th Battalion The Queen's, the remainder of the 2/5th marching on June 2nd to Tunbridge Wells, where the Home Service personnel of the 2/4th was amalgamated with that of the 2/5th and a new battalion, known at first as the 69th (Provisional) Battalion, and later as the 19th Battalion The Queen's, was formed on June 17th, 1915. All the officers and other ranks of the 2/5th, except about 15 officers and 100 non-commissioned officers and men, were posted to this new battalion. What officers and men remained continued to form what was still known as the 2/5th The Queen's, and the command was given in the first instance to Major de la Mare, and then to Lieutenant-Colonel St. Barbe Sladen, T.D., who came from the 1/5th in India, while Captain J. P. Sworder was appointed adjutant; both these officers were later killed in France.

Towards the end of 1915 the Battalion was sent to Reigate, arriving there very weak in numbers, and it was not until some months later that it began to be made up to strength, though it was only when the first groups of men were called up under Lord Derby's scheme that there was any real accession of numbers. The Battalion was now in the 200th Brigade of the 67th Division.

During March, 1916, there were several alarms by reason of Zeppelin raids, while Easter Monday, April 24th, proved an eventful day, when "special vigilance" was enjoined on account of the outbreak of the Irish Rebellion.

At the end of June the 200th Brigade left Reigate and marched to Wildernesse Camp, near Sevenoaks, but moved a fortnight later by Wrotham, Maidstone, Lenham, Charing, and Chilham to a camp at Westbere, on the main road between Canterbury and Margate, arriving here on July 17th, and sharing the camping ground with the 3/4th Battalion of the Regiment.

Early in August an "emergency striking force" was formed in the Brigade, composed entirely of trained men, the object being to have a body immediately at hand, in view of the possibility of an invasion of the coast of Kent; and on the 19th "special vigilance" was again declared owing to naval action in the North Sea. At the end of the month a large draft was sent to France.

On November 1st the Battalion moved again, marching to Margate, where the 2/5th was allotted a definite length of coast to patrol and man in case of emergency; this ran roughly from Margate Harbour to the village of Kingsgate, half-way to Broadstairs, and including the North Foreland. While at Margate the strength of the Battalion was increased by the arrival of personnel from different regiments in France, all consisting of boys under 19, whom it had been considered advisable to withdraw from service in the field.

During the night of February 25th-26th, 1917, the town of Margate was bombarded by ships of the German Fleet, but considering the size and weight of the shells fired, extraordinarily little damage was done. Later information showed that the enemy force consisted of three destroyers and that the object of the bombardment was the destruction of the wireless station at the North Foreland.

In April of this year Brigadier-General Marriott was succeeded in command of the 200th Infantry Brigade by Brigadier-General Gorges, who, after the Armistice, took a " Young Soldiers' Brigade " out to the Army of Occupation on the Rhine. Then at the end of this month the Brigade left Margate and went back to camp at Westbere.

In August preparations were pushed forward for sending the whole of the rank and file of the Battalion overseas, and on September 21st the camp was taken over by a Young Soldiers' Battalion nearly 1,700 strong ; and a few days later all the other ranks of the 2/5th The Queen's proceeded to France in two drafts, one of these joining the Royal Fusiliers, the other, another Battalion of The Queen's, the 2/5th, The Queen's then ceasing to exist as such.

### The 3/5th Battalion.

This Battalion was originally formed as a reinforcing unit to other Territorial battalions of The Queen's and came into existence at Guildford on June 1st, 1915, the first commanding officer being Lieutenant-Colonel J. Wyndham Wright. It was sent to Windsor on September 2nd, 1915, and to Purfleet on the 6th of the following month, while at the end of the year the Battalion was at Cambridge.

On April 4th, 1916, the 3/5th The Queen's was ordered to Crowborough, and remained here until October 27th, when another move took place, this time to Tunbridge Wells, where the Battalion was amalgamated with the 4/4th The Queen's, and was renamed the 4th (Reserve) Battalion.

### The 4th (Reserve) Battalion.

When this Battalion was formed in 1916 from the 4/4th and 3/5th Battalions of The Queen's, Lieutenant-Colonel Wyndham Wright was in command, but he was succeeded by Lieutenant-Colonel W. R. Campion, D.S.O., T.D., M.P. for Lewes, and on his returning to France, the command was assumed by Lieutenant-Colonel N. T. Rolls, who had served overseas with the 6th Battalion of the Regiment. He was appointed to command early in 1917, and on his arrival found the Battalion busily engaged in training new levies and in patching up and returning to the front the wounded men who were continually arriving from overseas. Even when the Armistice was arranged on November 11th, 1918, this work did not immediately cease, since the replacement of the forces in France and elsewhere still went on in order that war-worn men might be given leave home ; and as a result the disbandment of the 4th Reserve Battalion The Queen's did not take place until the summer of 1919.

### The 9th (Service or Reserve) Battalion.

Was raised as the 9th (Service) Battalion in October, 1914, by Captain L. M. Howard, and was renamed in April, 1915, the 9th (Reserve) Battalion, being used as a draft-providing unit for the other Service battalions of The Queen's. It was disbanded under A.C.I. 1528 of 1916 in August of that year.

### The 12th (Reserve) Battalion.

Was formed by Major S. B. Schlam, South African Defence Force, in October, 1915, from Depot companies of the 10th and 11th Battalions of the Regiment. In August, 1916, it became the 97th Training Reserve Battalion and in June, 1917, the 209th Infantry Battalion Training Reserve. In November, 1917, however, it was given not only a new number but a different territorial designation, becoming the 51st (Graduated) Battalion The Middlesex Regiment, and in February, 1919, the 51st (Service) Battalion of that corps. Finally, on April 8th, 1919, it was absorbed by the 7th Battalion The Middlesex Regiment, and ceased to exist as a distinct and separate corps. The headquarters of the Battalion was first at Coldharbour Lane, Brixton, then at Northampton, where Lieutenant-Colonel W. D. Wynyard, R.A.O.C., assumed command, then at Aldershot, and finally at Taverham, from which place it proceeded to Germany in April, 1919.

### The 16th (Home Service) Battalion.

This was raised at Basingstoke in October, 1916, and was in the first instance commanded by Lieutenant-Colonel E. W. B. Green, D.S.O., Royal Sussex Regiment. It was disbanded on June 21st, 1919.

### The 19th Battalion.

This was in the first instance formed at Tunbridge Wells, as the 69th Provisional Battalion on June 18th, 1915, by posting all officers and other ranks from the 2/4th and 2/5th The Queen's, who were not prepared to sign on for service overseas. Four officers and some 400 other ranks joined from the 2/4th and the initial strength of the Battalion was 16 officers and 944 non-commissioned officers and men.

On June 20th the Battalion was sent to Eastbourne and Seaford on coast defence duty, moving early in July to Lowestoft, where it took over from the Norfolk Regiment the area north of the harbour; the defences of Lowestoft included two semi-lunar systems of trenches north and south of the town, and other works on the beach, all covering the northern and southern approaches, and extending in each case to a length of about 1,000 yards. Later on a line of strong points on the cliff or beach was constructed at intervals of from 400 to 800 yards, with machine-gun emplacements, and to these were added a continuous wire entanglement covering the works. In places also there was a second line of defence, while there were protected headquarters for the Battalion and companies, with reserve ammunition and bomb stores, and bombardment shelters for garrisons and supports. All the main works were connected by field telephones, and during the last year of the war the Battalion had 48 Lewis guns and a battery of 8 Stokes mortars, for which deep emplacements, with cover for the guns crews, were constructed on the cliff at intervals of about 1,000 yards.

For some little time the Battalion had charge of the coast section from Lowestoft Harbour on the south to Corton on the north, but this was subsequently extended, first, from Pakefield to Hopton, and then to Gorleston.

Within a month of the formation of the Battalion a strong appeal was put forward by the Divisional General for further volunteers for service overseas, and the result of this and other pressure in the same direction was that nearly 300 more such volunteers were obtained from the Battalion before the end of 1915.

In April, 1916, the 71st (Provisional) Battalion was amalgamated with the 69th, the strength of the latter being thus raised to nearly 1,900 ; but in the autumn of this year drafts and discharges reduced the Battalion to about 450, though the arrival in November of 400 recruits restored matters again.

On April 25th the town of Lowestoft was bombarded by ships of the German Fleet, but though there was a good deal of damage to property there were very few casualties among either troops or civilians ; on this occasion Lieutenant A. J. Whittall and one private of the Battalion were wounded. Air attacks were also tolerably frequent, principally carried out by Zeppelins and occasionally by seaplanes. Then, in the winter of 1916, as also in that of the year following, an abnormal spring tide, coupled with a strong north-westerly gale, caused a kind of tidal wave, undoing in a single night the work of months by wrecking the defences and filling up the trenches.

On January 1st, 1917, the name of the Battalion was changed, and from the 69th (Provisional) Battalion it became the 19th Battalion The Queen's.

In June, 1918, when all available men were wanted for reinforcements in France, the strength of the Battalion dwindled down to some 400 effectives ; but in August when the establishment was raised to six companies, aggregating approximately 1,580 officers and other ranks, the effective strength rose for a time to nearly 1,700, and from this time until the end of the war the Battalion became officially a draft-finding unit.

In this year the town of Lowestoft was again bombarded from the sea, when Lieutenant W. H. G. Chapman, of the Battalion, was wounded.

Disbandment was ordered in November, 1918, and was completed in April of the year following.

The number of officers and non-commissioned officers who passed through the Battalion during the war amounted to over 400 officers and about 5,000 other ranks. Many drafts were sent overseas, and many more to reserve units ; the strength of the corps was added to from various sources, and during the latter stages of the war included men who had fought in most of the different theatres.

The Battalion was commanded from June, 1915, up to disbandment by Colonel W. J. Perkins, C.M.G., V.D.

THE END.

# POSTSCRIPT

By General Sir Charles Monro, Bart., G.C.B., G.C.S.I., G.C.M.G.,
*Colonel of The Queen's Royal Regiment.*

I have been asked to add a postscript to this War History. In doing so, I must first congratulate the author, Colonel Wylly, on having successfully achieved the most difficult task of comprising the record of the exploits of all the Battalions of the Regiment into one volume.

The History deals almost entirely with the hard work performed by all ranks overseas, but that is not all the story. The pages which follow unfold a tale of immense hard work on the part of our many friends in the County of Surrey who were compelled to remain at home and who undertook the great task of administering to the comfort, welfare, and encouragement of those who were fighting and to our prisoners of war.

All will agree that the organizations set up left nothing to be desired and contributed largely to the successful termination of the war.

To each and all of those who undertook this work I wish to express the appreciation and gratitude of the Regiment; their loyal and untiring service will be remembered as long as the Regiment exists.

# APPENDICES

## APPENDIX I.

### Parcels for Prisoners of War.

It will be remembered that the 1st and 2nd Battalions fought side by side during the last few days of October, 1914, and that both Battalions suffered heavy losses in killed, wounded, and prisoners.

During November it became apparent that our prisoners in German hands were being systematically ill treated and badly fed; it became necessary, therefore, to organize means for supplying them with food and comforts.

This work was inaugurated in November, 1914, by Mrs. Elias Morgan, wife of the Officer Commanding the Depot, who was responsible for the dispatch of the first consignment of parcels. As the needs of the prisoners increased, the assistance of Mr. H. Neden Harrison, of Guildford, was sought, and he threw himself into the work of organization with great energy.

For several months Mr. Harrison, assisted by Mr. H. Le Cocq and numerous ladies and gentlemen, carried on the organization at his private house, and a considerable sum of money was collected to defray expenses.

By August, 1915, the number of prisoners of war belonging to the Regiment had increased to about 600, and it was considered advisable to transfer the work, together with the balance in hand of about £600, to the Depot, where thenceforward it was carried on so ably by Mrs. Elias Morgan, and later by Mrs. Dawson Warren, assisted by numerous ladies and gentlemen belonging to and interested in the Regiment.

When the work was first started each one of the prisoners was adopted by someone in the county who undertook to supply him with comforts; as the number of prisoners increased, however, it became necessary to centralize the work, and every prisoner was then supplied once a fortnight by the Regimental Committee with a parcel containing food, tobacco, cigarettes, clothing, etc.

As a rule, the parcels were regularly received, and the gratitude of the recipients was fully expressed in the enormous number of letters (sometimes amounting to 900 in a week) received by the organization. There is no doubt that without these parcels many of the prisoners would not have survived the hardships they had to endure.

When the County Fund was started (*vide* Appendix II) the money received by the Regimental Care Committee was dealt with by the organization at the Depot, and the organization remained in being until 1921, the last two years of its work being devoted to the after-care of the returned prisoners.

## APPENDIX II.

### The Prisoners of War, Surrey Regiments, Relief Fund.

In the latter part of 1917 it became clear that the end of the war was not yet in sight and that the needs of prisoners of war must be regularly catered for. Mr. W. Shawcross (the Mayor of Guildford) conceived the idea of forming a fund which might be the means of assisting the organization already in being (*vide* Appendix I), by ensuring the provision of the necessary amount of money.

The first meeting to consider the scheme was held at the Guildhall, Guildford, on November 3rd, 1917, and was presided over by the Right Hon. E. S. Talbot, D.D., Bishop of Winchester. A subsequent meeting, held in London under the Presidency of the Lord-Lieutenant, Lord Ashcombe, decided to form a county fund with the title :—

> "The Queen's Regiment and the East Surrey Regiment Prisoners of War Relief Fund; Special County Appeal."

Mr. W. Shawcross was appointed Chairman and Mr. H. Le Cocq Organizing Secretary for the Western Area; Sir Charles Burge and Mr. Carter for the Eastern Area. Subsequently Mr. Le Cocq was appointed Organizing Secretary for the whole county.

The first duties of the two committees were to enrol workers, issue circulars appealing for donations, and organize flag days, entertainments, congregational and school collections, etc. Collecting cards were placed in all hotels, banks, boarding houses, etc., and all factories were asked to co-operate through their workmen.

The Fund was started by the Lord-Lieutenant, who gave £4,000 from his War Relief Fund; and the County Council, who contributed £2,000. The following figures give some idea as to how the appeal was supported in the Western Area of the county :—

| | |
|---|---:|
| Flag days | £3,200 |
| Entertainments, sales, etc. | £4,000 |
| Congregational collections | £3,000 |
| Elementary schools | £1,200 |

The money received was handed over to the Care Committees of the two Regiments, and in the case of The Queen's was dealt with by the organization set forth in Appendix I.

The Surrey Regiments were unfortunate in their casualties, and as the lists of prisoners increased daily, a meeting was held in October, 1918, at the Guildhall, Guildford, at which the Lord-Lieutenant presided, to discuss by what means the necessary funds could be raised for the coming year's demands for food and comforts for the prisoners of war. Happily, it proved unnecessary to proceed to the collection of this amount, and shortly after the signing of the Armistice a meeting was held to wind up the Fund. At this meeting it was decided to transfer, with the sanction of the Charity Commission, the balance of the Fund, amounting to about £3,400, to a Special Fund to relieve necessitous cases of the repatriated prisoners of war of the two Regiments. About £1,100 was expended in this way, and when all demands for relief ceased the balance remaining was, with the approval of the Charity Commission, paid over to the Old Comrades' Associations of the two Regiments, each receiving £1,000 5% War Stock and £367 7s. 9d. in cash.

Thanks to the generous response made by the public throughout the county, the total produced by the appeal amounted to £46,069 11s. 6d., made up as follows :—

| | | | |
|---|---:|---:|---:|
| Lord-Lieutenant's Fund | £4,000 | 0 | 0 |
| Surrey County Council | £2,000 | 0 | 0 |
| East Surrey Area | £17,735 | 11 | 4 |
| West Surrey Area | £22,334 | 0 | 2 |
| | £46,069 | 11 | 6 |

# APPENDICES

## APPENDIX III.

### Welcome Home to Repatriated Prisoners of War of The Queen's Regiment, held at Guildford on January 24th, 1919.

"Welcome home. With all kind thoughts and hearty good wishes for your welfare and future happiness."

So ran the memento card issued by the Committee of the Special County Appeal of West Surrey to 280 non-commissioned officers and men, repatriated from prisoners' camps in Germany, who were entertained in the County and Borough Hall, Guildford, on January 24th, 1919.

Although the idea of entertaining the repatriated prisoners whose homes are in West Surrey was initiated and carried through by the Committee of the Special County Appeal of West Surrey, the County Fund was not used for this purpose. A special appeal was made to cover expenses, which were necessarily very heavy, and the public made a generous reponse.

The invitation issued to the repatriated prisoners of war was extended to their wives and lady friends, 200 of whom accepted. Altogether the company numbered about 550, and it was found impossible to carry out the original intention of entertaining men of other regiments resident in the district.

The soldier guests, who came from no fewer than seventy-one towns and villages, had their railway fares paid for them. They assembled outside Guildford Station at 2.30, and, headed by The Queen's band, marched in procession to the Guildhall. The appeal to the residents to display flags and bunting was heartily responded to, and the High Street looked very gay. The pavements were packed with people, and as the men marched up the street to the strains of " See the conquering hero comes " cheer after cheer was given ; there was a fluttering of handkerchiefs and the waving of flags. At the Guildhall a halt was called, and the Mayor delivered an address of welcome from the balcony.

After the Mayor's address three cheers were given for the Regiment, a similar number for the Mayor, the proceedings closing with a verse of the National Anthem. The procession continued, via High Street and the Ram Corner, to the County and Borough Hall.

As soon as the company had assembled in the hall, an address of welcome was delivered by Lieutenant-General Sir Edmond Elles, G.C.I.E., K.C.B., on behalf of the Lord-Lieutenant, who was unable to be present. After this address, speeches were made by Major-General Sir E. O. F. Hamilton, K.C.B., Colonel of The Queen's, Brigadier-General F. J. Pink, C.B., C.M.G., D.S.O., and Mr. Henry Le Cocq.

Following the speeches a short concert was given

Owing to the limited space in the hall, it was necessary to divide the party for tea. The majority were accommodated in the Assembly Room, the others sitting down under the balcony.

Afterwards there was a distribution of cigars, cigarettes, tobacco, matches, chocolate and oranges. As a memento of the occasion each man received a bronze medal, to be worn on the watch-chain. One side bore the regimental badge, and the other the inscription, " Repatriated prisoners of war. The Queen's Regiment. Welcome Home. December, 1918." About 1,600 of these medals were subsequently sent as mementoes to those who were unable to be present at the Welcome Home.

## APPENDIX IV

### Regimental War Memorial.

In 1919 a committee composed of past and present officers and non-commissioned officers of the Regiment, under the Presidency of Major-General Sir E. O. F. Hamilton, K.C.B., then Colonel of the Regiment, was assembled to consider the erection of a fitting war memorial. Mr. Henry Le Cocq kindly consented to undertake the duties of organizing secretary, and circulars were distributed to all those interested.

As it was not possible to obtain a suitable site in the open air, it was decided that the memorial should be placed on the north wall of Holy Trinity Church, Guildford, close to the Regimental Chapel.

After consideration of several alternative designs, the committee accepted that submitted by Captain E. Stanley Hall, M.A., F.R.I.B.A., an officer of the 10th Battalion of the Regiment.

The work was completed in 1921, and the dedication and unveiling took place on June 4th. The memorial was dedicated by the Right Rev. E. S. Talbot, D.D., Bishop of Winchester, and unveiled by General Sir Charles Monro, Bart., G.C.B., G.C.S.I., G.C.M.G., Colonel of the Regiment. The address was delivered by the Right Rev. L. H. Burrows, D.D., Bishop of Sheffield, and fourteen local clergy assisted.

Before the service began the Colours of the 6th, 7th, and 8th Battalions were laid on the altar for safe keeping, and were afterwards placed in position over the Memorial.

The Memorial consists of a central niche in which rests the bronze and glass casket containing the book in which is inscribed the names of the 8,000 of all ranks who gave their lives during the war.

In the tympanum above the niche is placed the regimental badge, the Paschal Lamb, the mottoes and secondary badges being inlaid in the frieze and elsewhere. Below the badge is inscribed in inlaid letters :—

IN MEMORY THE QUEEN'S, 1914–1919.

Below the casket is the following inscription :—

TO THE GLORIOUS MEMORY OF 8,000 OFFICERS, WARRANT OFFICERS, NON-COMMISSIONED OFFICERS, AND MEN OF THE QUEEN'S WHO GAVE THEIR LIVES FOR THEIR COUNTRY IN FLANDERS, FRANCE, ITALY, GALLIPOLI, SALONIKA, MESOPOTAMIA, PALESTINE, EGYPT, INDIA, AFRICA, AND IN GERMANY, 1914–1919 WHOSE NAMES ARE IN THE BOOK OF LIFE.
THE MEMORIAL IS ERECTED BY THEIR RELATIVES, COMRADES, AND FRIENDS.

Two carved oak Corinthian columns support the tympanum. The Battle Honours of the Regiment are incised on panels on either side of the niche, and the whole of the central portion is raised on two steps of blue Honiton stone, while on each side oak panelling 36 feet long and 11 feet 3 inches high is placed.

Above the Memorial are situated three stained glass windows subscribed for by the 3rd, 8th, and 10th Battalions. The window on the left (8th Battalion) represents the Victory over the Devil—St. Michael slaying the Dragon. That on the right (10th Battalion) contains the figure of St. Catherine making her choice between the Crown of Laurels and the Crown of Thorns—the victory over the flesh. The centre window (3rd Battalion) depicts the victory of the Lamb, from the famous painting of Van Eyck. There is a dedicatory inscription at the foot of each window.

The total amount subscribed for the Memorial, including the amounts raised by the 3rd, 8th, and 10th Battalions for the windows, was £3,000. Some of the subscriptions were, however, earmarked by the donors for the Regimental Old Comrades Association.

REGIMENTAL WAR MEMORIAL.

[Photo: *Coppard & Kester, Guildford.*

# APPENDICES

## APPENDIX V

### Regimental Old Comrades Association

DURING 1913 Lieut.-Colonel Warren, then commanding the 1st Battalion, brought forward a proposal for the formation of a Regimental Old Comrades Association. Up to that time both Battalions and the Depot had their own Charitable Funds, which were administered separately by the Officers Commanding. Lieut.-Colonel Warren drew up a scheme for the whole Regiment on a contributory basis, providing for grants being made to N.C.Os. and men when they left the Colours. The scheme was approved by both Battalions and was actually brought into being early in 1914. The war interfered with progress, and when it began the money subscribed was placed on deposit.

Towards the end of 1919 the question of the re-constitution of the Old Comrades Association was taken up and a Committee assembled to draw up a comprehensive scheme.

The re-constituted Association came into being in 1920, having as its principal objects the maintenance of fellowship between past and present members of the Regiment and the obtaining of employment for members after leaving the Colours. All those then serving or who had at any time served in any Unit wearing or which had worn the Regimental Badge were eligible to be members; while anyone interested in the Regiment was invited to become an honorary member. Annual subscriptions were fixed according to rank for serving members, and at a flat rate for those who had left the Colours. In 1922 a Life Membership Subscription was introduced.

The Association has made steady progress, and at the end of 1923 the membership was 3,700. Its usefulness has been proved by the number of those who take advantage of their membership. Employment has been found for many applicants, and others have been enabled to make a fresh start in civil life by means of temporary loans or grants in aid. During 1923 over 2,000 letters were dealt with, ranging over a variety of subjects from employment to questions of pension, medals, etc.

The available capital of the Association in 1920 was about £1,700. Many of the Battalions formed during the war handed over the balance of their funds on demobilization, and at the end of 1923 the invested capital stood at over £6,000; the income for that year from all sources amounting to about £1,100.

The Association has its offices at the Regimental Depot, and any information required can always be obtained from the Secretary.

# INDEX.

Abbot, Lieut., 277
Abbott, Pte., 92
A'Bear, Capt. H. G., killed, 222
Abeele, 275
Abercrombie, Lieut. A. R., 34, 35, 37 ; Capt., 70
Adams, 2/Lieut. J. S., 225 ; wounded, 231
Adams, Bandmaster, 132
Aden, 2
Afghanistan, Amir of, 128 ; operations in, 144
Afridis, 144
Agra, 2
Aisne, Battle of the, 16 *et seq.* ; 1st Bn. crosses river, 17
Albert, 217
Albert Hall Commemoration, 117
Aldridge, Pte., 98
Aldworth, Capt. T. P., 23, 26
Ali Muntar, 160
Allan, Capt. A. M., 63 ; killed, 66
Allan, 2/Lieut. A. M., 92 ; wounded, 93
Allen, 2/Lieut. A. C., 44
Allen, 2/Lieut. L. T. M., missing, 273
Allenby, Gen., 8, 220
Alleyne, Capt. W. H., 83-85, 89 ; wounded, 91
Allinson, 2/Lieut., 242
Altivole, 2nd Bn. at, 118
Amiens, Battle of, 206, 207
Anafarta, 151
Ancre, River, 204, 205
Andrews, 2/Lieut. L. E., 252 ; wounded, Capt. 255 ; Major, 256 ; killed, 258
Andrews, Col. L. J., 280
Apted, Lieut., missing, 271
Ardagh, 2/Lieut. F. D., 179, 180
Armentières, 189, 190, 216
Armies—First, 28, 40, 56, 67, 96, 198, 203, 209, 256 ; Second, 28, 40, 56, 113, 173, 189, 224, 256, 257, 258, 263 ; Third, 40, 53, 56, 62, 67, 71, 110, 172, 195, 198, 204, 211, 216, 234, 245 ; Fourth, 40, 56, 71, 101, 193, 196, 209, 212, 231, 233-235, 253 ; Fifth, 53, 56, 62, 109, 194-196, 224, 225, 253 ; New, First, 189 ; New, Second, 211 ; New, Third, 237 ; French, Sixth, 193, 196 ; Tenth, 98, 166, 167 ; Italian, Third, Fourth, Sixth, Eighth, Tenth, 122
Armistice, 74, 168, 235, 265, 278
Armitage, 2/Lieut. A. C., killed, 30
Army Reorganization, Haldane Scheme, 2, 3
Arras, Battle of, 49, *et seq.*, 109 *et seq.*, 198 *et seq.*
Arras Offensive, 220 *et seq.*
Ashpitel, 2/Lieut. G. F., 55, 63, 64 ; Capt., 70
Ashton, 2/Lieut. A. L., killed, 206
Asiago Plateau, 120
Aslin, 2/Lieut. W. H., 113
Aspden, 2/Lieut. E. H., killed, 199
Aspden, 2/Lieut. F. H., wounded, 206 ; killed, 209

Aston, 2/Lieut. J., wounded, 222
Atall, 2/Lieut. E. E. F., 107
Atfield, C.S.M., 209
Atkins, Capt. H. R., 140 ; Major, 144 ; Lieut.-Col., 146
Atkinson, Capt. R. L., 113 ; wounded, 114, 115
Atkinson, 2/Lieut. W. L., wounded, 59 ; wounded, 231
Atkinson, Lieut. R. L. A., 179, 180
Aubers, fighting at, 94
Austin, 2/Lieut. A. McN., 45 ; wounded, 47
Austin, 2/Lieut. C. F., 92 ; killed, 95
Austin, C.S.M., 278
Authuille, 217
Aveluy, 204
Avery, 2/Lieut. N. B., 44 ; Capt., 63, 72

Babington, Lieut.-Gen. Sir J., 122
Bacon, 2/Lieut. S. F., 140 ; Capt., 146
Badcock, Lieut. F. T., 127, 130
Badge, Regimental, change in, 3, 4
Baghdad, 184, 189
Bailleul, 90
Bailey, Capt. L. D., R.A.M.C., 179, 180
Baily, 2/Lieut. E. D., 107 ; wounded, 113
Bain, 2/Lieut. L., 252
Baird, Brig.-Gen. A. W. F., 38, 43, 44
Baisieux, 250
Baker, 2/Lieut. L. C. E., 273, ; killed, 275
Baker, 2/Lieut. F., died of wounds, 254
Baker, Pte., swims Piave River, 119
Ball, Capt. F. S., 51 ; missing, 53
Ball, 2/Lieut. R. C., 183
Balne, R.S.M., 4
Bannerman, Lieut. R. R. B., 171
Barber, 2/Lieut. H. M., killed, 231
Barclay, Capt. W., 252
Barclay, Lieut. T. M., 146
Bareilly, 2nd Bn. arrives at, 128
Barley, 2/Lieut. G. W., 113
Barnard, Capt. M. F., 236
Barnard, 2/Lieut. J., 45, 50 ; wounded, 54
Barnes, Sergt., 26
Barnes, C.S.M., 210
Barre, Lieut. W. J., 278
Barrenger, Lieut. H. E., 146
Barrow, 2/Lieut. A. E., 172 ; Lieut., killed, 175
Barter, Lieut. E. H. G., 252
Bartlett, 2/Lieut. L. P. P. T., 225
Bartlett, Pte. F. W., killed, 268
Barton, Capt. E. de L., missing, 24
Basset, 2/Lieut. R. A. M., 5, 189
Basset, 2/Lieut. H., 68
Batchelar, 2/Lieut. R. T., wounded, 222, 225 ; missing, 227
Bates, Lieut. L. 146
Batten, 2/Lieut. E. V., 225 ; missing, 227

# INDEX

Battiscombe, Capt., 50
Battle Honours—"South Africa," 81; "Ghuznee, 1839," 2; "Tangier, 1662-80," 3; "Admiral Howe's Victory," 4; "Namur, 1695," 4; "Afghanistan," 6; Committee, 135
Battson, L./Cpl., 144
Bavai, 250
Baverstocke, Sergt., 26
Bayford, C.Q.M.S. G., 74
Baylis, 2/Lieut. R. H., 225
Baynes, 2/Lieut. W. H., 55; wounded, 59
Beach, Major L. H. F., wounded, 160; d. of w., 169
Beacon, Pte. H., 74
Beadle, Lieut. C. E. S., wounded, 196
Bearman, 2/Lieut., killed, 232
Beavis, 2/Lieut. R. E. G., wounded, 113
Beersheba, 158, 160
Behrens, Lieut. E. L., 136
Belcham, Lieut. and Qr.Mr., 105, 189
Bell, 2/Lieut., 201
Bennett, 2/Lieut. E. F., wounded, 213; Capt., 235
Bennett, 2/Lieut. L. E., killed, 44
Bennett, 2/Lieut. L. H., 37; wounded, 44
Bennett, Lieut. I. P. W., 211; Capt. 215; killed, 216
Bennett, 2/Lieut. M. P., 107; died of wounds, 113
Benson, Lieut. A. H., 146
Bentley, 2/Lieut. J., 186
Bermuda, 2nd Bn. at, 83, 84
Bernafay Wood, 215, 232
Bernard, Lieut. D. V., 70
Berrangé, 2/Lieut. R. F., wounded, 254; Capt., 257
Bessell, 2/Lieut. P., 225
Bessell, Capt. M., 252; killed, 254
Beswall, 2/Lieut. A. P., 218; wounded, 219
Bethell, Capt. E. W., 68; killed, 69
Bethell, 2/Lieut. E. W., 83; Lieut., 84, 85; wounded, 91
Béthune, 100, 192
Beynon, Brig.-Gen. W. G. L., 140-143
Bickell, 2/Lieut. E. G., 106
Binfield, C.Q.M.S. J., 85
Bingham, Capt. E. S., 68, 69
Bingham, 2/Lieut. E. S., 104; wounded, 105
Birch, Capt. T. I., 170, 171
Bird, 2/Lieut. E. H., 252; Capt., killed, 255
Bird, 2/Lieut. J. G. H., 84, 85
Birkett, Lt.-Col., 120
Birmingham, Cpl., 26
Bishop, Pte. A., 104
Blakeman, L./Sergt., 173
Blagden, 2/Lieut. M. B., 68; killed, 69
Blewchamp, 2/Lieut. H. A., 213; killed, 215, 216
Block, 2/Lieut. A. P., 128, 130, 133-136
Blount, 2/Lieut. C. H. B., 84, 85
Boddam-Whetham, Lieut. L. M., 104, 105
Boden, 2/Lieut., wounded, 199
Borst, 2/Lieut. C. L., wounded, 199, 201; killed, 203
Botterill, Mess Sergt., 98
Bottomley, Lieut.-Col. H. R., 82, 83-85; wounded, 91; killed, 97

Bottomley, 2/Lieut. G. D. G., 41; wounded, 43, 127
Botton, 2/Lieut. O. V., missing, 53
Bourne, 2/Lieut. C., wounded, 199
Bourne, 2/Lieut. J. W., wounded, 232
Bower, 2/Lieut. G. R., 41; killed, 43
Bower, 2/Lieut. F. J., 45; wounded, 53
Bower, 2/Lieut. W. F., 225
Bowden, Lieut. E. G., 267, 271, 273, 275
Bowman-Vaughan, 2/Lieut. J. G., 136
Bowring, 2/Lieut. T. J., wounded, 232
Boxall, C.S.M., 130
Boyd, Lieut. A. K., wounded, 169
Boyd, Lieut. J. D., 9, 24, 26, 27, 82, 83
Bradnock, 2/Lieut. G. N., 278
Bradshaw, 2/Lieut. A. W. A., 27; killed, 32, 33
Braham, 2/Lieut. D. C., wounded, 169
Brandt, Lieut. A. V., 146
Bray, Capt. F. E., 179-181, 185, 187
Bray, 2/Lieut. G. T., killed, 169
Brereton, Lieut. T. W., 252
Brewer, Sergt., 210
Brigades—Cavalry: 5th, 11; 6th, 13; Infantry; 1st, 12; 2nd, 12, 18, 21; 3rd, 6, 8, 12, 13, 26, 93; 4th, 13; 5th (1st Bn. joins), 30, 31, 33; 6th, 12; 13th, 114; 17th, 239, 241, 243, 246; 19th, 36, 38, 50, 54, (1st Bn. transferred to) 61, 66, 69, 71, 73; 20th, 99, 106, 111, 114; 21st, 87, 95, 100, 101; 22nd, 23, 84, 87, 96, 100, 101; 25th, 95; 35th, 193, 199, 200, 202, 207; 36th, 191, 193, 194, 196, 200; 37th, 193, 194, 195, 196, 199, 200, 202, 207; 50th, 212; 53rd, 216, 224, 231, 232; 55th, 211, 218, 224, 232; 71st, 239; 72nd, 237, 238, 239, 246; 91st (2nd Bn. transferred to), 100, 101, 107, 111, 114; 98th, 50-54, 57, 63, 66, 72, 73; 99th, 36, 38; 100th, 36, 38, 43, 50, 54, 57, 61, 69, 72; 110th, 50; 115th, 71; 123rd, 267; 124th, 252; Indian, 2nd, 140; 3rd, 142; 9th, 131; 12th, 184, 186; 18th, 130; 23rd, 130; 34th, 179, 181, 182
Brocklehurst, Capt. T. P., wounded, 99; killed, 103
Brodie, 2/Lieut. B. B., d. of w., 169
Brodhurst-Hill, Capt. R., 51; missing, 53
Brodrick, Lieut.-Col. Hon. A. G., 179, 180
Brooke, 2/Lieut. C. B., 27; Capt., 32; wounded, 33
Brooke, Lieut. J. J., killed, 175.
Brookes, Capt. W., wounded, 55
Brookes, 2/Lieut. L. J., 68; wounded, 69
Brooks, 2/Lieut. R. J., 63; wounded, 66
Brooks, 2/Lieut. J. A., 68; wounded, 69
Brooks, 2/Lieut. I. W., wounded, 97
Brooks, Lieut. J. C., wounded, 238, 248
Brotherton, Lieut. L., 146
Browett, Pte. A. J., wounded, 252
Brown, 2/Lieut. A. L., killed, 99
Brown, 2/Lieut. C. G., wounded, 219
Brown, Lieut D. A., 41; wounded, 43; wounded, 91
Brown, 2/Lieut. E. J., 140; Capt., 146
Brown, 2/Lieut. H. S., 252
Brown, Sergt. J., 210
Brown, 2/Lieut. J., 84
Brown, Capt. K. A., 68; killed, 69
Brown, 2/Lieut. K. A., 104, 105

# INDEX

Brown, 2/Lieut. R. S., missing, 273
Browning, 2/Lieut. T. G., 104
Buchan, 2/Lieut. T. O. M., 9; wounded, 23
Buchanan, Lieut., R.A.M.C., 91
Buck, Lieut. G. E., 133
Bucknall, Lieut. F. M. A., wounded, 172
Buckner, 2/Lieut. J. G., 37, 41
Buist, 2/Lieut. H. J., 41; gassed, 43, 48
Bullen, Pte., 274
Burdon, 2/Lieut. R. M., 106, 110
Burgess, 2/Lieut. P. G., missing, 238
Burgess, 2/Lieut. J. W. F., 252, 253
Burghope, 2/Lieut. G. H. V., 45; killed, 53
Burkitt, 2/Lieut. F. T., wounded, 93; wounded, 97
Burnaby, Lieut.-Colonel H. B., 267; killed, 268
Burnett, Pte., wounded, 182
Burnley, 2/Lieut. C. P., 240
Burr, Capt. R. C., wounded, 220, 252
Burrell, 2/Lieut. J., 41; wounded, 43; Capt., wounded, 59, 250
Burrows, Band-Sergt., 85
Burrows, 2/Lieut. J. D., 92
Burton, 2/Lieut. A., 27
Burton, 2/Lieut. R. M., 128, 130, 133, 134, 136
Bush, C.Q.M.S. W. H., 9; wounded, 21
Bushell, 2/Lieut. C., 9; wounded, 17; Lieut.-Col., 225; killed, 230, 231
Butler, Sergt., 25
Butler, 2/Lieut. H. A. R., 189; Capt., wounded, 194
Butler, 2/Lieut. W. J., 225
Butterworth, 2/Lieut. W. C., 41; killed, 43
Butterworth, 2/Lieut. H., 92; wounded, 93
Butaniyeh, 181, 182
Byng, General, 86

CADMAN, Lieut., 266
Cadre—1st Bn., names of, 76, 77; 2nd Bn., names of, 127
Caestre, 245, 271
Cambrai, Battle of, 202 et seq.
Campbell, 2/Lieut. A. M., killed, 44
Campbell, Major-General Sir F., 141
Campion, 2/Lieut. K. F., 179, 180-2
Campion, Lieut.-Colonel W. R., 284
Canal du Nord, 233
Cannon, Major H. C., 176, 189
Capper, Lieut.-General J., 239
Capper, Major-General T., 84, 86; killed, 100
Carlton, Major H. D., 120
Caroe, 2/Lieut. O. K., 140, 146
Carpenter, 2/Lieut. H. J., 51, 52; wounded, 53; Capt., 63; wounded, 66, 127, 130, 136, 239
Carpenter, 2/Lieut. J. W., wounded, 44
Carslake, 2/Lieut. W. B., 35; Capt., 41; wounded, 43, 55; wounded, 59
Carter, Lieut. H. W., 171
Cashel, 2/Lieut. J. S., wounded, 254
Castle, 2/Lieut. T. R., killed, 242
Cator, Brig.-General, 201
Caufield, 2/Lieut. J. L., wounded, 224
Cavan, General Earl of, 120, 121, 125
Cawston, 2/Lieut., 118
Chandler, 2/Lieut. H. E., 26, 37
Chapman, 2/Lieut. T. V., 99; Capt., wounded, 106; killed, 112

Chapman, 2/Lieut. W. H. G., 267; wounded, 286
Charles, 2/Lieut. L. B., 171
Charles, 2/Lieut. C. W. C., wounded, 59
Charlesworth, Lieut. E. F., 146
Charlton, 2/Lieut. R., wounded, 227
Chatterton, 2/Lieut. H. M. N., gassed, died, 240
Chichester, Major A. O. N. C., wounded, 261
Chitty, Lieut. F. G., 273
Chocolate Hill, 150
Christie, Capt. I. McI., 146
Clare, Lieut.-Colonel O. C., 224
Claret, 2/Lieut. A. E., missing, 273
Clark, Lieut.-Colonel W., 260; wounded, 261
Clark, Cpl. F. E., 61
Clark, 2/Lieut. C. S., 70, 72
Clarke, Capt. R. G., 6, 81
Clarke, 2/Lieut. H. P., wounded, 229; wounded 231
Clarke, Major, 255
Clarke, 2/Lieut. J. M., 240
Clark-Kennedy, 2/Lieut. A. E., 179, 180
Clausen, Capt. R. J., R.A.M.C., 37
Claxton, 2/Lieut. F. F. J., wounded, 232
Clayton, Capt., gassed, 240
Cleaver, Pte., 98
Clémenceau, M., inspects 33rd Division, 66
Clenshaw, Lieut. W. F., wounded, 56; missing, 59
Clerk, 2/Lieut. R. M., 189; Capt., 197; killed, 199
Cleverly, 2/Lieut. O. S., 179, 180; wounded, 183
Close, 2/Lieut. J. B., 27
Cloudesley, 2/Lieut. H., 211; killed, 213
Coad, Pte. J., 74
Coates, 2/Lieut. J. B., 93; wounded, 97; Major, 127, 130, 133, 136
Cockburn, Lieut. G. P., killed, 227
Cocks, Lieut. P. F. A., 182
Cohen, Lieut. W. R., 225; missing, 227
Colebrook, 2/Lieut. G. B., 27
Coles, Lieut. E. L., 231, 233
Coles, Major M. C., 81-85; Lieut.-Colonel, wounded, 91
Collings, 2/Lieut. E. d'A., killed, 44
Collis, 2/Lieut. J. G., 84, 85; wounded, 91
Collyer, Capt. G. F., 252
Cologne, 278
Combe, 2/Lieut. H. P., 128, 130, 133, 136, 249
Combles, 232
Conner-Green, 2/Lieut. W. R., missing, 24
Constant, Sergt. E., 103
Cook, Major W. C., 210
Cook, 2/Lieut. H. N. F., 267; killed, 270
Cook, R.S.M., 236
Cooke, Lieut. J. V., killed, 276
Cooke, 2/Lieut., 56
Cooke, Capt. C. A., killed, 238
Cooke, Lieut. H. d'A. M., 189
Cookson, Lieut. J. P. H., 267
Cooper, Capt. P. V., 225; wounded, 227; killed, 231
Cooper, Lieut. A. H. A., 172; killed, 175
Cooper, 2/Lieut. V., 9
Cooper, Sergt., 236
Cooper, L./Cpl., 89
Corkran, Brig.-General C. E., 31

297

# INDEX

Cornwall, Sergt., 232
Corps—I, 8, 11-16, 19, 20, 26, 28, 31, 35, 90, 98, 99, 189-192; II, 8, 12, 13, 19, 20, 195, 216, 263, 264; III, 31, 87, 101, 189, 193, 194, 202, 206, 207, 209, 225, 233, 234; IV, 20, 31, 35, 91, 94, 96, 98, 99, 189, 190; V, 31, 73, 74, 189, 194, 204, 206; VI, 50, 195, 196, 198, 200; VII, 50, 92, 101, 198, 202, 222; VIII, 62, 101, 195, 204, 209; X, 59, 101, 116, 167, 168, 173, 193, 195, 211, 257; XI, 190, 238, 257; XIII, 101, 176, 212, 214; XIV, 122, 125, 253, 258; XV, 101, 196, 203, 204, 214, 253; XVI, 66; XVII, 50, 172, 173, 198, 200; XVIII, 199, 200, 220, 224; XIX, 167, 263, 275; XXII, 206; Australian, 153, 154, 206; Canadian, 198, 206; Indian, 31, 189; German, VII, 94
Corry, 2/Lieut. J. E., 63, 65, 70
Cotgrave, Lieut.-Colonel E. C. B., 280
Cottrell, 2/Lieut. D. C., 225; wounded, 227
Courreaux, Capt. G. F., 127
Courthope, 2/Lieut. W. T. H. F., 269; wounded, 270
Cowan, 2/Lieut. T. R. G., 45, 50; wounded, 56
Cowan, 2/Lieut. J. A., 267
Cox, 2/Lieut. F., wounded, 254
Cox., Lieut. W. L. S., 267; Capt., wounded, 270
Cox, Sig./Sergt., 98
Crane, Lieut. L. F., 184
Crawley, 2/Lieut. H. C., 70
Crees, 2/Lieut. W., killed, 103
Cressy, 2/Lieut. C. H., killed, 238
Crichton, 2/Lieut. A. J., 37, 41; killed, 43
Crofts, Major L. M., 30, 37; Lt.-Col., 41; wounded, 44, 50; wounded, 59, 77, 82, 83-5, 88, 89; wounded, 91, 93, 127, 129
Croisilles, 111
Crompton, 2/Lieut. T., 63; missing, 66
Crook, 2/Lieut. L. A., 41; wounded, 43; killed, 59, 99
Crowe, 2/Lieut. P. C., 278
Crowley, Lieut. J. C., 140; Capt., wounded, 146; killed, 183
Crozier, 2/Lieut. T. A., killed, 273
Cuddon, 2/Lieut. P., 189
Cumberlege, 2/Lieut. E. C. W., 128, 133, 136
Cunningham, Cpl. W. H., wounded, 164, 169
Currie, 2/Lieut. G. D., 213; wounded, 216
Curtois, Lieut. P. A., wounded, 175
Cutler, Lieut.-Col. N. E., 138, 140, 144, 146
Cutler, Lieut. P. H., 146

DAKIN, 2/Lieut. E. H., 172; wounded, 173
Daly, Major-Gen. A. C., 250
Daly, 2/Lieut. C. E. St. F., killed, 201, 222
Damer, 2/Lieut. W., wounded, 219
Danby, Pte., 78
Dandridge, 2/Lieut. G. S., killed, 213
Daniel, 2/Lieut. E. E., gassed, 232
Daniels, Pte. W., wounded, 132
Danks, Capt. R. G., wounded, 204
Darlington, 2/Lieut. T., 274
Darke, Capt. L. J., R.A.M.C., missing, 273
Davidson, 2/Lieut. R. E. M., 189
Davie, 2/Lieut. J. C., 171; wounded, 178
Davis, 2/Lieut. C. H., wounded, 232
Dawson, Lt.-Col. R., assumes command, 82
Dawson, Lieut. H. A., 252

D'Eath, 2/Lieut. E., wounded, 169
De la Mare, Major L. S., 170, 283
Delville Wood, 43, 44, 105 et seq., 214, 242
Denny, 2/Lieut. H. B., 63, 64; wounded, 66
Denton, Lieut. F. W. H., 15; wounded, 17 Capt., 77
Denton, 2/Lieut. J. W. M., wounded, 276
Denyer, C.S.M. G. J., 211; wounded, 212
De Rougemont, 2/Lieut. M. H., killed, 97
Diaz, Gen., 122
Dibdin, Capt. L. G., 140; Major, 146
Dibdin, 2/Lieut. A., 140; Capt., 146
Dickebusch, 114; Lake, 173
Dickinson, Lieut. J. A., 63, 65; killed, 66
Dickinson, 2/Lieut. T. C., wounded, 220
Dillon, Lt.-Col. E. FitzG., 279
Dimmock, 2/Lieut. J. B., wounded, 112
Disbandment 6th Bn., 210; 10th Bn., 266
Divisions, British, reduction of Bns., 61
Divisions—British Cavalry, 3rd, 20; Infantry, 1st, 6, 8, 12, 15, 18, 20, 190; 2nd, 12, 30, 31, 36, 38, 96, 241; 3rd, 198, 199; 4th, 13, 82, 172; 6th, 239; 7th, 20, 31, 84, 91, 94, 96, 100, 101, 109, 121; 8th, 95, 96, 193; 9th, 31, 172, 263, 265; 10th, 148, 150, 162, 164; 11th, 148, 150, 151; 12th, 177, 181, 189, 192, 193, 194, 196-202, 206, 207, 208; 14th, 43, 196, 197, 221, 226, 253; 15th, 198, 199; 16th, 193; 17th, 71; 18th, 71, 101, 193, 207, 211, 221, 226; 19th, 193; 20th, 196; 21st, 53, 67, 71, 73, 103, 173, 177, 208, 221; 23rd, 43, 175, 257; 24th, 237, 239, 246; 25th, 222; 29th, 196, 202, 263; 30th, 167, 213, 214; 31st, 63, 100; 32nd, 108; 33rd (1st Bn. transferred to), 36, 38, 41-44, 50, 69, 71, 192; 34th, 165, 166, 193, 276; 35th, 263; 36th, 71, 276; 38th, 69, 204; 39th, 58, 199, 257; 40th, 148, 168, 242; 41st, 119, 196, 252, 253, 257; 42nd, 273; 46th, 34, 109, 190; 47th, 204, 207, 208, 269; 49th, 62; 50th, 59, 186; 53rd, 147-50, 156, 158; 54th, 148, 150, 156, 158-63; 55th, 202, 203, 241; 58th, 207, 226; 61st, 203; 62nd, 110; 63rd, 248; 66th, 70, 246; American, 27th, 275; 50th, 67; Australian, 4th, 110; French, 14th, 66; 17th, 49; German, 13th, 92; Indian, 1st, 148; 8th, 179
Dodge, Capt. J. B., 252; wounded, 254
Domoney, C.S.M., 130
Donne-Smith, 2/Lieut. L., wounded, 207
Dorrell, 2/Lieut. E. P., killed, 249
Doullens, 199
Dowling, 2/Lieut. F. L. W., 252
Drake, Capt. H. M., 237
Drew, 2/Lieut. E. D., 9; wounded, 33
Drowley, Pte., 182
Driver, Capt. B. H., 110; Major, killed, 113
Du Buisson, Lieut. J. M., 211; Capt., wounded, 218, 219, 222
Duke, Lieut. L. G., wounded, 238
Duncan, Lieut. P. C., 151; Capt., wounded, 160, 164, 168
Dyer, Major G. N., 77, 78

EAGLES, 2/Lieut. J. M., wounded, 273
Earl, Pte. W., 74
East, 2/Lieut. K. M., 45; Lieut., 63; Adjt., 70
East, 2/Lieut. L. C., 133, 136

# INDEX

Eastwood, 2/Lieut. F. M., 9 ; killed, 23
Eastwood, Lieut. & Qr.Mr. S. C., 211
Edenborough, Lieut. L. A. B., 146
Edenborough, 2/Lieut. E. H., wounded, 255
Edridge, Col. Sir F., 171
Edwards, Bandsman J., wounded, 131
Edwards, Capt. E. W., killed, 204
Edwards, Lieut. R. F., wounded, 276
Egypt, 153 et seq.
El Arish, 156, 158
Elder, Capt. K. W., 282
Elderkin, C.S.M., 52
Elliot, 2/Lieut. F. W., wounded, 194
Elliott, Regtl. Sergt.-Major C. J. M., 9, 24 ; Capt., 127, 130, 133
Elliott, 2/Lieut. C. W., 63 ; killed, 66
Elliott, Lieut. E. E., wounded, 205
Ellis, 2/Lieut. W. G. B., 252
Eltham, 2/Lieut. C. W., missing, 47
Embarkation for France, 1st Bn., 8
Endley, 2/Lieut. W. G., 146
Englefontaine, 72
Épéhy, attack on, 208
Ereckson, 2/Lieut. H. G. D., 252
Esdaile, Capt. P. C., 27, 30 ; Lt.-Col., 68, 81, 83, 85 ; wounded, 91
Evans, Capt. B. L., 140, 146
Evans, Lieut. G. C., 225 ; missing, 227, 228, 229 ; Capt., wounded, 232
Everett, 2/Lieut. W. T., killed, 250
Evetts, Lieut. E. F., 179, 180
Expeditionary Force, original, composition of, 8

FAIRCLOUGH, 2/Lieut. E. M., died of wounds, 255
Fairlie, 2/Lieut. A., 41 ; wounded 43
Fairtlough, Lt.-Col., 237 ; killed, 238
Fairtlough, 2/Lieut. L. H., 97 ; wounded, 98
Falcon, 2/Lieut. R. R. B., 140 ; Capt., 146
Farren, 2/Lieut. J., 211 ; wounded, 213
Farwell, 2/Lieut. C. W., 37, 41 ; wounded, 43
Faulkner, 2/Lieut. R. F., 41 ; wounded, 43, 48 ; Capt., 50 ; wounded, 59
Fearon, Lieut. P. J., 81, 82 ; Capt., 83 ; wounded, 93 ; Major, 133
Fearon, Lieut. J. G., 140 ; Capt., 146 ; wounded, 169
Featherstone, Lieut. O., 140 ; Capt., 146
Fellowes, Capt. E. A., gassed, 243, 249
Fendall, 2/Lieut. F. G., wounded, 217
Feneran, Lieut. E. C., 81
Fenn, Clr.-Sergt., 4
Ferguson, 2/Lieut. H. H. G., 213
Few, Major, 151
Field, 2/Lieut. C. A., died of wounds, 250
Field, 2/Lieut. E. A., 68
Filby, Lieut. T. C., 127, 130 ; Capt., 225 ; missing, 227
Finlayson, Cpl., 274
Fisk, 2/Lieut. H. E., 171
Fison, 2/Lieut. C. H., wounded, 186
Fitch, 2/Lieut. A. C., killed, 111
Fitch, Lieut. C. W., killed, 194
Flag, German, capture of, 240
Flanagan, 2/Lieut. G. A., killed, 206
Fleurbaix, 204
Flinn, 2/Lieut. O. S., 37, 41 ; Capt., wounded, 44

Flint, 2/Lieut. R. S., killed, 205
Foard, 2/Lieut., 239
Foch, Marshal, 74
Foley, 2/Lieut. R., 41 ; wounded, 43, 210
Foord-Kelcey, 2/Lieut. J. M., killed, 103
Forbes, 2/Lieut. A. H. D'E., wounded, 206
Ford, 2/Lieut. L. S., killed, 103
Ford, 2/Lieut. N. S., wounded, 271
Ford, Sergt. W. G., 176
Fortune, Lt.-Col. V. M., 279
Foster, Lieut. H. P., wounded, 33 ; Capt., 41, 42 ; wounded, 43
Foster, C.S.M. P., 9
Foster, 2/Lieut. P. G., wounded, 115
Foster, Capt. R. C. G., 102, 103, 104, 127, 129, 130, 136
Four-Company Organization, 6
Fowler, 2/Lieut. A. C. S., killed, 53
Fowler, 2/Lieut. C. D. M., 24 ; killed, 33
Fox, 2/Lieut. M. S., killed, 202 ; Capt., 237
Fox, Lieut. M. V., 9, 17 ; Capt., killed, 20
France, 10th Bn. returns to, 260 ; 11th Bn., 272
Franklin, 2/Lieut. C., wounded, 206
Freeman, 2/Lieut. N., 225
Freestone, 2/Lieut. C. A., 172 ; wounded, 175
French, F.-M. Sir J., 8, 19 ; resigns command of B.E.F., 37
Fricourt, 232
Friend, Lieut. S. J., 225
Fripp, 2/Lieut. P., wounded, 160 ; Lieut. 162, 169
Frost, Lieut. A. B., 172, 174, 175 ; missing, 227
Frost, 2/Lieut. E. G., 146, 244
Fuller, Capt. W. B., 84, 85, 90 ; killed, 97
Furness, Capt. F. L., 274 ; wounded, 275
Furze, 2/Lieut. E. K. B., 84, 85 ; wounded, 91, 97, 109, 110

GABB, 2/Lieut. G. M., 84, 85 ; wounded, 91 ; Capt., 127
Gabb, Capt. H. P., 179-81 ; wounded, 183
Gabb, 2/Lieut. J. D., 179, 180
Gadd, 2/Lieut. A. G., wounded, 217
Gadner, 2/Lieut., 111
Galbraith, Lieut. V. H., 179, 180
Gallipoli, 148 et seq.
Gammon, 2/Lieut. A. T., wounded, 243
Garbett, Capt. H. G., 246
Garden, 2/Lieut. J. J., killed, 222
Gardiner, Capt. H. D., 278
Garnier, Capt. J. W., wounded, 97
Garratt, C.S.M., 278
Garyne, 2/Lieut. W. T., 107
Gaynor, Capt. G. C., R.A.M.C., 63
Gaza, 156, 157, 160
German offensive of 1918, 24, 62, 204, 225, 247, 260, 272, 278
Germany, 11th Bn. advances into, 278
Gheluvelt, 1st Bn. at, 23-24 ; fighting at, 89, 90, 114
Ghent, 86
Gibbs, 2/Lieut. G. N., 252
Gibraltar, 2nd Bn. at, 82, 83
Gibson, 2/Lieut. W. G., 111 ; Capt., 113, 118, 121
Gibson, Pte., 74
Gibstone, 2/Lieut. H. C., 140 ; Capt., 146

# INDEX

Giles, 2/Lieut. W. J., killed, 205
Gillies, 2/Lieut. J., killed, 103
Gilliland, 2/Lieut. H. S., 171 ; wounded, 173
Gillott, Lieut. A., 147
Glasgow, Major W. J. T., 5 ; Lieut.-Col., 211, 212
Glencorse Wood, 222, 223
Goatcher, L./Sergt. W. N., 173
Godlonton, Lieut. B. G., 186
Godfrey, Lieut. F., 37 ; Capt., 38, 52, 53
Godley, Lieut.-Gen., 233
Goldberg, 2/Lieut. G. B., killed, 30
Golding, 2/Lieut. J. H., 213 ; wounded, 216
Gommecourt, 262
Gosney, Capt. H. J., 140 ; Major, 145, 146
Gosney, Lieut. L. L., 146
Graham-Clark, Major R. C., 267
Grant, 2/Lieut. A. F. M., gassed, died, 240
Grant, Capt. W. H. C., 225
Grave di Papadopoli, 122 *et seq.*
Gray, 2/Lieut. W. C., wounded, 232
Green, Drummer, 18
Green, R.S.M., 183
Green, 2/Lieut. B. de W., 63 ; killed, 66
Green, 2/Lieut. C. E., killed, 115
Green, Lieut.-Col. E. W. B., 285
Green, Lieut.-Col. H. W., 73 ; wounded, 74
Green, 2/Lieut. L. S. P., killed, 244
Green, Major and Qr.Mr. J., 140
Greener, Lieut. N. B., 146
Greer, Major and Qr.Mr. J., 140 ; Lieut.-Col., 146
Griffin, 2/Lieut. C. J., 104 ; Capt., killed, 106
Griffin, 2/Lieut. T. F., wounded, 160
Grigg, Major R. M., 48
Grinham, Cpl., 144
Gripper, Lieut. W. V. T., 92
Groombridge, Lieut. K. C., 146
Gross, 2/Lieut. W. H. B., killed, 47
Grove, C.S.M. H., 210
Groves, 2/Lieut. G. L., 140 ; Capt., 145, 146
Grundy, C.Q.M.S. J. F., 9
Grylls, Major A. R., 225, 237
Guards of Honour, Prince of Wales, 1
Gunner, 2/Lieut. H., 187
Gurrey, 2/Lieut. P., 39 ; Capt., 41 ; wounded, 43
Gwynne, Lieut.-Col. R. V., wounded, 256, 257

HADDON-SMITH, 2/Lieut. W. B., 81 ; Lieut., 82, 83 ; Capt., killed, 97
Haggard, Lieut. A. J. R., 68 ; gassed, 69 ; wounded, 213
Haggard, Lieut. B. C., 127, 130, 133, 211 ; wounded, 212, 215 ; wounded, 216
Haggard, Lieut. C. A., 211 ; wounded, 213
Haig, Lieut. A. L., 225
Haig, Lieut.-Gen. Sir D., 8
Haig, 2/Lieut. E. F. G., 104 ; wounded, 105
Haigh, 2/Lieut. C. R., 83, 85, 89 ; killed, 91
Hakes, 2/Lieut. F., wounded, 112 ; Capt., wounded, 206
Haldane, Lieut.-Gen. J. H. L., 200
Hall, Major A. K. D., 252
Hall, 2/Lieut. C. E., 225
Hall, 2/Lieut. C. S., killed, 194
Hall, 2/Lieut. S., 246
Hamilton, 2/Lieut. A. P., 81, 82 ; Lieut., 83
Hamilton, General Sir I., 147, 152

Hamilton, Major-Gen. E. O. F., 8 ; to be Col. of Regiment, 27 ; resigns colonelcy, 78
Hamilton, 2/Lieut. G. S. C., 242 ; Lieut., killed, 244
Hammond, 2/Lieut. C. C., wounded, 217
Hammond, Orderly-Room Sergt., 127
Hancock, 2/Lieut. G. O., wounded, 115
Handford, 2/Lieut. C. W., wounded, 206
Handscombe, Lieut. H. T., 186
Harding, 2/Lieut. R., wounded, 199 ; killed, 205
Hare, 2/Lieut. A. D. E. W., 258
Harker, 2/Lieut. J. G., 68 ; wounded, 69
Harland, 2/Lieut. R. E. C., 37, 41 ; wounded, 43 ; Lieut., 127, 130
Harper, Capt. R. H., 172
Harrild, 2/Lieut. R. A., 130
Harrison, Lieut. H. L., 37 ; Capt., 41, 54
Harrison, 2/Lieut. G. B., 179, 180
Harrison, 2/Lieut. R. J., 160 ; wounded, 169
Hart, C.S.M. T., 211
Hart, Capt. J. W., wounded, 261
Hartwell, Pte., 89
Harvey, 2/Lieut. C. L., 225 ; missing, 227
Harvey, 2/Lieut. H. E., wounded, 103
Harvey, 2/Lieut. V. C., 104, 105
Harwood, 2/Lieut. P., wounded, 169
Hassell, 2/Lieut. K. A. H., 225, 228, 229
Hasted, Pte. C., 105
Hastings, Lieut. C. H., 252
Havre, 252, 269
Hawes, 2/Lieut. R. A., 252 ; wounded, 254
Hawkins, 2/Lieut. L. T. S., wounded, 224, 236
Hay, 2/Lieut. A. F. A., 225 ; missing, 227
Hayes, Lieut. J. B., wounded, 22 ; Capt., 104, 105
Hayes, 2/Lieut. W., 5, 9 ; wounded, 17
Hayfield, Capt., 231
Hayley-Bell, Capt. F., wounded, 254 ; Lieut.-Col. 257
Haywood, 2/Lieut. B. G. T., wounded, 169
Hazebrouck, 220, 271
Hazell, Cpl., 275
Head, 2/Lieut. H. A., 267
Heath, 2/Lieut. F. J., 252 ; wounded, 254
Heath, Capt. M. G., 9, 14 ; wounded, 17, 27, 30 ; Lieut.-Col., killed, 99
Heath, Capt. R. L. G., 27, 30, 81-85 ; wounded, 91 ; killed, 99
Heaton, Lieut. D. R., 211, 212 ; wounded, 213 ; Capt., wounded, 217
Hebeler, Capt. R. S., 211 ; killed, 212
Hedley, 2/Lieut. J. C., wounded, 232
Hedley, Lieut. W. J., 267 ; Capt., killed, 270, 277
Heffer, 2/Lieut. A. B., wounded, 249
Helps, Lieut. M. D., 140 ; Capt., 146
Henderson, 2/Lieut. F. G. A., 81
Henderson, Capt. G. D., missing, 263
Henderson, 2/Lieut. J. F., wounded, 199, 225, 228
Heinekey, 2/Lieut. R. G., 93 ; wounded, 97
Henriques, Lieut. R. L. Q., 9 ; killed, 17, 81
Henriques, Lieut. W. Q., 238
Henson, Pte., 61, 62
Hepworth, Capt. A. M., killed, 169
Hepworth, Capt. P. M., 171 ; wounded, 175
Herbert, Lieut. A. S., 189
Herbert, Lieut. C. G., 208 ; killed, 213
Hewett, Capt. H. W., killed, 169
Hewett, 2/Lieut., 218

# INDEX

Hewitt, Capt. A. S., 92
Heyes, 2/Lieut. G. H., wounded, 169
Higgs, 2/Lieut. R. F., killed, 68
Higham, Capt. F. D., wounded, 241
Hill, Lieut.-Col. W. J. M., 165, 168
Hiller, 2/Lieut. A. M., killed, 97
Hillyer, 2/Lieut. S. G., wounded, 160, 169
Hindenburg Line, 204 ; battle of, 67
Hoare, C.S.M., 130
Hobbs, 2/Lieut. E., 102 ; killed, 103
Hodges, Capt. W. L., 179 ; Major, 180, 181
Hodges, 2/Lieut. J. D., wounded, 160, 169
Hodgson, Capt. A. S., 136
Hodgson, C.S.M. A., 9
Hodgson, Capt. C. B. M., wounded, 22
Hodgson, Lieut. H. E. A. 37
Hogan, Capt. A. J., 267 ; wounded, 268
Hogbin, 2/Lieut. E. B., 246
Hogg, Lieut. R. J. J., wounded, 232
Hoggett, 2/Lieut. F. R., wounded, 252
Hohenzollern Redoubt, 189, 191-93
Holden, Major V., wounded, 276
Holland, Lieut.-Gen. Sir A., 250
Holliday, 2/Lieut. J., 45, 51, 52 ; wounded, 53
Holliman, R.Q.M.S., 130
Holliman, Lieut. D., killed, 231
Hollis, Pte. W., 74
Home-coming, 1st Bn., 76, 77
Homewood, Pte., wounded, 173
Hooge Salient, 240
Hook, 2/Lieut. V., 211 ; wounded, 213 ; Capt., killed, 222
Hooke, Lieut.-Col. U. L., 170, 171 ; death of, 172
Hooker, Capt. W. S., 140, 146 ; Major, 164
Hooker, Sergt. J. H., 105
Hoole, 2/Lieut. R. H., killed, 241
Hope, 2/Lieut. P. R., 45
Hopgood, 2/Lieut. J. L., 239, 240
Hopkinson, 2/Lieut. J. A. L., wounded, 99, 253 ; Capt., wounded, 276
Hopoutre, 222
Horne, Major-Gen. H. S., 30
Horsell, C.S.M. W., 85
Horsford, Lieut. J. T., 209
Howard, Lieut. L. W. M., 211 ; killed, 212
Howard, Capt. L. M., 284
Howcroft, 2/Lieut. S. M., wounded, 54, 58
Howell, Lieut. L. B., 146
Howell, 2/Lieut. M. I. B., 27 ; killed, 33
Howell, 2/Lieut. W. J., wounded, 44
Howell, Lieut. R. E., 146
Howells, 2/Lieut. J., 246
Howells, 2/Lieut. J. P., 104 ; wounded, 104 ; Lieut., 105, 113, 115 ; Capt., wounded, 118
Hudson, 2/Lieut. E. H., wounded, 204
Hughes, Lieut. F. W. T., wounded, 160, 169
Hughes, 2/Lieut. I. T. P., 50 ; wounded, 57, 59 ; Lieut., 63, 66, 69 ; wounded, 128, 130, 133, 136
Hull, Lieut. H. C. E., 189
Hullcoop, 2/Lieut. E. F., 111 ; wounded, 112
Humphreys, 2/Lieut. D. F., 92 ; killed, 97
Hunt, Lieut. F. R. W., wounded, 22
Hunt, 2/Lieut. J. A., wounded, 227
Hunter, Capt. H. N. A., 9, 17, 20 ; wounded, 22
Hurry, Lieut. W. F., 146

ILOTT, Capt. C. H. T., R.A.M.C., gassed, 249

Incledon-Webber, Brig.-Gen., 201
India, 2nd Bn. embarks for, 127 ; trouble in, 129
Ingham, Sergt. E., 105
Ingpen, Lieut. N. C., 211
Ingram, Lieut. C. D., wounded, 183
Ingram, Lieut. C. G. F., missing, 160
Ingram, 2/Lieut. G. S., 84, 85, 88 ; killed, 91
Inkster, 2/Lieut. L., 252
Inman, C.S.M. H., 210
Innes, 2/Lieut. J., wounded, 111, 225 ; wounded, 233
Inverness Copse, 57, 222, 223
Inwood, 2/Lieut. D. L., 113 ; wounded, 115
Ionides, Capt. G. A., 172
Ireland, 1st Bn. proceeds to, 78 ; leaves, 79
Iremonger, Lieut. H. E., 9 ; wounded, 18 ; Major, 62, 63
Iron Crosses, 195
Ismailia, 154, 155
Ismail Oglu Tepe, 151
Italy, British force in, 116 ; 7th Division leaves for, 116, 117 ; King of, inspects, 125 ; 10th Bn. to, 258, 259 ; 11th Bn. to, 271
Ive, 2/Lieut. D., 84, 85 ; killed, 91

JACKMAN, 2/Lieut. O., 72 ; killed, 74
Jackson, 2/Lieut. C., 82
Jackson, 2/Lieut., 274, 275
Jacob, Lieut. F. A., wounded, 103, 127, 130
Jacob, Capt., 118
Jacobs, 2/Lieut. G. P. S., 48 ; missing, 53
Jakes, 2/Lieut. P. G., 63, 68 ; wounded, 69, 71
Jandola, 130
Jardine, Lieut. J. E. B., 179, 180
Jardine, 2/Lieut. L. W., 179, 180 ; wounded, 182
Jarvis, Major T. McL., 252 ; wounded, 254
Javes, 2/Lieut. R. C., killed, 254
Jebens, Bt. Major F. J., 136
Jeddere-Fisher, Major H. C., 211
Jefferis, Lieut. A. R., 140
Jeffreys, Lieut.-Col. J. W., 278
Jelley, L./Cpl. S., 223
Jenkins, Lieut. G. E., wounded, 232
Jennings, 2/Lieut. R. A. V., wounded, 169
Jephson, Lieut. C. M. W., killed, 169
Jerusalem, capture of, 164
John, 2/Lieut. A. H., 171
Johnson, Lieut. D. G. K., 146 ; wounded, 160, 169
Johnson, Lieut. R. E., wounded, 194
Johnson, 2/Lieut. P. W., killed, 30
Johnson, 2/Lieut. E. E., wounded, 103
Johnson, 2/Lieut. E. G., missing, 238
Johnson, Sergt. A., 242
Johnston, Capt. D. C., 252 ; wounded, 254
Joiner, 2/Lieut. A. E., 269
Jonas, 2/Lieut. L. N., wounded, 245
Jones, C.S.M., 65
Jordon, Capt. E., wounded,
Jordon, Lieut. and Qr.Mr. B. W., 267
Joynson-Hicks, 2/Lieut. R. C., wounded, 32, 33

KAILANA, 128
Kantara, 154, 155, 165
Katia, Oasis of, 154
Kavanagh, Rev. B., killed, 169
Kaye, 2/Lieut. W. E., 248

# INDEX

Keep, 2/Lieut. A. L., 267
Keith, Capt. S., 140
Kelly, Capt. S., 140, 267 ; killed, 270
Kelly-Kenny, Gen. Sir T., death of, 27
Kemp, 2/Lieut. C. G., 48, 50 ; wounded, 54 ; killed, 59
Kempster, Brig.-Gen. F., 100
Kemp-Welch, Lieut.-Col. M., 62, 63, 64, 65, 68, 82, 211, 212
Kenrick, Capt. G. E. R., 81, 82, 83
Kenny, Lieut. B. M., 9 ; wounded, 17
Khoja Chemen Tepe, 148 *et seq.*
King Edward, death of, 5
King George, accession of, 5
King, message from, 74, 125
King, Lieut. and Qr.Mr. G., 252
King-King, Major J. G., 82 ; Lieut.-Col., 83
King's Colour, 6th Bn., 210 ; 7th Bn., 236 ; 8th Bn., 250 ; 10th Bn., 266 ; 11th Bn., 278
Kirk, 2/Lieut. F. C. de L., 182
Kirkpatrick, Major H. F., 93 ; killed, 97, 98
Kitchener, F.-M. Lord, 10, 152, 188, 237
Kitchin, 2/Lieut. A. W. B., 211 ; killed, 212
Kitchingman, 2/Lieut. C. S., wounded, 271
Koebel, Capt. and Adjt. C. E. 5
Knight, 2/Lieut. J. O. C., killed, 204
Knight, C.S.M., 230
Knowles, Pte. A., 92
Kruiseecke, fighting at, 23, 89, 90
Kut, 180, 181

La Boisselle, 193, 195, 231, 232
Lacey, 2/Lieut. H. V., 53, 58
La Clytte, 256, 274
Ladha, 131, 133
Laing, 2/Lieut. W. W. A., 136
Lake, 2/Lieut. M. B. C., wounded, 245
Lakins, Cpl., 274
Lamond, Cpl. F., 92
Landon, Brig.-Gen. H. J. S., 6, 22, 25 ; Major-Gen., 36, 44
Lane-Nichols, 2/Lieut. D. W., 240 ; killed, 241
Lang-Browne, 2/Lieut. J. A., 82 ; Lieut., 83-85 ; wounded, 91 ; Capt., killed, 97
Langhorne, 2/Lieut. E. H., 45 ; wounded, 47
Langley, Capt. A. A., 267
Lansdowne, Lieut. E., wounded, 273
Lancaster, 2/Lieut. J. B., wounded, 224 ; wounded, 232
Lancaster, 2/Lieut. J. T., wounded, 231
La Panne, 271
Latham, Capt. A. T., 172
Laslett, Capt. W. H., R.A.M.C., 225
Laughlin, 2/Lieut. P. H., wounded, 160 ; killed, 169
Lawford, Brig.-Gen. S. T. B. 84, 93
Lawrence, Capt. and Adjt., 252 ; died of wounds, 254
Lawson, Pte. G., 74
Le Bas, 2/Lieut. O. V., wounded, 21, 27
Le Bas, Capt. R. S., 211
Leckie, Lieut. L. H., wounded, 124
Lee, Lieut.-Col. H. H., 69, 70
Lee, Major-Gen. R. P., 220, 223, 233
Lee, Lieut. R. T., 81, 82 ; Capt., wounded, 93 ; Lieut.-Col., 278, 279

Legge, 2/Lieut. L. St.C., 213 ; missing, 216
Leighton, Lieut. P. L., 128, 130
Lemnos, 150
Lennard, Lieut.-Col. E. W., 224
Lessels, 2/Lieut. R. M., killed, 166, 169
Lewis, Capt. H. F., 83-85, 87 ; killed, 91
Lewis, 2/Lieut. G. M., 267
Leuze Wood, 233
Liddell, Lieut.-Col. E. M., 225
Limbrick, 2/Lieut., 110
Lincoln, 2/Lieut. S. W., 146
Lindlar, 278
Lindup, 2/Lieut. C. A., 267
Lines, 2/Lieut. F. R., wounded, 217
Lippiatt, 2/Lieut. W. G., killed, 207
Livesay, Lieut. F. H., wounded, 233
Livesay, Lieut.-Col. R. O. H., 206
Lloyd, 2/Lieut. C., 213 ; wounded, 216
Lloyd, 2/Lieut. J. E., 104 ; wounded, 107
Lloyd, 2/Lieut. R. C., 45 ; killed, 47
Lloyd, 2/Lieut. R. S., 183
Lockwood, L./Cpl. G., wounded, 132
Lodge, 2/Lieut. A. P. D., wounded, 271
Lodge-Patch, Lieut., R.A.M.C., 244
Lofting, Lieut. F. C. G., wounded, 238
Lomax, Major-Gen. S. H., 6, 18, 25
Long, 2/Lieut. A. W. E., killed, 44
Longbourne, Capt. F. C., 9, 17, 18 ; wounded, 20, 81, 82, 99 ; Lieut.-Col., 104, 110, 279
Longbourne, Capt. H. R., 216, 217 ; killed, 222
Longbourne, Lieut. W. L. J., killed, 169
Looker, 2/Lieut. L., killed, 244
Loos, Battle of, 31 *et seq.*, 99 *et seq.*, 189 *et seq.*, 238
Love, 2/Lieut. R., 267
Love, 2/Lieut. H. O., wounded, 270
Lovell, 2/Lieut. A. H., 171 ; wounded, 175
Lover, Pte. E., 104
Lowen, Pte., killed, 119
Lucas, C.S.M., 85
Lucknow, 135, 136, 179
Ludd, 165
Luxmoore, 2/Lieut. E. C. L., 189
Lukyn, 2/Lieut. S. E., 37, 38, 41 ; Capt., wounded, 44
Lyndhurst, 2nd Bn. camped at, 84
Lys River, 263, 264, 276

Mabe, C.S.M. W. T., 211
McAfee, Lieut. W. G., R.A.M.C., 113
McArtney, C.Q.M.S. A., 9
McCabe, 2/Lieut. H. P., 172
McCabe, Lieut. A. W. E., 78
McCabe, Sergt. A., 48 ; Lieut., 97 ; wounded, 98
McCarthy, 2/Lieut. J., wounded, 205
MacDermott, 2/Lieut. L. A., killed, 249
McDonald, Lieut. W., 267
McGregor, Sergt., 236
McIver, Capt. C. D., wounded, 169
McKenzie, Lieut. A., 267 ; killed, 270
Mackenzie, Capt. A. E., R.A.M.C., 171 ; wounded, 175
MacLennan, Lieut. N. L., 146
McKinless, 2/Lieut. F. J., wounded, 232
McNair, Capt. F. R., wounded, 205
McNamara, Capt. A. E., 9 ; wounded, 17
McNaught, Capt. J. McG., killed, 169
McWhinnie, Lieut. C. R., died of wounds, 206

# INDEX

Mackworth, Lieut. J. W., 83
Maddock, Capt. R. H., 99, 104, 105
Mahon, Brig.-General, 1
Mahsuds, country of the, 129
Maisey, 2/Lieut. A. G., wounded, 196
Makin, 132
Mallett, Lieut. H., 63, 68; gassed, 69
Mametz, 212, 213; Wood, 104
Mance, 2/Lieut. H. E., killed, 254
Mangles, Capt. R. H., 81
Manicon, 2/Lieut. J. H., 201; wounded, 204
Mann, Major D., 210
Mann, 2/Lieut., 191
Manning, Sergt., wounded, 87
Mapleson, 2/Lieut. G. H., killed, 161, 169
Marsh, R.Q.M.S. H., 74
Marshall, 2/Lieut. H., 225
Marston, 2/Lieut. A. B., wounded, 216
Martin, Capt. H. L., 211; killed, 217
Martin, 2/Lieut. T., 269; killed, 270
Martin, C.S.M. W., 85
Martinpuich, 42
Mason, Lieut. H., 146
Mason, Lieut. S. J., wounded, 175
Master, Capt. C. E. H., 179
Master, Lieut. H. F. H., 81-83; Capt., 84; died of wounds, 88, 91
Matheson, Major-General T. G., 133, 134
Mathew-Lannowe, Capt. E. B., 9; wounded, 17; Lieut.-Colonel, 131, 133-136
Matthews, L./Cpl. H. P., wounded, 173
Matthews, 2/Lieut. H. J., wounded, 209
Maud, 2/Lieut. W. M., 140, 146
Maude, Gen. Sir S., 184-6
Maudling, Lieut. L. G., 276
Mawditt, Colour-Sergt., 4, 103
Maxse, Major-General F. I., 211; Lieut.-General, 213, 220
Maxwell, 2/Lieut. L. E. L., 130, 133
May, 2/Lieut. P. E., wounded, 276
Mayne, Brig.-General C. R. G., 61
Mellor, Capt. A. R. I., 261
Memorial Window, Guildford Church, unveiling of, 6
Menhinick, Lieut. J. S., 146
Menin, advance on, 87
Mercer, Lieut. J. L. C., 179, 180
Messom, 2/Lieut. H., 92; wounded, 97
Meteren, 63, 189, 241, 256
Middleton, 2/Lieut. G. C., wounded, 204, 209
Middleton, L./Cpl., 92
Middleton, R.S.M. A. C., 267
Millard, 2/Lieut. D. E. H., 45; killed, 53
Millard, 2/Lieut. E. J., wounded, 245
Miller, 2/Lieut. J. F., killed, 213
Miles, Pte. T., 74
Milner, 2/Lieut. J. S., 41; missing, 43; wounded, 59, 68
Mitchell, 2/Lieut. A. R., 225
Mitford, Brig.-General B. R., 237
Mobilization ordered, 8
Mohmands, operations against, 141 *et seq.*
Monchy-le-Preux, 201
Monro, Major-General C. C., 6; General Sir C., 28, 39; appointed Colonel of Regiment, 78, 80, 98, 128, 135, 152, 193
Mons, 11 *et seq.*; retreat from begins, 13

Montague-Bates, Capt. F. S., 91
Montauban, 106
Monteagle-Browne, Capt. E., 91
Montello, The, 118, 119
Monk, Lieut. F. J., wounded, 255
Monk, Sergt., 21
Moon, 2/Lieut. D., 274; wounded, 275
Moore, Capt. E. A., gassed, 249
Morgan, 2/Lieut. C. O. W., 113; Lieut., 128, 130, 133, 136
Morgan, 2/Lieut. W. J. C., wounded, 66, 68; gassed, 69
Morley, Pte. H., 104
Mormal Forest, 234, 235
Morris, 2/Lieut. F., killed, 183
Morris, 2/Lieut. W. T., wounded, 233
Morris, Cpl., 98
Morris, Pte. A. E., 230
Morrison, 2/Lieut. J. G. S., 37, 38; wounded, 39, 225, 228
Morse, 2/Lieut. W. S., 242
Morton, Lieut. G. C., 179, 180; Capt., 186
Moss, Capt. C. G., 172; wounded, 175
Moss, 2/Lieut. R. L., 140, 146
Moultrie, 2/Lieut. F. J. F., 72
Mountford, Lieut. E. W., 179, 180; Capt., wounded, 186, 187
Mundye, 2/Lieut. A., 37, 41, 104
Murray, 2/Lieut. C. P., 135, 136
Mushett, 2/Lieut. E., 127, 128, 130

NASARIYEH, 181, 183
Neale, Capt. G. H., 5
Nebi Samwil, 164
Needham, Capt. R., 26
Neilson-Terry, 2/Lieut. D., 211
Nelson, 2/Lieut. E. H., wounded, 219
Nevins, R.Q.M.S. R., 9, 26, 48; Capt., 63, 68
New, Capt. C. E., 26
Newman, Lieut. T., 279
Nicholas, 2/Lieut. W. L. J., 27, 37
Nicholls, L./Cpl., 274
Nieuport, 56, 57
Noble, 2/Lieut. A. T. L., wounded, 107
Nœux-les-Mines, 238
Norman, Lieut. J., 225
Norman, 2/Lieut. K. V., 45; wounded, 47
North, Lieut.-Colonel E. B., 262
North, Lieut. W. A., gassed, 69
Northover, 2/Lieut. H., wounded, 205, 209
Nowshera, 140
Noyon, 225

OAKLEY, Lieut.-Colonel R., 252; wounded, 254
O'Brien, 2/Lieut. R. H., 93
O'Byrne, 2/Lieut. D. C. H., 267
O'Connell, 2/Lieut. J. H., 239
O'Connor, 2/Lieut. D. R. J., 172; wounded, 175
Ogden, 2/Lieut. A., 225; missing, 227
Oldfield, 2/Lieut. G. C. O., 82; Lieut., 83
Olliver, Major (Temp.) G. K., 68, 84, 127, 130, 133-135
Ord, Capt. W., wounded, 204
Origin of the war, 7
Ormerod, 2/Lieut. T. L., wounded, 189, 194
Orpen, 2/Lieut. H. F., 189
Osborne, 2/Lieut. O. J. F., killed, 222

# INDEX

Osborne, Pte. J., 104, 105
Osmond, 2/Lieut. F. E., 187
Ost, 2/Lieut. J., 172; wounded, 175
Oswald, Major K. A., 170, 171; Lieut.-Col., 172; wounded, 175, 177
Otter, Major R., 268; Lieut.-Colonel, 269; wounded, 272; missing, 273
Owen, Lieut.-Colonel, 276
Owen, Pioneer/Sergt., 4
Oxley-Boyle, Lieut. R. F. C., 133, 135, 136

PAIN, 2/Lieut. M. W. H., 6, 9; Lieut., 26
Painter, Pte., 173
Parkes, 2/Lieut. J. W., 256
Parkes, 2/Lieut. L. O., 63, 64; wounded, 66
Parkhill, 2/Lieut. W., 248
Parkinson, Lieut. H. A., wounded, 196
Parnell, 2/Lieut. C., 104, 105
Parnell, Capt. G. B., 26, 27, 30, 32, 37; Major, 41; killed, 42, 43
Parsons, Capt. C., 189
Parsons, 2/Lieut. C. D. H., 136
Parsons, C.S.M. C., 85
Partington, 2/Lieut. O. J., 267
Pascoe, 2/Lieut. C. H., wounded, 91
Pash, Capt. A. L., 203; wounded, 204, 207
Patterson, Lieut. A. C., R.A.M.C., gassed, 69
Payne, 2/Lieut., 239
Pearson, 2/Lieut. D. H., 136
Pedder, Lieut. R. V., 267
Peden, 2/Lieut. G. E., 183
Peirs, Major H. J. C., 238, 239, 240; wounded, 241, 243, 246; Lieut.-Colonel, wounded, 247; gassed, 249
Pell, Lieut.-Colonel B. T., 19; wounded and missing, 24, 83, 89
Pelling, Lieut. F. W., 72
Pelly, Brig.-General R. T., 125
Pemble, 2/Lieut. C. A. L., killed, 169
Penman, 2/Lieut. G. E., 267
Penrose, 2/Lieut. G. A., 240
Penrose - Fitzgerald, 2/Lieut. M. J., 211; wounded, 213
Pentelow, Sergt., 196
Perkins, Col. W. J., 178, 286
Perkins, C.Q.M.S. A., 9
Perkins, 2/Lieut. L., 45; killed, 47
Perry, Pte. A., 83
Peshawar, 140
Petre, Lieut. L. J., 252
Peyton, Major W. R. B., 237
Phelps, 2/Lieut. G. P., 246
Philips, L./Cpl., 87
Philips, 2/Lieut. A. R. T., 160; Capt., wounded, 169
Phillips, 2/Lieut. H. C., killed, 259
Phillips, 2/Lieut. J. G. F., 216; wounded, 217
Phillips, Lieut. W. A., 14
Philpot, Capt. R. H., 69; wounded, 91, 97, 99; wounded, 103, 127, 130, 133-136
Phipps, 2/Lieut. W. G., 225; missing, 227
Piave River, 118; crossing of, 122, 259
Pickard, Capt. and Quartermaster F. B. B., 4, 83; Major, 211, 212
Pickering, 2/Lieut. B. M., 27
Pickering, Lieut. R. E., 128, 129-134

Pike, 2/Lieut. A. J., 189, 191; Capt., wounded, 199, 201, 202
Pilleau, Major H. C., 9; died of wounds, 17
Pilleau, Lieut. G. A., 41; wounded, 99
Pinchbeck, 2/Lieut. R. W., wounded, 113
Pink, Col. F. J., 1, 2, 81
Pinney, Major-General, 45, 53
Pitter, Pte., wounded, 132
Plant, 2/Lieut. P. G., killed, 33
Plowman, 2/Lieut. E., 248; wounded, 250
Plowman-Brown, 2/Lieut. C. H., 48
Plumer, General Sir H., 113, 116, 118, 256-258, 263, 278
Poelcappelle, action of, 224 *et seq.*
Poett, Brig.-General J. H., 211
Pope, 2/Lieut. W. A., 252; Capt., died of wounds, 254
Poperinghe, 222
Polygon Wood, 113, 175, 222; Beek, 174
Ponsford, Pte. C. W., 226
Porter, Lieut. M. C. L., 169, 267; Capt., wounded, 268
Portugal, King and Queen of, 82, 83
Potter, Lieut. A. G., 140; Capt., 146
Potter, 2/Lieut. D. R., 140; Capt., wounded, 146; killed, 169
Potter, Capt. R. W., 140; Major, 146
Pound, Lieut. M. S., 18; died of wounds, 21
Power, 2/Lieut. J. J., killed, 233
Powell, 2/Lieut. A. W., killed, 241
Powell-Jones, Capt. F. A. G., wounded, 206
Pratt, 2/Lieut. W. J., 68; wounded, 69
Pratt, 2/Lieut. G. L., killed, 97
Pratt, Cpl. P., 104
Prescott, Lieut. C. C., 128-130, 136
Pringle, Lieut. R. S., 9; died of wounds, 17
Price, Brig.-General G. D., 218
Price, Capt. C. W. M., 211
Price, Lieut. W. H., wounded, 238
Price, 2/Lieut. A. J., 276
Price, 2/Lieut. A. W., wounded, 270
Prior, Lieut. S. F., wounded, 60
Privett, Pte. J., 74
Protheroe, Major L. R., 280
Proven, 225
Pryce, Capt. W. H., wounded, 169
Puddicombe, C.Q.M.S. W., 85
Puddicombe, 2/Lieut. W. A., 172
Pulteney, General Sir W., 193, 195
Punter, R.Q.M.S. C. E., 211, 217
Purchase, 2/Lieut. G. T., killed, 59
Purdie, Pte., 61, 62
Purfleet, 211
Pym, 2/Lieut. J. S., killed, 197

QUILL, Lieut. B. C., 5

RAEBURN, 2/Lieut. W. A. L., wounded, 103
Rainsford-Hannay, Lieut. J., 81
Ramage, 2/Lieut. D. N., 107
Ramsay, 2/Lieut. D. G., 92; killed, 93
Ramsay, Major-General Sir J., 237
Ranger, 2/Lieut. E., 225; wounded, 227
Ranson, 2/Lieut. S. J., 252, 253
Rattey, R.Q.M.S. W., 4
Rawal Pindi, 1
Rawlinson, General, 87, 91, 193, 235

# INDEX

Rawlinson, 2/Lieut. A. R., 189
Rawson, 2/Lieut. F. P. S., 15
Raynham, 2/Lieut. H., 252
Read, 2/Lieut. M. R., 189
Read, Lieut. W. D. B., 146
Reeder, Lieut. and Qrmr. E. J. W., 179, 180; Capt., 187
Reeves, Lieut. E. E., 278
Reeves, Lieut. P. A., wounded, 249
Relf-West, 2/Lieut. T. P., wounded, 233
Reilly, 2/Lieut. H. D. R., 140; Capt., killed, 146
Regiments, British—Cavalry: Scots Greys, 13. Infantry: Bedfordshire, 2, 223; Buffs, 194, 196, 200, 205, 207, 209, 211, 214, 225, 232-239, 246; Cameronians, 61, 65, 66, 68; Durham L.I. 140, 267; E. Surrey, 194, 196, 200, 204, 211-214, 225, 232, 234, 237; Essex, 6, 36; Gloucester, 8; Highland L.I., 31, 41, 42, 57, 72; Irish Guards, 34, 88; King's Royal Rifle Corps, 41, 42, 51, 53, 72, 252; Lincoln, 196; London Scottish, 29; Manchester, 100, 103, 111, 114; Middlesex, 36, 214, 216, 267; Munster Fusiliers 26; Norfolk, 129, 140, 212, 213; Northampton, 214, 234; North Staffordshire, 239; Oxford and Buckinghamshire, 31; Rifle Brigade, 193; Royal Fusiliers, 241, 246, 252; Royal Inniskilling Fusiliers, 30; Royal Warwickshire, 84; Royal Welch Fusiliers, 84; Royal West Kent, 194, 196, 201, 207, 209, 211, 214, 216, 237, 267; Scottish Rifles, 61, 64-66, 68, 70, 71, 73; Sherwood Foresters, 114; Somerset L.I., 6, 140; South Staffordshire, 84, 100, 111, 113, 114, 174; South Wales Borderers, 8, 11, 15, 20, 23; Welch, 6, 8, 15, 16, 23; Worcester, 31, 36, 41, 42, 51, 57; Australian, 175; Indian, 4th Gurkhas, 130; 6th Gurkhas, 131; 11th Gurkhas, 132; 25th Punjabis, 131, 132; 28th 130; 30th, 130; 39th Garhwalis, 185; 44th Merwara, 181; 46th Punjabis, 140; 90th, 181, 185; 94th Infantry, 140; 109th, 131; 112th, 181; 114th, 181; 121st, 181.
Regiments, Infantry, German, 52, 92, 176, 242
Reutelbeeke, 57
Reynolds, 2/Lieut. F. D., 241
Ribton-Cooke, 2/Lieut. H., 50, 55; Capt., 63
Richards, 2/Lieut. H. H., 37, 41; wounded, 43; killed, 111
Richebourg l'Avoué, 96
Richman, 2/Lieut. L. V., gassed, 232
Rider, Capt. F. S., 243; wounded, 245
Ridpath, 2/Lieut. F. C. L., killed, 169
Riley, 2/Lieut. M. R., 146
Ritchie, Lieut.-Colonel Hon. H., 70, 71; died of wounds, 72
Roberts, Lieut. F. J., 81-83; Capt., 189
Roberts, Lieut. G. H., wounded, 164; Capt., wounded, 169
Roberts, Lieut. A. N. S., 82-84; wounded, Capt., 91; Major, 130, 133, 136
Roberts, F.M. Lord, presents Colours to 4th Bn., 138
Roberts, 2/Lieut. J. T., 102, 103-105; killed, 207
Robinson, 2/Lieut. A. G., wounded, 169
Robinson, 2/Lieut. W. A. L., 41; wounded, 43; killed, 270
Robinson, 2/Lieut. L. M., wounded, 222
Robson, Lieut.-Colonel H. D., 81, 82

Robson, 2/Lieut. A. F., 195, 196, 252; Capt., wounded, 254; wounded, 261
Rodger, Capt. F. McG., 146
Roe, Capt. E. A., killed, 167, 169
Roe, Major C. D., 130
Roffe, 2/Lieut. C. W., 37, 41
Roger, 2/Lieut. J. L., wounded, 169
Rogers, 2/Lieut. C. W., wounded, 217
Rolls, Lieut.-Colonel N. T., 284
Rolph, Pte. W., 4
Rope, 2/Lieut. J. A., killed, 44
Roper, Major S. D., 140, 142, 144; Lieut.-Col., 146, 164, 165
Rose, Capt. A. M., R.A.M.C., 9; missing, 24
Rosenbaum, Pte., 173
Rose-Troup, Lieut. J. M., 18; missing, 24
Roskilly, 2/Lieut. A., killed, 222
Ross, 2/Lieut. R. K., 84, 85, 90; Lieut., 91; Capt., 127, 130, 133
Ross-Hurst, 2/Lieut. K. W., 136
Rouges-Bancs, 96
Rought, 2/Lieut. C. S., 92
Roulers, 87
Rouquette, 2/Lieut. J. H., 41; killed, 43
Routley, R.Q.M.S. W., 85; R.S.M., 105
Rowland, Capt. R. H., gassed, 240; Major, 247
Royle, Capt. C. T., wounded, 273
Rudkin, 2/Lieut. J. A., 70, 72
Rudland, 2/Lieut. W. R., 70
Russell, 2/Lieut. J. E., wounded, 219
Russell-Stower, Major C. A., 211
Russen, 2/Lieut. F., 63, 64; wounded, 66
Rutherford, 2/Lieut. R. B., 189; Capt., killed, 194
Rutter, 2/Lieut. F. L., 104; killed, 105
Ryan, 2/Lieut. H. E., wounded, 270; wounded, 271; Capt., missing, 273
Rylands, Capt. F., 130

Sageman, C.S.M. F., 211
St. George, 2/Lieut. K. M., wounded, 169
St. Omer, 239
Salt Lake, Suvla, 150
Saltmarshe, 2/Lieut. O. E., 211; Lieut., killed, 213
Sambre River, 234
Samson, Lieut., 243
Samuelson, Capt. V. F., 171; wounded, 175
Sandells, Cpl., 275
Sanders, 2/Lieut. E. F., 239; gassed, 240
Sandiford, Capt. V. V. V., 189
Saunders, 2/Lieut. A. E., 76
Savereux, 2/Lieut. E., 186; wounded, 254
Sawyer, Lieut.-Col. G. H., 176
Scarpe River, 198, 200
Scheldt Canal, 209, 249; River, 264, 277
Scherpenberg, 66, 167
Schlam, Major S. B., 285
Schunck, 2/Lieut. R. S., died of wounds, 23
Schult, 2/Lieut. E., 107; died of wounds, 115
Schwaben Redoubt, 216, 217
Scott, Capt. G H. H., 211; killed, 213
Scott, Major-General A. B., 200, 202, 204, 206
Scott, 2/Lieut. A. N., 216; wounded, 217, 236
Scott, 2/Lieut. R. W., wounded, 254
Scrivener, 2/Lieut. E. R., wounded, 245
Secretan, 2/Lieut. H. B., 104; wounded, 105; Capt., wounded, 113

305

# INDEX

Selfe, 2/Lieut. B. C., 45
Selle River, 70, 71, 234, 248
Sells, 2/Lieut. A. J., wounded, 194
Semple, 2/Lieut. W. J., 189
Serley, 2/Lieut. W. F., 253
Servante, 2/Lieut. A. W., killed, 233
Shales, Sergt., 85, 130
Shakespeare, 2/Lieut. R. P., 136
Sharman, 2/Lieut. D. R., wounded, 196
Sharp, 2/Lieut. C. G., wounded, 273
Sharpe, Capt. W. C., 267
Sharpe, Lieut. A. J., 146
Shaw, Colonel A. G., 282
Sheppard, 2/Lieut. J. H., killed, 232
Shilcock, Lieut. J. W., 179
Ships, R.N.—*Carnarvon*, 84; *Europa*, 84; *Hyacinth*, 84; *Leviathan*, 84; *Minerva*, 139
Shipton, 2/Lieut. J. E., 55; gassed, 69
Shorncliffe, 81
Short, Lieut. R. H., 127
Short, 2/Lieut. W. J., killed, 217
Shortman, 2/Lieut. H. V., 252
Shoubridge, Major-General, 111, 113
Shuldham-Legh, Lieut. M. S., 128, 130, 211; wounded, 213
Shuter, 2/Lieut. F. P., wounded, 115
Sialkote, 1
Sillem, Lieut. J. H., 127, 128, 130, 134
Sillem, 2/Lieut. R. O., wounded, 99; Lieut., wounded, 113
Sillence, C.Q.M.S. H., 85
Simmons, Capt. W. G., 225, 230
Simmons, 2/Lieut. F. L., 189
Skeet, 2/Lieut. J. R., 172
Skeet, Lieut., killed, 228
Sladen, Major St. B. R., 179; Lieut.-Colonel 61; killed, 62; 283
Slatter, 2/Lieut. R. P., 37; Capt., 41; killed, 43
Smallpiece, Major F. W., 179, 180
Smith, Capt. H. W., 82; Major, 100
Smith, Capt. R. C., 267
Smith, Lieut. J. R., 238
Smith, 2/Lieut. A. J., killed, 271
Smith, 2/Lieut. G. G., wounded, 103, 110; killed, 112
Smith, 2/Lieut. L. P., 48
Smith, 2/Lieut. W., wounded, 91
Smith, 2/Lieut. T. B., 267; killed, 270
Smith, Pte., wounded, 172
Smith, Sergt., 18
Smith, R.S.M. W., 85
Smith, R.S.M. C. E., 211
Smith-Dorrien, General Sir H., 8
Snell, Capt. J. E., 225, 230, 231; wounded, 233
Snow, General, 53
Soames, Capt. C. F., 22; wounded and missing, 24, 89
Somme, Battles of, 41, 101, 108, 193, 212, 242, 253
Sowrey, 2/Lieut. J., 189
Sparkes, Lieut. R. B., 246
Spencer, 2/Lieut. E. W., missing, 273
Spens, Lieut. W. P., 179, 180
Spicer, Capt. R. W., killed, 160, 169
Spooner, Cpl., 52; Sergt., 55
Squarey, 2/Lieut. D. N. P., 118; Lieut., 127

Stacey, Capt. and Adjutant W. H., 146; wounded, 238
Stacey, Colour-Sergt., 4
Stacke, Capt. R. C., 93; Major, killed, 97
Stallard, 2/Lieut. H. J., 248
Stanley-Creek, Capt. S. F., wounded, 9, 17, 18, 21; missing, 24
Stanners, Sergt. H., 105
Stedman, Capt., wounded, 231
Stedman, 2/Lieut. H. A., wounded, 245
Stedman, 2/Lieut. L. G., wounded, 245
Stemp, C.S.M. A., 9
Stenhouse, Capt. H. W., 26, 27, 82, 83
Step, 2/Lieut. G. E., wounded, 224
Stevens, Pte. W., 74
Stevenson, 2/Lieut. J. C., killed, 207
Stevenson, 2/Lieut. G., 45, 63
Stewart, Lieut. W. A., R.A.M.C., 97; wounded, 98
Stilwell, Sergt., 26
Stone, Lieut. H. C., 146
Stones, 2/Lieut. W., 146
Stoop, 2/Lieut. A. D., 179, 180; wounded, 186
Storey, Capt. F. B., 37
Stovold, Capt. P. A., missing, 106
Stranger, 2/Lieut. W., 37; wounded, 47
Strawson, 2/Lieut. F. G., killed, 276
Streeter, Capt., 115, 118
Streeter, Sergt. E., 74
Strickland, Major-General Sir E., 78
Stringer, 2/Lieut. G. F., wounded, 169
Strode, 2/Lieut. M. G., wounded, 99
Strong, 2/Lieut. H. B., 9; killed, 23
Strudwick, 2/Lieut. J. M. K., wounded, 205
Sullivan, 2/Lieut. A. M., 236
Sullivan, R.S.M. G., 130
Sullivan, Pte., 21
Sundall, Lieut. C. E., R.A.M.C., 211
Sutherland, Capt. F., 252, 253
Suvla, 148; evacuation of, 153
Swain, Lieut. T. E., wounded, 249
Sweeney, C.S.M. E., 9
Sweet, 2/Lieut. H. G., 63; wounded, 66; killed, 169
Sweetman, Lieut. T. W., R.A.M.C., wounded, 254
Swindell, 2/Lieut. A. C., killed, 224
Sworder, Capt. J. P., killed, 283
Symons, 2/Lieut. I. W. S., 37; Capt., 136

TABUTEAU, Capt. T. H. B., 130
Tagliamento, passage of, 124, 125
Tank, 130, 133
Tanqueray, Lieut. T., wounded, 24
Tara Hill, 231, 232
Tasker, 2/Lieut. S. E., 276
Taylor, Lieut. A. J., 186
Taylor, Lieut.-Col. A. W., 5, 6, 81
Taylor, 2/Lieut. H. D., 44, 189
Taylor, Sergt. A., 6
Taylor-Jones, 2/Lieut. C., 97; killed, 99
Tedder, C.S.M., 130
Thatcher, Lieut. F. G., R.A.M.C., 85
Thatcher, 2/Lieut. H. D., wounded 217
Thatcher, Lieut. L. H. F., R.A.M.C., wounded, 91
Thiepval, 216
Thom, 2/Lieut. P. E., wounded and missing, 220

# INDEX

Thomas, 2/Lieut. A. G. I., wounded, 169
Thomas, Lieut. A. C., 84, 85; killed, 91
Thomas, 2/Lieut. D. J., killed, 169
Thomas, 2/Lieut. W. P., 171
Thomas, Lieut. R. O. V., 70, 71, 111
Thompson, 2/Lieut. H. J. P., 9
Thompson, 2/Lieut. H. M., missing, 53
Thompson, 2/Lieut. G. P., 26
Thompson, Capt. R. G., 238; wounded, 273
Thornycroft, Capt. J. R. M., killed, 21
Thornycroft, 2/Lieut. E. C., wounded, 103
Thrupp, Lieut. C. G. D., 41, 42, 50, 99
Tidy, 2/Lieut. S. E., wounded, 115
Tipper, C.S.M., wounded, 58
Title of Regiment, change in, 78
Titmus, 2/Lieut. A. H. J. M., wounded, 273
Todd, 2/Lieut. H. M., wounded, 269
Tollemache, 2/Lieut. J. E., 189, 239, 240; killed, 241
Toombs, 2/Lieut. C. J. O., 258
Tortise, 2/Lieut. H. J., 211; wounded, 213; wounded, 216; Capt., 225; Major, 236
Transports: *Alaunia*, 179; *Aronda*, 187; *Astraea*, 84; *Cesarea*, 267; *Balmoral Castle*, 84; *Braemar Castle*, 8; *Briton*, 84; *City of Calcutta*, 127; *City of Marseilles*, 127; *Cymric*, 85; *Dover Castle*, 84; *Dufferin*, 4; *Dunluce Castle*, 84; *Elephanta*, 180; *Haverfordwest*, 153; *Invicta*, 189; *Goorkha*, 84; *Grantully Castle*, 139; *Kenilworth Castle*, 84; *Mount Temple*, 211; *La Marguerite*, 171; *Malwa*, 165; *Port Lyttelton*, 187; *Rohilla*, 2; *Stephen*, 127; *Turkomania*, 85; *Ulysses*, 147; *Victoria*, 211; *Yale*, 127
Travers, Lieut. F., 211
Tredgold, Major, 151
Trench, 2/Lieut. P. R. O., 27
"Trench feet," 48
Trend, 2/Lieut. E. T., wounded, 200
Tringham, Lieut.-Col. A. M., 239, 246
Tron, Rev. M., wounded, 175, 177
Trônes Wood, 213, 214
Trotter, Lieut. B., 274; wounded, 275
Trythall, 2/Lieut. H. J., 55; wounded, 59
Tucker, 2/Lieut. F. D., killed, 59
Turberville, 2/Lieut. G., wounded, 206
Turl, R.S.M. G., 210
Turnbull, Lieut. P. M., R.A.M.C., 103
Turner, Lieut. E. L., 140; Capt., 146
Tweedie-Smith, 2/Lieut. A., killed, 35
Twigg, Brig.-General R. H., 36, 38
Twining, Capt., 147
Twining, 2/Lieut. R. H., wounded, 169
Twitchell, Pte. G., wounded, 132

Union Jack Club, 81

Valentine, 2/Lieut. M., 113; missing, 115
Van der Pant, Lieut. L. H., wounded, 209
Varndell, 2/Lieut. C. H. E., 189
Vaughan, 2/Lieut. H. W., wounded and missing, 220
Veasey, Lieut. H. G., gassed, 249
Vesey, Capt. and Adjt. I. L. B., 81
Versturme-Bunbury, Major J. K. N., 30, 32; wounded, 33
Victoria Cross, Lieut.-Col. Bushell, 226-230

Victory March, 127
Vidler, Lieut. L. J. C., 171; Capt., wounded, 175
Vignoles, Capt. F. C., 267
Villers Bretonneux, 246
Viney, Pte. E., 92
Vipan, 2/Lieut. G., 239
Vittorio-Veneto, Battle of, 122 *et seq.*
Voisin, 2/Lieut. G. H., 26

Wadson, 2/Lieut. S. P., killed, 207
Waite, Pte. S., 104
Waldie, 2/Lieut. C. P., wounded, 238
Wales, Prince of, speech by, 210
Walker, 2/Lieut. R. S., 45; missing, 53
Wallace, Major, 273
Wallich, Lieut. M. G. L., missing, 194
Wallington, Pte., 105
Wallis, Lieut. and Qr.Mr. G. H., 9, 25, 37, 41; Capt., killed, 69
Walmisley, 2/Lieut. A. E., 92, 93
Walpole, 2/Lieut. R. R., 81, 82; Capt., 211; killed, 213
Walsh, Lieut. P., R.A.M.C., 27
Walsh, 2/Lieut. J. B. W., killed, 99
Walter, 2/Lieut. J. S., 211, 215; Capt., 217, 218; wounded, 219
Walter, 2/Lieut. S. R. P., 99
Wanstall, Pte. J., 74
Ward, 2/Lieut. A. D. W., missing, 194
Ward, 2/Lieut. E. R., 104; wounded, 105
Wardell, Major H., 267, 268, 269; wounded, 270
Warden, Lieut.-Col. H. F., 77, 189
Wardroper, 2/Lieut. J., 267
Warren, Lieut.-Col. D., 6, 9; killed, 18
Waspe, C.S.M., 130
Watney, Col. F. D., 147, 151, 154, 170
Watson, Capt. A. S., wounded, 222, 225
Watson, Capt. C. F., 9, 15, 18, 19, 23-25; Lieut.-Col., 50
Watson, Lieut.-Col. S. T., 45, 81, 127, 129-136, 168, 189
Watson, 2/Lieut. W. M., 155, 157; wounded, 224; wounded, 231
Watts, Major-General H. E., 100, 108
Waziristan, operations in, 128, 129, 143, 144
Weare, 2/Lieut. F. G. C., 104; wounded, 106
Webb, Capt. E. J. G., 127
Webb, 2/Lieut. G. A., 252
Webb, Pte. J., wounded, 132
Webb, Pte., 275
Weeding, Capt. T., 84, 85; wounded, 91
Weeding, Major, 32; wounded, 34, 50; killed, 56
West, C.S.M. A., 105
Wheeler, 2/Lieut. G., 37, 41; wounded, 113, 114
Whetham, Capt. P., 81
Whibley, Pte. P., 104
Whiffin, Major G. G., 81
Whinfield, Lieut.-Col. H. C., 77-80, 84, 85; wounded, 91
Whinney, Major F. T., 172
White, Lieut. G. A., 84, 85; wounded, 91
White, Lieut. G. P., R.A.M.C., 267
White, 2/Lieut. F. C., wounded, 206
Whittaker, Lieut. H. L. C., 68; killed, 69
Whittaker, 2/Lieut. F. H. E., wounded, 74

# INDEX

Whittall, Lieut. A. J., wounded, 286
Whittet, 2/Lieut. G., 211, 213; killed, 216
Whittington, Lieut. L., 179, 180
Whittington, Lieut. P. R., 179, 180; Major, 187
Wigan, 2/Lieut. C. R., 179, 180, 182
Wigham-Richardson, Lieut. W., 211; wounded, 216
Wilcox, 2/Lieut. K. T. D., 239
Wilders-Lewis, Capt. H. C., killed, 256–257
Wiley, 2/Lieut. C. W., 267
Wilkins, Lieut.-Col. H. St. C., 26, 157, 162; wounded, 164, 169
Wilkins, Lieut.-Col. H. St. C., 26
Williams, Capt. E. H., wounded, 169
Williams, Major C. H., 189
Williams, Lieut. H. C., killed, 36; 84, 85; wounded, 91
Williams, Lieut. M. D., killed, 22
Williams, 2/Lieut. A. M., 136
Williams, 2/Lieut. F. C., 276
Williams, 2/Lieut. W. H., 278
Williams, Dmr., 25
Williamson, Pte., 98
Willis, 2/Lieut. N. A., wounded, 107
Willis, Pte. S., 74
Willmot, 2/Lieut. W. H. O., wounded, 115
Wills, 2/Lieut. A., wounded, 257
Wilson, Capt. C. E., 9; killed, 18
Wilson, Capt. R. E., 280
Wilson, Lieut. D. R., 84, 85; killed, 91
Wilson, Lieut. R. C., 127, 128, 130, 133, 136; wounded, 257
Wilson, 2/Lieut. J. H., 223
Wilson, Dmr. C., 74
Winnall, 2/Lieut. E. J., wounded, 111
Winter, Sergt.-Dmr. J., 37, 74
Wise, Capt. C. W., 140, 146

Wizernes, 271
Wodehouse, Lieut.-General, 2
Wolfenden, Lieut. J. R., 133
Wood, Capt. A., 22; wounded, 24, 25
Wood, Lieut. A. R. B., 146
Woodruffe, 2/Lieut. R. C., 202
Woods, Lieut. F. C., killed, 111
Woollatt, Capt. C. H., killed, 241
Woollatt, 2/Lieut. G. F., 213, 215; killed, 216
Wooster, 2/Lieut. C. D. H., 189; Capt., killed, 207
Worman, 2/Lieut. A. S., wounded, 199; wounded, 206
Wort, Lieut. and Qr.Mr. C. H. J., 81-85; Capt. 91
Wort, 2/Lieut. P. C., 92
Worthington, Capt. J. A., 252
Wright, Capt. E., killed, 194
Wright, Capt. W. D., 81
Wright, 2/Lieut. C. M., wounded, 112, 113
Wright, 2/Lieut. N. G., 213; missing, 216
Wyatt, Sergt., 228
Wyndham, 2/Lieut. G. H. S., 239
Wyndham-Wright, Lieut.-Col. J., 284, 285
Wytschaete Ridge, 167

YANDELL, Capt. W., 243; wounded, 245
Yeo, 2/Lieut. S., wounded, 69
Yetts, Lieut. L. M., 179, 180; Capt., 181
Yilghin Burnu, 150
Youl, Pte. H. E., wounded, 252
Young, 2/Lieut. E. J., 243; wounded, 245
Ypres, Battles of, 20, 56, 87, 94, 113, 173, 256, 257, 263, 270
Yser, 56, 57

ZEEBRUGGE, 2nd Bn. lands at, 85

Printed in Great Britain
by Amazon.co.uk, Ltd.,
Marston Gate.